CADOGANguides

PELOPONNESE & ATHENS

'A place that seemed ancient even in ancient times, that defies Greek stereotypes and gets under your skin in mysterious ways.'

Dana Facaros & Linda Theodorou

About the Guide

The **full-colour introduction** gives the authors' overview of the country, together with a suggested **itinerary** and a regional **'where to go' map** and **feature** to help you plan your trip. Illuminating and entertaining **cultural chapters** on local history, art, architecture, myth, food, wine and everyday life give you a rich flavour of the country.

Planning Your Trip starts with the basics of when to go, getting there and getting around. The **Practical A–Z** deals with all the **essential information** and **contact details** that you may need while you are away.

The **regional chapters** are arranged in a loose touring order, with plenty of public transport and driving information. The author's top **'Don't Miss'** sights are highlighted at the start of each chapter and there are also **short-tour itineraries**.

A **language and pronunciation guide**, a **glossary** of cultural terms, ideas for **further reading** and a comprehensive **index** can be found at the end of the book.

Although everything we list in this guide is **personally recommended**, our authors inevitably have their own favourite places to eat and stay. Whenever you see this **Authors' Choice** icon beside a listing, you will know that it is a little bit out of the ordinary.

Hotel Price Guide (*see also* p.71)

Luxury	€€€€€	€150 and above
Very Expensive	€€€€	€120–150
Expensive	€€€	€80–120
Moderate	€€	€50–80
Inexpensive	€	€50 and under

Restaurant Price Guide

The majority of tavernas will charge €15–20 a head for a meal with wine. Unless otherwise stated, taverna and restaurant prices in this guide fall within this range; if a particular place is more expensive or cheaper, we state the average cost per person for a two-course meal with wine.

About the Authors

Dana Facaros, whose father is from the Greek island of Ikaría, started her travel-writing career with Cadogan's *Greek Islands* in 1977. She recently celebrated getting Greek citizenship by breaking every plate in the house.

Linda Theodorou gave up teaching to live and work in Greece and follow in the footsteps of Pausanias. She has lived in the Peloponnese for more than 30 years and has never got over her love affair with the country and its people.

2nd Edition published 2008

01 INTRODUCING THE PELOPONNESE & ATHENS

...the place like a great plane-leaf that the sun's torrent carries away...

George Seferis

The improbable plane leaf of the Peloponnese, dangling from the mainland by a fragile, broken stem, was the cradle of ancient Greece. Not, mind you, of the democracy, mathematics, science or philosophy of ancient Greece, but of something else that claims an equal place in the cultural baggage of the West: the myths and legends. This is where Pegasus flew and Heracles laboured, where the curse of the House of Atreus devoured its victims (literally, at times), where the beautiful Helen hatched out of an egg, and where the Greeks themselves hatched a veritable rogue's gallery of monsters and gods – the Hydra, the Nemean lion, the Stymphalian birds, werewolves, Pan, Horse-headed Demeter, Wolf Zeus and more. Names like Mycenae, Tiryns, Arcadia, Argos, Olympia, Sparta, Troezen and the River Styx hover on the fine line of dream, and startle when you first see them on the road map, cheek by jowl with little symbols for campsites and petrol stations.

Níkos Kazantzákis called the Peloponnese 'the ancient acropolis of all Greece.' You can also look at it as the ultimate Greek theatre, scene of a great drama, each scene leaving behind a smattering of time-worn props. Act I opens with the long age of the pre-Greeks, an Aegean *Das Rheingold*. Act II sparkles with Mycenaeans and the Achaeans, a period of great art and cultural unity, before the curtain crashes down with the resounding boom of a dark age. Act III reveals the disjointed greatness of Classical times: of Corinth, Greece's first economic powerhouse; of Olympia, site of the greatest of all panhellenic games; of Epidauros, the most famed healing centre in the Mediterranean; of Sparta, mighty military

Previous page: Harbour at sunrise, Gýthio, Laconía, pp.403–405

Above, from top: Moní Taxiarchón, Achaía, pp.201–202; Kerameikós cemetery, Athens, pp.105–107

Above left: Orange and olive groves, near Spárta, Laconía, pp.370–71

Above right: Roadside shrine near Galatás, Argolís, pp.308–309

machine and in many ways the villain of the piece. St Paul and St Andrew convert it, but then it's curtains for the Peloponnese again, the curtain fabric being made of barbarian hordes. Act IV, starring the Byzantines, has a *Midsummer's Night Dream* interlude of French knights and chivalry in the Morea, as they called it, plus the Greek swansong at Mystrá, before the Turks bring down the curtain yet again. Then in Act V all is resolved: the indomitable clans and captains come down from their lairs to lead the War of Independence, and modern Greece is born, with a touch of *deus ex machina*. And the first tourists play Fortinbras, stepping over the bodies to get to the beach.

You could come here, like Fortinbras, and stay in some all-in resort complex, bathed in the spotlit clarity of the sun and sea, enveloped in the fragrance of pines, lemon blossoms and jasmine, and immerse yourself in the convivial 'eat, drink and be merry' atmosphere that is Greece. But to ignore the rest you may have to put blinkers on your sunglasses. The natural beauty of the Peloponnese comes in epic

proportions. The decorative and quaint have no place here; the land is as dramatic and magical as the myths that flowed from its pores, sensuous in the measure of the human imagination. Cool alpine pastures are disturbed only by the bells of cattle, sheep and goats while, all around, mountains claw at the sky, their bowels ripped up in chasms, their cliffs shattered by the sea; the sublime and awful Taíyetos range tails off into the Máni and ends at the entrance to Hell. When not impossibly vertical, the Peloponnese is astonishingly lush, with olives and vines and citrus groves.

There are two or three sides to every story here, and they are inextricably woven into the land, which is why photos taken of the Peloponnese often seem disappointingly flat. It has too many dimensions, too much history, too many monsters and heroes and gods. The latter may shy away from the busy holiday strips, but they are never very far when the noises of the modern world fall silent, either in the rosy-fingered dawn, or the stillness of the noonday demon, or the blazing bright starry nights where they were born.

Where to Go

The sea and mountains are in each other's pockets in the Peloponnese, and its shape and size naturally lend to touring in a circuit, with detours into the interior; for many people the first decision is whether to do it clockwise or counterclockwise. If you only stick to the most famous sites, you can probably whip around the old leaf in a couple of weeks (*see* the itinerary on p.16), especially now that the roads everywhere have been improved. But, while Olympia, Mycenae, Monemvasiá, Pýlos, Mystrá, Epídauros, Naúplio and the rest are must-sees, if you take time to explore, who knows what else you will find?

Most people start at **Athens**, with its sublime Acropolis and other relics of its golden age, its great museums and buzzing nightlife, then hire a car and cross over the Corinth Canal into the Peloponnese. After the capital we begin with **Corinthia** and its canal, and two major ancient sites: Corinth and Nemea, the latter, as a bonus, in the centre of one of Greece's top wine regions.

Achaía follows, a rim of lofty mountains and valleys along the Gulf of Corinth with its secret ancient cities, cliff-hugging monasteries, scenic railway at Diakoftó, ski centre, the river Styx and the big port of Pátras. In bucolic **Elís**, to the south, you'll find ancient Olympia with its excellent museum, sandy beaches, the Néda Gorge and the wonderfully remote Temple of Apollo at Bassae.

Argolís follows, home of the myth-laden citadels of Mycenae and Tiryns, of the perfect theatre of ancient Epidauros and of charming neoclassical Naúplio, as well as the big resort of Tólo and others along the Akte peninsula. Its ports offer excursions to three delightful Argo-Saronic islands hanging just off the shore: Póros, Hýdra and Spétses.

Arcadía, old even to the ancients, occupies the wild coast to the south and the mountainous heart of the Peloponnese, home to weird old religious shrines and traditional villages, especially around Gortynía and the Loúsios Gorge.

To the southeast of the region, **Laconía** was the beautiful stomping ground of the austere Spartans, where citrus groves grow under the tremendous Taíyetos range. Here you'll find the lovely Byzantine ghost town of Mystrá, the unforgettable, utterly unique peninsula of the Máni with its tower houses and prickly pear fences, and Monemvasiá, the Gibraltar of Greece. You can also sail to the lone Ionian island of Kýthera.

Messenía to the west is the land of lovely beaches, and of Kalamáta and its silvery olive groves, not to mention Nestor's Mycenaean palace at Pýlos, the awe-inspiring walls of ancient Messene, and old Venetian forts and ports at Methóni and Koróni.

Above, from top: Door, Spétses, pp.319–23; Corinth Canal, pp.155–6; Erechtheion, Athens, p.94

Opposite page: Hills, Messenía, pp.423–62

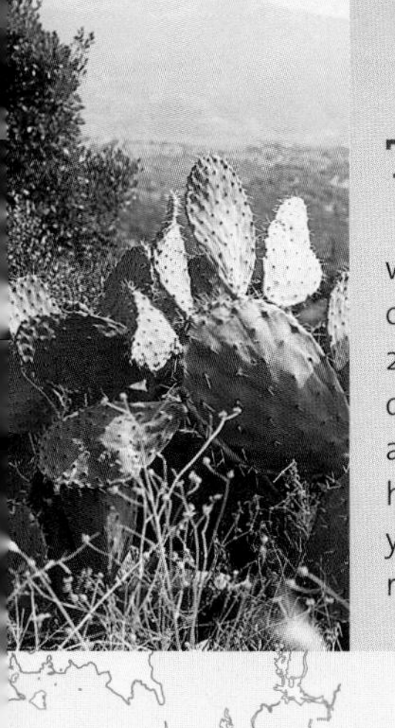

The 2007 Fires

The Peloponnese last made international headlines for the wrong reasons: the unprecedented wildfires in the summer of 2007 after a prolonged heatwave and drought that scoured 2.3 per cent of the country's surface. Other parts of Greece were destroyed as well, but the Peloponnese (especially Elís, Messenía and Arcadía) bore the brunt of the damage and loss of life. We have indicated the worst-hit areas in the text, but we do hope you'll visit them anyway; it will cheer up the locals as they try to rebuild their shattered lives.

Chapter Divisions

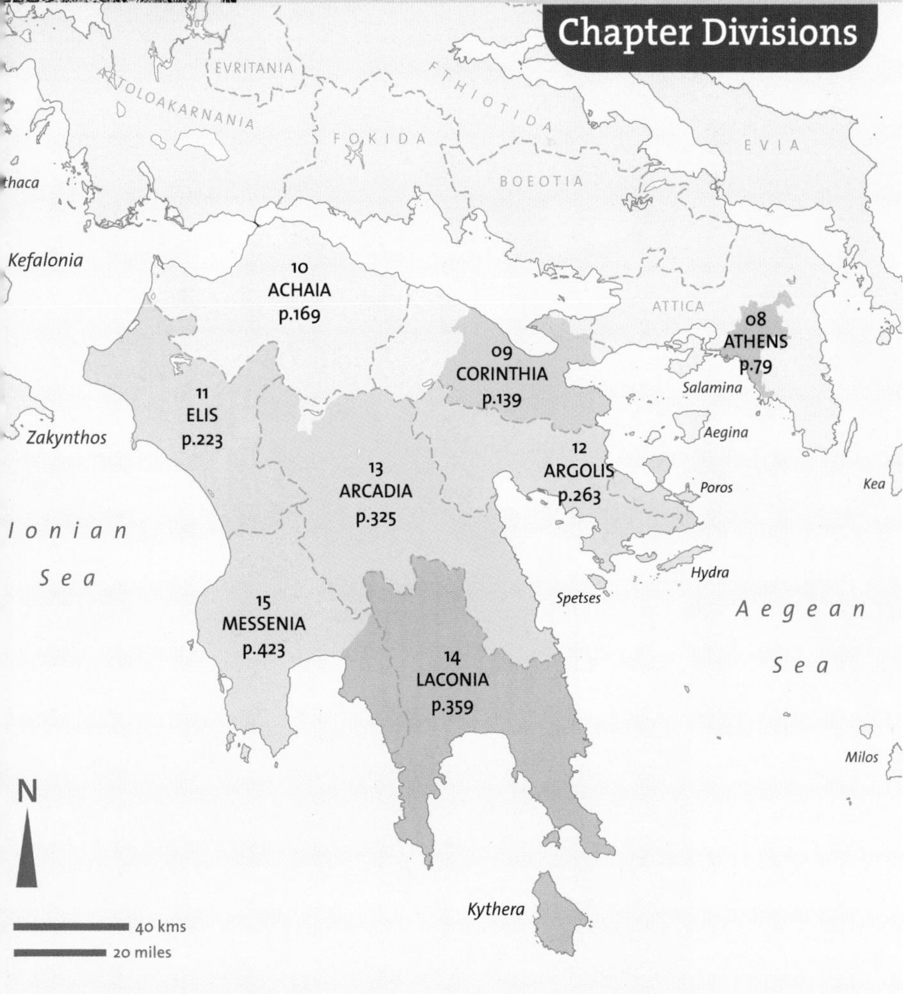

EVRITANIA
AITOLOAKARNANIA
FTHIOTIDA
FOKIDA
EVIA
BOEOTIA
Ithaca
Kefalonia
10 ACHAIA p.169
ATTICA
08 ATHENS p.79
09 CORINTHIA p.139
Salamina
11 ELIS p.223
Aegina
Zakynthos
12 ARGOLIS p.263
13 ARCADIA p.325
Poros
Kea
Ionian Sea
Hydra
Spetses
15 MESSENIA p.423
Aegean Sea
14 LACONIA p.359
Milos
N
Kythera
40 kms
20 miles

Clockwise from top left: Acropolis by night, seen from Philopáppos Hill, p.98; New Acropolis Museum, pp.94–6; iced coffee; restaurant, Pláka, pp.90–91; religious icons, Sýntagma Square, p.89

City Lights

Below the peerless Acropolis waits one of Europe's liveliest cities. The decade of primping for the 2004 Olympics was only the opening salvo in a series of urban improvements as Athens finds new ways to combine the preservation of its unique heritage with 21st-century style, perhaps best epitomized in the critically acclaimed New Acropolis Museum. Run-down industrial areas around the centre are coming back to life with edgy new clubs, restaurants, boutique hotels and museums such as the Pireos Street Annex and the forthcoming new National Museum of Modern Art, slated to fill the former Fix beer factory. But in spite of the changes the old Athens lives on – the ancient landmarks, now more beautiful than ever; the village feel of neighbourhoods; its love of late nights under the stars...

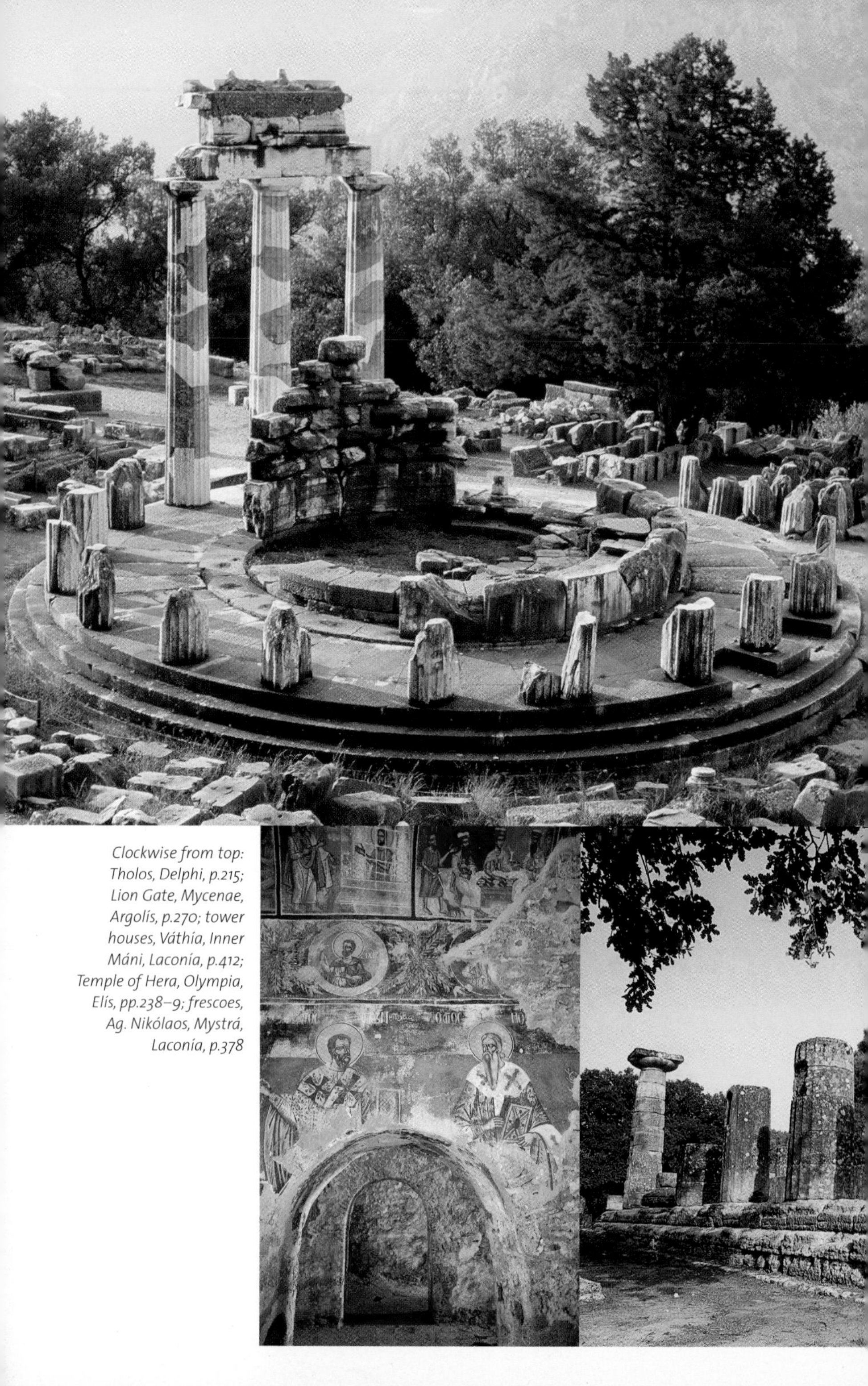

Clockwise from top: Tholos, Delphi, p.215; Lion Gate, Mycenae, Argolís, p.270; tower houses, Váthia, Inner Máni, Laconía, p.412; Temple of Hera, Olympia, Elís, pp.238–9; frescoes, Ag. Nikólaos, Mystrá, Laconía, p.378

Old Stones

Athens and the Peloponnese wear their old stones like crown jewels, in unforgettable settings. Between them they count seven UNESCO World Heritage sites: the Athenian Acropolis; the Temple of Apollo at Bassae; Olympia, where the games were founded in 776 BC; 'well-girt' Mycenae and Tiryns, linked in myth to Perseus, Agamemnon and Heracles; Epidauros, home to antiquity's most perfect theatre; and Mystrá, the last outpost of the Byzantine empire. But the region sparkles too with other gems: Homer's 'sandy Pylos'; Corinth, where St Paul preached; the legendary Argive Heraion, and Messene, with the best-preserved Classical walls in Greece. Not far away across the Gulf of Corinth are oracular Delphi and mysterious Eleusis. And jump ahead 1,500 years or so, and there's more: a hundred Crusader and Venetian citadel towns (Chlemoútsi, Karítaina, Koróni, Methóni, Monemvasiá and Naúplio are some of the most famous); the unique tower houses and frescoed chapels of the Máni; and the 18th- and 19th-century sea captains' mansions on the islands of Hýdra and Spétses.

Simple Pleasures

As grand and mythic as the Peloponnese is, you may well find that what you remember most fondly is a watching the sun set to the sound of sheep bells, or stumbling over the ruins of an obscure ancient city used as a playground by the local goats. Or perhaps you'll find a Frankish castle filled with lipstick-red poppies, or a secret waterfall in a gorge lined with impossibly old plane trees, or perhaps a *kafeneíon* in a tiny mountain village where an old woman gives you the best glass of water you've ever tasted. Take picnics, but most of all take your time. This god-haunted cradle of Western civilization still even has a few secrets up its sleeve: a species of dwarf land tortoise (*Testudo weissingeri*), unique to the Peloponnese, was discovered only in 1995, and who knows what else you might find if you take the time to look?

Left: Goat bells, Mystrá summer fair, Laconía, pp.373–80

Above: Roadside produce stall, near Pýrgos, Elís, p.229

Right: Honey for sale, Koúvela, Elís, p.258

Clockwise from top: Traditional barber's, Argos, Argolís, pp.274–8; seafood restaurant, old harbour, Naúplio, Argolís, pp.286–92; guard doll in pistachio nuts, Athens

Old but not Ancient Greece

For many of Greece's regular visitors, it's not only the Peloponnese's sandy beaches and historic monuments that make it a favourite destination: it's the fact that Old Greece, all but extinct on the more cosmopolitan islands, is alive and well here. You can find old fashioned *kafeneíons* and family-run tavernas (even a few very old ones, attached to butcher's shops), and a handful of hotels still stuck in the formaldehyde of the 1960s are a trip straight down memory lane. You can still find barber shops unchanged since the 1950s, working donkeys, and basil growing in blue and white painted cans outside people's doors. Best of all, you can still meet people who take the time to welcome visitors with old-fashioned and utterly disarming hospitality and kindness.

The Garden of Greece

The sea and mountains are in each other's pockets in the Peloponnese, but in between water and stone the land is immensely fertile. The citrus groves yield lemons the size of grapefruits and freshly squeezed orange juice for your breakfast. A sea of silvery olives at Kalamáta offers those delicious long purple-brown olives that stud a Greek salad; vines produce not only some of the most prestigious wines, but also currants for your scones. Higher altitudes yield mountains herbs and walnuts, and all summer long the Peloponnesians and their visitors delight in sun-ripened fruit and vegetables, from figs and the common melon to the *tsakóniikis melanzánas*, the exquisite little pale purple aubergines that only grow around Leonídio.

Above, from top: Orange groves near Epidauros, Argolís, p.302; figs, Kalamáta, Messenía, pp.425–6

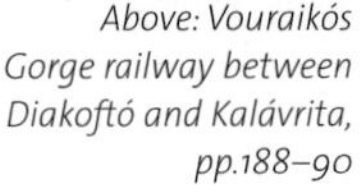

Above: Vouraikós Gorge railway between Diakoftó and Kalávrita, pp.188–90

Itinerary

The Best of Athens and the Northern Peloponnese in Two Weeks

Days 1–3 Fly into **Athens** and visit the must-sees: the Acropolis and the ancient sites along the new pedestrian walkway, and the National Archaeological Museum. At some point, have dinner on a roof garden overlooking the Parthenon, beautifully illuminated by night.

Day 4 Drive over the Corinth Canal, stopping for a look. Visit **ancient Isthmía** and **ancient Corinth**, and spend the night.

Day 5 Head south to **Epidauros**' theatre and archaeological site, then across to Naúplio.

Days 6–8 Visit **Naúplio**'s pretty centre, its archaeological museum and the Palamídi Fortress, and then use the town as a base for trips to **Tiryns**, **Argos**, **Mycenae**, and nearby beaches.

Day 9 Head north to **ancient Nemea**, then spend a leisurely day along the coast, perhaps heading into the mountains to visit **ancient Sikyon** or **ancient Aigeira**. Overnight in **Akráta**.

Day 10 In the morning, head over to **Diakoftó** and take the train or drive up the stunning **Vouraikós Gorge** to **Kalávrita**. Then continue west to see the new Río-Andírio bridge over the Gulf of Corinth, and bypass **Pátras** for the west coast. Visit the huge Frankish **Chlemoútsi Castle**. Overnight in nearby **Arkoúdi**.

Day 11 Visit **ancient Olympia**, where the Olympic Games were invented in the 8th century BC, and see its fabulous museum. Spend the night.

Days 12–13 Now for two days in the mountains, staying in country inns: from Olympia, drive north through the ancient oak forest to **Lála** and **Lámbia**; wander gradually eastwards via **Tripótama** and **ancient Psophis**, **Aronanía**, **Kleitoriá**, **Pheneós** and the **Stymphalian Lake**.

Day 14 Return to Athens.

CONTENTS

Maps and Plans

Reference

Contents

Peloponnese History

02

The face of Greece is a palimpsest bearing twelve successive inscriptions: Contemporary; the period of 1821; the Turkish yoke; the Frankish sway; the Byzantines; the Roman; the Hellenistic epoch; the Classic; the Dorian middle ages; the Mycenaean; the Aegean; and the Stone Age. Pause on a patch of Greek earth and anguish overcomes you. It is a deep, twelve-levelled tomb, from which voices rise up calling to you. Which voice should you choose?

Níkos Kazantzákis, *Travels in Greece*

One might add, which one is telling the truth? Much of Greek history is speculative, and fragmented regionally, or twisted and glossed over to fit a political agenda. This is not uniquely Greek by any means, only the Greeks have been doing it longer than most – since the 8th century BC. 'You enter Greece as one might enter a dark crystal,' Lawrence Durrell once wrote. 'The form of things becomes irregular, refracted.' As does their history (of which Athens gets its own, *see* pp.82–9).

20,000–3000 BC: The Stone Age: A Nice Time to Be a Goddess

Traces of the first Peloponnesians, from late in the **Middle Palaeolithic** period (35,000–20,000 BC), have been found in Argolís, Elís and Laconía. The large **Fráchthi** (Φραγχθι) **cave** in Argolís takes the prize for the greatest continuity of habitation; not only that, but the bottom of the Mesolithic deposit produced the earliest complete skeleton in Greece (*c.* 8000 BC). At this point, we can say Peloponnesian history set off. A gradual movement from a nomadic hunting life centred on cave dwellings, through rudimentary agricultural techniques and the introduction and domestication of sheep and goats, on to the discovery of pottery and simple house-building, brings us into the 6000s BC. By 3000 BC there were even small **Neolithic** settlements.

Aside from tools and the like, the most interesting artefacts of this Stone Age found in the Peloponnese are the small, squat, big-breasted, full-bottomed female figures, a type common in the Mediterranean, hinting at a widespread Mother Goddess cult.

3000–1200 BC: The Bronze Age: The Swing Plough Cuts a Wide Swath

This era has more holes than Swiss cheese. A slow, shadowy incursion of foreigners, bringing with them bronze metalworking techniques and the swing plough, occurred over the period from 2500 to 1800 BC. Or so they say. The current theory has two waves of migration, one in the **early Helladic** period of non-Greek-speakers, culminating in the building of the House of Tiles at Lerna (around 2200 BC), and another after its destruction, this time by horse-taming, chariot-riding, Greek-speaking **Indo-Europeans**, the people of the Minyan ware, whose civilization led up to the Mycenaean era. And all this while the indigenous population, so-called **Pelasgians**, hid in the remote corners of Arcadía, missing the sweeps of the new cultural brooms.

Bronze tools and the swing plough led to the stabilization of agriculture, allowing permanent settlements with lands radiating out several miles, about the distance it would take to travel in a day. Permanent settlements and prosperity led to sea trade, craft specialization and the first known use of symbols such as seals or pot marks, denoting a specific place, saying 'Here we are and this is ours'. This more 'civilized' situation allowed more time for art, more time for empire-building and more time for war. The swing plough would slowly put paid to the idea of female dominance of the agricultural cycle, dealing mother goddesses a blow from which they still haven't recovered. The Indo-European sky god cult, a social hierarchy that valued warriors, and a tendency to centre cult activity on hilltop or acropolis sanctuaries, all began to make their presence felt. In fact, we now have all of the makings of the **Mycenaean** culture, which seems to have exploded fully grown on to the Greek scene about 1600 BC.

Mycenaean wealth, as evidenced in their shaft graves and *tholos* tombs, is proof of their astonishing rise to power. While these settlements were not centred in the Peloponnese alone, Mycenae became so powerful that it gave its name to the era. Mycenaeans took over Minoan palaces in Crete and assimilated the culture. They dominated their fellow 'Mycenaeans' in some kind of loose federation, and much of the Mediterranean world as well. Their **palaces** were centres for the gathering and redistribution of agricultural and trading products, as well as headquarters for government and religion. Female goddesses were still important, but their male high priests were up-and-coming, and held the title of *wanax* or king. The Mycenaeans took the Minoan script Linear A and adapted it to create **Linear B** (*see* pp.454–6), making it the first written script in Greek. It was a syllabic language, suitable for documenting inventories in the palaces that were virtually storehouses of the culture's wealth. Mycenaeans sported armour and carried lances, not lilies like their Minoan counterparts; theirs was a warrior culture. One historian projects an image of a feudal-like system, with barons jockeying for place, which very soon produced too many younger sons looking for land or loot by stealing another man's wealth instead of by trade, and then inventing a warrior code that not only justified the process but idealized it. Certainly that is the image of Mycenaeans projected by Homer; whether or not Homer's idealization of the Mycenaean war culture is accurate or not, its literary reality became, for better or worse, the Greek *beau idéal*.

1200–500 BC: The Dark Age and the Archaic Age: Tribes, Scribes, Sculpture and the Dorian (K)not

After 1200 BC, the Mycenaean centres dwindled and disappeared one after the other, for reasons that are hard to determine – although increasingly the evidence from many fields is pointing to climate change, notably a massive, long-term drought. The traditional date of the fall of Troy is 1180 BC, and Mycenae, Tiryns and Pýlos collapsed not long after. Along with their palaces went the wonderful Mycenaean pottery with its lively animals, curved floral patterns and frescoes of everyday life. A much reduced population struggled on in isolated pockets of the Peloponnese. The Mycenaean word for 'chief' or 'baron', *basileus*, survived to become the Classical Greek equivalent of 'king', suggesting that these remnants were Mycenaeans, led by Mycenaean nobles. Linguists note the first inklings of the 'Dorian' dialect. Chieftains' houses and signs of cult activity at Asine in the Argolís and Nikchória in Messenía show that some kind of organization limped on. The Sanctuary of Athena Alea at Tegéa was founded in 950 BC. Pottery decoration became minimalist, abstract, seemingly in sync with a bleaker reality.

This period may have been a dark age, but a lot was happening while the lights were out. When the curtain rises on the **Archaic Age** in the 8th century BC, what do we find? Diverse groups of Greeks speaking different dialects in fairly recognized areas, who, while clearly understanding their cultural affinities with one another, were quite indisposed to any sort of wider political unity. Add to that the development of an alphabetic script, colonies in Asia Minor, the Black Sea and the western Mediterranean, and the founding of the Olympic Games in 776 BC marking the beginning of the Greek calendar, and you have another one of those amazing strides forward in history that seem to demand an 'invader' in order to explain them. Modern historians call them '**Dorians**', a group of somewhat rough and tough Greek-speakers arriving from points north who take over in Laconía, Corinthia, Argolís and Messenía, leaving the rest for refugees from the last era. If they came, they left very little archaeological evidence of their arrival. The Dorian debate continues. The existence of dialects is the most convincing evidence that they did exist, as well as the ancient Greeks' own insistence that the 'Sons of Heracles' entered the Peloponnese; the first recorded reference to them goes back to the work of the mid-7th-century BC Spartan poet Tyrtaios. Hard-drinking, club-wielding Heracles was a favourite Dorian hero.

In step with and nurturing all these 8th-century BC developments is that quintessentially Greek institution, the ***polis*** or city-state. The ideal of the free *polis* became the norm, and its development was one of the cardinal strengths of Greek culture. It allowed the social experimentation and group solidarity that would produce citizens, not just subjects, a development unique in that period in the ancient world. Art underwent a renaissance. Greek temples were turned into stone; monumental sculpture appeared; heroic story cycles developed. All these advances together shifted a confident Greek society from a rule of chiefs and tyrants towards the oligarchies and democracies which coalesced in the dazzling but all-too-short Classical Age.

500–323 BC: The Classical Moment

The **Classical period** started promisingly with the repulsion of the Persians. During this war of survival, the Greeks would band together (at least most of the time) to repel the common enemy; their victories at Marathon in 490 BC and Sálamis in 480 BC ensured the survival of Greek culture (the Persians did not just go belly-up, but would remain in the background well into the Hellenistic period, ever ready to be appealed to by one Greek faction or another). The great period of Athenian expansion followed: it formed an empire at the head of the Delian League, while polishing up the basics of Western civilization in art, poetry, drama and philosophy.

Over in the Peloponnese, the **Spartans** were marching to a different drum. Their political system, based as it was on the repression of a large majority, led to the creation of a military machine coupled with permanent political paranoia (*see* pp.51–5). Yet Spartan extremism was only taking the whole city-state ideal, with its emphasis on citizen loyalty and pride, to the limit, and it highlighted the system's most serious flaw: with loyalty to the *polis* the be-all and end-all, the possibility of a larger political unity was never seriously entertained. No Greek state ever trusted

Ancient Cities of the Classical Era

another; their inter-city policy was one of groupings into leagues for temporary advantage, with dissolutions and regroupings occurring whenever a new advantage was seen. No alliance was worth the stone it was carved on, in spite of the eternal friendship these ubiquitous *stelae* professed. Panhellenic shrines and games aside, the analogy that fits Hellenic culture is that of a not-too-well-adjusted family who got together on holidays, but who had nothing good to say about the family the rest of the year.

The tension between Sparta and Athens, a simmering blend of jealousy, mistrust and self-interest, led to the **Peloponnesian War** in 431 BC, the details of which are brilliantly described by Thucydides and Xenophon. Not for the last time, every other Peloponnesian city-state became a political football on the big boys' playing field, which more often than not was the Peloponnese itself. In 404 Athens finally lost and Sparta won but, like most bullies, Sparta could fight better than she could rule. Her hegemony lasted thirty short years before her former ally Thebes, under the great general **Epaminondas** (*see* p.432) shattered her army at Leúktra in Boeotía (371 BC). He then brought the war to the Peloponnese and liberated long-suffering Messenía from Sparta's tyranny. Theban power was crushed in turn by **Philip II of Macedon**, Alexander's father and a keen student of Epaminondas.

338–146 BC: The Hellenistic Age

Philip was a good organizer – more 'leagues' were formed – but his organizing days came to an abrupt end when he was assassinated. Alexander was too busy conquering the world to pay much attention to the Peloponnese. The Hellenistic and Roman rulers who followed often gave Greek cities their 'freedom', even if it was only the freedom to do as they were told. Paying lip service to the Greek city-state ideal meant you could get away with a lot. Resistance in the Peloponnese coalesced in the **First Achaean League** (280 BC), Greece's one significant attempt at a federation of states, but proved to be too little, too late. Most Peloponnesian states were members at one time or another, willingly or not, especially in the more powerful **Second Achaean League**, founded by Aratus of Sikyon in 245 BC. Macedonia eventually succeeded in regaining control, but the struggle weakened Greece, making it especially easy for **Rome** to deliver the knockout punch in 146 BC.

146 BC–AD 330: In Which The Romans Prove You *Can* Take It With You

Rome dissolved all leagues save the League of Free Laconians, hauled off as much art as she could cram into her ships, and created the province of **Achaía**. This included the entire Peloponnese, along with some of the mainland, and the Romans based its headquarters in Corinth. The Romans professed to having been 'conquered' by Greek culture, a pretty compliment, but, if the Romans considered themselves part of the Greek family, their Greek 'siblings' could never really have seen them as anything more than 'Big Brothers'. **Nero** entered the games and miraculously won all events. Roman tourists flocked to Greece; **Pausanias** wrote the first guide book. The Odeion in Corinth became a gladiatorial arena, and Sparta's Temple of Artemis Orthia, where boys were flogged, was especially popular.

Subsequent emperors handed out 'freedoms' like candy, and every city-state in the Peloponnese and beyond appealed to Rome to further its own local interests. Still, like every other era in history, people made the best of it, and Roman rule had its moments of peace, offering a better life than the **barbarians**, who began knocking at the Isthmus in AD 267. Under pressure, the Roman Empire divided itself like an amoeba into two parts. In 330 the emperor Constantine moved the eastern capital to Byzantium and changed its name to his own, **Constantinopolis**. Historians would call the resulting eastern half the Byzantine Empire, but to the Greeks (who even today refer to themselves as 'Romans') it has always been, simply, the 'Roman empire'.

330–1204: The Byzantine Empire, Greece Moves East

Under the empire, the Peloponnese became an unimportant Byzantine province with Corinth as its capital. Christianity spread early and pervasively, except in out-of-the-way places like the Máni. The remnants of pagan classicism were given short shrift. Ancient temples were razed to the ground to provide foundations for Christian churches, usually built from the same stone. Cities such as Corinth, Pátras and Lacedaemónia (ancient Sparta) kept their chins up, but the general picture is one of decline. Barbarian invasions continued, coupled with devastating outbreaks of plague; large populations from other parts of the Byzantine empire entered the picture. **Slavs** in particular changed the face of the Peloponnese as bureaucrats in Constantinople moved populations inside their large empire like dominoes in order to provide a lucrative tax base. One Byzantine map actually labelled the Peloponnese as 'the Land of the Avars'. But Greece absorbs invaders, and within several generations the vast majority of newcomers were assimilated linguistically and culturally. In fact, the greatest legacy of these incursions in the Peloponnese boiled down to place names: one third were Slavic in 1821. Like all newcomers, these people had nostalgically named their towns in their own language, and often after ones back home.

The Peloponnese deteriorated into a handful of large fiefs owned by absentee landowners interested only in taxes. By 1204, the empire at Constantinople was so remote that many Peloponnesians were not all that unhappy to see it taken over by the **'Franks'** (the Greek word at the time for any Catholic European) in the Fourth Crusade. This incursion was masterminded by Doge Dandolo and the merchants of **Venice**, who had a bone to pick over trading concessions in the east. As the Christian crusaders looted Christian Constantinople, the Venetians nabbed the best art and gained control of strategic ports along their trade routes, on the islands and at Methóni, Koróni and Monemvasiá in the Peloponnese.

1205–1821: Franks, Byzantines and Turks Build Castles in the Air

The **Latin empire** in Constantinople was a dud, reverting quickly to the Greeks. But in the **Morea**, as the Peloponnese was then commonly called, the situation was different, and all because of **Geoffrey de Villehardouin** and a few men in mail who had been stranded in the southern Peloponnese en route to the Fourth Crusade. The ease with which Villehardouin was able, with a little local help, to slice his way up from Methóni through Messenía, Elís and Achaía to join the French forces at Corinth led him to negotiate with the New Latin empire to form his own **Principality of Achaía** or *La Princée de l'Amorée*. This improbable outpost of medieval chivalry had its seat of government in Andreville (Andravída) and its principal castle at Glarenza (Kyllíni). Although Achaía was divided into twelve **baronies**, its lords flocked to Elís because it reminded them of home, and hung on long enough to write the most complete set of feudal law codes to come down to modern times, to build over a hundred castles, institute jousts, indulge courtly manners, marry Byzantine princesses and even produce their own *Chronicle of the Morea* to immortalize their conquest. But they kept losing control of bits of it, especially after the **Battle of Pelagonia** in 1259, when they had to give back Monemvasiá and the castles of the Máni and Mystrá to the victorious Greeks. The Byzantines then made **Mystrá** the seat of their despotate, from where they fitfully regained control over the rest of the Morea. More enduringly, they filled Mystrá with lovely churches – it would be the last capital of Byzantium, before the **Turks** took over in 1460, seven years after the fall of Constantinople, and did a little castle-building of their own.

The Turks were welcomed in some quarters simply because it was Ottoman policy to leave the Orthodox Church alone, something the interfering Pope in Rome was loath to do. But, religion aside, the Turkish turban was not an improvement over the Frankish mitre. Interested only in taxes, the Ottomans developed a *laissez-faire* policy except where money was concerned, combined with vicious reprisals if their authority was challenged. Through plague and indifference the population of the Peloponnese dropped to a mere 100,000. Significantly for the future, parts of the Peloponnese such as the Máni and western Arcadía never truly submitted to the Turks, and the pashas were constantly reduced to some form of power-sharing with local leaders, whom they could, of course, never quite trust. In spite of setbacks and disappointing efforts to oust the Turks by **Morosini** (Venice) in 1684 and **Orlov** (the Russians) in 1770, Greek freedom fighters, often in klephtic bands, fought and were defeated again and again, then headed for the hills and bided their time. Their numbers increased dramatically in the 1700s. An entire culture arose surrounding these free mountain spirits, who would take the lead in the War of Independence, although they found it hard to give up their independent lifestyle when real independence came.

1821–7: The War of Independence

Greeks both ancient and modern have often lived beyond their *polis*, and those at home kept their identity through the Turkish occupations. The revolutionary fires that swept through Europe in the late 18th century found plenty of kindling amongst Greeks; the secret **Friendly Society** (*Philikí Etairía*) founded by diaspora Greeks helped to co-ordinate activities between well-wishers abroad and Greeks in Greece.

In March of 1821, the War of Independence began. **Theodore Kolokotrónis** (*see* pp.344–5) took Kalamáta, and the flag of revolt was raised at the monastery of Ag. Lávra in Achaía by the Archbishop of Pátras on 25 March, the date later chosen as Independence Day. Kolokotrónis' successes pushed the Turks to the wall and in 1825 the Sultan called in **Ibrahim Pasha** of Egypt, promising him the Peloponnese if he could win it. He almost did, in the most vicious stage of the war. Luckily, in October 1827, in a victory the British would term an 'untoward event', the allied fleets of England, France and Russia sank the Turkish and Egyptian ships at the Battle of Navaríno in Pýlos (*see* pp.448–9), and virtually ended the war.

1827–1939: The Ship of State Sails Stormy Seas

The new country consisted of the Peloponnese and the mainland only as far north as Vólos, plus the Saronic and Cyclades islands. As the Powers searched about for a spare member of some neutral royal family to be king of Greece, the Greeks chose a president, **Iánnis Capodístria**, a former secretary of the Tsar. Capodístria offended the pro-British and pro-French factions in Greece with his pro-Russian policies, and he also offended the powerful **Mavromikális** clan, local warlords, who had him assassinated in Greece's first capital, Naúplio, in 1831. Before anarchy spread too far, the Powers found a king: **Otto**, teenage son of Ludwig I of Bavaria, who immediately offended Greek sensibilities by giving Bavarians all the official posts, including responsibility for the building of a new capital over the bedraggled village that was Athens. It was a prophetic choice: soon enough the locals would be as squeezed, not only by their foreign saviours, but also by Greek purists who looked to the past.

After the war, Greek cultural life was dominated by educated expatriates dreaming of returning to the days of Pericles. They had little taste for the 'fallen state' of their compatriots who had, through no fault of their own, missed the Renaissance and Enlightenment. Poverty reigned, and vast political problems awaited, such as the make-up of a new constitution and foreign policy; a more immediate problem was what to do with all of those freedom fighters who retained the medieval notion that, having won, they should be rewarded with territory, or at least be left alone to rule their old fiefs. A period of adjustment followed, as wily warlords slowly evolved into politicians, and vendettas entered the verbal arena (most of the time).

The fledgling Greek state was born with a special mission: the ***Megáli Idéa*** or 'Great Idea' of uniting all Greeks into a kind of *Byzantium Revisited*. It was not as absurd as it may seem today: in 1840, 26,000 Greeks lived in Athens, 120,000 in Constantinople. This goal was shared by Otto as well, but his arrogance and inadequacies led to revolts and eventually to his dethronement in 1862. The Powers found a replacement in **William George**, son of the King of Denmark (who learned of his new job in a newspaper wrapped around his sardine sandwich). He proved to be more tractable than Otto and more modern in his ideas. In 1864 the National Assembly made Greece a **constitutional monarchy**, a system that began to work practically under prime minister Trikoúpis in 1875. During the long reign of George I, Greece began to develop, with shipping as its economic base. Transport improved, most importantly the Corinth Canal (begun in 1882) and the Peloponnesian Railroad (1890s), which helped to make the traditional mainstays of agriculture and animal husbandry more profitable.

In 1910 **Elefthérios Venizélos** became prime minister of Greece for the first of many terms. He deftly used the two **Balkan Wars** of 1912–13 to further the Great Idea, annexing his native Crete, the North Aegean islands, Macedonia and southern Épirus. When the **First World War** broke out, the new king **Constantine I** (married to Kaiser Wilhelm's sister) supported the Germans while remaining officially neutral, whereas Venizélos set up his own separate government with volunteers in support of the Allies in northern Greece. The 'National Schism' went Venizélos' way when the Allies recognized the prime minister and bluntly ordered the king to leave; Venizélos then sent Greek troops to the Macedonian front to fight against Bulgaria.

During the Paris peace conference, Venizélos hoped to reap the rewards of his loyalty by claiming **Smyrna (Izmir)**, which at the time had a huge majority Greek population. Turkey was prostrate, and Britain, France and America agreed to a Greek occupation as a preliminary to a local plebiscite on the future of the area. Tragically, the Greek landings were accompanied by atrocities, and the Turks began to rally around national hero **Mustafa Kemal** (later **Atatürk**). Venizélos was defeated in elections, partly from disgust with all the foreign meddling in Greek affairs, by a royalist party promising a 'small but honourable Greece'. But Smyrna was too tempting a prize to give up. Encouraged by British prime minister Lloyd George, the Greeks marched on Ankara in March 1921. Kemal's armies routed them utterly, and by late August 1922 they threatened Smyrna; both sides committed atrocities, as thousands of Greek refugees fled the burning city. Turkish-Greek relations reached such an impasse that their leaders found a population exchange the only solution. Greece, then with a population of 4,800,000, was faced with finding housing and work for 1,100,000 refugees, while some 380,000 Muslims were sent to Turkey.

There were enough refugees to change the politics of Greece, and most of them supported Venizélos. The monarchy was abolished in 1924, and, after a bad interlude of military dictatorship under General Pángalos, Venizélos was elected prime minister again in 1928. Trade unions and the Communist Party, the **KKE**, gained strength. Venizélos made peace with Greece's neighbours (he visited Turkey in 1930 and even nominated Atatürk for the Nobel Peace Prize) and set the current borders of Greece, except for the Dodecanese, which Italy still 'temporarily occupied'.

The Second World War and the Greek Civil War

What Venizélos couldn't heal was the increased polarization of Greek political life, especially as the **Great Depression** led to violent labour unrest. Venizélos himself barely survived an assassination attempt; martial law was declared, coups were attempted, and in 1935, after a faked plebiscite, King **George II** returned to Greece, with General **Ioánnis Metaxás** as his prime minister. Metaxás assumed dictatorial control, exiled the opposition, and crushed the trade unions and the left. Although he imitated the Fascists in some ways, Metaxás prepared the Greek army against occupation, and on 28 October 1940, as the story goes, he responded with a laconic '*Óchi!*' (No!) to Mussolini's ultimatum that his troops massed on the Albanian border be allowed passage through Greece. The Greeks heroically pushed the Italians back, but refused British offers of assistance at first in the futile hope of preventing Germany from joining the conflict. But Hitler came to the Italians' rescue in April 1941, and by mid-month the severely outnumbered British, New Zealanders and Australians, along with the Greek government, were fleeing south to the sea and North Africa.

The miseries of Occupation – more civilians died in Greece than in any other occupied country; some 500,000 starved to death the first winter – led to vast support for **EAM**, the National Liberation Front, and its army, **ELAS**, that led the resistance. But their leftist politics were unpalatable to Churchill, who made a secret deal with Stalin to keep Greece within the British sphere of influence in the **'percentages agreement'**. Stalin, however, failed to tell Greek Communists about his deal, and the **Greek Civil War** – the first campaign of the Cold War – broke out three months after liberation. As Britain's containment policy was taken over by the USA under the Truman Doctrine, American money and advisers poured into Greece. The Civil War dragged on until 1949; leftists who were not shot or imprisoned went into exile. The whole affair, which often divided families, left a legacy of bitterness that is only just beginning to heal.

1950 to the Present: Interesting Times

Recovery was slow, even if orchestrated by America, and the Greek diaspora that had begun in the early 1900s accelerated. In 1951, Greece and Turkey became full members of NATO, an uncomfortable arrangement from the start because of Cyprus. General Papágos of the American-backed Greek Rally Party won the elections of 1952, but died in 1955, and **Konstantínos Karamanlís** replaced him, inaugurating eight years of relative stability. Agriculture and tourism grew, although the opposition criticized Karamanlís' pro-Western policy and his inability to resolve the **Cyprus** issue. Because one-fifth of the Cypriots were Turks, Turkey refused to let Cyprus join Greece – independence or partitioning was as far as Ankara would go.

In the early 1960s Greece was rocked with record unemployment, strikes and powerful anti-American feelings. In 1963 came the assassination of left-wing Deputy Lambrákis (see Costa-Gávras' film *Z*) for which police officers were tried and convicted. Karamanlís lost the elections of 1965 to centre-left warhorse **George Papandréou**, who gave a portfolio to his son Andréas, an economics professor at Harvard, whose mildly inflationary policies horrified the right. At the same time, the conservative 23-year-old **Constantine II** inherited the throne. The combination did not bode well; a quarrel with the king over reforming the military led to Papandréou's resignation in 1966. Massive discontent forced Constantine to call for elections, but, before they could take place, a coup by an obscure band of officers on 21 April 1967 caught both right and left by surprise. The **'Colonels'**, most of whom were of peasant stock and resentful of Athenian politicians, established a dictatorship. Colonel **George Papadópoulos** made himself prime minister; King Constantine fled to Rome.

The goal of the Colonels was a 'moral cleansing of Orthodox Christian Greece'. This pandering to the Greek *ethnos* included a revival of the *Megáli Idéa*, never far from the surface anyway. Censorship undermined cultural life, and the secret police tortured dissidents – or their children. While the regime was condemned abroad, Greece's position in the volatile eastern Mediterranean and in NATO were reason enough for America to prop it up. The situation went from bad to worse, and on 17 November 1973 students of the Polytechnic School in Athens went on strike. Tanks were brought in and many were killed. Popular feeling rose to such a pitch that Papadópoulos was arrested, only to be replaced by his arrester, the head of the military police, **Dimítrios Ioannídes**. In an insane bid for popularity, Ioannídes tried to launch a coup in Cyprus. It was a fiasco; the Turkish army invaded, occupying 40 per cent of the island. The Greek military rebelled, the dictatorship resigned, and Karamanlís returned from exile to form a new government and order a ceasefire.

Karamanlís and his Conservative **Néa Demokratía** easily won the November 1974 elections. The monarchy did less well in a plebiscite, and Greece became a **republic**. That same year Karamanlís anchored Greece to the European Economic Community, of which Greece became a full member in 1981. Karamanlís brought stability, but neglected the economic and social reforms Greece needed. These, along with a desire for national integrity, were to be the ticket to populist Andréas Papandréou's victories, beginning in 1981. His Pan-Hellenic Socialist Movement or **PASOK** promised much, beginning with withdrawal from NATO and the EU and the removal of US air bases. A national reconciliation with the resistance fighters from the war topped the agenda; women were given more rights, and even excess accents were kicked out of the written language as a heady liberalization swept the land. PASOK triumphed again in the 1985 elections, in spite of Papandréou's failure to deliver Greece from the snares of NATO, the USA or the EU. Inflation soared, and Greece had to be bailed out by a huge EU loan accompanied by an unpopular belt-tightening programme. In the end, scandals brought Papandréou down: corruption in the Bank of Crete, and the old man's affair with, and subsequent marriage to, a young airline hostess.

In 1990, Néa Demokratía leader **Konstantínos Mitsotákis** took a slim majority in the elections, but by late 1992 he also had his share of political scandals, and in October 1993 Papandréou was re-elected. He kept Greece in his thrall as Yugoslavia disintegrated, pushing nationalist buttons over Macedonia and siding (verbally, mostly) with the Serbs. As he played the gadfly, the once-reviled 'capitalist club', the EU, poured funds into Greece, resulting in new roads, and many in PASOK formed a new ruling class of 'socialist capitalists' with fingers in every economic pie. An attempt by Papandréou's wife's faction to take power was thwarted by a revolt led by trade minister **Kósta Simítis**, a bland technocrat. Refreshingly non-dogmatic and low-key, Simítis steadied the ship of state, and improved relations with Turkey (especially after each country leapt to the other's aid after the earthquakes in 1999). Infrastructure improved dramatically in the run-up to the **2004 Olympics**, which may have put Greece into debt, but were a resounding success on every other level. Greeks, however, were ready for a change, and in March 2004, just before the Olympics, voted in New Democracy's **Kósta Karamanlís** (the former prime minister's nephew). He has consistently proved himself more popular and trusted than George Papandréou (son of former prime minister Andréas – Greek politics is a family affair), who took over Pasok in 2004.

Problems remain. In the 2007 elections, Karamanlís and New Democracy managed a paper-thin majority in spite of a bond scandal, an inability to push through reforms in education and privatization, and the fact that 2.5 per cent of the country was incinerated in horrendous **wildfires** just weeks before the election, leaving over 60 dead and devastating large swaths of the western Peloponnese. A hardcore right-wing party gained support for the first time, using the battle cry of 'Greece for Greeks', and a return to Greek Orthodox values. The left gained too, leading one to suspect that the voting was more a protest against the two leading parties who have been labelled by one disgusted journalist as the 'twin towers'. Old-style polemics persist; Greeks have always liked to argue politics, and the press and television promote daily acrimonious debates with little substance. In spite of that, an increasingly sophisticated and aware population seems to want more matter and less rhetoric. There are voices crying out for improvement in the ecology – or at least a separation of the ministry of Public Works and Environment, which incredibly are one and the same at the time of writing. A plan backed by Greenpeace would make the Gulf of Corinth one huge marine park. There is an increased interest in integrating Greece's influx of foreign workers and asylum-seekers and an awareness, especially among the well-educated young, that Greece is not yet living up to its potential, that it should be looking forward.

Despite its famous attractions and natural beauty, tourism still takes second place to agriculture in the Peloponnese; wine in particular is now taken more seriously than ever. Emigration has slowed, although many mountain villages only have a few old-timers left to keep them from turning into ghost towns; after the 2007 fires, some may never return. The roads are improving yearly, and the beautiful Río suspension bridge over the Gulf of Corinth opened in 2004; at the time of writing the whole rail system is being overhauled. Yet the cosmopolitanism that now reigns on many Greek islands is far from the Peloponnese; you can still drive for miles in the mountains and not pass a single car.

Art and Architecture

03

Like many peoples, the ancient Greeks were inveterate storytellers, but with a twist: their focus was not so much on what happened but on how and why it happened, and here they founded one of the tenets of Western art. They were also our first over-achievers, fired with a 'divine discontent' and lust for fame that saw city-states jockeying to build the biggest temples, and votaries trying to outshine their peers with showy dedications. Architects, sculptors, painters and potters constantly innovated as they strove for an ideal that became the 'classic' standard by which other artists have since measured themselves; they were the first to become celebrities, the first to sign their work, and the first (in one case) to be worshipped as heroes.

5000–2000 BC: Neolithic and Early Helladic

Art in Greece begins in the Neolithic era, with simple paintings on the Diroú caves in the Máni and the lumpy little 'Venus' fertility figures common throughout Europe. The early Bronze Age, or Helladic period, began *c.* 3200 BC, and left tantalizing evidence of a sophisticated society in the two-storey **House of Tiles** at Lérna in Argolís (*c.* 2500–2200 BC) and in the pretty, interlaced seal impressions found there, now in the museum in Argos. Another Early Helladic palace, an enormous round one that once had a tile roof as well, was discovered at Tiryns. The similarity of Lérna and Tiryns to other sites around the Aegean suggests the rise of an indigenous civilization, identified with Herodotus' Pelasgians for lack of a better name. Two treasures hint at the luxury of this proto-palatial culture: gold jewellery discovered at Thyreatis (now in Berlin) and a golden sauceboat found 'somewhere' in Arcadía, and now in the Louvre.

2000–1600 BC: Middle Helladic

The Middle Helladic was coeval with the Middle Kingdom of Egypt and Stonehenge, but in the Aegean all the action was happening on Crete. The big island, unhampered by the Greek-speaking invaders, carried on evolving the brilliant civilization that Sir Arthur Evans named Minoan. Great palace complexes such as Knossos fostered the arts: frescoes, pottery, stone vases, jewellery, seals, bronze sculpture, ivories and more, all marked by love of nature, *joie de vivre* and a flowing line; the greatest Minoan works show an astonishing technical virtuosity. On the mainland, the Greek-speakers introduced their modest but well-crafted **Minyan ware**, first discovered by Schliemann at Orchomenos in Boeotía, the seat of the legendary King Minyas. Wheel-made pottery appears at the same time as in Troy, in the same style, leading to the intriguing possibility that the Greeks were really Trojans. Or vice versa.

1600–1100 BC: Late Helladic (Mycenaean)

In the late Bronze Age (*c.* 1600 BC), the Greek-speakers we call the Mycenaeans came into contact with the Minoans, and within 50 years Minoan art and culture underwent a sea change. Most of the earliest finds were simply imported. But as time went on, Cretan artists made goods to suit Mycenaean tastes, which leant towards the monumental and preferred simplified versions of their more exuberant motifs; scenes of hunting and war, almost unknown in Crete, were now popular. As the Mycenaean empire expanded and trade increased (they imported raw materials, mostly metals, and exported finished goods such as pottery, jewellery, aromatic oils and textiles), their distinct, remarkably homogenous style spread as far away as Italy and Egypt.

Palaces went up at Mycenae, Tiryns, Pýlos and Sparta in the Peloponnese, while traces of others have been found on the Acropolis in Athens. Although inspired by the Cretan labyrinths, the Mycenaeans built according to a more regular design that archaeologists call a ***megaron*** unit: this consisted of an ornamental gateway, a courtyard with an entrance porch or *propylon*, and a vestibule giving on to a large hall with a throne and circular hearth. The three Peloponnesian palaces (Pýlos is the best preserved) each had two of these *megaron* units, each supplied with a wine store. Off the *megarons*, two-storey residential quarters were built of wood and stone, supported by wooden columns, while beyond these were palace workshops. Exterior walls were dressed limestone; interior walls were plastered and the important ones painted with **frescoes**: battle and hunting scenes and processions, in which women, perhaps princesses or priestesses, have elaborate hair, bare breasts and flounced skirts. Floors were painted with gypsum tiles. Dressed stone (*ashlar*) was reserved for impressive gateways, and for the Mycenaeans' most spectacular architectural achievement: their corbelled ***tholos* tombs**, first built in Pýlos in 1550 BC, and reaching an apogee in the Treasury of Atreus in Mycenae. Most of the fabulous **gold treasure** discovered in Grave Circles A and B (1600–1550 BC) was made or inspired by Crete, although the method of burial was distinctly Mycenaean and the famous masks are very different from Minoan portraits. Native Mycenaean works in the Grave Circles show a vigorous, more barbaric technique, apparent in the energetic if awkward reliefs on the *stelae* that marked the tombs.

Some time around 1450 BC, the Mycenaeans of the mainland developed their own **Palace Style** of pottery. Stirrup-jars, with curious 'dummy spouts' in the centre, were the favourite storage jar, while squat, flat jars known as *alabastrons* (because they were first made of alabaster) were probably used to store essential oils and unguents. Another Peloponnesian creation is the 'Ephyrean goblet' (Ephyre was an old name for Corinth), where a single motif was placed in the centre of the goblet to striking effect. Mycenaean jewellers mass-produced gold-relief beads, and may have invented enamelling (fusing molten coloured glass to gold). They also adopted Minoan miniature techniques for their seals and gold signet rings, many of which are exquisite.

Towards the end of the period, potters in Mycenae experimented with pictorial scenes fumblingly copied from the palace frescoes, mostly showing chariots and warriors and mostly exported to Cyprus, although you can see a good example from 1200 BC in the Corinth museum. Others show symmetrical heraldic animals, perhaps derived from tapestry. A third type from Argolís is the **Close Style**, decorated with intricate bands and patterns incorporating birds. The same potters manufactured 'Mycenaean Dollies': highly stylized, minimalist **terracotta figurines**; with their arms folded over their breast, or held upright like a Ψ (psi), they look more like bud vases. The Naúplio museum has an exceptional group of 30-inch 'dollies', made on a wheel.

Deities in other materials, especially ivory, were more carefully made, although the quality points to Cretan manufacture, as in the case of the two ivory goddesses and the divine child (14th–13th century BC) found in the shrine next to Mycenae's palace. Another speciality, the gold, silver, copper and black niello-inlay work on the ornamental daggers found in Mycenae's graves, proves that Homer's description of Agamemnon's elaborate inlaid cuirass and Achilles' shield wasn't all fantasy.

1100–770 BC: The Dark Ages (Geometric Period)

In spite of their huge walls, the Mycenaean citadels (all except Athens) began to fall around 1200 BC. Communications broke down, and with them the stylistic unity of Mycenaean art. Although traditional pottery forms and motifs were reused, their meaning seems confused. Potters who attempted decoration were content with simple bands: this **'Granary Style'** would be the mainstay for a century or so.

The Classical Greeks knew this shadowy period as the less-heroic Iron Age, but in many ways this was the 'real' period of Homer; his description of the making of Achilles' bronze shield actually describes an iron-making process, and it was only after 1100 BC that cremation, Homeric-style, became common. Outside of Athens, at least one Mycenaean population survived the 'catastrophe' at Lefkandí, on Évia, where a royal couple were given a heroic burial in a shrine anticipating the Greek peripteral temple (1000–950 BC). Tripods found in a 'chieftain's house' at Nikchória in Messenía suggest that a similar situation may have existed there.

Although 'sub-Mycenaeans' still rattled about in the echoing halls of Mycenae and Tiryns, the Iron Age seems to have been a time of large-scale migrations, when it was every man for himself. There were no new communal buildings, no multiple graves, no writing, almost no contact with the outside world. Even communications with the gods dropped off; the dolly goddesses are forgotten, and until the late 10th century the only offerings at Olympia, Tegea and other Dark Age shrines were small clay animals. It seems the wheel was forgotten also. But when potters in Athens remembered (in the Proto-Geometric era, 1050 BC), their new wheels were faster than ever, their kilns hotter, their decoration completely abstract. One of their most successful designs was the typical Greek **running meander**. The best Geometric vases are meticulous – the invention of a compass with multiple brush-ends enabled potters to draw precise concentric circles that accentuate the forms of the vessels, their lustrous sheen glowing like metal. Late in the period (800–700 BC) figurative designs began; horses, fish and birds appeared, with a few lone humans. In Athens, vases were used as grave markers, with holes in the bottom for libations. On these, communal scenes appear, of stick figures wailing at funerals, warriors and hunters.

770–500 BC: Archaic

The peculiar Geometric interlude of self-effacement ended as abruptly as it had begun, with a reawakened interest in human figures and their doings – an interest that coincided with the first Olympiad and the adaptation of the Phoenician alphabet by the Greeks, both in the 770s BC. Mycenaean Linear B had been used by bureaucrats to record offerings and palace stores, but some of the oldest inscriptions in Greek show the stirrings of a new spirit: instead of lists there are dedications, curses, witticisms about wine and sly comments by men on male romantic interests.

The meaning of art itself changed as the Greeks redefined themselves and their *polis*. A 'citadel' in Homer (8th century BC), the word *polis* evolved in Archaic times into a city-state not unlike the medieval *comuni* of Italy. The *polis* superseded old attachments to family and tribe with communal sanctuaries, where local guardian deities were worshipped as part of a civic mythology. Mycenaean tombs were interpreted as the tombs of a *polis*'s heroes and demi-gods, and became legitimate claims in boundary disputes. Once defined on earth and in heaven, a *polis* could clone itself – and the 8th century BC was the great age of Greek colonies, across the Mediterranean and Black Sea. Or perhaps it was the pressure to colonize that focused attention on defining just what a *polis* was. Art and architecture were fundamental in expressing this new civic spirit.

One theory holds that it was the hero-worship at Mycenaean tombs that led to the rediscovery of figurative art, thanks to the Mycenaean grave goods. Another theory puts it down to renewed trading contacts, especially with the Hittites and Assyrians. Both may have inspired Corinth's beautiful polychrome **Proto-Corinthian ware** (*c.* 725–650 BC) with its orientalizing friezes and Mycenaean heraldic motifs of two animals facing one another. Designed for export, some of the finest Proto-Corinthian ware was found in Etruscan tombs, including the masterful Chigi Vase in Rome's Villa Giulia museum. The scene painted on it illustrates the new hoplite battle formation that replaced the Homeric military élite and cavalry (*see* p.21).

Corinth, at the vanguard of the age, invented **black figure painting** in *c.* 700, and produced quality work until Athens relegated her potters to provincialism. Athens had the advantage of the finest clay in Greece. Iron ore was added to create its characteristic red colour, and its painters specialized from the start in narrative scenes – the Proto-Attic amphora at Eleusis showing Odysseus blinding Polyphemos (650 BC) is one of their first masterpieces. The invention of **red figure painting** by Athenian potters in *c.* 530 BC (backgrounds were painted black, leaving inverted silhouettes, to which details were added with a fine brush) allowed painters to achieve a naturalism that no others could match; their vases were in demand across the ancient world.

The first Archaic essays into **sculpture** (*c.* 700–620 BC) are small, austere, flat figures with triangular heads, called **Daedelic** after their legendary Cretan creator. When the withdrawal of the Assyrians from Egypt in 672 BC reopened the country to Greek merchants, the monumental statues the Greeks saw there inspired their own version, the well-known ***kouros*** (young man). Like Egyptian models, the *kouros* has a stiff, formal posture, one foot placed before the other, arms down by the sides. The female version, the ***kore*** (maiden), clothed in drapery, evokes feminine grace and modesty, right arm extended to hold an offering.

Yet from the start the Greek approach was different. While Egyptians represented specific individuals or gods, decently clad, the naked *kouros* exists in that special Greek penumbra between the mortal and divine, an ideal rather than an individual, wearing an easy, confident 'Archaic smile' as if in on a secret joke. Nor did Greek sculptors feel compelled to repeat the same conventions over and over, but each added variations, striving better to represent nature. Towards the end of the Archaic period the Greeks learned the technique of hollow bronze casting; the Piraeus museum has the earliest examples, found, like most surviving Greek bronzes, in shipwrecks.

Most of the *kore* and *kouros* statues were dedicated at **sanctuaries**. In the beginning these were simply a sacred precinct (***temenos***) around an altar, where sacrifices were made. With the revival of sculpture, the need arose for a shelter to protect the cult statue. Clay models show that the earliest temples were simple houses with columned fronts. The first peristyle temples (with columns on all sides) were of wood. Corinth developed the **Doric style** and invented the 'classic' temple, with fluted stone columns, gable front and *metopes* (frieze panels); the oldest one still standing is, fittingly, in Corinth, the Temple of Apollo (550 BC). Its stout bunched columns are in marked contrast to the more graceful, airier works of the following century. But in essence the architecture of the Archaic age – buildings framed with columns and porches, so perfect for the climate – would remain the same throughout antiquity.

Adorning the temples were reliefs of battles or scenes from mythology. The Greek desire to narrate was a powerful impetus to realism, and some of the greatest Archaic works are temple tympanums and *metopes*, among them the three-headed Typhon in the Acropolis museum. Some bear traces of paint. The Greeks adored colour, and all that white marble of their temples and sculpture that we find so appealing would look bare to their makers.

Funeral *stelae*, first seen in Mycenae, returned to fashion at the end of the 7th century, often topped with concave finials evoking flowers on a grave. Sphinxes, as demon guardians of the dead, became the rage in the 6th century; tombs in Attica became so big and elaborate that Solon subjected them to sumptuary laws (laws controlling expenditure). These had the effect of making artistic qualities (rather than size) the focus, leading to the exquisite funerary *stelae* of the Classical era.

500–323 BC: Classical

The Greek fascination with maths, ideal proportions and pattern reached its apogee in the 5th century BC. For the first few decades the introspective **'Severe' Classical style** prevailed. Statues become much more naturalistic, breaking out of their stiff *kouros* poses, although their smiles are replaced by brooding glances. After the defeat of the Persians in 480 BC, however, confidence ran high. The sheer scale of the Temple of Zeus at Olympia proclaim the pride of the period. Iktinos perfected the Doric temple (and, many would say, all architecture) in his Parthenon, through the use of refinements such as *entasis* (*see* p.92). The Parthenon set the fashion for combining strong Doric elements with the more elegant Ionic order: the Temple of Apollo Epikourios at Bassae, also by Iktinos, is full of innovations, including the first known Corinthian column, its capital modelled on the curving volutes of the acanthus. Innovations continued during and after the Peloponnesian War, with the Erechtheion on Athens and its famous *caryatid* porch, and the beautiful, mysterious *tholos* building at Epidauros.

Sculptors vied to make figures more lifelike, on the verge of action. Yet, for all the new naturalism, their work retained the Archaic ideal, concentrating on archetypes. One of the greatest 5th-century sculptors, **Polyclitus of Argos**, was celebrated for his statues of athletes and for his treatise, the *Canon*, that mathematically defined the proportions of the body that constituted beauty, each in elegant relationship to another. Extremes, personality and emotion had no place here; the beautiful faces gaze off into a better world with calm Classical detachment. Bronze allowed sculptors greater freedom in their poses, and became the favoured medium for life-sized figures. Unfortunately it was also the favourite medium for melting by Christians or Turks, although a handful of superb exceptions escaped: the *Zeus/Poseidon* in the Archaeological Museum in Athens (and the *Charioteer* of Delphi, the horses of St Mark's in Venice and the *Riace Warriors*, in Calabria). Free-standing marble statues, on the other hand, are only known through Roman-era copies, although we still have a fair amount of Classical architectural sculpture. Panhellenic themes were popular: the Labours of Heracles and the battles of Centaurs or Amazons (i.e. the 'barbarian' Persians) against the Lapiths or men (representing the 'civilized' Greeks). **Phidias**, the first real celebrity artist, was responsible for the masterpiece of the genre, the Parthenon frieze, where the theme, the great Panathenaic procession, is a unique celebration of Athens in its heyday.

Greek cities also followed patterns. The geography is such that nearly all grew up by a hill, the **acropolis**, often with fortifications and the city's oldest shrines. Below, the centre of the city was the ***agora***, translated as 'marketplace', although it was much more: both the heart of civic life and a sacred *temenos*, marked by boundary stones, forbidden to the criminal and unclean. In the *agora* you'd find the Council House (*bouleuterion*), the presidential committee chamber (*prytaneion*), fountain house, and shrines, temples, altars and statues dedicated to civic gods or heroes. Along the sides, *stoas* housed shops and banks, their colonnades offering shelter from the sun and rain; one, the Stoa of Attalus in Athens, has been reconstructed. Here Greeks could indulge in their favourite pastime – talking. Planning became a science in the mid-5th century with the idealistic geometrician **Hippodamos of Miletus**, who laid out neat grids of streets to encourage *isonomia*, or social equality, as in the plan of Piraeus. In the early 4th century BC, Athens rebuilt its theatre in stone, and soon every city had one, many scooped into the convenient side of the acropolis hill; Epidauros has the most perfect remaining one (380 BC). Most cities had outer defensive walls, with the great exception of Sparta, which relied on its military prowess. Their helots or serfs, when they were liberated, were not about to rely on any such thing, and built the still remarkable walls at Messene (begun in 370 BC). Within the walls would be a quarter devoted to athletics and the body beautiful, with a gymnasium ('place where one goes naked') attached to various schools for young men, near to the stadium.

Vitruvius wrote that the Greeks discovered **perspective** in the 5th century, and the story goes that one painter, Zeuxis, even deceived the birds, who tried to pluck grapes from his picture. **Attic vases**, with their imaginative compositions, pure line, foreshortening and realism, reached their peak in the early 5th century, before the large-scale public works under Pericles lured artists away to bigger projects.

323–30 BC: Hellenistic

In the 4th century BC, after Philip II of Macedon put paid to the Greek city-state experiment, a quiet revolt against Polyclitus' *Canon* took place. Poses and expressions become more relaxed, and there was an increase in individual 'types', although compared to the warts-and-all Roman busts that followed they are still idealized. Alexander the Great was the first to use images of himself as propaganda. His favourite sculptor was **Lysippos of Sikyon**, who used less perfect but more lifelike proportions (with a notably smaller head) and statues meant to be seen in the round; together with his brother Lysistratos he invented the life mask and lost-wax method of casting. This was also the time of **Praxiteles of Athens**, who added charm and a sensuous grace to figures in *contrapposto* poses (with the weight resting on one leg); his only surviving work, the *Hermes* at Olympia, shows his exquisite modelling that conjures flesh from marble. Praxiteles carved the first life-sized female nude, of *Aphrodite*, which quickly became a tourist attraction in Knidos. Praxiteles may have been sculpting gods, but with him art had become pure art.

By the time Alexander died in 323 BC, the problems of pose, anatomy, proportions and drapery had been resolved. Now artists could only exaggerate; a Baroque sensationalism and complexity, all windswept drapery, violence and passion, became so prominent in works such as the bronze *Artemísseon Jockey* in Athens, the Louvre's *Winged Victory of Samothrace* and the Vatican's writhing *Laocoön* that reaction soon set in. The era saw the first wave of copies of older works, and others sculpted in Archaic or Classical styles, as in Damophon's statues at Lykósoura (now in Athens).

30 BC–AD 330: Roman

The *pax romana* not only ended the rivalries between the Greeks but pretty much dried up their inspiration as well, although a stream of workmanlike sculptors, architects and other talents found a ready employment in the Roman Empire, cranking out copies of earlier masterpieces. Romans bigwigs, notably the hellenophile emperor Hadrian and his wealthy friend Herodes Atticus, liked to show their appreciation for Greek culture with public buildings, especially in Athens and Olympia; the ruins of ancient Corinth are essentially Roman as well.

AD 330–1452: Byzantine

The founding of **Constantinople** at Byzantium in 330 coincided with the official recognition of Christianity. The first churches of the new faith were modelled on the three-aisle Roman basilica. The finest were decorated with mosaics – on the floors and, in a new departure, on the walls as well. In the 6th century, under the great Justinian, architects striving for a more Christian architecture placed a dome over a cruciform plan. Earthquakes and barbarian invasions over the next few centuries destroyed most of these early attempts; by the time the Greeks were ready to build again, the **Greek cross plan**, with a dome over the crossing supported on squinches or pendentives, had been mastered.

The **Middle Byzantine** or **Macedonian Age** (named after the Macedonian emperors, 844–1025), that followed the defeat of the Iconoclasts, brought a cultural revival and a vast building programme of new monasteries. Painted or mosaic decoration was often in the 'hierarchical' formulae that symbolically reproduced the universe; it was especially popular in *katholikóns* or monastery churches. Christ

Pantocrator ('all-governing') or the Christ of the Ascension reigns in the dome of heaven, surrounded by angels, while, just below, the Virgin and John the Baptist intercede for humanity. The Virgin and Child occupy the central apse. The surrounding vaults and upper registers show the *Dodekaorton*, the 'Twelve Feasts' of the Church, while in the lower, terrestrial zone are saints, prophets and martyrs (whose gory deaths are also a favourite subject in the narthex).

Yet even in the bloodiest Byzantine martyrdoms there is a certain trance-like detachment. Its saints reside on a purely spiritual plane; their most striking feature on church walls and icons is most often their intense, staring eyes. They never play on the heartstrings or ask the viewer to relive the pain of the Passion or coo over a baby Jesus; the Virgin (the *Panagía*, or 'all-holy'), cocooned in black like an Orthodox nun, has none of the charms of a Renaissance Madonna. 'The artistic perfection of an icon,' as Timothy Ware wrote, 'was not only a reflection of the celestial glory – it was a concrete example of matter restored to its original harmony and beauty serving as a vehicle of the spirit.' An intention wholly different from that of the ancient Greeks, in fact, who were infatuated with human beauty and intellect and made divinity in their own image. The calm Classical gaze of their gods was a reflection of earthly mathematical perfection; the Byzantine stare belongs to the visionary, abstract and ascetic. Curiously, this stare annoyed the Turks no end – in many churches you'll find frescoes more or less intact except for the eyes, gouged out by their knives. Others fell victim to superstitious peasants, who believed a saint's 'eyes', ground up, were good medicine for their own eye diseases.

Byzantine art under the **Comnene emperors** (12th–14th centuries) marked a renewed interest in antique models: the stiff, hieratic figures are given more naturalistic proportions in graceful, rhythmic compositions. Occasionally the emperors sent imperial mosaicists to decorate their foundations – leaving exquisite examples at Dáphni near Athens. The **Crusaders** for their part left castles as souvenirs of their stay, often built to keep their Greek subjects in line: Chlemoútsi, Platamónas, the Acrocorinth and Karítena (where they also left a fine bridge) are among the most impressive. The **Venetians**, who lasted longer, built impressive citadels at Naúplio, Pýlos, Methóni and Koróni.

The **Late Byzantine** period began in 1261, with the recovery of Constantinople by the Paleológos emperors. The humanist and naturalistic influences of the next century combined to produce, apparently independently, the Byzantine equivalent of the *trecento* art of Siena, with a greater attention to colour, perspective, landscape and architecture. At Mystrá, the lyrical frescoes in the churches are the great poignant might-have-been of Byzantine art. After the Turkish conquest the best painters (labelled 'post-Byzantine' in the museums, a period that extends to the present day) took refuge in Venetian-ruled Crete or the Ionian islands, or on Mount Áthos.

1460–1830: Turkish Greece (the Turkokratía)

The long centuries of Turkish rule left relatively few monuments in Greece. Much that the Turks themselves built was destroyed in the bitter War of Independence, or in its aftermath, or by earthquakes. Athens has a few mosques, hammams and public buildings, but the Peloponnese has next to nothing except for castles and forts. The Greeks of the Turkokratía are perhaps best represented by their defiant monasteries, often built on nearly inaccessible cliffs and ravines. The fiercely independent Maniátes built stone tower houses that remain one of the most startling sights in Greece. Ports with their own fleets, such as Hýdra and Spétses, have impressive captains' mansions.

Independence to Modern Times: 1830 to the Present

After the War of Independence, Greek cities were rebuilt with a modest neoclassical flair that seemed especially suitable. Athens, as the new capital, has the most lavish examples, while Naúplio basks in atmosphere and faded grandeur. One name to remember is **Ernst Ziller** (1837–1923), a German architect and friend of the archaeologist Schliemann (*see* 'Mycenae', p.265), who built some of the finest neoclassical buildings and mansions in Greece, including Schliemann's own villa in Athens (now the Numismatic Museum). Until the 20th century, however, traditional vernacular styles prevailed in most places. Earthquakes, neglect, the need to provide for a million refugees overnight after the Asia Minor fiasco in 1922 and the brutality of the Occupation and Civil War have all taken their toll, as has the rash of ugly apartments and hotels that mushroomed up in the 1960–70s to cash in on the honeypot of tourism. Prosperity in recent years, however, has brought an increased interest in traditional architecture: programmes are now in place to preserve the most beautiful villages, and new laws in many areas insist that new building conform to local styles. Yet there are spanking new things as well, beginning with the beautiful **Río-Andírio suspension bridge** over the Gulf of Corinth, completed in 2004 and the **New Acropolis Museum**, which, now completed, has had rave reviews after years of delays and controversy.

While modern Greeks have made names for themselves in **literature** and **poetry** (Cavafy, Kazantzákis, Rítsos, and the Nobel Prize winners Seféris and Elýtis) and in **music** and **film** (Maria Callas, Dimitris Mitropoulos, Mikís Theodorákis, Melína Mercouri, Elia Kazan, Costa-Gávras, Michelis Cacoyannis, Theodore Angelopoulos among others), most people would have a hard time naming a modern Greek artist or sculptor. To get acquainted with them, visit Athens' National and Municipal Galleries, and the Benáki Museum of Modern Art.

Topics

04

Losing their Marbles

Bonaparte has not got such a thing from all his thefts in Italy.

Lord Elgin, writing in 1801 from Constantinople

It is Greece's special sorrow that her War of Independence didn't begin two decades earlier, before the fad for antiquities swept Western Europe – a fad that became an international art race when the triumphant Napoleon pillaged Italy and Egypt to fill his newly created Louvre museum. But Thomas Bruce, the seventh Lord Elgin, ambassador to the Sublime Porte, trumped Boney to something even the Romans never thought of taking home: the sculptures of the world's most famous building. Admittedly Morosini was the first to try, in 1687 – after he bombed the then-intact temple (even though he knew the Turks were using it as a powder store), he added insult to injury by removing the great pediment showing the contest between Athena and Poseidon as a prize to take home to Venice. The ropes broke as it was lowered, and the statues shattered into bits.

Elgin got his turn in 1801 when the Turkish military governor in Athens refused to let his artist, Lusieri, erect scaffolding to sketch the Parthenon frieze. Elgin went to the Sultan to get a *firman*, or authority, and the Sultan, pleased that the British had just rid Egypt of the French, readily provided one, not only allowing Elgin's agents into the 'temple of idols' but to 'take away any sculptures or inscriptions which do not interfere with the works or walls of the Citadel.' Elgin interpreted this as a *carte blanche*, and sent Lusieri a long list of 'samples' to ship to London, all in the name of improving British arts by offering students back home a first-hand look at the greatest sculpture ever made. Besides, the Greeks 'have looked upon the superb works of Pheidias with ingratitude and indifference. They do not deserve them!' Considerable damage occurred to the marbles and to the temple's structure during the removal; some panels were even sawn in two. In the meantime Naploeon's agents were sniffing around Athens for any leftovers they could lay hands on. Byron was there when the last of the 120 crates were being loaded:

At this moment [3 Jan 1810], besides what has already been deposited in London, an Hydriot vessel is now in Piraeus to receive any portable relic. Thus as I heard a young Greek observe in common with many of his countrymen – for lost as they are, they yet feel on this occasion – thus may Lord Elgin boast of having ruined Athens. An Italian painter of the first eminence, named Lusieri, is the agent of devastation. Between this artist and the French Consul Fauvel, who wishes to rescue the remains for his own government, there is now a violent dispute concerning a car employed in their conveyance, the wheel of which – I wish they were both broken upon it – has been locked up by the Consul, and Lusieri has laid his complaint before the Waywode. Lord Elgin has been extremely happy in his choice of Lusieri. His works, as far as they go, are most beautiful. But when they carry away three or four shiploads of the most valuable and massy relics that time and barbarism have left to the most injured and most celebrated of cities; when they destroy, in vain attempt to tear down, those works which have been the admiration of ages, I know of no motive which can excuse, no name which can designate, the perpetrators of this dastardly devastation. The most unblushing impudence could hardly go further than to affix the name of its plunderer to the walls of the Acropolis; while the wanton and useless defacement of the whole range of basso-rilievos, in one compartment of the temple, will never permit that name to be pronounced by an observer without execration.

Another eye-witness, Edward Clark, wrote in his *Travel to European Countries* (1811):

The lowering of the sculptures has frustrated Pheidias' intentions. Also, the shape of the Temple suffered a damage greater than the one suffered by Morosini's artillery. How could such an iniquity be committed by a nation that wants to boast of its discretional skill in arts? And they dare tell us, in a serious mien, that the damage was done in order to rescue the sculptures from ruin...

Just as the *Hydra* sailed off to Britain with its cargo of marbles, another vessel arrived in Athens, carrying architect Charles Robert Cockerell, who, inspired by Elgin, was on his way to Aegina to strip the frieze off the Temple of Aphaia (which went to Munich instead). Even so, Cockerell managed to bag the marbles from the Temple of Apollo at Bassae; by then, Greek outrage at the plundering permitted by bribe-greedy Turkish officialdom had reached such a pitch that an armed band tried to hijack Cockerell's caravan, only to be thwarted by a forewarned Turkish army.

Nemesis, however, is a Greek goddess, and she saw to it that Elgin got no joy from his deed. One of his ships sank near Kýthera (although the marbles were expensively rescued by divers over the next two years). He faced constant ridicule from the British public, many of whom agreed with Byron on the issue; syphilis caused his nose to fall off, and he was divorced from his bubbly young countess. On his way home to Britain he was taken prisoner in France for three years, on Napoleon's orders. His marble-moving expenses totalled £63,000 (£10 million today), a quarter of which was bribes to Turkish officials (this was at a time when the contents of the *entire* British Museum were valued at £3,000), but he managed to get only £35,000 from Parliament when it finally agreed to the purchase, in spite of members who condemned him as a dishonest looter, and he died in poverty. The current Lord Elgin wishes his ancestor had never set eyes on 'the bloody stones'.

The issue of returning the Parthenon frieze comes up periodically, for instance in 1941, when several MPs proposed it as a reward for Greece's heroic resistance to the Nazis. Doubt, too, has been cast on old claims that Elgin 'saved' the fragile Pentelic marbles, by moving them into the London damp and smog (even Elgin noticed they were deteriorating, as he dickered with Parliament over the price). The current Greek campaign for the return of the marbles received a morale-boost in 1998, when William St Clair revealed in his *Lord Elgin and the Marbles* that the British Museum had 'skinned' away fine details and the patina of the marbles in 1937–8, when they used metal scrapers to whiten them. Polls say that a majority of the British public want to return the marbles, although that number doesn't include the director of the British Museum. The Greeks hope the truly beautiful viewing gallery on top of the New Acropolis Museum (*see* p.94) may change their minds.

A Greek Mythology Who's Who

Like all good polytheists, the Greeks filled their pantheon with a kaleidoscopic assortment of divinities. They may be more anthropomorphic than Egyptian or Indian gods but, having evolved over a thousand years, are nonetheless full of fathomless contradictions, subtleties and, above all, regional nuance. The Greeks had no 'Bible', no written book of dogma or ritual. About the only recognized higher authority was the Delphic oracle, which was famous for its ambiguities. The Olympians, the immortal dozen, became a recognized hierarchy by the Archaic period, mostly thanks to Homer and Hesiod, but even they were never cut and dried.

In reality, Greeks everywhere felt quite free to create their own peculiar perspective on their gods, and to hang on to any indigenous local ones they fancied as well. Naturally imaginative and idiosyncratic, they turned their stories of the gods into an art form as much as a religion. If one aspect of Zeus didn't appeal or fit the bill, he could be morphed by adding an epithet: Zeus of Oaths, Zeus the Saviour, Zeus of the Flies, *ad infinitum*. Different areas could claim the same divinity as their own home-grown god. If none suited, a god could be borrowed: even in ancient times, equating a minor local god or a foreign god with an Olympian or other deity was something of a parlour game, one that Plutarch and company especially enjoyed. Of course, the gods were conscripted to do duty on the political level, just as in Christianity. Every city-state had stories of the gods and goddesses fighting on their side, appearing on the ramparts, providing an idea, etc. Politicians have always had a nice appreciation of the usefulness of gods, especially in time of war.

And, like elderly aunts, the Greeks could never bear to throw anything out. Once a taboo, god or ritual became part of their religious furniture, it stuck around in one form or another, resulting in early chthonic deities rubbing shoulders with later, more rationalized versions of themselves. Local nymphs, naïads, river gods and dryads ran about; a whole host of early giants, heroes, half-animal deities such as centaurs, satyrs and snake men were constantly on the loose in the 'dream time' of the Greek collective religion. Over an incredible *one-third* of all days in the ancient Athenian calendar were important religious holidays just to accommodate the crowds. But we all have to start somewhere; the following is a short run-down of the big guns.

The one-time weather-god-turned-big-shot on Olympus was **Zeus** (or Dias, or Jupiter to the Romans), best known as a native of Crete. A version of the Indo-European sky god, he was lord of the thunderbolt, with a libido to match. Zeus was wedded to his sister **Hera** (Juno), the goddess of marriage, who had the handy knack of renewing her virginity annually in a river by her great temple on Sámos (it didn't improve their relationship). Although she began in Mycenaean times or earlier as a goddess of fertility, her special role in myth was as the wronged, jealous wife. Zeus had two brothers: **Poseidon** (Neptune), who ruled the sea, managed the rivers and caused earthquakes, and **Hades** (Pluto), god of the shadowy underworld and realm of the dead, who kept a low profile except when he went hunting for a wife and kidnapped Persephone, Demeter's daughter. **Demeter** (Ceres), goddess of corn and growing things, did not need to throw her weight around – when she was unhappy, nothing grew. She and her daughter were worshipped everywhere, especially in the Mysteries at Eleusis. **Aphrodite** (Venus), the goddess of love, is nearly as old as the earliest gods, and had a weird beginning. Born from the foam produced by the severed genitals of Uranos when his son Kronos castrated him, she was a force to be reckoned with: Corinth and Kýthera were her favourite abodes in Greece proper.

The second generation of Olympians were the offspring of Zeus. **Athena** (Minerva), the urbane virgin goddess of wisdom, handicrafts and ceramics, was born right out of the forehead of Zeus, his own ideal female; she was always associated with Athens in particular. **Ares** (Mars), a Thracian interloper, was the god of war. Oddly enough given Greek history, he was not a popular god, and often resembles a whining bully. **Hermes** (Mercury), born in the Peloponnese, was a one-man courier service, a go-between who watched over travellers and merchants and took everybody on their final journey to Hades. **Hephaestos** (Vulcan), son of Hera and crippled husband of Aphrodite, was ridiculed for his less than perfect body, but revered for his fire and forge which produced the weapons and baubles of the gods; Límnos was his special island. **Apollo**, patron of the Ionians, the god of light, music, reason, poetry and prophecy, was the *ne plus ultra* of a rationalized Greek god, but even he could lose his cool on occasion; his sacred places were his birthplace, Délos, and his oracle at Delphi. His twin **Artemis** (Diana), the tomboy, virgin moon goddess of the hunt, was a special favourite in the Peloponnese. The temperamental, cross-dressing **Dionysos** (Bacchus), god of wine, orgies and theatre, came from Phrygia and Thrace, but was popular everywhere.

And we forgot **Hestia** (Vesta), the virgin goddess of the hearth and Zeus' sister, and **Helios**, the sun god and patron of Rhodes – which makes 15 (so much for the magic number 12). Among the supporting cast, two in particular stand out: **Pan**, the Arcadian deity who gave his name to posterity in the word *panic*, and **Heracles** (Hercules), a god-hero in a class by himself, and a big favourite with the Dorians.

Poniría and the Island of Pelops

When asked by fellow Greeks from where they hail, Peloponnesians usually reply with a laconic *káto apt'avláki*, 'under the ditch'. Before visions of the Billy Goats Gruff take hold, know that the 'ditch' is the Peloponnesians' pet name for the Corinth Canal that separates them from other mainland Greeks. Although this land under the ditch was never a united political entity (except for a brief period under the Franks that hardly counts), and although it remains a patchwork quilt of regions and personalities, there is nonetheless one quality that clings to Pelops' island and separates its natives perceptually from their fellow Greeks. It is *Poniría* with a capital P.

Poniría translates rather badly into English as 'slyness', and may seem a strange quality to inspire pride. But it is an epithet that most Peloponnesians accept with a nod, at least when levelled at them by other Greeks, before they assign it in even greater quantity to some other place under the ditch: 'Yes, but they are even more so in Kalamáta', or Elís and so on. *Poniría* is the mental agility to assess any situation and somehow turn it to one's own advantage, especially in a way that makes boasting about it satisfying; the downside, of course, is forget everybody else ('*as tous allous*'), everybody else being people who are not family, close friends, or potentially useful people from politicians down to the lowliest bureaucrat. True, Greeks everywhere have admired and employed this 'trickster' quality, from Odysseus right up to Karagiózis, the clever underdog of the Greek shadow theatre, who always tries and often succeeds in getting the best of the Turks and his Greek neighbours, too. ***Ponirίa*** is not unique to the Peloponnese, but the Peloponnesians have always been considered to be the top of the line, the best of the best. Maybe that's because they have been at it longer than anyone else.

Consider the case of **Pelops**, the eponymous hero of the Peloponnese. Being chopped to bits, cooked and served in a stew to the gods might make anyone lean towards *ponirία*, of course, and that is exactly what Tantalos, his father, did to Pelops in one of the first empirical scientific experiments ever recorded. He wanted to see if the gods would notice. It turns out they did, all except for Demeter who, mourning the loss of her daughter Persephone at the time, absent-mindedly bit into his shoulder-blade. So when Pelops was reconstituted by the gods, he came sporting a nicely fashioned ivory chip on his shoulder. He settled in Elís and married Hippodamia, daughter of King Oenomaos, but only after using his supreme *ponirία*. In order to get the girl and win the kingdom, a suitor had to beat her father in a chariot race or die. Many had already tried and failed, but that was only because they hadn't thought of paying off the king's charioteer, Myrtos, to replace the lynchpins of Oenomaos' chariot with wax. Pelops did, got the girl, threw Myrtos into the sea to avoid paying him the promised bribe, and lived happily ever after, basking in universal admiration, honoured above all others at Olympia. Peloponnesian leaders in ancient times bent over backwards to link themselves to his family tree; and according to myth the true descendants of Pelops, the Pelopids, were born with the same chip on their shoulder.

Sisyphos (*see* p.144), the founder of Corinth, was so famous for *ponirία* that the ancient scuttlebutt claimed that he, and not the worthy Laertes, was the real father of Odysseus. *Ponirία* was actually seen as a desirable genetic trait, and it would have been a poor ancient Greek hero who did not employ it at every opportunity.

Almost two thousand years of history and the advent of Christianity have not altogether dimmed the lustre of *ponirία*. The long, galling centuries under the thumb of the Franks and Turks made *ponirία* a practical necessity for survival. Either of the great Peloponnesian heroes of the War of Independence, Theodore Kolokotrónis (*see* pp.344–5) or the cunning Petróbey (*see* p.402), could have written the book on it. It is also true that a disproportionate number of Greek politicians since independence have come from under the ditch, no doubt contributing to and perpetuating the legend. In recent Greek history, *ponirία* has been the necessary Peloponnesian political handicap (in a golfing sense) against the much wealthier regions of Attica and Northern Greece and the more socially unified islands.

And today? Now that life has settled down, democracy reigns, roads have opened up all the prefectures and Greece is a partner in the European union, surely *ponirία*, which after all is based on an 'us against them' premise, is dying out? Well...ask someone under the ditch!

Heracles and Sons

Grandson of Perseus, son of Zeus and Alcmene, Heracles was ancient Greece's most popular hero. Seven of his Twelve Labours occurred in the Peloponnese, and it had to be a very unimaginative Peloponnesian city-state that did not have at least one 'Heracles escapade' in its repertoire as time went on. Strong and resourceful, rarely modest and never faithful, this club-wielding superman appeared everywhere as a house guest from hell; he never stopped eating and drinking, and had trouble minding his manners. With the least provocation, he would go on a rampage and murder everyone, friend or foe. Then he would head to Delphi and demand to be absolved. Once, when the priestess refused, he stole her tripod, putting her temporarily out of business. On the other hand, he had his good points: he could bring your wife back from the dead, drain a lake or kill a monster, all before lunch.

His many moments of madness were blamed on Hera, who invented the role of the implacably evil stepmother. She even delayed his birth, by crossing her own legs so that Heracles' mother could not give birth at her proper time, meaning his cousin Eurystheus was born first and became Perseus' heir at Mycenae. Heracles killed snakes as a baby, went on to kill his flute master, and more. In one famous fit of madness he killed his own children, and to expiate the crime was sentenced by the priestess at Delphi to perform any twelve labours that Eurystheus, a coward and a bully, cared to set. She also changed his name from Alcides to Heracles or 'Glory of Hera', proving that she had a nice sense of humour.

Like all heroes, Heracles began as a cyclical nature god. In early depictions, his club bloomed; it was a tree branch. He even did a stint as a herm. The golden bowl he rode in was the sun. The fact that his labours were twelve reflected the twelve months of the year, and perhaps even the signs of the Zodiac – Leo is the Nemean lion, Cancer the crab that helped the Hydra, and so on. The Peloponnesian Labours were numbers one to six and the twelfth, if listed in their most time-honoured order:

1. *The killing of the Nemean lion*
2. *The killing of the Lernian Hydra*
3. *The capture of the Arcadian stag*
4. *The killing of the Erymanthian boar*
5. *The cleaning of the stables of Augeas*
6. *The killing of the Stymphalian birds*
7. *The capture of the Cretan bull*
8. *The capture of the mares of Diomedes*
9. *The theft of the Amazon Queen's girdle*
10. *The capture of the cattle of Geryones*
11. *The fetching of the golden apples of the Hesperides*
12. *Bringing Cerberus up from the Underworld*

By the Classical period, hundreds of other deeds had been added to 'Heracles lore'. He even did a turn in drag as the house servant of Queen Omphale, because he had murdered his friend Iphitos. (The queen's name, Belly Button, had Freud riveted.)

After innumerable adventures he was returning home with his new mistress Iole when he died in agony, seared by the Hydra's poison that his wife Deianira had smeared on his shirt. Deianira, poor thing, was under the mistaken impression that it was a love potion. He died a horrible death, railing against his wife, who committed suicide in despair. His reward, for all of this murder and mayhem? Instant apotheosis – and here his story departs from that of all other heroes worshipped by the Greeks. His was the only case of a human, or half-human, beating the system and becoming a god on Olympus, a hero-*theos* as Pindar called him. If Pindar were alive today, he might have made further comparisons with the careers of Jesus Christ, James Bond, the Godfather and Attila the Hun.

What it all means has kept a lot of great minds busy. Certainly Heracles reflected the ancient Greek male's distrust of women, his lust for glory, and, at least from a modern perspective, a strange kind of defeatism. His death was not really a promise of salvation for anyone else, but simply the ultimate superhero's perk that everyone could marvel at but never achieve. Some have argued, even in ancient times, that Heracles was a civilizing influence (they must have been reading the abridged version of his life!). But by and large the ancients loved him, forgave his rampages, gloried in his strength, appetites and virility, and empathized with his harsh, penalty-ridden life. In particular, he was the Dorian *beau idéal*, so much so that they appropriated his story and claimed to be his descendants, the Heracleidae. Of course, his rough and tough approach to problem-solving was right up their alley, but claiming him as an ancestor had political advantages, too.

The story goes that after the apotheosis of Heracles, Eurystheus banished his mother Alcmene and his sons from the Peloponnese, fearing they would one day depose him and claim Mycenae. Only the Athenians under Theseus dared to defy Eurystheus and give Alcmene shelter; Eurystheus marched against Athens, and was defeated and killed. But when the Heracleidae invaded the Peloponnese, which they regarded as their rightful inheritance, a great plague broke out. The Delphic oracle warned that they should wait for 'the third crop' before invading. Three years later they duly marched in, and their leader, Hyllus, fought a pitched battle with the King of Tegea for the prize. When Hyllus was killed, the Heracleidae blamed Apollo, but the god claimed they had misinterpreted the meaning of the oracle, which meant the third crop of men.

The conquest of the Peloponnese by the Heracleidae in the fourth generation after Heracles was billed by the Dorians as a homecoming. Their leaders divided the land by lot: twins Procles and Eurysthenes got Sparta (symbolized by a water snake), Kresphontes got Messene (a fox), and Temeus got Argos (a toad). By the 8th century, these three states had irrevocably fallen out with one another. The Dorian kingship in Argos quickly disappeared, and the subsequent rulers became mortal enemies of Sparta. In Messenía, the pre-Dorian natives absorbed the invaders and prospered. This made Sparta, which kept the Dorian faith, turn green with envy before she conquered the Messenians and turned all of them into helots or slaves, an act that the Spartans justified through an obscure adventure of Heracles in Pýlos.

Wine: From Symposia to Retsina

Bronze is the mirror of the form; wine of the heart.
Aeschylus

Greek settlement and the cultivation of the vine went hand in hand to such a degree that one scholar claims 'wine drinking was considered nothing less than a symbol of Greek cultural identity'. Mind, not just any old wine, any old way. The Greeks diluted it, with chilled water, and regarded drinking wine neat to be as boorish as drinking alone. There were rules of etiquette, from the topping up of your companion's glass when enjoying a tipple (still good manners in Greece) to the almost ritualistic forms observed during symposia. These all male get-togethers were such an important part of a city's social life that special rooms in public *stoas* were set aside to accommodate them. Women, good girls, anyway, were not supposed to imbibe; men firmly believed in keeping women sober and docile, and measures were taken to make sure they couldn't get at the amphorae on the sly.

At a symposium, men would not sit, but recline on couches or benches arranged around the walls, often wearing *stephánia* (flower or ivy garlands). After a symbolic toast to Zeus, drunk neat, the *symposiarch*, elected by his fellow drinkers, would preside over the distribution and mixing of the wine. The usual ration was two parts wine to five parts water, which would have given the wine about the same potency as beer. Half and half was not unknown, but considered rather greedy.

Wine was poured into the *krater*, a large cup-shaped mixing bowl, where the water was added. The diluted wine was then poured into an *oinochoe* or jug, and taken around by a slave to each guest's cup. Usually, the number of *kraters* was decided in advance – a one-*krater* party, a two-*krater* party and so on. There were variations on how many toasts, how big the *krater* or wine cups, but the idea was for each man to drink the same amount. A two- or three-*krater* party was great for producing good talk, songs and poetry. A ten-*krater* party was a wild shindig, no doubt with flute girls (prostitutes). As the evening disintegrated, guests would play a game called *kottabos*, in which a small bronze disc was placed on a pedestal in the centre of the room. Drinkers would leave wine in the bottom of their cups, and flick it at the disc while reclining on their couches. The winner knocked it off. In practice everyone got splashed. Perhaps we shouldn't be surprised to find Grecian urns (not the kind Keats wrote odes to) that show symposium guests vomiting all over the place.

Now that we know how they drank, what did they drink? As today, every house had its own humble supply of inexpensive wine. But islands like Chios and Lesbos were famous for their vintages, and in plays and literature the ancients waxed eloquent about their fruitiness, aroma and quality. Exporters shipped their wine all over the Aegean in distinctive amphorae, each shape instantly recognizable in the same way as bottles of Bordeaux or Chianti are today. Since cork was unknown in Greece, the amphorae were sealed with supple plugs of newly cut pine. Its fresh resin inevitably affected the taste of the contents as they sloshed about during transport, and retsina was born. Nowadays, to duplicate the flavour, which is as popular today as it was back then, a dollop of pine resin is added to the barrel of wine. That is the only difference between retsina and ordinary white wine. Of course, aside from its value in restoring faded frescoes (it *is* turpentine, after all!), it also tends to make the habitual retsina drinker think any other wine, dry by European standards, too sweet.

Pausanias and the Golden Age of Guides

Guide writers today can hardly help envying Pausanias, the man who first put Greece on the tourist map. When he did his research some time after AD 150, during the peaceful reign of the Antonine emperors, Greece was a backwater, the Roman province of Achaea (Thermopylae was the northern frontier), but the monuments of more glorious times were still in place. Stories and facts were unencumbered by entrenched scholarly controversy, his readers could be counted on to plough through whatever boring bits he indulged in, and history was two thousand years shorter.

Very few details of his life are known except that he was a Greek, born in Asia Minor, but based in Rome. He travelled extensively, spending twelve of his middle years in Greece, taking copious notes. His *Guide to Greece* was aimed at the well-heeled Roman élite who wanted to soak up a little culture. The fact that he wrote in Greek rather than Latin separated the sheep from the goats; only seriously interested and educated Romans could read Greek at all. His *modus operandi* was simplicity itself: he would settle in one area, such as Corinth, and radiate out in all directions until he had covered the local ground. This was not only efficient, it was also about the only method possible in an age when roads were mule paths, and inns were few and far between. Pausanias didn't bother with minor details such as how he got to places, food or accommodation. His wealthy readers could count on the hospitality of city officials. That meant he could concentrate on what he liked best: history and religion.

Before describing the physical details of a city, Pausanias always wrote an exhaustive history, from the first inhabitant right down to his own time. Local *cicerones* were well informed back then and supplied him with genealogies, important historical data at that time. Pausanias was a stickler for who begat whom. Christianity was still a century and a half away, so there were plenty of priests he could pester, charm or cajole to give him the lowdown on local rites. He loved any ritual, any oracle, no matter how obscure, and, happily for us, he was a pushover for the weird and offbeat. He was perfectly capable of passing a landmark temple such as the one to Apollo in Corinth with scarcely a mention, in order to expound on Glauke's fountain, where the poor girl had landed trying to douse the flames of Medea's poisoned cloak. He did give lengthy descriptions of a temple that caught his fancy, like the ones at Olympia, but fancy is the key word. He left out a lot, in order to keep in what he liked. Where he had the edge was that, since no other guide survived, his every description became definitive by default.

He also had personality, which sometimes burst out beyond the confines of his impersonal style. Clearly fed up on the way from Corinth to Sikyón, he mentioned a memorial to Lykos the Messenian, and then grumbled, in the kind of aside that today's editors would certainly cut, 'whoever he was'. He often took his sources with a grain of salt: 'People who enjoy listening to mythical stories are inclined to add even more wonders of their own.' He hedged his bets by giving alternative versions of stories, or else staunchly defending his favourite against all comers. He sometimes affected a cynical, scientific approach, laconically offering a particular myth for those 'who want a more god-haunted version'. He wouldn't fall for just any old line, although what to his mind was acceptable and what wasn't may seem idiosyncratic nowadays – 'The story of giants having serpents instead of feet is ridiculous,' he blustered at one point, and yet he sat by an Arcadían river hoping to hear the trout sing. He could be pedantic, and thank goodness for that. He is amazingly accurate, not that that has satisfied today's armchair scholars; doctorate theses are written on how Pausanias erred on some minor point. His guide has affected not only the way we see Greek history, but also what we see. Scores of archaeological sites have been discovered solely because of his painstaking details, and much of our knowledge of Greek religious practice is a result of his writing. Every Greek guide writer since has, to some degree or another, followed in his footsteps – and cursed the fact that he did not cover northern Greece, too.

Well aware of his impact, areas all over the Peloponnese use his name freely. Any very old plant will do. There is Pausanias' plane tree in Éghio, his grape vine south of Kleitoriá, and so on. And the precedent for that? The man himself, of course. Pausanias was deeply impressed when he was himself shown 'Menelaos' plane tree' in Arcadía. Like any good guide writer, he was himself the archetypal tourist: canny yet credulous, intrepid, hopeful, dogged and, above all, infused with endless enthusiasm for Greece itself.

Spartan Habits

Stand straight in the front rank with your shield before you
and see your life as your enemy; the darkness of
death should be welcome as the light of the sun.

Tyrtaios (fl. 685–668 BC)

Sparta's poet Tyrtaios was the first Greek poet after Homer and Hesiod whose name has come down to us, but, in contrast to the wide-ranging humanity of his predecessors, his words reverberate with a fanaticism that haunts us to our terrorism-ridden day, echoed perhaps most memorably in the Nationalist slogan in the Spanish Civil War *¡Viva la muerte!* (Long live death!). As the Athenians invented democracy, the Spartans invented ideology, and their much-lauded state of *eumonia* (well ordered and under good laws) was not only the first but one of the longest-lasting and most successful totalitarian regimes of all time. Even today, when science fiction writers need an extra-galactic baddie, it's usually the Spartans who get the call. They're the spooky aliens in the space pyjamas who suck the life out of innocent humans, only now they improve their race with genetic engineering rather than tossing weaklings over the ravine.

The Spartans weren't always quite so warped. Herodotus wrote that in the 7th century their *polis*, fresh from the conquest of Messenía, was not the best- but the worst-governed city-state in Greece. This was also the time when it seemed to be happiest, or at least a time when poetry and art flourished. As a contrast with Tyrtaios, obsessed with courage and the beauty of dying in battle, there was Alkman, a native of Sardis and one of the fathers of the choral lyric, who lived in Sparta and wrote fondly of nature, wine, flowers and girls. Although the Spartan élite were forbidden to manufacture or trade, from the early 7th century BC until 550 BC their underclass *perioikoi* made fine pottery; although frivolous arts were forbidden (they didn't give us the word 'spartan' for nothing), ancient accounts say they made functional things like tables and beds beautifully. The Spartans loved music. This about sums up the extent of their cultural life. To all the achievements of the day, in science, mathematics, the theatre and poetry, in philosophy, art and architecture, they may as well have been Teflon-coated.

By 600 BC Sparta emerged as the strongest state in the Peloponnese, and the exhortations of Tyrtaios to a beautiful death triumphed over the sweetness of Alkman. War and preparedness for war became obsessions. The Spartans sacrificed dogs to the war god Ares, and bound the feet of his statue to keep him from ever leaving Sparta. They built a temple to the son of Ares, Phobos, or fear. They purposely buried their dead in the middle of their villages to accustom people to the sight of dead bodies. Like the Nazis, they were fitness freaks, and dominated the list of victors at Olympia for decades.

The authority for nearly all aspects of life in Sparta was Lykourgos, although, as Plutarch wrote, every fact about him was disputed even in ancient times. Many historians today doubt his very existence; his name sounds altogether too werewolfy. But in Sparta he was credited with a number of reforms, besides his famous constitution (*see* p.363). His other laws, however, were never written down, as in other city-states, but *sung* at festivals. One can just imagine how much fun one of these Spartan hoedowns must have been.

Lykourgos instituted the *agoge*, or state education system, where short rations and two cold baths a year were the rule. Staying lean was believed to make the boys grow taller. If they survived until the age of twelve, they were more or less expected to be wooed by an adult. As with everything in Spartan life, there was also a military reason behind this army of lovers: bonds of affection encouraged a tighter phalanx.

At age 20 a Spartan joined a supper club (*syssition*). These *syssitions* each had 15 members, who were expected to attend their communal meals every night. This again was one of Lykourgos' great ideas, and legend says that, when he announced it, it so infuriated the aristocrats that one of them poked out his eye. It didn't do any good; all Spartans had to spend the rest of their lives dining with their messmates on black pig's blood broth with vinegar and very diluted wine, with little of the sparkle of an Athenian symposium. An inhabitant of Sybaris once quipped that the Spartans didn't fear death because death was preferable to their diet.

Lykourgos also took everyone's land and divided it into equal shares for the Spartans, but then he went even further and banned gold and silver, allowing only coins made of iron, tempered in vinegar to become useless even as iron. This was to make Sparta immune from luxury, vices and commerce. 'No rhetoric-master, fortune-teller, harlot-monger, jeweller or engraver would set foot in a country which had no money,' as Plutarch commented. But iron served them well enough: the best mines in Greece were nearby, and one theory behind their military successes was the fact that they may have invented steel in the 7th century BC and used it to tip their spears. Yet the first recorded protest against the mechanization of war occurred in Sparta in 365 BC when a catapult dart was shown to King Archidamos III, who exclaimed, 'O Heracles! The valour of man is extinguished!'

To keep his Spartans pure, Lykourgos kept them isolated. They had to have a good reason to travel, and strangers were only allowed into Sparta if they had a good reason to be there. One law forbade fighting the same enemy over a period of time, lest they learn Sparta's secrets and weaknesses. King Agesilaos was much blamed, when he went to war so often against the Thebans, for the fact that the Thebans copied the Spartans with their own army of lovers, the Sacred Band, and defeated them soundly.

But while the myth of Spartan invincibility lasted, they scared the living daylights out of the Greek world. They called themselves the Lacedaemonians, or 'Lake Demons', wore dog-skin caps or helmets with tall, frightening plumes, and marked their shields with a simple L that struck terror in their enemies. When the Spartans were at war, rations were increased. 'They were the only people in the world to whom war gave repose,' remarked Plutarch.

Spartan athletes trained naked, and passed the custom on to the other Greek states at the Olympics. Yet, when they had clothes on, Spartan fashion was the opposite of asceticism: they wore luxurious scarlet cloaks – which were so out of the norm that they too were accredited to Lykourgos – to teach them to despise the flow of blood or to hide the fact they were wounded from their enemies. Their shoes were very fine. Most of all, they were noted for their long flowing locks, which elsewhere in Greece were considered effeminate after first youth. Again the Spartans referred to Lykourgos, who said 'it made a good-looking man more beautiful, and an ill-favoured one more terrifying'. Before going into battle, the Spartans primped; when the Persians found Leonidas and his Three Hundred at Thermopylae, they were astonished to find them calmly working on the finer points of their coiffure.

Like the Nazis, the Spartans were superstitious in the extreme. An army would not march out without a seer, and they would not go into battle until the auguries were good. They camped wherever their mascot goat sat down (a kinky custom, but not exclusively Spartan). They sacrificed to Zeus before they left Sparta, then again on Sparta's boundaries, every evening and before battle (sometimes stopping their forward march to do so). It was essential that they always use the same flame of the initial sacrifice in Sparta. Yet with the gods on their side, discipline among the rank and file was so great that they would sit under a direct arrow attack if ordered to do so, then later comment that it made 'great shade'. They did have a certain laconic wit. But if they lost a battle, which was rare, it was no laughing matter. The relatives of the dead were all smiles; of survivors, all gloom.

With all their wars, the Spartans had a hard time keeping up their population. They had to make their *perioikoi* fight with them, and later even the helots. An ancient saying has it that, while no man was freer than a Spartan, no slave was more repressed than a helot. It was legal to kill them. They would be forced to get drunk, and do low dances and sing vulgar songs to make the Spartan youth despise them; when the Thebans liberated them and tried to teach them some noble songs, they couldn't get the helots to sing them, at least at first. 'The masters wouldn't like it,' they said. There was one occasion when the helots actually thought the masters meant them well. They were made to fight in the Peloponnesian War and, when it was over, the Spartans asked the helots to choose the 2,000 bravest men among them. The Spartans put garlands on their heads and took them about the temples as if they were going to enfranchise them, then executed them to a man.

Food and Drink

05

Life's fundamental principle is the satisfaction of the needs and wants of the stomach. All important and trivial matters depend on this principle and cannot be differentiated from it.

Epicurus (3rd century BC)

Epicurus may have lent his name to gourmets, but in reality his philosophy advocated maximizing simple pleasures: rather than continually seeking novelty, Epicurus suggests making bread and olives taste sublime by fasting for a couple of days. In that way Greeks have long been epicureans: centuries of poverty taught them to relish food more than 'cuisine'. What has changed, especially in Athens, is that cuisine has arrived. The influx of international tourists is partly responsible, but so is the rise of a well-travelled generation of Greeks. Where they travel, fusion is the rage, with a broad Mediterranean slant; Athens and major resorts now have Italian, Chinese, Mexican, Indian, Japanese and Turkish restaurants.

Of course most restaurants and tavernas are still Greek, serving fish from the seas, free-range chicken, lamb, fresh herbs and honey from the mountains, wild young greens from the hills, olives, fruits and nuts from the groves. Cooking methods tend to be simple, with strong Turkish and Italian influences that enhance natural flavours. A good cook almost never resorts to canned or frozen ingredients, or even the microwave – one criticism levelled at Greek food is that it's served cold, but once you get used to it, you realize that many dishes are actually tastier once they're left to cool in their own juices, especially in the summer. Anyway, the natives may be right – recent studies show that eating like a Greek is remarkably healthy.

Greek Dishes

Many Greek dishes need no introduction – *tárama*, moussaka, *gýros*, feta, retsina, vine leaves, Greek salads with feta, Greek yoghurt and baklava have achieved the universality of lasagne and chicken tikka. But although some of the food may be familiar, if you've not been to Greece before, you may find eating different from what you're used to, with a big emphasis on informality. A typical meal begins with bread (usually excellent) and starters (*mezédes*) to be communally shared: olives, *tzatzíki* (cucumbers and yoghurt), prawns, *tírosaláta* (feta cheese dip), *koponistá* (pungent smoked or salted fish), roasted sweet peppers, cheese or spinach pies, meatballs, or *saganáki* (fried cheese sprinkled with lemon). These are followed (often within minutes) by a shared salad and potatoes, and your own main course. This could be a gorgeously fresh omelette, or an oven dish or stew (called 'ready dishes', as they're already prepared) such as moussaka, *pastítsio* (cooked macaroni, layered and baked with ground meat, cheese, cream and topped with béchamel sauce), roast lamb or chicken, *makaroniá* (spaghetti with meat sauce), *yemistá* (stuffed tomatoes or peppers), *stifádo* (spiced beef stew with baby onions), *lagostifádo* (rabbit stew, similar but flavoured with orange), *kokinistó* (beef cooked with tomatoes and a hint of cinnamon), lamb or veal *youvétsi* (baked with tomatoes and with teardrop pasta), *chirinó me sélino* (pork with wild celery, in egg and lemon sauce), or *kréas stin stámna* (lamb or beef baked in a clay dish). Meats grilled to order come under the heading of *tis óras* ('the On-Times') – pork chops

Vegetarian Dishes

Of all the people in the EU, the Greeks now eat the most meat per capita, but they also eat the most cheese, more than even the French, and follow only the Italians in eating pasta. Basically they eat a lot, which means there are plenty of dishes for vegetarians and vegans, especially if you go to a *mezedopoleíon*, where you can make a meal out of an array of little non-meat starters (a 'vegetarian' is a *chortofágos*).

Because of historic poverty and the demands of Orthodox fasts (which forbid animal and dairy products), Greece has many traditional vegetarian dishes, and if you're a vegan Lent is an ideal time to come, because restaurants go out of their way to prepare them (especially artichokes, *aginádres*). At any time of the year you should find pulses, in starters such as *gigántes* (giant butter beans in tomato sauce), bean soups (*fasoláda*), *revíthia* (chickpeas, baked or in soups or fritters) and occasionally lentils (*fakés*).

Other vegan stand-bys are ratatouille-like *laderá* (vegetables cooked in olive oil), a host of salads, sometimes enlivened with *kápari* (pickled caper plant), *pantsária* (beetroot drizzled with olive oil and vinegar), *yemistá* (peppers or tomatoes stuffed with rice), *briáms* (potato and aubergine/courgette, baked with olive oil), *imams* (aubergine stuffed with tomato and onion), *keftédes* (vegetable fritters of carrot, tomato, chickpeas or courgette, which are the most popular but also the hardest to pronounce, *kolokythiakeftédes*), *dolmádes* (rice- and dill-filled vine leaves), or potatoes roasted with lemon, olive oil and garlic; tavernas offer endless chips, although of late many use frozen. *Skordaliá*, the classic garlic dip, is traditionally made with puréed potatoes and olive oil, though some places now do it with soft cheese.

(*brizóles*), lamb cutlets (*paidákia*), kebabs (*souvláki*), minced steak (*biftéki*), meatballs (*keftédes* or *sousoukákia*), sausage (*lukániko*), or grilled chicken (*kotópoulo skára*).

Seafood is fresh and delicious but relatively expensive (blame overfishing), but you can usually find reasonably priced whitebait (*marídes*), fresh sardines (*sardínas*), cuttlefish stew (*soupiá*) and squid rings (*kalamári*). Baked or fried *bakaliáros* (fresh Mediterranean cod) is always a treat and shouldn't break the bank. Some places serve soups – *psarósoupa* (with potatoes and carrots) or spicy tomato-based *kakávia*, a meal in themselves with hunks of bread and a bottle of wine. Prawns (*garídes*) are lightly fried or baked with garlic, tomatoes and feta as *garídes saganáki*, a dish invented in the 1960s; spaghetti with lobster (*astakomakaronáda*) is another recent addition to many Greek menus. Note that fish is usually priced by the kilo; often you'll be asked to pick out the one you want cooked and the owner puts it on the scale in front of you.

Desserts are rare, although many places offer complimentary watermelon or sliced apples sprinkled with cinnamon or nutmeg; Greeks make lovely sweets, puddings, cakes and ice creams but tend to eat them in the late afternoon, after the siesta.

Eating Out

In resort areas and the touristy parts of Athens, there are plenty of places offering familiar breakfasts, lunches and dinners at familiar hours for visitors, but you may find getting into the Greek pace of life more enjoyable. This means a light **breakfast** (many bars sell yoghurt and honey), supplemented **mid-morning** with a cheese pie (*tirópitta*). At 2 or 3pm, indulge in a long al fresco **lunch** with wine, followed by a siesta or *mesiméri* to avoid the scorching afternoon heat. Get up at 6 or 7pm for a swim and an **ice cream**. Around 8pm, it's time for a *vólta*, the see-and-be-seen evening stroll, and a sunset drink, while deciding where to go. Greeks rarely eat before 10pm and **evening meals** can go on into the small hours. Children are welcome (they too nap in the afternoon) – toddlers crawl under the table, while the adults become increasingly boisterous, punctuating the meal with fiery discussions and bursts of song or dance. The more people round the table the merrier, and the more likely the meal will turn into a spontaneous cabaret. After dinner, have a brandy in a café or hit the tiles until dawn.

Restaurants and Tavernas

The sociable Greeks eat out more than most Europeans – twice a week is the national average – and they usually order more than they can eat. But it's only recently that they've paid much attention to the food (witness all the cookery shows and celebrity chefs on Greek television).

At the older ***estiatória*** (restaurants), now becoming rare, all the Greek standards wait on the steam table for you to choose from, and are served up faster than McDonald's. Newer ones tend to be like those back home, although it's worth looking out for ones that do traditional regional dishes. **Tavernas** are more numerous and more like family-run bistros, and can range from beach shacks to barn-like affairs with live music in the evening. Waiters will reel off what's available; if there's a menu, home-made translations may leave you more baffled than ever.

Mezedopoleíons specialize in tapas-like *mezédes*, a host of little dishes, served with ouzo, *rakí*, beer or wine. Of late, there's been a revival of the old-fashioned cookshop or ***mageireftá*** (μαγειρευτά) with pots simmering on the stove and casseroles such as moussaka; these are often open only for lunch.

At the seaside you'll find fish tavernas, ***psarotavérnes***, specializing in all kinds of seafood from sea urchins and octopus stew to red mullet, swordfish, bream and sardines – some of the best of these are owned by fishermen. Most carry a meat dish or two for fish-haters who get dragged along. If you're a red-blooded meat-eater then head for a ***psistariá***, specializing in charcoal-grilled chicken, lamb, pork, beef or *kokorétsi* (lamb's offal, braided around a skewer). In some places you can still find a ***hasapotavérna***, a grill room attached to a local butcher's shop, with fresh carcasses on display to entice in the clientele (usually with the tail attached, as proof of freshness). Besides chops and steaks, they often offer kebabs, home-made sausages and sometimes delicious stews, usually served by the butcher's assistant in a bloodstained apron for added carnivorous effect.

Other eateries in Greece need no introduction: the pizzeria (often spelled ***pitsaría***), American fast food (with local adaptations, such as non-meat meals on offer during Lent) and Goody's, the Greek chain (with lots more variety). Even the smallest islands have at least one ***gýros*** or *souvláki* stand for cheap greasy fills, many now offering chicken as well as the usual pork.

Bakeries sell an array of sweet and savoury hot pies; a ***bougatsaría*** (μπουγατσαρια) specializes in them. For something sweet, just look at the lovely displays in any ***zacharoplasteío*** or pastry shop. In resorts and towns, you can also find shops run by Greece's favourite ice-cream maker, Dodóni (Δωδώνη).

Kafeneíons and Cafés

Every village has a *kafeneíon*: a coffee house but, more importantly, a social institution where men (and increasingly women) gather to discuss the latest news, read the papers, nap or play cards and incidentally drink coffee. Some men seem to live in them. The bill of fare features thick Greek **coffee** (*café ellinikó*), prepared in 40 different ways, although *glykó* (sweet), *métrio* (medium) and *skéto* (no sugar) are the basic orders. It is always served with a cold glass of water. Other coffees in Greece, unless you find a proper Italian espresso machine, won't make the earth move for you. '**Nes**' (aka instant Nescafé) has become a Greek word, and comes either hot or whipped and iced as a frappé. Soft drinks, brandy, beer and ouzo round out the old-style *kafeneíon* fare.

Smart newer cafés with cosy chairs usually open earlier and close much later, and are much more expensive – a coffee can cost €3, although remember you are paying to sit in the grandstand of local life and can lounge about there for hours. In resort areas they offer breakfast, from simple to complete English, with rashers, baked beans and eggs. They also serve mineral water, ice cream concoctions, crêpes, milkshakes, wonderful fresh fruit juices, cocktails, and creamy Greek yoghurt and honey.

Bars (*Barákia*) and Ouzeries

Even the most flyspeck town tends to have at least one music bar, usually playing the latest hits (foreign or Greek). They come to life at cocktail hour and again at midnight; closing times vary but dawn isn't unusual. Standard cocktail prices have now risen beyond the €4–5 mark in ordinary bars, even in the wilds of the Peloponnese. The price is a lot higher in urban areas, especially so if any kind of live entertainment is on offer. But before you complain, remember that the measures tend to be triples by British standards. If in doubt stick to **beer** (Amstel or Heineken, although Greece has its own brand, the slightly sweet Mýthos), ouzo, *soúma* (like ouzo, but sweeter), wine and Metaxá.

A grand old Greek institution, the **ouzerie**, features the national *apéritif*, **ouzo** (the *rakí* drunk by the Byzantines and Venetians, renamed ouzo in the 18th century from the Latin *usere*, 'usable'). Clear and anise-flavoured, it is served in tall glasses or a *karafáki* holding three or four doses which habitués dilute and cloud with water or ice. If you dislike aniseed, the Greeks also make an unflavoured **grappa** called *tsikoúdia* or *rakí*). As Greeks look askance at drunkenness – as in ancient times, when they cut their wine with water and honey – ouzo is traditionally served with *mezédes*; for an assortment, ask for a *pikilía*.

Wine

Grapes are native to Greece, and there could be something to the myth that wine was invented here during a moment of divine inspiration.

Wine is a vital part of Greek social life. This is not immediately obvious at the height of summer when Greeks unaccountably switch to beer, despite the fact that chilled white wine is more cooling. But for the rest of the year wine is always

Wines of the Peloponnese

Several Peloponnesian wines have *appellation* (AO) status. Neméa, the best known, is a noble dry red wine cultivated from the local *agiorítiko* grapes. The hill country around Pátras yields mainly dry whites from *rodítis* and also velvety Mavrodaphne, one of Greece's great dessert wines, blended with *korinthiaki* grapes and similar to port. A third area, Mantinía, produces dry whites made from *moschofílero*, cultivated on the slopes of Mount Mainalo.

Below are some estates to look out for, that also welcome visitors (do ring ahead). Also see *www.enoap.gr*.

Ktima Pappaioánnou (Ancient Neméa, Corinthia, **t** 274 602 3138). Any one of his wines is worth the effort, but try his new dry red Pappaioánnou Erythrós 1999 (Παππαιοάννου Ερυθρός) made from 100 per cent native *agiorítiko* grapes.

Domain Skouros (Maladéndri, Neméa, Corinthia, **t** 275 102 3688). Their dry red Agiorítika Skoúra (Αγιορίτικα Σκούρα), made from 100 per cent *agiorítiko* grapes, is excellent, but also try the dry white Chardonnay Skoúra, made from the grapes that have taken to Greek soil like ducks to water.

Gaia (Koútsi, Neméa, Corinthia, **t** 214 602 2057) produces a wonderful rosé: 14–18h Paraskevyopoúlou (14–18η Παρασκευοπούλου), again from *agiorítiko* grapes.

Oenofóros (Selinoús, by Éghio, Achaía, **t** 269 102 9415). Besides a good chardonnay and cabernet sauvignon, Oenofóros has taken the *lagorthi* grape, indigenous to Kalávrita, and resurrected it from the dead in their white Lagorthi, hinting of lemon and spices. Their best-known wine is the dry white Aspolíthi made from *rodítis* grapes, the most widespread grape in Achaía.

Achaia Clauss (Pátras, Achaía, *see* pp.209–10).

Paparoúsis Estate (Patrás, Achaía, t 261 042 0334 or **t** 261 027 7673). They recommend their new Epilegménos reserve red, their Pátras Drosállis (Πατρα Δροσαλλις) from *rodítis* grapes, and Moscahatos Riou-Patron (Μοσχηατος Ριου Πατρον), a sweet wine.

Ktima Merkoúri (Korakochóri, north of Katákolo, Elís, **t** 262 103 4891). This, the most famous winery in Elís, began decades ago, but each new generation innovates and keeps the winery on its toes. Their newer red Avgustiadis Mourvedre Merkoúri is made from a blend of their own grapes, while their better-known Ktima Merkoúri comes from *reosco* and *mavrodaphne* grapes. From higher-altitude *rodítis* grapes they also produce Foloe (Φολοε), a dry white.

Tsélepos (by Rízes near Tegea, Arcadía, **t** 271 054 4440). Arcadía has ideal growing conditions, so expect to see major national growers Cambas and Boutari. Tselepos is a smaller estate giving them a run for their money, creating magical vintages from *moschofílero*.

Spirópoulos (at Artemísion, north of Trípolis, Arcadía, **t** 279 606 1400) is a going concern just southwest of the Artemísion tunnel. They concentrate on vintages (red, white, rosé and sparkling) made especially from the local *moschofílero* grape. They welcome visitors, so give them a ring if you're in the area (going south, take the first right after the tunnel and continue for 5km; look for the traditional tower).

present, accompanying a humble dish of olives and cheese or the most elaborate dinner, and drunk by everyone from the old folks to the children, in small amounts, of course. Which estate produces the best wine, or whose barrel was the most successful, is as hotly debated as who has the best beans, or olive oil.

As in ancient times (*see* p.49), etiquette is still important. It would be a poor host who did not fill every guest's glass and then his own, with plenty of toasts along the way (*yámmas* is the easiest to remember). As today's wines are much less potent than ancient ones they are are no longer mixed with water by most drinkers, although it is by no means an uncommon practice. Every family outside of Athens either has a barrel of wine, or a connection with a local who provides cheap bulk wine. The ancient Greeks stored their wine in clay amphorae sealed with resin; the disintegration of the resin helped prevent oxidation and lent the wine a flavour that caught on (and is now supplied by pieces of resin). Like ouzo, though, young Greeks are turning their backs on it, and draught ***retsína*** (*retsína varelísio* – the best kind) has to be sought out. Koutali is a reliable bottled variety and widely available. It is admirably suited to Greek food, and after a while you may find non-resinated wines bland. Order it by the *kílo* (about a litre), *misó kiló* (half) or *tétarto* (250ml).

In the past 30 years, the Peloponnese has seen the birth of the small, knowledgeable, passionately committed **wine estate**, equipped with spotless stainless steel, temperature-controlled fermentation vats, and a store room full of oak barrels where their premium or signature wine is slowly maturing. These vintages may not have the Californians or even the French trembling yet, but they're getting better at an astounding pace and challenging the average person's loyalty to the homely barrel of wine sitting in his store room. Corinthia, Achaía, Arcadía and Elís have the optimal growing conditions: above 1,300 and under 2,600ft, where grapes can mature slowly in lots of sunlight and are irrigated only by rain. Head for a local ***cava*** (wine shop) or ask at a restaurant. If you're really keen, visit the **vineyards** (the ones in the box below welcome visitors if you ring ahead). Most of these produce a variety of wines, and all experiment. The material is certainly there: Greece has over 300 indigenous grape varieties, not to mention many introduced international standbys.

The Greek Menu (*Katálogos*)

Ορεκτικά (Μεζέδες)	***Orektiká (Mezédes)***	**Appetisers**
τζατζίκι	*tzatzíki*	yoghurt and cucumbers
ελιές	*eliés*	olives
κοπανιστί (τυροσαλάτα)	*kopanistí (tirosaláta)*	cheese purée, often spicy
ντολμάδες	*dolmádes*	stuffed vine leaves
μελιτζανοσαλατα	*melitzanosaláta*	eggplant (aubergine) dip
σαγανάκη	*saganáki*	fried cheese with lemon
ποικιλία	*pikilía*	mixed hors d'œuvres
μπουρεκι	*bouréki*	cheese and vegetable pie
τυροπιττα	*tirópitta*	cheese pie
αχινοί	*achíni*	sea urchin roe (quite salty)
Σούπες	***Soópes***	**Soups**
αυγολέμονο	*avgolémono*	egg and lemon soup
χορτόσουπα	*chortósoupa*	vegetable soup
ψαρόσουπα	*psarósoupa*	fish soup
φασολάδα	*fasoláda*	bean soup
μαγειρίτσα	*magirítsa*	giblets in egg and lemon
πατσάς	*patsás*	tripe and pig's foot soup (for late nights and hangovers)
Λάδερα	***Ládera***	**'Cooked in Oil'**
μπάμιες	*bámies*	okra, ladies' fingers
γίγαντες	*yígantes*	butter beans in tomato sauce

μπριαμ	*briám*	aubergines and mixed veg
φακηες	*fakés*	lentils
Ζυμαρικά	***Zimariká***	**Pasta and Rice**
πιλάφι / ρύζι	*piláfi/rízi*	pilaf/rice
σπαγκέτι	*spagéti*	spaghetti
μακαρόνια	*macarónia*	macaroni
πλιγγούρι	*plingoúri*	bulghar wheat
Ψάρια	***Psária***	**Fish**
αστακος	*astakós*	lobster
αθερίνα	*atherína*	smelt
γάυρος	*gávros*	mock anchovy
καλαμάρια	*kalamária*	squid
κέφαλος	*kéfalos*	grey mullet
χταπόδι	*chtapóthi*	octopus
χριστόψαρο	*christópsaro*	John Dory
μπαρμπούνι	*barboúni*	red mullet
γαρίδες	*garíthes*	prawns (shrimps)
γοπα	*gópa*	bogue (boops boops)
ξιφίας	*ksifías*	swordfish
μαρίδες	*maríthes*	whitebait
συναγρίδα	*sinagrítha*	sea bream
σουπιές	*soupiés*	cuttlefish
φάγγρι	*fángri*	bream
κιδόνια	*kidónia*	cherrystone clams
σαρδέλλα	*sardélla*	sardines
μπακαλιάρος (σκορδαλιά)	*bakaliáros (skorthaliá)*	cod (with garlic sauce)
σαργός	*sargós*	white bream
σκαθάρι	*skathári*	black bream
στρείδια	*stríthia*	oysters
λιθρίνια	*lithrínia*	bass
μίδια	*mídia*	mussels
Εντραδες	***Entrádes***	**Main Courses**
κουνέλι	*kounéli*	rabbit
στιφάδο	*stifádo*	casserole with onions
γιουβέτσι	*yiouvétsi*	meat baked with pasta
συκώτι	*seekóti*	liver
μουσκάρι	*moskári*	veal
αρνί	*arní*	lamb
κατσικι	*katsíki*	kid
κοτόπουλο	*kotópoulo*	chicken
χοιρινό	*chirinó*	pork
Κυμάδες	***Kymádes***	**Minced Meat**
παστίτσιο	*pastítsio*	mince and macaroni pie
μουσακά	*moussaká*	meat and aubergine baked with white sauce
μακαρόνια με κυμά	*makarónia me kymá*	spaghetti Bolognese
μπιφτέκι	*biftéki*	hamburger, usually bunless
σουτζουκάκια	*soutzoukákia*	meatballs in sauce
μελιτζάνες γεμιστές	*melitzánes yemistés*	stuffed aubergine/eggplant
πιπεριές γεμιστές	*piperíes yemistés*	stuffed peppers
Της Ωρας	***Tis Óras***	**Grills to Order**
μπριζόλα	*brizóla*	beef steak with bone
μπριζόλες χοιρινές	*brizólas chirinés*	pork chops

σουβλάκι	*souvláki*	meat on a skewer
κοκορέτσι	*kokorétsi*	offal kebabs
κοτολέτες	*kotolétes*	veal chops
παιδάκια	*paidákia*	lamb chops
κεφτέδες	*keftéthes (th as in 'th')*	meatballs

Σαλάτες — *Salátes* — Salads and Vegetables

ντομάτες	*domátes*	tomatoes
αγγούρι	*angoúri*	cucumber
ρώσσικη σαλάτα	*róssiki saláta*	Russian salad
σπανάκι	*spanáki*	spinach
χωριάτικη	*choriátiki*	tomato and cucumber salad with feta cheese and olives
κολοκυθάκια	*kolokithákia*	courgettes/zucchini
πιπεριεσ	*piperiés*	peppers
κρεμιδι	*kremídi*	onions
πατάτες	*patátes*	potatoes
παντσάρια	*pantsária*	beetroot
μαρούλι	*maroúli*	lettuce
χόρτα	*chórta*	wild greens
αγκινάρες	*anginármes*	artichokes
κουκιά	*koukiá*	fava beans

Τυρια — *Tiriá* — Cheeses

φέτα	*féta*	hard sheep's milk cheese
κασέρι	*kasséri*	hard buttery cheese
γραβιέρα	*graviéra*	Greek 'Gruyère'
μυζήθρα	*mizíthra*	soft white cheese
πρόβιο	*próvio*	another sheep's cheese

Γλυκά — *Glyká* — Sweets

παγωτό	*pagotó*	ice cream
κουραμπιέδες	*kourabiéthes*	sugared biscuits
λουκουμάδες	*loukoumáthes*	hot honey fritters
χαλβά	*halvá*	sesame seed sweet
μπακλαβά	*baklavá*	nuts and honey in filo pastry
γιαούρτι (με μελι)	*yiaoúrti (me méli)*	yoghurt (with honey)
καριδοπιτα	*karidópita*	walnut cake
μήλο	*mílo*	apple
μπουγάτσα	*bougátsa*	custard tart

Miscellaneous

ψωμί	*psomí*	bread
βούτυρο	*voútiro*	butter
μέλι	*méli*	honey
μαρμελάδα	*marmelátha*	jam
λάδι	*láthi*	oil
πιάτο	*piáto*	plate
λογαριασμό	*logariasmó*	the bill/check

Drinks

κρασί	*krasí*	wine
άσπρο	*áspro*	white
κόκκινο	*kókkino*	red
κοκκινέλι	*kokkinéli*	rosé
ρετσίνα	*retsína*	wine (resinated)/retsina
νερό (βραστο/μεταλικο)	*neró (vrastó/metalikó)*	water (boiled/mineral)
μπύρα	*bíra*	beer

Drinks (*cont'd*)

χυμός πορτοκάλι	*chimós portokáli*	orange juice
γάλα	*gála*	milk
τσάϊ	*tsái*	tea
σοκολάτα	*sokoláta*	chocolate
καφέ	*kafé*	coffee
φραππέ	*frappé*	iced coffee
πάγος	*págos*	ice
ποτίρι	*potíri*	glass
μπουκάλι	*boukáli*	bottle
καράφα	*karáfa*	carafe
στήν γειά σας!	*stín yiásas* (formal, pl)	To your health! Cheers!
στήν γειά σου!	*stín yiásou* (sing)	

Planning Your Trip

06

When to Go

Climate

Greece enjoys hot, dry, clear and bright Mediterranean summers, cooled by winds. Winters are mild, and in general the wet season begins at the end of October when it can rain 'tables and chairs' as the Greeks say.

Any time is a good time to visit the Peloponnese. Winter offers wild, world-class clubbing in Athens, or a chance to play in the snow on the high peaks, or see archaeological sites in lonely splendour. Landscapes that seem barren in August are often lush in January. Spring is a marvellous time for wild flowers, and for participating in the Pátras Carnival or Greek Easter, the biggest holiday on the calendar. Late spring or September and October are the best for hiking or travelling by car on the small unpaved roads in the mountains, since they tend to wash out in the winter rains and are rebulldozed in the spring. September and early October tend to be calm and warm without being stifling, the swimming is still excellent and the Greeks are laid back (it's also the best time to find bargains). That leaves July and August, the most popular months for sun-lovers and people with children. This includes the Greeks themselves, so it's always the busiest time and prices are at their highest.

Average Temperatures in C°/F°

	Athens	Pátras	Trípolis	Kalamáta
Jan	11/48	10/50	5/41	11/48
April	16/60	16/60	12/52	16/60
July	28/82	26/79	24/74	27/80
Oct	23/74	19/66	15/58	20/68

Average Rainfall in mm

Jan	130	108	124	141
April	55	49	56	46
July	6	3	18	3
Oct	92	87	80	91

Festivals

Every village has its *panegýri*, or patron saint's festival, some celebrated merely with a special service, others with events culminating in a feast and music and dancing till dawn. The main events throughout the year are listed in the box below, and you'll find others listed in the text. For **national holidays**, *see* p.76.

Tourist Information

Greek National Tourist Offices

UK and Ireland: 4 Conduit Street, London W1S 2DJ, **t** (020) 7495 9300, *www.gnto.co.uk*.

Calendar of Events

Before Lent

10 days before Lent on the Greek calendar Pátras Carnival starts up.

March

17 Maniate independence, Areópolis.

23 Kalamáta celebrates independence.

April

Greek Easter Trípolis has a very lively party; Leonídio with its small hot-air balloons is unique; the Friday after Easter sees celebrations in Éghio and at Kefelári near Argos.

June–September

Athens Festival Theatre, jazz, classical music and dance, in the Herodes Atticus Odeion.

Epídauros Festival Ancient drama and music.

Sainopoúlio Amphitheatre Festival Sparta, featuring drama and music events.

July

23 Liberation from the Turks, Monemvasiá.

Mid-July–mid Aug International dance festival, Kalamáta.

August

1–15 Navarínia celebrations in Pýlos.

15 Monemvasiá fishermen's festival, Týros.

15–17 Festival of Apollonia Tyritou.

Late Aug Aubergine Festival, Leonídio.

September

23 Liberation from the Turks, Trípolis.

Spartathlon in Sparta, and ultra-marathon.

October

20 Very lively celebration of the Battle of Navarino in Pýlos, with allied sailors.

USA: Olympic Tower, 645 Fifth Avenue, Suite 903, New York, NY 10022, **t** (212) 421 5777, *www.greektourism.com*.

Canada: 1500 Don Mills Road, Suite 102, Toronto, Ontario, M3B 3K4, **t** (416) 968 2220.

Australia and New Zealand: 37–49 Pitt Street, Sydney, NSW 2000, **t** (02) 9241 1663.

In Greece

The multilingual tourist information number in Athens, **t** 171, is good for all Greece (outside Athens, **t** 210 171). Many towns have local tourist offices.

Embassies and Consulates

Foreign Embassies in Athens

UK: 1 Ploutárchou St, **t** 210 727 2600.

USA: 91 Vassilías Sofías, **t** 210 721 2951.

Canada: 4 Ioan. Gennadíou, **t** 210 727 3400.

Ireland: 7 Vass. Konstantínou, **t** 210 723 2771.

Greek Embassies Abroad

UK: 1A Holland Park, London W11 3TP, **t** (020) 7229 3850, *www.greekembassy.org.uk*.

USA: 2217 Massachusetts Ave N.W., Washington DC, 20008, **t** (202) 667 3169/ **t** (202) 939 1300, *www.greekembassy.org*.

Canada: 76–80 Maclaren Street, Ottawa, Ontario, K2P 0K6, **t** (613) 238 6271, *www.greekembassy.ca*.

Ireland: 1 Upper Pembroke St, Dublin 2, **t** (01) 676 7254.

Entry Formalities

Passports and Visas

All **European Union** members can visit and stay in Greece indefinitely.

Most **non-EU tourists** entering Greece don't need a visa (including American, Australian, New Zealand and Canadian citizens) for stays of up to 90 days on presentation of a valid passport. Anyone staying in the Schengen zone beyond the 90-day period may be subject to a fine at the time of departure and will be barred from entry into any other Schengen country for 90 days. In Greece, fines for overstaying the three months run from €587 to a whopping €1,174. To stay longer, get a visa before you leave home or take your passport, photos and bank statements (or other proof that you can support yourself) and lots of money – €464 at the time of writing – 20 days before your time in Greece expires to the **Aliens Bureau**, 173 Leof. Alexándras, ✉ 11522 Athens, **t** 210 770 5711, or your local police station.

Customs

EU nationals can now import a limitless amount of goods for their personal use.

For travellers entering the EU from outside, the duty-free limits are 1 litre of spirits or 2 litres of liquors (port, sherry or champagne), plus 2 litres of wine, 200 cigarettes and 50 grams of perfume. Much larger quantities – up to 10 litres of spirits, 90 litres of wine, 110 litres of beer and 3,200 cigarettes – bought locally and provided you are travelling between EU countries, can be taken through customs if you can prove that they are for private consumption only and taxes have been paid in the country of purchase.

Disabled Travellers

The big bonus of Athens' having hosted the 2004 Paralympics has been a vast increase in awareness: laws are now in place to increase accessibility in museums, transport and hotels. Athens got the bulk of the improvements (there's even a lift to the Acropolis), and it may be a while before the rest of Greece catches up. Access on trains, buses, small planes, ferries and hydrofoils poses

Advice for Disabled Travellers

In the UK

RADAR, 12 City Forum, 250 City Rd, London EC1V 8AF, **t** (020) 7250 3222, *www.radar.org.uk*.

Holiday Care Service, **t** 0845 124 9971, *www.holidaycare.org.uk*.

Disability Now, 6 Markets Road, London N7, **t** (020) 7619 7323, *www.disabilitynow.org.uk*.

In the USA and Canada

Mobility International USA, **t** (541) 343 1284, *www.miusa.org*.

SATH (Society for Accessible Travel and Hospitality), **t** (212) 447 7284, *www.sath.org*.

Emerging Horizons, *www.emerginghorizons.com*.

challenges, and the steepness of the terrain means that many villages have steps for streets and/or cobblestoned pavements.

Insurance and EHIC Cards

EU citizens are entitled to free medical care at the basic **IKA** (Greek NHS) **hospitals** with their **European Health Insurance Card (EHIC)**; apply at post offices, online at *www.ehic.org.uk*, or by calling **t** 0845 606 2030. Unlike the old E111 forms, you'll need to apply for a card for every member of the family .

Consultations with Greek dentists and doctors are free, but you will have to pay part of the cost of X-rays, etc. If you have a prescription, expect to pay a small standard charge plus 25 per cent of the actual cost of the medicine, which is non-refundable. If you are charged in full, obtain a receipt and keep the prescriptions as well as the self-adhesive labels from the medicines. (If you obtain any medicine or treatment privately, you pay the full cost.) Take the original receipts and your EHIC to the nearest IKA office within one month, and they will reimburse you. If you are staying where there is no IKA office, you must pay the full costs and apply for a refund on return to the UK. Keep all original prescriptions, self-adhesive labels and receipts.

In any case, consider a **travel insurance** policy with adequate repatriation cover.

Non-European nationals should check their health insurance schemes to see if they are covered in Greece.

Money and Banks

The official currency in Greece is the **euro**, pronounced *evró*. Cents are *leptá*.

The word for **bank** is *trápeza*, derived from the word *trapézi*, or table, used back in the days of money-changers. **Banking hours** are Mon–Thurs 8.20–2, Fri 8.20–1.30. The number of **ATMs** grows every year.

Major hotels, luxury shops and resort restaurants take **credit cards** (look for the little signs), but smaller hotels and tavernas certainly won't, and many petrol stations don't either. Visa is the most widely accepted.

Traveller's cheques are always useful as a back-up. The major brands (Thomas Cook and American Express) are accepted in all banks; take your passport as ID, and shop around for the best rates (which are usually in banks).

You can have money sent to Greek post offices via the **Girobank Eurogiro system**.

Getting There

By Air

From the UK and Ireland

Scheduled flights direct to **Athens** operate from the UK on British Airways, easyJet, KLM, and Greece's national carrier, Olympic (which may be renamed when – if ever – it's sold). There are scheduled flights from Dublin to Athens on Malev Hungarian Airlines.

Charter flights fly direct from many UK and Irish airports to **Athens**, the southern Peloponnesian airport of **Kalamáta**, and the air base at Aráxos west of **Pátras**. If you don't want a package you can usually book just the flight. Most run from May to mid-October but there are also early specials, in March and April, depending on when Greek Easter falls.

Make sure to **confirm your return flight** prior to departure; *see* box, opposite.

From the USA and Canada

Olympic, Delta, Continental and Lufthansa have daily flights from the USA to Athens in summer; Olympic also flies direct from Toronto and Montreal, but check the Internet for deals.

Airline Carriers

UK and Ireland

British Airways, UK **t** 0870 850 9850; Ireland **t** 01 890 626747, *www.ba.com*.

easyJet, **t** 0905 821 0905, *www.easyjet.com*.

KLM, **t** 08705 074074, *www.klm.com*.

Olympic Airlines, UK **t** 0870 6060 460, *www.olympicairlines.com*.

Malev Hungarian Airlines, Ireland **t** (01) 844 4303, *www.malev.hu*.

USA and Canada

Air Canada, Canada **t** 1 888 247 2262, *www.aircanada.com*.

British Airways, USA **t** 800 AIRWAYS, *www.ba.com*.

Continental, USA **t** 800 231 0856, *www.continental.com*.

Delta, **t** 800 221 1212, *www.delta.com*.
KLM (Northwest), USA **t** 800 225 2525, *www.nwa.com*.
Lufthansa, **t** 800 609 9976, *www.weflyhome.com*.
Olympic Airways, *www.olympicairlines.com*.

Charters and Discounts

UK and Ireland

Avro, **t** 0870 458 2841, *www.avro.co.uk*. Cheap flights to the islands.
Budget, **t** (01) 631 1111, *www.budgettravel.ie*. Last-minute bargains/charters from Ireland.
Charter Flight Centre, **t** (020) 7854 8434, *www.charterflightcentre.co.uk*.
Fly Thomas Cook, *www.flythomascook.co.uk*.
Just the Flight, **t** 0870 758 9589, *www.justtheflight.co.uk*. Charters to the islands.
STA Travel, **t** 08701 630 026, *www.statravel.co.uk*. Student discounts.

UK Websites

www.cheapflights.co.uk
www.expedia.co.uk
http://travel.kelkoo.co.uk
www.lastminute.com
www.opodo.co.uk
www.skyscanner.net
www.travelocity.co.uk
www.travelrepublic.co.uk

USA and Canada

Air Brokers International, USA **t** 800 883 3273, *www.airbrokers.com*. Discount agency.
Homeric Tours, USA **t** 800 223 5570, *www.homerictours.com*. Charter flights and tours.
Last Minute Travel Club, USA **t** 877 970 5400, *www.lastminuteclub.com*. Annual membership fee gets you cheap stand-by deals.
Travel Cuts, Canada **t** 1866 246 9762, *www.travelcuts.ca*; USA **t** 800 592 2887, *www.travelcuts.com*.
STA Travel, **t** 800 781 4040, *www.statravel.com*. Student travel discounts.

US/Canadian Websites

http://greeceflights.com (specializes in Greece)
www.cheapflights.com
www.cheapflights.ca
www.ebookers.com
www.expedia.com
www.orbitz.com
www.travelocity.com

Getting from the Airport

For connections from Athens airport to the city centre, Piraeus, and bus and train stations to the Peloponnese, *see* p.83.

By Train

The best route by train from the UK to Greece is through Italy. Starting with the **Eurostar** from London to Paris, the furthest port, Brindisi, is about 24 hours away, but it also has the shortest ferry journey to Pátras.

For information on trains from the UK to Greece, and the various **rail passes** available for the British (e.g. Inter-Rail) or for North Americans (e.g. Eurail), contact Rail Europe.

Rail Europe (UK): 178 Piccadilly, London W1, **t** 08708 371 371, *www.raileurope.co.uk*.

Rail Europe (USA and Canada): **t** 877 257 2887 (USA), or **t** 800 361 RAIL (Canada), *www.raileurope.com*.

Eurostar, **t** 08705 186 186, *www.eurostar.com*.

Airlines in Athens

Aegean Airlines, **t** 210 353 0101.
Air France, **t** 210 353 0380.
Alitalia, **t** 210 353 4284.
British Airways, **t** 210 353 0453.
Cyprus Airways, **t** 210 353 4312.
Delta, **t** 210 353 0116.
Easyjet, **t** 210 356 8120.
KLM, **t** 210 356 8120.
Lufthansa, **t** 210 353 0155.
Malev, **t** 210 324 1116.
Olympic, **t** 210 936 8424.
Singapore Airlines, **t** 210 353 1259.
Thai Airways, **t** 210 353 1237.

By Sea

The most common route to Greece by sea is from Italy; routes are well established, with daily overnight ferry services from various east coast ports (*see* box, overleaf). Check timetables, compare prices and book tickets on all the lines on these general websites:

Greek Ferries Club, *www.greekferries.gr*.
Hellas Ferries Center, *www.hellasferries.gr*.
Paleologos, *www.ferries.gr*.

Italy–Greece Ferries

In Pátras, these companies all have a counter in the new terminal by Gate 6 (the Melina Gate).

ANEK, **t** 261 022 6053, *www.anek.gr*. Venice and Ancona to Igoumenítsa and Pátras.

Superfast, **t** 261 062 2500, *www.superfast.com*. Ancona and Bari to Igoumenítsa and Pátras.

Minoan, **t** 261 042 6000, *www.minoan.gr*. Venice and Ancona to Igoumenítsa and Pátras.

Ventouris, **t** 210 482 8001, *www.ventouris.gr*. Bari to Corfu, Igoumenítsa and Kefaloniá.

Maritime Way, **t** (00 39) 040 676 0411 (Italy), *www.maritimeway.com*. Brindisi to Pátras, Kefaloniá and Igoumenítsa.

Endeavor Lines, **t** 261 062 0061, *www.endeavor-lines.com*. Brindisi to Pátras and Igoumenítsa.

Agoudimos, **t** 261 046 1800, *www.agoudimos-lines.com*. Bari to Pátras and Igoumenítsa. Pátras to Kefaloniá, Igoumenítsa and Bari

Blue Star, **t** 261 063 4000, *www.bluestarferries.com*. Bari to Pátras and Igoumenítsa.

You can also book ferries through:

UK: **Viamare Travel**, **t** 0800 0681 676.
Canada: **Omega Travel**, **t** 604 738 3433.
USA: **Amphitrion Holidays**, **t** 800 424 2471.

In high summer, reserve – you'll also save money by booking at least 45 days in advance. There are special rates for families, children under 12 and seniors over 60, and sometimes for holders of Eurail/Inter-Rail cards. Many offer camping on board.

By Car

Driving from London to Athens (and taking the ferry from Italy to Greece) at a normal pace takes around 3½ days.

An **international driving licence** is not required for EU citizens. Other nationals can obtain one at home, or at an Automobile Club (ELPA) office in Greece by presenting a national driving licence, passport and photo.

Drivers' Clubs

For more information on driving in Greece, contact the AA, RAC or, in the USA, the AAA:

AA, general enquiries, **t** 0870 600 0371, *www.theaa.com*.

RAC, general enquiries, **t** 08705 72 27 22, *www.rac.co.uk*.

AAA (USA), **t** 800 222 4357, *www.aaa.com*.

The **Motor Insurance Bureau**, **t** 210 322 3324, *www.mib-hellas.gr*, can tell you which Greek insurance company represents your own, or provide additional cover for Greece.

The **Greek Automobile Club** (**ELPA**), in Athens, **t** 210 606 8812, gives advice.

Customs formalities for bringing in a car are easy. You're allowed six months' free use of a car in Greece (or 15 months by paying a fee) before it must leave the country. To avoid difficulties when you leave, make sure your car is stamped in your passport on arrival.

Getting Around

By Train

To date, Greek rail (**OSE**) has been somewhat patchy, slow and old-fashioned, but this is changing. A new fast suburban train, the **Proastiakós** (**t** 210 527 2000, *www.proastiakos.gr*) already links Athens, Piraeus and its airport to Corinth and Kiáto in the Peloponnese; work is being done to extend it to Pátras at the time of writing. The line south of Corinth to Trípolis will still follow the existing tracks, but is being updated, as is the scenic rail line to Kalávrita. For information on tickets, their progress and what is completed, the **national information** number is **t** 1110 (If you press '2', you can ask in English); also see *www.ose.gr*.

In Athens, the station for northern Greece is Lárissa, on Deligiánni St. The station for the Peloponnese is behind it, reached by a pedestrian bridge. In Piraeus, the Proastiakós station for the Peloponnese and Lárissa station is near the metro on Konanós Street.

By Bus

Domestic buses (**KTEL**) are useful for reaching the main towns in the Peloponnese. In August, reserve seats in advance on the long-distance buses. The website, *www.ktel.org*, has long been in transition; to get reliable **bus information**, phone **t** 171 inside Athens or **t** 210 171 outside; they are happy to reel off the bus schedules. Athens to Olympia takes around 5½hrs, Tripolis 1½hrs, Kalamáta 4½hrs, Naúplio 2½hrs, Kalavríta 3½hrs.

To get to the **terminal** at 100 Kifissós Street (**t** 210 512 4910 or **t** 210 512 4911), take bus E93 from the airport or bus 051 from Omónia Square (Zínonos and Menandroú Streets).

By Sea

Athens' port, **Piraeus**, is the launchpad for Hellenic Seaways services to the Saronic Islands and the Peloponnesian ports of Méthana, Portochéli and Ermióni. Departures are from Aktí Posidonos (near Plateía Karaiskáki). As a rule hydrofoils and catamarans travel at least twice as fast as slow ferries and are twice as expensive. On most hydrofoils you can sit outside in the back, but on the catamarans and fast ferries you have to stay inside. In the peak season they're often fully booked, so buy tickets early. Beware: if the weather is very bad, they won't leave. Check with the Piraeus port authority, **t** 210 422 6000.

Hellenic Seaways, t 210 417 1190, *www.hsw.gr*.

By Car

At the time of writing, hiring a small car averages around €20–30 a day, and open-air Jeeps at least a third more. Most require that you be at least 21, some 25. In the off season, negotiate. **Fuel** at the time of writing is around €1.10 per litre.

While driving in the centre of Athens may be a hair-raising experience, the rest of Greece is fairly pleasant. There are few cars on most roads, and most **signs**, when you're lucky enough to find one at all, have their Latin equivalents as well as the names in Greek. **Traffic regulations** and signalling comply with standard practice on the European continent (i.e. driving on the right). Where there are no right-of-way signs at a crossroads, give priority to traffic coming from the right, and always beep your horn on blind corners. You may want to take a spare container of **petrol** along, as stations can be scarce and only open shop hours.

ELPA (the Greek automobile club) have a toll tourist helpline in English, **t** 901 124 1600. They also operate a **breakdown service** (**t** 10400); if you belong to an affiliated automobile club at home, it's free anywhere.

By Motorbike

Motorbikes and scooters (and increasingly quad bikes) are popular summer modes of transport. Rental **rates** vary (€12–20 a day for a scooter, anything over 250cc will be similar to a car), and include third party **insurance** coverage. You will need a valid **driving licence** and for anything over 125cc a full **motorcycle licence**. The downsides: many of the bikes are poorly maintained, many of the roads are poorly maintained, and everyone takes too many risks: hospital beds in Greece fill up each summer with foreign and Greek casualties. Most islands have laws about operating motorbikes after midnight but they are as enforced as often as the helmet requirement.

By Bicycle

Cycling has not caught on in the mountainous Peloponnese, either as a sport or as a means of transport, though you can usually hire a bike in major resorts to pedal to the beach. Trains and planes carry bicycles for free or a small fee. Several companies offer cycling tours, *see* overleaf.

Where to Stay

Hotels

Prices are posted in every room. Off season (i.e. mid-September–July) these are much lower and often very negotiable, which is why prices are not always displayed on websites; although note that for many mountain hotels the prices are higher on winter weekends. Check for online discounts. In season there may be a 10 per cent surcharge for stays of only one or two days, an air-conditioning surcharge, as well as a 20 per cent surcharge for an extra bed. If you have any reason to believe all is not on the level, complain to the tourist police. For complete listings of hotels in Athens and the Peloponnese, see the Hellenic Chamber of Hotels' site, *www.grhotels.gr*.

Hotel Price Ranges

Price ranges in this guide are for a double room in peak season (July and August by the sea, winter weekends in the mountains, when breakfast is usually included in the charge) and for low season; sometimes they vary enormously. Rates are almost always negotiable.

luxury	€€€€€	€150 to astronomical
very expensive	€€€€	€120–150
expensive	€€€	€80–120
moderate	€€	€50–80
inexpensive	€	less than €50

For budget hotels and bargains, try:

www.hostelworld.com.

www.hostelbookers.com/hostels/greece.

Rooms, Studios and *Xenónas*

Privately run **rooms** (ΔΟΜΑΤΙΑ, *domátia*) are generally cheaper than hotels and sometimes more pleasant. Many have basic kitchen facilities, which turn a room into a '**studio**'. Until June and after August, rates are negotiable; owners will nearly always drop the price per day the longer you stay.

In the alpine regions of the Peloponnese (mostly), you'll find ***xenónas***, country inns, built in the traditional style; some are basic, others are quite lavish, equipped with not so traditional Jacuzzis and other goodies. Open all year, they are the key to winter tourism in the Peloponnese; Athenians love to come to play in the mountain snow and sit around the fireplace, so prices are always highest on winter weekends.

Camping

Greece's summer climate is perfect for camping, especially close to the sea, where breezes keep the mosquitoes at bay. Unauthorized camping is illegal, although each village enforces the ban as it sees fit.

Specialist Tour Operators

In the UK

Andante Travels, **t** 01722 713800, *www.andante travels.co.uk*. Guided archaeology tours of the Peloponnese, e.g. 'From Homer to Hadrian'.

Exodus, **t** (020) 8675 5550, www.exodus.co.uk. Cultural holidays and ancient sites.

Explore, **t** 0870 333 4001, *www.explore.co.uk*. Guided tour all around the Peloponnese.

GAP Adventures, **t** 0870 999 0144, *www.gapadventures.com*. Cultural tours.

Headwater, **t** 01606 720 199, *www. headwater.com*. Walking holidays.

Inntravel, **t** (01653) 617755, *www.inntravel.co.uk*. Walking, fly/drive holidays, villas and hotels.

Martin Randall, *t* (020) 8742 3355, *www. martinrandall.com*. Medieval and Classical Peloponnese guided tours.

Naturetrek, **t** 01962 733051, *www.naturetrek. co.uk*. Butterfly-spotting.

Neilson, **t** 0870 333 3336, *www.neilson.co.uk*. Sailing, watersports, mountain bike holidays.

Ramblers, **t** (01707) 331133, *www.ramblers holidays.co.uk*. Walking and wild flower tours.

The Travelling Naturalist, **t** 01305 267994, *www.naturalist.co.uk*. Flowers, birds, history.

Walks Worldwide, **t** (01524) 242 000, *www. walksworldwide.com*. Self-guided walks in the Máni.

In the USA and Canada

Breakaway Adventures, **t** 800 567 6286, *www.breakaway-adventures.com*.

Classic Adventures, **t** 800 777 8090, *www. classicadventures.com*. Cycling tours.

Cycle Greece, **t** 800 867 1753, *www.cyclegreece. gr*. Pedal to the sacred sites and spas.

Ya'lla, **t** (503) 977 3758, *www.yallatours.com*. Guided tours of Athens and the Peloponnese.

In Greece (t + 30)

Athens Centre, **t** 210 701 2268, *www.athens centre.gr*. Learn modern Greek in Athens.

Triumph Bike Tours, **t** 229 409 4905, *www. triumphbiketours.com*. See the Peloponnese on a 900cc Hinkley Triumph; group or self-guided.

Trekking Hellas, **t** 210 323 4548, *www.outdoors-greece.com*. A wide choice of special-interest holidays: rafting, trekking, tapestry-making, food, tours for cherry lovers...

Self-catering Operators

Telephone numbers are for the UK, unless specified otherwise.

Direct Greece, **t** 0870 191 9244, *www.direct greece.co.uk*. Hotels, villas and flats in the Máni.

Greek Options, **t** 0870 241 8668, *www.greek options.co.uk*. Villas and apartments in Stoúpa.

Hidden Greece, **t** (020) 8758 4707, *www.hidden-greece.co.uk*. Athens and the Argo-Saronic Gulf.

Iglu, **t** (020) 8544 6401, *www.igluvillas*. Villas.

Kosmar, **t** 0871 7000 747, *www.kosmar.co.uk*. Self-catering package holidays.

Manos, **t** 0871 664 7983, *www.manos.co.uk*. Self-catering holidays to the major resorts.

Simply Travel, **t** 0870 166 4979, *www.simply-travel.co.uk*. in the Máni, Messenía, Ástros.

Sunvil, **t** (020) 8568 4758, *www.sunvil.co.uk*. Villas and apartments.

Vintage, **t** 0845 344 0449, *http://vintagetravel. co.uk*. Houses with private pools.

Practical A–Z

07

Imperial–Metric Conversions

Length (multiply by)

Inches to centimetres: 2.54
Centimetres to inches: 0.39
Feet to metres: 0.3
Metres to feet: 3.28
Yards to metres: 0.91
Metres to yards: 1.1
Miles to kilometres: 1.61
Kilometres to miles: 0.62

Area (multiply by)

Inches square to centimetres square: 6.45
Centimetres square to inches square: 0.15
Feet square to metres square: 0.09
Metres square to feet square: 10.76
Miles square to kilometres square: 2.59
Kilometres square to miles square: 0.39
Acres to hectares: 0.40
Hectares to acres: 2.47

Weight (multiply by)

Ounces to grams: 28.35
Grammes to ounces: 0.035
Pounds to kilograms: 0.45
Kilograms to pounds: 2.2
Stone to kilograms: 6.35
Kilograms to stone: 0.16
Tons (UK) to kilograms: 1,016
Kilograms to tons (UK): 0.0009
1 UK ton (2,240lbs) = 1.12 US tonnes (2,000lbs)

°C	°F
40	104
35	95
30	86
25	77
20	68
15	59
10	50
5	41
-0	32
-5	23
-10	14
-15	5

Volume (multiply by)

Pints (UK) to litres: 0.57
Litres to pints (UK): 1.76
Quarts (UK) to litres: 1.13
Litres to quarts (UK): 0.88
Gallons (UK) to litres: 4.55
Litres to gallons (UK): 0.22
1 UK pint/quart/gallon = 1.2 US pints/quarts/ gallons

Temperature

Celsius to Fahrenheit: multiply by 1.8 then add 32

Fahrenheit to Celsius: subtract 32 then multiply by 0.55

Greece Information

Time Differences

Country: + 2hrs GMT; + 7hrs EST

Dialling Codes

Greece country code 30

To Greece from: UK, Ireland, New Zealand 00 / USA, Canada 011 / Australia 0011 then dial 30 and the full 10-digit number

From Greece to: UK 00 44; Ireland 00 353; USA, Canada 001; Australia 00 61; New Zealand 00 64 then the number without the initial zero

Operator: 132

International operator: 139

Emergency Numbers

European emergency number in English 112
Police: 100
Ambulance: 166
Fire: 199
Car breakdown (ELPA) 10400; tourist helpline in English 174

Embassy Numbers in Greece

UK: 210 727 2600; **Ireland** 210 723 2771;
USA: 210 721 2951; **Canada** 210 727 3400

Greek Measurements

Two uniquely Greek measurements you may come across (especially if you are looking at property) are the ***strémma***, a Greek land measurement (1 *strémma* = ¼ acre); and the ***oká***, an old-fashioned weight standard, divided into 400 *drams* (1 *oká* = 3lb; 140 *drams* = 1lb)

Shoe Sizes

Europe	UK	USA
35	2½ / 3	4
36	3 / 3½	4½ / 5
37	4	5½ / 6
38	5	6½
39	5½ / 6	7 / 7½
40	6 / 6½	8 / 8½
41	7	9 / 9½
42	8	9½ / 10
43	9	10½
44	9½ / 10	11
45	10½	12
46	11	12½ / 13

Women's Clothing Sizes

UK	6	8	10	12	14	16	18	20
USA	2	4	6	8	10	12	14	16

Children

Greeks love children, and children usually love Greece. Depending on their age, they go free or receive discounts on ships and buses. However, don't count on pharmacies stocking your brand of milk powder or baby foods – it's safest to bring your own supply. Disposable nappies are widely available.

Greek children usually have an afternoon nap (as do their parents), so it's quite normal for Greeks to eat *en famille* until the small hours. Even so, finding a babysitter is rarely a problem: just ask at your hotel.

Crime and Safety

Police t 100/**t** 112
Fire t 199/**t** 112

With one of the lowest crime rates in Europe, Greece is a safe country for travellers, although you should be cautious in busy tourist hotspots. As you would anywhere, lock your car and don't leave valuables on show inside, and don't leave personal possessions unattended. If you have a theft and you intend to make an insurance claim, report it to the police in order to get paperwork to show. Unscrupulous taxi drivers overcharging tourists, however, is rife; if it happens, write down the licence number and threaten to complain and the issue is usually resolved.

Women travelling alone will not usually be harassed, but should be prepared for a fusillade of questions. Greeks tend to do everything in groups or pairs and can't understand people who want to go solo.

It is advisable, as events in recent years have proved, to avoid taking photographs anywhere near airports or military sites.

Eating Out

Eating out in Greece gets better all the time, as the Greeks themselves are becoming more demanding. If you join them for dinner, there's no Western nit-picking over who's had what. You share the food, drink, company and the bill, *to logariasmó*, although hosts will seldom let guests part with a cent.

Waiters are often paid a cut of the profits (which is why some obnoxiously tout for custom in busy resorts); tipping is discretionary but much appreciated. By law, there's a book for registering any complaints.

Restaurant and Taverna Prices

A meal at the huge majority of tavernas – if you don't order a major fish – usually runs at around €15–20 a head with generous carafes of wine. Prices at simple tavernas are lower; sophisticated restaurants can be much higher.

In this guide, if the prices for tavernas and restaurants fall within this usual range, no price is mentioned, but for higher-priced or much cheaper places we state the average cost for a two-course meal for one with wine.

For more about dining, including local specialities, wines and a menu decoder, *see* the **Food and Drink** chapter, pp.55–64.

Electricity

The electric current in Greece is 220 volts, 50Hz; plugs are continental two-pin. Bring an adaptor/transformer from home, as they are rare in Greece.

Health and Emergencies

Ambulance t 166/**t** 112
Hospital/pharmacy t 1434

For **first aid**, go to the nearest Local Health Centre (**ESY** or 'kentro eEas'), which are well equipped to deal with snake bites, jelly fish stings, grippe, etc., and treat foreigners for free. Where there are no ESYs, **rural doctors** (*iatrós*) do the same work, also free..

For more serious illnesses or accidents, you'll need the **hospital** (*nosokomío*); helicopters act as ambulances when necessary.

Most doctors pride themselves on their English, as do the **pharmacists** (found in the *farmakeío*), whose advice on minor ailments is good, although their medicine is not particularly cheap. Pharmacies also sell condoms (*kapótes*), seasickness remedies, sunscreen, tampons, insect repellent, etc., and you can get the morning-after pill and the Pill without a prescription – show your old packet. However, bring extras of any prescription drug you need, and stock up before heading off to remote areas.

The strong sun is the most likely cause of grief, so be careful, hatted and sunscreened.

National Holidays

1 Jan New Year's Day
6 Jan Epiphany, *Ta Fóta/Theofánia*
Feb–Mar 'Clean Monday'
25 Mar Greek Independence Day
Late Mar–April Good Friday and Easter Monday
1 May Labour Day
40 days after Easter Pentecost (Whit Monday)
15 Aug Assumption of the Virgin
28 Oct 'Ochí' Day (in celebration of Metaxás' 'No' to Mussolini, *see* p.28)
25 Dec Christmas
26 Dec Gathering of the Virgin

If anything else goes wrong, do what the Greeks have done for centuries: pee on it.

Greek **tap water** is perfectly safe to drink, and inexpensive plastic bottles of spring water are widely available (and responsible for untold pollution in landfill sites).

National Holidays

Museums, archaeological sites, offices and shops close down on these holiday dates (*see* box, above); many businesses and shops also close down for the afternoon before and the morning after a religious holiday. If a national holiday falls on a Sunday, the following Monday is observed.

In Greece, Orthodox Easter is the equivalent in significance of Christmas and New Year in northern climes – the time when far-flung relatives return to see their families back home. It's a good time of year to visit for the atmosphere, feasts and fireworks – but beware that the buses and roads are packed.

After Easter and 1 May, spring (*ánixi* – the opening) has officially come, and the tourist season begins.

Opening Hours

For **banks**, *see* p.68. For **post offices** and **shops**, *see* the relevant sections below.

Museums and Sites

In Greece, **archaeological sites** and **museums** are generally closed on Monday, and hours are shorter in the winter. **Admission fees** are usually between €1.50 and €7; if they cost more, this guide will say '*adm exp*' instead of '*adm*'. **Students** with valid ID get a discount, and in state museums EU visitors under 18 or over 65 with ID get in cheaper or often free.

Churches and Monasteries

Because of a surge in thefts, **churches** only open when there is someone around, often in the late afternoon (6–7pm); at other times you may have to hunt down the key (*kleethEE*). **Monasteries** close for a couple of hours at midday. Note that visitors are expected to dress respectfully – long trousers for men, knees covered for women. Many provide long skirts or robes for the scantily clad.

Post Offices

Offices of the **Hellenic Post/ELTA**, which is also useful for changing money, are **open** Mon–Fri 7.30am–2pm, although in large towns they may be open till 7.30–8pm and on Saturday morning as well. Signs for **post offices** (*tachidromío*) as well as **postboxes** (*grammatokivótio*) are bright yellow and easy to find. On two-slot boxes, *Esoterikó* is for domestic mail, and *Exoterikó* is for overseas.

Stamps (*grammatósima*) can also be bought at kiosks and in some tourist shops. **Postcards** cost the same as letters and are given the same priority (about three days to the UK, unless posted from a remote village).

If you do not have an address, mail can be sent to you *poste restante* to any post office in Greece, and picked up with proof of identity (you'll find the postal codes in the text). After one month all unretrieved letters are returned to sender.

Shopping

Official **shopping hours** are Mon and Wed 9–5, Tues, Thurs and Fri 10–7 (in Athens, it's usually 9pm), Sat 8.30–3 and Sun closed, except for many food shops and bakeries. Tourist shops stay open much later in season. Leather goods, gold and jewellery, traditional handicrafts, embroideries and weavings, onyx, ceramics, alabaster, herbs and spices and tacky knick-knacks are favourite buys.

Non-EU citizens tempted by big ticket items can justify their indulgences by having the sales tax (VAT) reimbursed – this is 18% of the purchase price. Make sure the shop has a TAX FREE FOR TOURISTS sticker in the window, and pick up a tax-free shopping cheque for your purchases, along with instructions for reimbursement at the airport as you depart (allow an extra hour).

Sports and Activities

Water Sports

Greece was made for water sports, and by law, all the **beaches** are public. Hundreds fly the European Blue Flag. Resort beaches have parasols and sunbed concessions and snack bars, and if there's a breeze you'll probably find a **windsurfer** to rent (favourite spots are Páros, Lefkáda, Rhodes and Kárpathos). Bigger beaches have **paragliding**, **kite surfing** and **jet skis**.

Naturism is tolerated in designated or out-of-the-way areas. On the other hand, topless sunbathing is legal on the majority of popular beaches as long as they're not smack in the middle of a village; exercise discretion.

Scuba-diving, once strictly controlled, is as of 2006 open everywhere, which should soon translate into more diving centres in the Peloponnese. Contact the **Owners of Diving Centres**, 67 Zéas, Piraeus, **t** 210 922 9532. Also see the ***Hellenic Underwater Times***, *www.huts.gr*.

Land Sports

The Peloponnese, with its dramatic mountains, gorges and exceptionally rich flora and fauna, is made for hiking. **Trekking Hellas**, 7 Filellínon St, Athens ✉ 10557, **t** 210 331 0323, *www.trekking.gr*, offers a wide range of excursions in the mountains.

If you like altitudes, the Greek **mountain clubs** (**EOS**) have marked trails and refuges for spending the night on the Peloponnese's highest mountains: at Kyllíni (7,788ft) and Chelmós (7,670ft) in the north; Maínalo (6,496ft) in the centre; and Taíyetos (7,887ft) and Párnonas (6,345ft) in the south. For more information, contact **EOS**: 3 Plateía Ag. Theodoron, Athens ✉ 10561, **t** 210 323 8775, or see the following places:

Éghio: K. Theodóroi, ✉ 23100, **t** 269 102 2308.

Kalamáta: 23 Evripídou, ✉ 24100, **t** 272 102 2129.

Corinth: 30 Koliátsou, ✉ 20100, **t** 274 102 9970, **t** 274 102 5694.

Xilókastro: 11 Adamópoulos , ✉ 20400, **t** 274 302 2918.

Pátras: PO Bs 1346, ✉ 26110, **t** 261 027 3912.

Sparta: 97 Gortsóloglou, ✉ 23100, **t** 273 102 2574.

Trípolis: 6 A. Konstantínou St, ✉ 22100, **t** 271 023 2243.

Kalávrita: SOXA Kalavríton, ✉ 25100, **t** 269 202 2611 or **t** 269 202 2346.

And **skiing**? Why not, on the snowy slopes of Chelmós or Maínalo? It ain't the Alps, but how many people can say they've been on a ski holiday in southern Greece? For skiing on Chelmós, **t** 269 202 4451, *www.kalavrita-ski.com*; for Maínalo, **t** 279 602 2211.

Paragliding (*anemopterismós*) is very popular, and some of the updraughts in the Peloponnese are ideal. For more information, try *www.paragliding.gr* or the **Hellenic Air Sports Federation**, PO Box 70262, Glyfáda 16600, Athens, **t** 210 964 9788.

Tennis is very popular in Athens, with numerous clubs from Glyfáda to Kifissiá, and at all major resort hotels (many are lit up at night so you can beat the heat); often non-residents are allowed to play in the off season.

Most resort areas, by the sea or in the mountains, are near **riding stables**.

Telephones and the Internet

Operator **t** 132 (Greek), **t** 139 (international)

The **Organismós Tilefikinonía Elládos**, or **OTE**, operates public card phones. **Phone cards** (*télekartas*), sold in kiosks, come in

Average Sea Temperatures in °C/°F

Jan	April	May	July	Aug	Sept	Oct	Nov	Dec
15/59	16/61	18/64	24/75	25/77	24/75	22/72	18/64	17/63

denominations from €4 to €12. OTE also offers a *Xronocarta*, which is cheaper for long-distance calls, but involves dialling more numbers. Some **kiosks** have a telephone with a meter. These are getting rare, as all Greeks own mobiles.

British and Irish **mobile phones** work in Greece if they have a roaming facility; check with your service provider. Frequencies on the country's four networks are 900 and 1800 MHz. If you're going to be in Greece a while and using your mobile a lot, and as long as your mobile is not locked to a UK network, avoid the astronomical roaming charges (both outgoing and incoming) by temporarily replacing your UK SIM card with a local or international one (see *www.0044.co.uk*), or buy a pay-as-you-go phone locally. You can also rent a mobile phone in Greece: try **Cellular Abroad**, *www.cellularabroad.com*, or **Planet Omni**, *www.planetomni.com*.

To **phone Greece from abroad**, the country code is 30. To **call home from Greece**, dial the international prefix (UK 00 44, Ireland 00 353, USA and Canada 00 1, Australia 00 61, New Zealand 00 64).

All Greek **phone numbers** are 10-digit and you must dial all 10 digits wherever you are, and when phoning from abroad. Numbers that begin with 2 are landlines; numbers that begin with 6 are for mobiles.

Any popular tourist destination will have at least one **cybercafé**, charging between €4–6 an hour; many hotels and offer Internet access as well. Just ask.

Time

'God gave watches to the Europeans and time to the Greeks,' they say, but if you need more precision, Greek time is Eastern European, 2hrs ahead of Greenwich Mean Time, 7hrs ahead of Eastern Standard Time in North America.

Tipping

This is discretionary in restaurants and bars but, if the service has been good, a tip is appreciated. In taxis, one generally just rounds up, or adds an extra euro or two depending on the fare. During certain holidays such as Greek Easter, an extra euro is built into the price.

Toilets

Tavernas, *kafeneíons*, museums, bus stations and sweet shops almost always have facilities (it's good manners to buy something), and occasionally you'll find public toilets (usually pretty grotty) in the towns. 'Women' is ΓΥΝΑΙΚΑ (*gynéka*), 'men' ΑΝΔΡΟΣ (*ándros*).

In older *pensions* and tavernas, do not tempt fate by disobeying the little notices 'the papers they please to throw in the basket', or it's bound to lead to trouble.

If you stay in a private room or *pension* you may have to have the electric water-heater turned on for about 20 minutes before you take a shower. In most smaller *pensions*, water is heated by a solar panel, so the best time to take a shower is in the late afternoon or the early evening. In larger hotels there is often hot water in the mornings and evenings, but not in the afternoons.

Transliteration and Pronunciation

There is no general agreement on a standard method of transliterating the Greek alphabet into Roman letters, which means that you will constantly come across variations in the spellings of place names and words, on maps, in books and on road signs.

When transcribing, in this guide we have used D for the Greek *delta* (Δ), which you may see elsewhere as DH or TH; CH for *chi* (X), which is pronounced like the 'ch' in 'loch' and which you may see written as H, e.g. in Portochéli (Porto Heli); F for *fi* (Φ), which you may see elsewhere as PH; and G for the Greek *gamma* (Γ), which sounds more like a guttural GH verging on a Y when followed by *i* or *e*, as in *agios* (saint), pronounced '*ayios*'. Exceptions are made where there is a common ancient name or accepted modern English spelling such as Corinth.

Stressing the right syllable is vital to pronunciation, so the stressed letter of each word is accented with an acute (´) accent.

See also **Language**, pp.463–7.

Athens and Piraeus

Athens is rarely love at first sight – under the sublime Acropolis, the modern city pales into an urban crazy quilt. At second glance, however, you realize that it may not be pretty but it can be an awful lot of fun; Athens' redeeming features were always its innumerable oases tucked away amidst the bustle, its feverish nightlife, its summer festivals – and the Athenians themselves, whose friendliness belies the reputation of most urbanites.

08

Don't miss

1. The most famous building in the world
   The Parthenon p.92
2. Ancient beauty
   National Archaeological Museum p.110
3. Ouzo and *mezédes*
   Psirrí pp.108 and 125
4. Where Socrates walked
   Ancient Agora p.100
5. The view from the top
   Lykavitós Hill p.116

See map overleaf

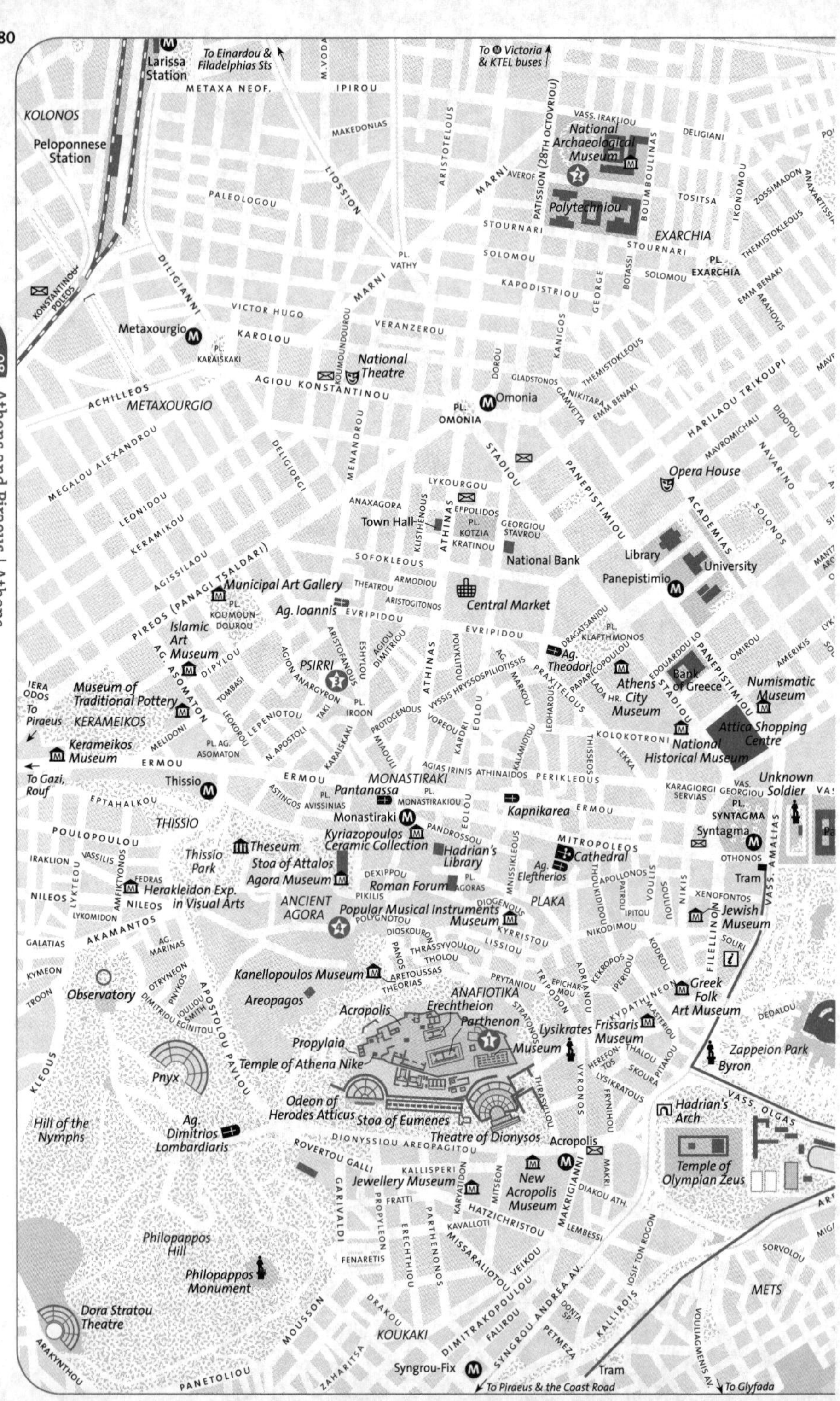

Larissa Station
To Einardou & Filadelphias Sts
To Victoria & KTEL buses
KOLONOS
Peloponnese Station
National Archaeological Museum
Polytechniou
EXARCHIA
PL. EXARCHIA
Metaxourgio
National Theatre
Omonia
PL. OMONIA
METAXOURGIO
Opera House
Town Hall
PL. KOTZIA
National Bank
Library
University
Panepistimio
Municipal Art Gallery
Central Market
Ag. Ioannis
Islamic Art Museum
PSIRRI
Ag. Theodori
Athens City Museum
Bank of Greece
Numismatic Museum
Museum of Traditional Pottery
KERAMEIKOS
To Piraeus
Kerameikos Museum
National Historical Museum
Attica Shopping Centre
To Gazi, Rouf
Thissio
MONASTIRAKI
Pantanassa
Kapnikarea
Unknown Soldier
PL. SYNTAGMA
Syntagma
THISSIO
Monastiraki
Kyriazopoulos Ceramic Collection
Hadrian's Library
Cathedral
Theseum
Thissio Park
Stoa of Attalos
Agora Museum
Roman Forum
Ag. Eleftherios
Tram
Herakleidon Exp. in Visual Arts
ANCIENT AGORA
Popular Musical Instruments Museum
PLAKA
Jewish Museum
Kanellopoulos Museum
ANAFIOTIKA
Greek Folk Art Museum
Areopagos
Observatory
Acropolis
Erechtheion
Parthenon
Lysikrates
Frissaris Museum
Propylaia
Museum
Zappeion Park
Temple of Athena Nike
Byron
Pnyx
Odeon of Herodes Atticus
Stoa of Eumenes
Hadrian's Arch
Hill of the Nymphs
Ag. Dimitrios Lombardiaris
Theatre of Dionysos
Acropolis
Jewellery Museum
New Acropolis Museum
Temple of Olympian Zeus
Philopappos Hill
Philopappos Monument
METS
Dora Stratou Theatre
KOUKAKI
Syngrou-Fix
Tram
To Piraeus & the Coast Road
To Glyfada

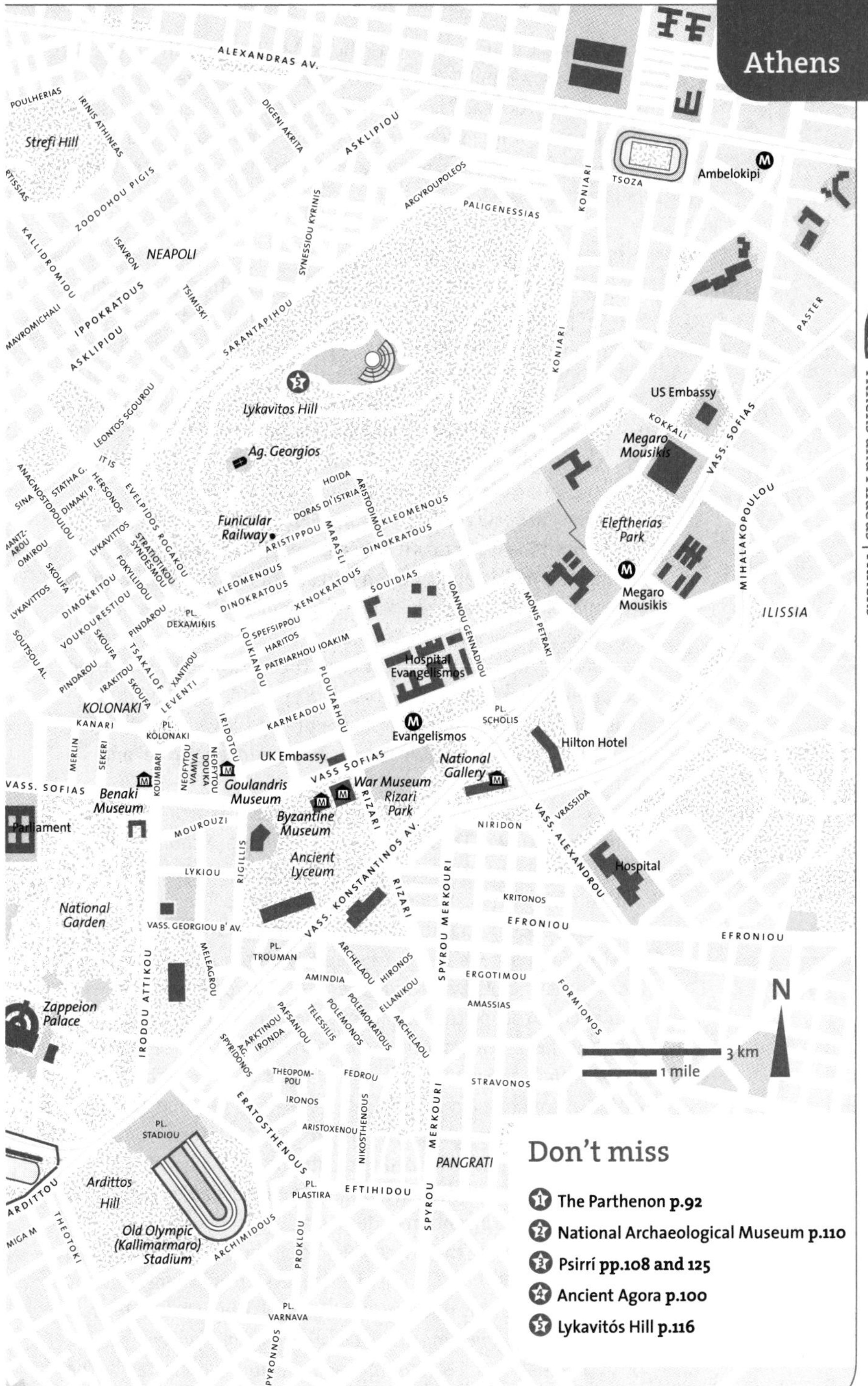

Don't miss

1. The Parthenon **p.92**
2. National Archaeological Museum **p.110**
3. Psirrí **pp.108 and 125**
4. Ancient Agora **p.100**
5. Lykavitós Hill **p.116**

As well as its original charms, the 2004 Olympics left Athens with vastly improved public transport, pedestrianized streets, overhauled museums and archaeological sites, renovated neoclassical buildings, revitalized squares and gardens, new hotels and restaurants – and the changes are continuing apace: Athens gets better all the time.

History

Who doesn't desire to see Athens is stupid; who sees it without liking it is even more stupid; but the height of stupidity is to see it, like it, and then leave it.
Lysippus
(4th century BC)

Athens was inhabited by the end of the Neolithic Age (*c.* 3500 BC), but her real debut on to history's stage began in the second millennium BC, when invaders, probably from Asia Minor, entered Attica and established small fortified enclaves. Their descendants would claim they were 'the children of Kecrops', a half-man half-snake who founded Kecropia on the future Acropolis. Kecrops, whose sacred bird was the owl, gave them laws and taught them the cultivation of that all-important crop, the olive.

The next act saw the birth of **King Erechtheos**, 'the earth-born'. Snake from the waist down himself, Erechtheos was the official founder of Athens, and through him and his mother, the earth, Athenians would claim an inalienable right to Attica. Erechtheos introduced the worship of Athena; later versions of the civic myth would claim her as *his* foster mother. The snake and the owl then become her symbols and, by extension, the city's. Nor did the real thing leave the Athenian stage entirely; Classical Athenians firmly believed that their Acropolis was guarded by a real and benevolent snake.

The city's Mycenaean rulers had a fortified palace on the Acropolis. Her hero **Theseus** dates from this era. Although best known for killing the Minotaur in Crete, Theseus was also credited with unifying Attica under Athenian leadership. The city's politicians would scramble to be associated with his exploits; at the height of Athens' glory in 475 BC, **Kimon** brought his bones back from the island of Skýros and gave them a hero's burial. Athens managed to escape the Dorian invasions after 1200 BC and, although her culture declined and many of her people emigrated to Asia Minor, the escape was a great point of pride with Athenians, who as a result considered themselves more Greek, more legitimate and certainly more refined than their Dorian neighbours. All of this helped to create the amazing self-confidence and sense of difference that would lead to, among other things, the invention of democracy.

Some time during the 8th century BC all the towns of Attica were indeed peaceably united under the leadership of Athens. This large city-state was jointly ruled by a *basileus*, the king who doubled as the chief priest, a *polemarch* (general) and an *archon* (civil ruler), positions that by the 6th century BC were annually elected by the

Getting to Athens

For details of flights to Athens from the UK and USA/Canada, *see* **Planning Your Trip**, pp.68–9.

Elefthérios Venizélos airport is 25km northeast of the centre of Athens. **Airport information**, **t** (+ 30) 210 353 0000, *www.aia.gr*, 24hrs a day in English and Greek. The airport has up-to-date facilities for the disabled, and a five-star Sofitel Hotel outside the main terminal. English is spoken in the **information booths**, which also have a complimentary phone service to every airport facility and airline, plus brochures about public transport in Athens.

Most of the action is on **level 0** (Arrivals): a **post office** (*open daily 7am–9pm*); an **Internet-fax** office (*open 8am–10pm*); **Pacific Baggage Storage and Courier, t** 210 353 0352 (*open 24hrs*), a **pharmacy** (*open daily 6am–midnight*); **exchange bureaux** (*open 24hrs*) and several **banks**, all bristling with automatic tellers; plus an office of the **EOT** (the Greek National Tourist Office), **t** 210 353 0448, with brochures and maps (*open Mon–Fri 9–6, Sat, Sun and hols 10–3*).

Getting to and from the Airport

Athens airport is linked to the city every 30mins by metro and bus and the suburban rail line (*see* p.70).

By metro: Line 3 goes to Sýntagma and Monastiráki, where you can make connections to Piraeus (1hr from the airport), or take the Suburban Railway, the Proastiákos, to Piraeus. Airport metro tickets are €6, or €10 return. The first metro from Sýntagma leaves at 5.38 am, the last at 10.59pm.

By airport bus: Express buses (*www.oasa.gr*) from the airport run to the nearest metro station, Ethnikí Amyna (X94), Sýntagma (X95), the Kifissós bus station (X93) and Piraeus (X96). Buses depart from the airport's main terminal. A good safe time-estimate from the terminal to the end of their lines might be an hour, slightly more in peak traffic periods. Every stop has a sign showing exact timetables. One-way tickets cost €3.20. Validate your ticket on the machine in the airport bus to mark the time and date. Children under six travel free.

By car: A toll road, the Attikí Ódos (€3) links the airport to the centre of Athens and on west to Kifissós and the Lamia–Piraeus highway, and to Elefsína and the Peloponnese.

By taxi: *See* 'Getting around Athens', overleaf. Taxis to Athens centre cost around €25, to Piraeus port €30, and the fare is doubled between midnight and 5am (so if you arrive near to 5am, it's best to wait until 5).

---

aristocracy in an assembly on the Areopagus. Conflict arose between the aristocrats and rising commercial classes, and reached such a point that **Solon**, an aristocrat elected *archon* in 594 BC, was asked to re-establish 'good order'. He complied, writing new laws in exquisite poetry. Slavery as a result of debt was abolished, existing debts forgiven, trade and crafts encouraged, and the **Council of Four Hundred** established to include a broader base of citizens in government. Solon's laws were carved on rotating wooden tablets and placed in the Agora. This public display of laws and notices would become a hallmark of Athenian democracy; 7,500 inscriptions were found in the Agora alone.

But Solon's good start didn't stop his kinsman **Pisistratos** from making himself a 'popular' dictator or *tyrannos* in 560 BC. He began the naval build-up that first made Athens a threat to other Greek city-states. He reformed the Panathenaic Games in an attempt to rival the Olympics, instituted grandiose building projects and encouraged the arts and the planting of olives. Later, Athens would vilify his name, but there is no doubt that Pisistratos was a one-man chamber of commerce for the Archaic city. His increasingly despotic son **Hippias** ruled until 510 BC, when **Kleisthenes**, a member of the aristocratic Alcmaeonid clan, paid for a new marble temple at Delphi, and then 'suggested' that the oracle command

Getting around Athens

By Metro, Tram and Bus

The **metro** (*www.ametro.gr*) operates from 5.30am to 12.20am and is an important means of getting across Athens. The air-conditioned **Athens Tram** links the city to its seaside suburbs. The terminal is on Leofóros Amalía a couple of streets south of Sýntagma, with spurs along the coast to Piraeus/Falíro, and from Glyfáda to Voúla, putting Athens' beaches within 20 minutes or so of the centre. See *www.tramsa.gr*.

Tickets are 80¢. Purchase bus and tram tickets (50¢) at the kiosks before boarding, and punch them in the machine; if you're caught without a ticket the fine is 60 times the fare. Transfers good for 90 minutes on metro and bus or tram routes cost €1. It is possible to buy a day ticket for €3, or a week ticket for €10, valid on all buses, metros and trams.

Note that all city transport, except the Piraeus–Athens bus, stops at midnight, so plan to arrive at your destination before then. For metro or bus info within the city, call **t** 185, Mon–Fri 7am–9pm, Sat–Sun 9–5.

By Taxi

There are stands in some squares, at the airport, train station and bus stations, but most taxis cruise the streets. Sharing is common (*see* below). The minimum fare (Tariff One) is €2.50; the almost double Tariff Two is for the period between midnight and 5am. If you travel on the Attikí Ódos, you'll be charged an extra €2.70 for the road tolls. Each bag over 10kg is 30¢. The charge for being picked up at the airport is €3 and 80¢ for the bus or train stations. On major holidays, such as Easter, the driver gets a mandatory 'present' of €1. Taxis are regulated by the **Athens Traffic Department**, 24–6 Deligiánni St, Metaxoúrgio, **t** 210 523 0111. Not all drivers are honest, but merely showing this address to a driver usually solves disputes.

Radio taxis charge €2.50 from the moment you call, and slightly more if you book in advance. In many cases, especially if you're going to the airport, it's worth it. Try: **Athens** 1, **t** 210 921 7942; **Parthenon, t** 210 532 3300; **Enotita, t** 210 645 9000; **Ikaros, t** 210 515 2800 and **t** 801 112 4000.

Because fares are so low and demand so great, Athenians often **share cabs**. Usually, the cabbie leaves his flag lit, even if he has passengers, to indicate that he is willing to take more. Hailing a cab this way is not for the faint-hearted; the usual procedure is to stand by the street, flag down any passing cab, and, if they slow down and cock an ear, shout out your general destination. If the taxi is going that way, the driver will stop; if not, he won't. Check the meter when you board, and pay from there, adding €1 (the minimum fare), plus any baggage charges. If the cabbie asks for the full fare, start writing down his licence number and ask for a receipt; that usually settles the issue on the spot.

By Car

Not fun. Besides the traffic jams, the one-way system is confusing and parking is almost impossible. If you need assistance, call **ELPA** (the Greek Automobile Club), **t** 10400.

---

the Spartans to liberate Athens from the tyrant. In the aftermath, as the aristocrats squabbled, Kleisthenes proposed reforms to check their power. They responded by trying to dissolve the Council of Four Hundred, and before they knew it they were cornered on the Acropolis by a spontaneous uprising; after 50 years of tyranny, the people were ripe for a new order.

Kleisthenes' reforms were revolutionary. For the first time, government would no longer merely reflect the social order, but base itself on the concept of *isonomia*, or equal rights (at least for all male citizens). Ignoring previous divisions by clan or geography, Kleisthenes divided the population of Attica into ten political *phylae* (tribes); each of the ten would draw lots to select 50 members to serve in the new **Council of Five Hundred**, from which a further lot was drawn to select ten *archons*, all of whom were meant to spend a tenth of the year in Athens. Motions for new laws were debated first by the Areopagos (the aristocrats' old

Athens Metro

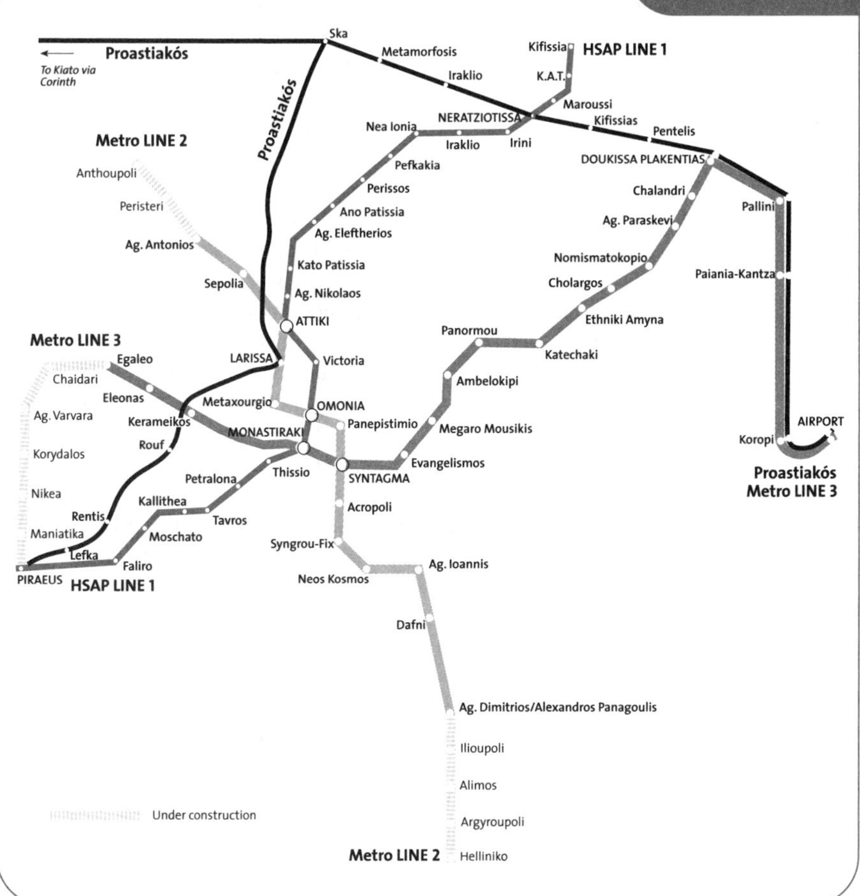

assembly, surviving as a kind of House of Lords) and then by the Council, and then presented to the popular assembly for a vote. Kleisthenes also introduced ostracism – if any man was deemed too powerful, the citizens could vote him into exile for a decade.

Meanwhile, Ionian Greeks in Asia Minor (whom the Athenians regarded as cousins) urged Athens to come to their aid against the mighty Persian Empire, which was forcing them to pay tribute. Recklessly, Athens agreed, and sent an army that burned the Persian city of Sardis and returned home. It was provocation enough to land the city in the soup with **Darius**, the Persian king of kings, who in 490 BC sent an expeditionary force to **Marathon**, where it was defeated by the Athenians under **Miltiades**. Although Sparta and the other Greek states recognized the Persian threat, Athens was the only one seriously to prepare for it, thanks to

Themistocles, a 'new man' (his father was a greengrocer), who persuaded the Athenians to invest in a much bigger navy. Perhaps even more astonishingly, in 480, when Darius' son **Xerxes** duly returned with the greatest army and navy the ancient world had yet seen, Themistocles convinced the Athenians to abandon their city altogether and trust in their fleet. Rumours had it that even the Acropolis snake was seen beating a fast retreat, a sure sign that the rock would fall. Xerxes occupied Athens and razed it, just before he snatched defeat from the jaws of victory at **Sálamis**.

After the allied Greeks defeated the Persians at **Plataea**, Themistocles engaged in a diplomatic war of nerves with Athens' powerful ally **Sparta**, hastily building **city walls** in 478 BC. The Spartans strongly believed that Athens should have no such thing, ostensibly in case the Persians returned and used them to their advantage. But Themistocles kept Sparta distracted until the walls were a *fait accompli*; Athens, from then on, would be much harder to capture from land. In 477 BC Themistocles made its fleet – the only one in Greece capable of resisting the constant Persian threat – the foundation of a web of alliances modern historians call the **Delian League**. Headquartered on the holy island of Délos, its membership eventually reached 200 city-states (but significantly, not Sparta), who contributed money, men or ships in return for protection. Athenian triremes challenged the Persians in Egypt and elsewhere, not always with success. Trade followed the flag, and one thing led to another; to keep the navy in fighting shape and justify its existence (and its expense), the Athenians were soon sticking their fingers in every pie around the Aegean and beyond. And what began as a league became a *de facto* empire.

The Athenians were sailing in some uncharted social and political waters, and **theatre** played a fundamental role in helping them cope with it all psychologically; prisoners were even released so they could attend the plays. The oldest tragedy to come down to us is Aeschylus' *The Persians*, from 479 BC. Sculptors might have achieved the calm Classical ideal in art, but political change in Classical Athens continued at a breakneck pace: in 470 or so the brilliant but prickly Themistocles was ostracized, much to his surprise, and the popular, easygoing aristocrat **Kimon**, son of Miltiades, became the leading politico. In 465 BC, wealthy Thássos, objecting to Athenian meddling in northern Greece, became the first major state to defect from the Delian League. Kimon took it after a two-year siege, and settled Athenians there in a *cleruchy*, or self-supporting garrison. In a far more controversial move, Kimon sent troops at Sparta's request to help it subdue the rebellious helots holed up on Mount Ithóme (*see* p.437). But Sparta suspected the Athenian hoplites were too sympathetic to the helots and sent them home again, a rejection that Athens took as a great insult.

In 463–462 BC, while Kimon was away on Thássos, a younger generation, led by **Ephialtes**, pushed through a motion that abolished nearly all the powers of the aristocratic Areopagos and established an annually elected council in its place. Now the people were in control from top to bottom; even the courts, until then run by officials, adopted a jury system. More conservative Greek states viewed the Athenian experiment in radical democracy with the same fascinated horror as Europe would the French Revolution. Now it was Kimon's turn to be ostracized; Ephialtes was assassinated and **Pericles** emerged as the popular leader when he proposed the final democractic touch: pay for jurors, for members of the Council of Five Hundred and other public servants, making it possible for even the poorest *thetes*, the lowest class who rowed the triremes, to participate.

'Born into the world to take no rest themselves and to give none to others,' was Thucydides' description of his fellow Athenians. Their wealth, feeling of unlimited potential and addiction to novelty attracted all the greatest artists and intellectuals of the time to the city: Phidias and others revolutionized sculpture; Sophocles, Euripides and Aristophanes saw the first night performances of their plays in the Great Dionysia; Herodotus wrote his *History*; Anaximander and Socrates philosophized. And the Athenians agreed with their brilliant Pericles, that now that they ruled the Aegean they could only keep going forward, wherever their momentum might take them. They would use the dues of the Delian League to do it, with enough left over to rebuild the temples destroyed by the Persians, beginning with the greatest of them all, the Parthenon, completed in 438 BC.

While she was busy creating the fundamentals of Western culture, Athens never passed a year without a war somewhere, and as often as not it was Athens herself stirring the pot. The day of the independent *polis* was over: Athens signed a 30-year peace treaty with Sparta in 446 BC, each recognizing the other's sphere of influence in Greece. But Pericles always suspected a showdown between the two big powers was inevitable. He linked Athens to Piraeus with long walls, ensuring the city's lifeline in a siege, and then followed policies designed to provoke the Spartans. War-weary Athenians would later come to blame him for everything.

In 431 BC, the uneasy *détente* in Greece unravelled into the cataclysmic **Peloponnesian War**. Although fighting Sparta and Sparta's allies as well as rebellious members of the Delian League (eager to slip away from Athens and the 300 per cent increase in dues she demanded), it was still Athens' war to lose, and she lost it. The first year saw a Spartan army occupy Attica. Everyone took refuge behind Athens' new walls, only to suffer the **Great Plague** of 430 BC, which carried off thousands, Pericles among them. The city's new leader, the demagogue **Kleon**, refused every chance for peace, leaving the Spartans, especially their young and just general **Brasidas**, to pose as the liberators of Greece; when both Kleon and Brasidas were killed in the battle for Amphipolis, the exhausted sides signed the **Peace of Nicias** (421 BC). It wasn't worth the stone it was carved on. Egged on by flattering, irresponsible politicians, especially the mercurial **Alcibiades**, nephew of Pericles and student of Socrates, the Athenians overreached themselves by attempting to conquer **Syracuse**, the biggest city in Magna Graecia, where they suffered their gravest defeat (413 BC). An oligarchic *coup d'état* in 411 exposed Athens' internal divisions, though full democracy was eventually restored. Athens battled on for another seven years, still refusing all offers of peace. Revolts of allies and a Spartan alliance with Persia sealed her doom; Lysander and the Spartans brought the city to her knees with a crushing naval defeat at **Aegospotami** in 405 BC.

The Spartans resisted calls from Corinth, Thebes and other cities to destroy Athens, content merely to raze the long walls and the fortifications of Piraeus. The brutal regime they installed, the **Thirty Tyrants**, killed over 1,500 citizens and *metics* (resident foreign merchants) with the help of the Spartan occupation force, before they themselves were executed in a revolt.

Democracy made a quick recovery. By 378 BC the city had set up a **second Delian League**, but the Peloponnesian War had struck a blow from which ancient Athens would never recover; though still the most important city in Greece, it would never again be a political force. Although **Socrates** was put to death (399 BC), partly as a scapegoat for his wayward pupils (besides Alcibiades, another one, Critias, had been a ringleader of the Tyrants), Athens' intellectual traditions held true in the 4th century, the age of Praxiteles, Menander and Plato.

When **Philip II** made a great power of **Macedonia**, Athenian patriotism was kept alive by the orator Demosthenes even as Philip subdued all of Greece (338 BC). Losing control of its own destiny, the city would become a prize fought over by Alexander's generals, beginning with **Demetrios Poliorketes**, who captured the city in 294 BC and made it the backdrop to his playboy escapades. In the new Hellenistic world, Alexandria, Rhodes and Pergamon gradually displaced Athens as cultural centres. In 168 BC Rome captured Athens, but in honour of past glory left her with many privileges; 80 years later, though, Sulla punished the city for supporting Mithridates of Pontus by destroying Piraeus, the Agora and the city walls. Later Romans would remember their cultural debt; while the city dwindled, they came to attend the academies and endow the city with monuments. **St Paul** started the Athenians on the road to Christianity in AD 44. In the 3rd century **Goths** sacked the city; in

529, **Justinian** closed the philosophy schools, and converted the Parthenon into a cathedral.

Now a backwater, Athens re-enters history as the plaything of the **Franks** after they seized Constantinople in 1204. **Guy de la Roche** was made the Duke of Athens, a dukedom held at various times by the Catalans, Neapolitans and Venetians. In 1456 it was the turn of the **Ottomans**, who converted the Parthenon into a mosque and the Erechtheion into a harem. The Venetians made several attempts to wrench it away; in **Morosini**'s siege of 1687, a shell struck the Parthenon, where the Turks had stored their gunpowder. In 1800, Lord Elgin looted much of its surviving frieze.

In 1834, after the **War of Independence**, Athens – population 200, living in a clutch of houses under the Acropolis – was declared the capital of the state for the grandeur of its name. **Otto of Bavaria**, the first king of the Greeks, brought his own architects with him to lay out a new city, based on a grid running northeast of Stadíou and Panepistimíou (El. Venizélou) Streets. Neoclassical public buildings, evoking ancestral glory, went up everywhere, many of the more elaborate ones financed by wealthy Greeks of the diaspora, keen to show off their Hellenic credentials. By 1860 the population had risen to 30,000. Yet even the best-laid plans could not cope with the flood of people from the countyside who came looking for jobs and the thousands of Greek refugees who arrived after the population exchange in 1922, and much of the rest of city was built quickly on the cheap. Today Athens resembles a dense domino game stacked over the dry hills of Attica. The metropolis squeezes in four million lively, opinionated inhabitants – over a third of the population of Greece – who are now more prosperous than they have been since the age of Pericles, and enjoying all the post-2004 Olympic improvements that have made their home, after 2,000 years, a world-class city again.

Sýntagma Square and Pláka

Unless you sail into Piraeus or arrive by metro from the airport, approaching Athens means a long slog through its seemingly eternal 'burbs. Deep within this outer urban husk, Athens' very new and very ancient personalities begin to unfold at their classic intersection, Sýntagma.

Sýntagma Square

Sýntagma or 'Constitution' Square is the centre and crossroads of the modern city, where bus, trolley, tram and shiny new metro lines converge, *períptera* sell newspapers from around the world, and Greeks who don't give a hang about cultural pollution pack the great big McDonald's, drinking McFrappés. The square was designed to set off the large neoclassical royal palace, now the **Parliament Building** (Voulí), fronted by the **Monument to the Unknown Soldier**, whose guards in *evzone* uniform astonish passers-by every hour with some of the strangest steps ever invented by the military mind. Stretching beyond the Parliament are the **National Gardens**, a cool haven of shade to escape the summer heat. Finds discovered during the construction of the metro are displayed in the Sýntagma **metro concourse**; a glass wall offers a view of the historic strata of subterranean Athens.

Pláka

A short walk up Filellínon Street on the south side of Sýntagma Square will take you to Kydathinéon Street, the main artery into Pláka, the old neighbourhood gathered under the skirts of the Acropolis. Arvanites (Christian Albanian speakers) who settled here in the 15th century apparently called it *Pliak Athina*, 'old Athens'– hence 'Pláka'. On Filellínon, have a look at the 11th-century Byzantine church of **Ag. Sotíra**, restored in the 1850s by Tsar Alexander II and now serving the city's growing Russian community, and the small, rather dour neo-Gothic **St Paul's**, serving the Anglicans (who incidentally do a lovely carol service if you're in Athens on Christmas Eve). The atmosphere, however, changes abruptly when you turn down Kydathinéon: the streets of Pláka are narrow and, as they follow the city's ancient and medieval plan, seem to go where they please, with no room for cars. Pláka is the Athens that became Greece's capital in 1834; since then its houses have been converted into hotels, tavernas or souvenir shops, making it the vortex of tourist Athens.

Jewish Museum
*39 Níkis St, **t** 210 322 5582, www.jewishmuseum.gr; open Mon–Fri 9–2.30 and Sun 10–2; adm*

Greek Folk Art Museum
*17 Kydathinéon St, **t** 210 322 9031; open summer Mon 12–7, Tues–Sun 8–7; winter Tues–Sun 8.30–3; adm*

Frissíras Museum
*3–7 Monís Asteríou St, **t** 210 323 4678, www.frissirasmuseum.com; open Wed–Fri 11–7, Sat and Sun 10–3; adm exp*

Amid the hubbub wait a smattering of museums. A handsome neoclassical building houses the **Jewish Museum**, with one of the most important collections in Europe, arranged by theme. Though Jews lived in Greece since Hellenistic times (and became assimilated as Romiótes), the Sephardic majority arrived from Spain after 1492; only a fraction survived the Holocaust. The **Greek Folk Art Museum**, opposite the Byzantine church of the Metamorphósis, offers several floors of needlework, carvings, silver, weapons, jewellery, shadow puppets (*karaghiózis*), bridal costumes and a delightful room from a house on Lésbos painted by Theóphilos Hatzimichaíl, Greece's great naïf master, complete with Alexander the Great and two volcanoes. For something completely different, the **Frissíras Museum**, around the corner, offers an important collection of 20th-century art gathered together by Vlássis Frissíras; one building is used for rotating displays from the permanent collection, the other for temporary exhibitions.

Further east, Kydathinéon runs into Adrianoú, the oldest street in Athens still in use, now chock-a-block with tourist shops.

Kydathinéon next meets Tripodón and Séllei streets, once an important intersection for theatre-lovers. On the fifth day of the Great Dionysia festival (*see* pp.96–7), in Academy Award fashion, a panel would choose best actor, best playwright and best producer/ sponsor (*choregós*). Every winner was allowed to put up a monument – usually a tripod – to his victory in this area and, being typical Greeks, each one did; Tripodón Street, as its name suggests, was lined with them. One of the more elaborate is just to your left along Séllei Street: the **Monument of Lysikrátes**, put up by a winning *choregós* of 334 BC. Its Corinthian columns stood under a frieze depicting Dionysos and the Tyrrhenian pirates. Much later, the monument was incorporated into a Capuchin friary to serve as a library. When Byron stayed, he was wont to do his reading there by lamplight; the ghost of Lysikrátes, recognizing a great histrionic type, would probably not have minded. In 1818 the friars were the first in Greece to grow what would become an essential ingredient of the national salad – tomatoes – in their garden.

Continuing south of the Pláka, Séllei Street turns into Výronos and runs into pedestrian-only Dionysíou Areopagítou Street, part of the wonderful new 4km **walkway** between the chief monuments of ancient Athens. There are many routes you can take from here, but you can't do better than to start at the top and visit the Acropolis itself.

The Acropolis

Acropolis
***site** (**t** 210 321 0219) and **museum** (**t** 210 323 6665); open May–Sept 8–7.30; Oct–April 8–5; ticket for both costs €12 and includes adm to the ancient Agora, Temple of Zeus (Olympeion), Roman Agora, Theatre of Dionysos and Kerameikós – all the sights on the pedestrian walkway – so visit the Acropolis first; there's a lift to the top for the disabled (ring ahead)*

Acropolis means 'top of the town', and although many Greek cities grew up around similar natural citadels, Athens has *the* Acropolis, a sheer limestone rock standing a proud 300ft over the city, visible for miles around. It is the key to the city; Athens would not be Athens without it. Inhabited by the end of the Neolithic era, it later supported a Mycenaean palace with a Temple of Athena inside it, surrounded by Cyclopean walls. Before democracy, the tyrants lived here as well, sharing the rock with a Temple of Poseidon and Athena, built after their famous contest to become patron of the city. Poseidon struck the Acropolis with his trident to create the salt spring Klepsydra; Athena invented the olive tree, and won. In 480 BC her wooden cult statue was hurriedly bundled off to Sálamis, just before the Persians burnt everything. This allowed for renovations and the creation of the Acropolis as we see it today, a showcase dedicated to the wealth and glory of Athens.

Themistocles rebuilt the processional ramp leading to the **Propylaea**, the majestic entrance gate built in Pentelic marble by Pericles' architect Mnesikles in the 430s BC to complement the Parthenon. Take a close look at it; ancient (and many modern) architects considered the Propylaia the equal of the Parthenon itself, ingeniously built over an uneven slope, its five gates with enormous wood and bronze doors big enough to admit horsemen and chariots for the annual Panathenaic procession. On either side of its entrance are wings; the one to the north held a picture gallery (*pinakothéke*) which also served as a VIP lounge, where notables could rest after their climb up, while the smaller one to the south is a *trompe l'œil* work that appears to have the same dimensions as the *pinakothéke*, although in fact it is little more than a façade because the priests of Athena Nike refused to have a wing in their precinct.

To the right of the Propylaia, on a stone-filled bastion of the Mycenaean wall, stands the pretty little Ionic **Temple of Athena Nike**, built of Pentelic marble by Kallikrates in 478 BC. In 1687 the Turks dismantled it to build a nearby wall, making it easy to rebuild it with its original material in 1835 and again in 1936, when the bastion threatened to crumble away; it has recently been dismantled and rebuilt again, reinforced by a titanium skeleton. A cast replaces the frieze. From the temple platform, once the site of a statue of Wingless Victory, King Aegeus watched for the return of his son Theseus from his adventure with the Minotaur. Theseus was to have signalled his victory with a white sail but forgot; at the sight of the black sail Aegeus swooned, fell off the precipice and gave his name to the Aegean sea.

The Parthenon

⓫ Parthenon

The Parthenon, the glory of the Acropolis and probably the most famous building in the world, is a Doric temple constructed between 447 and 432 BC by Iktinos and Kallikrates, supervised overall by Phidias, the Michelangelo of the Periclean age. Originally called the Great Temple, brightly painted and shimmering with gold, it took the name Parthenon (Chamber of the Virgin) a hundred years after its completion. An estimated 13,400 blocks of Pentelic marble went into its construction, each cut to precise mathematical calculations; the largest weighed 10 tons and no two blocks were alike. Its architects wrote the book on *entasis* or 'tension' to imitate nature, shaping the columns so that they swelled very slightly in the centre, as if they were live things supporting the weight. As there are no straight lines in nature, there is none in the whole building: the foundation is slightly curved to prevent the visual illusion of drooping caused by straight horizontals. The columns bend a few centimetres inward, and those on the corners are wider. These minute details, many invisible to the naked eye, give the Parthenon its incomparable life, harmony and bounce.

The Doric order, symbolic of strength, was used in the outer colonnade of 46 columns. It was decorated with 92 *metopes*, carved with scenes of conquests over 'barbarians' that echoed the recent triumph over the Persians: the east side portrayed the Battle of Giants and Gods, the south that of the Lapiths and Centaurs, on the west were the Athenians and the Amazons, and on the north the Battle of Troy. Only fragments (mostly in the British Museum) survive of the pediment sculptures of the birth of Athena and her contest with Poseidon – after shelling the Parthenon, Morosini tried to remove the pediment as a souvenir for Venice but the ropes broke and the whole thing shattered. The inner colonnade was Ionic, symbolic of Athens' culture, and had a more peaceful and spiritual decoration: a sublime 524ft continuous frieze of 400 human figures and 200 animals in low relief designed by Phidias, depicting the quadrennial Panathenaic Procession in which the wooden cult statue of Athena in the Erechtheion was brought a golden crown and a new sacred garment, or *peplos*. Here, too, subtle calculations (the lower bits are sculpted to a depth of 3cm, the upper to 5.5cm) and a slight downward tilt gave the figures added life. An early British traveller, Edward Daniel Clark, remarked on how 'all the strength and impression of the composition depend on the viewing of the work in relation to that exact distance and optical angle which Phidias himself had calculated'. After the passing of Lord Elgin's agent Lusieri (*see* p.42), only an inscription remained on the wall: *Quod non fecerunt Gothi, hoc fecerunt Scoti* (What the Goths did not do, the Scots did here).

The Parthenon was designed to hold Phidias' chryselephantine (ivory- and gold-covered) statue of Athena, which stood over 36ft high; small surviving copies give an inkling of its majestic appearance. Altogether, the Parthenon, with its masterful perfection and unusually elaborate decoration, was a temple not so much to the gods (it lacked even the most basic cult necessity, a permanent stone altar) as to the glory, genius and wealth of Athens, leader of the Delian League. The statue of Athena was clad with 44 talents of gold, a big part of the state treasury – the goddess's robes as Fort Knox. (The Romans later did the same with their statue of Juno on the Capitoline Hill.) In order to see it in all its glory, the Parthenon had a unique roof, tiled with white marble slabs sliced so thin that light could actually filter through.

The Parthenon later found a religious role as a church and mosque, remaining intact until 1687, when Morosini's bomb hit the Turks' powder stores and blew off the roof; an earthquake in 1894 was another serious blow. Entrance within the Parthenon has been forbidden to save on wear and tear; preserving it from smog has been part of an intense rehabilitation programme since 1983, with the scaffolding removed in time for the Olympics. While discovering how to clean off a century of pollution with lasers and microwaves and using hot, pressurized carbon dioxide to re-harden stone surfaces, Greek engineers have learned a good deal about ancient building techniques and will reconstruct as much as possible, using rust-free titanium rods.

The Greek flag flying on the belvedere beyond the old museum building has a special meaning to Athens. The first thing the Nazis did in their occupation was replace it with the swastika. On the night of 30–31 May 1941, two teenagers crept up the secret Mycenaean stair and stole it right from under the guards' noses, in what became the opening salvo of the Greek resistance.

The Erechtheion

The last great temple of the Acropolis, the Erechtheion, was completed only in 395 BC, after the Peloponnesian War. This complex Ionic temple with three porches and none of the usual Classical colonnades owes its idiosyncrasies to the much older holies of holies it encompassed – the sanctuaries of Athena Polias, Poseidon Erechtheus, Kekrops and the olive tree planted by the goddess – yet such is the genius of its structure that it appears harmonious. The southern porch facing the Parthenon is supported by six *caryatids* (now casts), designed to complement the Parthenon opposite. Lord Elgin nicked one; the other girls were said to weep every night for their missing sister. Behind the East Portico, with its six Ionic columns, the *cella* was divided up to serve both Athena Polias and Poseidon Erechtheos, and held the biggest juju of them all: the primitive cult statue of Athena Polias, the wearer of the sacred *peplos*. Down the steps is the Erechtheion's best side: its north porch, defined by six tall and elegant Ionic columns. Part of the floor and roof were cut away to reveal to the gods the marks left by Poseidon's trident; when the Turks made the temple a harem, they used the sacred place as a toilet. This porch was the tomb of Erechtheos, some say Kekrops, and the traditional home of the Acropolis guardian snake. A small olive tree replaces the Athena-created original in the western court of the temple.

New Acropolis Museum
by Acropolis metro station, between Makrigiánni and Mitséon Sts, **t** *210 924 1043; www.newacropolismuseum.gr; due to open partially in late 2008, and fully in 2009; hours and adm still undecided at time of writing*

New Acropolis Museum

The Swiss-born architect Bernard Tschumi had hardly won the design competition for this museum when the controversies began; critics lambasted it for its size, its modernity and its location – a mere 800ft – from Athens' crown jewel. Now, after a hundred lawsuits and four years of delays, even the harshest critics have had to admit the result is breathtaking. The New Acropolis Museum doesn't shout 'Look at me!', but speaks with the rare quiet beauty of a building that fits its function like a glove, engaging the Acropolis in a dialogue of form and beauty spanning 3,000 years.

Symmetrical, however, it ain't. When the archaeologists, sent to do rescue digs, unearthed once crowded and vibrant streets of the Hellenistic and Roman city on the site, the architects went back to the drawing board to realign the building on the ancient streets and raise it on a hundred columns to preserve the site and many of the artefacts left in situ. The spectacular glass top floor, however, is aligned to match the Parthenon, its stellar *doppelgänger* across the way.

The logic and elegance of the interior is apparent as soon as you enter. With ten times more space than the old Acropolis museum on the rock, objects that have been in storage for decades will finally be put on display. Artefacts discovered around the Acropolis hill are to your right as you enter, and to your left a long, wide ramp leads to an impressive staircase echoing the grand entrance to the Acropolis itself. Most of the floor is glass to reveal the ruins below. At the top of the stairs awaits a spectacular 6th-century BC pediment showing Heracles wrestling Triton and three snake men, a fitting welcome to the lofty, columned hall of Archaic art that runs along the south side of the building. Even when Pericles refurbished the rock and built the Parthenon, dedications to the gods could not by law leave the sacred precinct, so many of these artefacts were either buried inside the Acropolis or embedded in its fortification walls. The stars are the *kouroi* and *korai* and the *Calf-Bearer* (*Moschoforos*) from 570 BC, all smiling their famous Archaic smiles and yet each one remarkably individual. Other figures once decorated the 'Old Parthenon' and Temple of Athena Polias. Many still have traces of their original paint – and all are bathed in natural light through the glass walls and ceiling.

Stairs lead up to a mezzanine floor (with a restaurant, VIP room, and a lovely balcony overlooking the Archaic statues), and then continue up to the atrium of the third floor, which echoes the inner *cella* of the Parthenon itself, and houses epigraphic material and artefacts from the Temple of Nike. From here you enter the south end of Tschumi's *pièce de résistance*: a glass gallery, built in the exact dimensions of the Parthenon to house Phidias' sublime 525ft frieze of the Panathenaic Festival, displayed just above eye level, the panels arranged in the same order as they were on the Parthenon itself (colour coding and drapery indicate which marbles are originals and which are copies). As you turn the west corner the Parthenon itself comes dramatically into view, offering a unique chance to visualize what it originally looked like. The gallery is simply so much more beautiful, luminous and evocative than the fusty old Duveen Gallery where the marbles are kept in the British Museum that it is in itself a compelling argument for their return.

The final exhibition area contains Hellenistic and Roman finds and takes you again to the stairs and the glass ramp. There is one final surprise: the *caryatids* from the Erechtheion porch are lined up on the balcony watching your descent, a perfect final touch in a museum where modern form and ancient content blend so seamlessly.

South of the Acropolis

The neighbourhood around the New Acropolis Museum, Makrigiánni, was named after the likeable general of the Greek War of Independence, who wrote a colourful autobiography in spite of being illiterate (he devised his own code) and whose **statue** is on Dionysíou Areopagítou Street, near the metro. Just up from here, the **Ilías Lalaoúnis Jewelry Museum** is where Lalaoúnis (b. 1920), the only jeweller ever admitted into the French Académie des Beaux Arts, displays his collection of jewellery based on designs going back to the dawn of European civilization.

Ilías Lalaoúnis Jewelry Museum
4a Karyátidon St and Kalispéri, **t** *210 922 1044, www.lalaounis-jewelrymuseum.gr; open Mon, Thurs, Fri and Sat 9–4, Wed 9–9, closed Sun and Tues; adm; free Wed after 3*

Theatre of Dionysos

Theatre of Dionysos
t *210 322 4625; open May–Sept daily 8–7; Oct–April daily 8–5; adm*

From the Acropolis metro station, the first ancient monument you come to, built into the side of the big rock, is probably the oldest playhouse in the world. But its stone seats never saw a first-night performance of the great tragedies of the Classical period. In fact no stone theatre in Greece existed before the 4th century BC; Aeschylus, Sophocles and Euripides made do with seats dug into the hill or wooden bleachers. The existing and much modified theatre was begun from 342 to 326 BC and reached its present form by the time of Nero when it seated 17,000.

Each spring in this precinct, Athenians, since the time of Pisistratos, attended the **Great Dionysia**, an *agon* or contest in which playwrights presented plays to honour the god and to be judged by their peers, a five-day theatrical extravaganza accompanied by plenty of schmoozing over the wine *krater*. On the first day, all citizens, plus aliens and colonials, took part in a huge parade displaying the hundreds of cows and bulls about to be sacrificed to the god. The custom was for each participant to hold up and wave an enormous phallus, a reminder that Greek drama sprang from much earlier fertility rites. There were political overtones as well. Dionysos' cult statue was brought 'home' to Athens every year from his stomping ground Eleutherai, the area of Attica closest to Thebes and Mount Kitherónas, to watch the performances in his honour, and to remind the Thebans and everyone else that Athens was *numero uno*. Day two also started with a parade in front of the audience, beginning with bearers each holding aloft the equivalent of a talent in silver, until all of that year's tribute to Athens from her subject allies was lined up on display. This was meant to assure the subject states that their money was being well looked after. Then came the orphans, the state-supported children of citizens killed in battle, and so forth. Then treaties were announced and special honours given to citizens. Only then were that day's plays performed. No event shows the total unity of Athenian civic and religious ritual better than the Great Dionysia.

There were four days of plays. Each of the first three consisted of three tragedies and a satyr play. On the fourth day, five comedies were performed, one after the other. Each year's plays were under the jurisdiction of the *archon*, the annually elected leader. He chose the *choregoi*, or producers, one for each play. These ancient angels had to pay for the production for the good of the state and were also expected to fork out for a big banquet for their troupe after the performance. The *archon* chose the plays, and the lead actors presumably chose the rest of the cast. All were amateurs, but it can be assumed that the same group participated regularly. All in all, well over a thousand men and boys would be rehearsing each year. From this festival emerged comedy that even the Marx brothers could only approach, and dramas whose lyric power and brilliance has seldom been equalled.

No one is really sure whether women attended these all-day performances. Audiences were rowdy at times, and on occasion threw bits of their lunch on stage. After all, most of the masked actors were neighbours, and the plays often raised thorny contemporary issues, although after one playwright, Phrynichus, got in hot water in the 490s for openly referring to the fall of Athens' ally Miletus and making the audience cry, the dramatists took care to veil their comments in myth.

Stoa of Eumenes and Odeion of Herodes Atticus

Such was the reputation of Athens after its heyday that it had a slew of wealthy benefactors, all keen to enjoy a bit of reflected glory. One was Eumenes II of Pergamon (d. 159 BC) who built the long **Stoa of Eumenes** next to the theatre, where the audience could relax and buy drinks and snacks; its roof supported a road, the *peripatos*, that encircled the Acropolis. Off this was an **Asklepeion**, dedicated to the healing god Asklepios, founded afer Athens was decimated by plague in 429 BC. Next to the Stoa of Eumenes is the **Odeion** (AD 161), another gift, this time from the Rockefeller of his day, Herodes Atticus, whose life reads like something out of the *Arabian Nights*; he inherited his extra-ordinary wealth from his father, who found a treasure outside Rome. Famous in its time for having no interior columns to support its long-gone cedar roof, the 6,000-seat *odeion* hosts the excellent

Festival of Athens, where modern European and ancient Greek cultures meet in theatre, ballet and classical concerts performed by companies from all over the world.

West and North of the Acropolis

The Areopagos, Pnyx and Philopáppos Hill

Below the Acropolis entrance and slightly to the north is the bald **Areopagos**, or hill of the war god Ares, the seat of original assembly. Here the High Council heard murder trials, in the open, so that the councillors could avoid the pollution of being under the same roof as a murderer. It figured prominently in Aeschylus' *Eumenides* where the rule of law (albeit a shockingly patriarchal law by today's standards) defeated vengeance for the first time in history during the trial of the matricide Orestes. Although Ephialtes removed much of the power of the Council, it continued to advise on the Athenian constitution for hundreds of years. One of its tasks was to judge foreign religions, including Christianity and its Unknown God as expounded by St Paul in AD 52 (verdict: not impressed, although a certain Dionysos converted and became Athens' first bishop and saint, Dionysos the Areopagite).

Below the Areopagos and across Apostólou Pávlou Street (the continuation of the new pedestrian promenade), archaeologists have uncovered an ancient Athenian neighbourhood under the olive trees. Another lane south of here leads to the lovely Byzantine church of **Ag. Dimítrios Lombardiaris** (a favourite late afternoon rendezvous for Athens' gilded youth) while various paths, paved with stone and ancient marbles, wind up to the lofty **Philopáppos Monument** (AD 114), built in honour of Caius Julius Antiochos Philopappos, a Syrian Prince and friend of Athens. Philopáppos Hill is one of the beauty spots of Athens, where you can hear the cicadas over the traffic; as the Acropolis is almost level with the monument, you can even pretend that modern Athens doesn't exist. The sunsets are famous – but after dark it's very isolated, so take care. Signs point the way down to the **Dora Stratou Theatre**, where the city's professional folk dance troupe (*see* p.127) performs nightly in summer; note that you can also get there by taxi.

To the right of Ag. Dimítrios, another path leads to the shallow bowl of the **Pnyx**, where the democratic assembly, the *Ekklesia*, met 30 to 40 times a year and heard the speeches of Pericles and Demosthenes, or of any citizen (i.e. any free Athenian male over the age of 20 who had performed military service) who donned a wreath and mounted the steps of the rostrum. To make sure even the poorest could attend, Pericles paid a wage of two *obols*. Even so, it was sometimes necessary to summon the police (Scythian slaves, who were crack archers and excused from the taboo of laying hands on a citizen) to lasso the Athenians – literally, with a rope dipped in red paint as a mark of shame – to fill the minimum attendance quota of 5,000; for important debates 18,000 sat here. What you see dates from the 4th century BC; in Roman times the assembly moved to the Theatre of Dionysos. Today there are still Pnyx assemblies – of tourists watching the Sound and Light Show. Beyond this is the **Hill of the Nymphs**, where the magical maidens have been replaced by the **Observatory** (signposted Αστεροσκοπειο), designed by Theófilos Hansen in 1842.

Anafiótika and the Roman Forum

North of the Acropolis, you can descend into Pláka through its upper quarter, **Anafiótika**, a residential enclave left by the builders of Otto's palaces, who came from the island of Anáfi and, homesick, tried to recreate their village here. Still mostly residential, one handsome neoclassical mansion on its edge now holds the Kanellópoulos Museum. This private collection is a sampler of Greek civilization, from Neolithic times to the 19th century, with choice *objets d'art* from every period: ancient vases; Tanagra figurines from Thebes – the first Dresden shepherdesses, but less cloying – that were the rage in the ancient world in the 4th and 3rd centuries BC; 2nd-century portraits from El Fayyum in Egypt, icons by some of the best-known painters, and intricately carved crosses.

Kanellópoulos Museum
*corner of Theorías and Panós Sts, **t** 210 321 2313; open Tues–Sun 8.30–3; adm*

From here Itanós Street will take you down to Thólou Street, which leads shortly to the **Kleánthes House** (1831) – one of the very few surviving buildings that predated Athens' appointment as capital; it served as the first home of the University of Athens from 1837 to 1841. From here Klepsýdras Street descends to the Romaïkí Agorá, or Roman Forum. Feeling uncomfortable in the Greek Agora after wasting it (*see* p.101), the Romans built their own marketplace that kept its role up into Ottoman times. They knew the time day and night, thanks to a *klepsydra* (hydraulic clock) in the octagonal 1st-century BC **Tower of the Winds**. Once a bronze Triton weathervane spun on top, over the frieze of the eight winds; Vitruvius wrote that its builder, the astronomer Andronikos Kyrrestes, wanted to prove there were eight winds, not four. At its west end, the forum contains the **Gate of Athena Archegetis**, built by Julius and Augustus Caesar; one of its posts, still in place, has the market-pricing rules imposed by Hadrian. There is also a court and ruined *stoa*, and the **Fethiyé Tzamí**, the Victory or Corn Market Mosque, now used as a store room. Opposite the Tower of the Winds, the **Medresse** (with Arabic script running over the door) was an Islamic seminary (1721), later used as a prison.

Roman Forum
__t__ 210 324 5220; open May–Sept 8–7.30; Oct–April 8–5; adm

Near the Tower of the Winds, at 8 Kyrrístou Street, is the 17th-century Bath House of the Winds, the only surviving hammam in

Bath House of the Winds
__t__ 210 324 4340; open Wed and Sun 10–2

Athens, complete with domes and marble baths. In operation until 1965, it now belongs to the **Greek Folk Art Museum**, and has exhibits on public bath houses in the Balkans and shows how the ancient city's water supply worked. It's a pity they just didn't reopen it as a functioning bath house. At the top of Diogénous, the next street down, the **Popular Musical Instruments Museum** offers a fascinating collection of old and new Greek folk instruments with headphones to listen to what they sound like.

Popular Musical Instruments Museum
t 210 325 0198; open Tues and Thurs–Sun 10–2, Wed 12–6; closed Mon

Plateía Agorás, just north of the forum, is a pleasant place to sip a drink while contemplating the ancient walls of **Hadrian's Library**, an enormous building (400ft by 269ft) donated by that most philhellene of emperors, equipped with an inner peristyle courtyard and garden with a long pool; after renovation, it may be opened to the public. A walk west down around the ruins will take you to the bustling, renovated Monastiráki metro station. It shares the square (one of several spruced up for the Olympics) with the charming little 10th-century Byzantine basilica of the **Pantánassa** (the Queen of Heaven) that was the *katholikón* of the monastery that gave its name to the area, and with the large **Tsizdaraki Mosque**, built by the governor of Athens in 1759. This now houses the **Kyriazópoulos Ceramic Collection**, another annexe of the Greek Folk Art Museum, with a display of traditional ceramics and pieces from some of the country's best-known living potters.

Hadrian's Library
open Mon–Fri 8.30–3

Kyriazópoulos Ceramic Collection
t 210 324 2066; open Wed–Mon 9–2.30; closed Tues; adm

Monastiráki is also the name of the area west of the square, where bulging shops sell antiques, fake Timberland boots, Thai trinkets and second-hand books and fridges; **Plateía Avissinías**, at the centre, is chock full of old furniture, and on Sunday comes to life with a bustling outdoor antiques and flea market. But this part of Athens has always been a market: the Agora is only a block away.

The Heart of Ancient Athens: The Agora, Kerameikós and Around

The Agora

(4) Agora
*entrance on Adrianoú St, **t** 210 321 0185; open May–Sept daily 8–7.30; Oct–April daily 8–5; **museum** open May–Sept Mon 11–7.30, Tues–Sun 8–7.30; Oct–April Mon 11–5, Tues–Sun 8–5; adm*

The Agora was the living heart of ancient Athens: not just a market, but a stage for public life, for elections, meetings, festivals and court proceedings. It had many of the characteristics of a *temenos* (sacred precinct), marked with boundary stones, with water available for purification at its entrances, and was strictly off limits to draft-dodgers, convicted murderers, traitors and other political outcasts. For citizens, the news, political manoeuvrings, verbal gymnastics and social contacts available in the shade of its *stoas* were life itself. By citizens, of course, we mean men. Only flute girls (prostitutes) and poor women selling fish or other goods were

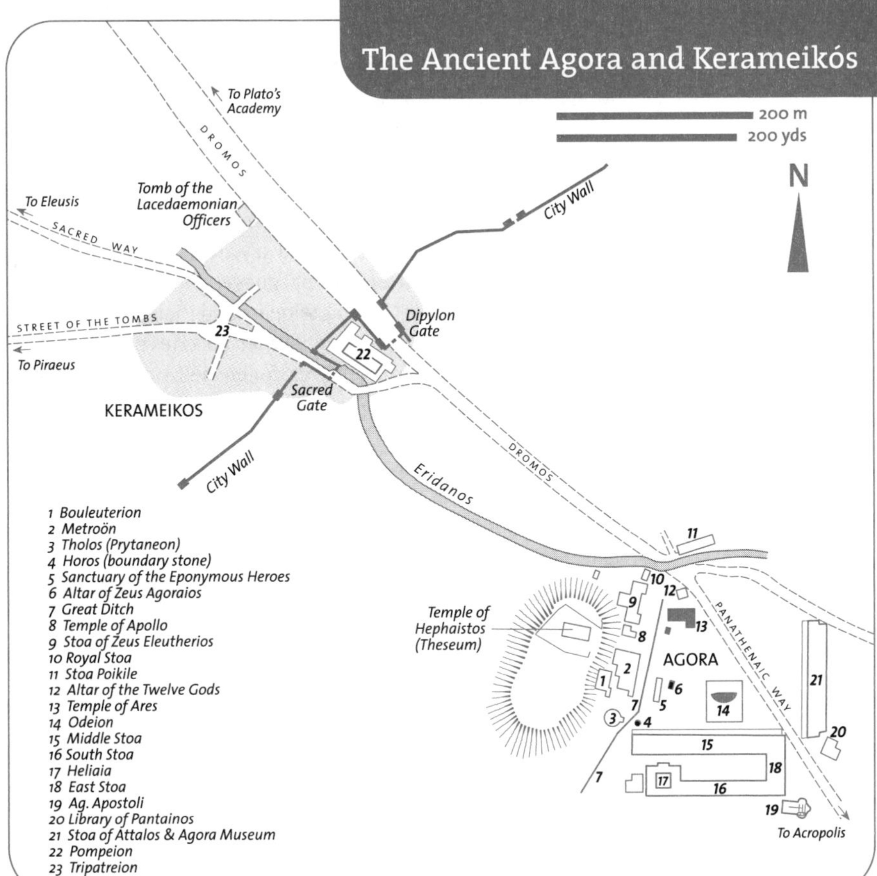

regulars in the Agora. Good girls stayed at home; men even did the shopping. Aristophanes satirized the way they looked as they sashayed about during the Peloponnesian War, parcels dangling from their spears and knocking against their armour. Here a man could get lucky, and be buttonholed by the likes of Socrates or Demosthenes. The conversations in this highly charged public arena changed the course of Western civilization.

The Agora started out as a large open space, with *stoas* and buildings around its perimeter. After the Persians razed it in 480 BC, it was rebuilt on a much grander scale. Once again, after suffering desecration at the hand of Sulla's Romans, most of the structures were rebuilt, and then more added to create a clutter a 5th-century Athenian would scarcely have recognized. Firebug barbarians didn't rebuild, however, and Athenians in need of cut stone pirated the ruins for centuries to build walls, churches and houses.

What's left covers every era of ancient history. Only foundations remain of the council house or **Bouleuterion**, built in the late 6th century BC after its establishment by Kleisthenes, and the neighbouring Temple of the Mother of the Gods, the **Metroön**, built by the Athenians as reparation for the slaying of a priest from her cult. Rooms on either side served as the public records archive and citizens' registry (to this day *mitroön* in Greek means 'register'). The annually elected *prytanes* governed from the round **Tholos** or **Prytaneon**. Since some had to be on call day and night, it had kitchens and sleeping quarters. Official guests were fêted here, and honoured citizens, such as Olympic winners and their descendants, were given dining rights in perpetuity. When Socrates was on trial, he was asked to choose a just sentence for himself. He replied that he should be given the right to eat free at the Prytaneon, meaning that he regarded himself as a valuable member of the state. He got to drink hemlock instead, in a building further south that has been tentatively identified as Socrates' Prison.

Near the Tholos is a **Horos**, one of the Agora's boundary stones still in situ. Opposite the Metroön, a stone fence and statue bases mark the remains of the **Sanctuary of the Eponymous Heroes of Athens**, which once contained the statues of the ten heroes instituted by Kleisthenes to give their names to the ten tribes of Athens. Since each tribal ward was spread shotgun fashion all over Attica to avoid one large geographical area taking precedence, members came here to read announcements (on stone *stele* or painted boards) concerning their tribe. The nearby Altar of Zeus Agoraios received the oaths of the new *archons*, a practice initiated by Solon. Running between the enclosure to the ten heroes and the Metroön is the **Great Ditch**, engineered in Kleisthenes' time; it still dutifully drains rainwater from the Acropolis through the Agora to the Eridanos river that flows through the Kerameikós cemetery.

The small 4th-century BC **Temple of Apollo** by the Metroön was dedicated to the forebear of the Ionians, who believed themselves descended from Apollo's son Ion. Almost nothing remains of the **Stoa of Zeus Eleutherios**, one of the recorded haunts of Socrates. It was partly built into the rock in 430 BC in honour of Zeus the Saviour for his role in saving the city from the Persians. Some of it disappears into the metro tracks. Walk over (or have a look over, if the guards haven't opened the gate) the bridge to the pathetic little strip of ruins between the tracks and Monastiráki shops to the small **Royal Stoa** (*stoa basileios*) where Athenian laws were written in stone for all to see; Socrates faced them when the indictment was read out against him. A massive slab built into the stoa's step, believed to be a lintel from a *tholos* tomb, was the traditional oath stone where the Athenians swore their most sacred vows.

In front of the Royal Stoa is a small, square enclosure of waist-high stone slabs, an early crossroads shrine apparently dedicated to the daughters of Leos who were sacrificed to save the city from famine way back when. It was *avaton* (forbidden territory), but Athenians threw small tokens into it and in an adjacent circular well to honour the deified daughters – votives that offer clues into the city's religious life. If walking through the embankment north at this point were possible, you would come to the once-famed **Stoa Poikile**, decorated with paintings of the Battle of Marathon, where Zeno of Kition taught in the late 4th century; hence 'Stoic' philosophy. Now it and a temple share a dismal hole on the other side of Adrianoú Street, where the Agora made a turn towards the gate that divided it from the Kerameikós cemetery.

Back over the bridge, in front and beyond the Stoa of Zeus, stands the **Altar of the Twelve Gods**, from which all distances in Attica were measured, although this too was partially obliterated with the laying of the Piraeus–Thissío train tracks in 1868, when no one knew exactly where the Agora was; ruins lay everywhere. Beside the Altar of the Twelve Gods, right at the main entrance, is part of the **Panathenaic Way**, the ceremonial path from the Dipylon Gate to the Acropolis, laid out by Pisistratos at the consecration of the Panathenaic Festival in 566 BC. In Athens' heyday, it was a gravel path; the fancy stonework that appears further up is 2nd century AD Roman.

South of the Altar of Twelve Gods stood a 5th-century BC Doric **Temple to Ares**. But it wasn't always here: it was dismantled stone by stone, just like London Bridge, and brought to town from the suburbs by the Romans and placed here, making the Agora just that much less open. The Romans also filled in other blanks to the south. The three giants standing sentinel nearby were originally part of the **Odeion of Agrippa**, built in 15 BC; parts of the orchestra remain intact, but the massive roof collapsed in AD 190. Both the site and giants were reused in the façade of a 5th-century gymnasium. Near the 2nd-century BC **Middle Stoa** are ruins of a Roman temple and ancient shops. On the other side of the Middle Stoa was the **South Stoa**, where the rooms used for symposia can still be made out. The doors of each are slightly off-centre, allowing a long couch to fit on one side of the 'door'. Small, but intimate, these were for stag parties, complete with wine, women and song. Beside it, to the west, is the large, square people's court, or **Heliaia**, organized by Solon in the 6th century BC to hear political questions. It has been identified as one of the possible sites of the jury trials; since the jurors could number in the hundreds in the radical democracy, a big space was required. It was used well into Roman times.

Between the South and **East Stoa** (2nd-century BC) is the 11th-century cross in the square church, **Ag. Apóstoli**, built on the site where St Paul addressed the Athenians; it was restored, along with its fine paintings, in 1952, and sports a tall, elegant octagonal dome held up by four Roman columns. The Holy Apostles are the patron saints of the used goods vendors' association, the members of which attend a special service on 3 June. Across the Panathenaic Way run the remains of **Valerian's Wall**, thrown up in AD 257 against the barbarians, made of stone from buildings wrecked by the Romans. Between Valerian's Wall and the Stoa of Attalos are higgledy-piggledy ruins of the **Library of Pantainos**, built by Flavius Pantainos in AD 100 and destroyed 167 years later. Beside it, the **Stoa of Attalos** was built in the 2nd century BC by one of Athens' benefactors, King Attalos II of Pergamon, and carefully reconstructed in 1953–5 with funds from the Rockefellers; all the materials used replicate the original except for the rafters, which are concrete painted to resemble wood. It now houses the Agora Museum in one large hall; the original building was divided into 42 luxury shops on two floors, leading off the shady *stoa* – exactly like a shopping mall. And, in case you are wondering, the public **latrines** were at the south end of this *stoa*, en route to the newer Roman forum (*see* p.99).

The Agora Museum

Well laid out and varied, this museum is a far better introduction to everyday Athenian life than the blockbuster Archaeological Museum. Among its delights are a complex balloting mechanism for choosing jurors that resembles a Japanese *pachinko* machine, a Spartan shield that some Athenian soldier hauled home as a trophy from Sphakteria (which put paid to the 'come back with it or on it' legend) and a 4th-century BC child's training potty.

Also on display are the *óstraka* (potsherds) used to ostracize anyone whom the Athenians thought was getting too uppity. It worked this way: once a year, a referendum took place when voters were asked if they thought any citizen a danger to the state. If a majority said yes, another vote was held. On this occasion, a citizen could write the name of anyone he chose on an *óstrako*, the scrap paper of the day. If 6,000 people voted, then whoever got the most votes, no matter what the actual count, was exiled for ten years. Although it was not often used, Themistocles was a victim, and Pericles used it to get rid of a rival. The system was also abused. Of the 190 *óstraka* found in a well, only 14 different handwritings can be discerned: someone was producing his enemy's name wholesale on pottery pieces and handing them out to anyone he could persuade to vote.

The Theseum (Temple of Hephaistos)

On the west edge of the Agora, the mid-5th-century BC Theseum is nothing less than the best-preserved Greek temple in existence. It was given this name by archaeologists who thought it was the tomb built by Kimon for the supposed bones of Theseus, but they were wrong. This Doric temple was dedicated to Hephaistos, the god of metals and smiths. It is constructed almost entirely of Pentelic marble and decorated with *metopes* depicting the lives of Heracles and Theseus. Converted into a church in the 5th century, it was used as a burial place for Protestants until 1834.

Herakleidon Experience in Visual Arts
*16 Iraklidon St, **t** 210 346 1981, www.herakleidon-art.gr; open Tues–Sat 1–9pm, Sun 11–7; closed Mon, adm*

The now mostly pedestrianized neighbourhood west of the temple, **Thissío**, has trendy cafés and restaurants with lovely Acropolis views. It also has a spanking new private museum in a beautifully restored neoclassical mansion, the **Herakleidon Experience in Visual Arts**, with special exhibitions and a permanent M.C. Escher collection.

Kerameikós: the Graveyard Shift

Kerameikós
*148 Ermoú St, **t** 210 346 3552; open May–Sept daily 8–7.30; Oct–April daily 8–5; adm; guide book on sale at the site*

Extending from the Agora was the ancient Athenian West End, a large quarter known as Kerameikós, or 'pottery district'; it too is now linked to the rest of the ancient centre by a pedestrianized promenade (the west end of Ermoú Street). The great landmark in Kerameikós was the recessed 'two-towered' or **Dipylon Gate**, the city's front door and the largest gate in ancient Greece, complete with a vast courtyard for public gatherings. The marble floor of the *de rigueur* **fountain house**, where travellers abluted before entering the city, survives just inside its double doors. South of the gate stretches a marvellous section of **city walls**, then the smaller, but more imposing **Sacred Gate**, where the Sacred Way and the Eridanos stream made its exit.

When German archaeologists started digging here after 1913, they found the Eridanos had covered Kerameikós in 26ft of silt. They dug to the bedrock, as archaeologists do, and then did an incredible thing: they replaced just enough to recreate the area as it was in the late 5th century BC. Even the boundary stones are still in place, as are the contemporary tombs and the (now filled in) moat, with the remains of the small wall or *proteichisma* in front to deter siege engines. The result is a peaceful bit of the Athens of Socrates' day, with a view back to the Acropolis just as an ancient traveller would have seen it. The value of the finds here is incalculable – not in gold but pottery, the articles of everyday life, as befits a city that made her wealth from the exceptional clay found here and the brilliance of her potters.

Kerameikós was originally much larger, extending 1.5km west to Plato's Academy. Its residents were used to living cheek by jowl with the dead. Potters potted and prostitutes hung about the gates trolling for custom (rates were regulated by law, and depended on the service on offer). Meanwhile, in the **Pompeion**, located just inside the walls, officials either organized the parade (*pompe*) for the Panathenaea Festival, or lolled about on one of the 60 dining couches in rooms off the main courtyard. The Panathenaic ship carrying the *peplos* for Athena was stored here. And annually, thousands streamed through the Sacred Gate on to the **Sacred Way** (Iéra Ódos) leading to Eleusis (*see* p.133). Plato must have strolled and philosophized on the **Dromos**, the wide street leading through the Dipylon Gate to his academy. Merchants and sailors would have gone down the Sacred Way to the **Tripatreion**, an easy-to-spot triangular enclosure honouring all of the dead, and then left on the **Street of Tombs**, to Piraeus and beyond. And punctuating all this: funerals and burials, over 2,000 years' worth.

The Cemetery

Mycenaean Athens used the present Agora as a cemetery, but by the sub-Mycenaean period the dead were laid here in stone-lined trenches, heads orientated towards the Eleusis road, accompanied by pitchers, amphorae and mugs filled with food and drink for the afterlife, and then covered with a mound. The Geometric period saw an increase in burials, both cremated and not (it seemed to be a matter of choice), but now the mounds were topped by vases; some of these were monumental, culminating in the enormous Dipylon Amphora in the National Archaeological Museum. Offerings became ever richer to showcase a family's wealth.

By the Archaic period, clay-offering trenches were the norm. Some extended as long as 36ft from the grave, allowing ever more pots with food and other offerings to be burned and buried with the body (the link between food offerings, regeneration and the afterlife continues today; seed offerings, *spermá*, are still part of Orthodox rites of the dead). Grave *stelae* very like our tombstones, carved with human figures, appear. Feeling things were getting out of hand, Solon wrote a law curbing ostentatious funerals, but aristocratic tombs remained showy nonetheless. By the time of Pisistratos, the distinctive amphorae, prizes of the Panathenaic Games, were placed over the graves of the victors. This was the cemetery's grandest period and many monuments survive, mostly because they were used to build Themistocles' city walls, thrown up on the double in 478 BC. Henceforth, all burials were outside the walls.

By the Classical period, inhumation prevailed, and white ground *lekythoi*, jugs and clay figurines were popular grave goods. Babies, and there were many, were buried in amphorae. There were both family enclosures and collective state burials. The long narrow **Tomb of the Lacedaemonian Officers**, whose deaths in 403 BC were described by Xenophon, is still on the Dromos. Large marble *stelae*, some in situ, depicting departing ladies or soldiers, became the vogue until yet another law in 317 BC prohibited ostentatious monuments. This one stuck. Little *kioniskoi*, the stubby columns you see around the museum, became the norm in the Hellenistic period. The Romans revived the splendour for a time, but slowly Kerameikós was abandoned, even by the potters who had squatted in the ruined Pompeion.

The newly renovated **museum** is a treasure house of pottery from every era, beginning with lovely Proto-geometric bits and pieces with Mycenaean designs visibly melting into Geometric patterns, such as a little *caryatid* with an Archaic smile, and a wonderful elaborate offering vase with three cockerels. The nested offering plates with the elaborate filigreed handles seem to be unique to this museum and would tempt any hostess today, as would the dainty 'tea cups' with saucers on display. Sadly there are lots of children's toys, a poignant reminder of the high infant mortality rate and the pain this must have caused. There are many artefacts from the Classical and late Classical period, especially white *lekythoi* and painted Tanagra figurines. Look for the *katára*, a sinister oval lead box containing a manacled lead doll, scratched with the names of people to be cursed – a message sent express to Hades with the corpse. The many painted clay rosettes had been placed on the deceased's breast and coins were placed on the corpse's mouth to pay the boatman Charon.

Maria Callas Museum
t 210 346 0981; open Mon–Fri 10–3

Pireos Street Annex
t 210 345 3111; open Wed, Thurs, Sun 10–6, Fri and Sat 10–10

Beth Shalon Synagogue
t 210 325 2823

Museum of Traditional Pottery
t 210 331 8491; open Mon–Fri 9–3; adm

Islamic Art Museum
corner of Ag. Asomáton and Dipylou Sts, t 210 325 1311, www.benaki.gr; open Tues and Thurs–Sun 9–3, Wed 9–9; closed Mon; adm

Around Kerameikós: Gázi and Psirrí

One project for the 2004 Olympics was the greening of Kerameikós: the grimy workshops once piled against its walls have been razed and planted with gardens to enhance the ancient setting. This should also give a boost to Athens' 'Technopolis' just west, occupying the skeletons of the old gasworks of **Gázi**, a former industrial slum finding a new life with galleries, clubs and some of the city's top restaurants. Along Piréos Street there's **Technópolis**, a multi-function cultural space in the old foundry, with a Maria Callas Museum. Just south on Piréos Street, the spanking new Pireos Street Annex, part of the Benáki art empire (*see* pp.114–15), has become a top venue for temporary art and photography.

Heading east from Kerameikós on Ermoú back towards the centre, the first street you come to is Melidóni, site of the Beth Shalon Synagogue and the small Museum of Traditional Pottery, dedicated to the art of Greek pottery. Although the emphasis is on the last century, techniques have hardly evolved for the big pots since the heyday of Kerameikós. While in the neighbourhood, don't miss the new Islamic Art Museum, housed in two neoclassical buildings in a complex that incorporates part of the ancient wall and a tomb. This houses the Benáki family's fabulous collection of 8th–19th-century Islamic art, one of the ten most important in the world, acquired during their residence in Egypt.

Psirrí

Just east begins **Psirrí** (Ψυρρη), a neighbourhood of winding lanes, where Byron courted Teresa Makri, 'the maid of Athens'. Its name comes from the slang for 'shaved' or 'fleeced', a reminder of its days as a tough district famous for gangs, where entering was something of a risk. It's now one of the trendiest spots to eat and play in Athens, and the city is fixing up the streets radiating out from Psirrí's centre, **Plateía Iróon**. They are almost perfect, like stage sets, an effect heightened by the squalor of the ungentrified edges and sparks cascading from body shops whose elderly owner-welders have stayed put. If you continue north on Aristofánous Street and turn right on Evripídou Street (Athens' spice street), you'll find **Ag. Ioánnis**, a tiny church with a Corinthian column sticking out of its roof that probably came from a temple to Asklepios. People visited it to cure their fevers, the idea being to tie the fevers to the column. Some bits of string and wool still dangle behind the iconostasis.

Municipal Art Gallery
t 210 324 3022; open Mon–Fri 9–1 and 5–9, Sun 9–1; closed Sat

Evripídou Street leads west to large Koumoundoúrou Square, where the former foundlings' hospital of 1874 is now the **Municipal Art Gallery**, devoted to Greek art since 1821, offering a fine introduction to modern Greek painting, engraving and sculpture.

Ermoú Street and Athens Cathedral

Hermes was the conductor of dead souls at Kerameikós, but he was also the patron of commerce, and you may have already noticed that the pedestrianized east end of his street, Ermoú, beyond Monastiráki, is dedicated to shopping, serenaded by old men playing old songs on barrel organs, or *latérnes*. The Byzantine church sunken in the middle of the street – King Otto's father, Ludwig of Bavaria, just managed to spare it from the destruction decreed by his son's planners – is the late 11th-century **Kapnikaréa**; it has a charming central cupola supported by four Roman columns, fine frescoes from a later period, and old bas reliefs and inscriptions embedded on the outer walls. Its name, referring to smoke (*kapnós*), goes back to its founder, an official who collected the hearth tax.

The next parallel street south of Ermoú, Mitropóleos, passes large Mitropóleos Square, with its two churches side by side. The little one is the 12th-century Ag. Elefthérios, better known as **Panagía Gorgoepíkoös**, 'Our Lady who Grants Requests Quickly'. Nicknamed 'the little cathedral', this is the loveliest church in Athens, built almost entirely of ancient marbles, one carved with a calendar of state festivals and another with the zodiac. The adjacent 'big' cathedral or **Metrópolis** was built in 1840–55 with the same collage technique, using bits and pieces from 72 destroyed churches around Athens. The Kings of Greece were crowned here between 1863 and 1964, and it contains the tomb of the unofficial saint of Greek independence, the Patriarch of Constantinople Gregory V, hanged by the Sultan in 1821 for failing to prevent the uprising.

North of Sýntagma to Omónia Square

From Sýntagma Square, Otto's planners laid out two parallel streets, Stadíou and Panepistimíou, to link up to Omónia Square in the north. If you take the latter from the top of Sýntagma, you'll soon find at No. 12 the **Numismatic Museum**, with one of the most important coin collections in the world, aptly residing in Heinrich Schliemann's neoclassical mansion, the Ilion Megaron (1881). This was designed by Schliemann's architect friend Ernst Ziller, who had accompanied the man to Troy and later became a Greek citizen. Inside and out, motifs recall Schliemann's momentous discoveries at Troy and Mycenae – don't miss the delightful salon frieze of baby archaeologists, merrily digging up pots. Detailed English explanations and computers relate the long history of money (the ancient Greeks, amongst their other achievements, were behind that as well), from the bronze weights used in exchange back in the 16th century BC, to the first silver and gold coins minted in the 7th century BC, in Lydia and Ionia in Asia Minor, to the often beautiful coins minted in Classical and Hellenistic times. One shows what Cleopatra really looked like: a prim, old-fashioned Greek schoolmarm.

Numismatic Museum
t 210 364 3774; open Tues–Sun 8–3; adm

If you cross from here to Stadíou via Amerikís Street, you'll meet the imposing Old Parliament Building (1875–1935), guarded by a flamboyant equestrian statue of Kolokotrónis (*see* pp.344–5). This now houses the **National Historical Museum**; all around the old deputies' chamber are exhibits on Greek history, concentrating on the War of Independence: famous ships' figureheads, named for ancient heroes (many wear thick coats of paint – when sailing through the Bosphorus they had to be painted black to avoid offending the Turks); the Zográfos paintings – 25 colourful scenes narrating Greek history from the fall of Constantinople to the War of Independence, commissioned by General Makrigiánnis, who described the events to the painter Dimítri Zográfos (another set of the paintings are in the Windsor Castle library); memorabilia of war heroes and of Byron, along with items and engravings used to rouse the world to the Greek cause; and a sumptuous collection of folk costumes from across Greece.

National Historical Museum
t 210 323 7617; open Tues–Sun 9–2; adm, free on Sun

Two streets up Stadíou, flanking large Plateía Klafthmónos, a former residence of King Otto and Queen Amalia now houses the

Athens City Museum
*7 Paparigópoulou, **t** 210 324 6164; open Mon and Wed–Fri 9–4, Sat and Sun 10–3; adm*

Athens City Museum, with models, memorabilia and romantic paintings of Athens as it was (it's startling to see how built up the Acropolis and Agora were before the archaeologists went to work), as well as furnishings from Otto's bumpy reign. Among the paintings, don't miss the anonymous portrait of Byron, Turner's *Allegory of Enslaved Greece* (1822) or Nikólaos Gýzis' charming *Carnival in Athens* (1892). Diagonally opposite, on Plateía Klafthmónos, the 11th-century church of **Ag. Theódori** has a beautiful door. You may be tempted to stop for a drink or lunch in its pretty little oasis; many Athenians do.

Across Stadíou from the square is the Panepistimíou metro station and, beyond that, on Panepistimíou Street, the 'Trilogy' – three huge neoclassical buildings, designed by two Danish brothers, Theophilos and Christian Hansen. The **Academy of Athens** (1886) on the right, with its huge statues of Athena and Apollo, was built with funds donated by Simon Sinas, a Vlach from Albania, who founded the National Bank of Austria in Vienna; the others are the **University** (1846) and the **National Library** (1901).

At the north end of Panepistimíou, traffic spins around **Omónia** ('Concord') **Square**, or 'ammonia' as Henry Miller called it in *The Colossus of Maroussi*. Once Athens' Times Square, with 24-hour dives and porn-peddling *períptera*, only a few whiffs of the old Omónia linger after a dull revamp, although at least the fountains and trees have returned. One busy street, Athinás, leads south to the palatial **Dimarchíon** or City Hall, next to a handsome mansion by Ziller, before it divides the fruit and vegetables from the meat and fish stalls of the city's colourful **Central Market**.

Central Market
open Mon–Sat until 3

National Archaeological Museum

27 National Archaeological Museum
*Patissíon (28 Oktovríou) and Tossítsa Sts (a 10min walk north from Omónia), **t** 210 821 7717; open April–mid-Oct Mon 1–7, Tues–Fri 8–7.30; adm*

This is the big one, totally revamped for 2004, and containing some of the most sublime works of the ancient Greek world, housed in a vast neoclassical edifice begun in 1866. But note: some exhibits may be moved.

The museum's oldest artefacts are **Neolithic**: small schematic figures going back to the 5th millennium BC from Sésklo and finds from Troy and its close cultural cousin, Polióchni on Límnos, the oldest site in the Aegean. The **Cycladic** civilization that blossomed in the 3rd millennium BC was famous for its startlingly contemporary-looking marble figurines; the museum has the largest complete figure ever found, the famous 4,500-year-old harpist, and the 'frying pans' found in Early Cycladic graves (were they mirrors filled with water, or drums, with skins stretched over them, or did they hold offerings for the dead?), and a unique silver diadem decorated with rosettes and animals from Sýros. The longest-lasting Cycladic settlement was Phylokopi on Mílos; under the influence of the nature-loving Minoans it produced the delightful frescoes of flying fish and lyrical vases shaped like birds in song.

Among the museum's chief glories is the most important **Mycenaean** collection in the world – the treasures that convinced Schliemann that he had truly found the fief of his Homeric heroes 'rich in gold': gold masks, including the one Schliemann dubbed the 'mask of Agamemnon', bronze niello-work and cloisonné daggers, a magnificent bull's head rhyton, a boar's tusk helmet, lovely ivories (note especially the two goddesses with the child), frescoes from Tiryns and Pýlos, Linear B tablets, the deathly white Sphinx mask from Mycenae, delightful gold seals and signet rings, the 12th-century BC warrior *krater*, showing soldiers marching to war, a mini-fresco of ass-headed demons and the two exquisite gold cups found in a tomb at Vapheío, probably of Minoan manufacture, with vivid *repoussée* scenes of capturing a bull.

After the collapse of the Mycenaeans (*c.* 1150 BC), Greek art began its revival with ceramics: don't miss the striking monumental **Late Geometric** grave amphorae from Dipylon (760 BC) and one of the earliest inscriptions in Greek (740 BC) on a vase found at Kerameikós. The museum also has rare examples of the sculpture of the day, flat, linear 'Daedalic' figures with their triangular heads, a prelude to the mid-7th-century introduction of the **Archaic** figures of the *kouros* and *kore* with their haunting smiles, as if they had 'known Divinity', as John Fowles put it. The collection spans the oldest extant *kouros*, a colossus from Soúnion (from 610 BC), to the perfect *Phrasikleia Kore* by Aristion of Páros, holding a mushroom, her dress painted with rosettas and solar-symbol swastikas, then to the *Aristodikos Kouros* (510 BC) whose vigour, muscles and relaxed pose points directly to the Classical age. Other key Archaic works include the earliest known *Nike* or *Victory* (550 BC) from Délos, a magnificent *krater* of 640 BC showing Apollo's return to Délos after his annual confab with the Hyperboreans, a beautiful Parian marble relief of a dancer or athlete in motion, the grave stele of the hoplite Aristion (510 BC) signed by Aristokles, and the bases of *kouros* statues found in Athens, with fascinating reliefs of athletes – wrestlers, long jumpers, hockey players and two punters egging on a cat and dog.

After the Persian Wars, the Archaic smiles are replaced by the early **Classical** 'severe style', epitomized in the relief from Soúnion of a serious-looking boy crowning himself. The museum has an unsurpassed collection of Classical funerary art, including the *Stele of Hegeso*, an Athenian beauty, enveloped by the delicate folds of her bridal gown; its discovery at Kerameikós inspired a poem by Palamas. Another highlight are two exquisite votive reliefs: of *Hermes and Nymphs* and *Dionysos and the Actors*, both *c.* 410 BC.

Roman copies of works by the great sculptors of the age offer hints of what's been lost; one is a lifeless copy of Phidias' *Athena* from the Parthenon, another, the marble *Diadoumenos*, is a copy of a famous bronze by Polykleitos, author of the 'canon' on the proportions of Classical beauty. Surviving Greek originals have mostly been found on shipwrecks: one is the splendidly virile bronze *Poseidon* (*c*. 460 BC) about to launch his trident, found off Cape Artemísion.

The same wreck yielded the bronze *Jockey* (*c*. 140 BC), one of the most dramatic works of the **Hellenistic** era, the horse straining and the boy's face distorted by the speed; other rescued bronze originals are the *Marathon Boy*, attributed to Praxiteles, and *Antikýthera Youth*, attributed to Euphranor of Corinth. Other Hellenistic masterpieces are the beautiful and melancholy *Ilissos stele* by the school of Skopas and a striking relief of a young Ethiopian groom, trying to calm a horse, found in 1948 by Larissa station. Also look for the bust of Plato (a Roman copy) and a bizarre double herm head of an elderly Aristotle; the *Wounded Gaul*, the base of a statue by Praxiteles, showing the music contest between Apollo and Marsyas; busts of Demosthenes and his enemy Alexander the Great in a lion helmet, with graffiti on his face; the giant heads from the Temple of Despoina at Lykosoúra in Arcadía by Damophon; and a charming group of Aphrodite, raising her slipper to whack a pesky Pan. Small votive reliefs and illustrated decrees offer fascinating insights into religious life, involving plenty of bearded snakes.

From the 500 years of **Roman** rule in Greece, there's a bronze Augustus from an equestrian statue, found in the Aegean and looking very much like Roddy McDowall, and a group of 2nd- and 3rd-century AD portrait herms from the Diogeneion, an Athenian gymnasium, offering a unique look at the upper-class Athenians of the day. Roman busts include ones of Hadrian and Antinous, the favourite he deified, and Marcus Aurelius, whose portrait shows a last attempt at psychological analysis before inspiration dried up altogether. A peculiar one is the bust of Julia Mamaea, mother of Emperor Alexander Severus (AD 232–5), who was sentenced to death, which required that all her portraits be hammered.

And that's not all. Upstairs, the museum has one of the finest collections anywhere of Greek vases, and another of small bronzes going back to 1000 BC: votives from Dodona, Olympia and the Acropolis, as well as the Antikýthera Device (59 BC). This mass of clockwork, recovered from a Rome-bound shipwreck in 1900, was a mystery until 1958, when it was shown to have been an astronomical computer, in all likelihood the 'future-telling astronomical device' of Rhodes described by Cicero; it surprised the many people who thought the ancient Greeks, for all their cleverness, never applied themselves to technology. There's an excellent **Egyptian collection**, and the **Stathátos Collection** with exquisite *objets d'art* and jewellery from all periods, including an egg-shaped red-figure vase showing a woman dowsing. Another special section is devoted to **Minoan Akrotíri**, on the island of Santoríni: lovely vases and frescoes of *Boxing Children*, the *Antelopes* and *Spring* with dancing swallows (18th–17th-century BC), enough to make all those Atlantis stories seem true.

Around the Museum

Epigraphic Museum
t 210 821 7637; open Tues–Sun 8.30–2.30

In the same big building, but with a separate entrance at 1 Tosíta Street, the **Epigraphic Museum** has an enormous collection of ancient inscriptions, mostly from Attica. Until the 6th century, all were written in *boustrophedon*, 'as the ox ploughs', back and forth (binders in the rooms have easier-to-read transcriptions, although they aren't translated into English). Stone-carvers must have worked fast; one stele has the decree of Themistocles in 480 BC, ordering the evacuation of Athens.

South of the museum is the **Polytechníon** school (1880), where students began the uprising against the military junta in 1973, and met tanks in response. The neighbourhood behind this is Exárchia, Athens' Latin Quarter, home of trendies, students and literati. *Terra incognita* for tourists, its leafy heart, **Plateía Exárchia**, is lively after dark, with traditional ouzeries, hip-hop music bars and smoke-filled *rembétika* clubs. Exárchia was once nicknamed 'Anarchia', but now its square shelters a huge FloCafé, which in Greece is as middle class as you can get. Above the square, there are lovely views of the Acropolis from **Strefi Hill**.

East of the Acropolis: The Záppeion and Zeus

East of the Acropolis and south of Sýntagma Square, off busy Leofóros Amalías, **Záppeion Park** is an extension of the National Gardens, surrounding the handsome horseshoe-shaped **Záppeion Palace** (1888), designed by Theophilos Hansen and now used for summit meetings and other big events. On the corner of Amalías and Vass. Ólgas, don't miss the **statue of Hellas to Lord Byron**, in which a maiden representing Greece hugs the poet while sticking her hand in his pocket – a fairly accurate allegory of what occurred during the War of Independence, which Byron was the first Western celebrity to support. Since then he has been the National Favourite Brit; the first philhellene to have loved live Greeks as much as if not more than the ancient ones, and one who blasted Elgin for vandalizing the Parthenon.

Temple of Olympian Zeus
t 210 922 6330; open May–Aug daily 8–7; Sept–April daily 8–5; adm

Across from here, in Leofóros Vass. Ólgas, is the entrance to the **Temple of Olympian Zeus**. Fifteen enormous columns and one prone and broken like spilled breath mints recall what Livy called 'the only temple on earth of a size adequate to the greatness of the god'. The spot was long sacred: not far away stood a very ancient temple to the Earth, with a cleft in the floor said to be the drain for the deluge sent by Zeus to punish humanity, killing all but Deucalion and his wife. The ambitious foundations were laid by Pisistratos, but work ground to a halt with his son, only to be continued in 175 BC by a Roman architect, Cossutius. It was half finished when Cossutius' patron, Antiochos IV of Syria, died, leaving Hadrian to complete it in AD 131. Nearby are the ruins of a well-appointed Roman bath and bits of other temples. The view to the east is tranquil, closed by the violet-tinted slopes of Mount Hymettos, while to the east, where traffic hums down Amalías, stands **Hadrian's Arch**, in Pentelic marble, erected by the Athenians to thank him for his benevolence. The complimentary inscription reads, on the Acropolis side: 'This is Athens, the ancient city of Theseus', while the other side reads: 'This is the city of Hadrian, not of Theseus'.

Further east, Vass. Ólgas turns into Leofóros Vass. Konstantínos, where the landmark is the big white horseshoe of the **Kallimármaro Stadium**. Another benefactor, good old Herodes Atticus, built a marble stadium for the Panathenaea Festival in AD 140; it was restored for the first modern Olympics in 1896 by yet another benefactor, Georgíos Averoff, and used again in 2004 Olympics for the last lap of the marathon.

West of the stadium lies **Mets**, a neighbourhood popular with artists and media folk, with some fine old houses and tavernas. On its south end (just off the map) is modern Athens' oldest cemetery, the evocative, cat-filled **Próto Nekrotafeío**, its monuments resembling a modern Kerameikós: look for Schliemann's temple tomb, and the more modest graves of Melina Mercouri, Andréas Papandréas, and Kolokotrónis.

East of Sýntagma Square

The Benáki Museum

Benáki Museum
*Koumbári St, **t** 210 367 1000, www.benaki.gr; open Mon, Wed, Fri and Sat 9–5, Thurs 9–midnight, Sun 9–3; adm; book ahead for lunch or the Thurs night buffet*

Another main artery, Leofóros Vass. Sofías, begins next to the Parliament and heads east, passing ministries, embassies and the excellent Benáki Museum at the corner of Koumbári Street. Antónios Benáki, born in 1873 into a prominent family in Alexandria, spent 35 years amassing Byzantine and Islamic treasures, and in 1930 was the first individual in Greece to open a museum, here in his beautiful neoclassical mansion. Hundreds of donors since have made this the best place in Athens for a complete overview of Greek civilization, beginning with Cycladic figurines, Minoan, Mycenaean and Cypriot Bronze Age ceramics, Early Helladic gold cups, Mycenaean jewellery from Thebes and a lovely gold kylix decorated with running dogs from Dendrá. Next come fine Archaic and Classical sculpture and vases and some exceptional Hellenistic and Roman artefacts, including the intricate gold jewellery of the 'Thessaly Treasure'. The Christians follow, with 3rd-century El Fayyum portraits, 6th-century Coptic textiles, Byzantine earrings (that match those worn by the Empress Theodora in the mosaics at Ravenna), frescoes, illuminated manuscripts and a superb collection of icons, including two painted by El Greco before he left Crete for Venice and Spain. A Florentine *Madonna* attributed to Nicoló di Pietro Gerini keeps them company; some icons show how close the Greeks themselves came to adopting the Renaissance before the Turkish conquest.

The first floor offers an overview of what the Greeks were up to under the Ottomans. There's a superb collection of costumes, jewellery, painted wooden chests, religious items, ceramics and embroideries, including a spectacular silk embroidered *spervéri* (a tent hung over the matrimonial bed) made on Rhodes. Among the marble reliefs, don't miss the one showing Constantine the Great amid trophies of Greek victories. There's a reconstructed traditional room from the plate-collecting-mad island of Skýros, and two exquisite 18th-century rooms from a wealthy merchant's mansion in Kozáni, full of intricate carvings and painted decoration. Rooms 22 and 23 contain items made by visitors to Greece, including two pretty watercolours by Edward Lear. The second floor has a large room for special exhibits (which are usually excellent), folk pieces and items from the pre-War of Independence period.

The third floor covers modern Greece, from 1821 to the present: here you'll find Alí Pasha's silver and gold rifle (a gift from Britain's George IV); Byron's portable desk (the size of a laptop computer); the original score to Dionýssios Solomós' *Hymn to Freedom*, the Greek national anthem; the swords, flags and portraits of the Greek heroes; and 32 lithographs by Peter von Hess on the liberation of Greece, all that survives of the murals commissioned by Ludwig I in the (now destroyed) Royal Palace in Munich. Other exhibits include the court dress of his son King Otto, memorabilia of Venizélos, Cavafy's notebook, manuscripts and first editions, the Nobel Prizes won by George Seféris (1963) and Odysséas Elýtis (1979), and the Lenin Prize won by Yánnis Rítsos in 1977.

Kolonáki and Lykavitós

Koumbári Street, next to the Benáki Museum, leads up a block to **Kolonáki Square**, Athens' Knightsbridge in miniature, complete with fancypants shops, upmarket restaurants, big cafés, the British Council and plenty of 'Kolonáki Greeks' – Athenian Sloane Rangers – to patronize them.

Above **Plateía Dexamení**, the Roman aqueduct ended in a reservoir; in 1840 it was rebuilt, and still serves the city. From here, two flights of stairs lead up to the **funicular** at the corner of Aristippoú and Ploutarchoúis, which every 10 minutes ascends the city's highest hill, **Lykavitós** (Lycabettos), 980ft and illuminated like a fairytale tower at night. The summit offers a 360° view over greater Athens; here too is the white 19th-century chapel of Ag. Geórgios, a restaurant/bar, a lovely outdoor theatre and a cannon fired on national holidays.

Lykavitós Hill

Besides boutiques, Kolonáki has more museums, beginning with the sleek **Goulandrís Museum of Cycladic and Ancient Greek Art**, two blocks east of the Benáki Museum. The collection of Cycladic art (3200–2000 BC) rivals that of the National Archaeological Museum: a beautiful display of some 300 white marble statuettes as they evolved from the earliest abstract violin-shapes. Although most are female, the delightful *Toastmaster* who has been raising his glass now for around 4,500 years steals the show. The second and fourth floors have a choice collection of art from Mycenaean to early Christian times: well-preserved Corinthian helmets offered to Zeus at Olympia and exquisite vases. A glass corridor leads to the lovely **Stathátos Mansion**, designed by Ernst Ziller and now used for temporary exhibits.

Goulandrís Museum of Cycladic and Ancient Greek Art
4 Neofýtou Doúka St, ***t*** *210 722 8321; open Mon, Thurs, Fri 10–4, Wed 10–8, Sat 10–3; closed Sun and Tues; adm*

Near here, a French philhellene, Sophie de Marbois, Duchesse de Plaisance, had her beautiful **Villa Ilissia** (1848, by Stamátis Kléanthes) on the once idyllic banks of the Ilissos. Even the river is now underground, but the villa now houses the **Byzantine Museum**, the most important collection in the country – not only icons but marble sculptures, mosaics, woodcarvings, frescoes, manuscripts, ecclesiastical robes, the 7th-century Mytilíni treasure, and some exquisite pieces from Constantinople brought over by refugees in 1922. Two rooms on the ground floor are arranged as chapels: one Early Christian (note the 4th-century statue of Orpheus as Christ, from Aegina) and another Middle Byzantine. The icons include the superb 14th-century *Crucifixion* from the church of Elkómenos in Monemvasiá. A new extension under the museum will be linked to the recently excavated **Lyceum**, where Aristotle, angry after failing to become Plato's successor at the Academy, set up his own school.

Byzantine Museum
22 Vass. Sofías, ***t*** *210 721 1027; open Tues–Sun 8.30–3; adm*

Just down Vass. Sofías, at the corner of Rizári Street, fighter planes mark the **War Museum of Greece**, containing weapons and battle relics from earliest times to Greece's expeditionary force in the Korean War; there's a display on the ancient beacons that just may have informed Mycenae that Troy had fallen. Opposite is the

War Museum of Greece
t *210 724 4464; open Tues–Sun 9–2*

British Embassy, and next to that **Evangelismós Park**, with a useful metro; the British and American archaeological schools are above this and, at the top, the impressive neoclassical Gennadeion Library, one of the city's best; cases along the walls have assorted treasures, including a lock of Byron's hair.

Further east on Vass. Sofías, **Rizári Park** is unmissable for its huge statue of *The Runner* by Kóstas Varotsós; turn right here for the National Gallery on Vass. Konstantínou, just across from the Hilton.

National Gallery (Ethnikí Pinakothéki)

National Gallery
50 Vass. Konstantínou, **t** *210 723 5857; open Mon and Wed 9–3 and 6–9, Thurs, Fri and Sat 9–3; Sun 10–2; closed Tues; adm exp*

The National Gallery offers a thoroughly enjoyable journey through five centuries of secular Greek art, even if El Greco is the only Greek artist you've ever heard of when you walk through the door. Nor is it exclusively Greek. On the ground floor, highlights of the museum's Western European collection include the likes of Lorenzo Veneziano's *Crucifixion*, two fine paintings by Luca Giordano (*The Healing of the Lame* and *Esther and Ahasuerus*) that show his vast range, a memorable 16th-century *Self-sacrifice of Marcus Curtius* attributed to Lambert van Noort, showing the brave Roman plummenting into the Forum's abyss, with nonchalant beetles in the foreground, and the only-known *Rest during the Flight into Egypt* that stars guinea pigs, painted in the 17th century by Jan Breugel II and Hendrich van Balen.

But the focus is on Greek art, and there are some gems. The oldest works are by El Greco from his Toledo days (the shimmering, immaterial *Concert of Angels*, *St Peter*, and the *Burial of Christ*), and by Greeks living on Venetian Crete and the Ionian islands during Turkish rule. After independence, many Greek painters went to Bavaria for training and, in the polished academic style, the 'Munich school' supplied the portraits, charming genre scenes of picturesque Greeks, landscapes and romantic views of the east demanded by the bourgeoisie: especially the delightful works of Nikólaos Gýzis (*The Engagement*) and Geórgios Iakovídis (*Children's Concert*). Gýzis in his last decades (d. 1901) moved on to symbolism (the vampy *Spider*) and large mystical paintings with a Blakean intensity (*Behold the Celestial Bridegroom Cometh*).

The upper floor is dedicated to the 20th century, when attempts were made to found a national school, led by the astonishingly versatile Konstantínos Parthénis, whose best-loved work is of the martyr for freedom, *Athanássios Diákos*. But most artists went their own way. Nikifóros Lýstras was a harbinger of a back-to-basics Greek modern style (*The Kiss*). The great Níkos Hadzikyriákos-Ghíkas, internationally the best-known modern Greek painter, was a 'Phototropic Cubist' and is well represented here, while others drew their inspiration from folk themes and fairytales (Iánnis Tsaroúchis and Theóphilos Hatzimichaíl). Giórgos Gounarópolous was the Greek Odilon Redon, and Níkos Egonópoulos became the leading Surrealist. The last section contains postwar works by Iánnis Móralis, Spýros Vasilío and others.

To Moní Kessarianí and Mount Ymittós

South of the National Gallery lies the essential Athenian neighbourhood of **Pangráti**, a good place to get a feel for everyday life in Athens. To escape the city altogether, take a taxi or bus 224 from the Byzantine Museum (on Leoforós Vass. Sofías) up the long humpback slopes of **Mount Ymittós** (Hymettos), where fragrant shrubs produce a honey famous since antiquity for increasing longevity. The bus leaves you a 1.5km walk from the 11th-century **Moní Kaisarianí**, built over an ancient sanctuary at the source of the Ilissos. The oldest Byzantine baths in Greece remain visible through a grille (they were later used as an olive press) and the pretty stone church is coated in early 18th-century frescoes inspired by the Cretan school. The monastery was abandoned in the late 1700s; during the War of Independence the Turks took its once famous library to the Acropolis to use the paper for cartridges. The Nazis used this remote corner to execute hostages; now there are picnic tables and the lovely groves planted by the Athens Tree Society. A Roman ram's mouth fountain in the outer wall still gushes out water, and two minutes above the monastery a cistern by a cave holds the **Kallopoúla spring**, whose waters in ancient times were considered sovereign against sterility, while a bit further up, by the ruins of a Palaeo-Christian basilica and Frankish church, is a superb viewpoint over Athens, stretching as far as the Peloponnese on a clear day.

Moní Kaisarianí
t 210 723 6619; open Tues–Sun 8–3; adm

Into the Northern Suburbs

Beyond the museums, Leofóros Vass. Sofías continues past the **Mégaro Mousikís** concert hall (1992) with its nearly perfect accoustics, and then the US Embassy and the big crossroads at Ambelókipi. To the left, Leofóros Kifissiás heads north towards **Maroússi**, a pleasant suburb famous for its clay and pottery, where the 80,000-seat **Olympic Stadium** was built in 1982, in anticipation of the 1996 games which ended up in Atlanta. For the 2004 games, it was given its striking roof of sweeping steel arches designed by Santiago Calatrava. It's now home to two Athenian football squads, AEK Athens FC and Panathinaikos. Just don't look for any giants – Henry Miller's 'Colossus of Maroussi' was a real man, the unforgettable Katsímbalis – but you may want to seek out the **Spathario Shadow Theatre Museum** in Plateía Kastalías, dedicated to the art that the Greeks know by its lead character, Karaghiózis, who came to them by way of the Turks, who came to *them* by way

Spathario Shadow Theatre Museum
Plateia Kastalías, t 210 612 7245, www.karagiozismuseum.gr; open Mon, Tues, Thurs and Fri 10–2, Wed 10–2 and 6–8

Goulandrís Natural History Museum
13 Levídou, t 210 801 5870; www.gnhm.gr; open Mon–Sat 9–2.30, Sun 10–2.30; adm

Gaia Centre
100 Othónos St, t 210 801 5870; open Mon–Sat 9–2.30, Sun 10–2.30; adm

of 14th-century Arab merchants, who saw the shadow puppet plays in Java.

Further north, at the terminus of the metro, is **Kifissiá**, a wooded suburb under the slopes of Mount Pendéli favoured by the élite ever since the fabulously wealthy Herodes Atticus built his villa here. The **Goulandrís Natural History Museum** has won awards for its displays related to Greece and the rest of the world (with explanations in English). The **Gaia Centre** is an autonomous wing of the Goulandrís museum devoted to ecology, loaded with audio-visual systems, and inventive and informative displays.

Other Sites around Athens

Railway Museum
4 Siokoú St, Sepólia, t 210 512 6295; open Tues–Fri 9–1, Sat and Sun 10–1

Hellenic Cosmos Cultural Centre
254 Pireós St, Távros, Ⓜ Kallithéa or bus 049 from Omónia Square, t 210 254 0000, www.fhw.gr; open winter Mon, Tues, Thurs 9–2, Wed and Fri 9–9, Sat 11–4, Sun 10–4; summer Mon, Tues, Thurs, Fri 9–4, Wed 9–9, Sun 10–3, closed Sat

Pierídis Museum
34–6 Kastoriás, Athinais Conference Centre, Votanikós, t 210 348 0000; open daily 9.30–1; adm

Plato's Academy (Akadimías Plátonos) was in a sacred wood, west of Lárissa station on a spot identified in 1966 by a boundary marker. The philosophizing here may have changed the world, but the archaeologists have yet to find anything worth seeing: just a few foundation stones in the trees.

The **Railway Museum**, in Sepólia, houses Greece's only collection of its retired iron-horses, including the original Diakoftó-Kalávrita train (*see* p.189), wagons made for George I and the smoking car that the Empress Eugénie gave to Sultan Abdul Hassiz.

The **Hellenic Cosmos Cultural Centre**, in Távros, midway to Piraeus, is the non-profit Foundation of the Hellenic World's high-tech look at Greek civilization, offering a range of special exhibition and virtual reality experiences in the new **Tholos theatre**; their website offers a tour of Greek history.

Pierídis Museum of Ancient Cypriot Art, in the Athinais Conference Centre just off the Iera Odos in Votanikós, is a former silk factory converted to hold the Pierídis Foundation's excellent collection, dating from 8000 BC to Classical times.

ⓘ Athens ›
EOT: 26 Amalías, near Sýntagma Square, t 210 331 0392, www.gnto.gr; open Mon–Fri 9–8, Sat and Sun 10–7

Useful Information in Athens

The **tourist police** have a 24hr magic number: **t** 171. A voice in English will answer any question you may have, including lost property queries. From outside Athens, ring **t** 210 171. Athens' **municipal tourist information, t** 195, is also very helpful.

At the **National Tourist Organization (EOT) office**, pick up their free *Athens–Piraeus Public Transportation* pocket map and booklet *Athens/Attica* with excellent maps. The helpful weekly *Athens News* comes out on Fridays and is on sale at most kiosks. Save money at Athens' ancient sites with an all-inclusive ticket (*see* p.91).

Emergencies

First aid (ambulance): t 166.

Police: t 100.

Fire: t 199.

Hospital: t 1434.

Pharmacies on duty: t 1434.

European emergency number (all cases, in English): **t** 112.

Useful Addresses

Main post office (ELTA): Sýntagma Square, **t** 210 323 7573, *www.elta.gr. Open Mon–Fri 7.30am–8pm, Sat 7.30–2, and Sun 9–1.30.*

Aliens Bureau (for non-EU passport-holders who need visa extensions): 173 Alexándras, **t** 210 770 5711.

Traffic police: 24–6 Deligíanni St (behind the Archaeological Museum), **t** 210 528 4121. For towed cars.

Left luggage: Besides the airport's 24hr left-luggage facility, you can leave your bags in central Athens at **Bellair Travel**, 40 Voúlis St, **t** 210 323 9261, *www.bellairtourism.com.gr*. *Open Mon–Fri 9–6, Sat 9–2.*

Launderette: 10 Ángelou Géronda St in Pláka, **t** 210 321 3102. Wash, dry and fold for €9 a load; they advertise a 2hr service. *Open Mon–Sat 8–7, Sun 8–1.*

Shopping in Athens

A new law has decreed that **shopping hours** in Greece are Mon–Fri 9–9, Sat 9–6.

Ermoú Street is the centre of mid-range fashion shopping; for designer fashions, prowl the boutiques of **Kolonáki** and **Kifissía**. **Pláka** and **Monastiráki** are the places to go for light-up Parthenons, but are also not bad for casual clothes, accessories, leather, ceramics, rugs, some real antiques and genuine junk. The **Central Market** on Athinás St (*open Mon–Sat 8–3*) is fun, even if you don't need any food. **Evripídou St**, west of Athinás St, is Athens' spice street.

Attica on Panepistimíou Street near Sýntagma is central Athens' shopping heaven, with eight floors of mostly designer goods.

The Athenians themselves have fallen for **The Mall**, at 35 Papandréou St, Maroússi, **t** 210 630 0000, *www.themallathens.gr*, with well over 200 shops, restaurants, cinemas, cafés. etc.; it's next to the Neratziótissa station, served by both the metro and suburban rail line. *Open Mon–Fri 9–9, Sat 9–8.*

For books in English: try **Eleftheroudákis**, 17 Panepistimíou St, **t** 210 325 8440, or 20 Níkis St, **t** 210 322 9388, the latter with a good selection of guide books. **Compendium**, 5 Nikidímou and Níkis Sts, **t** 210 322 1248, is a cosy English-only shop, with an eclectic selection of used paperbacks to buy or swap.

Where to Stay in Athens

Athens is a big, noisy city, especially so at night when you want to sleep – unless you do as the Greeks do and take a long afternoon siesta. Note that during slow periods you can get great deals, even in the luxury hotels: below, low-season prices appear in brackets after the hotel name if they are different from the category in which they fall for high season.

Luxury (high season) (€€€€€)

Grande Bretagne, 1 Vass. Georgíou, on Sýntagma Square, **t** 210 333 0000, *www.grandebretagne.gr*. Built in 1862 to house members of the Greek royal family who couldn't squeeze into the palace (the current Parliament building). It was used as a Nazi head-quarters, then by Winston Churchill, who had a lucky escape from a bomb while spending Christmas here in 1944. Totally renovated, it offers style and service that the newer hotels may never achieve. It now has a spa as well. Ⓜ Sýntagma.

St George Lycabettus, 2 Kleoménous (Plateía Dexaménis, Kolonáki), **t** 210 729 0711, *www.sglycabettus.gr*. An intimate atmosphere and wonderful views of the Parthenon or out to sea, and a pool, too. Ⓜ Evangelismós.

Athenian Callirhoe, 32 Kalliroís and Petmezá, **t** 210 921 5353, *www.tac.gr*. Friendly, soundproofed boutique hotel near the Temple of Zeus, with a delightful modern look and a rooftop restaurant with a view of the Acropolis. Ⓜ Acropolis.

AVA, 9–11 Lyssikrátous, Pláka, **t** 210 325 9000, *www.avahotel.gr* (*low season* €€€€). Very comfortable central apartments and suites with balconies and broadband. Ⓜ Acropolis.

Divani Palace Acropolis, 19–26 Parthenónos St, **t** 210 922 2945, *www.divanis.com* (*low season* €€€€). A great location near the Acropolis, with a pool, and part of the ancient city wall in its lobby. Ⓜ Acropolis.

Athens Baby Grand, 65 Athínas and Lykoúrgou Sts, near Omónia, **t** 210 325 0900, *www.classicalhotels,gr* (*low season* €€€€). Ten international artists (some of them graffiti) have contributed to the décor of this hip new hotel in a great location for walking. Ⓜ Omónia.

Achilleas, 21 Lékka, **t** 210 323 3197, *www.achilleashotel.gr* (*low season* €€€€). Small, cosy, renovated, central; suites for families. Ⓜ Sýntagma.

Zinon, 3 Keramikoú St, practically in Omónia Square, **t** 210 325 1106, *www.hotelsofathens.com* (*low season* €€€€). Excellent location with the Best Western tradition (and special offers) behind it. Ⓜ Omónia.

Pláka, 7 Kapnikaréas and Metropóleos (Ermoú–Pláka area), **t** 210 322 2706, *www.plakahotel.gr* (*low season* €€€€). Homey, small, totally renovated, right in the shopping district, with a roof garden view of the Acropolis. Ⓜ Sýntagma.

Eridanus, 78 Piréos, **t** 210 520 5360, *www.eridanus.gr*. Hip hotel near Technopolis that opened for the Olympics, with French (**Jerome Serres**) and Greek (**Varoulka**) gourmet restaurants. At the lower end of this price category. Ⓜ Thissío.

Titania, 52 Panepistimíou, **t** 210 330 0111, *www.titania.gr*. Practically on top of lively Omónia Square. Pleasant rooms with broadband and a rooftop restaurant, the **Olive Garden**, planted with old olives, and gorgeous views. Prices are at the bottom of this category. Ⓜ Omónia.

Very Expensive (high season) (€€€€)

Ochre & Brown, Leokouríou 7, **t** 210 331 2950, *www.ochreandbrown.com*. Small (11 rooms) and very, very hip urban hotel, with a lounge/restaurant to match. Ⓜ Thissío.

Astor, 16 Karagiórgi Servías (just off Sýntagma Square), **t** 210 335 1000, *www.astorhotel.gr*. Standard A-class hotel in a great location, with a view of the Acropolis with breakfast. At the lower end of this price category. Ⓜ Sýntagma.

★ Magna Grecia >

Magna Grecia, 54 Mitropólis, **t** 210 324 0314, *www.magnagreciahotel.com* (*low season* €€€). Small boutique hotel in a neoclassical building with wooden floors and high ceilings next to the Pláka, with lovely views. Ⓜ Sýntagma.

Parthenon, 6 Makrí (Makrigiánni), **t** 210 923 4594, *www.airotel.gr*. Great location and a pretty outdoor breakfast area. Ask for the rooms with balconies. Ⓜ Acropolis.

Austria, 7 Moussón-Filopáppou, **t** 210 923 5151, *www.austriahotel.com* (*low season* €€€). In a great location facing the Philopáppos Hill close to the Acropolis entrance. Makes the complicated navigation required to reach it by car worth it. Book online for discounts. Ⓜ Acropolis.

Art Gallery Pension, 5 Eréchthiou and Veíkou Sts, **t** 210 923 8376, *ecotec@otenet.gr* (*low season* €€). A quiet, well-run, old-style hotel which has raised its rates into the stratosphere for what it offers. Each room has its own bathroom, it is quaint, and Pláka is a 15min walk away. Ⓜ Syngroú-Fix.

Expensive (high season) (€€€)

Acropolis Select, 37–39 Fálirou St, Koukáki, **t** 210 921 1610, *www.acropoliselect.gr*. Tucked away on a quiet street, an easy walk to the Acropolis, this is a charming boutique hotel (renovated in 2000) that offers a lot that higher-category hotels offer, including family rooms, babysitting service and private parking. Ⓜ Syngroú-Fix.

★ Acropolis House >>

Acropolis House, 6–8 Kódrou (off Kydathinéon St in Pláka), **t** 210 322 2344. A neoclassical house with modernized rooms but in a traditional style, with antique furnishings, frescoes and a family welcome. Ⓜ Sýntagma/Acropolis.

Byron, 19 Býronis, Pláka, **t** 210 323 0327, *www.hotel-byron.gr*. Small, on a quiet street. Ⓜ Acropolis.

Jason Inn, 12 Asómaton, by Asómaton Square in Psirrí, **t** 210 325 1106, *www.douros-hotels.com* (*low season* €€). This modest hotel has been renovated and is perfect for excursions to Monastiráki, Psirrí, the Acropolis and Kerameikós. Ⓜ Thissío.

Carolina, 55 Kolokotrónis (Sýntagma–Pláka), **t** 210 324 3551, *www.hotelcarolina.gr* (*low season* €€). A classic since 1934, but old hands won't recognize anything but the old-fashioned 'cage elevator' and its friendly owner: it was all spruced up for the Olympics. At the bottom of this price category. Ⓜ Sýntagma.

Dióskouros >>

Adonis, 3 Kódrou, Pláka, **t** 210 324 9737, *www.hotel-adonis.gr* (*low season* €€). Central and renovated; all rooms have balconies, and there's a breakfast roof garden and bar with views. Ⓜ Sýntagma.

Arethusa, 6–8 Mitropólis, **t** 210 322 9431, *www.arethusahotel.gr*. Typical hotel in a great location, just around the corner from Sýntagma Square, and a roof garden with Acropolis views. Ⓜ Sýntagma.

Oscar, 25 Filadelphías and Samoú, by Lárissa station, **t** 210 883 4215, *www.oscar.gr*. A standard hotel good for train connections and with a small pool and roof garden. Ⓜ Lárissa.

Moderate (high season) (€€)

Dryades, Emm. Benáki (Exárchia, by the Stréfi Hill), **t** 210 330 2387. All rooms en suite and the top three and roof garden have lovely views; the adjacent **Orion** (same owners) has smaller, cheaper rooms.

Metropolis, 46 Mitropólis, **t** 210 321 7871, *www.hotelmetropolis.gr*. Cute, homey and old-style air-conditioned rooms with TV, right opposite Athens cathedral. Ⓜ Sýntagma.

Phaedra, 16 Herefóndos (Pláka, near the Lysikrátes Monument), **t** 210 323 8461, *www.hotelphaedra.com*. Renovated with air-conditioning and TV, but still 'old-style', quiet on a lovely pedestrian square with a Byzantine church. Some balconies and rooms overlook the Acropolis. An old standby. Ⓜ Acropolis.

Adam's, 6 Herefóndos (Pláka), **t** 210 322 5381, *adams@otenet.gr*. Quiet, central, just 3mins from Hadrian's Arch; the rooms are comfortable and the location's great. Ⓜ Acropolis.

John's Place, 5 Patróu (behind the large Metropólis church), **t** 210 322 9719 (*low season* €). An old-fashioned classic, basic, with bathrooms down the hall. Ⓜ Sýntagma.

Kouros, 11 Kódrou (off Kydathinéou St, Pláka), **t** 210 322 7431 (*low season* €). In an attractive old house near the Greek Folk Art Museum. Prices may be up for discussion if not full. Ⓜ Sýntagma.

Nefeli, 16 Iperídou, Pláka, **t** 210 322 8044 (*low season* €). Adequate, charming little hotel. Ⓜ Sýntagma.

Inexpensive (high season) (€)

Dióskouros, 6 Pitákou (near Hadrian's Arch, Pláka), **t** 210 324 8165, *www.hostelworld.com*. Delightful, old-fashioned place with high-ceilinged rooms in a neoclassical building in a fairly quiet spot. Ⓜ Sýntagma/Acropolis.

Marble House, 35 A. Zínni (Koukáki), **t** 210 922 8294, *www.marblehouse.gr*. A comfortable Greek-French-run hotel, a bit of a hike south of the Syngroú-Fix metro; air-conditioning extra. Ⓜ Syngroú-Fix.

Pella Inn, Ermoú and Karaskáki, **t** 210 321 2229, *www.pellainn.gr*. En suites and non-en suites, clean and in a good spot. Ⓜ Monastiráki.

Tempi, 29 Eólou, **t** 210 321 3175, *www.travelling.gr/tempihotel*. Nothing special, but it has pleasant management and a terrific central location. Prices plummet out of season. Ⓜ Monastiráki.

Hostel Aphrodite, 12 Einhárdou and Micháil Vóda, **t** 210 881 0589, *www.hostelaphrodite.com*. Private rooms sleeping up to four and a dorm, a bar, laundry service and Internet café. Ⓜ Lárissa/Victoria.

The Student and Travellers' Inn, 16 Kydathinéon (Pláka), **t** 210 324 4808, *www.studenttravellersinn.com*. Hostel with air-conditioned private rooms sleeping up to four, some en suite, and Internet facilities. Ⓜ Sýntagma/Acropolis.

Victor Hugo Hostel, 16 Victor Hugo, **t** 210 523 2540, *www.aiyh-victorhugo.com*. Renovated in 2006. En suite double rooms and quads and Internet facilities. Ⓜ Metaxourgeío.

Eating Out in Athens

Athenians rarely dine out before 10 or 11pm, although most places are open by 8pm. Also note that many restaurants close in August.

As elsewhere in this guide, assume a cost of €15–20 per head with wine unless otherwise stated.

Sýntagma and Around

Aigli >>

Aigli, Záppeion Park, **t** 210 336 9363 (€50). Far from the traffic, near Záppeion Palace, in the restored Aigli complex, which also includes a music bar and outdoor cinema. A lovely place to feast on taste-packed delicate Mediterranean dishes while contemplating the Acropolis. Book.

Cellier Le Bistrot, 10 Panepistimíou (in the *stoa*), **t** 210 363 8525 (€30). Old restaurant revamped into a stylish bistro, with an Italian chandelier and the biggest mirror in Greece; Greek and international classics and a good wine list.

Pasaji, in the Spiromilíou Arcade and Voukourestíou St, **t** 210 322 0714 (€25–30). Sophisticated décor plus a good chef, N. Ismirnólou, and a pleasant ambience make this a winner. The restaurant looks out into the renovated glass-roofed *stoa* where it also has tables. Very quiet for the centre of Athens. *Open Mon–Sat 1pm–1am, Sun 7pm–1 am.*

Lullaby Café-Lunch Bar, in the Aígli area by the Záppeion Palace, **t** 210 336 9302. On a nice day this is the perfect spot for coffee, ice cream or snacks (try Aliki's *pítsa*), with a view of the grass and park. *Open daily from morning to late.*

Delphi, 13 Níkis, **t** 210 323 4869. Reasonably priced traditional Greek food served in air-conditioned surroundings all year round. It has been a standby for more than 30 years. No smoking policy.

Kentrikón, 3 Koloktrónis, **t** 210 323 2482. In a quiet *stoa*, a large, airy dining room, a favourite of local business types; the varied menu includes both meat and fish. *Open Mon–Sat 12–6.*

Furin Kazan, 2 Apóllonos, **t** 210 322 9170 (€12). Really good sushi and other oriental fast food in a simple setting – or try one of the other noodle bars and Chinese restaurants on the street.

Dorís, 30 Praxitélous, by Ag. Theodóri behind Plateía Klafthmónos (off Stadíou), **t** 210 323 2671 (€12). A little lunchtime gem, the favourite of the local business people who choose from a large glass case and then repair to marble tables either in its air-conditioned rooms or outside in a pretty courtyard. The best of quite a few good places in this area. Excellent *loukomádes*. *Open Mon–Sat 7.30am–6.30pm.*

Pláka

Pláka, the traditional tourist ghetto, is still fun, and it caters to the non-Greek urge to dine before 10pm. Touts, however, can be real pests; a blank stare tends to discourage them.

Daphne's, 4 Lysikrátous (by the Lysikrátes monument), **t** 210 322 7971 (€45). In a neoclassical mansion with Pompeiian frescoes and beautiful courtyard – a rarity in Athens – serving generous, refined Greek and international dishes. *Closed lunch.*

Mostru Live, Lissíou and 22 Mnissikléous in upper Pláka, **t** 210 322 5337. Live music, big prices (€25+ a head), fantastic view of the city.

Kuzina, 9 Adrianoú and Thissío, **t** 210 324 0133. In a neoclassical building, with a very modern interior, displaying new artists' work, Kuzina offers a gourmet experience for €30 – two starters, two mains, pudding and a bottle of wine. The chef, Áris Tsanaklídis, set up Spondi (*see* Pangráti), and here the idea is to fuse world and Greek tastes with dishes such as ribeye steak with a coffee and cumin crust, or scallops with pea fava. *Open daily for lunch and dinner.*

Byzantino, 18 Kydathinéon, **t** 210 322 7368 (€20–22). In the heart of Pláka, serving big portions (the fish soup and lamb fricassée are excellent) under the trees. It's also one of the few decent places open for Sunday lunch.

Tou Psarrá, 16 Erécthios and 12 Erotokrítou, in Upper Pláka, **t** 210 321 8733 (€20–22). A pretty setting with two floors indoors and an open space outside, this taverna specializes in tasty *mezédes*, fish and good desserts; more of a local haunt than a tourist one, especially in the off season.

Bakaliarakiá >>

Bakaliarakiá, 41 Kydathinéon, **t** 210 322 5084 (€14). Great old-fashioned Greek atmosphere in a cellar supported by an ancient column; good snacks, fried cod and barrel wine since the 1900s. *Open eves only; closed summer.*

Diogénis, Plateía Lysikrátes, **t** 210 324 7933. The outdoor part of this old standby for good Greek food is just lovely – right beside the ancient monument. The prices can pinch a bit but careful choices, or just stopping for brunch, can be very reasonable. Serves coffee and cakes too. *Open all day, every day.*

O Théspis, 18 Thespídas, **t** 210 323 8242. Little hole in the wall above the Diogénis with a wonderful little multi-layered terrace; quiet and charming.

Eden, 12 Lissíou, **t** 210 324 8858. Athens' oldest vegetarian restaurant and very popular, even with carnivores, with vegetarian quiches and soya moussakas. *Closed Tues and Aug.*

Platanos, 4 Diogénis, **t** 210 322 0666 (€13–15). The oldest taverna in Pláka, near the Tower of the Four Winds, serving good wholesome food in the shade of an enormous plane tree. *Closed Sun.*

To Kafeneío, 1 Epicharmoú, **t** 210 324 6916. Excellent *mezédes* (e.g. famous meatballs in sauce), snacks and sweets till 1am in a building from 1836. *Closed Aug.*

Trístrato, Áng. Gérondo and Daidálou Sts, off Kydathinéon, **t** 210 324 4472. A cosy spot for coffee, tea, and fabulous fresh cherry cheesecake. Not cheap, but very popular for a *tête-à-tête*. *Open daily 11am–midnight.*

Monastiráki

Monastiráki is more for snacks than dining. If you have a hankering for *souvláki* and *gýros* any time of the day or night, get yourself to the bottom of Mitropóleos Street to either **Thanássis**, **t** 210 324 4705, or **Sávas**, **t** 210 324 5048.

Brachera, Plateía Avissínia, **t** 210 321 1720 (€35). Art Deco design and roof garden with superb Acropolis views, with Mediterranean cuisine that attracts ship-owners, web designers and fashionistas. *Open 8pm–1am; closed Mon.*

★ Ouzo Melathron >

Ouzo Melathron, 50m from entrance to Agora at Ag. Filíppou & Ástiggos, **t** 210 324 0716 (€22). Packed with Athenians grateful to get a seat by mid-afternoon on a Saturday, feasting on mussels cooked in several different ways, Arabic pie with pine nuts, seafood dishes and free chocolate crêpes with cream for dessert. Great wine and friendly service from helpful young staff.

Abyssínia Café, 7 Kinetoú St by Plateía Avissínia, **t** 210 321 7047 (€20–22). An institution – a former antiques shop serving baked sardines, beer on tap, *halloúmi*, snails and spinach moussaka, with live music (Fri–Sun), attracting a trendy local crowd. *Open noon–1am; closed Sun eve and Mon.*

Koutí, 23 Adrianoú, **t** 210 321 3029. Come here to linger over great *mezédes* with a stellar view of the *stoa* of Attalos; right beside the Monastiráki metro. *Open 11am–1am.*

Thissío and Áno Petrálona

Thissío's infinite watering holes line Apostólou Pávlou, Iraklídon and Níleos streets opposite the ancient Agora. Note that the farther you go along Iraklídon, the more authentic the bar, and that a 10–15min walk south on Demofóndos St from Níleos will lead you into the heart Áno Petrálona, a new Greek-only hotspot for little tavernas and bars, especially those on Tróon Street, one block east of Demofóndos after the park.

Pil-Poul, 51 Apostólou Pávlou, Thissío, **t** 210 342 3665 (€65–90). Luxurious, romantic setting with lovely Acropolis views from the terrace, to go with some of the finest French cuisine in Greece, with wine list to match. *Open Mon–Sat eves only, 8.30pm to 3am.*

Stavlos, 10 Iraklídon, Thissío **t** 210 346 7206 (€20). Housed in the old Royal Stables, an art gallery, bar and restaurant with the old stable yard beautifully decorated to look like an old square in the Pláka.

Oikonomou Tavern, 41 Tróon and Kydantídon Sts, Áno Petrálona, **t** 210 346 7555. Here forever, with some tables on the street. Great casserole dishes, *stifádo*, and plenty for vegetarians at bargain prices. Costa-Gávras is an *habitué* when in Athens. *Open from 8.30pm; closed Sun.*

Chez Lucien, Tróon, Áno Petrálona, **t** 210 346 4236. Lucien and his Greek wife run a tiny hole in the wall where you share three or four excellent French specials at large wooden tables, or at a few small tables out on the narrow pavement. Very reasonable prices. Go close to 8.30pm because Lucien refuses to take reservations. *Open eves only.*

Psirrí

Although still popular, Psirrí now must take second place to Gázi, Kerameikós and Roúf as the in-place for Athenians. Perhaps its very fame has caused the 'in-in' crowd to move on. Still it is lovely, and has some beautiful restaurants, bars and tavernas; live music is most often on the menu on Sundays at noon and Friday and Saturday evenings.

Hýtra, 7 N. Apostóli, **t** 210 331 6767 (€45). The 'Stewpot' is one of Athens' finest, where a new head chef from France takes a refined look at Greek tradition. *Closed lunch and Sun in Oct–May*.

Avalon, Leokórou 20 and Sarrí (one block north of Lepeniótou), **t** 210 331 0572 (€25–35). Good food served on long shared tables in a woody, yet modern space with an interior terrace. Small steamed clams are their signature dish. *Open eves only*.

Taki 13, 13 Táki St, **t** 210 325 4707 (€25). The first, and still fun. It has a superb atmosphere and, although the food is simple, it's a great party bar, with live Greek music on Thurs, Fri and Sat nights starting at 10.30pm, Sun from 4pm. *Open Tues–Sun eves*.

Zeidoron, 10 Táki and Ag. Anárgyro, **t** 210 321 5368 (€18–30). Always crowded for their changing selection of *mezédes*. Good if you arrive on the right day; try the *kolokythiakeftédes* – courgette rissoles. *Open Mon–Thurs eves only; Fri, Sat and Sun from 11am*.

Pak, 13 Menandroú, **t** 210 321 9412 (€10–17). Indian classics for a change of pace.

Taverna tou Psirrí, 12 Aischýlou, **t** 210 321 4923 (€10–15). The last workaday taverna that has somehow so far resisted gentrification; it's small, plain, but homey, and good.

Gelato Mania, 21 Aísopou. The best ice cream in Athens – and great waffles in winter.

Gázi, Roúf and Kerameikós

Some of the best restaurants in Athens have parked themselves in this former industrial area and gasworks, a short walk west of Kerameikós.

Varoulko, 80 Piréos, **t** 210 522 8400 (€50–60). One of Greece's most imaginative seafood restaurants, long in Piraeus, is now linked to the Eridanus Hotel, where Michelin-starred chef Leftéris Lazaroú has added kid, rabbit and tripe to his repertoire. *Open eves only; closed Sun*.

Kítrino Podílato, 116 Keramikoú and Iéra Ódos, **t** 210 346 5830 (€30–40). The 'yellow bicycle' may serve the most inventive *nouvelle* Greek *cuisine* in the country and a great Greek wine list, too. *Closed lunch, all day Sun and June–Sept*.

Dirty Fish, 12 Tripotopolemoú, **t** 210 347 4763 (€30). Popular restaurant with nice décor, a pretty garden, friendly service and innovative Greek delights from both sea and land. *Open Tues–Sun 8.30–1.30; live music on Sun from 4pm*.

Butcher Shop, 19 Persephónis (right outside Technópolis), **t** 210 341 3440 (€25–35). Modern carnivore restaurant with meat hanging in 'the window', tables outside and a small balcony too. *Open noon until late every day*.

Sardelles, 15 Persephónis, **t** 210 347 8050 (€15–25). If you prefer fish, this one is a few doors down with seafood and a modern décor. *Open daily 12.30pm–midnight*.

Mamacas, 41 Persephónis, **t** 210 346 4984 (€25–30). Greek classics in an updated setting; great views of the Acropolis from the top level.

Prósopa, Ierá Odós and Konstantinoúpolis, Roúf, **t** 210 341 3433 (€25–30). A Mediterranean kitchen – try the shrimps and pasta, and an arty décor that attracts the young and trendy to its sidewalk tables by the train tracks. *Open eves only*.

Bátraxos, 3 Evrimédondos, off the Ierá Odós in Keramikós, **t** 210 341 1662 (€17–22). Popular for its tasty organically raised products. *Open eves and Sun lunch; closed Mon*.

Skoufias, 50 Megálou Basilíou, Roúf, **t** 210 341 2252 (€10–17). Good food behind a salmon pink storefront. A local favourite. *Open eves only; closed Mon*.

Kanélla, 70 Konstaninopóleos and Efmolpidón Sts, Gázi, **t** 210 347 6320 (€9–20). Home cooking behind a pretty window full of coloured bottles. Kyria Lítsa really knows her stuff. *Open lunch only.*

South of the Acropolis, Makrigiánni, Koukáki, Néa Smyrna

Edodi, 80 Veíkou, **t** 210 921 3013 (€45). The restaurant that put Koukáki on the map. Superb *haute* Mediterranean *cuisine*, down to the desserts – just let your waiter guide you through the day's delights. Rated one of the five best in the city. *Closed lunch and Sun, plus Aug.*

Calirrhoe, Kalliróis 32 and Petmezá in Koukáki, **t** 210 921 5353 (€30–40). This summer restaurant, on the terrace atop the hotel, offers a stellar view of the Acropolis and some very good Greek cuisine as well. *Closed Sun eve.*

Cook – Eat, 72 Megálou Alexándrou and 2 Aidiníou, Néa Smýrni (by the Ag. Fotiní tram stop), **t** 210 931 3108 (€22–35). Owners Maria Koutroupi and Kostas Dimitellos mean what they say at this fun, contemporary restaurant. Watch the chefs on a video screen, and if you're inspired, go into a second kitchen and cook for your table under a chef's supervision. There's a wide range of dishes, and some unusual starters such as Manouri cheese with pistachio and almond in mashed quince. *Open lunch and eves.*

Claudios, 38 Veíkou, **t** 210 923 514 (€20–25). Small and casual, specializing in good, filling Italian dishes. No garden, but it's air-conditioned. *Open Tues to Sat 7–12.30, Sun 12–5.*

MániMáni, 10 Falírou, **t** 210 921 8180 (€20). Taverna serving delicious courgette fritters and other 'cooked dishes' from the Máni. *Open eves Tues–Sat, also lunch on Sat and Sun; closed Aug.*

The Oinomageireio ton Theon, 23–27 Makrigiánni St, **t** 210 923 3721 (€12–15). It may be mistranslated as 'God's Tavern' on their card, but there are no mistakes in the taverna food, on display inside. Right by the Acropolis metro on a pedestrian street with tables outside. *Open daily 10am to midnight.*

Ambrosia, 3 Drákou, Koukáki, **t** 210 922 0281 (€12). This busy and inexpensive *psistariá*, a local favourite, has lots of choices.

Psitopoleío, 16 Drákou, **t** 210 922 5648. Some of the best grilled chicken in Athens.

Omónia

Ideal, 46 Panepistimíou, **t** 210 330 3000 (€20–30). Historic restaurant, which has been making diners happy with well-prepared Greek classics for over 40 years. *Closed Sun.*

Meat Me, 65 Athínas, **t** 210 325 0906 (€20–25). On the ground floor of the Baby Grand Hotel. Burgers, T-bone steaks, lamb chops and some vegetable dishes, too, served in an arty designer setting.

Hell's Kitchen, 13 Kleisthénous, by Plateía Kotziá, **t** 210 524 1555 (€12–20) New, modern place with a varied menu including ribeye steak and baked salmon, all served up by its American-Greek owners with great *élan*. A perfect casual lunch or dinner spot.

★ Diporto >>

Díporto, Central Market, **t** 210 321 1463, opposite the parking garage (€12). An institution that needs no sign; it's down some steps and has remained unchanged for at least 50 years, serving Hellenic soul food. *Patsás* (tripe soup), the traditional hangover cure, is served on paper-covered tables set on a bare cement floor. If not the tripe, try whatever soup is on offer (the chickpea soup is delicious); portions are huge. *Closed after 6pm and all day Sun.*

Athinaikón, 2 Themistokléous, **t** 210 383 8485 (€11–14). A golden oldie and a great place to fill up on tasty *mezédes* and swordfish or lamb kebabs while watching the passing crowds. *Closed Sun.*

Andréas and Sons, 18 Themistokléous, **t** 210 382 1522 (€11–14). Tasty seafood at marble-topped tables in a cosy setting at reasonable prices. It is in a quiet narrow street with some outside tables. *Open Mon–Sat 11am–11.30pm.*

Diethnés, 5 Nikitará St, just off Themistokléous, **t** 210 383 9428 (often under €8). So old-fashioned that the printed menu is unchanged since the early 1980s. Elderly waiters in white jackets serve a steady crowd of regulars with delicious 'ready food' – great stewed dishes and tasty fish; there are a few tables out under the ivy. *Open 6am–6pm.*

Exárchia

Giántes, 44 Baltetsíou, near Plateía Exárchia, **t** 210 330 1369 (€21–24). Minimal décor, a delightful closed-in terrace, and mostly organically grown food.

Fasóli, 22 Ippokátous and Skoufá, **t** 210 330 0010 (€15–25). Modern, unpretentious, with classic Greek baked and pasta dishes cooked fresh daily and on display. Good food and a nice atmosphere. *Open Mon–Sat 1pm–3am.*

Barbara's Food Company, 63–65 Emm. Benáki, **t** 210 380 5004 (€10–14). Fresh salads and a wide choice of dishes on display to choose from. *Open Mon–Sat 12 noon–1.30am, Sun 2pm–10pm.*

Kolonáki and Around

Boschetto, Evangelismós Park off Vass. Sofías, **t** 210 721 0893 (€60). Lovely Italian delicacies in a bosky setting, outside in the summer or in a winter garden. *Open eves exc Mon.*

Sale e Pepe, 34 Aristippoú, **t** 210 723 4102 (€60). One of the best wine cellars in Greece to go with exquisite Mediterranean cuisine – try the oysters with *sabayon* sauce. *Closed lunch and all day Sun.*

Orizontes Lykavitou, Lykavitós Hill, **t** 210 722 7605 (€50). Under St George's Chapel, with tables on the terrace and views over all of Athens. Excellent modern Greek cuisine.

L'Abreuvoir, 51 Xenokrátous, **t** 210 722 9106 (€40–60). Athens' oldest French restaurant, and still going strong with all the classics.

Frame, Deinokrátous 1, Plateía Dexamenís, **t** 210 271 4368 (€30–35). Bright colours with a 1960s and '70s atmosphere and good Greek food, with an emphasis on salads, risotto, and a fish fillet with *plygoúri*, a Greek treat you can ask them about.

Fillipou, 17 Xenokrátous, **t** 210 721 6390. (€12). Where Kolonáki moms take the family when they want home cooking they did not have to produce; just point at what you want. An old standby. *Open Mon–Fri eves, Sat 12–5.*

Pangráti (east of the Kallimármaro Stadium)

Spondi >>

Spondí, 5 Pýrronos (off Plateía Varnava), **t** 210 752 0658, *www.spondi.gr* (€60). By common acclaim, Athens' best restaurant. True *haute cuisine* with imagination and flair in a lovely old mansion with a garden courtyard. Extraordinary desserts, and huge wine list. Book. *Closed Sun in summer.*

Vlássis, 8 Pastér, **t** 210 646 3060 (around €20). Out towards the US Embassy, a superb family-run taverna, the place to find true Greek cuisine and one of the rare ones with excellent wines and desserts, too. Book. *Closed Sun eve and mid-July–Sept.*

Vyrinis, 11 Archimídou, Pangráti, **t** 210 701 2153 (€15–20). Classic taverna with a large garden, owned by the Konstandinos family since the 1940s that draws a mix of arty types, families and foreigners. Try the beef or rabbit *lemonate* and *rakómelo – rakí* and honey – a good drink in winter. Reserve at weekends. *Closed Sun eve, and all day Sun in July and Aug.*

Taverna Kavarítis, 35 Arktinoú and 4 Pausaniou, **t** 210 721 5155 (€15). Friendly and authentic neighbourhood favourite for al fresco dining under the vines.

Entertainment and Nightlife in Athens

The summer is filled with festivals, headlined by the eclectic **Athens Festival**, **t** 210 928 2900, *www.greekfestival.gr*, which attracts big names from around the world.

At other times, **classical music** fans should try to take in a performance at the **Mégaron Musikís**, on Vass. Sofías and Kokkáli, **t** 210 728 2333, Athens' acoustically wonderful concert hall. Maria Callas got her start at the **Greek National Opera House**, 59–61 Akademías St, **t** 210 361 2461, which is shared with the national ballet.

From May to Sept there are nightly **folk dance** performances at the **Dora Stratou Theatre** on Philopáppos Hill, **t** 210 921 4650, not far from the **Sound and Light Show** on the Pnyx (*April–Oct*).

Rembétika, the Greek blues, is in full revival in Athens; for the real thing try **Stoa Athanaton**, upstairs in the Athens' meat market at 19 Sofokléous, **t** 210 321 4362 (*closed Sun*).

For **jazz**, try **Half Note**, 17 Trivonianoú in Mets, **t** 210 921 3310 and **Upstairs at the Bar Guru**, Plateía Theátrou, Omónia, **t** 210 324 6530, *www.bargurubar.gr/jazzupstairs.htm*; **Cafe Alavastron**, 78 Damaréos, Pangráti, **t** 210 756 0102, has jazz and ethnic sounds by local musicians but closes in summer.

For **salsa** try **Cubanita**, 28 Karaïskáki, in Psirrí, **t** 210 331 4605. **Discokafeneio** on Miaoúlis St in Psirrí is lively late into the night; nearby, **Soul**, 65 Evripidoú, **t** 210 331 0907, has tasty international cuisine and a very hip music bar upstairs.

Some of the best live **rock** happens at the **Gagarin Live Music Space**, 205 Liosíon near Ⓜ Attikís, **t** 210 854 7600. **Toy Café Bar**, near Sýntagma at 10 Karýtsi, just off Stadioú, is a favourite informal hangout of media types. In Gázi, a former kindergarten, **Nipiagogeio**, 8 Kleanthoús, **t** 210 345 8534, is one of the city's hottest freestyle dance bars. **Stavlos**, 10 Iraklídon, in Thissío, **t** 210 345 2502, offers live music, sometimes soul, sometimes rock; **Club 22**, Akadamías and 3 Z. Pigís, **t** 210 922 2244, is a favourite for rock and hip hop, and sometimes even stand-up comedy. **Banana Moon**, B. Konstantínou 2, by Plateía Stadíou (near the Kallimármaro Stadium) has mainstream music all year round.

Gay Athens has moved to Gázi as well. Try the dance bars **Máyo**, Persephóne 33, **t** 210 342 3066, and **Sodáde**, Triptólemou 10, **t** 210 326 8657.

In summer, **clubs** in Glyfáda and Voúla are favourites as others in the city close down. Find out what's going on in the magazine *LIFO*, distributed free at almost all metro stations (although you'll need Greek help); the English-language *Athens News* also lists the clubs every Friday.

Athens' **outdoor cinemas** are a treat in summer and all the films are in their original language. Two of the nicest are in Kolonáki: **Dexamení**, in Dexamení Square halfway up Lykavitós, **t** 210 360 2363; and **Athinaía**, 50 Haritós St, **t** 210 721 5717. Also try **Ciné Paris** on Kydathinéon in Pláka, **t** 210 322 2071 (next to wonderful old-fashioned **Brettos Bar and Distillery**, which distils its own ouzo); **Thissíon**, 7 Apostólou Pávlou St, **t** 210 342 0864 (with an Acropolis view); and **Aigli** in the Záppeion Gardens, **t** 210 336 9369, which has the best sound system.

Piraeus

While its tall grey buildings and hurly-burly, Piraeus (ΠΕΙΡΑΙΑΣ / Πειραιας) may not win you over at first glance, but, in a country that derives most of its livelihood from the sea, it's in some ways Greece's true capital, while Athens is a sprawling suburb where the bureaucrats live. It has a buzz, and excellent seafood, two good museums and some interesting corners in between. Another thing to do in Piraeus: try not to think of the song from *Never on a Sunday*, which was filmed here in 1960.

History

In 479 BC, when Fáliron could no longer meet Athens' needs, Themistocles made Piraeus the city's chief port. Security was foremost in his mind: he surrounded its three harbours with walls and left plans for the famous Long Walls – a 7km corridor to

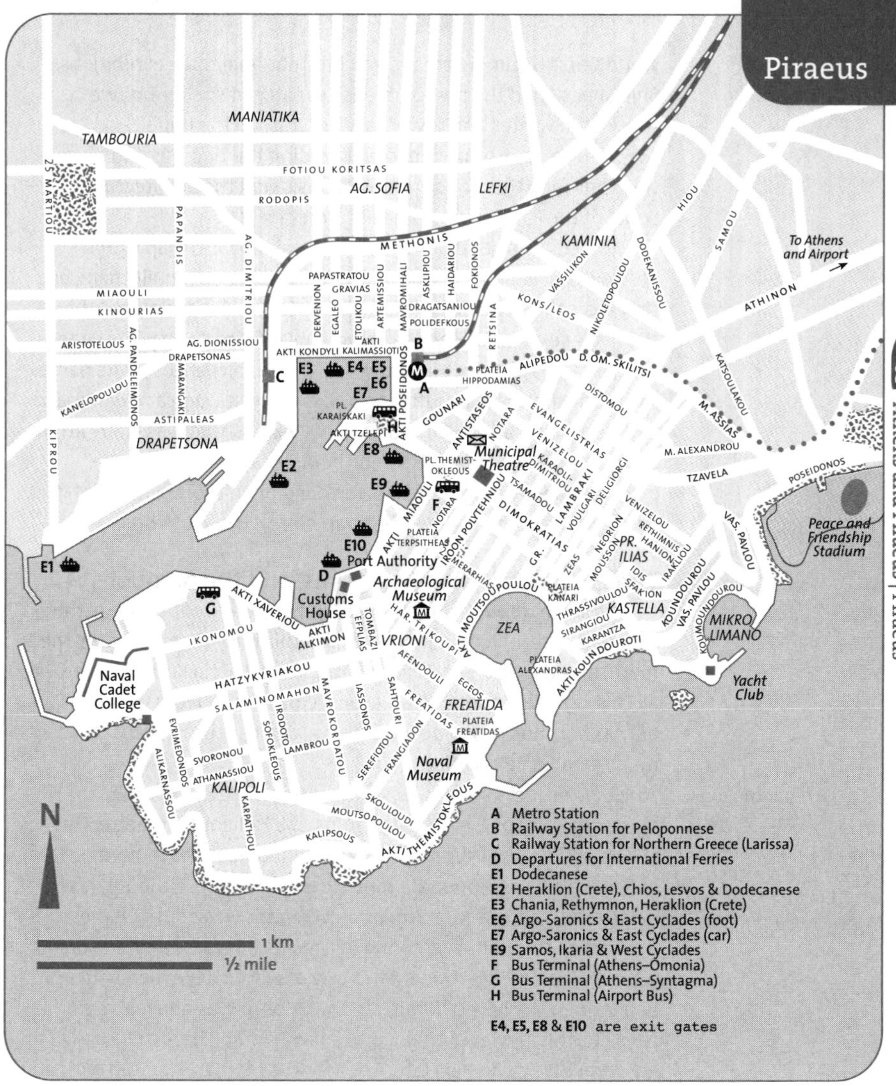

Athens. These were completed by Pericles, who, being Pericles, also wanted to make the port a showcase, and hired the geometer Hippodamos of Miletus, a proto-hippie with long hair and outlandish dress, to lay out the city. The grid plan Hippodamos chose (and which still exists) was not designed like modern grids, to make land easy to parcel out and sell but to promote equality among citizens, and for a while at least he succeeded. Piraeus quickly became the business district of Athens. All religions were tolerated, and women were allowed for the first time to work outside the home. Hippodamos also designed a huge *agora*, for the world's first commercial fairs and international trade exhibitions. Ship sheds lined the harbours, each capable of sheltering two triremes in winter, and near Zéa Marína stood the huge Skeuotheke, an arsenal capable of holding the riggings and weapons for a thousand triremes, considered the architectural equal of the Parthenon in ancient times.

In 404 BC, at the end of the Peloponnesian War, the Spartans destroyed all Piraeus' fortifications. Admiral Konon rebuilt them, but they weren't good enough to keep out Sulla, who decimated the city in 88 BC, nor Alaric, who sacked it in 396. For 1,900 years Piraeus dwindled away, with a population as low as 20, even losing its name to become Porto Leone (after an ancient lion statue, carved in 1040 with runes by Harald Hardrada and his Vikings, that was later carted off by Morosini to embellish Venice's Arsenale). As port to the capital, Piraeus has regained its former glory, although much of it dates from after 1941, when German bombs blew it to bits.

Three Harbours, Two Museums, and the Acropolis

The main **harbour** of Piraeus was known in ancient times as the Kantharos or 'goblet' for its shape, and this busy sheet of water, the metro and the ticket agencies surrounding Plateía Karaiskáki are all that 99 per cent of visitors ever see of the city. From here it's only a short bus ride or 20-minute walk across the isthmus to much smaller **Zéa Marína**.

Archaeological Museum of Piraeus
31 Har. Trikoúpi St, ***t*** *210 452 1598; open Tues–Sun 8.30–3; adm*

Just two streets in from Zéa is the excellent **Archaeological Museum of Piraeus**, next to the ruins of a Hellenistic theatre. This is a museum full of suprises: on the ground floor the tomb *stele* of Pancharis is exceptional, standing over 11ft high, although it's dwarfed by the 24ft **Monument of Nikeratos** (325 BC), the largest funerary monument ever found in Greece. Nikeratos and his son were *metics* (foreign residents), many of whom were merchants and formed the bulk of Piraeus' population. It was nouveau riche piles like this, however, that led to a law banning monster monuments a few years later. Look for the marble engraved with a foot, arm and finger, used as standard measures, a Mycenaean pig's head rhyton, Minoan finds from Kýthera, the bronze beak and 'eye' from an ancient trireme, an ancient harp for the Tomb of the Poet, and marble plaques manufactured for the Roman market in the 2nd century AD, pandering to the Roman vision of ancient Greece (the nymphs in particular would look perfectly at home in the Italian Renaissance). The stars of the museum are upstairs: five large bronzes found by Piraeus' cathedral in 1959, including two statues of Artemis, a majestic Athena, a tragic mask and an exquisite *kouros*, the *Apollo of Piraeus*, the oldest known Greek hollow-cast bronze statue (*c.* 500 BC).

Naval Museum of Greece
Plateía Freatída, **t** *210 451 6264; open Tues–Sun 9–2; adm*

The **Naval Museum of Greece** is a few blocks down Aktí Themistokléous, by Plateía Freatída. Built around a section of ancient walls, the museum has plans of Greece's greatest naval battles, a model of the triremes used at Sálamis and a host of maritime mementoes. Don't miss the exquisite tiny ships made of bone by French prisoners in England during the Napoleonic Wars, which Aristotle Onassis used to keep on his yacht *Christina*.

Heading in the other direction (east), Thrasyvoúlou Street leads directly to **Kastélla**, the ancient acropolis, where the terrace of the Bowling Club café has views over the city and coast. Snug in a pretty amphitheatre below, **Mikrolímano** is an almost perfectly round harbour filled with yachts and fish restaurants. The landmark on the reclaimed land east of Piraeus at **Paléo Fáliro** (Athens' original, pre-Piraeus port) is hard to miss because of the dramatic ship-shaped **Peace and Friendship Stadium** (1985), used for basketball games and concerts, and for volleyball in the 2004 Olympics.

Where to Stay in Piraeus

Savoy, 93 Iróon Polytechnioú, **t** 210 428 4580, *www.savoyhotel.gr* (€€€/€€€). A few minutes from the port, renovated, smart, well-run hotel with broadband in the rooms.

Triton, 8 Tsamadoú, **t** 210 417 3457, *users.otenet.gr/~htriton* (€€€/€€€). Standard hotel within walking distance of the docks.

Ideal, 142 Notára (in from Gate E10), **t** 210 429 4050, *www.ideal-hotel.gr* (€€/€€). Pleasant air-conditioned rooms, recently renovated, plus Internet service.

Glaros, 4 Chariláou Trikoúpi, **t** 210 451 5421, *www.glaros-hotel.gr* (€€/€€). Near the Ideal, same friendly owners.

Pireaus Dream, 78 Notára, **t** 210 411 0555, *www.piraeusdream.gr* (€€/€€). Just in from Gate E9, a contemporary and comfortable haven.

Ionion, 10 Kapodistrioú, **t** 210 417 7537, *www.ionionhotel.com* (€€/€). The classic One Onion, only 2mins' walk from the Metro; recently renovated rooms with air-conditioning.

Achillion, 63 Notára, **t** 210 412 4029 (€/€). The cheapest in Piraeus but not bad at all – air-conditioned rooms 5mins from the quay.

Eating Out in Piraeus

Chryssopsaro, 61 Al. Papanastasíou Street, Kastélla, **t** 210 412 0333 (€40). Tasty, trendy seafood.

Η ΦΩΛΙΑ, 30 Aktí Poseidónos, **t** 210 412 0781 (€10). Family-run restaurant in business since 1968: pick what you want from the pans of home-cooked 'ready' dishes and sit down at one of the Formica tables. *Closed eves.*

Jimmy the Fish, 46 Aktí Koumoundoúrou in Mikrolímano, **t** 210 412 4417 (€35). Great salads, octopus, spaghetti with lobster, or the fish of your choice, perfectly prepared.

Margaró, 126 Chatzikyriákou, **t** 210 451 4226 (€14–17). Unpretentious but wonderful fish taverna near the naval academy; attracts locals and the élite.

Nine Brothers (Énnea Adélfi), 48 Sotiros (behind Plateía Kanári at Zéa Marína), **t** 210 411 5273 (€9–12). A taverna popular with lots of locals, and a big choice of dishes.

Piraeus Yacht Club, Aktí Mikrolímanou, **t** 210 413 4084 (€36). Pretty setting, and *numero uno* in Piraeus for innovative Mediterranean cuisine – starring an exquisite cuttlefish risotto.

Tony Bonanno, 63 Panapastasíou, **t** 210 411 1901 (€28). Art Deco atmosphere, superb Italian food. *Open eves only.*

West of Athens

Dafní and its Byzantine Mosaics

Dafní Monastery
due to reopen some time in 2008; ring the tourist office to be sure

The busy multi-lane National Road west of Athens passes an endless array of forklift retailers before reaching Dafní park and the once-grand walled **Dafní Monastery**, a World Heritage Site, judged by Byzantine art historian David Talbot Rice to be nothing less than 'the most perfect monument of the 11th century'. At this very point, the **Sacred Way (Iéra Ódos)** from Athens to Eleusis began its descent to the sea, and the Temple of Apollo Daphneios ('of the laurel'), an important stop on the road, supplied both the building stone and its name for the monastery in the 6th century. The existing cross-in-square church of 1080 was decorated with superb mosaics by masters from Constantinople, an unusually extravagant gesture on the part of the emperor who knew full well how vulnerable this area was to attack. After 1204, the Frankish Dukes of Athens gave the monastery to the Cistercians and made it their ducal mausoleum (hence the fleurs-de-lys and Latin crosses on the two sarcophagi). It functioned again as an Orthodox monastery under the Turks, but declined after the War of Independence, serving as a barracks, a lunatic asylum and a sheep pen; at one point pirates lit a fire under the dome, thinking the mosaics were of solid gold and would melt. Restoration began in 1887, and has been continuing on and off ever since, most recently after the 1999 Athens earthquake caused serious structural damage.

Each mosaic in Dafní is a masterpiece, made during the golden age of the Comneni and touched with Classical grace. Your eye, however, is drawn up at once to an implacable vision of Christ that makes even Michelangelo's stern Jesus of the Sistine Chapel's *Last Judgement* seem amenable in comparison. Below him are the 16 prophets, and, in the squinches and along the walls, scenes from the lives of Christ and the Virgin, including a *Crucifixion* (with a heartrending Virgin), a majestic *Transfiguration* and a wonderful *Descent into Hell*, with Christ shattering the door.

If one were to pin down a setting for Shakespeare's *A Midsummer Night's Dream*, Dafní's park, scene of the late lamented Athens wine festival, is the most logical candidate. Further west on the Sacred Way/busy highway, the sharp-eyed may spot a few remains of a **Temple of Aphrodite**. Beyond that at **Skaramangás** are Greece's largest shipyards, founded in 1956 by Stávros Niárchos. Broad views of Elefsína Bay and its refinery open up to Sálamis and the narrow strait where the famous naval victory over the Persians took place in 480 BC. The **Lake of Reiti** to your right was once the fishtank of the Hierophant of Eleusis; the Sacred Way crossed it on a causeway. The road then crosses into the Thirasian Plain (the Rarian Plain of myth), where there's a turn-off to the right for Elefsína.

Getting West from Athens

The A16 **bus** from Plateía Koumoundoúrou (Eleftherias) stops at Dafní and Elefsína. Orange buses from Athens' Thissío metro station depart every 30mins for Mégara, and stop in Dafní and Elefsína as well.

Elefsína (Ancient Eleusis)

Many are the sights to be seen in Greece, and many are the wonders to be heard; but on nothing does heaven bestow more care than on the Eleusinian rites and the Olympic games.
Pausanias

Now known as Elefsína, this Greek holy of holies and birthplace of Aeschylus (525–456 BC) is a busy industrial city at the crossroads of the new Attica highway with the E94 to the Peloponnese. In the centre of town, residential streets surround the ruins of its famous sanctuary and low acropolis. This had a Mycenaean settlement, and it is during that era that Demeter became associated with the city. Tradition has it that King Eumolpos, the very first celebrant of her Mysteries, had Thracian origins (the Thracians were famous for believing in life after death). Afterwards Demeter's priests were chosen from two aristocratic families, the Kerykes and the Eumolpidai, the latter providing the chief priest, the Hierophant (the 'displayer of sacred things').

The cult became truly panhellenic after 600 BC, when Athens assimilated the Mysteries into her increasingly grandiose civic religion. Pisistratos built huge fortification walls and towers around the site to emphasize its importance, and a 20km road known as the Sacred Way was laid out from the Dipylon Gate to the sanctuary. Now that Eleusis was in their territory, Athenians could boast that *they* had introduced cultivation and the Mysteries to the world. The hereditary priests continued in office, but the Athenian *archon* took charge of the annual event. Initiation was open to all Greek-speaking men and women, slave or master, and the penalty for telling what occurred on the last night was death; Aeschylus was nearly lynched for supposedly revealing too many details in one of his plays. Subsequent leaders added grand buildings and expanded the sanctuary's boundaries. Under Pericles, the Hall of Initiation was doubled in size, and the Mysteries remained so popular into Roman times that one writer called it 'the common precinct of the world'. Emperors, especially Hadrian and Marcus Aurelius, funded building sprees. But Theodosius' anti-pagan edict in 379 and the sanctuary's destruction by Alaric and the Visigoths in 395 marked its end. The town itself survived into the Middle Ages, and then was abandoned until the 18th century.

The Mysteria

'Thrice blessed are those mortals who see these mysteries before departing to Hades; for they alone have true life there. All that is evil besets the rest,' wrote Sophocles, and although the secret was

The Myth of Demeter and Kore

Kore (or Persephone) was out gathering flowers when the earth suddenly opened up, a dark chariot emerged, and its driver Hades, the god of the Underworld, made off with her. Her mother, the goddess Demeter, disguised herself as an old woman and searched the world for her, and when she came to Eleusis she sat disconsolate on the 'mirthless rock'. Keleus, the king of Eleusis, took her in, and Iambe, his daughter, tried to cheer her up by telling jokes. Touched by their hospitality, Demeter decided to make Keleus' youngest son immortal by immersing him in fire; his frightened mother intervened, thus dooming him to immediate mortality. Demeter then angrily revealed her true self, and ordered Keleus to build her a house ('Eleusis', according to some, means the 'temple of her in dark rage lurking'). Eventually Keleus' older son Tripolemos told Demeter that he had witnessed Hades stealing her daughter Kore. In her fury, Demeter ordered the world to stop bearing fruit until Kore was returned. Humanity was on the point of starvation when Zeus intervened with a compromise. As Kore had eaten six pomegranate seeds (symbol of the marriage bond) in the gardens of the dead, she would have to spend six months down below as Persephone, queen of Hades, but could spend the other six months on earth with her mother. Demeter then rewarded Tripolemos with agricultural know-how: seed corn, a plough, and a winged chariot pulled by snakes to travel and spread the word. With the seasons and farming taken care of, she then introduced her Mysteries to Eleusis.

kept too well to know what the initiates saw (one assumes, with Demeter as the focus, that it involved the regenerative cycle of nature), the build-up to the great revelation is known in detail. In March, initiates would participate in the Lesser Mysteria on the banks of the Ilissos river in Athens, a necessary preliminary to the Great Mysteria that lasted for nine days in September, which ran like this: on the first day the sacred objects in baskets (*kistai*) were taken from Eleusis to the City Eleusinion in Athens' Agora. On the next day, the Herald would proclaim the opening of the festival, with the proviso that murderers, desecrators and non-Greek-speakers abstain. The next day the initiates went to the sea at Fáliro, where they each sacrificed a piglet, bathed in a ritual purification, and donned new clothes. The next day was in honour of Asklepios, for latecomers (usually VIPs). On the fourth day, the sacred objects were returned to Eleusis, followed in procession by the initiates bearing a statue of Iacchos (Dionysos, as the lord of the dance), crying 'Iacchos! Iacchos!'. To stress the civic aspect of the rite, they were followed by the members of the Areopagos, the Council of Five Hundred, and Athenian citizens ordered by tribe and *deme*. There were frequent stops along the Sacred Way, to sing and sacrifice at shrines, and at the Kephisos bridge, where insults and jokes (*gephyrismoi*, or 'bridgery') were hurled at leading members. On their arrival in Eleusis at dusk, the initiates would be regaled in the forecourt and dance around the Kallichoron, the fountain of good dances.

The secret rites took place during the next two nights, when each initiate would be guided by his or her *mystagogue* (sponsor). The little that we do know (derived from art, literary hints and hostile Christian writers) suggests that the entire experience with its dramatic tension was just as important as the 'secrets' revealed. The effects may have been heightened with drugs; the poppy, after all, is one of Demeter's symbols, and ergot, a fungus that attacks her grain rye, is the base ingredient of LSD.

At some point the initiates were blinded with a hood; a winnowing fan was passed over them, and they wandered about in the dark, disorientated, while the Hierophant beat a gong, summoning Kore from the earth. The Mysteries culminated in the Telesterion, illuminated by thousands of torches held by the Epoptai ('the beholders' or second-year initiates), when 'things shown' by the Hierophant offered a transcendental moment that united the initiate with the divine, in a mystic communion that provided some kind of hope for the afterlife. Then the Epoptai witnessed 'the ear of corn, silently cut' and perhaps the epiphany of Demeter's child Ploutos ('wealth)', bearing a cornucopia. The eighth day was for sacrifices and celebrations, and on the ninth day the initiates returned to Athens.

The Site

Ancient Eleusis
t 210 554 6019; open Tues–Sun 8.30–3; adm

Trying to evoke the enactment of the Mysteries in modern Elefsína in broad daylight requires some imagination; the ruins wrapped around the acropolis are a confused palimpsest from Mycenaean to Roman times, surrounded by views of cranes, smokestacks and rusting tankers. At the site entrance is a portion of the **Sacred Way**, which ended in the large **forecourt** outside the walls. This was redone by the Romans, who also rebuilt the **Temple of Artemis Propylaea** and its two altars (note the gameboards carved in the steps, perhaps by idle initiates). Identical **triumphal arches** (copies of Hadrian's in Athens) stood to the right and left of the forecourt, the latter leading into the town; the inscription 'All the Hellenes to the Goddesses and the Emperor' is still in place. Beyond are remains of hotels and baths. The ornate **fountain** near here was the Kallichoron 'of the beautiful dances', although the original was elsewhere.

Marble steps lead up to the sanctuary's monumental entrance, the **Great Propylaea**, built by Marcus Aurelius. It was modelled after the Propylaea on the Acropolis and built of the same Pentelic marble, but during the barbarian invasions in the 3rd century AD its colonnade was walled in; you can see the track in the stone where the doors opened. The large medallion bust, probably of Marcus Aurelius, came from the pediment. To the right of this were the houses and meeting rooms of the priests. Further up, the **Lesser Propylaea** was a walled 40ft passage built with funds from Cicero's friend Appius Claudius Pulcher after 50 BC. Again, grooves remain where the doors opened on their rollers. Beyond lay the **sacred precinct of the Mysteries**, where only initiates could enter. To the

Ancient Eleusis

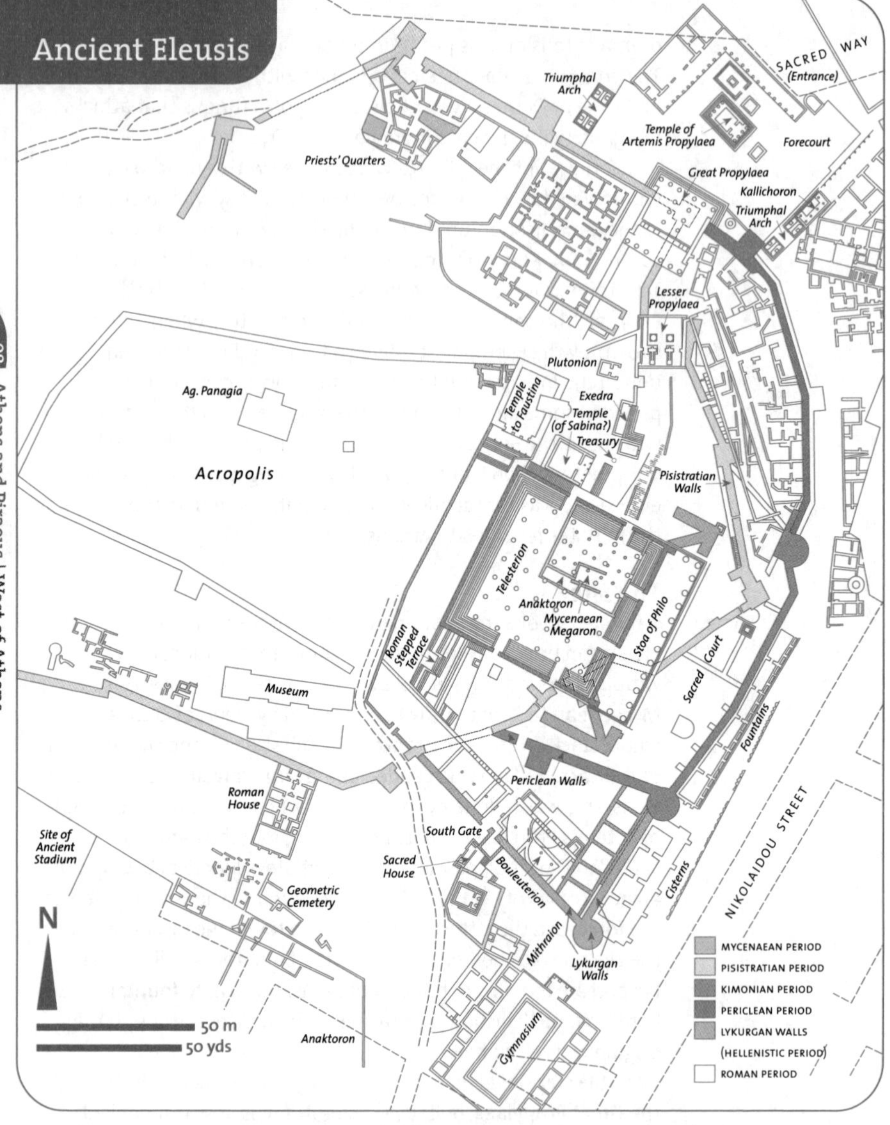

right, the small cave called the **Plutonion** is now thought to have been the location of the Mirthless Rock; a natural rock here fits the bill, and as initiates entered they would have a glimpse of 'Demeter' grieving by the flickering torchlight. The rock-cut ***exedra*** beyond may have been a stage for a scene in the re-enactment drama; to its left stood a **treasury** (another candidate for the Mirthless Rock) and a **temple**, perhaps dedicated to Hadrian's wife Sabina.

Beyond is the great square platform of the Hall of Initiation, the **Telesterion**. Solon built the first proper *telesterion* in 590 BC, but as the cult grew it had to be enlarged, first by Pisistratos and then by Pericles, who ordered the design from Iktinos, the architect of the Parthenon, although it was only completed after both had died. Iktinos' *telesterion* was a hypostyle hall supported by 42 columns and solid exterior walls (except for six doorways) with eight tiers of seats on each side, capable of holding 3,000 initiates. In the centre, the **Anaktoron** held the sacred objects displayed by the Hierophant at the climax of the ceremony. In all reconstructions of the Telesterion, the Anaktoron was always exactly here, right on top of the Mycenaean *megaron*, which according to the Hymn to Demeter (*c.* 600 BC) was the house built by King Keleus for Demeter. Only one layman was ever allowed inside the Anaktoron: the Roman emperor Marcus Aurelius, to thank him for all his contributions. The massive **Stoa of Philo** on the outer (southeast) side was added in *c.* 310 BC. Around this was a court, gradually filled in over the centuries but which has now been excavated to reveal the older defensive walls. Southwest of the Telesterion is a Roman stepped terrace, perhaps used for performances, leading up (on the north end) to scant ruins of a **Temple to Faustina**, wife of Antonius Pius, known by the Greeks (who knew how to flatter their overlords) as the New Demeter.

Eleusis museum
same hours as site; separate adm

Up the steps, the **museum** has a model of Eleusis in its heyday and items associated with the cult, including copies of two reliefs from the National Archaeological Museum: one of Demeter, Kore and Tripolemos, and the 'Ninnion tablet' that shows the initiate Ninnion being led by Dionysos to Kore at the Lesser Mysteria and, on top, being led by Kore to Demeter in the Great Mysteria. There's an endearingly bizarre amphora from the mid-7th century BC showing the *Blinding of Polyphemus* and *Perseus Slaying Medusa*, with her sisters in dancing pursuit. Painted before the gorgons' faces had become standardized with crossed eyes and protruding tongues, the artist imagined their heads as cauldrons, with snakes emerging like handles. The same room has a striking Archaic *Fleeing Kore* from 490 BC; also look for a headless *Demeter*, attributed to Agorakritos, student of Phidias; Antinous dressed as Dionysos; a *caryatid* from the Lesser Propylaea, bearing on her head the sacred basket decorated with the ears of corn, poppies, rosettes and *kernoi*; and the only piece of linen to survive from Classical times. The last room has ceramics, including *kernoi*, with their many little cups and holes for offerings of grains, wine, honey or oil.

Above the museum is the **acropolis**, whiskered with prickly pear, now crowned by a little church, bell tower and flag. Below the museum is a Hellenistic-Roman **Bouleuterion** by the well-preserved 4th-century BC Lykurgan walls and towers. Within the walls here was the Geometric-era **Sacred House**, dedicated to an unknown hero worshipped into Archaic times.

Along the Coast to the Corinth Canal

West of Elefsína the main (toll) highway next passes into the **Megarid**, the ancient state north of the Isthmus and powerhouse in the first millennium BC.

The chief city of **Mégara** was one of the few in the Bronze Age to have a Greek rather than pre-Greek name ('the big houses'), and its Dorian population was unusually well organized; like the Corinthians they soon made their city a mercantile centre, specializing in woollen cloaks. But as Mégara's territory was small, it was one of the first to colonize, beginning with Megara Hyblaea in Sicily in 728 BC, followed in 660 BC by Byzantium. It produced the aristocratic poet Theognis (*c.* 570–485 BC), who wrote elegant verse for dinner parties (including the first great body of homosexual poetry); in Classical times it held annual games that featured a kissing contest between boys. Clashes over the control of Sálamis led Mégara to be squeezed like a pimple between Corinth and Athens (which eventually dominated), but it had a last hurrah under one of Socrates' pupils, Euclides, founder of the Mégaran school of philosophy (440–380 BC). The modern city is still famous – for chickens. Almost nothing of its past has survived above ground besides its street plan (although there are a few ruins at Páxi); its ancient port, along with some terrific fish tavernas, is worth stopping at to explore. An **Archaeological Museum**, in Mégara's former town hall, has items from rescue digs – a Classical lion spout, grave *stelae*, vases and finds from an Archaic cemetery in Aleppochóri.

Archaeological Museum
22 G. Menidiáti, **t** *229 602 2426; open by request*

West of Mégara, the old and new roads and the railway pass on the narrow corniches of the **Kakia Skala** ('evil stair'), laboriously carved in the flanks of the **Geranía** massif, here plunging sheer into the sea – the mythic landscape where Theseus performed his labours en route from Troezen (*see* pp.305–307) to Athens. The old road by the sea is more fun to take if you have the time; at the 50km mark from Athens are the **Skironian Rocks**, where the nasty brigand Skiron used to kick travellers into the sea and into the jaws of a man-eating turtle, until Thesues gave him a dose of his own medicine. Here sculptor Kóstas Polychronópoulos opened the **Skiróneio Museum**, with his own and other contemporary works; a sweet little amphitheatre overlooking the sea is used for concerts.

Skiróneio Museum
t *229 606 1270; open Fri, Sat and Sun 10–7*

Kinetta, with its gardens descending to a white shingle beach, marks the end of Attica. The next village, **Ag. Theódori**, was ancient Krommyon, the lair of the man-eating sow, which Theseus also dispatched. On the highway bridge, you can pass the **Corinth Canal** (*see* p.155), a dramatic ribbon of blue under sheer walls, before you know it. Beyond lies the Peloponnese.

Corinthia

Corinth's natural citadel, the formidable 1,863ft limestone rock of the Acrocorinth, is one of the great landmarks of Greece, and in ancient times a thousand sacred prostitutes plied their trade on its summit. In the last 2,000 years, the Romans, St Paul and his followers, plus countless earthquakes, have scoured the city clean of its fleshpots, but the fascination lingers: ancient Corinth was as wealthy and artistic as it was naughty, and its remarkable ruins near the poignantly ephemeral modern city that bears its proud name offer a touching reminder of human frailty.

Mighty as it was, Corinth was not the only city-state in these parts: the fertile plains and valleys sheltered smaller independent neighbours such as Sikyon, Neméa, Phlious and Kleónai. Exploring these is just as rewarding, and takes you through some great wine country.

09

Don't miss

1. The ruins and citadel of a commercial giant
Ancient Corinth **p.145**

2. Reliving the ancient games
Nemea **p.160**

3. Emperor Nero's grand dream
Corinth Canal **p.155**

4. A topographical poem to swim in
Perachóra **p.157**

5. Ruins decorated with springtime wild flowers
Ancient Sikyon **p.164**

See map overleaf

Corinthia

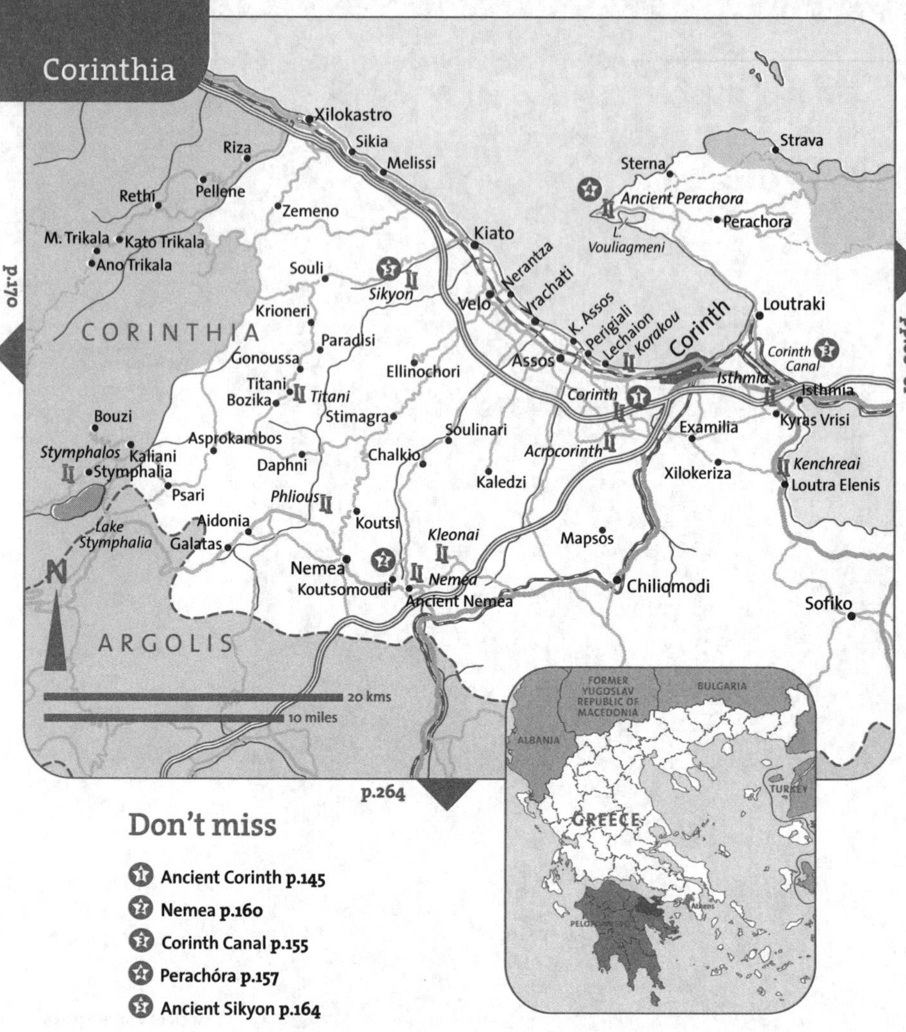

p.170
pp.80–81
p.264

Don't miss

1. **Ancient Corinth p.145**
2. **Nemea p.160**
3. **Corinth Canal p.155**
4. **Perachóra p.157**
5. **Ancient Sikyon p.164**

'Wealthy' (αφνειος) was Homer's word, but 'decadent' is the epithet that has stuck to the great city at the gateway to the Peloponnese. The city-state of Corinth (Κορίνθος) included the Isthmus – *the* Isthmus that gave its name to all isthmuses – as well as a pocket of mainland around Loutráki. The modern prefecture, however, continues south to the Dervenáki pass, and encompasses the Kyllíni range to the west (*see* pp.173–5), giving Corinthia a beautiful mountain hinterland that it did not possess in ancient times. Agriculture is the mainstay, especially the growing of Greece's finest wine grapes and currants (the English word is derived from 16th-century *raisins of Corauntz*, or Corinth). And with modern systems of irrigation in place, the prefecture once again fits its Homeric description.

Corinth

A Historical Outline

The area's first inhabitants, back in 5000 BC, left scant remains near the sea at Léchaion, and signs of continuous settlement from 5000 to 3000 BC on the eastern slopes of the Acrocorinth. Although the Mycenaeans later lived throughout Corinthia, there was not a significant presence on the big rock itself; they preferred the lower seaside hill of Korákou to the north.

Corinth emerged out of the dim cocoon of the dark ages some time in the 9th century BC as a wealthy, precocious Dorian *polis* that would eventually extend north to the Corinthian Gulf port at Léchaion, then across the Gulf to include Perachóra, and then eastward to the newer port of Kenchreaí on the Saronic Gulf. Perfectly placed to control the north–south land route between the Peloponnese and the rest of Greece, and to expand its maritime influence to the east and west, Corinth, under an aristocratic family called the Bacchiads, had the talent to exploit its unique position.

According to Thucydides, the Corinthians invented the trireme, a ship with three banks of oars in tiers, equipped with an outrigger in the upper bank of oars to keep these clear of the lower rowers; this gave the trireme a lot more oomph for the length of the ship and gave Corinth's famous mariners an early boost. One of their first tasks was to clear the seas of pirates. They were arty as well: Pliny, in his *Natural History*, even claims drawing was invented in Corinth, when a girl, knowing her lover was sailing away, used a piece of charcoal to trace his shadow on the wall. Corinthian ware, decorated with birds, flowers and monsters, dominated Mediterranean markets from the 8th to the 6th centuries BC.

Although the Bacchiads had masterminded Corinth's rise to power, things began to go wrong for them when they were drawn into the first ever sea battle, with their own colony, Corcyra (Corfu), in 664 BC. A few years later, their refusal to share power led to their overthrow and exile by a popular leader named Kypselos (Cypselus), one of the first 'tyrants' in what would become an era of tyrants in Greece. Kypselos and his son Periander (625–585 BC) founded colonies in northwest Greece to secure a supply of timber and flowers for the manufacture of perfume; they cultivated the friendship of Miletus to assure trade links with Asia Minor and made Corinth the most prosperous city in Greece. Periander instituted the Isthmian Games, built the *diolkos* (ships' towpath) across the Isthmus and built the great Temple of Apollo in stone, becoming the first Greek politician to translate the hitherto wood or clay brick temples into permanent monuments, reflecting civic prestige as well as piety.

Getting to and around Corinth

By car: Corinth is an easy one-hour drive from Athens or Trípolis. Note that ancient Corinth lies 5km west and slightly inland from the modern city. Exits for ancient Corinth are well signposted except on the highway from Pátras which just says 'Corinth-Argos'. For **car hire**, try **Vasilpoulos** (**t** 274 102 5573, *www.cars-hire.gr*) at Admántou 39, near the main *plateía*.

By train: Corinth's new **train station** (**t** 1110), part of the Athens suburban (*proastiakós*) rail network, is in Examília south of town; taxis and an hourly bus link the centre of Corinth to Examília. Trains to Athens and Kiáto (west) run hourly from 6am to 11pm. To points further west, service is less frequent and on the old line. Trains south to Argos and Trípolis also leave from the new train station.

By bus: Buses for ancient Corinth leave hourly from the **city depot** (**t** 274 102 5425) at 4 Demókritas (opposite the old train station) from 6am to 11pm. Buses for Loutráki leave every half-hour from the corner of Ethnikís Andistássios and Arátou (**t** 274 102 5645) from 5.30am until 10pm. This bus (do tell the conductor) can drop you off at the inter-provincial **KTEL bus depot** (**t** 274 107 3980) just west of the canal on the old national highway, if you need connections to points beyond Corinth (over 20 buses to Athens from 5.30am–9.30pm, hourly to Pátras, or elsewhere).

By taxi: For a radio taxi, call **t** 274 107 3000. These charge about €8 or €9 for ancient Corinth, €4.50 for the train station, and €12 to Loutráki; luggage is extra.

For all that, Periander's private life was unspeakable (necrophilia with his wife and incest with his mother is only some of the gossip); he had to be talked out of castrating 300 youths of Corcyra upon the death of his son. And yet he came to be called one of the Seven Sages of Ancient Greece, perhaps because the Fortune 500 had yet to be invented. The truth is that Corinth was never an intellectual centre. The arts that flourished here were the decorative and commercial ones. Political development would stop at the stage of oligarchy, a style of government well suited to both aristocrats and merchants, the usual beneficiaries of post-colonial booms.

Corinth became vulnerable when her economic dominance was challenged by Athens, another naval power, particularly after the expulsion of the Persians in 480 BC. Increasingly wary of Athens, she opted for the Spartan sphere as the lesser of two evils. Corinth gained little from this alliance and, after Athens' defeat in the Peloponnesian war in 404, she switched sides again and again, as did every other city during this turbulent period.

In Hellenistic times Corinth continued to act as a magnet for travellers and merchants, providing all the raunchy pleasures one might expect in a city with two ports of call and a great Temple of Aphrodite on the Acrocorinth. The young Alexander came to see the sights. One of these was Diogenes, the sour-tongued Cynic, who lived in a storage pot, berating the foibles of rich and poor alike. The urbane and fun-loving Corinthians didn't mind having a few pet ascetics about for their entertainment value, and Diogenes certainly delivered. When Alexander asked him if he desired some favour, he is reputed to have replied, much to Alexander's amusement, 'Stand a little out of my sun.' Alexander was impressed. 'If I weren't Alexander, I would like to be Diogenes,' he declared. (Coincidentally they would die on the same day 13 years later, one having conquered the world, the other still in his pot.) Diogenes' grave near the Kenchreaí Gate was a tourist attraction into the Roman period, as was the nearby grave of Laïs, the city's most renowned courtesan. Her grave-marker sported a lioness with a ram between its paws – a common symbol of Corinth, but to use it in this context shows a certain genius.

Corinth joined the Achaean League after 243 BC, led it in 200 BC, and dared to thumb its nose at Rome. At one point the citizens dumped excrement on the heads of the Roman envoys to show just what they thought of them. The Romans failed to see the joke and sent Mummius to sack and destroy the city in 146 BC, appropriating its treasures and monuments for Rome and selling its saucy citizens into slavery.

Corinth lay a deserted ruin until Julius Caesar rebuilt it in 46 BC. By the 1st century AD it was booming again and 'famous for being famous', proof that nothing succeeds like excess. This attracted Paul in AD 51, who doubtlessly saw a golden opportunity to preach the new religion, and he remained in sin city for eighteen months, teaching and plying his trade as tent-maker, a sojourn that would inspire his two Epistles to the Corinthians. He did not have an immediate effect on the population at large, although he did gather followers. His message of the Messiah irritated the local Jewish minority to such an extent that they took him to court for corrupting their faith. The Roman governor Gallio declined to prosecute, probably considering Paul just another small-time troublemaker trying to introduce yet another new god.

As Rome's hold weakened, Corinth attracted the barbarians, and what they did not destroy, frequent earthquakes, especially in 375 and 521, did. The city would continue to exist, as the Acrocorinth's Byzantine fort testifies, but it sank into obscurity during the Byzantine period along with the rest of the Peloponnese. The Franks wrested it from Greek defenders in 1210 after a five-year siege; the Isthmus was vital to the creation of their principality of Achaía and their hopes of uniting the Peloponnese politically. In 1458 the Turks took over, and added little to the fortifications, concentrating instead on building an entire city inside the fortress walls. In the 1680s the Venetians took over for 28 years, then the Turks returned until 1822, when they were turned out during the Greek War of Independence.

Modern Corinth: A Hub but not a Centre

Modern Corinth stood on the ruins of the ancient city until 1858, when a devastating earthquake caused it to relocate five

Corinthian Civic Mythology

Every Greek city-state worth its salt produced an official history tracing its origins to various gods and heroes, even if some parts of it were sneered at by rivals. The resulting 'political myth' is one Greek innovation that politicians have emulated ever since. The *nouveau riche* citizens of Corinth had a little trouble establishing a credible family tree; unlike other populations in the Peloponnese, they lacked a Mycenaean story cycle to hang their mythological hats on. But after a few false starts during the Archaic period, and with some help from the poet Eumelos, Corinth came up with a patchwork civic dream team: two patron deities, a witch, a founding father, a hero and a horse. The fact that **Poseidon**, god of the sea and earthquakes, and **Helios**, the sun god, vied with each other for the top job probably reflects the fact that each was an earlier, local deity before the city expanded. In a nice compromise, Poseidon got the Isthmus and the Sun got the Acrocorinth and the city, where his worship soon seamlessly merged with his Olympian counterpart, **Apollo**.

After obtaining the Golden Fleece, they say that **Jason** beached the *Argo* at the Isthmus and dedicated it to Poseidon. His wife **Medea**, as a granddaughter of Helios, became the legitimate ruler of Corinth, with Jason as king. When, ten years later, Jason threw her over for the younger **Glauke**, Medea sent the girl a flesh-eating poisoned cloak and left Corinth in a huff, in grandad's chariot pulled by winged serpents. In the local version of the story, the Corinthians then stoned her children to avenge the loss of Glauke. Centuries later, rumour had it that Euripides was paid off by the Corinthians to write that Medea had killed them herself. As for Jason the vow-breaker, he became an outcast and beggar, and returned to the Isthmus to hang himself on the prow of the *Argo*, only it broke off first and fell on his head.

Before flying off, Medea handed over the reins of power to **Sisyphos**, 'the very wise'. Sisyphos, a great promoter of navigation and commerce, was also fraudulent, avaricious, and above all cunning (*ponirós*, *see* pp.45–6) – in short, the perfect founding father for Corinth. His qualities were much admired. The unfailing Spring of Peirene on the Acrocorinth was his reward from the Asopos river for finding his daughter whom Zeus had kidnapped. He even tried to cheat death, and succeeded twice, but his efforts to keep the good times rolling caused him to be punished eternally in Tartarus, pushing a boulder up a hill until it almost reached the top, only to have it roll down again to the bottom, a fate that made him patron saint of Existentialists.

Before he died, Sisyphos handed over the reins to his grandson **Bellerophon**. No matter that he got his name 'killer of Bellerus' because he did kill a fellow named Bellerus; a lot of Greek heroes had homicidal moments, something that didn't seem to detract from their status at all – in fact, it was a handy way to get them off on their adventures. An oracle usually declared that in order to expiate their crime, they had to serve some other king in some other place, who would send the hero off to kill an outlandish monster or two. In Bellerophon's case it was the **Chimaera**, equipped with a lion's head, a goat's body and a snake's tail. To accomplish this, an oracle told him he would need the help of **Pegasus**, the flying horse born of the blood of snake-haired Medusa when Perseus struck off her head. The goddess Athena, helper of heroes, gave Bellerophon a golden bridle to harness the magic horse when he lighted to drink from the spring on the Acrocorinth. Aboard Pegasus, he flew over the Chimaera and dropped lead arrows into the monster's flaming mouth to melt inside its innards, ensuring it as gruesome a death as any invented by Hollywood.

Once a basic story was in place, exploits could be added and embellished until each hero was good for both civic self-congratulation and many evenings around the communal hearth. Bellerophon tempted fate by trying to fly to Olympus. An angry Zeus unseated him and hurled him to earth where he spent his last days lame and miserable. Greek heroes rarely had a happy end, an interesting subject in itself. But Zeus immortalized Pegasus as a constellation and the Corinthians placed him on their coins throughout their long history.

kilometres closer to the canal. It didn't help much. Destroyed and rebuilt several times because of more earthquakes (1928 and 1981 were the big ones), most of the buildings and houses are businesslike concrete boxes, hunkered down as if waiting for the next blast of Poseidon's trident. Of course, in a Greek city of 30,000 souls you'll find one or two pleasant squares. The *plateía* in front of the large church of St Paul is one, and so is seaside Elefthériou Venizélou Square, better known as **Plateía Touristikoú Kéntrou**. But Corinth's proximity to other towns and resorts has almost extinguished any effort on its part to attract visitors. It does have a good **Folk Art Museum** on Plateía E. Venizélou, displaying traditional costumes from all over Greece, the labour of love of a Corinthian who not only collected the costumes, but also donated the modern three-storey building. Other than that, you could give Corinth a miss.

Folk Art Museum
t 274 102 5352; open Tues–Sun 8.30–1.30; adm

Ancient Corinth

Ancient Corinth is now no larger than a village, with an attractive *plateía* that has not changed much in the past thirty years, except that more shops have been added. It is quiet at night when all the tourists have gone home.

The Archaeological Site and the Museum

Archaeological Site and Museum
t 274 103 1207; open daily April–Oct 8–7.30, Nov–Mar 8–5; adm exp

With a few notable exceptions, the ruins you see today are of the Roman city rebuilt by Caesar and visited by Pausanias in the 2nd century AD. Roman visitors arriving at the port of Léchaion would enter the city on the 40ft-wide **Léchaion Road**, its long commercial main street, built in the 1st century AD and paved with large limestone slabs, with the luxury of paved sidewalks on either side. Handy for freshening up on the left were the once sumptuous 2nd century AD **Baths of Eurykles**. The nearby public latrines, with their tiny keyhole openings, suggest a broad sense of communal spirit along with awfully small bottoms, but these multi-holers were the ancient norm; for toilet paper there was a sponge on a stick, dipped in sea water between customers.

Just after the latrines, the road is lined with **small shops** on the east and rather posher ***stoas* with shops** on the west. Confirming Corinth's commercial fame, the archaeologists found an extraordinary number of these boutiques, once filled with perfumes, silks, jewellery and oils, both locally made and imported from the east. The northernmost, semi-circular *stoa* dates from the 4th century AD, while the long southern one replaces an earlier *stoa* from the 1st century AD. Directly behind the row of shops to the east was the large sacred precinct or **Peribolos of Apollo** (1st century AD), its internal courtyard surrounded by Ionic columns.

The Léchaion Road still evokes the flavour of this Romanized Greek metropolis. Holy places stand shoulder to shoulder with commercial and public buildings in a seemingly haphazard order that is as typically Greek as the straight road is typically Roman.

This habit of combining density and diversity in communal living has endured well into this century, even in towns without space problems. Greeks have always liked their civic life up close and personal. Where the Léchaion Road enters the Agora, there stands a large public fountain, a feature found at the entrance of most Greek cities and markets. This particular one, the lower **Fountain of Peirene** (the upper is on the Acrocorinth), was one of the most famous. Rebuilt and renovated from the 6th century BC to Byzantine times, it still does the business (trickling water is audible behind the arches of the fountain) even if drinking deep might not be advisable today. Behind the arches are tunnels dug way back into the rock, with reservoirs to gather the water, a technique that is still used today in Greece. An ancient and less prosaic explanation claimed that the waters were really Peirene's tears, which flowed eternally after her two sons Lechaios and Kenchreas, fathered by Poseidon, were killed. At least it has the advantage of explaining the names of the ports. Most of what you see today is the 2nd-century AD work of Herodes Atticus, that wealthy Roman philhellene, who had the entire front clad with marble and added the large vaulted apses that are so prominent on three sides. In ancient times, Corinth's famous mirrors and weapons were tempered in its waters.

Just west of the fountain are three steps, followed by a landing and more stairs. This marks the spot of the once grandiose **main entrance** to the Forum/Agora. It started out as a *propylaea* and ended up, by the 1st century AD, as a large Roman triumphal arch with smaller ones on each side. The few remaining stones make this difficult to visualize. If you think along the lines of the Arc de Triomphe, only topped with horses and two bronze chariots carrying Helios and his son Phaeton, you will be in the conceptual ballpark. The large open rectangle of the **Roman Forum/Agora** measures 690ft by 300ft. On the west it is bounded by a row of shops fronted by six small **Roman temples** and on the east by the large **Julian basilica**. Its east–west dimensions were determined by the length of the huge 4th century BC **South Stoa** which forms its southern boundary on the higher of its two levels. Corinth's only Greek civic building still standing proud in Roman times, it had 71 Doric columns on its façade and 38 Ionic columns inside those. It originally consisted of shops on the ground floor. All but two of these came equipped with wells, suggesting that they served refreshments, from jugs chilled in the water. The second floor was probably a hostelry. The back of the *stoa* was altered over and over again; one part eventually housed the Roman **Bouleuterion** and the **Kenchreaí Gate**, punched through in AD 35 to mark the beginning of the Roman road to Corinth's Saronic Gulf port. The east–west retaining wall holding up the higher level in front of the

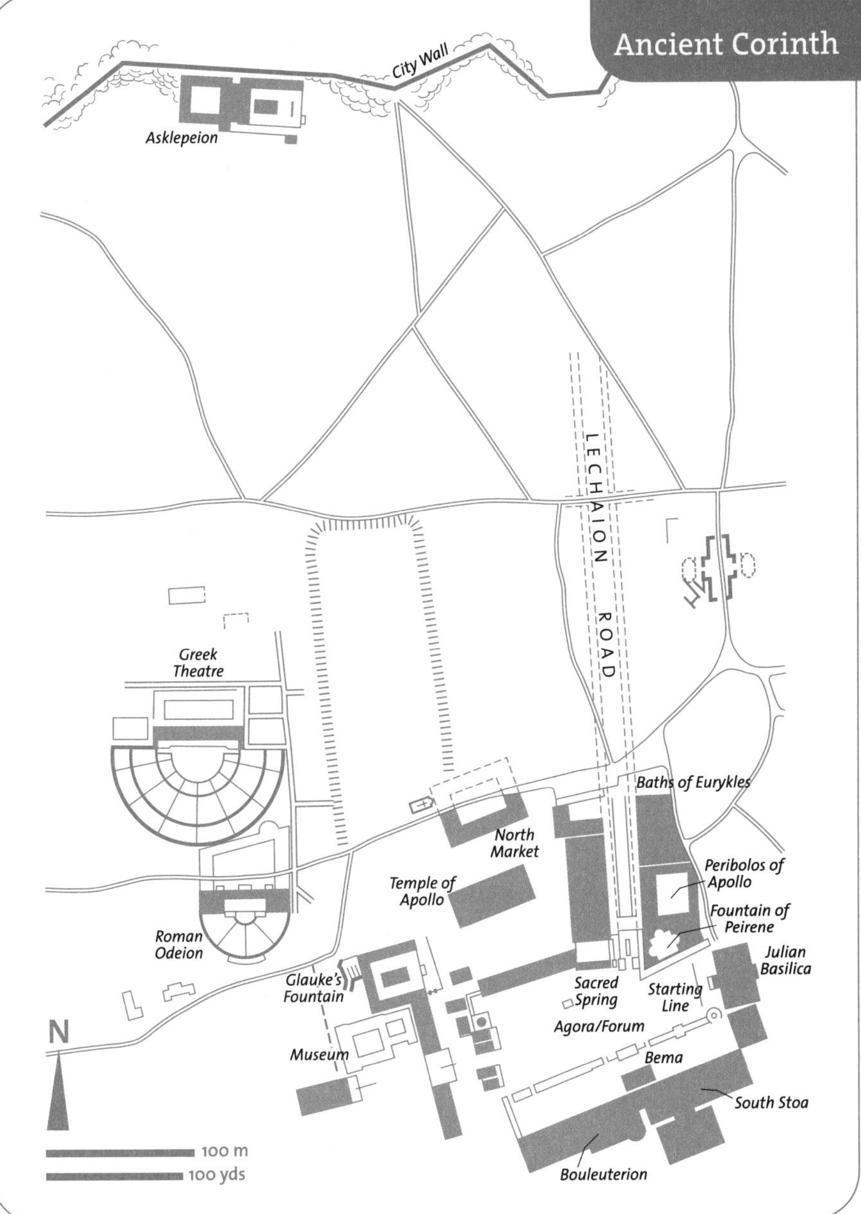

South Stoa contains a rostrum or ***bema***, a large platform with six stone courses, from which the Roman governors and other dignitaries would address the people. On either side of it were rows of shops matching those on the north side of the lower Agora. It was probably in front of this *bema* that the apostle Paul was brought before the Roman governor Gallio.

To the right of the triumphal arch as you enter the Agora is an area with quite a few depressions and some pieces of a triglyph wall. If you look hard, you will see the entrance and stairs to a **sacred spring**, an important source in Greek times. It is the most obvious reminder that, under all that Roman paving, the ancient Greek city lies unseen except for a few traces exposed here and there by probing archaeologists. One such probe revealed 6th-century BC **race starting lines** in front of the Julian basilica.

The remnants of the austerely beautiful Doric **Temple of Apollo** still dominate this Roman city. One of the oldest stone temples in Greece, it was completed around 550 BC. It had a peristyle of 38 monolithic limestone columns, 24ft high, six on the short sides and 15 on the long, and, although only seven remain in place, its sheer bulk and simple lines make an impressive sight. It once had a larger precinct, but parts of it kept being appropriated for other buildings, mainly shops, especially towards the Léchaion Road. To the north of the temple are the remains of the **North Market**, another Roman *agora*, and one used into Byzantine times. Just west of the Temple of Apollo is **Glauke's Fountain**, a huge cube hewn out of natural rock, dating from the Archaic period, with a multi-cistern design like the Fountain of Peirene. Tradition had it that the unfortunate Glauke threw herself in here, trying to escape the burning poison of the infamous poisoned wedding cloak sent to her by Medea.

The Museum

Starting with the room to the right of the entrance, you'll find Corinth's earliest finds displayed more or less chronologically, with the exception of a delightful Archaic *kore* still wearing some of her paint, who holds court among the Roman artefacts. Note the unusual square painted terracotta house altars and the figures of a bridal couple sitting demurely in a wagon drawn by horses, also on the room's right side. In the centre, cases display lovely examples of Corinthian ware, ceramic moulds, and shards used to hold paint. The room to the left of the entrance has a fascinating collection of Roman glass, three well-preserved Roman floor mosaics, and Frankish and Byzantine ceramics, most famously an exuberant 12th-century *sgraffito* plate showing Diogenis Akritas and a princess seated in a complex yet simple design that foreshadows Picasso – note the feet added outside the 'frame'. The courtyard has the usual headless statues and leads to a room displaying some of the many clay ex-voto body parts found in the Asklepeion.

The Theatres and the Asklepeion

Just outside and to the north of the site entrance are the ruins of the **Roman Odeion** and the **Greek theatre**. The Odeion was built around AD 100 and later redecorated by Herodes Atticus, antiquity's

Andrew Carnegie. It seated 3,000 spectators in seats carved out of the natural rock. Not much is left and, although it may have started out with concerts, by AD 225 it had been converted to accommodate gladiatorial contests and fights with wild beasts in accord with the tastes of Corinth's Roman residents. Corinth offered the only such entertainment ever in the Peloponnese. Times must have been tough for tourism because the **theatre**, which started out modestly in the 5th century BC, also ended up as an arena for gladiators, exotic beasts and mock naval battles at about the same time.

Anyone who over-indulged could head for the **Asklepeion**, 400m north of the theatre next to the Lernian fountain and remnants of the north wall. *Asklepeions*, dedicated to Asclepios, the god of healing, abounded in Greece. A stone offering-box with a few coins was found at the entrance. Many clay body parts – feet, hands, breasts, genitalia, etc. – were found there, testaments of hope or satisfaction. These tokens are now displayed in the museum.

The Acrocorinth: Flying Horses and Memorable Knights

Acrocorinth
t 274 103 1266; open daily 8–5

The road to the Acrocorinth begins at the lower site entrance and winds up to the massive gates on the west side of the citadel. The big rock is just far enough away from the lower city to have had a few historical moments of its own during the Middle Ages, when for defensive reasons these fortified heights were 'downtown' Corinth. One of these, surprisingly, involved another flying horse and rider. In 1205, the Franks, under Geoffrey de Villehardouin, besieged the Acrocorinth and, suspecting they were in for a long haul, built their own tiny, picturesque Pendeskoufi castle on its own little peak (you'll see it as you come up the road; the intrepid can scramble over for a visit). Although the Acrocorinth would hold out until 1210, by 1208 the Greeks' bold but frustrated commander, Leon Sgouros, unwilling to live to be a famous 'loser' of battles, decided on an spectacular exit strategy. In a grand gesture much appreciated by allies and enemies alike, he galloped his horse off the castle walls and both plunged to their deaths on the rocks below.

In 1305 the Acrocorinth was an important Frankish stronghold with a bishopric and nine dependent castles when it witnessed another landmark performance: a great medieval tournament hosted by Isabelle and Philip of Savoy. There is something delightfully incongruous about this 'Greek' feudal society fête, held at one of the few peaceful moments during the Franks' tenuous, tempestuous hold on the Morea; it is surprising that the gentry had the leisure and security for such a meeting. Philip announced to the lords and ladies of the Latin empire that seven champions from France had challenged the chivalry of Achaía. They responded by coming, a thousand strong, from all over the Peloponnese, and from farther north as well. For 20 days there was feasting and jousting, the likes of which that huge primordial rock had never seen before and would never see again. Today the Acrocorinth is home to wonderful large green lizards, a hawk or two and some shy partridges.

Touring the Citadel

The mainly Frankish outer wall, almost two miles long, encircles the entire summit, and was later enhanced by the Venetians with crenellated ramparts, watchtowers and a moat.

The first gate is Turkish, and the second, arched and buttressed, is Frankish, with a now-empty niche created by the Venetians for their Lion of St Mark. The most impressive gate is the third, massive, square and Byzantine, although a good deal of it dates from the 4th century BC. Once through the gates, ruined Venetian buildings and the extensive ruins of the Turkish city are pretty much all that remain; the Turkish barracks mark the site of the Temple of Athena Chalintida, 'the bridle-holder'. The upper Peirenean Spring, where Bellerophon caught Pegasus, is to the south, not far from the square Frankish keep; if you attempt to reach it, then the value of a flying horse to get around here does not need to be laboured. Next to nothing survives of the numerous sanctuaries that Pausanias records, including ones to Violence and Necessity. According to a command from the Delphic oracle, Medea's children were buried here in the precinct of a temple of Hera; and, in atonement for their murder, seven Corinthian girls and seven boys were chosen yearly to be dressed in black and immured in the temple precinct for twelve months.

A path from the third gate ascends beyond the ruins of the mosque, to the Acrocorinth's highest point, the eastern summit where the Archaic **Temple to Armed Aphrodite** stood. 'Disarming Aphrodite' would have been more accurate, since anyone with enough cash for the offering plate could join the steady stream of worshippers up the hill to visit the sacred prostitutes. There is a maddening lack of practical information as to just how this functioned. That it had the blessing of the city fathers and was a five-star attraction with all the sailors passing through the two ports goes without saying. There seems to have been no stigma attached to the profession in Corinth, but there was a hierarchy among the thousand priestesses. Laïs, whose tomb was mentioned earlier, was a high-class courtesan, or *hetaera*, yet one famous for her sliding scale of fees; she had a soft spot for Diogenes the Cynic, who enjoyed her favours on the house. Artists vied with each other to paint her breasts and poets struggled to capture her charm: 'She was more glittering than the clear water spring of Peirene' was one effort that has survived. Today this temple is a mere rectangle of stones baking in the sun, but the view over all Corinthia is climactic.

Léchaion, Ancient Corinth's Northern Port

To reach ancient Léchaion (Λέχαιο) from ancient Corinth, drive north to the old east–west coast road, turn right, and after 150m turn left at the sign. From Corinth, take the old coastal road west for 3km. The harbour is easily spotted from this road.

The port of Léchaion made Corinth a powerhouse in the Archaic and Classical periods, even though it was superseded by Kenchreaí afterwards. It was largely artificial, a cluster of boat bays excavated and protected from the sea by what is now a large sand dune. The eastern entrance can still be clearly seen. In the 5th century BC, the port was connected to the city by long **walls**. Back then it was quite built up; Pausanias describes a temple to Poseidon. What is so striking is the small size of the bays. These can be easily traced, especially in winter when they are full of water, a reminder that ancient vessels could be hauled up on beaches with enough willing hands. These protected boat bays were a tremendous advantage because the winds in the Gulf of Corinth come up quickly and make beaching a boat tricky even today.

Léchaion is now in the middle of an unkempt industrial area. Swampy in winter, bleak in summer, it is hardly ever visted, although there is a beach in front of the dunes. The site is littered with debris, but of a more interesting variety than that usually found around Greek shores; Léchaion is still virtually unexcavated, so bits and pieces of ancient cargoes and Greek and Roman refuse litter the ground along with the usual plastic rubbish. While here, visit the ruined **Basilica of Ag. Leonídas**, built in AD 450 and promptly toppled by an earthquake in 551. At 610ft by 150ft, it was nearly as big as St Peter's in Rome. Its entire floor is intact, with polychrome marbles galore, showing that this port was still important at this late date.

Basilica of Ag. Leonídas
t 274 103 1443; open Tues–Sun 8.30–3

Where to Stay and Eat in Corinth

Modern Corinth ✉ 20100

Ephira, 2 Ethnikís Andistássios, **t** 274 102 2434, *www.ephirahotel.gr* (€€/€€). Convenient, recently renovated, efficient, and helpful.

Akti, 1 Ethnikís Andistássios, **t** 274 102 3337 (€). Right on the noisy main square; strictly for bargain-hunters. Some rooms with air-conditioning. *Open all year.*

Neon, in Touristikí Plateía; the best bet for a quick bite. This upscale Greek chain has self-service counters for food, salads, wine, desserts and coffee. If that doesnscattered around the square.

★ Marinos Rooms and Taverna >

Ancient Corinth ✉ 20100

Marinos Rooms and Taverna, t 274 103 1209, *marinosrooms@icn.gr* (€/€). A pleasant modern building set in the pines on the south edge of town. The adjacent taverna is one of the best; and the food, inspired by mama Elizabet, is delicious. *Open Mar–Oct.*

Shadow, t 274 103 1481 (€/€). On the northeast edge of town coming in from the highway, a plain building on the edge of town. The rooms have fridges and Mr Papaiouánnou, the new manager, promises a restaurant on the ground floor. *Open all year.*

Tassos, t 274 103 1225 (€/€). 9 rooms with air conditioning and TVs, a good bargain choice and over a nice taverna too. *Open April–Oct.*

Diónysos, right across the street. A no-frills, but good, *psistariá.*

The Ancient Korinth, t 274 103 1361. On the main square for years and, while as touristy as it gets, it's a great place to people-watch while eating or drinking.

Léchaion ✉ 20006

Léchaion is the sort of place to stay in briefly in order to see ancient Corinth. It can be reached frequently by local buses.

Simi, t 274 102 0461, *www.simihotel.gr* (€€/€€). On the sea with an outdoor pool in the garden, well maintained although not in a particularly attractive area. Very good value for money. *Open April–Oct.*

Blue Dolphin Camping, t 274 102 5766 (€/€). Has been here for years on the sea, right beside the Hotel Simi. *Open April–Oct.*

Ísthmia, the Canal and Kenchreaí

The Isthmus of Corinth, a scoured land of thistles blasted by earthquakes, won't win any beauty prizes, although the blue ribbon of the canal with its vertiginously vertical walls is a memorable sight. Long before it was even conceived, however, the Isthmus had a reputation for express transport; a certain Sinis used to get his jollies by waylaying travellers, asking them to help him bend a pine tree back to the ground, only to release the tree at just the right moment and catapult his helper into the sea. Theseus, on his famous road-improvement hike from Troezen to Athens, gave him a taste of his own medicine.

The extensive ruins of Ísthmia and the Sanctuary of Poseidon lie close to the Saronic Gulf by the modern village of **Kyrás Vrísi** (Κυράς Βρύση). The sanctuary was Corinth's first, founded in the dark ages. By the 8th century BC, it began to serve a much wider audience passing by on one of the busiest (and safest) roads in Greece. The Isthmian Games, in prestige second only to Olympia, were instituted by Periander in 582 BC; here in 336 BC Alexander was declared the champion of the Greeks against the Persians. For all that happened here, however, this site is not for the archaeologically faint-hearted. Continually rebuilt, altered and added to during its long history, it also suffered total destruction, once by the Romans in 146 BC, and after that by the barbarians.

Ancient Ísthmia
Site and museum, t 274 103 7244; open daily 8–2.30; adm; do phone ahead: the excellent museum has been closed for several years for renovations but it should be open by now

Ancient Ísthmia

As you enter the fenced-in part of the site, the **Sanctuary of Poseidon** stands just on your right. First constructed with wooden

Getting to Ísthmia, the Canal and Kenchreaí

By bus: buses leave the centre of Corinth four times a day from Ethnikís Andistássios and Aratou Streets for Ísthmia. Consider a **taxi**.

By car: Follow the signs from the canal zone to Ísthmia. Almost immediately you will see the ruins on your right beside the road. The turn-off is signposted; the main road continues south past Kenchreaí and Helen's Baths on its way to Archaía Epídauros.

To get to Ísthmia and Kenchreaí from ancient Corinth, follow the road towards Argos and then towards Examília (Εξαμίλα) and Ísthmia (Ισθμια), passing by way of the extensive limestone quarries used to build Corinth. They are now planted with trees and are very attractive, at least where the locals have not dumped their garbage. To bypass Ísthmia for Kenchreaí, turn southeast at Examília, through Xilokériza (Ξιλοκέριζα).

columns in the 7th century BC, it was replaced by a Doric stone temple in the 5th century BC with a peristyle of six by 13 columns; the ruin you see today is its replica, built a century later. As at Olympia, its early votive offerings included the most conspicuous signs of wealth of the 8th century BC: armour and tripod cauldrons.

At the southeast corner of the sanctuary are the only visible remains of the original **classical stadium**: a good portion of the **starting line** for foot races. Since the games were held in honour of the god, the stadium's proximity to the temple isn't odd. Look for the triangular-shaped pavement of stone slabs scored with radiating grooves. There is a circular pit at the apex where the starter stood, holding ropes that, when released, opened each of the 16 starting gates at the same time, much the same way as they do in modern horse or greyhound races.

Just northeast of the Temple of Poseidon are the paltry ruins of a 4th-century BC **theatre**, where Nero addressed the citizens. East of here are the remains of Justinian's **Byzantine fortress**, which abutted the tremendous **trans-Isthmian wall**, first built by the Spartans in 480 BC against Xerxes, in case the Greeks failed to hold the Persians at Sálamis and Plataea. The wall stretched six Roman miles and was known as the Hexamilion – hence the town of **Examília** – and followed the line of low bluffs. They can still be traced almost in their entirety, thanks to Justinian's massive refortification and addition of 153 towers, which cannibalized all the stone from the temple and theatre. Unlike the Spartans' wall, these defences were tested by the barbarians, and failed miserably. In the early 15th century they were restored by Emperor Manuel II, and failed again when the Turks breached them for the first time in 1423. East of the Byzantine fortress, eight or nine courses of the Spartan wall can still be seen.

Further east down the road from the museum and to your right is the **new stadium**. Built in a natural depression, it functioned from about 390 until 146 BC, and again when Corinth was rebuilt after 46 BC. Both the start and finish lines have been discovered, so we know that the classic one *stade* race here was 181.5m (198yds).

The Isthmian Games and the Boy on a Dolphin

The Isthmian Games were one of the four *stephaniteis* or crown athletic events, referred to by athletes as the *Períodos* or circuit. The others were Olympia, Delphi and Nemea. At all four, victors were crowned with wreaths: wild olive at Olympia, bay at Delphi, wild celery at Nemea and pine at Ísthmia. With the 'quadruple crown' and a lot of smaller athletic events, an athlete could be on the move representing his city a good deal of the time. Those who prevailed at all four games were *Periodonikes*, circuit winners, and there was no greater honour.

The Isthmian Games occurred every two years and, as at Olympia, they were cause for a truce. Although held to honour Poseidon, they also commemorated the youth Melicertes-Palaimon, who had died tragically when his mother leapt with him into the sea after a series of adventures that would cause even a daytime soap to take pause. The important part is that a dolphin brought his body to Ísthmia and Sisyphus, who happened to be his uncle, recognized him. At the time Corinth was suffering a famine and an oracle declared that it would stop and never occur again if Palaimon was properly buried and games were held regularly in his honour. Sisyphus buried him under a sacred pine. Melicertes (from the Phoenician *Melkarth*, the 'guardian of the city') may have been a title of the King of Corinth. All the crown events were funeral games, perhaps because there were funeral games in Homer, always the Greeks' ultimate authority. In any case, Palaimon's death created the required situation, tied the story in neatly with the legend of Sisyphus, and gave artists lots of scope in depicting the pathetic scene of a boy stretched out artistically on the dolphin.

It was a theme that particularly appealed to Roman sensibilities; they used the motif in their circular temple and enclosure of Palaimon right beside the Temple of Poseidon and depicted it on the Roman coins of Corinth. Only the square base of the temple can be seen today. Plutarch tells us there were mystery rites for Palaimon at this temple that involved many lamps; some are now in the museum.

No two stadiums had the same length marked for the one *stade* race, the distance varying by as much as 10m. Southeast of the new stadium are the remains of a **Cyclopean wall**. No one is sure of its purpose, but it is proof that low-lying Ísthmia, with its gentle slopes and sea view, was just right for Mycenaean tastes.

The Museum

This houses finds from Ísthmia and Kenchreaí, including a fascinating Archaic lustral basin (*perirrhanterion*) found in the Temple of Poseidon and which looks for all the world like an elaborate bird bath. There are also well-preserved helmets dating from 700 to 480 BC, a strikingly contemporary-looking Hellenistic clay bathtub, and beautiful glass panels in *opus sectile* with architectural and floral motifs from the 4th century AD. Made of coloured glass and plaster, they were found under water at Kenchreaí, still in their packing cases, their delivery interrupted by an earthquake – a good thing for us, because they are lovely, and give an idea of the kind of wall decorations of the period. The natural formaldehyde of the sea preserved an even rarer find: the wooden doors from the Temple of Isis, practically unique and alone worth the visit. This Temple of Isis is the same as described in Book XI of the *Golden Ass* of Apuleius, where the goddess transforms the hero back into a man. Isis, who may have been in Greece very early on (*see* 'Troezen', p.306), made a big comeback with the Romans.

Her temples often had pools, with Nile vegetation painted on the walls; the more elaborate Italian ones even had crocodiles.

Kenchreaí: Corinth's Eastern Port and Helen's Baths

When St Paul sailed to Ephesus from Kenchreaí, just over 7km south of Ísthmia, it was horseshoe-shaped with moles at its northern and southern end, each of these equipped with port facilities as well as temples. The Temple to Isis stood on the south mole, as did a later Christian basilica. There is not much to see unless you are prepared to go snorkelling: rising sea levels have left a good many of the ancient buildings under water. A little farther on are **Helen's baths** (Λουτρά Ελένης), still a little seaside bathing area today. The most beautiful woman in the world probably didn't bathe here, but the Romans certainly did, although in their day the warm spring was on land, forming a reservoir and baths. The spring bubbles up under water now; test its temperature for yourself.

The Ditch and the *Diolkos*: The Great Ship Passages at Corinth

How difficult it is for human beings to force what the gods determine.
Pausanias

Corinth Canal

Pausanias was commenting on failed efforts in antiquity to turn 'Pelops' island' into a geographical reality by digging a canal across the 6km-wide umbilical cord that linked it to the rest of mainland Greece. Periander was the first to see the advantages of the 'ditch', as the locals call it: it would cut the trip from Piraeus to the Ionian sea by about 200 nautical miles, nothing to sneeze at then or now, and allow shipping to avoid the treacherous winds around Cape Matapan in the south Peloponnese. Traces of Periander's efforts have been found at the western end of the canal. The project was too expensive, so Periander opted for the ***diolkos***, the stone carriageway, over which ships could be towed from gulf to gulf, although experts differ on whether they went on rollers, pulled by a winch, or by a wheeled cart. All agree, however, that the cargo had to be offloaded before the ship could be hauled overland. This sat fine with Corinth's merchants, who made a mint out of transporting goods between the two ports. According to the chronicles, the *diolkos* was still in service in the 9th century AD, for ships with a 300-passenger capacity. The most accessible traces are signposted, on the southwest bank of the canal near the iron bridge that links Corinth to Loutráki. Other traces of the *diolkos* appear further east, on the other bank; unlike the canal, it wasn't straight. The *diolkos* was especially useful for war ships; Octavian used it to chase Antony and Cleopatra after their defeat at Actium.

An old prediction by the philosopher Apollonius of Tyana augured ill to anyone who toyed with an idea of digging a canal. Julius Caesar and Caligula did, and had studies taken; one by Egyptian experts in AD 40 claimed that the water level of the Corinthian

Where to Stay in Ísthmia

Ísthmia ✉ 20100

This area offers pretty good swimming, but enthusiasm may be dampened by the proximity of oil refineries on the mainland. The Saronic Gulf is not as clean as the Corinthian, but here the sea is not polluted.

Kalamaki Beach, **t** 274 103 7653, *www.kalamakibeach.gr* (€€€€€/€€€). Between Ísthmia and Kenchreaí. Impersonal, but offers a big pool, nice grassy grounds, tennis and a pretty strip of beach. *Open April–Oct.*

Sea View, Loutrá Eléni, **t** 274 103 3551, *seaview@kor.forthnet.gr* (€/€). On the busy main drag; basic rooms with air-conditioning, TVs and fridges, which have the advantage of overlooking a charming little cove, perfect for a swim. *Open April–Oct.*

Isthmia Beach Camping, **t** 274 103 7447, *www.campingisthmia.gr* (€/€). Attractive; shares the beach with the Kalamaki Beach Hotel. *Open April–Oct.*

Gulf was higher than the Saronic, and putting through a 'ditch' would result in the island of Aegina being inundated. But in AD 67, Nero, not one to miss a Greek island or two, went ahead anyway. He inaugurated his effort in grand style by personally loosening the first clod of earth with a golden axe as the citizen population cheered him on. His axe struck an oozing red substance, which Nero, naturally superstitious, interpreted as blood. He remembered Apollonius but decided to disregard the omen. For three months, 6,000 slaves from Judea excavated along the same line as the modern canal; work started at each end and everyone was supposed to meet in the middle. They might have done so, but Nero suddenly got word of conspiracies in Gaul and Rome, and was soon killed by his own secretary. The canal project died with him.

Canal Vista *docked off the old National Rd,* **t** *274 103 0880, www.corinthcanal.com; May–Sept, Mon, Thurs, Fri, Sat and Sun; ring ahead for times*

After a gap longer than most European projects, work was resumed in 1881 by a Hungarian whose reward was to be the control of the canal for 99 years. When he went bankrupt, a Greek company financed by Andréas Sýngros continued. The first ship passed through on 25 July 1893 and Aegina had nothing to fear: the Egyptian experts had been wrong. When it first came into use the canal was 92.5ft wide (69ft at the bottom), the water was 26ft deep, and the sides at their highest point were 180ft. **Cruises** lasting just over an hour are offered on the *Canal Vista*.

North of Corinth: Loutráki and Perachóra

Loutráki (Λουτράκι)

Although on the north side of the canal, this bit along the Gulf has been an integral part of Corinth since ancient times. It offers the prefecture's biggest resort, and one of its most evocative ancient sites. The resort, **Loutráki**, with its long arc of shingle beach, water sports, casino and spa, has a Riviera glow. Crowded

Getting to and around Loutráki and Perachóra

Loutráki is 6km west of the Canal Zone. The **bus** station, **t** 274 402 2262, is at El. Venizélou Av and Korínthou St. Buses come and go frequently from Athens (nine a day), Corinth and the canal, but only one bus a day goes in summer to Vouliagméni. **Taxis**, **t** 274 406 1000, congregate near the bus station; they will take you to the local sights and wait for you. Signs abound for **car** and **bike rentals**. For **mopeds**, have your hotel call **t** 697 064 8487; for a car, contact LM Tours, *see* p.158.

---

with hotels (and in the summer just plain crowded), it is still compact enough to walk from end to end. The fountain-filled esplanade offers wonderful views of the Gulf and the surrounding mountains. Excursion boats depart from a lovely waterside park, and a 50ft artificial waterfall rushes dramatically down stone terraces over by the spa. The latter existed in Roman times when Loutráki was called Therma because of its saline waters, flowing at a constant 30°C. Enter the spa's temple-like confines and sip a cupful, just to see the décor, probably a pretty accurate reconstruction of the original Roman establishment.

Northwest of Loutráki, the coastal road leads to the lovely 2km-wide lagoon of **Lake Vouliagméni**, joined to the sea by a canal in 1880. Although often crowded in July and August, the swimming is always good, and there are tavernas to make a day of it.

Perachóra: 'Over There'

Perachóra

Heraion of Perachóra
always open

Two km beyond the lake, tucked on the westernmost point of a narrow peninsula, the ruins of the small **Heraion of Perachóra**, with its precipitous rocky shore and lighthouse, form a topographical poem. From here, the Gulf of Corinth resembles a mountain lake ringed by mighty Mount Kyllíni to the south, and Mounts Helicon and Kithairon to the north. The lighthouse, set within the precincts of the sanctuary, stands near vestiges of polygonal and ashlar walls.

The **Sanctuary of Hera Akraia** was established here by the Corinthians in the 8th century, inspired by the even older Argive Heraion (*see* p.278). It was a strategic necessity for Corinth to control the peninsula in one fashion or another (the name Perachóra, meaning 'the land over there', comes from the perspective of the big city). The Heraion was a popular site, reaching its peak in the 7th and 6th centuries when it outstripped Ísthmia, receiving hundreds of offerings such as Phoenician scarabs, metalwork from Italy and the Near East, and specially made votives of thin gold – almost as if Hera's worshippers were showing off their exotic tastes. Here, in contrast to Ísthmia, the votives were of a peaceful, domestic nature, including female jewellery and clay models of the bread rings (*kouloúria*) that the Greeks eat today.

Perachóra had a setback in 390 BC when Sparta, at odds with Corinth, destroyed both it and Ísthmia. During the Hellenistic period it was again a going concern until the Romans sacked it in

146 BC. It never fully recovered; subsequent residents were more interested in the warm waters of Loutráki. But what a spot this must have been when it was functioning, with boats coming in and out of what is really the only possible landing place in the area. Some of the ruins are under water and on a calm day the little cove that was Perachóra's port is perfect for snorkelling. Standing in the centre of this, with the mole to your right, you will see before you the **Temple to Hera Akraias** of *c.* 525 BC. 'Akraias' was a common epithet for Hera; her earliest temples were built on heights or hilltops, reflecting her first important role as a sky goddess; the *acro* in acropolis comes from the same word. To your left is an L-shaped building, once a two-storey ***stoa*** built around 400 BC. Between it and the temple are a few square stones, the foundations of the **altar**. Over behind the mole was the **Greek *agora***, and, superimposed on it, some later Roman houses.

Overlooking the port, behind the little church of **Ag. Ioánnis**, are the remains of a Hellenistic **apsidal temple**, built over an even earlier water source. What remains is the long, narrow cistern about 7ft deep, with rounded ends and rough stone steps to the bottom. Immediately beside it, to the south, is the floor plan of a two-roomed building used for banquets or symposia. The shaded porch of the church is a great spot for an al fresco symposium of your own, but bring your own water; the cistern is dry. Beyond it, to the east as the ground level rises, are the hard-to-decipher ruins of **Hera Limenia** (Hera of the Port) built in the 7th century BC. Over 200 unique bronze flasks with rounded, belly-buttoned shapes were found here. Just up a bit and to the east are the ruins of a small settlement and some polygonal walls.

Perachóra is a reminder of the long centuries that these sanctuaries functioned, of the exquisite sense of place of their builders and of the integral part a sanctuary played in civilized life. The site was excavated by the British School between 1930 and 1933; for an account of the digs and life in the nearby village of Perachóra – now prosperous, but impoverished and completely isolated at the time – read *An Affair of the Heart* by Dilys Powell, the wife of the archaeologist.

Tourist Information North of Corinth

There is no tourism office currently open in Loutráki, but it does have a superb website, *www.loutraki.gr*, which can tell you all about just about everything.

Tourist police, at Venizélou and Lékka Sts, **t** 274 406 5678.

LM Tours-Cruises, 8 Plateía 25 Martíou, **t** 274 406 4919, *lmtours@ otenet.gr*, offer tours, car hire, and a cruise to the Saronic Islands.

Activities North of Corinth

Loutráki's **waters** cure stress, or will make you feel and look more beautiful: for info contact the **Hydrotherapy Centre** opposite the Peace park at G. Lékka St, Loutráki ✉ 20330, **t** 274 402 2215. **Alpha Cruises**, **t** 274 402 1937 or **t** 694 488 2216, offer day **cruises** in the Saronic Gulf via the Canal three times a week. **Watersports** include windsurfing and canoes. Or go for broke at Greece's biggest and oldest casino, the swish **Club Casino Loutraki**, 48 Posidónos, **t** 274 406 0300, *www.clubhotel loutraki.gr*.

Where to Stay North of Corinth

Loutráki ✉ 20300

Palace, 19 G. Lékka St, **t** 274 402 6695, *www.hotelpalace.gr* (€€€€€/€€€€€). Built in 1923, this neoclassical wedding cake by the sea is in the centre, beautifully renovated *à la* Bath with chandeliers, brass beds and gilt. The dining room is worth a look and the lounge serves snacks in elegance more affordable than the rooms. *Open all year.*

Poseidon Club, 3km west, **t** 274 406 7938, *www.poseidonresort.gr* (€€€€/€€€€). Upscale holiday village with every imaginable service. *Open April–Oct.*

Pappas, 1km west, **t** 274 406 2782, *www.hotelpappas.gr* (€€€/€€). Standard seaside hotel with a pool and private beach. *Open April–Oct.*

Cristina Maris, 77 Posidónos, **t** 273 306 9490, *www.hotel-cristina-maris.gr*. (€€€/€€). New waterfront hotel a bit south of the centre, extremely pretty with a lovely pool embedded in a courtyard and parking.

Mandas, 1 Económou St, **t** 274 402 2575, *www.mantashotels.gr* (€€/€€). Near the bus station; friendly and with a small rooftop pool. *Open all year.*

Segas, 8 Ag. Ioannoú, **t** 274 402 2623, *hotelsegas.netfirms.com* (€/€). Charming, eager-to-please family-run hotel on a pedestrian street near Plateía 25 Martiou; book online and get a free breakfast.

Le Petit France, 3 Márkou Botsári St, **t** 274 402 2401, *lepetitfrance@yahoo.com* (€/€). A *pension* near the bus station, with a small garden, run by a delightful French-Greek family. Cheaper rooms on the first floor. *Open April–Oct.*

Eating Out North of Corinth

Loutráki

Try these, or simply walk along the esplanade and choose.

Plaza, 9 Posidónos St, **t** 274 402 2798. Has a good name for seafood.

To Karvágio, 99 Posidónos, **t** 274 406 6230. Among a clutch of tavernas en route to the casino south of town. Good food, warm atmosphere, and a singing group on weekends.

★ Rigáni >>

Rigáni, 5 Papanikoláou, **t** 274 406 6744, *www.rigani.gr*. Set back two streets from the Casino (a 3min walk), this cosy, family-run restaurant is a local year-round favourite – with good reason. It's a member of the Slow Food movement, and the authentic tastes shine through in their dishes. Try their delicious mushroom soup, grilled meat, or try whatever casserole dishes have been cooked fresh that day, served with organic Nemean wine.

South of Corinth: Lion's Blood and Grape Vines

With the exception of Nemea itself, it might be fair to call the ancient cities in this valley 'drive-by' sites, strictly for the archaeologically obsessed. But do drive by. *Nemea* means meadow or pasture, an apt description of this charming landscape of rolling hills swathed in grape vines; it is at its very best in spring, but October during the harvest is good fun, too. The fields bearing

Getting around in Grape Country

Providing you are forewarned, getting to ancient Nemea and nearby sites like Phlious, Kleónai and Aidónia is easy. There are five approaches:

1 There are exits from the Corinth–Trípolis highway and from the Corinth–Argos secondary highway for Neméa and ancient Nemea (Αρχαία Νεμέα). Even if you get lost, one is only 4km from the other. A bus joins Corinth and the Nemeas seven times a day.
2 A lovely secondary road from Vracháti (Βραχάτι) on the Corinthian Gulf takes you south via Soulinári (Σουληνάρι) to ancient Nemea.
3 From Kiáto on the Corinthian Gulf, drive south to Soúli (Σούλι), and then southwest to Gonoússa (Γονούσσα), drop in to ancient Titane/modern Titáni (Τιτάνι) and continue via Boziká (Μποζικά) and Dáphni (Δάφνι). Pass by ancient Phlious (Αρχαία Φλειούς) on your left just before you meet the bigger road and turn left to Neméa and ancient Nemea.
4 You can even come over the hills from Stymphalía (*see* p.175) via Psári (Ψσ,ρι), Galatás (Γαλατάς), Aidónia (Αηδόνια) and Petrí (Πετρί), pass by ancient Phlious on your left, to Neméa, and ancient Nemea.
5 Go to ancient Kleonai (Αρχαία Κλεώνα), passing by the temple to Heracles and then south of town to ancient Nemea.

raisin grapes have telltale flat cement platforms with bits of scaffolding where the grapes are laid out to dry in the sun, and quickly covered over should it rain. The raisins are wonderful, but it is wine, specifically fine red wine, that has made the area famous.

Nemea has come a long way since lurid labels like Lion's Blood and Blood of Hercules were the only ones flogged in roadside stands. Nemea's native *agiorgítiko* grapes are named after the Phenean Monastery of Ag. Geórgios (*see* p.178), which at one time owned all the land hereabouts. Thanássis Papaioánnou (Παπαιωάννου) is the biggest landowner now, and his family have put Nemea on the international wine map. His son has studied viticulture in France, and the family constantly experiments to improve native Peloponnesian varieties. Their current award-winning red wine is Palaiá Klímata, and Aristócracy is their excellent new white. But don't neglect smaller Nemean wine estates and their products either, especially at the bargain prices they charge. (For more information, *see* p.60.)

This fertile area has been busy since prehistoric times. On the hill of Tsougiza immediately west of ancient Nemea are the remains of a Neolithic and Early Helladic settlement, and the Mycenaeans were here, too, as their graves at Aidónia show. Locals claim the cave on Tsougiza's south slope was the lair of the Nemean lion of the spear-, arrow- and stone-proof hide, who feasted on Greeks until Heracles, in his First Labour, strangled it with his bare hands, henceforth making use of its invulnerable pelt as a handy anorak. That made growing grapes a lot safer.

Ancient Nemea

Like Olympia, Nemea was a sanctuary dedicated to Zeus, not a city. Its games, held every two years, were one of the 'big four' in ancient Greece (*see* p.154). Originally local races attached to Kleónai, a cult centre for Heracles under the aegis of powerful Argos, the games were instituted as panhellenic in 573 BC. They were interrupted in 415 BC when the temple burned, and moved to Argos, resuming in Nemea in 330 BC when the temple was rebuilt. Contests included the usual: horse and foot races, wrestling, musical contests and drama. Since 1974 the University of California at Berkeley has been conducting excavations at Nemea under the direction of Stephen G. Miller. If they have less to show than, say, Olympia, they have certainly compensated for that by making it most interesting, beautifully laid out, welcoming, and more attractive than any other small site in the Peloponnese.

The Museum and Sanctuary of Zeus

Museum and Sanctuary of Zeus
t 274 602 2739, www.nemea.org; open May–Oct Tues–Sun 8–7.30 (note museum opens at 12.30 on Mon in summer); Nov–April Tues–Sun 8.30–3

Finds from Nemea, Kleónai and Phlious from prehistoric to Roman times fill Nemea's modern museum. Large photographs show how artefacts were found and used, and there are models of the important structures in the sanctuary. Of special interest are the many items relating to the games themselves, and the room displaying the rich and beautiful finds from the 15th-century BC Mycenaean cemetery at Aidónia near Nemea. This treasure represents an important victory for the Greek archaeological service. When excavations began in Aidónia in 1978, it transpired that 10 of its 18 tombs had been looted just a short time previously. Usually that would be the end of it, but in 1993 a New York gallery published a catalogue featuring a collection of Mycenaean jewellery, valued at $1.5 million, that was about to go to auction. The archaeologists at Aidónia took one look at it and cried foul; the Greek government obtained a court order to halt the auction, then showed, through stylistic similarities with items found in the unlooted tombs, that the collection was most probably stolen from Aidónia. In an out-of-court settlement, the gallery donated the collection to a Greek foundation in exchange for a tax write-off, and the gold was brought home to Nemea.

Leaving the museum in the direction of the temple, the first ruins you see belong to an early **Christian basilica and cemetery** dating from 400, superimposed on what is assumed to be a much earlier hotel for athletes or visitors. Beyond that is a row of **small buildings**, side by side, that probably belonged to the various participating city-states. These may have been treasuries, but a kitchen out front suggests that they could have also been early versions of the hospitality suite. In the second to last one on the right are traces of a bronze-working establishment. Victors often commissioned statues on the spot, so these sanctuaries attracted itinerant artists.

Three columns used to be all that remained of the original 36 of the Doric **Temple of Zeus** (140ft by 72.5ft), designed by Scopas in *c.* 330 BC and built over an earlier, smaller 6th-century BC temple. Restorers have upped the number to seven, and plan on more. You can descend stone steps into this temple's 6ft-deep *ádyton* under the *cella*, but beware of Zeus' anger: it was an underground holy of holies where only priests were allowed, suggesting an oracular temple like Delphi's. What went on, no one knows.

The **altar** to the east was 132ft long. Like all other temple altars, this low-lying table received the blood of the sacrificial animals and served as a base for burning the offering to the god. The sacrifices at the Nemean Games must have been huge affairs to have required an altar this long. Of course, since the meat was immediately cut up and roasted on spits or boiled, it serves as a reminder that a communal feast was part of the religious ritual. Usually the meal took place by the altar so that the cult statue could 'view' the sacrifice and be satisfied. In some cases, meat was actually charcoal-broiled on the altar itself! The Greek word for the official who butchered the carcass was *mageiros*, the modern Greek word for 'cook', and before the animals were led in procession to the altar he was ready with his knives and had a good fire on the go. The **baths**, built in the 4th century BC, are so beautifully designed and so complete that they seem to beg for water and mosaic tiles, especially the pool. Since the games were held in summer (one event was a sprint in full armour), this must have been a popular spot.

The 4th-century BC **stadium** is 500 yards east of the temple. Both starting lines have been found. Two were needed because each race, no matter what its length, had to finish at the horseshoe end of the stadium in front of the judge, seated on a special bench low in the stands. A longer race involved running around turning points placed in front of both starting lines. As at Ísthmia, strings attached to the starting gates were held by one person behind the starting line, so that runners would all get off at the same moment. They had toe-holds, too. A water source, originating at the horsehoe end, was sent all around the stadium perimeter in a stone trough, so that thirsty spectators coud easily refresh themselves. If that's not enough, then surely the underground tunnel leading from the 'undressing' room into the stadium will convince you that this place was state-of-the-art! Graffiti on the tunnel walls recorded the names of the most handsome athletes, inscribed by their admirers.

Like the others, the Nemean Games were funeral games (*see* p.154). In spite of an earlier tradition that Heracles started the games after killing the Nemean lion, the story that stuck was one that claimed they were started by heroes of Argos (the famous Seven against Thebes) led by Adrastus. On their way to Thebes they passed through Nemea looking for water. A palace nurse was out walking with the king's son Opheltes, whom she had in her arms because an oracle said that if he touched the ground before he walked he would die. Eager to help the soldiers, she laid Opheltes on a bed of wild celery to lead them to the spring. A snake bit the child and the oracle was fulfilled. This was a bad omen, and a seer told the Seven that they must institute games to Opheltes to ward off evil luck. The prizes were wreaths of wild celery, and the officials of the games would wear black as a sign of mourning. The opening ceremonies, with mourning city officials, naked athletes and 40,000 spectators, must have been quite a sight. In 1996, there was a reopening of the stadium, complete with celery and black-robed judges, and the American ambassador. The athletes, however, opted for white robes, a regrettable deviation from historical accuracy.

A Brief Look at Other Ancient Cities in the Area

Kleónai (Κλεώναι) lies 6km northeast of ancient Nemea and is joined to it by an asphalt secondary road that passes by the stadium. Kleónai reached its peak in the Mycenaean and Archaic periods and then faded into oblivion, except for a small Hellenistic **Temple of Heracles** in the middle of a vineyard. A famous drunkard, Heracles would have loved that. Note that the prosperous town of Kondostavlí has taken to calling itself 'Ancient Kleónai', even though it is several kilometres away. For that reason, a lot of people get lost trying to find ancient Kleónai while actually standing in it! If you follow the signs for modern Ancient Kleónai from the Corinth–Argos road, you will cross railway tracks, and then the Corinth–Trípolis highway. Immediately beyond, look for the sign that says 'Temple of Heracles'. The temple's entire substructure is intact a short way off the road.

Titáni (Τιτάνι) had a famous ***asklepeion***, but all you can see today are its acropolis walls on three sides of a hill, now topped with the cemetery and the church of Ag. Tryphón, made of ancient stone blocks. Set in the cypress groves, it is very picturesque, overlooking the Asopós Valley and south to the Phleiasian plain.

Ancient Phlious (Φλειούς) doesn't get a sign, although the entire valley was named after it. Phleiasian wine was famous all over ancient Greece, and some of its vines must have been the great-granddaddies of Nemea's *agiorgítiko* grapes. But *sic transeunt flores*... If you want to see the acropolis, it's just south of the road about 3.5km west of modern Nemea on the Pétri–Aidónia road, just before the turn-off to Dáphni. The little church of the Panagía on the hill marks the site of its ***asklepeion***.

The Corinthian Gulf Coast to Xilókastro

On the coastal strip, one town flows seamlessly into another, so much so that you can only tell you are in a centre when the cluster of shops selling food, clothes and agricultural products gets denser, the church gets bigger and an often spiffy-looking town hall appears. Mainly serving the farming communities of the fertile coastal plain, these market towns have slid into tourism by the accident of their proximity to Athens and their narrow shingle beaches. A villa went in here, then there, and then the weekenders wanted a coffee shop, a taverna, something to do, and suddenly the farmers who owned those sandy, infertile plots by the sea realized that they were onto a good thing. Condos and apartments sprang up like mushrooms and were snapped up by Athenians, so used to urban density that living in close quarters even in the country seemed normal and, at least here, there was a clean sea and no smog.

With its mélange of styles, the strip is a great place to see the natives in action. Every town is busily planting palm trees and enriching its facilities. Greeks, including all those prosperous farmers with the citrus groves, olive trees and market gardens behind the towns, are getting more demanding, too. Nor do these towns close down for the winter as they do in the south. Restaurants and bars line most beaches and change hands with the speed of light. Ask at your hotel to find the latest culinary hot spot or join the Greeks in their *vólta*, the evening stroll up and down the seafront, to find one that suits your fancy. The views over the Gulf of Corinth are spectacular and all towns are within easy distance of Sikyon, Stymphalía and Mount Kyllíni.

Kiáto (Κιάτο) is a prime example. Palms are going in everywhere, and the restaurant strip (2km west of town) gets ever more swish. It has a fair-sized port and processes currants, citrus fruits and tomatoes. The shopping centre is great fun too, especially on a Saturday when all the villagers come to town. But the main reason to come is Sikyon, one of the most spectacular minor archaeological sites in the Peloponnese.

Ancient Sikyon

Sikyon means 'Cucumberville' and is at its best in spring, when thousands of red poppies compete with other wild flowers to decorate the Hellenistic and Roman ruins. Homer called its lofty table land *evrichóro* or 'wide open', and stupendous views of the Corinthian Gulf and northern plain compete with those of the

Getting around the Corinthian Gulf Coast

Local **buses** serve the whole strip west from Corinth several times a day, as do **trains**.

Kiáto has an exit from the Corinth–Pátras toll road and, beside it, a new **train station** (**t** 1110), part of the suburban rail system. The **bus station** (**t** 274 202 2243) is in the town centre, with many connections both east and west. There is a bus three times daily to ancient Sikyon. **Taxis**: **t** 274 202 2600. The road for **ancient Sikyon**, 6km south, begins in Kiáto's central Plateía Ploumistoú, opposite the large brown and beige church of the Metamórphosis. It is not well signposted, but you know you're on the right track if you pass the Hotel Pappás. Or ask for the village of Vasilikó. Once outside Kiáto, the road is well marked; you know you've arrived when you see the museum.

Xilókastro has an exit from the toll road and a **train station**, **t** 274 302 2297, with trains several times a days from Athens and Pátras. **KTEL buses**, **t** 274 302 2218, arrive 14 times a day from Athens, and can take you to Corinth, Loutráki, and mountain villages such as Tríkala, Stymphalía and the Pheneós area. **Taxis** congregate in the main *plateía*, **t** 274 302 2663.

mighty Acrocorinth and Pendeskoufi etched on the eastern horizon. It is a lovely drive and the picturesque ancient theatre offers a perfect spot for a picnic.

Although Sikyon was too close to Corinth to break through into the top division of city-states, it wasn't for a lack of talent. It was here, or so they say, that Prometheus gave the gift of fire to brutish humankind. Herodotus wrote that Adrastos, the famous king of Argos (*see* p.275), had an important shrine in the *agora* of Sikyon, and some say that tragedy was born in the local choral recitals of Homeric verses in honour of the unfortunate hero.

Sikyon prospered under the rule of its first tyrant, **Orthagoras**, the son of a cook; his brother Myron built the famous Treasury at Delphi to commemorate his Olympic victory in 648 BC, putting Sikyon on the artistic map for the first, but not the last, time. In his *Politics*, Aristotle wrote that the tyranny of Orthagoras and his family was the longest-enduring of any in Greece, owing to their moderate behaviour (although other accounts describe Myron as an adulterer and rapist). Orthagoras' grandson **Kleisthenes** became prominent on a panhellenic scale after defending Delphi in the First Sacred War and winning the chariot races at Delphi and Olympia. His sympathy for the poor made him harsh to Sikyon's aristocrats, to the extent of breaking off ties with Argos and abolishing the cult of Adrastos (only to earn Delphi's disdainful opinion of the move: 'Adrastos was King of Sikyon, but you are merely a stone-thrower.'). Nevertheless, in 572 BC Kleisthenes held an old-fashioned Homeric competition for the hand of his daughter Agariste, drawing suitors from all over the Greek world, including one from Sybaris, Smindyrides, who was decadent even by Sybaritic standards, astonishing the locals with his entourage of a thousand attendants, including his own private fishermen, fowlers and chefs. But it was Megacles of Athens who won the tests of character, wisdom, athletics and Agariste's hand, and it was their son Kleisthenes who set Athens on the road to democracy (*see* pp.83–4). Old Kleisthenes' successor, Aeschines, was deposed in 556 BC, and afterwards Sikyon fell into the Spartan sphere.

This small city-state, growing olives and almonds, was one of the most important art centres in Greece. Aristocles, Kanachos, Polykleitos (some say) and Lysippos (Alexander's favourite sculptor) were natives who made its school of bronze-working famous. Its ceramics were famous into the Classical period, and Sikyon (like Corinth) was said to have invented drawing, a story supported by the discovery in the nearby Cave of Pitsá of a trove of painted wood panels from 530 BC (now in the National Archaeological Museum in Athens). In the Hellenistic era, it produced the painter Pamphilos, whose famously expensive school produced two of the most celebrated artists of the time, Apelles and Melanthios. Sikyon was even famous for its clothing and shoes.

Sikyon's most famous son was **Aratos**, who became a great leader of the Achaean League in 245 BC and navigated the dangerous water of Macedonian politics until his luck ran out and the Macedonian king ordered his death by poisoning. Sikyon then fell under the sway of Rome and hosted the Isthmian Games from 146 to 46 BC when Ísthmia lay in ruins. After that Sikyon seems to have simply faded gracefully into ruins around its Roman baths.

The Site and Museum

Sikyon Site and Museum
t 274 202 8900; open Tues–Sun 8.30–3; adm

Archaic and Classical Sikyon lay somewhere towards Vasilikó, until 303 BC, when Demetrios Poliorketes 'the Beseiger', son of Alexander's successor Antigonas of Syria, moved Sikyon to its present site for reasons of defence, although it is hard to imagine why. True, the triangular table land stands on small bluffs and has rivers both east and west, but the little acropolis doesn't look as if it could have held out under a serious siege.

Sikyon's **theatre** is small. Its side entrances at stage level are very well defined, as is its *skene* in front. Nine tiers of seats of the *koilon* are intact, as are many of the throne-like armchairs in the first row. There was an even shorter route to the theatre from the acropolis: two vaulted passages led to the upper seats, both of which can be clearly seen, especially the eastern one.

The dirt road just in front of the theatre ascends to the acropolis. Just beyond the theatre, a retaining wall of the stadium may be seen: downtown Sikyon was very compact. Go right on the first dirt road on the way up the hill and you come to the depression where the **stadium** was, on your left. The Roman baths, built in the 2nd and 3rd century AD, now house the attractive museum.

Cross the road from the museum, pass through a gate and on your left is the long, 125ft by 36ft foundation of an Archaic **temple**, which was here long before the city moved to join it. It may have been dedicated to Apollo. Beyond it to the right is the **gymnasium**, built on two levels, containing a well-preserved **fountain** with two columns on the landing to the upper level. Beyond the temple foundations in a straight line and a bit to the left is the square ***bouleuterion*** where 16 inner columns once supported the roof, and beside it a 350ft ***stoa*** that had 20 shops behind its double-columned porch.

Xilókastro

Xilókastro (Ξυλόκαστρο), the westernmost town on Corinthia's coastal strip, is in a class by itself. It has a lovely shingle beach on the east side of town, backed by 2km of peaceful pines, which the citizens voted to preserve early in the 20th century. That foresight alone sets Xilókastro apart. Two km west of the centre, along a beach road lined with restaurants and cafés, the **Marina Sports Complex** offers public clay tennis courts, and a lovely square pond with a tiny amphitheatre for concerts. Always a popular Greek resort, Xilókastro is encouraging foreign tourism, and succeeding, although some may think that the holiday apartments going in to accommodate foreigners and Greeks alike are becoming too dense and too many. One reason why is its beautiful mountain hinterland; you'll have to turn to the next chapter for that.

Panagía Faneroméni – A Warp in Time

There's an unusual sight on the outskirts of Xilókastro, 500m west of the toll road exit on the Old National Road: a large **basilica church** – in itself not unusual, but with a huge outdoor space or atrium defined by massive marble blocks. The marble lustral **basin** in the colonnaded courtyard is a perfect reproduction of the basins used for purification that once stood outside ancient temples (*see* p.154). Note the massive doors, resembling the ones that guard ancient Macedonian tombs. These accentuate the essential otherness of this church, begun in the 1970s by Father Nikkon, an unmarried village priest (but that is another story).

Panagía Faneroméni is still a work in progress. An array of glittering **mosaics** wait inside, replicating on one side the mosaics at Ravenna; others show the usual saints and images but, unlike most Greek churches, Christ rather than his mother has pride of place in the central apse. The marble iconostasis is as low as the altar rail in a Catholic church, and the pulpit is a miniature marble ambo with stairs, set amid the congregation. The whole, in fact, is as close to an intact early Christian church as you'll ever see. Father Nikkon has no time for domes, high iconostases, or Mary taking precedence over Jesus, and he has made it his life's work to recreate a 'proper' church, including the vast atrium, where the non-baptized could retire during the mystery of Communion. The cost of it all is almost as staggering as the concept, but donations come in and slowly every grey interior wall will be covered in mosaics. One will show the Ascension of Alexander the Great, a not unheard of but rare subject (there's one in St Mark's in Venice). Panagía Faneroméni is a delightful and impressive reminder that early churches incorporated compatible architectural and spiritual elements from ancient temples, and that Orthodoxy today, in spite of its seeming seamlessness, has plenty of room for individuality.

Useful Information along the Gulf Coast

Xilókastro Tours, 2 I. Ioánnou, **t** 274 302 4137, *www.xylokastrotours.gr*. Can help with room rentals, car hire, and excursions.

Where to Stay and Eat along the Gulf Coast

Vracháti ✉ 20006

Best Western Alkyon, 100m from the sea, **t** 274 105 2010, *www.alkyonhotel.gr* (€€€€/€€€). A tad hard to find, but all mod cons including underground parking and a pool in a lovely garden. *Open all year.*

Kokóni ✉ 20002

Karava's Village, **t** 274 203 2861 (€€/€€). Tucked between Vracháti and Nerántza, this little oasis with a pool is sometimes block-booked but well worth a call to see if they have any vacancies. *Open April–Oct.*

Periandros >>

Nerántza ✉ 20200

Nerántza, **t** 274 203 2329 (€€/€€). A moderate sized hotel right on the sea if a little crowded by adjacent buildings; has fridges, air conditioning and TVs. *Open all year.*

Kiáto ✉ 20200

Triton, 2 Metamorphosis, **t** 274 202 3421 (€€€/€€). By the port; the best on offer. All rooms have mini bars, TVs and air-conditioning. *Open all year.*

Touristiko Periptero >>
Karamaliki >

Karamaliki, 9 Miaoúli, on the waterfront, **t** 274 202 4000. Shaded by tamarisks, and much favoured by the locals who call it Angelo's, this is the place to head for. He often closes in the late afternoon for a siesta.

Ellinikon, in the centre, **t** 274 202 5026. This is the one for Greek cuisine.

Xilókastro ✉ 20200

Le Convivial,2 Vagená, **t** 27430 29103, *www.leconvivial.com* (€€€€€/€€€€€) Luxury suites, furnished with antiques from Tuscany and Umbria, and a spa.

Daphne's Club Apartments, on the east end of the forest, **t** 274 302 2966, *www.daphnesclub.com* (€€€€/€€). Spacious, well designed and equipped with large balconies, a stone's throw from the sea. Reserve. *Open all year.*

Fadira, 2 Ag. Makáriou, **t** 274 302 2648, *www.hotelfadira.gr* (€€€/€€). Friendly, functional pile with a bar and restaurant right by the waves. *Open May–Oct.*

Apollon, 105 Ioánnou, **t** 274 302 2239, *www.apollonxylokastro.gr* (€€/€€). Attractive neoclassical house and modern annexe, with a pool, surrounded by high hedges. A bargain for its class. *Open all year.*

Periandros, 3 Ag. Makáriou, **t** 274 302 2272 (€/€). Small, tidy, cheap and friendly, two steps from the sea. The café-restaurant (lunch only) is immersed in pines. *Open May–Oct.*

Xilókastro must have a mile of sea-front tavernas and restaurants all vying for your attention. They are popular and noisy, although things get quieter at the marina end. There is one really worth recommending, though, because of its setting and atmosphere:

Touristiko Periptero (aka Touristiko Pefkiás), 1 Karamanlís, **t** 274 302 8554. On the sea by the forest, lovely setting and ambience: well-run café and restaurant with reasonable prices and lovely cakes. There is parking, and showers on the beach. *Open all year.*

Achaía

Achaía, the Riviera of the Peloponnese, stretches along the north coast from Aigeíra to Kalógria. It possesses 'a strange, suggestive power,' according to Níkos Kazantzákis, 'something feminine, fecund and dangerously fascinating.' Much of this fascination is concentrated in eastern Achaía, where the coast, hemmed in by fantastical hills hedgehogged with pinnacles of stone and pine, is only a prelude to the enchantment of the mountains, so close and yet so rarely breached by foreign tourists.

The Gulf of Corinth, rimmed by formidable peaks on the north shore as well, resembles a majestic if slightly dishevelled Italian lake, one where seigneurial villas and gardens on the shore have been replaced by white Greek towns swathed in bougainvillaea, and vines, olives, and emerald citrus groves that produce lemons the size of Mohammed Ali's fist.

10

Don't miss

1. A railway trip through Heracles' spectacular gorge
Diakoftó railway p.189

2. Secrets revealed
Ancient Aigeira p.182

3. Sink holes, lovely views, and a monastery
Pheneós Valley p.177

4. A lost valley with a temple and cave lakes
Lousí p.193

5. Apollo's oracle under Parnassos
Delphi p.211

See map overleaf

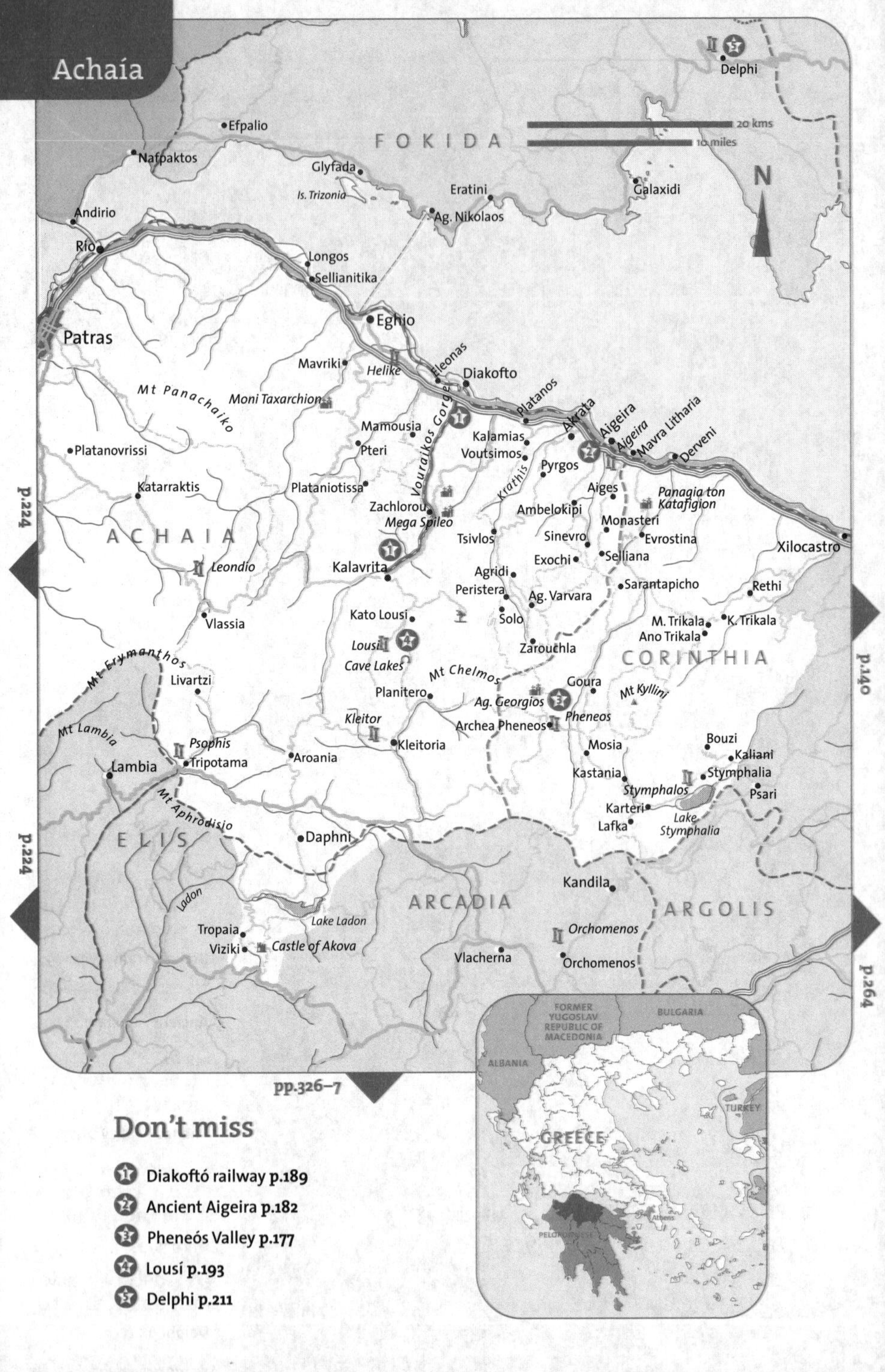

Don't miss

1. Diakoftó railway p.189
2. Ancient Aigeira p.182
3. Pheneós Valley p.177
4. Lousí p.193
5. Delphi p.211

The name Achaía was given to this area because so many Mycenaeans – Homer's Achaeans – came here as refugees after the lights went out in 1100 BC. They had plenty of talent – in Archaic times, they colonized Sybaris and Croton, two of the wealthiest and weirdest cities in Magna Graecia. Back home, Achaía managed to stay pretty much out of the history books until Hellenistic times, when its Achaean League, one of the only efforts at federalization ever attempted by the fractious Greek states, made both Sparta and Macedon sit up and take notice. In 245 BC, Aratus of Sikyon was its illustrious leader, and a parliament of member states was regularly convened in Éghio. The league could not unite sufficiently to counter the Romans, however, and in 146 BC they devoured the entire Peloponnese as *their* province of Achaía in the same half-baked way that they re-named all of Hellas 'Graecia' after the first tribe they met. The Franks followed suit when they, in turn, named the Peloponnese the principality of Achaía.

Modern Achaía, birthplace of some of the most significant figures in 20th-century Greece – George Papandréau senior and his enemy, George Papadópoulos, and Kostís Palamás (national poet and author of the 'Olympic Hymn', still performed at the Olympics today) – tends to get short shrift in books because it defies neat definitions and lacks a major brand-name attraction. Topographically and historically, it is a patchwork quilt of separate areas within separate areas. Even now, although politically a prefecture with its capital at Pátras, it is not a psychological unity. Eastern and western Achaía go their own ways. Alpine Achaía has far more in common geographically with alpine Corinth than it does with Pátras and the flat dunes and marshlands of western Achaía. And since no one travelling through mountain passes gives a fig about a prefecture's boundaries, Corinth's Mount Kyllíni is here, keeping company with its eastern Achaían cousins.

The North Peloponnesian Mountains: Off the Beaten Track

Speeding along the seaside highway between Xilókastro and Pátras, tourists note the crenellated and folded hillsides that make the north coast so attractive, and not much else. And yet, five minutes driving on any road south of the highway lies a magnificent and underexplored area of Greece. From east to west, the three great mountain ranges of **Kyllíni**, **Chelmós** and **Erýmanthos** line up, just waiting to be discovered. Back in the mists of geological time, Erýmanthos rolled over the Chelmós range and settled in its present location behind Pátras. The results of this geographical arabesque are everywhere in evidence.

How to Explore the Area

These mountains can be approached from any direction, but the easiest access is from the north coast. With the exception of the rail line to Kalávrita, all public transportation is by local buses or taxis. Coastal trains from Pátras to Kiáto are currently being upgraded to join the Proastiakós (Suburban Rail Line) to Athens. New tunnels, new tracks, and bridges may cause interruption of services. Inter-provincial buses on the toll road will drop you in (or in the vicinity of) coastal towns. Almost any of these can be used as a base for day trips. They stay open all year, and if their pebble beaches cannot rival the sandy beaches of the west coast, the swimming and the view across the Gulf are always wonderful. The sea is remarkably clean because so few of the worst floating polluters can navigate the Corinth canal.

Exploring can take longer than a map distance might suggest. Because all three mountain ranges are oriented north–south, travelling east and west usually involves detours in search of passes. That, of course, is part of the area's charm. To avoid the 'Cinerama Syndrome' where you drive all day, see lovely spots but have no time to enjoy them, consider either an early start or an overnight mountain stay.

For sheer variety of magnificent views in a short distance, it would be difficult to beat the north Peloponnese. Mountain villages sit precariously on heights, and ambush you in unexpected places as you turn corners on the twisting roads. And while small churches dot every Greek landscape, the ones you'll find here are particularly profuse and picturesque. Out-of-the-way archaeological sites can be visited in lonely splendour: rivers rush through the valleys even in the heat of summer, while, all along the Corinthian Gulf, busy towns are set on small coastal plains formed by mountain streams on their way to the sea.

These three mountain ranges are user-friendly; high, at about 7,500ft, but not too high, wild and rugged in places, but not inaccessible, sparsely populated, but not deserted, and crisscrossed by an impressive network of roads, most of which are passable except in the dead of winter. Lotus-eaters can explore while staying in comfort by the sea; the more adventurous can find rooms in the mountain villages. Walkers and cyclists at all levels can find the right mountain to climb or an easy stretch to saunter. You can even ski. And best of all, you can pick and choose what to do. It is hard to find a road not worth taking.

Another plus is the people, lovely and hard-working who, except in the coastal areas, are not yet inured to tourists. That fact alone makes the mountain villages a pleasure. Stops at village coffee shops should be an important part of the itinerary. Most of these watering holes resolutely turn their backs on the view and look inward, at the single main road running through the village, a fact that puzzles first-timers to Greece. But working in the fields offers quite enough vistas for the inhabitants, so when relaxing they would rather focus on each other and see who is going where with whom. When you stop to have a coffee or ouzo, and people-watch, you will notice that the villagers are sitting there having a good look at you, too. This is the perfect moment to haul out the phrase book and say hello. More often than not, someone will speak English anyway. These villages are just isolated enough to have fascinating local histories. If you do find English-speakers, from Chicago, or Sydney, or wherever, make the most of it and ask them about their village.

Mount Kyllíni

Born at the dawning of day, at midday he played the lyre, and in the evening he stole the cattle of far-shooting Apollo.

Homeric hymn to Hermes

Kyllíni (Κυλλήνη), with its twin peaks and two names, crowns western Corinthia, its foothills dipping into Achaía as far as Aigeíra. Known as Mount Zíria in the days before independence, its ancient name was restored by the Greek government as part of its effort to make the modern map reflect the Classical period. Sometimes these new 'old' names stuck, sometimes they didn't; co-ordinating your map with the names used by locals can be an adventure. Kyllíni/Zíria settled for both and the names are used interchangeably.

In ancient times, this mountain and these foothills were sacred to **Hermes**. The son of Zeus and the nymph Maia, he was born on Kyllíni, and after driving Apollo's cattle from Thessaly to Olympia he hopped back in the cradle and pretended to be a regular old baby until Zeus forced him to confess himself as a cattle-rustler; to make it up with Apollo he gave him the lyre he had just invented from a tortoise shell. **Hermes' birth cave** is off the road, half an hour's walk from the Alpine Club refuge. No one has bothered to signpost it, but ask any local for the '*speeliá tou Ermí*'. Some think that the god's name originated from the word 'wind', and that he started his career as a mountain-haunting wind spirit. Sit under any plane tree in the mountains and you'll understand why; the wind sings through its branches, a unique, soporific and soothing sound. Perhaps it was this manifestation of Hermes that led to his skill in charming even the gods to sleep. So while visiting Mount Kyllíni, try some of the local retsina, spinach pie or roast lamb, lie back under the trees and see what happens.

Áno Tríkala, the Convent, and the Ring Road

There are several Tríkala villages on the road, but the one to aim for is just below the western summit of Mount Kyllíni: little **Áno Tríkala** (Υνω Τρίκαλα), occupying a spectacular 3,600ft balcony overlooking the Gulf of Corinth. In spite of its position on the north face of the mountain, it catches the winter sun all day. Fruit and nut trees surround it; beneath them lie acres of terraced grape vines, and below these stretch the olives, and then the orange and lemon groves of the river valley, the entire spectrum of Greek agriculture spread at your feet. Just behind you, the scenery switches as abruptly as a stage set to dense spruce and pine forest,

Getting to and around Mount Kyllíni

By **car**, Kyllíni's most accessible route is from Xilókastro (*see* p.167). The road that leads to the toll road will take you to the Tríkalas, through curious sandy cliffs and dune-like hills which extend along the coast for miles. Beyond Ríza (Ρίζα) a secondary road goes up to Pelléne, above which lie the scarce ruins of ancient Pellene, a member of the Achaean League and a site for the cognoscenti. The Pelléne side road joins the Tríkala road farther up the mountain.

A **bus** from Xilókastro, **t** 274 302 2218, goes up to Áno Tríkala at 5.30am and 12.30pm but only on Fridays, returning to Xilókastro almost immediately each time. Consider a **taxi**.

---

even more dramatic in winter when covered in snow. This unique overview made Áno Tríkala a resort in the early 1900s; the stone shell of a hotel built in 1934, which saw the likes of King Farouk of Egypt and King Paul of Greece, is being renovated to cash in on the mountain village mini-boom. Stone weekend houses are sprouting up to replace the ruins of the many abandoned houses, and mountain inns are added yearly.

If the year-round residents' houses seem architecturally cacophonous, not to say ugly, in comparison, therein lies a reality of the Greek character and a village economy that has operated up until the present. Thirty years ago, a bare reinforced concrete balcony or naked brick bathroom tucked up against the old stone house made life easier, and aesthetics be damned. Greece has hitherto been a cash economy. People added what they could afford, and if that was not a lot, they began and then...waited. That is why so many homes of the older villages all over the Peloponnese seem perpetually *in medias res*. Villagers used to laugh outright when visitors told them about the 30-year mortgages on their finely finished homes. To them, this was not ownership at all; it was debt, a pitiful situation that only a fool would willingly accept. Times have changed but these proud debtless owners may yet have the last laugh.

No Greek mountain village would be complete without a huge spreading plane tree, a fountain or running water, a crispness and clarity in the air and a little stone church. Look for those immediately east of Áno Tríkala's old hotel. The tiny church of **Ag. Nikólaos** was built in 1750 and is unusual because a residence was added on to the back; take a close look at its little arched doorway and you will see a small hole in the stone lintel. This was to accommodate a rifle barrel poked through from the upstairs room, aimed to blow an unwelcome visitor to smithereens: Greek hospitality is legendary, but it had its limits and was rarely extended to the Turks. The small windows are typical of old mountain houses. In times of trouble, these villages became armed camps. Each man's house, no matter how small, was his fortress.

Ag. Vlasíou
t 274 309 1210

A road winds up through the forest to the wealthy convent of **Ag. Vlasíou** (Αγ. Βλασσίου), just one km above Áno Tríkala, which

Where to Stay and Eat around Mount Kyllíni

Áno/Méso Tríkala ✉ 20400

Katafígio Ermís, Áno Tríkala, **t** 274 309 1121, *www.katafigioermis.gr* (€€€€€/€€€€). Nine cabins at the top of the village, each with its own fireplace. The restaurant serves good home cooking: try any lamb dish or spinach pie. *Open Sept–May.*

Helydorea, Méso Tríkala, **t** 274 309 1444, *www.helydorea.gr* (€€€€/€€). The first of the many elegant stone-built inns now in town, all perfect down to the duvets on their brass beds; fireplaces in the suites for four and biologically grown local wine. As with many mountain inns, prices plummet in midweek and summer. *Open all year.*

Mysaion, Méso Trikala, **t** 274 309 1141, *www.mysaion.gr* (€€€/€€). In the traditional style, run by Greek-Americans; it has a restaurant, and a fireplace in each room. *Open all year.*

Ta Tríkala, Áno Tríkala, **t** 274 309 1260 (€€/€). Mr Korkari's modest hotel in the centre is not at all fancy, but has good-sized rooms, balconies, minibars and fireplaces in the big dining room. *Open all year.*

There are two mountain refuges on Kyllíni-Zíria. Book in advance through the **Corinth Mountain Club** (31 Ag. Pávlos, Corinth 20100, **t** 274 102 5694) and the **Eghion Mountain Club** (Éghio 25100, **t** 269 1022 308).

Psistariá Apostóli Deláris, Áno Tríkala, **t** 274 309 1358. The villages are full of small *psistariás*. This one is popular with the locals and day-trippers. *Open all year.*

boasts a pretty garden, picnic tables, water, a lovely view and an icon of the saint dating from 1400, responsible for many healing miracles. The nuns are in residence only at weekends during the winter, preferring a warmer setting near the sea during the week, something of a new wrinkle in the monastic tradition. The road continues on to two **refuges** run by the Greek Alpine Club, resting under Kyllíni's western summit. The walk to the highest **peak** (7,130ft) takes about two hours from the refuge. A 28km, as yet unpaved ring road around the western peak starts from the first mountain refuge (the road is newly paved to here), perfect for mountain- or motor-bikes, walkers or four-by-fours. Mountain bikers say the easiest way is clockwise. Unpaved tracks diverge from it to points south and west, but are not always passable by car. Two small mountain lakes, which dry up in the summer, can be reached on foot from the first mountain refuge or by car, one from each of the roads branching out and up above Ag. Vlasíou.

Stymphalía and Pheneós: Where Still Waters Run Deep

Tucked around Mount Kyllíni's southern slopes, the Stymphalía and the Pheneós valleys are so close together that if you stand on the road to the Xénia Hotel above Kastaniá you can look down into both of them from the same vantage point. These unusual valleys are prime examples of a peculiarly Peloponnesian phenomenon:

Getting to and around Stymphalía and Pheneós

One daily **bus**, leaving from Kiáto at 12.30pm, **t** 274 202 2240, passes through Stymphalía's villages, up to Kastaniá and over to Mosiá (Μοσιά) until Goúra (Γούρα).

Cars can come from Nemea or coastal Dervéni via Rozená (Ροζενά), from coastal Xilókastro via Zemenó (Ζεμενό), or from the more travelled Kiáto road via Soúli (Σούλι) and Kaliáni (Καλιάνοι). Main roads are reasonably well signposted. From Kaliáni, it's a 4.5km drive up to the village of Boúzi (Μπούζι), from where you can hike up to Kyllíni's eastern peak. It is possible to reach Pheneós from the Kalávrita–Trípolis road via the Pheneós pass from the west. A good paved road links Stymphalian Kartéri and Phenean Mosiá.

water from the mountains runs down to form lakes, their size depending on how much of the water finds its way out through porous limestone passages called *katavóthres* (sink holes or dolines). If these work well, the result is flat, usable and very fertile land around a lake that is substantial in spring and sometimes non-existent by autumn. Catastrophe can and does occur if these sink holes become blocked.

In ancient times both valleys harboured cities by their respective lakes and flooding was attributed to the gods. One legend has it that an angry Artemis blocked the sink hole at Stymphalía with wood because her worship was not being properly observed. Only when a hunter, following a fleeing deer into the rising water, was swept up and carried down into the earth was her thirst for revenge satisfied and the drain cleared. Today blockages are attributed to earthquakes or human carelessness, and the sink holes are covered with grilles to prevent hunters, deer or anything else from being washed down. Both valleys can be visited in a day – enough to see, but not to explore, and they are worth exploring. The lakes look their best in the spring, but any time is good for the scenery.

The Stymphalía Valley

Stymphalía is rimmed by Mount Trachí on the south, Mount Pharmakás to the east and towering Mount Kyllíni to the west, but is more open to the north, where a series of cultivated valleys shelve down towards the reed-ringed shallow lake. In spring it measures about 2km by 6km, culminating in the west under **Láfka** (Λάυκα) and **Kartéri** (Καρτέρι). A ring road now circles the lake.

Stymphalía saw one of the **Labours of Heracles**. Foul-smelling man-eating birds, so numerous they blotted out the sky whenever they rose from their marshy roosts, were terrorizing the inhabitants with impunity because their formidable beaks, claws and feathers were made of bronze. Heracles outsmarted them by shaking rattles made by Hephaestos and then shooting them with arrows as they rose up in confusion. Today the lake is home to herons and other species of birds now protected from hunters. The only 'monsters' to look out for are the many snakes that sun themselves on the rocks surrounding the lake in spring. If you haven't any rattles, just make noise.

Ancient Stymphalos stood on the lake's west side, on a low hill immediately south of the prominent ruins of the 13th-century **Cistercian abbey church**. Classical stones abound in this Frankish ruin. There is no sign, but you can reach the low **acropolis** by turning east on the first dirt road south of the church. At times, the ruins are partly submerged in the lake. Artemis' Sanctuary and Temple, described by Pausanias, must have been somewhere here. Its roof was festooned with statues of the Stymphalian birds, which were imagined to look rather like egrets. These temples must have been wonderful sights when they were freshly painted in bold bright colours, decorated with statues of local heroes or legends, much the same way as churches today depict their patron saints.

Ancient Stymphalians seemed to have birds on their mind. Pausanias recorded that behind the temple there were white statues of virgins with birds' legs. It is hard to know which detail is more interesting, his confident identification of statues as 'virgins', or the fact that humans were sporting ornithological appendages. These less than anthropomorphic details are a reminder that this city was part of Arcadía in the old days, and primitive Arcadía is the home of gods who did not quite evolve to human form.

Not a very dependable water source in recent years, the lake dried up completely in the summers of 1997 and 1998. When it filled up again in 1999, it was immediately full of good-sized fish, which puzzled the locals. Their theory is that there must be underground reservoirs where the fish can survive, but no one is sure where they are.

The Pheneós Valley

3 Pheneós Valley

The wild and spectacular Pheneós valley is entirely hemmed in by high mountains – Kyllíni on the east and the highest and most rugged peaks of Chelmós on the west. Pheneós' present lake is much smaller than Stymphalía's, although the long valley floor is as flat as an ironing board, a sure indication that it has been much bigger at times. The mountains, especially to the southwest, have a water line marking a previous level of the lake, looking for all the world like a bathtub ring. Its sink holes are in the south and southwest corners. The villages, all well above the old water line, are working villages, with beautiful stone houses and churches built hard up against a garage, a cement and brick bungalow with flat roof and rusting iron rods for a projected second floor, or a chicken shed, typical of prosperous farming communities that expanded in the 1960s and '70s. The major crop is potatoes. There are lots of shepherds too.

Ancient Pheneos is a knob-like hill at the north end, in front of the village of **Kalívi** which now calls itself 'Ancient Pheneós'. There are various ancient stones and excavated pits, all pretty obscure except to archaeologists. Pheneans claimed that Heracles passed a winter here between Labours, piercing the valley's sink holes and dredging a channel to drain the plain while fathering yet another local mini-hero on a princess – altogether a Phenean version of the American folk hero Paul Bunyan, with a libido as big as Babe, his blue ox and sidekick. Certainly traces of an ancient drainage effort have been detected in aerial photographs. Apparently Odysseus also visited and was so impressed by the flat grassland that he established a herd of horses here. But Pheneós, like Stymphalía, was Arcadian, and Arcadians in particular had a tendency to claim just about any god or hero as their own, or at least as a visitor.

Hermes was worshipped here, of course, since he was born on Mount Kyllíni, and games were held in his honour. Demeter's sanctuary contained a rock with a cunningly fashioned top housing a sacred mask which the priest wore once a year while beating the ground with rods. This primitive fertility ritual had its roots in the deep past. Anyone swearing an oath in Pheneos swore 'by the rock'. Alas, it is no more, not even in the tiny museum of ancient Pheneos, which is hardly open anyway.

The valley boasts a delightful spot of relatively recent origin. On a pine-clad mountainside, a short drive north of ancient Pheneos (well signposted: Μον Αγ. Γεωργίου), is the large 18th-century **Monastery of Ag. Geórgios**, rugged and not at all dressed up for tourists. The beams supporting its overhanging third floor are made from large, naturally curved boughs. The inner courtyard has a rough wooden cross with no decoration at all, quite a rarity in Greece. The buildings look older than the date would suggest, and its four sides enclose a small church. The tiny cells with their low doorways are many, and recently the last three monks to use them have seen their numbers swell because the monastery is undergoing renovations. The small door to the church is one-third elaborately carved wood and two-thirds bronze, embossed with St George, in relief, slaying the dragon. The frescoes of 1768 are worth a look, but today it is the setting that sets this monastery apart, as well as the monks' love for their cats. They are known to hang a long woven rug out of the window, so that their tabbies can grab hold and climb in when the big doors are locked.

A good-sized artificial lake has been created just below, putting the small chapel of **Ag. Nikólaos** on a tiny islet, reached by a short causeway from the shore. It is a beautiful sight.

Where to Stay in Stymphalía and Pheneós

Stymphalía/Pheneós Valleys ✉ 20016

Xenía Kastaniá, Kastaniá, **t** 274 706 1283, *www.xeniakastania.gr/hotel.php* (€€€/€€). An attractive stone hotel set high in the forest above the village with a big reception area and stone fireplace. *Open all year.*

To Kartéri, Kartéri, **t** 274 703 1203, *www.agrotourismos.com.gr* (€€/€€). Simple, clean rooms. Mrs Dalavángkas radiates competence and good cheer. New rooms out back (*expensive in winter, moderate in summer*) have kitchens and fireplaces. *Open all year.*

Xenónas Seméli >

Xenónas Seméli, Goúra, **t** 274 705 1319, *www.hotelsemeli.gr* (€€/€€) A new guesthouse with 10 good rooms in town with a fabulous view over the Pheneós valley. There's a lovely terrace for coffee breaks as well. *Open all year.*

To Stéki, Kastaniá, **t** 274 706 1270 (€€/€). At the top of the village; a bit impersonal but with five big rooms, balconies, views, and a good restaurant with fireplace. *Open all year.*

Eating Out in Stymphalía and Pheneós

There are restaurants and cafes around Stymphalía and two or three in Goúra as well.

Leonídas, Kartéri, **t** 274 703 1203. Good country food and huge barrels of local wine.

To Patrikó, Kaliáni, **t** 274 702 2224. Old-fashioned service and good food in a newly renovated taverna.

South of Dervéni: Evrostína and Two Churches with a Difference

Just west of coastal Dervéni, a road branches south via **Rozená** (Ροζενά) and climbs up 12km to **Evrostína** (Ευροστίνα), or Zácholi as the locals call it. This area was called the Switzerland of the Peloponnese until the devastating fire of 2000. Evrostína itself was spared and offers an attractive millpond, a cool shady path beside its stream, restaurants and, in June, the best cherries anywhere. It also offers two unique churches with fascinating stories.

Two and a half kilometres north of Evrostína on the edge of a sharp turn, an arched gateway in natural stone has a sign saying Παναγία των Καταφυγείων, which could easily be dismissed as just a rather grandiose roadside shrine. But if you walk through the gate, and down and down a narrow path, you will soon catch sight of the white walls and red roof of **Panagía ton Katafigíon**, Our Lady of Refuge. This is a church with a difference. Built into a cleft in a sheer limestone rock face, it is definitely not for vertigo-sufferers. The famous hanging monasteries of Metéora in northern Greece come to mind, but this one has as much sheer rock above it as below. Clinging to the cliff, totally hidden from the road, it would seem like an early medieval monastery or hermitage for a misanthropic saint. But no. It was built in the 1780s. A decade earlier, the Russians under Orlov had entered the Peloponnese to 'liberate' the Greeks from the Turkish yoke. Like so many other foreign efforts, this one was half-hearted and lasted only until Catherine the Great kissed and made up with the Sultan. Turkish reprisals began, and the soldiers were ordered to wipe out all mountain bastions of resistance. The villagers fled into this valley and took up residence for years in the many caves that dot the cliff.

Our Lady of Refuge was built to answer the need of every Greek community, no matter where, to have a church. It was deserted after the people returned to their villages, but is now being restored and visitors are welcome. From the ante-room, before the church itself, you can ascend a metal staircase (if you dare) into one of the large cave refuges. They were once reached by wooden ladders as depicted in the wonderful painting at the road entrance. The church itself is tiny, modest in the extreme, but still containing the little silver *támata* votives with arms, legs and other appendages that attest to miracles or hoped-for ones. A sign in Greek asks visitors to snuff out candles before leaving, a wise precaution given the isolation. As you climb back up to the road and through the gateway again, the reason for its large size, incorporating a stand for votive candles, becomes clear. Many elderly who would like to pay their respects could not possibly make the steep 15-minute trek down to the church.

Beautiful **Ag. Geórgios** in Evrostína is a 'gift' of the Turkish occupation, too, but in a very different way. In the 18th and early 19th centuries, Evrostína was a thriving community with a population of over 6,000 and no church large enough to house them all. This suited the Turks fine. Their strange relationship with Orthodoxy was a matter of policy. As long as the Church kept the Greeks in line, they tolerated it, but church-building permits were hedged with restrictions either to discourage construction or to ensure that churches remained tiny. If a permit could be wrested from the Turkish government at Corinth, it was a 40-day permit only. If the basic church construction, walls and roof, were not completed in 40 days, then the church was razed to the ground or, worse, turned into a mosque. No construction was allowed after sunset. The Evrostinians got their permit, and cleverly built only one third of the church, ensuring that the Turks would order its destruction. Whereupon they carefully numbered the dismantled stones and hid them in village houses. They then applied for another permit starting from 1 June 1811, the month with the longest daylight hours. This gave them a head start for a truly ambitious project – a sublime monument to their Maker and a splendid rebuke to the Turks.

It was to be 98ft by 50ft, and to have 17 cupolas or *troulí*: 12 for the Apostles, four for the Evangelists and one for God. The plan came from a Greek architect in Constantinople, and is so unusual that it is still studied at the Athens Polytechnical School; the only similar one is on the island of Sými. In 39 days, the church that you see now was built. A chain of 1,000 men passed each stone from hand to hand from the quarry; sandstone was chosen for its lightness and the relative ease with which it could be worked. The massive iconostasis was carved from a single tree and is ornate even by Greek standards. Note the 'flames' supporting religious icons and the censers suspended from the beaks of eagles. If the priest is not there, Ag. Geórgios is locked, although it doesn't hurt to check the back door. Keys can be got from Mr Golfinópoulos' *psistariá* in the village at the base of the long staircase to the church. A road winds up to the church as well if those stairs intimidate. And besides Golfinópoulos', you can have lunch at Evrostína at **H Zachóli** and even sleep over at the town's *xenónas*.

H Zachóli
t 274 303 2847

Xenónas
t 274 303 2122

Between Kyllíni and Chelmós: Akráta and Ancient Aigeira

Seaside Akráta makes an ideal base for delving into the mountains. Aigeíra, one of the most attractive ancient sites in Achaía, is close by, as is the hellbent river Styx.

Akráta and Around

Akráta (Ακράτα) is a town that leaves you wondering if developers have any sense at all. Twenty-five short years ago, there were two or three buildings by the sea. The rest of the town was three kilometres inland. During the tourist boom of the late 1970s and early '80s, everyone who owned a piece of seaside land decided to cash it in all at once, and the results are only too evident. Now Akráta has huge apartment blocks, three supermarkets, banks, a little shopping centre, very trendy coffee shops, night spots, an outdoor cinema, and a short six-week season during which all of those apartments fill up. Having said that, there are pluses. Akráta has a beautiful curving pebble beach, and the mountains offer a stupendous backdrop. It is lively during the summer and businesses still function in the off season when it becomes a very nice town indeed. Seven km west of Akráta, on the hillside, the picturesque village of **Plátanos** (Πλάτανος) overlooks the sea and has managed to remain more traditional in spite of the many new villas sprouting up.

The Mountains Southeast of Akráta: Ancient Aigeira

One of the 12 great cities of the Achaean League, Aigeíra occupies an isolated hillside overlooking the Gulf of Corinth. The Roman port, still visible at present day Mávra Lithária, is nearly 3km from the theatre. The space in between was all part of the city, currently

Getting to Akráta and Aigeira

If you are travelling by **car**, **Akráta** has an exit from the toll road. There is a **train** station, **t** 269 603 1291, 500m from the centre (there's a card-operated phone at the station to call a taxi). An hourly **bus** between Pátras and Athens will leave you on the toll road, not far from the town **taxi** stand, **t** 269 603 1892. Local buses operate several times a day to/from Éghio. Get tickets for Éghio, Kalávrita, Athens or Pátras at the newspaper shop cum KTEL station of Ioánna Roumeliótis; near the traffic lights in Akráta, **t** 269 603 1204.

There is a **bus service** to Selliána at 6am and at 1.30 pm on Tuesday and Thursdays from the KTEL cum newspaper shop of Mr Doúmouras in **Aigeíra**, **t** 269 603 1022. It is possible to ride to ancient Aigeira on the ascent, view the site, and return as the bus descends from Selliána. For a **taxi** in Aigeíra: **t** 269 603 2433. By **car**, go 1km east of modern Aigeíra and past the river, where a sign (Αιγές 9, Μοναστήρι 14, Σελιάνα 18) directs you left and left again under the road and railway, and then up towards ancient Aigeira. Set your kilometre gauge to zero under the railway bridge; 5.2km places you directly behind the theatre on your left exactly at the point where the paved road turns south. At this spot, a small dirt road descends towards the sea (hopefully the sign προς Αρχαίο θεατρο ('to the ancient theatre') will still be there).

being excavated at a snail's pace by the Austrian School. A Mycenaean palace-like structure graced its acropolis, but we will have to take the archaeologists' word for that.

History

Little has been written about Aigeira except by Polybios and Pausanias in the Roman period. This is typical of many ancient cities in Achaía: a lot went on, but no one recorded it. As late as 688 BC, the city was called Hyperesia and as such you'll find it in the Homeric list of ship-senders to Troy. How it became Aigeira is a lesson in ancient military tactics: the Sikyonians, informed that the bulk of the Hyperesian army was off on a foray, massed by the sea near the city preparing for a dawn attack. The fast-thinking Hyperesians herded all of their nanny goats on to the city walls and paraded them about with torches attached to their horns. The Sikyonians took one look at the torchlight parade, assumed reinforcements had arrived, packed it in and went home. In inter-city raids, discretion was often considered the better part of valour. In honour of their close call, the Hyperesians renamed their town Aigeira, its root meaning being 'goat', and planned a new temple to Artemis, to whom they attributed the success of their plan. To determine its location, they let the beautiful lead nanny goat wander about and built the temple where she sat down to rest. This temple has yet to be found, perhaps because no one has considered borrowing a nanny goat and having another go.

Ancient Aigeira
the gardening guard Lítsa Demopoúlou, ***t*** *269 603 1717, is normally there Tues–Sun 9–2.30; 9–6 in July and Aug but suggests that you ring first to be safe; at other times the site is fenced in but visible*

The Site

The **theatre** was built around 280 BC. The orchestra and most of the seats were chiselled directly into the rock on the slope, so their outline becomes a little fuzzier each year as rain and wind erode it. In its heyday it seated 10,000. Like most theatres in Greece it reflects Roman alterations, distinguished by the brickwork. The acoustics are wonderful, and the view from the centre of the top row is magnificent. The mountains of Parnassos and Helicon to the north, 'stretched out like naked athletes' as Kazantzákis wrote, provide a purple-tinted backdrop to the Gulf of Corinth.

Just in front of the theatre are several **basins** in a row, protected by a tile roof. Water was fed into the first basin by a single pipe, filling it until it overflowed into the second basin, then into the third, and draining away only after having passed through the entire row. There was no technological reason why these basins could not each have had their own water supply and drain, and yet the same system existed in surrounding villages until very recently, as in Plátanos. One was expected to wash what was dirtiest at the farthest basin and move up to the one nearest the water source in methodical stages. This must have led to 'kitchen sink' dramas more immediate and gripping than anything offered on the big stage to the south. Older villagers today will tell you that anyone jumping the queue was grist for the gossip mill and immediately labelled a *kakí neekokeirá* (bad housekeeper), still about the worst label a woman can acquire in a small Greek village. Only indoor plumbing ended the 2,500-year run of this type of local communal washing area, just one more example of the unchanging fabric of everyday life in Greece, especially evident in mountain villages built on ancient settlements. In some ways, this adherence to tradition is more impressive than a temple or statue could ever be.

Besides the theatre, the largest structures are the two **temples** to its left, both covered by an unattractive tent to preserve their plaster. In the larger temple, a huge marble head of Zeus was found, now in the archaeological museum of Athens. It is unclear whether either of these temples was actually dedicated to Zeus, despite the discovery of the head. It seems too large for this temple, but then again in Hellenistic times, large statues were in vogue. In front of the theatre and to the right as you face the Gulf is the more evocative waist-high ruin of the tiny **Temple to Fortune**, with hollows for the nine small statues mentioned by Pausanias. Tyche or Fortune is one of the most appealing goddesses, and the enthusiasm with which she was worshipped is a reflection of the fatalism mixed with hope that is still so much a part of the Greek character. Temples to Fortune sprang up with particular frequency in the Hellenistic and Roman period when life was very precarious and worshipping Lady Luck seemed as good a way as any to keep body and soul together. There is something very 'human' about the scale of this temple, rather like the many tiny Orthodox churches scattered about today's Achaía.

Move south through the fields towards the sea: that flat area you see low on the horizon from behind the guard's kiosk is the **Agora**, which is still largely unexcavated. Notice that the retaining walls of the descending fields are quite often ancient walls, and some small 'fields' are actually enclosed by the foundation walls of a large building, their 'gates' an ancient doorway.

To walk up to the **acropolis**, follow the first sign on the road (as you approach the site) that says 'Mycenaean Acropolis', then clamber up a road built between the remains of the city walls, some of which have crumbled picturesquely beneath a pine tree. The view is excellent, but the ruins are hard to decipher. Water was brought by an aqueduct from farther up the mountain and collected in the clay **cistern** covered with a tile roof. A bit of it forms the back wall of a small farmhouse on the left of the road, less than a kilometre beyond the theatre. Water is still brought down the mountains to the lower villages, only now in ubiquitous serpentine black hoses that slither down most of these mountain roads.

Vlovoká, Monastéri and Selliána

The road continues south to **Vlovoká** (Βλοβοκά), spectacularly situated at the base of a massive reddish cliff-face. This escarpment is a remnant of the huge, Nile-like fan delta that graced this area aeons ago and deposited the fantastical, dune-like hills you see along the coast from Xilókastro to Akráta, along with the aggregate rock of the theatre. Vlovoká guarded the southern pass into the mountains and, if you look carefully, you will spot a classical wall supporting a flat threshing floor and three tall cypress trees just north of the first houses. This platform offers an unobstructed view of the ancient acropolis and the pass, and was no doubt a look-out post in the old days. The view can be duplicated in comfort at the little summer coffee shop by the church lower down in the village.

Vlovoká, like so many places in the Peloponnese, has recently been renamed after a nearby ancient settlement and is now called **Aigés** (Αιγές) on many maps. Most villagers persist in calling it Vlovoká, a name with a less grand but more interesting pedigree. It is related to the word 'damaged': in the past, people with contagious diseases were left here to fend for themselves in the perpetual winter shade of the cliff-face. The custom of isolation, in the case of tuberculosis, persisted into the 19th century. Renaming villages in Greece is a pervasive and ongoing process; most small towns have probably changed their name at least once, and sometimes more often depending on invasions or even political whims. Someone once said that to have a place named after you in Greece was nothing; to have it stay named after you was a miracle. Continue past Vlovoká and you come to **Monastéri** (Μοναστήρι) whose monastery is not especially beautiful or old, but, like every other of its kind in Greece, shows real genius in its placement. A cypress-lined path leads up to it. There are two tavernas in town if you feel peckish.

Transhumance, Then and Now

Most Achaían villages over the 2,600ft mark are virtually deserted in winter, filling up again in spring and summer, reflecting the ancient transhumance patterns that probably go right back to Neolithic times. Shepherds and farmers stayed in villages like Selliána for the summer grazing months and went down to the coastal plains with their flocks for the winter. Therefore, mountain Selliána became seaside Sellianníitika ('little Selliána'), mountain Porovítsa became seaside Porovítsina, and so on. This phenomenon explains some of the similar-sounding names on the map of the Peloponnese. It also explains why so many Greeks have more than one house.

Many mountain houses were abandoned along with this way of life, but have now been bought by city folks, and are being renovated as summer retreats, thus reviving transhumance, albeit in another form. A walk through Selliána or almost any mountain village will reveal handfuls of these sometimes tacky, but usually lovely, reconstructions. They have added life again, at least in summer, to many villages which were practically abandoned a few short years ago.

The road continues to the village of **Selliána** (Σελλιάνα), placed at the north end of a lovely alpine valley. In Selliána traces of **ancient Phelloe** can easily be seen by the church of **Ag. Vassílios** in the lower village. Apparently Phelloe was a substantial town; inscriptions at Delphi record the gifts it sent. There is a push by classicists to rename the village Phelloe and to get rid of its present Slavic name, but 'Selliána' is winning out at the moment. Like so many Achaían towns at this altitude (2,600ft), Selliána is lush and well-watered, an oasis surrounded by sterner, barren peaks. The bowl-shaped valley, planted with fruit and walnut trees, is wonderful for walking or cycling. For a good view of the valley, either walk up on the small dirt road opposite the *kafeneíon* for five minutes, or drive to **Perithóri** (Περιθώρι), which hugs the mountain to the south.

Beyond Selliána

From the Selliána valley, the adventurous can try the road east to Pheneós via **Sarantápicho** (Σαραντάπηχο), or west to **Ag. Varvára** (Αγ. Βαρβάρα) and **Zaroúchla** (Ζαρούχλα), via **Exochí** (Εξοχή). Be warned; these are unpaved, seldom travelled roads, and, though passable, they are not usually in great shape after heavy rain, and should probably only be attempted by car in summer. See what the local Toyotas and Datsuns are doing. In the summer months, it is possible to return from Selliána to modern Aigeíra via **Sinevró** (Σινεβρό), **Óasi** (Οαση) and **Ambelókipi** (Αμπελόκηποι). It is paved except for the bit to Sinevró. There, pay a visit to the tiny and exquisite Armenian church built by Martik Manikián, a Greek architect of Armenian descent. Churches with pointed domes and handmade stained glass in the Art Nouveau style are thin on the ground in Greece, not to mention the eagles on the altar. He has beautifully renovated several houses and created a cantilevered balcony over the gorge as well. The church is on his property but he has so far always welcomed tactful visitors.

Where to Stay and Eat around Akráta

Akráta has the lock on seaside hotels and they are open all year. Akráta's beach is about 1km long, and crowded with fast food, cafés and restaurants, so a half-hour *vólta* will reveal all its charms. In July and August the shore road is closed in the evening, making it all much nicer.

Akráta ✉ 25006

Akráta Beach, t 269 603 1180, *www.akratabeach.gr* (€€€/€€). In the middle of the seaside strip, fully renovated; the rooms have all mod cons and the seaside café is a local favourite. Ask for a quieter room at the back.

Antónios Stravrópoulos, t 269 603 2339, *www.antonios-hotelrooms.gr* (€€€/€€). Ten apartments on the strip, with kitchens, TV, air-conditioning and parking.

Xenónas Melíti, t 269 603 2320 (€€€/€€). Tasteful studios for up to five on the seaside beside Antónios'. All have air-conditioning, DVDs, and CD players. There is a small garden. *Open all year.*

★ Caposáldo >

Caposáldo Paralía Porovítsas, **t** 269 603 9170/**t** 694 760 9032, *www.caposaldo.gr* (€€€/€€). Well signposted 1.5km west of Akráta, with a lovely garden pool by the sea, these seven studios offer a peaceful friendly setting, good for families. Open for coffee and a swim too. *Open all year.*

Akráta Beach Camping, t 269 603 1988, *www.akrata-beach-camping.gr* (€/€). Near town, on the sea by the river. Has a very pleasant and helpful manager. *Open April–Oct.*

Lámbros, t 269 603 1414. Offers good Greek food in a pleasant setting by the sea.

Thomás, at the west end of beach, **t** 269 603 2450. Good food, friendly service, all under a canopy of mulberry trees.

Veggéra, t 269 603 3000. Pleasant Italian restaurant by the sea that has made quite a splash with the locals. Also pizza takeaway, and a terrific house salad.

Ammos Club, t 269 603 2279 and **La Corte, t** 269 603 3760. Side by side and hard to tell apart, these are the current café favourites.

Plátanos ✉ 25006

Foliá, t 269 606 1211. Popular family-run taverna right on the sea.

Agápe, t 269 606 1312. A local favourite in the cool shade. Try the fried *kalamáres* or the cheese-filled meat patties.

Aigeíra ✉ 25006

Mouriá, t 269 603 1772. Right on the sea and favoured by many. It offers traditional fare and grilled meat.

Katsoúris (Κατσούρης), **t** 269 603 1327. On the main road in Aegeíra, complete with fountain and excellent food.

Nightlife in Akráta

The **Cosmic Club**, by the river with the other clubs, is the current hot spot, with cars still in the car park at breakfast time. After a court battle with the neighbours, it's soundproofed too.

Mount Chelmós: South of Akráta

This drive into the mountain fastness of Chelmós is beautiful at any time of the year, with its pine forests and lofty peaks, and is truly gorgeous in the snow. In winter the road from Akráta to Zaroúchla is ploughed every day. Each tiny village on this route has its own personality, with at least one picturesque stone church and heart-stopping view. Turn off for Tsivlós and in one kilometre you come to its lovely little mountain lake. This area has not been geared to mass tourism, but this may change because of the new

Getting to Mount Chelmós

No buses here. **Taxis** are available in Akráta, **t** 269 603 1892. By **car**, leave the old national road at the traffic lights in Akráta, follow the straight road to upper Akráta as far as it will go and then follow the signs to Pýrgos (Πύργος), Valimí (Βαλιμί) and Zaroúchla (Ζαρούχλα). After Pýrgos and Valimí, descend to the valley – passing the turn-off to Tsivlós (Τσιβλός) – and on through to Zaroúchla. For Sólo (Σόλο) and Peristéra (Περιστέρα), branch off from this road after Agrídi (Αγρίδι) and before Zaroúchla. There is an unpaved road from Zaroúchla to Pheneós for the daring. Ask about its condition in Zaroúchla.

---

road from Peristéra to the Kalávrita ski centre. Still, it is lovely and those wandering on foot will find tiny churches squeezed into niches on a cliff-face and can stroll along the Kráthis river that runs from Zaroúchla to the sea. Cyclists will enjoy the road from Tsivlós to Zaroúchla. This route also offers the walk of all walks to the sheer rock-face scoured by the falls of the infamous Styx.

The River Styx

The Styx ('the Abhorrent') was one of the five rivers of Hades. By its waters the Olympian gods would swear their most sacred oaths; here Achilles was dipped by his mother to ensure immortality. She forgot to let go of his ankle, of course, bequeathing us the expression 'Achilles' heel'. Ancient gossip held that only the hoof of a horse could hold its water (a clue that it was sacred to Horse-headed Demeter), and that any other container, whether glass, agate, stone or gold, would disintegrate on contact. Rumours flew that Alexander the Great was poisoned by water from the River Styx. The apparent paradox, that immortal water (*athánato neró*) could kill, is a reminder of the double meaning of 'sacred': something to be worshipped was also something to be feared, and approached only with proper preparations. The same attitude comes in good stead if you want to hike to the source of the Styx.

A number of roads purport to lead to the Styx, but the road to hell is paved with bad directions. If you just want to say that you, like Achilles, dipped in the Styx, take the road past the village of **Sólo** with its pretty church, and follow it down to the river (you can approach the source this way, too, but it is trickier to find the trail). Real tenderfeet should follow the signs from Sólo's centre towards the **Fountain of Gólfo** (Γκόλφω). This takes you round a bend or two until, just before the fountain, the massive cliff and waterfall come into view. The water stains the rock face, giving the Styx yet another name, *mávro néri* or black water.

The walk to the source is a good two hours each way from the point where the marked trail starts. Don't try it in the winter. From **Peristéra's** *plateía*, follow the sign to Áno Mesoroúgi (Ανο Μεσορπούγι) and continue along the narrow road until it ends (2km or so). Parking is tricky as this road just peters out into a path. When it does, follow the trail marked by the Alpine Club with red

Where to Stay and Eat around Mt Chelmós

The villages fill up at weekends, especially in the winter and on major holidays, and then relax into relative quiet. All the tavernas are good here. Be sure to ask for the local specialities: bean soup, pittas with cheese or greens and roasted meat, all served with home-made country bread.

Tsivlós ✉ 25006

To Pétrino >

To Pétrino, t 269 603 4190 or t 697 362 0237, *www.limnitsivlou.gr* (€/€). Four small rooms, with a common sitting room. Cosy and well run. It also has an excellent restaurant with fireplace and terrace, presided over by Mrs Vlákou, a lovely lady and a great cook. *Open all year.*

Peristéra ✉ 25006

Anagnostopoúlou Rooms, t 269 603 3988 (€/€). This hospitable family literally welcomes guests into their own living room. *Open all year.*

Xelmós, t 269 603 4076. Good food, including their speciality, charcoal-grilled trout from the fishery below the village.

Zaroúchla ✉ 25006

Dryádes, t 269 603 4840, *www.driadeshotel.gr* (€€€€/€€€). At 3,713ft in the pines, stone and wood-clad hotel offering a pool, hammam, DVD, Internet and two common rooms with fireplaces.

Aroánia, t 269 603 5090, *www.aroania-hotel.gr* (€€€/€€). New large traditional-styled hotel with a fire-place in every room, large lobby with fireplace, and more. *Open all year.*

Xenónas Helmós, t 269 603 3959 (€€/€). Five plain rooms run by the Psariádi family. *Open all year.*

Tou Ioánnis, t 269 603 3939 and the **Ydata Stygós t** 269 603 5050. Both good tavernas.

circles and arrows. Towards the end, when the path becomes very steep, you can opt to go down along the river and then climb up to the trail again. Shortly after this, you'll reach the bottom of the waterfall with its little cave. It's at its most spectacular in spring and early summer, but don't stand directly under the cliff-face. Pieces of the rock wall often come tumbling down, proving once again that Styx and stones can break your bones.

Diakoftó to Kalávrita: The Vouraikós Gorge, the Railway and Cave Churches

Coastal **Diakoftó** (Διακοφτό) ① occupies a large spit of sandy river land. Its pretty, narrow shingle **beach** is a good kilometre from the train station, and stretches out far beyond its port. But what Diakoftó is famous for is the awesome and rather terrifying red cleft in the mountains just behind it known as the **Vouraikós Gorge**. Sir James

Getting to Diakoftó and into the Gorge

The Diakoftó **train station, t** 269 104 3206, is on the Pátras–Corinth line, and is served by daily buses from Akráta and Éghio. It is a local line and therefore reasonably priced. A popular move is to take the train to Zachloroú, the last station in the gorge, and then either walk up to the Méga Spíleo monastery (a good steep hike on a well-marked path) or hike back along the rails for 3hrs to Diakoftó (check the train times if you do this). Or have a coffee in Zachloroú, and wait 20 minutes or so for the same train on its return from Kalávrita.

Fraser, gazing at it in 1900, thought the entrance 'might pass for the mouth of hell'. Its spectacular scenery has always encouraged poetic hyperbole. The ancients attributed its origin to Heracles, who cut the narrow swath through the mountains with his sword in an attempt to join up with Voura, a local girl who caught his fancy. Geologists say it was formed aeons ago when earthquakes, water pressure and erosion forced a passage through the mountain valley of Kalávrita, draining what had been a very large mountain lake into the Gulf of Corinth.

① Diakoftó railway

The famous **train** up the gorge to Kalávrita begins its journey in Diakoftó. One of the most spectacular rail journeys in the world, this small gauge line was begun in 1889 by an Italian company and completed in 1895, opening the hitherto inaccessible area around Kalávrita. The original plan was to extend the line to Trípolis, but the money ran out. The train is due to reopen some time in 2008 with spiffy new cars already waiting at Diakoftó station; the fact that they are wider than some of the tunnels may cause a longer delay. It is worth waiting for. In the hour and 10 minutes it takes to get to Kalávrita, the train wends its way through six tunnels, over 40 bridges, and climbs up to dizzying heights, a staggering 2,300ft in 14 miles, through wild and tremendous scenery. The train is aided by a rack-and-pinion system on very steep grades, for a distance of 2.2km. The locals use it as well, and it has been known to stop in its tracks more than once at Easter when local villagers have offered the passengers and crew a glass of wine, a red egg, and a snack.

Zachloroú (Ζαχλωρού) ② is a romantic spot right by the tracks, deep in the gorge, under the shadow of Méga Spíleo Monastery (*see* p.191). Its name means 'green' in Greek, and 'behind the

An Alternative Way into the Gorge

If the train is full or not working, take this alternative route south into the gorge. Go west of Diakoftó on the Old National Road, crossing the river. Just beyond it, take the first road left – a yellow-tented kiosk marks the spot. Paved at first, but good all the way, it takes you 6km into the gorge, beside the river (with good picnic spots). After the town dump, it gets truly beautiful, with caves, canyons, and dizzying possibilities for rock-climbing and hiking detours. By kilometer five, the effects of the 2007 fire are evident. Still, this gorge, even at this point, is spectacular. Many huge rocks look poised to make the plunge, but then again, they always have.

mountain' in Slavic. Both fit. Refugees from Épirus settled here to escape the Turks, creating an unexpectedly large settlement. It is a perfect spot for a 'village experience', either for an extended lunch or an overnight stay.

Kalávrita and Around

The terminus of the rack-and-pinion railway, Kalávrita, 2,460ft above sea level, is a pretty, well-watered town of 2,000 souls, famous for its cheeses and pastas, especially *xilópittas* (tiny squares) and *trachaná*, a dry mixture of goat's milk and flour. It is the market town for the dozens of mountain villages which surround it, and the hub of the somewhat sporadic bus service for the entire area, as well as the site of the district court. Given the Greek penchant for litigation, that in itself ensures a large daily influx of visitors. Kalávrita is also the closest town to the increasingly popular Chelmós Ski Centre. This has brought trendy cafés, *pensions* and hotels, including one building with a glassed-in pool. Its Ag. Lávra Monastery is one of the most visited in Greece, while Méga Spíleo has a more stunning location, and the church in Plataniótissa is totally *sui generis*.

Kalávrita

Kalávrita (Καλάβρυτα) ③ is a town with too much history. It sits directly on the ruins of ancient Kynaitha, which left only traces of its acropolis inside the ruined Frankish fortress on the hill to the east. Its modern name, *Kalí Vríssi* or 'Good Fountain', is derived from an ancient tale about a spring by a plane tree which was said to be a sure cure for the bite of a rabid dog. The lives of the people here were changed forever on 13 December 1943, when the occupying Germans, in retaliation for the death of four soldiers, gathered the entire male population of the village together on the hillside below the castle and gunned them down. Over 1,200 men and boys were killed. The women and children had been gathered together in the local school to be burned alive, but a single Austrian soldier baulked at this atrocity and allowed them to escape. Kalávrita subsequently became a town of widows and children, as did many of the neighbouring villages where similar reprisals were taken. The **school** has recently been made into a museum and the hillside is dominated by a huge cross marking the site of the 'sacrifice'; the clock in the village square has been stopped at 2.34 since that day to mark the hour of the massacre.

Kalávrita school
t 269 202 3646; open Tues–Sun 10–5

At **Ag. Lávra**, 6km west of Kalávritra, the flag of independence was first raised against the Turks. It now resides in the monastery's church and has become a pilgrimage site for modern Greeks. Ag. Lávra was founded in AD 961, but its present attractive monastery was built in 1827 (although frankly, by Peloponnesian

Ag. Lávra
t 269 202 2363; open 8–6, but closed for 2hrs at lunchtime

Getting to and around Kalávrita

Kalávrita is small, so getting around and getting acquainted takes 10 minutes flat. A **bus** from Athens arrives once a day via Akráta, **t** 269 603 1204, once a day from Éghio, **t** 269 102 2424; and several times a day from Trípolis. For bus information in Kalávrita, **t** 269 202 2224; for train information, **t** 269 202 2245.

There are many **taxis**, **t** 269 202 2127, in the main *plateia*, but no bus service to the ski area. A taxi one way costs about €20 in good weather. Icy conditions demand danger money! Of course, a bus for skiers would be a good idea, but the taxi lobby disagrees. Their monopoly will end if the plan to extend the railway to the ski centre ever gets under way. The taxis are also handy if you want to visit some of the neighbouring villages. The cost of a trip to either the Méga Spíleo or Ag. Lávra Monastery, with a half-hour stop and a return, is between €20 and €25.

Méga Spíleo is accessible on the Kalávrita coast road, or by leaving the train at Zachloroú (*see* p.189). From there, however, it is a steep 45min walk. If you do hike up, turn left at the highway to get to the monastery. Plataniótissa can be reached from the Méga Spíleo–Kalávrita road on the east, via Kerpiní (Κερπινή) on a so-so road, from the Éghio–Ftéri–Kalávrita road in the west on a good road, or in the summer on an even more direct newly paved road from the old coast road 600m west of the turn-off for Mamousiá (Μαμουσιά). The closest you can get by bus is Válta (Βάλτα), 5.4km from the village on the Éghio–Kalávrita run (weekdays only).

Chelmós Ski Area
t 269 202 2174, www.kalavrita-ski.com

standards, it's a bit dull). The bus from Kalávrita to Kleitoriá can drop you off near it. The **Chelmós Ski Area** (5,480–7,670ft), Greece's second-largest, is wonderfully situated on the mountain's north slope, 14km southeast of Kalávrita. With its chair lifts, and twelve runs offering 20km of skiing, it has a resolutely international atmosphere. No lurking Greek gods or malevolent bogeys could possibly compete with all that colourful ski-wear, and the trendy wooden cafés and restaurants. Snowboards, toboggans and skis can be rented either on the slopes or in town.

A new 8km road goes south from the ski area to **Neraidórachi**, a bare rock that is host to the shiny white **Aristarchos**, Greece's eye on the universe, inaugurated in 2007 and the second-largest telescope in Europe. With its 2,340m lens, it can spy both vertically and horizontally on three-quarters of the universe, and has a range of 8–12 billion light years. Security staff have a lonely chalet nearby; the telescope can be operated by remote control from Athens. Why Neraidórachi? It is the darkest, clearest site in all of southern Europe. You can glimpse it from the top of the valley road leading down to Lousí.

Near Kalávrita: Méga Spíleo

Méga Spíleo
t 269 202 3130; closed briefly in the afternoon; dress respectfully

The monastery of the 'Big Cave', **Méga Spíleo** (Μέγα Σπίλαιο) ④, is 7.5km north of Kalávrita. Wedged into the spectacular cliffs of the Vouraikós Gorge, 3,300ft above sea level, the present monastery is not as beautiful as its setting; the original burned down in 1934, when a powder keg stored since the War of Independence (in case of emergencies) caught fire. Behind the ugly façade is the cave where Euphrosyne, a shepherdess, discovered the miraculous wax and wood icon of the Mother of God (Theotókos) in AD 362. It was supposedly made by St Luke and quickly proved its worth by

Cave Worship

The tradition of cave worship goes way back. Greece's limestone cliffs are riddled with clefts and holes, and many were shrines to gods long before the first temples were even conceived of. When Christianity prevailed, the caves were rededicated. The usual way for this to happen was for a shepherd, goatherd or young woman to 'discover' an old icon, most often of the Virgin for some reason, which had miraculous healing properties. The cave would then become a centre of Christian worship, with the icon, sometimes the worse for wear because of its burial, becoming the focus of worship. The countless discoveries of 'icons' in this manner is nothing short of miraculous in itself.

Somewhere in or near the Vouraikós Gorge was the famous Cave of Heracles belonging to ancient Voura, the city that gave the Vouraikós river its name. This cave was featured on its coins. It contained a small statue of Heracles and a basket full of goat and sheep knucklebones, the ancient equivalent of dice. For a small fee, the interested party would cast the knucklebones and a board at the back of the cave would list a fortune according to the number cast. If there is something of the old-time fairground game to this, the culture that produced church bingo can certainly not cast the first stone (or knucklebone)! And the ancient Greeks had a better reason to worship with dice than the Catholic Church. A cast of the die, or the choice of a white or black ball in a lottery, was truly allowing the gods to decide. That is why so many major decisions in Athenian democracy were made by lot. The choice was not random, but the gods' choice – fate. This cave has been tentatively identified and signposted, immediately above the old national road near the entrance road to Eleóna, just west of Diakoftó. But the gorge offers hundreds of other candidates.

zapping a dragon with a proto-laser beam. The icon is on display along with many more relics and treasures, some of them very old, in the monastery's museum.

The Tree Church at Plataniótissa

That churches in Greece are varied in terms of size, magnificence and choice of building materials is readily apparent to the most casual visitor, but the church at Plataniótissa (Πλατανιότισσα) ⑤ adds a new wrinkle. It is contained entirely in the bole of a huge plane tree, can accommodate 20 people and is surely the only tree anywhere with a floor tiled in blue and white. The nave, complete with chandelier, measures 10ft by 13ft. This is also, understandably, the only church where lighting candles is strictly forbidden. But rules are made to be broken in Greece, and a no-nonsense fire extinguisher stood at the ready outside the 'door' for years until recently, when exasperated church officials simply placed inviting candle holders outside, beside the tree's 'door'.

Notice that, while having one root, the tree appears to be three separate trees from the outside, a perfect symbol of the Trinity. That, of course, was just the icing on the theological cake. One stormy night in 840, the icon of the Theotókos from Méga Spíleo was hung inside the tree during a tour of the area. To the amazement of all, an exact replica of the icon appeared in the wood opposite where it had been hung. Sceptics may claim it was carved, but the relief has kept its shape throughout 1,160 years of tree growth (the face of Mary is quite hard to make out, but it is there) and that is only one of its score of miracles.

Where to Stay and Eat around Diakoftó and Kalávrita

Diakoftó ✉ 25003

Chris-Paul, t 269 104 1715, *www.chrispaul-hotel.gr* (€€/€€). Handy for the train station and, though rooms are small, the garden is large and there is a pool; parking. *Open all year.*

Panorama, t 269 104 1614, *www.greecepanorama.gr* (€€/€€). Plain, but with TV and air-conditioning; on the sea, with terrific views and a good restaurant. *Open all year; in winter, weekends only.*

Kochili, t 269 104 1844. Right by the port and known for its seafood.

Kostas, t 269 104 3228. By the train station; the locals' favourite winter taverna.

T'Agnantio >

T'Agnantio, in Trápeza 4km east of Diakoftó, t 269 104 1340. Toúla and Vassíly serve great cheese balls, *dolmádes*, giant beans and grilled fish, all served up with one of the best views ever. Go at sunset.

Zachloroú ✉ 25003

Romántzo, t 269 202 2758 (€/€). Eight plain rooms beside the station with an excellent terrace restaurant under tall trees in the heart of the gorge.

Kalávrita >
www.kalavrita.gr

Kalávrita ✉ 25001

Kalávrita is buzzing all year round. While there are no bargains during the ski season, rates plummet in summer when accommodation is easy to find.

Aphrodite, t 269 202 3600, *www.aphroditeinn.gr* (€€€/€€). Well-decorated rooms dramatically perched above the town, with the beds tucked up in a loft.

Filoxenía, t 269 202 2493, *www.hotelfiloxenia.gr* (€€€/€€). Standard rooms in a pleasant setting right in town.

Maria, t 269 202 2296, *www.kalavrita.net/maria.htm* (€€/€€). Comfortable and dead central. The good news is the recent renovation; the bad is the colour scheme.

Chríssa, t 269 202 2443, *www.xrissa.gr* (€€/€€). Six air-conditioned rooms opposite the train station. There are hot plates in each room for coffee and tea.

Karabéllas, a street behind the train station, t 269 202 2189 (€€/€). Small spotless en suite rooms with a common kitchen in a garden setting.

It used to be that a stop in Kalávrita meant a cup of 'Nes', excellent yoghurt, or *patsá* (sheep's stomach soup) at the restaurant opposite the court house. No more; Kalávrita has gone upscale (and still has great yogurt). Try it at the **Gri-Gri café** opposite the schoolhouse (as well as their *crémas*, and *baklavá*).

Stani, t 269 202 3000. Opposite the National Bank, offering good taverna fare (shown in a glass case) in a cosy *après-ski* atmosphere.

Taverna Elatos, t 269 202 2541. Has been there for years, more 'traditional' and with a nicer terrace in summer.

Plataniótissa

There are three small summer restaurants near the tree church, open from Easter to October. Specialities are delicious goat dishes, either boiled or roasted. Plataniótissa's valley is especially lovely in the early spring.

South of Kalávrita: Lousí, the Cave Lakes, Planitéro and Kleitoriá

A good road leads out from the centre of Kalávrita, up past the turn-off for the ski area, to **Lousí** (Λουσοί) and the Cave Lakes (16.5km). Almost immediately after the fork to the ski area, the scenic alpine valley of Lousí spreads out before you, with the Chelmós range providing a dramatic wall to the east. Many hikers

Káto Lousí coffee shop
t 269 208 3331

use the tiny village of **Káto Lousí** (Κάτω Λουσοί) as a starting point to climb Mount Chelmós; the local **coffee shop** has a few rooms, and there's a small taverna.

This valley belonged to **ancient Lousi**, a city with enough wealth to have hosted its own games in Hellenistic times, and old enough to have accumulated one of the earliest Greek legends, when it was the site of a healing miracle performed by Melampos, a famous magician. The story goes that the daughters of King Proitos of Tiryns had been turned into cows by Dionysos and were running amok in the area. Melampos cured them by purifying them in the waters of a cave, thus giving Lousi its name which means 'washing' or 'bathing'. The legend of the cave and stream was pooh-poohed until 1964 when the the cave and the waters running through them were rediscovered – today's **Cave Lakes**, signposted on the road south of Lousí. This ancient underground water course runs for 6,500ft, its 13 small 'lakes' linked by tunnels. The tour, however, may disappoint, unless they actually open up one or two of the larger lakes to visitors as promised. The Romans knew all about the cave; archaeologists found a sign written in Latin inviting visitors to take a drink but forbidding them to bathe in the water. This water was said to make you give up alcohol altogether, so think twice before you sip.

Cave Lakes
t 269 203 1001; open all year, 9.30–4.30; adm

Lousí's other sight is the floor plan of the **Temple of Artemis the Tamer**, the protectress of herds. The entire valley was sacred to the goddess, another example of pragmatism and religion joining hands. This made sheep- and goat-rustling a religious crime, and therefore subject to penalties harsh enough to act as a deterrent. To visit this temple (well signposted), take the road from Káto Lousí for about 4km until a small sign to **Lousikó** (Λουσικό) directs you left and up the hill. Keep going until you come to the large floor of the temple on your left, set in the shade of towering trees, affording a fine view of the valley. This is the perfect picnic spot. They say that water was piped directly to this temple from the cave. This is no longer true, so bring your own (and some wine too if you didn't drink that cave water).

South of Lousí and the Cave Lakes you come to the end of the road and are faced with a choice: Planitéro, 3.5km to the east, or Kleitoriá, 5km west.

Planitéro: Giant Trees and Singing Trout

The narrow canyon leading to Planitéro is formed by the Aroánios river. It gushes out from the foot of a limestone cliff and in no time at all becomes a rushing stream heading pell-mell to join the Ládon, whose own source starts in exactly the same abrupt fashion a few kilometres south, just off the road to the Pheneós pass. Many rivers in the Peloponnese start from nowhere like this, the resurgent outflow of the waters that disappeared into sink holes in valleys like Pheneós and Stymphalía. The well-watered plane trees here have assumed fantastic proportions and shapes straight out of a Gustave Doré illustration. This impression is marred only slightly by stall owners noisily flogging local produce – nuts, oregano, mountain teas, honey, and dried plants in colours that nature has never produced.

On the rocks behind the 'source' is Planitéro (Πλανητέρο), once quite an extensive mountain village and charming even now. It is on the E4 trail which goes from central Europe to Kalamáta, in case you feel like wandering off. Trout farms take advantage of the clean, fast waters, and restaurants have sprung up to take advantage of the trout. Pausanias travelled to the banks of the rivers here because he was intrigued by the legend that they contained spotted fish that sang like thrushes. Of course he meant trout. He tells us that he sat for a whole evening when they were supposed to be in best voice, but heard nothing. You can try your luck.

After lunch, stroll past the stone mill at the entrance to the village. It is still used today to grind corn and wheat and has a side room on the right as you enter to wash heavy village *flokati* rugs, a process that is best done with a torrent of water.

Kleitoriá: Sheep Bells, Quiet Nights, and Country Life

Kleitoriá (Κλειτοριά), or Mazéika, is a sleepy village in an attractive valley, where the peace and quiet is broken only by roosters, sheep bells, the odd tractor and the two daily buses from Kalávrita. It has more often been passed through than stopped at until recently, when a new hotel and growing interest in mountain tourism have made it an increasingly popular destination. There are scant ruins in the valley bottom at **ancient Kleitor**, on the north side of town. It makes a lovely stopover in quiet surroundings; just don't expect much nightlife. South of Kleitoriá, let yourself be tempted by signs for the **Historic Pausanias Vine Tree** just off the road: an extraordinary grape vine that occupies several terraces, with trunks over a foot in diameter, that uses full-grown holm oaks to support its heavy branches.

From Kleitoriá into the Boondocks

Kleitoriá is a good base for mountain forays. Besides the obvious trips to Planitéro, Lousí and Aroanía (*see* below), you can go 7.5km south to the well-marked **Pheneós pass**, and then east to Stymphalía and Pheneós (*see* pp.175–8). Kleitoriá can also be a stepping stone for a trip to **Dáphni** (Δάφνι), 30km southwest, and to the **Ládon Dam and Lake**. Dáphni has a cluster of circular *alónias* (threshing floors) on the hill opposite the town to the east, threaded with still-discernible mule paths. The clustering of

Where to Stay and Eat South of Kalávrita

Áno Lousí ✉ 25001

Sperchos, **t** 269 208 3348 (€€/€€). This new apartment hotel is neat, clean (some suites have fireplaces), much cheaper in season than its counterparts in Kalávrita, and has a good restaurant too. It is very welcome to the 'I love Lousí' fan club because of the view.

Planitéro ✉ 25007

Varvára Militopoúlou, **t** 269 203 1831 (€€/€). Five brand new rooms with kitchens, and a communal fireplace. *Open all year*.

Laléousa, **t** 269 203 2385. On the edge of the village as you enter, and certainly the most upscale place to eat, with a waterfall and a view in a shaded spot of the river. *Open weekends only*.

Farma Rigóyianni or 'Swan Lake', **t** 269 203 1654. Built over a shady pond about 1km before Planitéro (it moved from town), it always had geese and ducks, but now they have added swans.

Kleitoriá ✉ 25007

Mount Helmos, **t** 269 203 1221 (€€/€€). A pleasant, small, newish hotel catering to mountain- and ski-lovers. *Open all year*.

Georgia Rápanou rooms, **t** 269 203 1308 (€€/€€). Nine newly built rooms 100m from the hotel, each with a small kitchen and bath, and a common room with fireplace. *Open all year*.

Pétrino, **t** 269 203 1857. This small, nicely decorated bar and restaurant is as upmarket as it gets around here.

alónias on non-productive hillsides (so the useful arable land would not be wasted) is typical of many Peloponnesian villages.

This area is very out-of-the-way, and leads into Arcadía via **Trópaia** (Τρόπαια) and the really obscure and wild ruins of the Frankish **Castle of Akova**, a few kilometres west of **Vizíki** (Βιζίκι), on a poor but passable unpaved road (ask for directions in Vizíki). This one is also for people looking for an adventurous route to or from the main Pýrgos–Trípolis road.

Deep into Erýmanthos to the Innermost Edge of Achaía

Clusters of wild and beautiful peaks, culminating in Mount Erýmanthos, rise dramatically from dense forests where animals seem to lurk – or would, if the rapacious hunters were controlled more effectively. The isolated, precipitous hamlet of Aroanía and the site of ancient Psophis at Tripótama form the perfect introduction to the area. The urge to dart down a side road here and there may be almost overwhelming.

Aroanía and the Church of St Paul

Leave the Kalávrita–Kleitoriá road, 18km south of Kalávrita. At that point, you will be 'on top of the world' and looking at a sign pointing west to Aroanía. The road clings to the perpendicular rock-face, as the Kleitoriá valley unfolds itself dramatically for several kilometres, and then snakes down to the isolated little

Getting to Innermost Achaía

A **bus**, **t** 269 202 2224, leaves Kalávrita at midday for Aroanía, Psophis and on to Dáphni where it spends the night, retracing the route in the morning. Other buses to Psophis pass on the main road en route to Kalávrita or Athens, and sometimes to Olympia or Pýrgos. The paucity of public transport here is the price for being at the back of beyond in the first place, and for straddling three provinces in the second. Ask at the Psophís supermarket.

By **car**, Psophís can be approached from Pátras, from Amaliáda to the west, and even from Olympia via Lála in the south.

---

hamlet of **Aroanía** (Αροανία), which must have more churches than inhabitants. Nonetheless, a beautiful new slate-grey stone one dedicated to **Ag. Pávlos**, complete with a guest house for the faithful, is almost completed. Churches like this one are privately funded, usually by devout locals who have made good. Remarkably, long after they have left their villages, many, many Greeks still endow churches in this way, despite the fact that they are only likely to be full on their name days once a year, in this case 29 June.

Ancient Psophis and the Erymanthian Boar

From Aroanía, the road follows the Aroánios river 16km to **Tripótama** (Τριπόταμα, 'Three Rivers'), a village of 450 souls, where the Aroánios meets two other rivers to form the large Erýmanthos, at the picturesque confluence just south of the road.

Tripótama is built on the southern tip of the much larger ancient city of **Psophis**, an impressive situation which would have been even more impressive in its heyday when the surrounding hills were oak forests full of wild boar, bears and huge land tortoises. Psophis, which existed from Mycenaean into Roman times, was named after Psophis, whom Heracles obligingly impregnated when he passed through en route to one of his Twelve Labours: the killing of the Erymanthian boar which had been ravaging the countryside. Historically somewhat obscure, Psophis was nonetheless famous for a fact so unbelievable that Pausanias rejected it out of hand: the city claimed to be the home of a truly happy man, one Aglaos by name. Pausanias, who had had no problem with giants, singing fish or visiting Greek gods, simply could not swallow the idea of a happy man. His conviction speaks volumes for the ancient view of man's place in the scheme of things. Fame and glory might be achieved if the gods were kind, but complete happiness – never.

The **ruins** of Psophis are easily approached from the little walled monastery of **Koímesis tis Theotókou**, on the northern edge of the village beside the Kalávrita road. Take the unpaved driveway up to its gate and you are in the middle of a city that up until now has scarcely been excavated. The extensive ruins go up the hill to the west and down the other side to the river. Squared-off blocks and

Where to Stay and Eat in Innermost Achaía

Aroanía ✉ 25007

Archondikó >>

Xenónas Aroanías, **t** 269 206 1414 or **t** 697 427 2225 (€€/€€). Simple 'traditional' rooms with TVs and fridges in a pretty stone building, presided over by Mr Petros, who knows this leafy out-of-the-way area well. Try bargaining in summer. *Open all year*.

Taverna of Kyría Ióta, in a lovely little town of Livártzi, 13km northwest of Aroanía, **t** 269 205 1195. Good home cooking under huge plane trees at the head of a gushing river. *Open all summer and on winter weekends*.

Tripótama ✉ 25007

Archondikó, **t** 269 205 1222. Opposite the supermarket in the main *plateía*, and so much the local favourite, they do not even put their name outside. Try the local boiled goat and other succulent meats, all served under a modernistic metal and canvas shade.

bits and pieces of columns are scattered everywhere; sections of its city walls can be seen on the Kalávrita road. The monastery itself was built on a temple, whose truncated columns survive in its courtyard. Workmen renovating the building in 1999 decided that the tallest column could use a sprucing up and completely sanded down its outer layers, proving not only how white all of that apparently grey lichen-coloured stone is, but also how vulnerable these unguarded, unsung sites really are. The little house beside the monastery is full of ancient stones and columns. After 2,000 years or so of local attention, the archaeologists who have planned extensive excavations here had better hurry up if they want to find anything at all. There is a flat piece of column under a tree near the entrance to the monastery for a picnic or a few thoughts on happiness in Arcadía. Alternatively, you could try the excellent restaurant in town.

West of Diakoftó: Eleónas and Kyreneia (or maybe Ancient Voura)

On the coast west of Diakoftó and the Vouraikós Gorge, the next chance to turn into the mountains is by **Eleónas**. Its beach, one of the best in the area, is lively in the summer, with tavernas and good swimming. From here you can make the short ascent up the mountain towards Mamousiá with great views, some scanty ruins and an intriguing controversy. There is a bus to Eleónas from Éghio, but to go inland you'll need your own transport. The turn-off south to **Mamousiá** (Μαμουσιά) is 4.5km west of Diakoftó on the Old National Road. Just as you approach Mamousiá, at the 7.1km mark, you will see a sign to 'ancient Kyreneia' and a 'Hellenistic Funerary Monument'. Turn left and park by the tiny church of Konstantinós and Eléni. There is a spectacular descent into the Vouraikós Gorge from the dirt road just before the church to the secondary road along the river (*see* p.191). You can take either fork; the roads meet further down. As long as you choose roads that descend you can't get lost, although you may have some scary moments. Much of this route's natural beauty will take time to recover from the devastating fire of July 2007, a fire so rapid that it burned 8km of forest road in under two hours.

East of the church are the remains of a roofed **Hellenistic cemetery**, discovered when a water pipe was being laid. The tomb (now waist-high) has a temple façade, only here the 'doors' were carved in the stone. On the other side of the church, to your right, is the footpath to the **acropolis**. This has just a few meagre traces of buildings and a theatre, but the path itself, partly carved into the rock, was the ancient mule track. It offers a precarious, but glorious, perch to view the countryside and to marvel yet again at the evocative settings of these ancient cities.

The question is – is it ancient Voura or Kyreneia? In topographically obscure Achaía, where there are far more ruins than known ancient place names, no one can be sure. Some scholars put Voura at Katholikó on the road to Kalávrita, but that takes it a long way from the gorge and the Cave of Heracles (*see* p.192) that was engraved on Voura's coins. Leave the head-scratching to the archaeologists and brave the dirt road beside the monument that leads up to a plateau that was downtown to the ancients. Now covered with *rodítis* vines, these grapes, unlike the pines, survived the fire and are at just at the right altitude to mature at the slow rate that makes them so perfect for top-notch wines. The view across the gulf is stupendous.

Helike: the Greek Pompeii

If you descend to the coast by the paved road (affording a great view of the coastal plain), you can ponder the fate of **ancient Helike**, which once graced the coast hereabouts. During the earthquake of 373 BC that destroyed Voura, Helike and all its inhabitants slipped into the sea and were submerged under the waves of a tsunami. Just prior to the earthquake the people of Helike had killed some Ionian envoys in a Sanctuary of Poseidon, and its demise was attributed to his wrath. If so, he still has moments of irritation because this slippage into the sea is a phenomenon that still occurs here when the earth shakes. The sudden disappearance of Helike was one of the most celebrated disasters of antiquity, and may well have been in Plato's mind when he described Atlantis.

Half-sunken, the ruins of Helike were visited by Roman tourists in boats, but attempts in the last hundred years to locate it in the sea proved futile. In 1988, Dora Katsonopoúlou, working on a hunch that the *poros* ('strait') Helike fell into was more like a lagoon

Where to Stay West of Diakoftó

Eleónas ✉ 25003

Africa, Eleónas, **t** 269 104 1751 (€€/€€). 100m from a good beach; has kitchens in the family rooms, fridges in all rooms, TV, parking and a pool. It has the best facilities for the price of any hotel in the area. *Open all year.*

Eden Beach, Rodiá, **t** 269 108 1195, *edenbeach@yahoo.gr* (€€€/€€). Upmarket for the area, more of a hideaway than a family place, with good amenities and a small, isolated beach quite close to Eleónas.

rather than the gulf, joined forces with Steven Soter and began looking much further inland. It was a while, however, before they struck gold. First they uncovered a Roman settlement erected in honour of Helike. Next they found a rich Early Helladic settlement, the first ever found in Achaía, which may have suffered the same fate as Helike, only *c.* 2000 years later. Then they found the nice straight Roman coastal road. Finally in 2001, with the aid of ground-penetrating radar, they found what they were looking for: Classical Helike. There are hopes that it may prove to be a Classical Greek Pompeii and that some of the wealthy city's bronze and marble statues may be found as Katsonopoúlou, Soter and the Helike Project bring the city to the light. For the latest news, or to volunteer at the dig, try *www.helike.org*.

Éghio and its Ferry

Legend has it that Agamemnon gathered the Achaean leaders in Éghio (Αίγιο) to debate the expedition to Troy. It seems like a long way from his base, but Mycenaean culture was far more widespread in the Peloponnese than was first thought. In 276 BC, Éghio became an important member of the Achaean League, but its substantial ancient monuments were destroyed in a succession of earthquakes. The Slavs demolished the rest in 800 and Éghio became 'Vostítsa', a name which it retained during the Frankish occupation when it was the seat of a barony held by Guy de Charpigny, a fact worth mentioning because the area near Kalávrita where Guy had his summer house is still called 'Kerpini', although few of the residents remember why. After independence, Vostítsa became Éghio once more.

Now the second city of Achaía, it is the commercial and administrative centre for the surrounding villages, and really hums during its Saturday market. Few tourists stay here, preferring the beaches on either side, but it is still the place to go for clothes, doctors, dentists and foreign periodicals, not to mention local buses, the train and the ferry across the Gulf of Corinth. Another place to go is **Psilá Alónia** at the top of Metropóleos Street for coffee, ouzo or snacks in summer. This large square and park provide a wonderful view of the Gulf. The ferry port is slowly

Getting to and around Éghio

Éghio is 92km from Corinth and 41km from Pátras. It is served by **train**, **t** 269 102 2385, from Pátras and Athens several times a day, as well as by KTEL **buses**, **t** 269 102 2424, to and from Athens hourly.

City buses, **t** 269 102 8787, stop at the beaches of Lóngos and Sellianítika several times a day.

At the port, **t** 269 102 8888, the **car ferry** for Ag. Nikólaos on the north shore of the Gulf leaves 4 times a day from 7am–5pm. Cars cost €12.50; passengers, €2.5.

---

becoming more attractive as some of the old warehouses, used to store currants in the 19th century when Éghio's port was a going concern, are being renovated. This is the spot to have a bite while waiting for the ferry. **Pausanias' Plane Tree** grows in the *plateía* just east of the docks; magnificent though it is, the AD 150 date may be a slight exaggeration and it is highly unlikely that our man ever scribbled in its shade. The church of **Panagía Trypití** is also by the ferry dock. Climb its 150 steps to a small cave where yet another icon of the Virgin was found, this time by a shipwrecked sailor, who swam to safety by following a mysterious light emanating from the cave. The feast day, the Friday after Easter, draws huge crowds.

Éghio museum
t 269 102 1517; open Tues–Sun 8.30–3

The **museum** is housed in the beautifully renovated marketplace built by Ernst Ziller in the centre of town. It is not large, but houses the finds from Éghio as well as other Achaean League cities; there would be plenty more to see if modern Éghio hadn't been built on top of the ancient city, obscuring its illustrious past. Don't forget to stop at the **Oinofóros Winery**, in Selinoús, an eastern suburb of Éghio, to look around and try the wine made from local grapes.

Oinofóros Winery
t 269 102 9415

Beaches West of Éghio: Lóngos and Sellianítika

The two resorts, Sellianítika and Lóngos, are side by side but **Lóngos** (Λόγγος) is by far the prettier of the two. Set well away from the two national roads, the lush atmosphere resembles an Ionian island, with a tiny, round *plateía*, shaded by a huge plane tree beside the church of Ag. Demétrios. It has an outdoor cinema nearby. Three access roads go down to the beach, but there's no road along the shore, so the waterfront is very pleasant.

Sellianítika is not to everyone's taste; a road runs between all the hotels and restaurants and the sea, although there are relatively quiet places at either end. The people of mountainous Selliána (above Aigeíra) transported themselves and their animals here for winter, unable to find a spot directly north of their summer village, and then proceeded to turn it into a resort.

Around Éghio

Moní Taxiarchón
t 269 105 6208

The cliff-hanging **Moní Taxiarchón** (Μονή Ταξιαρχών) is one of the most striking monasteries in Greece, and well worth the effort it takes to get there (*see* overleaf). If you're driving from Éghio, you come first to the **lower monastery**, first built in the early 1600s.

Getting to Moní Taxiarchón

There is a twice-daily **bus** from Éghio (**t** 269 102 8787) to Melíssia that can drop you at the road for the monastery, but it is still a good 4.5km walk, so consider a taxi. If you're driving, look on the east side of Éghio, not far from the centre, for the sign (Μονή Ταξιαρχών). Drive through the village of Mavríki (Μαυρίκι) and continue across the river, bearing right until you come to the lower monastery.

The **present monastery**, with its church in the courtyard, dates from 1782 and offers a library of some 4,000 books plus its famous rose-petal jam. For a few years, the roses will need to be imported. This lovely valley was devastated by fire in 2007, although the monastery itself was untouched.

From the picnic area you can see up to the real attraction: the upper **Monastery of the Blessed Leóndios** (*c.* 1377), glued high on the side of a cliff and partially dug into the living rock. As extraordinary as it is, this is not unique in the area; there is another slightly less accessible one above Trápeza. Two small churches grace the monastery, and a dizzying flight of 55 stairs ascends to the tiny shrine of Leónidas, looking out over the mountains upon mountains that surround the valley, fading endlessly into the distance as far as the eye can see. When you descend the stairs, take note of the tiny roadside-style shrine in front of the churches. For years, it was lit, not by the usual wick- and oil-filled container, but by a bare 40-watt light bulb, a practical move on the part of the elderly monks in the monastery below to avoid tramping up the hill to keep the lamp burning. Well, perpetual light is perpetual light, and, while there, it must have been attached to the longest electrical cord in Greece. The Orthodox Church has always displayed a kind of elasticity that allows it to add a few new flourishes now and then. But perhaps the few younger monks from Áthos, now on the scene, thought it was too big a stretch: the light bulb has been replaced by the traditional oil and wicks.

Mount Panachaikó and the Éghio–Pátras Ring Road

Mount Panachaikó is a high, 6,319ft knob at the northern tip of the Erýmanthos range. A scenic 100km ring road from Éghio to Pátras, which separates Panachaikó from Erýmanthos' highest peaks, offers a fine introduction to alpine Achaía. It passes **Ptéri** (Πτέρι), a pleasant mountain village (not far from the tree church at Plataniótissa, *see* p.192), and passing the turn-off to Kalávrita (12km, *see* p.190) continues on to **Vlassía** (Βλασία). The peaks of Mount Erýmanthos loom to the south and a footpath from Vlassía leads to one of its summits. Next comes **ancient Leondio** (Λεοντιο) with its tiny theatre and then the villages of **Katarráktis** (Καραρράκτης) and **Platanóvrissi** (Πλατανόβρυση), and then on to Pátras. If you start early enough, trips up some of the more interesting side roads are possible.

Where to Stay and Eat in and around Éghio

Éghio ✉ 25100

Galini, **t** 269 102 6150 (€€/€€). Has the monopoly and the view. It is best for winter stays really, with minibars and TV, and has a cosy bar area overlooking the Gulf. *Open all year.*

Tasos/Stathis, in the main square, Polyxroniádou, **t** 269 102 8998. Éghio does better in the food department: this tiny restaurant is one of the best *souvláki* places in Greece and has been popular for well over 30 years.

Oinomageirión of Demétris Pléssas >

Oinomageirión of Demétris Pléssas, down by the port, just west of Pausanias' Plane Tree, **t** 269 602 8691. A terrific restaurant with home-cooked meals, run by the same family since 1960.

Lóngos ✉ 25100

Long Beach, **t** 269 107 2196, *www.longbeach.gr* (€€€/€€). With tennis, pool and lots of water sports, this holiday-village style hotel is Lóngos' biggest and best. All rooms face the sea, and weekdays are cheaper than weekends. *Open April–Oct 15.*

Lóngos has lots of little bars and coffee shops, and one very good fish restaurant.

Paradis, **t** 269 107 2313. This coffee shop in the main *plateía* is a local hang-out and a good source of information about rooms to rent.

Beau Rivage. A trendy bar on the sea, popular day and night.

To Baltáki, **t** 269 107 2307. Lóngos' reasonably priced seafood emporium and taverna, also right on the sea. Follow the signs from the square.

Sellianítika ✉ 25100

From the Beau Rivage, you can walk east over to livelier and much noisier Sellianítika, full of little bars, cafés and places to eat.

Kanelli, **t** 269 107 2213, *www.hotelkanelli.gr* (€€/€€). At the western end of the beach, closest to Lóngos, this seaside hotel is quite new and has everything in miniature, except the pool. Its prices jump all over the place. A good chance to bargain?

Panagíotis, at the east end, **t** 269 107 1840 (€/€). Has good-sized air-conditioned rooms on top of a very popular restaurant at the east end of the beach. *Open all year.*

The Northwest Coast: Río and Pátras

Río, the Ferry and the Bridge

Like Brazil, Greece has its Río, but most tourists stay only long enough to line up for the car ferry, and that is only if they haven't skipped Río altogether by going via the stunning new white suspension bridge, dominating the skyline and Río itself. Still, Río is something of a resort area in its own right, as well as a wealthy suburb of Pátras. The lovely villas here bring to mind a comment made by an envious Englishman, that 'Greece is a poor country full of rich people'.

The seaside **Río Casino**, oozing the ersatz splendour of the genre, is one reason why Río is so popular. Greeks are the biggest gamblers in the EU, but the queue for the casino on New Year's Eve, a traditionally popular evening's gamble for *goúri* or good luck all year, can be three kilometres long. No wonder they paved over the tennis courts to create more parking spaces. The entire shoreline west of the ferry dock is chock-a-block with cafés, restaurants, bars

Getting to and from Río

Río is 6km east of Pátras, with very well-marked exits, if you are travelling by **car**. It has a **train station**, **t** 261 099 1244. Right by the docks is the glass-canopied **bus stop** where a no.6 bus will take you to the centre of Pátras in less than half an hour.

The **ferries** at Río, **t** 261 099 1203, are a virtual extension of the highway, taking cars and passengers day and night for the 20-minute run to Andírio, over the narrowest stretch of the Gulf of Corinth. A well-marked road takes you the 2km from the main road to the docks. Passenger cars cost €5. Passengers do not pay. The bridge is faster, but costs €11.

and discos patronized by most of Pátras in the evenings and on weekends. The décor is distinctly African and/or tropical, as if one emporium's thatched roofs and potted palms took hold and infected the entire strip. Perhaps visions of big Río are dancing in their owners' heads. After all, Pátras holds the biggest carnival in Greece (*see* p.205).

The **Kastelli**, or little castle down by the docks, while fairly complete, can hardly compete with the new *carioca* look. Used as a prison for a while, it sits, forlornly, its moat still full of water, waiting for action. It was built in 1499 by the Turks to match the one across the narrow strait at Andírio and saw the last stand of Ibrahim Pasha's troops in 1828 before their defeat by a combined English and French force.

Where to Stay in Río

Río ✉ 26500

Porto Río, **t** 261 099 2212, *www.portoriohotel.gr* (€€€€/€€€). The Casino's hotel, always crowded with gaming outsiders, but the pool is quiet. *Open all year.*

Rion Beach, **t** 261 099 1422 (€€/€€). This seafront hotel would have been the last word in the 1960s; it has a garden in front and parking, is close to the ferries without being on top of them and is just a 5min walk from the Río train station. *Open all year.*

George, 9 Ionías, **t** 261 099 2627 (€/€). Several blocks in from the sea, and perhaps a tad too close to the bridge, this small, friendly hotel is being renovated and tries hard to keep the prices low and its clientele loyal. *Open all year.*

Eating Out in Río

Río's cafés and restaurants are lined up for inspection along the shore.

Naútoíko, Posidónos 12, **t** 261 099 5992. This seaside taverna serves delicious food in a lovely setting, with good service too. Many students from a local cooking school earn their stripes here, and it is a great favourite of the Pátras crowd.

Rementzo, **t** 261 099 3829. With a pine-filled terrace and fireplace inside, this is also popular.

Kalypso, **t** 261 099 4770. Slightly more modest, with a pleasant terrace as well.

Entertainment and Nightlife in Río

Río, with its **casino**, is a main playground for Pátras; the **nightclubs** are clumped together, each one more exotic and bizarre than the next. Ask around. The type of music offered changes even more rapidly than the façades.

Pátras: Always a Bridesmaid

Beautifully situated between sea and mountain, Pátras (Πάτρα) is the marine gateway to the Peloponnese and its largest city. Byron first set foot in Greece at Pátras in 1824, but left almost immediately, pretty much setting the pattern for future tourism. Today's problems include traffic snarls, the near-impossible parking situation, and the prevailing box-like architecture that only an anti-seismic expert could love.

History

Pátras was substantial enough in Classical times to have long walls from its acropolis to the sea *à la* Athens. But, in spite of its historical prominence and key location, the city has somehow never achieved real star status during its long history. It was a going concern in Roman times when its bizarre festival to Artemis was in full swing and the Apostle Andrew came to be martyred. Rich enough to attract Saracen raids in the 9th century, it became the seat of a Frankish barony and a Latin archbishopric in 1205. Sold to the Venetians in 1408, retrieved by the Greeks in 1429, it was seized by the Turks in 1460, who misruled it and then burned it down in 1821 during the initial stages of the War of Independence. The present city plan, designed on a grid system with arcaded pavements (some of which survive), was initiated by Greece's first president Capodístria, who recognized its potential importance to the fledgling state.

Modern Pátras, now Greece's third city, is making Herculean efforts to modernize and attract business and tourism. It contains trendy corners, a huge university and quite a large industrial base, but somehow it still retains the old-fashioned atmosphere of a small provincial town except by the seaside, where the mammoth

Carnival Time

The city changes radically in the ten days or so before Lent, when the Pátras Carnival turns the entire town into a playground for thousands upon thousands of home-town party-makers and revellers from all over Greece. In this city of 200,000, it would be hard to find someone not involved in the Carnival, an orgy of mad costumes, wine-drinking and street parties that culminates in a parade so long it takes hours to pass through the city. Originally a series of pre-Lenten balls held in the houses of rich merchants in the 1840s, the Carnival assumed a wilder and more popular form when it took to the streets in 1870 and ladies began arriving unescorted, masked, dressed from head to foot in black. They chose their own unmasked male partners for the evening or for the night, with an abandon that only a rigid and puritanical society can produce. A masked ball is still held in the Municipal Theatre during the festivities, and whether the old tradition is entirely observed or not remains the secret of those who are lucky enough to be invited. The festival ends with the burning of King Carnival at midnight by the port, a fiery ritual that is not the first of its kind to occur in Pátras, and makes one wonder if the origins of carnival do not date back to even earlier times.

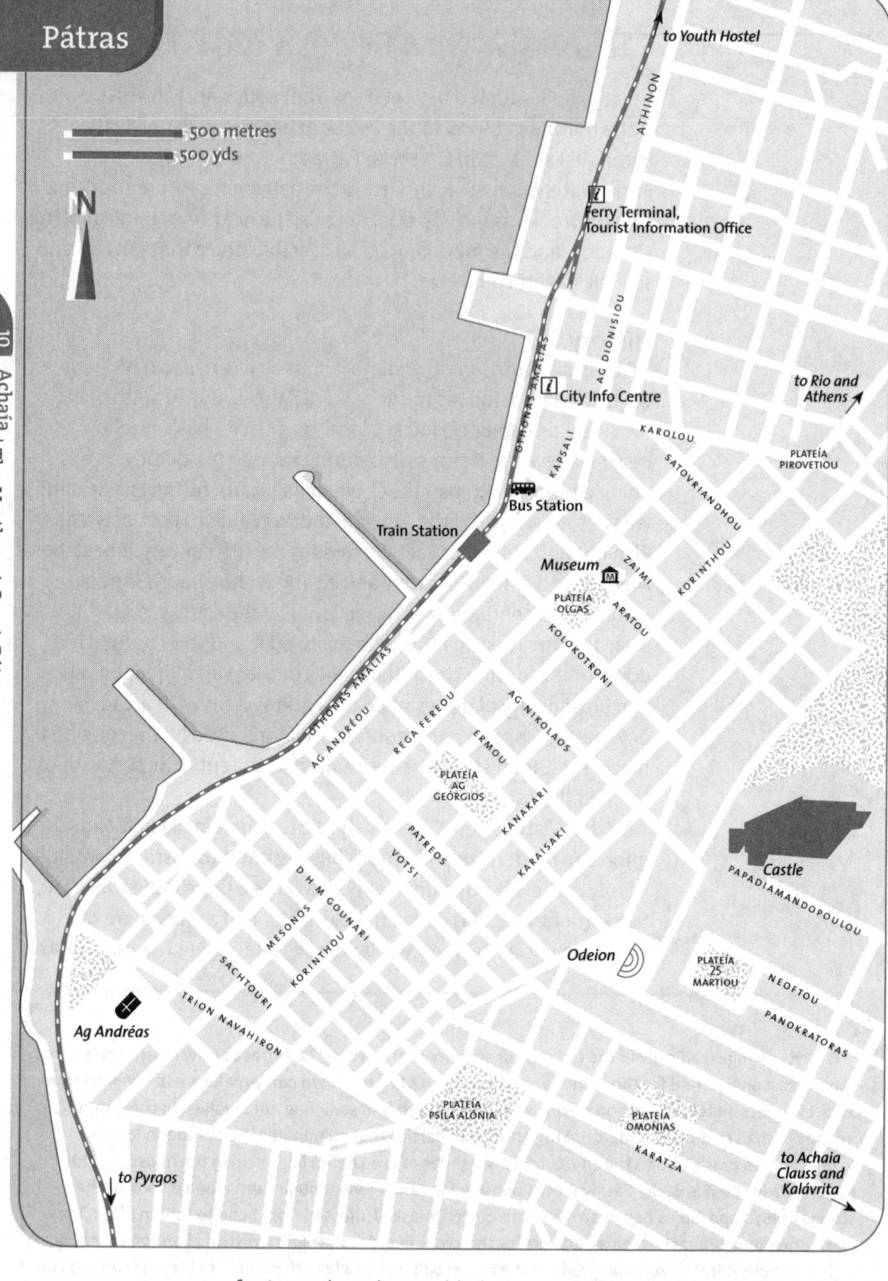

ferries and a palm-studded square give it an indeterminate international flavour. Somehow, words like 'sophistication' or 'world class' don't come to mind in Pátras. Its many hotels are adequate, but convey the same feeling that pervades the rest of the city: they know you are not going to stay any longer than you have to.

Getting to and around Pátras

By Car

Arriving by car from the east is easy. Follow the sign for the port, 2km from the highway into town. Coming from the west is a bit more complicated because of one-way streets. If you get lost, keep going east until you can turn left to the port (*to Limáni*) just past the bus station. Traffic woes have been alleviated slightly by the new toll road bypass south of town (three exits for Pátras) and the creation of vast free car parks by the shore just west of the Ag. Andréas church.

By Bus and Train

The portside KTEL **bus station**, **t** 261 062 3887, is on Óthonos Amaliás St between Arátou and Zaími Sts, just east of the train station. For **information** on city buses, call **t** 261 027 3936.

The depot for buses to Kyllíni (three a day) is at 48 Óthonos Amaliás St and Ermoú, four blocks from the KTEL station, **t** 261 022 0993.

The **train station**, **t** 261 063 9108, virtually in the port, has a left-luggage facility and a glassed-in café, which is not a bad spot to sit and contemplate your next move.

Car Hire

Many car rental agencies have offices right around the port.

National, 1 Ag. Andréou, **t** 261 027 3667, *www.nationalcar.com.*
Hertz, 2 Karólou, **t** 261 022 0990, *www.hertz.gr.*
Sixt, 5 Ag. Dionýsou, **t** 261 027 5677, *www.sixt.gr.*

Waiting in Pátras?

For most tourists, Pátras means waiting: in lines at shipping offices, for a bus or train out, for a parking space, or for a ferry that maddeningly leaves at midnight. Luckily, there is lots to do in Pátras during that period between buying a ticket and leaving.

The port area is good for shopping, but natives prefer the streets off **Plateía Ag. Geórgios** and further up towards the castle where the old market still exists, albeit barely. While in the square, look out for the ornate **municipal theatre**, built in 1872 by Ernst Ziller, with an interior like a miniature La Scala. Two **AB supermarkets**, the *crème de la crème* of Greek supermarkets, at the east and west exits of the town, offer plenty of parking and are a good place to stock up before taking a ferry or heading into the interior. Both have lunch counters, too.

Pátras museum
*corner of Maízonos and Arátou Sts, facing Plateía Olga, **t** 261 027 5070; open Mon–Fri 8–3*

Pátras castle
main entrance open Tues–Sun 8–7; in winter Tues–Fri 8–5, Sat–Sun 8–2.30; adm free; the small entrance at the top of the stair closes 30mins earlier; a pleasant path joins the two entrances

The small neoclassical building housing the **museum** is far too small for the archaeologically rich area of Achaía. But for people-in-waiting it is a pleasant and not too demanding distraction. All eras are covered, and there's a pretty 2nd-century BC Roman mosaic pavement displayed on the first floor. Give **swimming** a miss in Pátras: if you have time, go instead to the noisy, but unpolluted, beaches at Río (6km east) or towards Vrachnéika (10km west).

The Castle, the Odeion and Psilá Alónia

For walkers, the **castle**, on the site of the ancient acropolis, is best reached via Ag. Nikoláos Street. The ascent involves a hundred steps and is tough going on a hot day, but the view is great and the area very peaceful and pleasant. (It is possible to drive up by taking

Dim. Goúrnari Street to Boukaoúri Street and then left. Parking is relatively easy here.) The castle has an attractive keep and is a mélange of Byzantine, Frankish, Venetian and Turkish architecture. The north wall, which dates from the 9th century, contains column drums and other paraphernalia from ancient temples, including the famous Temple to Artemis.

These embedded relics bring to mind Pausanias' description of the annual **Festival of the Laphria**, dedicated to Artemis and held on this very spot. Every year, a grand procession wended its way to the temple from the lower town. The last member of the procession was the priestess of Artemis, resplendent in a chariot pulled by yoked deer. Huge logs were placed in a circle around the goddess' altar the day before and, when the priestess arrived, vast numbers of wild and tame beasts – birds, bears, deer, wolf-cubs, wild boar and more – were herded or thrown into the circle, and the logs set aflame. The resulting holocaust, the pride of the city fathers, must have originated as a ritual to ensure fertility since the altar was also heaped high with fruits from the orchards. Whether it was once less bloody and then became debased to cater to depraved Roman tastes is anyone's guess. But that would be small consolation for the animals that every citizen helped to collect for the special day. Pausanias notes with satisfaction that there was no record of anyone being injured by the animals. A pity.

Roman Odeion
Sotiriádou St, t 261 027 6207; open Tues–Sun 8.30–3

The **Roman Odeion** is hard by the castle to the west. Extensively renovated, the *odeion* was built around AD 150 and seated 2,300 spectators; it is now a venue for the **International Pátras Festival** in summer, offering music, theatre and dance (call the Odeion number for information). When the festival is in progress, there is also a ticket kiosk in Plateía Ag. Geórgios.

A stroll west along Sotiriádou Street and then right on Karatzá Street will bring you to **Plateía Psilá Alónia**, Pátras' smartest watering hole, offering cafés and a panoramic view of sea and city: a great spot to people-watch and have a drink.

The Church of St Andrew

On the western end of Ag. Andréou Street, within easy walking distance of the port, the church of **Ag. Andréas** (Aγ. Aνδρέας) was begun in 1908 and finished in 1974. It is fashionable to sneer at its cream and yellow reinforced concrete façade with its mixture of styles, but it's grand in its own way, and earthquake-proof, too. It can accommodate 8,000 worshippers under a 130ft-high dome, complete with a huge wooden chandelier. Note the *Virgin and Child* behind the white iconostasis with the unusual folk art depiction of the city of Pátras itself running along the bottom, together with castle and miniature cathedral. Beside the church is the earlier basilica-style church built by Kolokotrónis in 1835, which itself replaced an earlier church, and is where Andrew's grave is said to be.

Tradition has it that Andrew, the Apostle of Greece and Asia Minor, was martyred on this spot for refusing to deny Christ. He asked to be crucified on an X-shaped cross because he was too humble to be crucified on the same cross as Jesus; pieces of it are displayed in the cathedral (front-right) behind the glass case containing his cranium. Andrew was one of the first Christians to be praised as a hero by Greek writers; an early popular epic described him leaving Pátras to save his people from evil cannibals called the Myrmidons (the followers of Achilles at Troy), with Christ captaining his vessel in true Greek heroic tradition. Alas, its echoes of the *Odyssey* were not to the early church's liking, and it was suppressed, leaving Andrew with a famous name, but few stories to go with it. The treatment of his remains, however, is an odyssey of sorts. According to one story, his headless body was taken to Scotland in the 4th century and shipwrecked near Fife, thus explaining the Scots' particular affection for the saint and the cross on their flag. Others say his body was taken to Constantinople, stolen in the Fourth Crusade in 1204, and now rests in Amalfi. His head, on the other hand, remained in Pátras until it was hauled off to Rome by the fleeing Thomas Paleológos in 1460. Pope Paul VI returned it in 1964. Andrew became the patron saint of Pátras after 805, when his shining (and intact) apparition appeared miraculously on the castle's battlements and saved the city from the Slavs.

Like so many Christian churches in Greece, this cathedral is built over an ancient temple, this one to Demeter. It contained a famous oracular **well** which could tell the sick whether or not they would survive. Petitioners would tie a mirror on a string and lower it to just above water level where it would mist up, then look in the mirror to see themselves either alive or dead. It was believed to be infallible, so consider carefully before you dangle any mirrors over. It is now a Christian shrine (down some stairs immediately west of the small basilica beside the main church), complete with candles and icons because Andrew was said to have both slept here and baptized the first Christians using its water. Water can still be drawn by means of a metal cup attached to a chain. Beyond the metal doors beside the well lie ancient ruins.

Pátras in a Bottle

Achaía Clauss Winery
t 261 036 8100; open summer daily 11–6; winter daily 11–5

About 9km from the port, the Bavarian-style **Achaía Clauss Winery** offers free, hour-long daily tours and tastings from 11am to 7pm. To get there, head out of town on Dim. Goúnaris Street, following the signs for the village of **Saraváli** (Σαράβαλι) and eventually the signs for the winery, and the winery itself will appear on the hill; the no.7 bus from Óthonos Amaliás Street, via Yerokostopoúlou and Kanári Streets, leaves every 30 minutes for the 25-minute trip, but leaves you at the gate, facing an 800m walk. Try hitching up the drive.

The winery was the brainchild of Gustav Clauss, who saw the possibilities of all of those rolling hills around Pátras. It produced its first commercial batch of Mavrodaphne, a sweet, red port-like wine (named after a Greek woman Clauss admired) in 1873. Achaía Clauss never looked back. It produced the first bottled table wine in Greece when it inaugurated its legendary, and now much improved, Demestica brand in 1901. The newer Achaía Clauss Pátras wine is even better.

ⓘ Pátras ›

*EOT: Melina Gate (Gate 6), port area, **t** 261 043 0915; also 26 Filopímenos, **t** 261 062 0353, one street east of Goúnari*

*City Info Centre: 6 Óthonas Amalías, near Karólou, **t** 261 046 1740, www.infocenterPátras.gr; open daily 8am–10pm*

Useful Information in Pátras

The small **EOT bureau** at the Melína Gate is often closed. A much better bet is the **City Info Centre**.

Tourist police, 52 Goúnari, **t** 261 069 5191. Information and brochures.

Central post office, at Mézonas and Zaími Sts, **t** 261 062 0594. *Open Mon–Fri 8am–8 pm, Sat 8–2.*

Port authority: **t** 261 034 1002. For information about ferries to Italy or the Ionian islands.

Where to Stay in and around Pátras

Pátras ✉ 26500

The hotels here are all close together, making comparison easy, but Pátras is not the town to stay in unless in a pinch; you'll do far better to go to points east or west.

Primarolia, 33 Óthonos Amaliás, **t** 261 062 4900 (€€€€€/€€€€). Fantastic and well-run 'art hotel' where each room is an individual delight.

Astir, 16 Ag. Andréou, **t** 261 027 7502, *www.greekhotel.com/peloponnese/patra/astir* (€€€/€€). A marble pile right at the port with a rooftop pool.

Adonis, Zaími and 9 Kapsáli, **t** 261 022 4213 (€€/€€). Directly opposite the bus station; a stone's throw from the train station and port.

El Greco, 145 Ag. Andréou, **t** 261 027 2931 (€€/€). Central enough if the Adonis is full.

Pension Nicos, Patréos 3, at the corner of 145 Ag. Andréou, **t** 261 062 3757 (€/€). This is a cheap and clean bargain with en suite rooms. Walking up its small curving marble staircase is like walking back in time 30 years to some quiet Greek village – until the traffic noise intrudes, of course. The owner has cleverly placed his reception on the third floor where he has a bar overlooking the traffic. By the time you have navigated the stairs, any urge to clamber back down and try elsewhere vanishes.

The Coast West of Pátras

Although dotted with beauty spots, most notably the extensive pine forest of Strofiliás near Kalógria, as well as wetlands, grassy dunes and sandy beaches, the Achaian coast west of Pátras holds surprisingly little charm. The seaside road west to Vrachneíka is a solid line of villas, cafés, ouzeries and restaurants and, while the swimming may not be wonderful, it beats the beaches closer to Pátras. From Kamínia and on to Cape Áraxos, the water gets cleaner and the beaches, at certain points, more appealing.

There are several luxury resorts, the kind that look great in brochures, and are so well-equipped that you needn't venture out into the surrounding countryside at all.

The hotels below are listed in order of their distance from Pátras.

Poseidon, 14km west at Kaminía, ✉ 25002, **t** 261 0671602, *www.poseidon-hotels.gr* (€€€/€€€). Fairly new, in a fairly built-up area by the sea. International in flavour, well appointed and well run,with TV, small pool, and buffet breakfast. Mostly business clients.

Castella Beach, 18km west at Alissós, ✉ 25002, **t** 269 307 1477, *www.castella-beach.gr* (€/€). Pleasant family-run hotel by the sea. Negotiate if you wish to stay a few days. *Open all year.*

Camping Golden Sunset, Káto Alissós, ✉ 25002, **t** 269 307 1276, *www.patras campings.gr* (€/€). A popular choice as well, offering a pool, water slides, and a narrow beach. *Open Mar–Oct 15.*

Achaios, 22km west at Niforéika, ✉ 25200, **t** 269 302 5370, *www.hotel achaios.gr* (€€€/€€). Impressive, large modern hotel with TV, pool, tennis.

Dyme, 25km west at Káto Achaía, ✉ 25200, **t** 269 302 5310 (€€/€). Just off the main square, a lovely provincial hotel, with a tiny garden and a blue façade, now offering TV and air-conditioning.

Grecotel Lakopetra Beach, 35km west at Lakópetra, ✉ 25200, **t** 269 305 1713, *www.grecotel.gr* (€€€€€/€€€€€). With indoor and outdoor pools, tennis, the works. Full board required. *Open April–Oct.*

Kalogria Beach, 12km west of the Grecotel at Kalógria, ✉ 27052, **t** 269 303 1380, *www.peloponnesetravel.gr* (€€€€/€€€€). Offers the whole round of facilities and has the best beach in the area. The dunes and reeds are lovely at sunrise and sunset. *Open April–Oct.*

Eating Out in Pátras

Mourágeios, 8 Themistokléous, Kastellókambos, **t** 261 099 1729. Pátras' premier restaurant up by the castle, serving such delicacies as octopus with lemon and caramelized onions, smoked salmon, and duck fillets, in a quiet, sophisticated setting complete with an olive tree.

Ichthyóskala, **t** 261 033 3778. Well-priced seafood by the sea in front of Ag. Andréas. Fish are displayed in wooden boxes as if at a market and you choose the one you want.

Fayoúm, 7 Vas. Roúgou, up near the castle, **t** 261 027 0557. Run by a German couple using good Greek ingredients to create traditional and not so traditional dishes; try their unique meat, goat's cheese and fruit. *Eves only.*

There is a potpourri of fast food places around the port, and one or two pleasant spots for a snack near the north entrance to the castle that offer a view.

A Trip into Central Greece: Delphi

Delphi, one of Central Greece's most spectacular ancient sites, is now an easy day (or overnight) trip from the Northern Peloponnese, via the Río–Andírio bridge or the Éghio–Ag. Nikólaos ferry; you can also go directly from Athens.

Excavations by the French began in 1891 – but before they could excavate the antiquities they had to move the newer village on top of the ruins to its present site. **Modern Delphi**, filled with hotels, is a small, rather ordinary town split by the highway into two frumpy one-way streets, Vas. Pávlou & Frideríkis and Apóllonos. Parking is not easy, so take what you can get.

Ancient Delphi

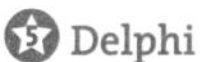

The greatest oracle of the ancient world occupies one of the most spectacular, lyrical settings in Greece: a shelving ledge below the sheer Phaedriades (the Shining Cliffs), with a wild glen and

The Myth

Gaia, or Earth, had the first oracle here, with her consort Poseidon. Her daughter Themis, goddess of justice and order, inherited it, then Phoebe the moon goddess, who 'as a birthday gift' gave it to Phoebos Apollo – a succession that mirrors the interests of religion itself, from early fertility cults to the great cosmic patterns of the sun and stars. The oracle's first name was Pytho, and it was watched over by Earth's guardian, Python, who like the Athenian Kekrops was a hero-snake, a sacred king, who had to be killed to make way for the new. To get there from his natal Délos, Apollo turned himself into a dolphin (*delphinos*, hence Delphi) and hijacked a Cretan ship; he shot Python and erected the Omphalos, the navel, the holy of holies, over his tomb.

Apollo evolved into what must have been the ideal of every Greek man – handsome, lusty, arty, an ace at the bow or lyre, the ultimate Olympian, the god of truth and light. Although the rationalizers made Python into an evil monster, Apollo had to be cleansed of the murder, and he spent eight years in self-imposed exile as a slave of the King of Thessaly in the Vale of Tempe, tending his flocks. When he returned to Delphi, he instituted the Pythian Games to celebrate. His first priests were Cretan captains from Knossos' fleet, recalling the Minoan roots of his cult.

Apollo, however, didn't spend the whole year at Delphi, but in November went north for his annual confab with the Hyperborians. For the three months in his absence, when no oracles were given, Apollo's youngest brother Dionysos took over the sanctuary. Women from Athens and Delphi, known as the Thyiads, would join in orgiastic rites on Mount Parnossós, culminating every nine years in a festival called the Herois, in which the Thyiads 'brought up Semele' (the mother of Dionysos, who was really Gaia) from Hades to bless the earth. The priests would later downplay this side of Delphi, better to promote the Apolloine message of truth and light; the Romans, who lacked the psychological fine-tuning of the Greeks, would deny it altogether.

dense olive groves at its feet, and the Gulf of Corinth 2,000ft below. Like Olympia, Delphi was a holy place that all Greeks shared; it was the centre of the world – when Zeus released an eagle in the east and an eagle in the west, Delphi is where they met. It was *the* great authority, appearing somewhere in nearly every Hellenic myth and saga. And the whole – the stories, the temples, the art in the treasuries – was a masterpiece, albeit with a pinch of humbug.

History

The long continuity of the sanctuary in myth is reflected in Delphi's Minoan finds, traces of Mycenaean building under Apollo's Temple and a cache of 200 Mycenaean terracotta statues found under the Temple of Athena Pronaia. This Athena superseded a Bronze Age goddess, who was remembered perhaps in the fact that it was always a woman, the Pythia, who spoke for Apollo. The oracle, originally in the middle of a village, was in business by the time of the *Iliad*. It gained more than local importance in response to a very precise need in the late 8th–7th centuries BC: to offer guidance to the newly emergent land-hungry city-states, especially in sanctioning the founding of colonies abroad. Delphi was the first shared oracle, and as such specialized in community issues, legitimizing crucial decisions made by oligarchs, kings and tyrants alike. Although remote (which helped maintain its neutrality), the frequent comings and goings made Delphi the

Getting to and around Delphi

By car: Delphi is a 2hr, 111km drive along the coast from Andíro, just over the Río bridge, or a 43km drive from the ferry port of Ag. Nikólaos opposite Éghio (*see* p.200).

By bus: There are two buses a day from Pátras, and four from Ag. Nikólaos (ferry across the Gulf of Corinth) via Itéa, There are also six buses a day to Delphi from Athens' Liossíon terminal, **t** 210 831 7096, via Thebes, Livadiá and Aráchova. Delphi's **bus station**, **t** 226 508 2317, is at the west end of modern Delphi at Apóllonos and Vas. Pávlou & Frideríkis St.

Taxis: **t** 226 508 2000.

---

central switchboard of the Greek world. Its festival, held every eighth year, featured a competition of songs performed on the lyre.

The first Temple of Apollo was built between 650 and 600 BC, when the Delphians were forced to move outside the holy precinct. It marked a crisis in relations between the local and outside interests in the sanctuary – the so-called First Sacred War of 600–590 BC – which may not even have really happened, but which nicely explained the rise of the Amphictyony ('those who dwell around') of 12 tribes (the Ionians, Dorians, Achaeans, Thessalians, etc.) that took control of the sanctuary, declared Delphi an independent city, put the fertile Crisaean plain below off limits to the plough, and reduced the locals to temple servants. The Amphictyonic League, a kind of proto-United Nations, met twice a year, once at Delphi and once at Thermopylae. The *Homeric Hymn to Apollo* also appeared at this time, and emphasized the panhellenic aspect of the cult; the old Delphic festival was reorganized as the quadrennial Pythian Games, one of the four crown events of Greece (*see* p.154). But the music competitions remained as important as the usual athletic contests and chariot-racing on the Crisaean Plain. Winners were crowned with bay from the Vale of Tempe.

Although participation in the Pythian Games was limited to Greeks, the Delphic oracle acquired international prestige: Egyptians, Etruscans and Persians all made the arduous journey to consult it. In 548 BC, the sanctuary was destroyed by fire, but the temple and the treasuries were soon rebuilt on a grander scale with money sent from all over the world. No one, however, contributed as much as the Alkmaeonids of Athens, who took over the temple project and paid for it to be faced in Parian marble. The grateful oracle then ordered the Spartans to oust the Alkmaeonids' enemies, the Pisistratids, from Athens. This serious breach of ethics was followed by a second scandal in 490, when the Spartan king Cleomenes I paid the oracle to declare his fellow king Demaratus illegitimate, but he was caught and committed suicide.

Trying to preserve its reputation, the oracle became cautious, and took the Persian side in the wars. Xerxes showed his gratitude by sending an expedition to pillage Delphi, but Apollo knew how to 'protect his own' with a miraculous rock slide. The whole saga of the oracle's advice to Athens, to rely on its 'wooden walls' and 'divine Sálamis', may even have been invented by Themistocles to increase support for his plans; many prophecies were made up after the fact, back at a time when a *polis* had time to 'improve' history. By the time of the Peloponnesian War, when historians like Thucydides interviewed eye-witnesses, oracles became less useful as a propaganda tool; keeping records on stone, as in Athens, also made the past harder to tweak. But perhaps most importantly, the Greek city-states, especially the democracies, felt sufficiently legitimate to not want any second-guessing from Apollo.

In spite of the fall-off in big state oracles, Delphi continued to be honoured as the ultimate authority on religion. Victors in war felt obliged to send Apollo a tithe of the spoils, which were used to create works of art in a fever of one-upmanship. In 448 BC a Second Sacred War broke out for local control of the sanctuary, with Athens taking the Phocian side and Spartans the Delphian side. In 373 rocks from the Phaedriades cliff fell on the Temple of Apollo, and in 356, while contributions came in for its rebuilding, the Phocians started the Third Sacred War by rifling the treasuries to pay their army; after their 15 minutes of fame, Philip II of Macedon smashed them and made them repair the damage (346 BC). In 279 BC the Galatians tried to seize Delphi, but a combination of local heroics and another timely landslide from the Phaedriades saved the day. The Romans did some repair work when they weren't pillaging (Sulla took all the gold and silver in 83 BC; Nero, who competed in the games and naturally won a music prize, pinched 500 statues). In the 2nd century AD, Hadrian and Herodes Atticus restored it all and the Pythia spoke again, mostly for Roman tourists. The last oracle was given to Julian the Apostate in the 360s, whose envoy received the apocryphal reply: 'Tell the king, the fair-wrought hall has fallen to the ground. No longer has Phoebus a hut, nor a prophetic laurel, nor a spring that speaks.'

The Sanctuary of Athena Pronaia

Pausanias, as usual, was the first to leave a traveller's account of Delphi, and today the traditional tour follows in his footsteps. There are two sacred zones, roughly a mile apart, and if you approach from the east you'll come first to the area called **Marmária** with the Sanctuary of Athena Pronaia; steps lead down to it from the road.

The Mycenaean finds here indicate that this was the original pre-oracle sanctuary of the village. On the terrace are two ruined temple-like buildings, one of which was dedicated to Philakos, a local hero who helped rout the Persians from Delphi in 480 BC. Below are remains of altars and the **Old Temple of Athena Pronaia**,

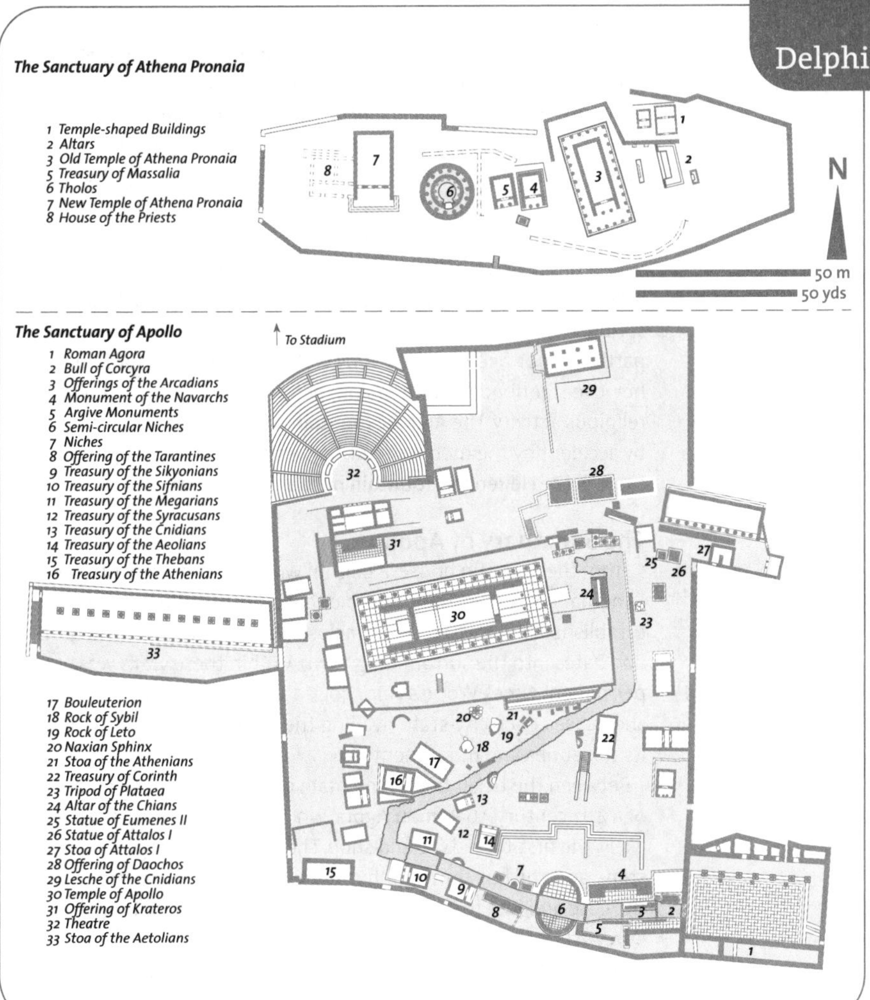

'the Temple Guardian', which was built of porous stone in the mid-7th century (the surviving capitals are among the oldest in Greece). It was a particularly unlucky building, rebuilt in *c.* 500 BC, damaged by the landslide in 480 and then the earthquake in 373; even when it was excavated, another landslide ruined all but three columns. Next to it was a Doric **Treasury** (*c.* 480 BC), the Parian marble **Treasury of Massalia** (Marseille) from 530 BC, and the loveliest and most mysterious building in Delphi, the partly reconstructed **Tholos** (*c.* 390 BC). A rotunda in Pentelic marble, topped with a conical roof and surrounded by a ring of 20 Doric columns, with an inner circle of 10 Corinthian columns, it resembles the equally mysterious Tholos in Epidauros and could be by the same architect. Old Pausanias didn't mention it, however, leaving us clueless as to its purpose. Next to it stood the **New Temple of Athena Pronaia**, from *c.* 360 BC, built in the local limestone. A path west of here leads to the 4th-century BC **Gymnasium**, which was rebuilt by the Romans. The steepness of the site forced them to build on two levels: on top was the *xystos*, a covered running track, while below was the *palaestra*, built around a court with a circular pool. The nearby café has lovely views.

Back on the road, where it bends around the ravine that separates the cliffs of the Phaedriades, rises the clear, cold **Castalian spring**. Here pilgrims, priests and the Pythia bathed and in particular purified themselves by wetting their hair (murderers, however, required full immersion) before participating in any religious activity. The **Archaic fountain house** (*c.* 590 BC) was found by accident by the modern road; some 50 yards further up the slope is the **Hellenistic fountain house**, cut out of the rock.

The Sanctuary of Apollo

Sanctuary of Apollo
t 226 508 2312; open summer daily 8–7.30; winter daily 8.30–3; adm exp but includes adm to the museum; bring a bottle of water

From the fountain house, a pilgrim would continue east to the Sanctuary of Apollo. The trapezoidal perimeters of its precinct, established in *c.* 600 BC, were enclosed by a wall or ***peribolos*** that had gates into the surrounding town. Within these walls was a permanent Greek World's Fair, chock-a-block with magnificent showcases, each city-state rivalling the others in the splendour of its treasuries and monuments.

Between the ticket booth and main gate are extensive remains of a 4th-century AD **Roman Agora**, where the last pilgrims (or more likely, the first tourists) could shop. The **Sacred Way** begins up a few steps, and still has some haphazard paving from Roman times. Past the gate and just to the right is the base of the bronze **Bull of Corcyra** (480 BC), dedicated by Corfu after it landed an enormous catch of tuna. This has a certain innocent charm compared to what follows. Opposite stood the overweening **Monument of the Navarchs**, dedicated by Lysander in 403 BC to celebrate Sparta's victory over Athens at Aegospotami with 37 bronze statues of Spartan admirals and gods. Facing them (and in their face) were the **Offerings of the Arcadians**, nine bronze statues erected to celebrate a successful invasion of Sparta in 369 BC. Back on the left side, the Athenian **Offering of Marathon** (460 BC) was erected as a tardy tribute to Miltiades. It set a lofty standard for victory monuments with 13 bronzes by the great Phidias (the 10 eponymous heroes of Athens plus Miltiades, Apollo and Athena); three more were added later. Next to this are remains of two **Argive Monuments**, showing the Seven against Thebes and the revenge of their sons, the Epigonoi (the large semi-circular niche) erected after a victory over Sparta in *c.* 460 BC. For Argos, any thumping of Sparta was worth celebrating: to mark her defeat by Epaminondas of Thebes they erected the niche on the left, with statues of the 10 mythical kings. The colonies got in on the act too – next to the 10 kings is a large rectangular base that supported the **Offering of the Tarentines**, donated by Sparta's colony in southern Italy.

Next come the first of 27 once dazzling treasuries, most now reduced to rubble. On the left beneath the Sacred Way lie the square foundations of the **Treasury of the Sikyonians**, built *c.* 580, and rebuilt after the big fire; it had an open pavilion that may have displayed the chariot of the Sikyon tyrant Kleisthenes, victor of the first Pythian Games. Next to it are the huge foundations of the **Treasury of the Sifnians** (*c.* 530 BC), the most splendid of all, an elegant Ionian building in Parian marble funded with tithes from the island's gold mines; its magnificent frieze is in the museum. At a bend in the Sacred Way stands the platform (on the right) of the **Treasury of the Megarians**; there are scanty remains of the **Treasuries of the Syracusans** (erected after their great upset victory over Athens), **Cnidians** and **Aeolians**; on the right, half of the foundations survive of the **Treasury of the Thebans**, built after they defeated Sparta at Leúktra (371 BC). Just up from here on a triangular platform stands the Doric **Treasury of the Athenians** in Parian marble, where Athens proudly displayed the spoils of Marathon. It offers a general idea of what the others looked like; in 1906, the city of Athens paid 35,000 gold drachmae for it to be reconstructed.

Next to this are the damaged rectangular foundations of the **Bouleuterion** or council house of the Delphians, and the **Rock of the Sibyl**, a chunk fallen from the Phaedriades where tradition has it that the first Pythia, Herophile, stood and sang when she came from Troy. Another of the boulders here is the **Rock of Leto**, where Apollo's mother stood and gave him the encouragement he needed to slay Python, whose lair was the nearby crevice. Part of the mighty Ionic column of the **Monument of the Naxians** (570 BC) is in place on another rock; its crowning Sphinx is in the museum. Behind this was the **Sanctuary of Gaia-Themis**, the original oracle where a spring once flowed, its traces covered in part by the **retaining wall of the Temple of Apollo**. This wall, made of irregular rounded polygonal blocks fitted together without mortar, is a unique work of masonry that stood up to the area's many earthquakes. In the late Hellenistic era, the Delphians used it for a municipal noticeboard.

On the left, the long structure against the retaining wall was the **Stoa of the Athenians**, built in 478 BC to house Persian trophies – the massive cables of linen and papyrus, 3ft thick, that had bound Xerxes' famous boat bridge over the Hellespont and the figure-heads from his ships; the inscription is intact on the lower step. The circular space up the steps in front of the *stoa* was the **Halos**, or threshing floor, where every ninth year the *Stepteria* mystery play was held. A lane off to the right passes the remains of the **Treasury of Corinth**, the oldest at Delphi, built to house gifts given by Croesus, hoping to butter up Apollo for a favourable divination.

The Sacred Way, now well paved, rises past the circular base that once supported the 18ft gilded bronze **Tripod of Plataea**. Inscribed on the bottom with the names of the 31 cities who joined to defeat the Persians in 479, the tripod's legs twisted like a giant rope and ended in three snake heads, supporting a great golden basin. The basin was pillaged by the Phocians in the Third Sacred War, while the tripod was taken by Constantine the Great as a bauble for Constantinople, where it remains in the Hippodrome, minus a snake head, lopped off by Mehmet the Conqueror in 1452. The plinth nearby held the **Chariot of Helios**, a dedication from Rhodes (*c.* 304 BC); there is some evidence that the magnificent Horses of St Mark's in Venice may have started their varied career pulling the chariot here. North of this are two **pedestals** for gold statues of Eumenes and Attalos of Pergamon, and the ruined Stoa of Attalos.

At the top of the Sacred Way are the bases of the **Tripods of Gelon and Hiero**, all that remain of four huge golden tripods on a vast monument commemorating Syracuse's victory over the Carthaginians at Himera in 480 BC – but they too fell victim to the Phocians in 353 BC. To the left is the 28ft **Altar of the Chians** in black and white marble, offered in the 5th century BC in thanksgiving for their liberation from the Persians. In 1920, after being liberated from the Turks, the islanders paid for its reconstruction.

In spite of all the competition, the Doric **Temple of Apollo** dominated Delphi and still does today, with its six re-erected columns. Tradition says the first temple was built of bay wood and leaves, the second in feathers and beeswax, and the third in bronze, before the legendary architects Agamedes and Trophonios built it of stone in the 7th century. After the fire in 548 BC this was replaced by the splendid Alkmaeonid temple, on the same scale as the Parthenon; after rocks fell on it in 373 BC, it was rebuilt in local limestone, with pediment sculptures of Parian marble that have curiously vanished without the slightest trace. The French excavators dismantled the temple, searching for signs of the famous cleft and the *adyton* – where the Omphalos was kept, where the sacred spring Kassiotis was piped, and where the Pythia sat on her tripod – and for all their pains found only hints of a small underground structure.

Delphi's moralizing bent was concisely expressed by the two famous maxims inscribed in the *pronaos*: 'Know Thyself' and 'Nothing in Excess'. The first one didn't quite have the meaning we give it today, but advised knowing one's limitations before the gods, while the second expressed the moderation, the *sophrosýne* that the Greeks idealized, perhaps because they so rarely if ever achieved it outside of art. Pausanias on his visit saw an altar of Poseidon, a gold statue of Apollo, statues of Homer, the Fates and the iron throne of Pindar (who, to the chagrin of Greece, had supported Delphi's defeatism in the Persian Wars; nevertheless his ghost was invited to an annual feast with Apollo). Here too was the hearth of the eternal flame, made of fir branches and tended by women past menopause. If any Greek city's sacred fire was somehow religiously 'polluted', all the fires in the city would have to be extinguished and a messenger sent on the double to bring back a new clean flame from Delphi.

The Sacred Way follows the length of the temple; to the west, a gate in the *peribolos* led to the large **Stoa of the Aetolians**, dedicated after their victory over the Galatians in 278 BC. Before that, to your right, is the rectangular *exedra* that held the **Offering of Krateros** (320 BC), dedicated by the companion who saved Alexander the Great's life during a lion hunt in Susa. A Roman stair next to it ascends to the 4th-century BC **Theatre**, which hosted the musical and poetry contests of the Pythian Games. It is beautifully preserved (the Romans were the last to restore it, in grey limestone) and it enjoys a magical view, at its best in late afternoon. The orchestra still has its irregular pavement and water channel; the 35 tiers of seats are divided two-thirds of the way up by a *diazoma* (landing). A path to the east leads to a rectangular *exedra* that was the **Offering of Daochos of Thessaly** (330 BC) – some of its statues are in the museum – and the site of the **Temenos of Neoptolemos**, honouring the son of Achilles who was killed here by a priest of Apollo. The ruins further on belonged to the **Lesche of the Knidians** (*c.* 450 BC), a ritual dining-hall/clubhouse that once had an extraordinary painting by Polygnotos, of which Pausanias' lengthy description is all that survives; it was so complex that it included 'viewing instructions'.

Two fountains that once held the water of the now dry Kossotis spring lie between the Theatre and **Stadium**. The latter is at the top of Delphi, proof that even spectators in ancient times had to be fit. It too is one of the best preserved in Greece, and was last renovated by the ever-generous Herodes Atticus, who added the triumphal arch on the end. Stands seating 7,000 on the north and west sides were cut into the rock, while the south side (with no seats) was made level by a support wall in the 5th century BC. The track here was 177m, or 600 Roman feet.

The Museum

Delphi Museum
open summer daily 8–7.30; winter daily 8.30–3; entrance included in site ticket

Located just west of the site, this museum, full of beautiful things, is Delphi's modern treasury. A large **floor mosaic** of animals at the entrance came from a 5th-century church on the site. At the top of the **stairs** an iron tripod and bronze cauldron from the 7th century BC offer an example of the favourite votive offering of Archaic times. Next to it is a Hellenistic copy of the Omphalos, the navel of the world, found just outside the Temple of Apollo (it was definitely an 'outie'); marble fillets and knots represent the wool and jewels that covered the original. Even Delphi's earliest votives had an aristocratic quality: **Room II** has three bronze shields from the 8th century BC and a small Daedelic *kouros* perhaps representing Apollo (*c.* 650 BC). The next room, **Room III**, has two bold early 6th-century BC *kouroi* from Argos, *Kleobis* and *Biton* (*see* p.278), signed by Polymedes, a small bronze *Apollo* and five damaged but intriguing Archaic *metopes* on the story of the Argonauts from the first Sikyonian Treasury (560 BC).

Once an item had been dedicated to a god, it had to stay in the holy precinct, and if damaged it was buried in a dump. One of these dumps, from the mid-5th century BC, yielded the beautiful works in **Room IV**: a life-sized bull made of silver sheets, originally attached to a copper frame, and ivories, including the heads of Artemis and Apollo (with long golden tresses) from chryselephantine statues, along with some of the golden sheets, decorated with animals, that adorned their garments (6th century BC). **Room V** has the enigmatically smiling Naxian Sphinx, young and lithe on her very fluted Ionic column; sphinxes were frequently placed on Archaic tombs as guardians, and this one may have served the same role, replacing Python as the oracle's protector. Here, too, is some of the liveliest Archaic sculpture to come down to us, from the Treasury of the Sifnians (*c.* 535 BC), which justifies the building's reputation – a delightful *caryatid*, the great pediment sculpture of the impetuous Heracles stealing Apollo's tripod while Athena tries to referee, and the two surviving friezes by an unknown master. On the east frieze, the gods are assembled (pro-Trojan deities on the left, pro-Greek on the right) while the Greeks and Trojans fight over a body. The north frieze shows the Gigantomachy, where the gods do battle with the giants.

The next room, **Room VI**, has the original *metopes* (*c.* 490 BC) from the Treasury of the Athenians, showing the labours of Theseus and Heracles, notable for their daring composition. **Rooms VII and VIII** contain the remains of the Archaic Alkmaeonid Temple of Apollo, and two hymns to Apollo from the 2nd century BC, found engraved in the wall of the Athenian Treasury; they are among the few to survive complete with their musical notation in Greek letters. **Rooms IX and X** have grave *stelae* and fragments from the Tholos – its Hellenistic *metopes* are remarkable, sadly damaged. **Room XI** contains statues from the *Offering of King Daochos of Thessaly* (330s BC) celebrating his boss Philip II's victory at Chairóneia. The five, representing Daochos' ancestors, are copies of bronzes; at least one, Agias (14 times victor in the Olympic, Pythian, Nemean and Isthmian Games), was by Lysippos. Here, too, is the giant 4th-century BC acanthus column topped with three dancing girls, who once held a tripod.

The museum's star, the bronze *Charioteer* of *c.* 475 BC, stands in **Room XII**, along with bronze fragments from the rest of the monument, which was smashed in the earthquake of 373 BC. It was dedicated by Polyzalos of Gela in Sicily, who won the chariot race – a sport that became an obsession among Gela's tyrants. A great work of the Severe Classical style, the charioteer is calm, having already won his victory; even the eyes of magnesium and onyx, with their eyelashes, are well preserved and slightly uneven, which combined with other slightly less-than-perfect features give the cool figure his individuality. His body, which resembles a fluted column, was disproportionately elongated, perhaps because it was meant to be seen from below. The last room, **Room XIII**, is dedicated to the handsome Parian marble figure of Antinous (2nd century AD), a laughing little girl (3rd century BC) and a fine Hellenistic portrait bust, believed to represent Titus Q. Flamininus, who defeated the Macedonians in 197 BC. Small bronzes and ceramics are here too, some going back to Mycenaean times and some from the Corycian Cave. A new modern mausoleum-style museum has been built, tucked under the road, which will display some of Delphi's many other finds.

ⓘ **Arachóva >**
on the short road to the Xenia Hotel, **t** *226 702 1630; open Mon–Fri 8am–10pm, Sat and Sun 8–12*

ⓘ **Delphi >>**
12 Vas. Pávlou & Frideríkis, **t** *226 508 2900; open Mon–Fri 7.30–2.30*

Where to Stay in and around Delphi

Aráchova ✉ 32004

With its handsome traditional-style inns, nearby Aráchova is a terrific alternative to staying in Delphi. In summer and on winter weekdays, prices plummet without any effort on your part.

Besides the following, there are 200 rooms through the **Women's Rural Tourism Cooperative, t** 226 703 1519.

Santa Marina Arachova, t 226 703 1230, *www.santa-marina.gr* (€€€€€/€€€€). Luxurious new boutique hotel with sumptuous rooms, gorgeous mountain views, and a cosy bar. The restaurant serves dishes using organic ingredients brought in from the Santa Marina farm on Mýkonos.

Xenónas Generális, t 226 703 1529, *www.generalis.gr* (€€€€€/€€). Beautiful restoration of an old mansion: colourful rooms done up in a mix of modern design and folk tradition, plus an indoor heated pool and a brand new spa. Popular with weekending Athenians, but weekday prices very reasonable all year round.

Villa Filoxenia, t 226 703 1406, *www.villafiloxenia.gr* (€€€€/€€). Opposite the Sfaláki below, on a quiet street; attractive appartments with traditional décor, and fully equipped with sitting rooms, bedrooms and kitchens.

Xenónas Sfaláki, just after the turn for the ski area (look for the signs), **t** 226 703 1970 (€€€/€€). Cosy, quiet, well run; with charming rooms for four; a cute breakfast area with tiny fireplace.

Delphi ✉ 33054

Hotels here are nondescript but comfortable, and every one above D class has room for a tour bus or two. All are open all year.

Amalía, Apollónos St, **t** 226 508 2101, *www.amalia.gr* (€€€€€/€€€€€). At the west end of town, with views. Garden setting, breakfast in the large restaurant and spacious lounges. Outdoor pool.

Apollonia, 37–39 Ifigenías and András Syngroú, **t** 226 508 2919, *www.hotelapollonia.gr* (€€€€/€€€). New hotel built in the traditional style, with spacious rooms (including connecting rooms for families), helpful staff and a good restaruant. Parking 100m away.

Pythia Art Hotel, 6 Vas. Pavlou, **t** 226 70 508 2328, *http://delphihotels.eu* (€€€/€€). Delphi's boutique hotel, decorated with contemporary Greek painting, had a thorough renovation in 2004; bright airy rooms have lovely views, but the bathrooms are small.

Hermes, 27 Vas. Pávlou & Frideríkis, **t** 226 508 2318 (€€€/€€€). Neat, modern, white with brown trim; some rooms with view. Bargain gently in the off season.

Vouzás, 1 Vas. Pávlou & Frideríkis, **t** 226 508 2232 (€€€/€€). At the east end; a marble pile spilling down the hill with superb views from the rooms that need a serious revamp.

Pan, 53 Vas. Pávlou & Frideríkis, **t** 226 508 2294, *www.panartemis.gr* (€€/€€). Not new, but clean, and many rooms have a view. Some sleep five, so it is a great family choice.

Varónos, 25 Vas. Pávlou & Frideríkis, **t** 226 508 2345 (€€/€€). The jungle of potted plants helps to obscure the boring furniture in the spacious lobby. Clean and modern.

Sun View Rooms, 84 Apollónos, **t** 226 508 2349 (€/€). Friendly Mr Kalénzis' seven new rooms may be Delphi's best bargain, with TVs and balconies with unimpeded views. They claim they spend €20 a week on cleaning products, and it shows.

Pension Sibylla, 9 Vas. Pávlou & Frideríkis, **t** 226 508 2335, *www.sibylla-hotel.gr* (€/€). A bargain with a friendly English-speaking owner. High-ceilinged en suite rooms.

Eating Out in and around Delphi

Aráchova

Taverna Agnantio, towards the east end of town on the main road, **t** 226 703 2114. Specializes in grilled meats. *Closed July and Aug.*

Taverna Karathanási, on the main street in the centre, **t** 226 703 1360. Plain but cosy, specializing in casserole dishes since 1930; in summer, dine on the upstairs terrace.

Delphi

Taverna Váchos, 31 Apollónos, **t** 226 508 3186. Pink tablecloths, an expanse of marble floor and a great terrace form the backdrop for this upmarket, reasonably priced family taverna.

Epíkouros, 33 Vas. Pávlou & Frideríkis, **t** 226 508 3250. This elegant restaurant with a terrific view belongs to the Acropole Hotel; it is well cared for and caters for groups. *Open weekends only in Nov–Mar.*

Lechariá, 33 Apollónos, **t** 226 508 2864. A few steps west of Váchos. Nicely decorated with blond wood and red-checked curtains; this cosier spot has good food and the killer view.

Elís

If the seven prefectures of the Peloponnese were Snow White's dwarves, soft green Elís would be Sleepy. Elís has done its best to sit it out on the periphery of the great events of the Peloponnese, rarely throwing its weight around. Its very unobtrusiveness and political insignificance made it ideally suited to host the greatest of all panhellenic games at Olympia which, over time, made all of Elís neutral holy ground. If you're looking for the Arcadía painted by Poussin, of wandering shepherds watching flocks grazing in oaken groves, come here.

The sweetness of Elís turns to high drama in the south on the frontiers of Arcadía and Messenía, where the Temple of Apollo at Bassae and the Néda Gorge are the highlights: the first an awesome work of man, the second a well-kept natural secret and a slice of vanishing Greece.

11

Don't miss

1. A bucolic setting and a great museum
Olympia p.230

2. A Frankish castle by the sea
Chlemoútsi p.225

3. A brooding, austere temple
Apollo's temple at Bassae p.253

4. Nature's enchantments
Néda Gorge p.255

5. Traditional village charms
Andrítsaina p.252

See map overleaf

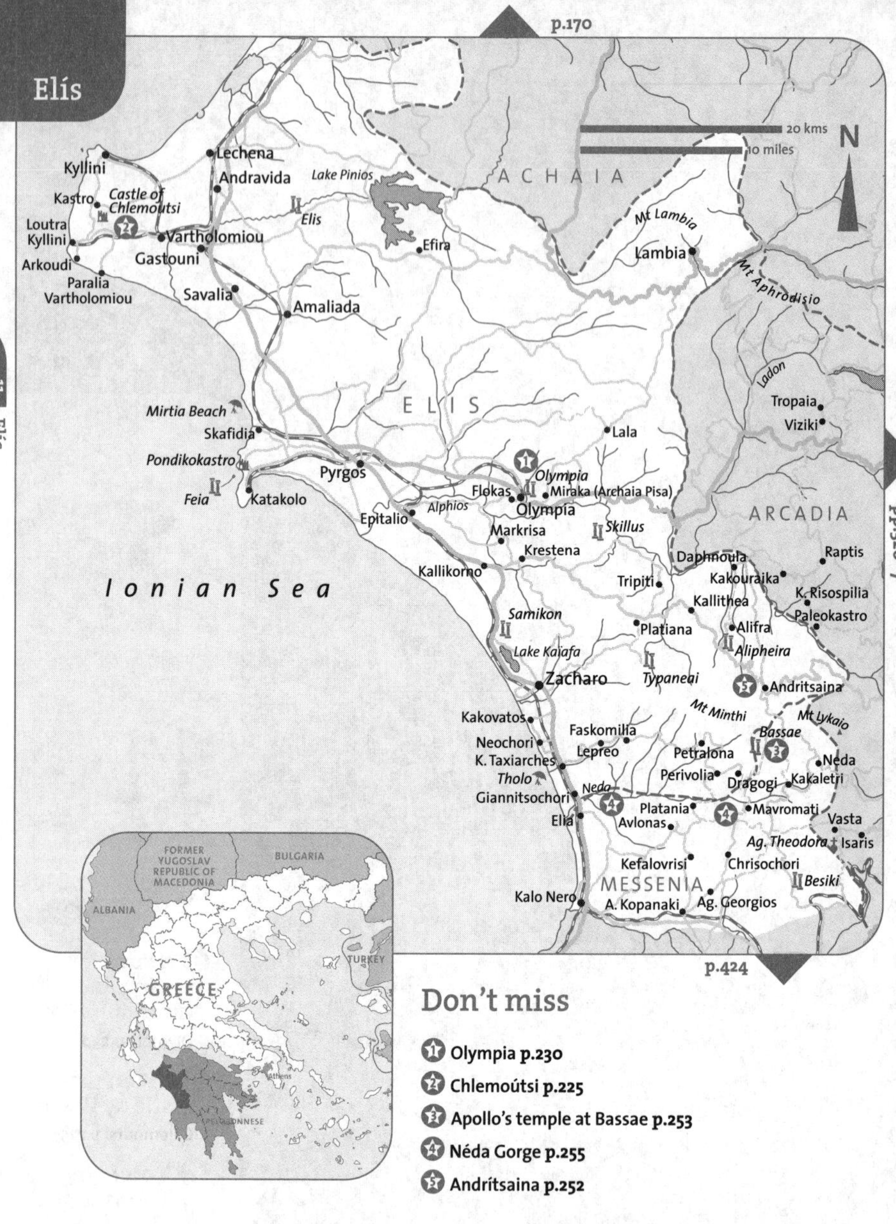

Don't miss

1. **Olympia p.230**
2. **Chlemoútsi p.225**
3. **Apollo's temple at Bassae p.253**
4. **Néda Gorge p.255**
5. **Andrítsaina p.252**

If Elís didn't stir the pot, it may be because it was singularly contented. The Eleans never founded a colony, perhaps because their own land was so rich and well-watered. Homer calls it 'goodly'. Although it had the usual ancient problems with neighbours, it was far enough away from the worst of them, Sparta. When the sons of Heracles landed on the coast of Elís to invade the Peloponnese, they were, according to the Delphic oracle, to seek the guidance of a certain Triops, 'the three-eyed'. They soon came across an Aetolian named Oxylus riding a one-eyed horse and decided he would do. Now Oxylus had been exiled in Elís for a year to expiate a murder, and he knew how fertile it was, so he craftily diverted the Dorian invaders around Elís and led them on their victorious march through the rest of the Peloponnese. As a reward for his services, the Dorians made him king of the bit they never saw – Elís. Like Pelops, another king of Elís (*see* p.46), Oxylus had the *ponirία* to do what needed to be done. Centuries later, Elís was beloved by the Franks, who called it the 'milk-cow of the Morea' and made their capital here: it reminded them of a slightly dishevelled France, and they found it one of the few places in southern Greece suited to growing flax and grazing cattle. Sand dunes and beaches line its gentle coasts, although neglect and wasteful farming under the Turks made them malarial until after the Second World War and the advent of DDT.

Northern Elís

The green, low hills in this northwesternmost corner are not what first spring to mind when you think of Greece, but they are the bee's knees if you're a cow or a grapevine or a watermelon or a lazy cyclist. Otherwise it's all a bit ho-hum.

Andravída and Chlemoútsi

Following the main highway southwest from Pátras, you may well be buzzed over by pairs or threesomes of training jets from the air base at Áraxos. Closer to ground, you may be more intimately plagued by humming little vampires; this, after all, is the Peloponnese's Mosquito Cape, or Aktí Kounoupéli.

The first likely place to stop for a coffee is **Andravída** (Ανδραβίδα). This was Andreville, the once flourishing Frankish capital of the entire Morea (as they called the Peloponnese), complete with royal palace and princely funerary chapel, now all dust in the wind. Only the transept of the 13th-century Gothic cathedral of **Ag. Sophia** remains, fenced in a lot by the school. The adjacent town square offers the requisite cafés and a bust of the dashing mustachioed Kapetan Konstantinídes, a local hero of 1821.

Castle of Chlemoútsi
open Mon–Sat 8–8, Sun 8–2.30; closed Mon in winter

The scenery improves west towards the rolling hills of the coast, nor do you have to go far before the mighty landmark **Castle of Chlemoútsi** (Χλεμούτσι) looms into view. The name of its distinctive hill derives from its resemblance to a turtle shell, and it has drawn people since Palaeolithic times. The physiognomy changed for good in the 1220s, when Geoffrey I de Villehardouin, Prince of Achaía, demanded that his Latin clergy part with some of its gold to pay for a proper *château-fort*, which he called Clermont.

Getting to and around Northern Elís

Three **buses** a day leave for Kyllíni from Pátras (*see* p.207); look for the one saying 'Zákynthos'. Pýrgos is Elís' main transportation hub, with several **trains** (**t** 262 102 2576) daily to and from Pátras, Katákolo and ancient Olympia. The Pýrgos bus station, just below the main *plateía*, **t** 262 102 2592, has 10 daily buses to Athens, hourly to Olympia, and several to Kyllíni, Katakólo and Kalamáta. Buses to the beaches or to ancient Elis depart infrequently from Amaliáda, which is also on the Pátras–Pýrgos train route.

The furious pope excommunicated him, but Geoffrey didn't bat an eyelid. The result is the finest and largest Latin building ever built in Greece, dwarfing the little village of **Kástro** that clings to its skirts. Geoffrey's brother William later built a mint in its walls, to stamp the coin of the realm, the *tournois* ('tails' showed the cathedral of St-Martin de Tours), confusing the Venetians, who called Chlemoútsi Castel Torense. The walls of the castle have recently undergone a five-year restoration and are quite complete, although for some silly bureaucratic reason you can no longer walk along the top for the famous view over all of Elís and Zákynthos. Inside, the massive outer curtain wall is a hexagonal keep bearing a plaque to the 'Marble King' Constantine Dragatses, the last and future emperor of Byzantium (*see* p.373), who took Chlemoútsi in 1427 as part of his campaign to capture Pátras and put an end to the Franks' pirating ways. The keep's six lofty vaulted halls of fine ashlar masonry are impressive, even if their floors have caved in, leaving their fireplaces suspended on the walls. Panels in English explain what's what. Although the restorations have tidied things up, one almost misses the uncanny atmosphere of Chlemoútsi in the 1960s, when the walls still bore the yawning hole smashed through by Ibrahim Pasha and dead ravens hung upside down from the tower, flapping to and fro in the wind.

Kyllíni, Loutrá Kyllíni and Arkoúdi

Six kilometres north of the castle was Clarence, or Glarentza, in knightly days of yore the chief port of Frankish Greece. Now restored to its ancient name **Kyllíni** (Κυλλήνη), it's merely the chief port for the island of Zákynthos, sitting on the horizon. Pausanias found the usual temples in place when he visited Kyllíni as well as a 'Hermes statue that the people there worship so devoutly which is just an erect penis on a pedestal'. You can almost hear him mutter 'the hicks!' to himself. The Hermes is long gone, of course, but so are medieval Clarence's banks, merchants' palaces, monasteries, artificial port and other institutions that made it one of the richest towns in Greece; when Constantine Dragatses captured it, he razed it to the ground to prevent the Franks from returning while he concentrated on conquering Pátras. Just behind the banana-lined beach is a weedy lot with some very meagre remains of the Frankish castle. Of the ancient city, zilch. There are some nice fish tavernas, but the waiting-to-go-somewhere-better air hangs as heavily over Kyllíni as Pátras.

Graced with stunning dunes, eucaplytus groves, hot mineral waters and a long sandy beach, **Loutrá Kyllíni**, 12km south, now hosts a vast Grecotel resort complex. For something more intimate, carry on just south to a delightful little oasis called **Arkoúdi** (Αρκούδι), which piles down a hill to meet a sandy beach, a pretty horseshoe curling out to sea rocks, rimmed with a banana hedge. The coastal road east of here passes other beaches and the piney **Thinon** (Θινών) **Forest** by the **Paralía Vartholomioú**, with a big car park and a pleasant club on the sands to provide snacks by the sea.

Ancient Elis

To the east, **Gastoúni** (Γαστούνι), a prosperous livestock-rearing village, derives its name from the Frankish barony of Gastogne. The Turks were fond of it too. It has a pretty cross-in-square Byzantine church, **Koímisis tis Theotókou**, built in the 12th century, and renovated and frescoed in 1702.

The first Elean villages were probably much like Andravída or Gastoúni and scattered all over the region. After a period of political upheaval, they united in 472 BC to belatedly form a *polis* with a democratic government and founded a new capital, **ancient Elis**, 15km east of Gastoúni. Exclusive Elean control over the Olympic Games was confirmed at the same date with the building of the great Temple of Zeus at Olympia. There isn't anything half as grand here, although many athletes would come up here to train in the city gymnasium and *palaestra* for the required nine months before the games, along with their relatives and friends, lending Elis a very cosmopolitan air once every four years. Because of the Sacred Truce, the city had no walls until 312 BC. And by the 3rd century AD it was utterly gone.

Elís museum
t 262 204 1415; open Tues–Sun 8.30–2; adm

The **museum** has finds from the site, including some rare theatre tickets (made of stone) which would admit you into the early Hellenistic-Roman **theatre**, the most intact of ancient Elis' remains. This was already in ruins when Pausanias saw it, and unusually it never had seats, although the side entrance to the right is well marked, while to the left of the stage are stones that resemble a bar stool. The view, as always, is rather pretty, in this case over cows in the meadows. The modern road cuts through the *agora*; there are overgrown foundations of a single and a double *stoa*, two Sanctuaries of Aphrodite (right next to each other – perhaps the Eleans needed double help in affairs of the heart), baths and other buildings, some identified, none particularly compelling. The most popular shrine was a *temenos* to Achilles, while the most unusual one was dedicated to Hades, the god of the underworld, and only open once a year.

Where to Stay and Eat in Northern Elís

Kástro Chlemoútsi/Kyllíni

✉ 27050

Staying up in the little village hunkered under the castle offers a quiet change of pace.

Paradise, 100m from the beach at Kástrou Kyllínis, **t** 262 309 5450, *www.killiniparadisehotel.com* (€€/€€). Balconied rooms, two pools, playground, tennis, a garden and a pleasant taverna. *Open May–Oct.*

Catherine Lepída's Apartments, **t** 262 309 5224 or **t** 262 309 5380, *www.8ung.at/apartments* (€€/€€). The lovely Mrs Lepída speaks excellent English. Her studios are surrounded by greenery. *Open May–Oct.*

Kastro, **t** 262 309 5434 (€/€). Simple rooms but a bargain. *Open June–Sept.*

★ Castello >

Castello, **t** 262 309 5360. Family-run taverna with tasty home cooking.

Sou Mou, Kyllíni, **t** 262 309 2396. The best of many near the beach and ferry docks, with traditional fare.

Loutrá Kyllíni ✉ 27050

Olympia Riviera, **t** 262 306 4400, *www.grecotel.com* (€€€€€/€€€€). The Grecotel chain has converted this run-down spa straggling under the trees into a smart, 500-acre complex of four resort hotels, including a boutique hotel and villas (**Mandola Rossa**) and a thalassotherapy-spa complex.

Arkoúdi/Vartholomío

✉ 27050

Akti Rooms, Arkoúdi, **t** 262 309 6100, *pankath@otenet.gr* (€€/€). The classiest choice, a minute above the beach; fresh, airy rooms, marble baths, kitchenettes and mosquito screens. *Open all year.*

Soulis Apartments, Arkoúdi, **t** 262 309 6379, *www.soulisgroup.com* (€€/€). Lovely views and a courtyard paved with slate. *Open all year.*

Dougas, Arkoúdi, **t** 962 309 6432, *www.hotel-dougas.com* (€/€). Way back from the sea but with a pool, restaurant and grassy lawn; a good family choice. *Open all year.*

Alfa, Vartholomío, **t** 262 304 1707 (€/€). Near the Thinon forest; pleasant, family-run, with TVs and mini-fridges. *Open all year.*

Just east of Arkoúdi there are two campsites:

Anginara Beach, **t** 262 309 6211, *www.camping-aginara.gr* (€/€).

Ionion Beach, **t** 262 309 6395, *www.ionion-beach.gr* (€/€). *Open all year.*

Akrogiáli, Arkoúdi, **t** 262 309 6379. Good food on a big shady terrace, with glimpses of Zákynthos through the banana fronds. *Open all year.*

Arquoudi, Arkoúdi, **t** 262 309 6167. Right on the beach, serving snacks, drinks and meals.

Central Elís

Katákolo, Pýrgos, and Alph the Sacred River

The coast south of the 'snout' of Elís is one sweeping sandy beach dotted with campsites reached by little access roads off the main Pátras–Pýrgos highway. The beaches stop at the hilly nub of **Katákolo**, dangling like the proverbial hair from the chinny chin chin. It shelters a convenient port for cruise ships, behemoths that dwarf the little town as they disgorge passengers for Olympia. The pedestrian street in front of Katákolo's portside bars and restaurants has an old-fashioned charm. Stairs in the village lead to the attractive headland surrounding the castle, if you feel like wandering.

The main port of ancient Elis was located around on the other side of the little peninsula, at **Feia**. This is where Olympic-goers from Italy landed, but in the 6th century AD an earthquake caused most of it to subside into the sea. Only its former acropolis, the **Pondikókastro** or 'Mouse Castle', survived, and was transformed by the Villehardouins into the **Castle of Beauvoir** (to see it by car, loop around the back of the little peninsula by following the sign to Ag. Andréas, 1km before Katákolo; it is right above the Hotel Vriniótis). The castle has a romantically overgrown keep and pretty sunset views. A good beach is an added incentive to visit; with a snorkel you may find some of the walls of the ancient port.

Of the sandy beaches to the north of Katákolo, **Mirtiá**, north of **Skafidiá**, is especially nice. Skafidiá is named after a 12th-century monastery, built for an icon of the Panagía. It resembles a little castle, complete with a Venetian tower, and contains a fine library.

East of Katákolo, **Pýrgos** (Πύργος) is probably the dullest capital in the Peloponnese, founded around 1687 during the brief Venetian interlude. Traditionally linked to the currant trade, it isn't a bad place really, but there isn't much to say about it. If you're taking a train or bus to Olympia, you may find yourself here. Try to avoid driving in the centre. At the top of the town, the stately *plateía* with a big white church of Ag. Nikólaos, neoclassical buildings and bars draws most of the 28,700 inhabitants in the evening.

South of Pýrgos lies the mouth of the **Alphiós**, the longest river in the Peloponnese and the favourite of Zeus; its prestige was such that the Greeks put the letter *alpha* first in their alphabet. In the mid-7th century BC, as the Olympics began to draw competitors from the Greek colonies in Italy, the story was told that the lusty river god Alphios fell in love with the nymph Arethousa, and pursued her all the way under the Ionian sea, 'through caverns measureless to man' to Syracuse in Sicily, where he finally caught up, their waters mingling in the seaside springs of Arethousa. Shelley unkindly labelled the Alphiós a 'brackish, Dorian stream' and it must have been murky too when it played its other starring role in mythology, during Heracles' Fifth Labour, the cleaning of the stables of King Augeias of Elís. Under Athena's guidance, Heracles diverted the river through the mass of accumulated manure, sweeping it away in a single day.

The coastal area south of the Alphiós, once a shallow lagoon, is now usually dry; **Epitálio** on its banks has some remains of its Hellenistic-Roman namesake, and scant traces of Homeric Thryon up on the hill of Ag. Geórgios. To continue south along the coast, *see* p.249.

Where to Stay and Eat around Katákolo and Pýrgos

Katákolo/Ag. Andréas ✉ 27067

Olympian Village, on Skafídiá Beach, **t** 262 108 2000, *www.aldemarhotels.com* (€€€€€/€€€). One of those luxurious, 'all in' resorts that are springing up like toadstools. The prime minister and his entourage like this one. It has indoor and outdoor pools and an acclaimed restaurant, the Artemis. *Open May–Oct.*

Iónio, Katákolo, **t** 262 104 1494 (€€/€). Simple quiet rooms in a little neoclassical building. *Open all year.*

Zéphyros, Katákolo, **t** 262 104 1170 (€€/€). Traditionally-styled, and a bit fancier. *Open all year.*

Vriniótis, Ag. Andréas, **t** 262 104 1294, *www.vriniotis.gr* (€€€/€€). A great location by the castle; newly renovated, with air-conditioning. *Open all year.*

Pýrgos ✉ 27100

These hotels are near the train station and *plateía*, and most were upgraded for the 2004 Olympics. All are *open all year*.

Ólympos, Patrón and Karkavítsa 2, **t** 262 103 3650, *www.hotelolympos.gr* (€€/€€). Like its rivals, it's had a recent facelift, and offers TV, minibars, and air-conditioning.

Pantheon, Themistokléous St 7, **t** 262 102 9748 (€€/€€). Renovated, and similar to the Ólympos.

Letrina, inner edge of town on the Pátras road, **t** 262 103 3644 (€€/€€). Done up for the business crowd, with parking and a restaurant.

There are cafés and tavernas in the town's main *plateía*, a short stroll away.

Olympia

Olympia

The Olympic Games were the most prestigious in the ancient world, and lasted for over a thousand years. The low wooded hills in a triangle formed by the Hill of Cronus and the rivers Alphiós and Kladeos provided a congenial setting for those great panhellenic meetings and to this day, no matter how many tour buses descend on the site, it retains a peaceful, detached quality. The presence of people from around the world and the monologues of their cicerones even adds a note of realism: in ancient times it was much the same, as visitors from around the Mediterranean were shown around the marvels by official local guides and masters of ceremonies called *exegetés*.

Olympia epitomizes the spirit of *agon*, the agonistic or competitive drive first recognized by Nietzsche as a prime force in Hellenic culture. Lovers, politicians, warriors, philosophers, beautiful girls, weavers, musicians, dramatists and artists all 'competed for the prize' *agonizesthai*; in Mégara there was even a contest for the sweetest kisser (among boys). But no contest counted for as much as Olympia. The Sacred Truce that commanded the Greeks put aside war in favour of sport is an attractive concept our modern nation-states still have trouble replicating, although the modern Olympic Games, now that they are completely commercialized and professionalized, are a pretty fair replica of the ancient games. The Greeks never did believe in anything as warm and fuzzy as

Getting to Olympia

Olympia is 322km from Athens, 115km from Pátras. For **trains**, change at Pýrgos; five a day will take you to and from Olympia (Olympia Station, **t** 263 402 2677). There are 16 **buses** from Pýrgos, 3 direct from Athens (Kifissoú terminal **t** 210 513 4110), 2 from Trípolis, and 2 per day from Lálas.

For a **taxi** call **t** 262 402 2555 or **t** 262 402 2788.

---

amateur good sportsmanship. Ancient athletes were as professional and well rewarded as our modern celebrities, and winning was everything, no two ways about it; the last man to finish was hooted at, not clapped home.

History of the Olympic Games

Finds from the sanctuary show that Olympia was first inhabited in 4000 BC, while the first apsidal houses were built in the north part of the Altis by 2000 BC. Although a Mycenaean presence is noticeably absent in the sanctuary itself, Mycenaean graves discovered near the museum at least show they were in the neighbourhood. There is even a name for their as yet undiscovered city: **Pisa**, the home of King Oenomaos, who disgusted the gods by planning to build a temple with the skulls of the young men who lost the chariot race for the hand of his daughter Hippodameia. Pelops' victory, of course, put an end to such carryings-on (*see* p.46), but it certainly wasn't a very sporting start for Olympia.

After the collapse of the Mycenaeans, settlement in the valleys of Elís was dispersed. Olympia itself was never a town, and its first role may have been as a central meeting place and shrine for Elean community leaders. The date for the **first cult activity** has been pushed back to around 1000 BC; by the 9th century, in addition to the terracotta votives, there are bronze dedications and jewellery from Messenía and Arcadía as well as Elís, suggesting that meetings had expanded to include western Peloponnesian chieftains; the wealth of their offerings would have enhanced their status with one another and with the folks back home. As the decades passed, these bronze dedications grew in scale; in the Early Iron Age, there is a great increase in large tripods, horse figures, wagons and charioteers, indicative of aristocratic interest in Olympia.

The 776 date for the **first Olympic Games** was first recorded in the list of victors by the 5th-century BC Sophist, Hippias of Elís. The date became especially important for later Greeks. 'From this time Greek history is believed accurate in the matter of chronology. For before this, as anyone can see, they hand down various opinions,' wrote Byzantine historian Eusebios in the 4th century AD (Eusebios also pinpointed the fall of Troy to 405 years prior to the first Olympiad, spot on by today's reckoning).

Mythic Founders and Funeral Games

The rise of a state religion with shared values, expressed in panhellenic shrines such as Olympia and Delphi, was essential in taming not only aggressive aristocrats but also aggressive states. The myths that gave the Olympics their legitimacy and prestige meant the games had to have origins from the dawn of time: the story goes that **Zeus** and his father **Cronus** wrestled for Elís, and Cronus was killed and buried under the conical hill that still bears his name. According to Plutarch, to celebrate his victory, Zeus founded the first games – a foot race and a fight to the death. The winners of the first six games were crowned with apple leaves, symbol of immortality. Mirroring this is the Elean story of **Heracles** who stopped here after cleaning out the Augean stables. He sacrificed to Pelops and Zeus, and marked out the boundaries of the sacred precinct or ***altis*** around the barrow of the hero Pelops: 'he set apart the plain right round as a resting-place for the banquet', as Pindar put it. Heracles also introduced the wild olive to Olympia as a gift from those northern magicians the Hyperboreans, and founded games in honour of Pelops and Zeus. His younger brothers ran the first race and he crowned the victor Paeonius with a spray of **wild olive**. Other stories say that Zeus himself appeared to compete in the wrestling with Heracles, and it was a draw.

All panhellenic games, at Olympia as well as at Ísthmia, Nemea and Delphi, were **funeral games** (*epitáphios agón*), harkening back to the games that Achilles held for Patroclos in the *Iliad*. These were seen as prestigious not only for the memory of the dead, but also for whomever held the games, determined the rules and awarded the prizes. Yet funeral games seem odd to us today. One explanation has it that, in the switch from a matriarchal religion to the patriarchal Olympian cult, the afterlife turned dismal. For Homer's heroes, life was everything; death, especially the death of a young person, caused not only great grief but rage. It was a tear in the fabric of the cosmos; order was upset; the games allowed for a physical release of the rage while confirming the struggle and victory of life. Throughout their history, the ancient Olympic Games would begin with death – the slaughter of oxen on the altar of Zeus.

Last but not least, Pausanias mentions that the first races at Olympia were run by girls, competing to become the priestess of Hera. Hera's temple, after all, is the oldest at Olympia, reputedly founded by Hippodameia, in celebration of her marriage to Pelops. This very ancient race or ***agon*** suggests that the origins of all games were not funereal at all, but seasonal fertility rites. These had three cycles: the sun represented by Zeus, the moon by Hera, and the earth, or lost underground cycle, represented by Demeter Chamyne. With the later dominance of Zeus at Olympia, a quadrennial foot race began among youths to see who would be consort of Hera's priestess and the King of Elis, and the meaning of the games shifted to fit into the Homeric mould. But the girls' race was not forgotten, and continued to take place every year as part of the **Heraia**, an event open only to young women of Elis, who wore short *chitons* with one shoulder bared, and ran a distance just under a *stade*. The winner was crowned with an olive wreath, and had the right to a prime portion of the cow sacrificed in Hera's honour, and to dedicate a statue of herself to Hera.

The archaeological evidence would push the date up to about 720 BC, based on items found in the wells of the Altis. These wells were dug every four years and filled in at the end of the festival with junk and discarded votive offerings (according to sacred law, votives were inalienable possessions of the god, and, even when they were thrown out, they had to be thrown out within the sanctuary). Around 720 BC, the wells show a massive increase in jewellery dedications, imports from Italy, and the first pottery used for eating and drinking. Hippias' list of victors, even if his date is uncertain, does confirm that the games gradually caught on. Although early winners all came from the west and central Peloponnese, cities from the Corinthia and Mégara regions posted their first victories in the late 8th century BC, Sparta in 720. The first Athenian win was 696, and the first from Italy was 672.

Until 724 BC there was only one event, a foot race that ended at the Altar of Zeus. The games always started with the sacrifice of a black ram to Pelops, followed by massive sacrifices of oxen to Zeus. Philistratos describes what happened next:

The consecrated portions then lay on the altar, but had not yet been set alight; the runners were one stadion [about 200 yards] away from the altar; in front of the altar stood a priest who gave the starting signal with a torch. The victor put fire to the sacred portions and so went away Olympic victor.

The first winner of this race to light the barbecue was, fittingly, a local cook named Koroibos. By 708 BC there were five events. All in all, Olympia's panhellenic status was a slowly evolving process. Sparta's enslavement of Messenía in 710 seems to have added some urgency to the process, as the other city-states saw it was in their interests to meet on a regular basis. The games offered the perfect excuse, and it became the custom to send not only athletes to the Olympics, but *theoroi*, official diplomats.

The development of the *polis* led directly to the institutionalization of the Olympics. The games were an important showcase for the members of the élite, allowing them to cut a fine figure before the entire Greek world. As the city-states 'tamed' their great families, the Olympics offered individuals glory without power and states triumphs without swords. But thoughts of real war were never far off. Weapons and armour, which were formerly buried in the tombs of aristocratic warriors, became favourite dedications at Olympia after 700 BC, while tripods went out of fashion by 600. Dedicating arms rather than pots was also a nice way for each city-state to advertise its prowess to the greater Greek world.

Weapons for non-votive purposes were strictly prohibited. According to legend, the **Sacred Truce** or *Ekecheiriá* dated from the 8th century, when King Iphitos of Elis, Kleothenes of Pisa and Lykourgos of Sparta agreed to its terms. It was inscribed on the famous bronze **Discus of Iphitos** in the Temple of Hera, and declared that Elis and Olympia were sacred; that no armies were allowed to set foot in their territory; that every four years a truce would be announced by three special heralds to the entire Greek world, during which all hostilities had to cease for three months.

The privilege of running the games (and resulting economic benefits) did not go uncontested. At first run by Elean aristocrats, the games were taken over in 668 BC, in the 28th Olympiad, by an underclass of Pisatans, with the military help of Pheidon, the tyrant of Argos. Herodotus described Pheidon in shocked terms as 'the man who carried out the most arrogant action ever of all the

Greeks when he expelled the Elean presidents from the Olympic Games and presided over them himself'. In 572 BC, Sparta defeated the Pisatans, and the Eleans took over the games again (with Sparta looking over their shoulders). Curiously enough, this did not help Sparta's athletes, who had previously dominated the list of victors. After 578 BC their victories decline, in spite of the fact that the Spartans were famous for only participating in the events they felt they could win.

A Day at the Races: the Games in their Final Form

As the years passed, the games became highly regulated, with an Olympic committee setting the rules, although these were never written down: everyone just knew them. There were divisions for boys and grown men. To participate one had to be a free Greek, and have a clean record (no murderers or temple robbers allowed). The Macedonians, for instance, were snubbed until they brought proof of sharing common ancestry with the Argives; similar genealogical gymnastics were later performed to admit the Romans. **Women** were banned from the games, although unmarried girls were apparently very much on the periphery of Olympia, attracted by the aphrodisiacs of wealth, glory and toned pectorals.

The custom of competing naked dates from 720 BC. Some said it was introduced by the Spartans; others say it began after someone's pants fell down during the foot race. Coaches had to be in the altogether as well after one athlete's mother penetrated the all-male bastion disguised as his coach, until she was found out and tossed off the Typaean rock. If other women succeeded in sneaking in, they never told. While open to all free Greeks, the rules in effect limited participation to the wealthy, or those with a wealthy sponsor. All athletes had to spend 10 months **training** and were required to spend a month prior to the games at the sanctuary itself, observing a strict vegetarian diet and sexual abstinence – which may have been the reason behind the banning of women. Coaches were highly respected, and they kept a close eye on their charges, watching their diet (fish and cheese were in, starchy food out) and even forbidding conversation at mealtimes to prevent the jocks from straining their brains. The monkishness of the regime was assuaged by the crowds of admirers and agents who swarmed around the athletes, who were already the most conceited creatures in the world. Fashionable young men came to see and be seen, beggars to beg, actors to recite, and no doubt punters to bet. Herodotus came to read from his *Histories* – young Thucydides was a captive listener.

The athletes and their coaches at least had roofs over their heads; nearly everyone else below VIP status slept out of doors, in conditions that make Woodstock sound cosy. Significantly, one sacrifice offered at the Olympic festival was to Zeus Averter of Flies. There was a famous anecdote of a master, faced with an unruly slave, who threatened to free him and take him to the Olympics unless he behaved.

The **umpires** were called *Hellanódikai*. Originally there was only one, a hereditary office held by an Elean, but after 584 BC others were added until there were 10, all from Elís, and all selected by lot. They bore not whistles, but rods to whack athletes who jumped the gun or otherwise played dirty, and levied large fines on states and athletes who wilfully cheated. The Spartans (it *would* be them) were banned from the games in 420 BC for attacking Lepreon during the Sacred Truce, and forced to pay 2,000 *minas*. The cheaters' fines were used to finance bronze statues of Zeus, known as **Zanes**. In some 292 Olympiads, there are only 16 of these, which isn't a bad record.

The games took place over five days in July, at the first full moon after the summer solstice. The **first day** saw the opening ceremonies, the sacrifices to Pelops and Zeus, the registration of athletes and their vows to obey the rules at the statue of Zeus Horkios, the god of oaths. The **second day** was dedicated to the boys' events: running, boxing (with thongs of ox-hide wrapped around the hands, and punches directed to the head; matches were only decided when someone conceded), wrestling and the *pankration* (a sport similar to WWF wrestling) in which the only rules were no biting or gouging out of eyes; boxing, hitting, strangling, kicking and stomping on one's opponent were all acceptable. It too ended when one party surrendered. Or died.

On the **third day**, there was the extremely popular chariot-racing in the hippodrome, which began with charioteers sacrificing to the Taraxippus or horse-scaring ghost of Myrtos, the charioteer of King Oenomaos whom Pelops kicked into the sea (*see* p.46). On the same day the men's pentathlon (discus, javelin, long jump – with weights in each hand – wrestling and a sprint) was held in the stadium. The **fourth day** was devoted to the other men's sports: racing, wrestling, boxing, *pankration*, and a race in full hoplite armour, huge shield in one hand, always held at dawn to keep the competitors from dying of heat exhaustion. On the **fifth day** the winners were handed a palm frond, crowned with their olive wreaths and fêted. Sacrifices were made to the gods in thanksgiving for their victories. There were moonlight processions and, apparently, a general orgy after all that abstinence.

The victors, the ***Olympioníkai***, were permited to erect votive statues in the sanctuary. If they won three times, the statue could bear their own features. Itinerant craftsmen set up workshops to make these on the spot; they also produced thousands of little bronze figurines as votives and souvenirs. The prize of an olive wreath may have been nominal, but the prestige attached to it was overwhelming. The *Olympioníkai* returned home like triumphant Caesars dressed in purple robes, at the head of a procession of horse-drawn chariots. A winner might even be invited to knock down part of the wall of his home town, as having such men obviously precluded the need for any other defences. He would dedicate his wreath on the altar of the city's patron god, and receive countless gifts and an ode in his honour, perhaps by the divine Pindar. More concretely, he could expect free meals in perpetuity at the local *prytaneion*. An insufficiently honoured victor could cause trouble: Oibatas of Dyme in Achaía felt slighted and put a curse on all Achaians, so that they remained victory-less until they erected a statue in his honour. The glory of victory was so exaggerated that the whole purpose of the games, at least from the point of view of the city-states, sometimes backfired; rather than tame aristocrats, an olive wreath granted political clout to those who knew how to use it – Alcibiades' outrageous career began with winning the chariot race. The *Olympioníkai* were antiquity's darlings, and only a few voices in the wilderness, among them Plato's, ever questioned the sense of it.

The End

As time went on, the lists of victors were dominated by colonists: the Olympics assumed a special importance for them, not only in confirming their Greekness, but also in demonstrating their independence from their mother colonies with their rich dedications. By the time of Philip of Macedon the games had taken on a distinctly more secular character; Philip even erected a monument to himself and his family in the Altis. The stadium, originally in view of the Altis to emphasize the religious aspect of the games, was now hidden with the new Echo Stoa. Bribing officials was not unknown, and the athletes were highly paid prima donnas. A luxury hotel and baths went up to lodge them in comfort.

Standards declined even further when they let the Romans in. Their senses dulled by the brutality of gladiatorial fights, most weren't very interested, and left the Olympics to the philhellene élite. The games reached their nadir in AD 67, when they were delayed two years to enable Nero to participate. He insisted on inaugurating a new musical competition for himself to win, and raced a 10-horse team in the chariot race, fell out twice and failed to finish, but won anyway, and gave the judges an ample reward for their good judgement. Meanwhile, the thousands of statues that once crowded the Altis were slowly filtered off to Rome and later to Constantinople. In AD 392 Theodosius the Great banned the games, along with every other whiff of paganism in the empire. Christians briefly occupied the complex and used some of the stone to build a wall against the Vandals. Earthquakes knocked the temples over, and the fickle Alphiós and Kladeos rivers overran their banks, altered their course and buried the sanctuary in mud, supplemented by landslides off the hill of Cronus. Soon only the name and memories remained, while Olympia lay under 12 feet of mud – deep enough to protect its temple sculptures from most of the Lord Elgins of the world, at least until 1829 when the French found the Temple of Zeus and whipped some of its *metopes* off to the Louvre. In 1875, a Prussian scientific mission took over, signing an agreement that all the finds should remain in Greece. One of the biggest enthusiasts and contributors to the digs was Kaiser Wilhelm, who fancied himself a new Achilles. The Germans have been there practically ever since, with an interlude during the war years. In 1961, the International Olympic Academy was founded here to promote the Olympic spirit – it's just east of the site, near the memorial to Pierre de Coubertin (1862–1937), the prime mover behind the revival of the games and whose heart is contained in a *stele*.

The Site

Olympia Site
t 262 402 2517; open April–Oct 8–7.30; Nov–May 8.30–3; adm exp, but you can save money by purchasing the combined site and museum ticket

In the Altis

The Altis, a super-*temenos* or sacred precinct enclosing several temples, is an irregular quadrangle measuring about 200 yards on each side, surrounded by a low wall and bounded on one side by the Hill of Cronus. As you enter the site, with the river Kladeos flowing down below to the right, the Altis is just to your left, and the gymnasium and other secular buildings (*see* below) on your right.

Altis means 'grove', a word which goes back to Olympia's origins: the oldest sanctuaries were often just that, set in leafy groves, in caves or on hilltops. Dedicated to the gods, they were also safe neutral zones for humans. The modern entrance in the northwest corner corresponds to an ancient one, where the first building you see is the **Prytaneion**. This was the headquarters of the *prytaneis*, the priests who were in charge of administering the sanctuary and offering sacrifices on its many altars. The Altar of Zeus in particular required one blood offering a day. To cook all that meat, the Prytaneion had a useful feature – an eternal flame dedicated to Hestia, goddess of the hearth. It also had kitchens and a banquet room, where the victors feasted at the end of the festival.

The circular building nearby was the **Philippeion**, erected by Philip II of Macedonia after his victory over the united Greeks at Chairóneia in 338 BC. The Altis may have been sacred and panhellenic but it was no UN-prototype, and this wasn't its first monument celebrating a Greek victory over Greeks. But it must have been the most galling, even though it was a rather pretty

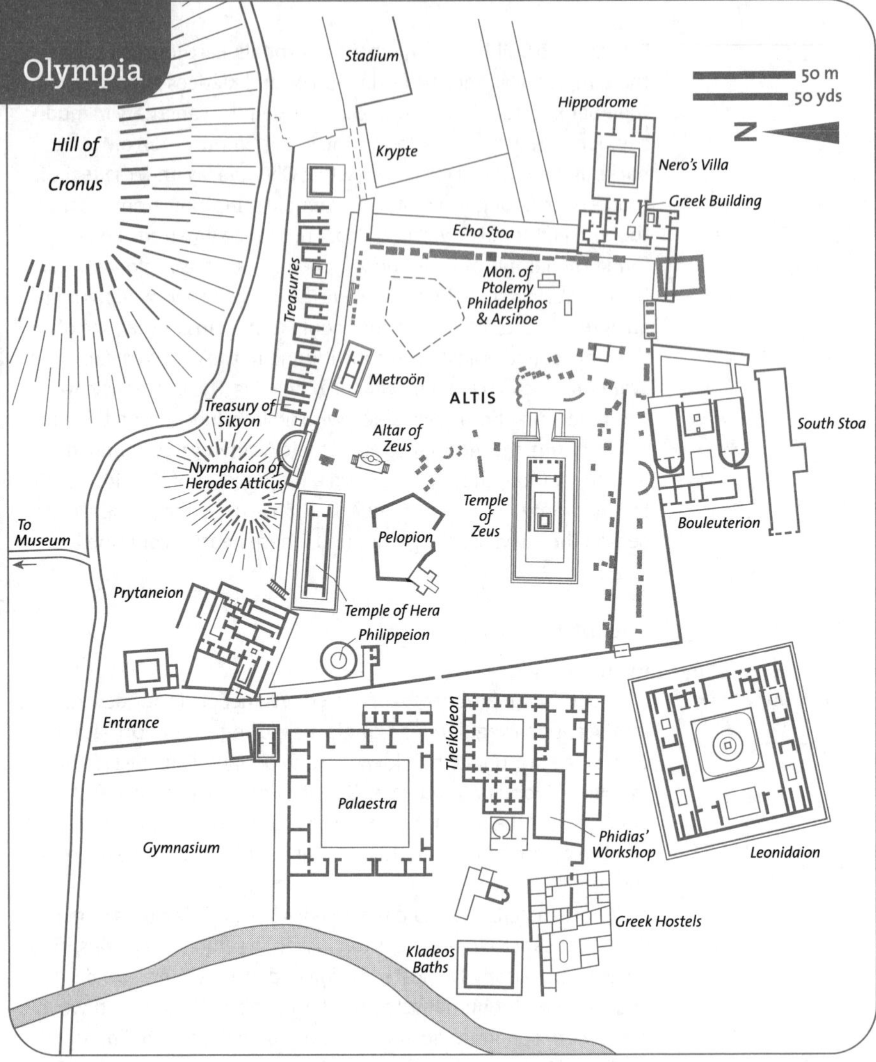

gazebo with 18 Ionic columns around the porch, eight Corinthian columns around the wall, and a bronze roof crowned with a poppy-shaped boss. If the door were open, you would have seen five gold and ivory statues of the Macedonian royal family by the sculptor Leochares, including one of Alexander, whose immortality was proclaimed here during the games in 324 BC. How many Greeks gagged as they heard that is not recorded.

Nearby, the **Temple of Hera** is the oldest at Olympia, as well as a key work in the evolution of the Greek peristyle temple. The original was built of wood in the 8th century BC but, beginning in 590 BC, it was rebuilt as a long and narrow Doric temple with six by 16 columns supporting a weighty entablature of wood and a tile roof. The first columns were of wood, but these were replaced with stone as they rotted; their different styles show that even a Doric column can alter with fashion. When Pausanias visited in AD 160, there was still one last wooden column in place. Four stone ones have been re-erected. Crowning all was a terracotta *akroterion* shaped like a disc, 8ft in diameter and decorated with concentric bands of coloured decoration. It looked a bit like a giant dartboard rising out of the middle of the roof.

The temple had two interior rows of columns and an Archaic statue of Hera enthroned, with Zeus standing by her side. It also served as a treasury, holding some of Olympia's holies of holy: the Discus of Iphitos, the gold and ivory Table of Kolotes where the victors came to receive their olive wreaths, and the cedar Chest of Kypselos. This was donated by the 7th-century BC tyrant of Corinth, who had been locked in it as a child by his mother to hide him from the aristocratic Bacchiads whom he later overthrew (*see* p.141). The chest was lavishly decorated with every conceivable mythological scene, and merited a long description by Pausanias. He also briefly noted a certain statue of Hermes and Dionysos by Praxiteles that was found in the *cella* in 1877.

In front of the Temple of Hera was the **Pelopion**, the low burial mound of Pelops, which appears to have been worshipped in some way since 1100 BC, when the precinct around it was first laid out. During the Archaic period, this precinct was made into an irregular pentagon, surrounded by a stone wall. It was open to the sky, with trees and a few statues scattered within, and was given a monumental entrance in the southwest corner in the 5th century BC. Here the Eleans opened the games with a sacrifice of a black ram on a fire of white poplar. Looking back towards the Temple of Hera, the great ash **Altar of Zeus** is believed to have stood to the right. This was elliptical, the curve filled with a 22ft-high pile of ashes of tens of thousands of victims. The new ashes would be moistened with water from the Alphiós, and given a fresh coat of plaster every year.

To the right of the Temple of Hera, the semi-circular building under the Hill of Cronus is the **Nymphaion of Herodes Atticus**, which Herodes, one of Rome's wealthiest men, built in AD 150 in honour of his wife Regilla. This was an elaborate fountain built on three levels, with two little round fountains on either end and a two-storey *exedra* in the back, with niches to hold statues of the Antonine emperors. Herodes also installed the pipes and aqueducts that brought water to this fountain, and the grateful Eleans added statues of Herodes and his missus to the ensemble as a way of saying thanks.

Next to the fountain, overlooking the Altis from the wooded Hill of Cronus, are the twelve **treasuries** or *thesauroí*, all in a line. These were erected by Dorian states between 600 and 480 BC including Byzantium, Cyrene (Libya), Metapontum, Elipamnos (whereabouts unknown), Sybaris, Selinunte, Gela and Syracuse (all Italy), Sámos, Mégara and Sikyon (the only three in Greece proper). The usually reliable Pausanias miscounted and listed only 10 treasuries, which has made their identification problematic. Enough material has survived from four of them to form an idea of their appearance, basically mini-Doric temples: the **Treasury of Sikyon**, with the column and capital, is the best preserved, made from stone specially brought from Sikyon. As at Delphi they served as little showrooms for their city-states, containing both gifts to Zeus and votive offerings for Olympic victories. Syracuse used hers to display trophies from the Battle of Himera, where she led the victory over the Carthaginians in 480 BC, on the very same day as the Battle of Sálamis.

The little ruined building in front of this row was a ***metroön***, a late 4th-century BC temple dedicated to the Mother of the Gods. The Romans didn't have much time for her, and divided her temple up to hold statues of their emperors. The row of stone pedestals between the *metroön* and the treasuries once held the **Zanes** (the plural of Zeus), the statues erected to stigmatize incidents of wanton foul play, paid for by the cheaters' own fines. Like the sacrifices, this is another ancient custom that has fallen by the wayside, but an interesting one that could be revived if the Eleans got their wish to hold the modern Olympics permanently in their territory again. Beyond the stone arch is the ***krypte***, the vaulted passage into the stadium built by the Romans.

The Germans located the **Stadium** during their first digs in 1875–81, and completed the excavations in 1960. The original stadium was 90 yards to the west and had only one embankment; this new one, laid out in the 5th century BC, had two embankments capable of seating 45,000 spectators. It must be the most famous, and the most simple, stadium in the world. There were never any seats: everyone sat on the ground except for the umpires or *Hellanódikai*, who sat on the dais at midfield. Opposite is the stone altar of Demeter Chamyne, whose priestess was the only woman allowed to attend the games as a last nod towards the games' original meaning (*see* p.232).

The track is 35 yards wide, sufficient for 20 racers, and 210 yards (192m, or one *stade*) long. The starting and finishing lines are marked by low slabs; on the west end you can see the indentations made for the runners' toes. The classic race was the one *stade* sprint, but there were also the *diaulos* (two *stades*) and the *dolichos* (as many as 24 *stades*, or about three miles). A low stone parapet separated the athletes from the spectators; an open stone water channel, with basins at intervals, provided refreshment. To the south, in an open valley of the Alphiós, the **Hippodrome** has been washed away or buried under a deep layer of mud. Pausanias left a long description of its elaborate starting gate, invented in the 6th century BC. Both chariot races and horse races with professional jockeys were held; Argos was the first city to establish a national stud for the Olympics.

In the 4th century BC the Stadium was almost completely cut off from the Altis by the building of the 308ft double-colonnaded **Echo Stoa**, attributed to Philip II or Alexander. Little remains of it, but in its day it was one of the wonders of Olympia: any word pronounced here would echo seven times. The walls were lined with paintings (hence its other name the Stoa Poikile), which gave the spectators something to look at as they queued up to enter the stadium. The Archaic-era starting line was found under this *stoa*. In front of the *stoa* are the ruins of the **Monument of Ptolemy Philadelphos and Arsinoe**, his wife (and sister), both of whom had a gilt statue on top of a 33ft column. The Ptolemys, descendants of the Macedonian general who ruled Egypt after Alexander's death, were keen to confirm their Greekness in spite of their Egyptian-style marriage, and were great ones for showy dedications to themselves in panhellenic sanctuaries.

At the end of the *stoa*, a bit was tacked on after 373 BC, which became known as the **Stoa of Hestia**, made of stone that had fallen from the Temple of Zeus in an earthquake. A building of unknown import was added behind this (outside the Altis) known as the **Greek building**, and behind this are the remains of **Nero's villa**. Eager to curry favour with the locals, the emperor decreed that all northern Peloponnesians were free. The locals, forced to foot the huge bill to build the villa and entertain Nero, weren't impressed.

Dominating the southern half of the Altis is the massive platform and shattered columns of the **Temple of Zeus**, one of the largest Doric temples ever built. Designed in 460 BC by Libon of Elís, the stone is the local grey nubbly shell aggregate, and it was originally covered with fine white stucco to resemble marble. Because of the low-lying area, Libon made the platform unusually high and supplied a ramp on the east side – a typical Peloponnese feature. Although on a massive scale, it was otherwise a textbook classical peristyle temple, six by 13 columns, each 34ft high, with a base diameter of 7ft. The mighty capitals supported an entablature over 13ft high, punctuated with lionhead spouts, while the pediments framed the superb statues in the museum – the *Battle of Lapiths and Centaurs*, and the *Chariot Race of Pelops and Oenomaos*. You can see the foundations of the *cella*, with its two vestibules, the *pronaos* (in front) and *opisthodomos* (at the back). Six *metopes* on the *Labours of Heracles* decorated each end. The roof tiles were of marble.

Inside the *cella* was a pair of colonnades, supporting an upper gallery, and one of the Seven Wonders of the Ancient World: the chryselephantine (gold and ivory) **statue of Zeus** by Phidias. Its black marble base occupied a whole third of the *cella*. Previous statues of Zeus showed him with thunderbolt in hand; Phidias, taking his cue, he said, from the *Iliad's* description of Zeus who nods to grant the request of Thetis 'and shook great Olympos', showed the father of the gods enthroned in majesty, serene and aloof, his sceptre in his left hand and a figure of Nike, or Victory, in his right. At 38ft high, the figure was so big that had Zeus risen from the throne he would have gone straight through the roof. But 'over-the-top' was the keynote: the statue was made of wood, covered with pieces of carved ivory to form the flesh, while all the rest, including his hair and beard, was covered with sheets of gold. The throne was covered with gold, ivory and ebony, inlaid with jewels and glass, and decorated with mythical scenes, some carved, some painted by Paionios on screens stretched between the sides of the throne. All who saw it were overwhelmed.

To keep it from warping, olive oil was kept in a shallow trough in the surrounding tiles. A bigger threat came in the form of Caligula, who ordered the head of Zeus replaced with one bearing his own features. As the imperial agents were about to accomplish the dirty deed, the statue 'burst into such a roar of laughter that the scaffolding collapsed and the workmen took to their heels,' wrote Suetonius. Three hundred years later, it wasn't laughing when Theodosius II took it to Constantinople, where it burned in AD 475.

According to Pliny, some 3,000 votive statues once surrounded the Temple of Zeus. A few pedestals for the dedications remain. One of the largest was the dedication of Mikythos, a former slave who vowed an enormous pedestal lined with statues if his son recovered from an illness. The greatest statue was the *Nike* of Paionios (now in the museum).

Outside the Altis

The chief processional gate of the Altis was southeast of the Temple of Zeus. Outside and to the west of this are the rather confusing remains of the **Bouleuterion**: two apsidal buildings linked by a colonnade, begun in the 6th century BC and transformed over the years. This was the seat of the *Boulé* or Olympic Committee, elected from the Elean aristocracy. Between the buildings stood the statue and altar of Zeus Horkios, 'of the oaths', where all the competitors had to swear on gobbets of raw boar meat to follow the rules. To emphasize the consequences, the statue held menacing thunderbolts in each hand. South of the **Bouleuterion** stretched the **South Stoa** (mid-4th century BC), which may have been the *proedria* from where officials watched the procession of athletes. It probably contained shops as well. Directly west are the ruins of the 3rd-century BC **Baths**.

Next to these begin the vast jumble that was once the **Leonidaion**, a large hotel built by Leonidas of Naxos in *c.* 330 BC. It measured 246ft by 265ft and was enclosed by four *stoas*, with a peristyle courtyard within. It burned and was restored by Hadrian, who made it into an ancient Hyatt hotel, enlarging the rooms and surrounding them with gardens complete with canals and islands and flowerbeds; guests could watch the processions and ceremonies from the comfort of their balconies. Further west, along the banks of the Kladeos stream, are remains of more modest **hostels** built by the Romans and an older Greek bath-house topped by the more up-to-date Roman **Kladeos Baths** (2nd century AD).

In 1958, the archaeologists uncovered a well-preserved **paleo-Christian basilica**, a bit ho-hum in this setting, until they realized that it was built over the **Workshop of Phidias** mentioned by Pausanias. Here, in a room the exact same size as the *cella* of the Temple of Zeus, the greatest artist of the ancient world made his statue of Zeus. If there was any lingering doubt of its identity after the discovery of a mass of artist's materials – tools, clay moulds for the folds of the robe, and the slivers of gold and ivory – it was laid to rest with the discovery of the sculptor's cup, his coffee mug as it were, inscribed on the bottom 'I am the property of Phidias'. Phidias had come to Olympia under rather shadowy circumstances after making the chryselephantine statue of Athena for the Parthenon. Enemies of his friend and patron Pericles accused Phidias of stealing gold intended for the Athena statue; he was cleared, but then accused of the impiety of depicting Pericles' and his own features on Athena's shield. The Athenian democracy may have been the least grateful or most jealous of its great men of any government in history. But making Phidias *persona non grata* in Athens was Olympia's gain.

The ruins north of here, heading back towards the entrance of the site, are all Hellenistic. The **Theikoleon**, the square building that survives only in outline on the northeast corner of Phidias' workshop, was the parish house for the priests of Olympia, the *Theikoloi*. Next to this is the charming square ruin of the **Palaestra** where wrestlers, boxers and jumpers trained. The *stoas* surrounding the courtyard held dressing rooms, a room where the athletes scraped their bodies and were anointed with oil, and small seating areas for spectators; 32 of the original 72 Doric columns with their simple capitals have been re-erected. Directly abutting on this is a double row of stumpy columns and the remains of the monumental entrance, all that survives of the massive **Gymnasium** (2nd century BC), where training for running, javelin and discus took place. The walls were inscribed with the names of victors. The West Stoa, where the athletes had their rooms, subsided into the river, along with an all-weather covered track.

Museum of the History of the Olympic Games in Antiquity

Museum of the History of the Olympic Games in Antiquity
t 262 402 9119; open summer Tues–Sun 8–7.30, Mon 12–7.30; winter daily 8.30–3

The old archaeological museum building on a hill between the site entrance and town now houses this relatively new museum. The vestibule has mock-ups of the ancient site; the large central room has displays on the different ancient events, with statues, descriptions in English, and artefacts for each event. A great bronze chariot wheel has pride of place. Other rooms contain fascinating leftovers from the games and an exhibit on women and physical exercise. Lots of tripods are in evidence. Don't miss the room dedicated to the other big games at Delphi, Nemea and Isthmia (*see* p.154).

Museum of the History of the Excavations
t 262 402 9119; open summer Tues–Sun 8–7.30, Mon 12–7.30; winter daily 8.30–3

Beside this neoclassical building are the **toilets** (not a bad thing to know in this vast site) and a small, pantiled building housing a **Museum of the History of the Excavations**, which offers an idea of how complex an undertaking this was.

The Archaeological Museum

Archaeological Museum
t 262 402 2742; open April–Oct daily 8–7.30; Nov–May Tues–Sun 8.30–3, Mon 12.30–7.30; adm exp, but a combined site and museum ticket is cheaper

This is one of the top archaeological museums in Greece, housing the most spectacular of the thousands of finds the Germans have unearthed since the 1860s. The new anti-seismic building is almost invisible, discreetly tucked in the pines and cypresses on the northwestern flank of the Hill of Cronus. Displays start in the vestibule with scale models of the Altis and a reproduction of a Geometric-era tripod dedication.

Other rooms are laid out more or less chronologically. **Room I** houses Neolithic tools and pottery, Mycenaean grave goods and a splendid collection of bronze votives from the 12th–9th centuries bc found in the wells of the Altis: the oldest bronze animal figurines, culminating artistically in a trio of dogs attacking a deer (800 BC), and then the bronze tripods. Tripods were the Ferraris of the Geometric age, and are the first evidence of the sumptuous level of dedications that would set Olympia apart. Unlike later votives, many of which were manufactured by itinerant craftsmen at Olympia, these three-legged cauldrons were made in different parts of Greece, each more elaborate than the next: note especially the leg of a Corinthian one from around 820 BC showing *Heracles and Apollo fighting for the Delphic Tripod* (*see* p.403). Some scholars believe scenes such as this didn't illustrate myths, but *inspired* them once the original meaning was long forgotten. Others believe the scene proves that tripods were the prizes for the first games. No one knows.

Later bronzes fill **Room II**: tripods and tripod fragments decorated with orientalized motifs of animals, monsters and Sirens, influenced by trade with the East and dating from 700–625 BC. The engraved, *repoussée* sheets of bronze that once covered wooden boxes and wooden tripod legs offer fascinating 7th-century BC vignettes, including a warrior bidding farewell to his wife and his child as he departs in his chariot, and another depicting the *Murder of Clytemnestra*. An especially well-worked one from around 670 BC shows the kinky *Myth of Kanieus*, the story of a Lapith woman named Kanis who was loved by Poseidon. When Poseidon offered to grant her her heart's desire, she confessed to being bored with being a woman, and asked the god to turn her into an invulnerable man. Now named Kanieus, he became king of the Lapiths, but offended Zeus by telling the Lapiths that they had to worship his spear as their only god. During the famous wedding of Peirithous, attended by Theseus and the gods, the Lapiths' cousins, the Centaurs, tasted their first wine, got drunk and tried to rape the wedding guests. The ensuing tussle, in which civilized humans defeated the irrational horse-men, was a key symbol for the Greeks, but there was one human casualty: the invulnerable Kanieus. The Centaurs, armed with tree trunks, pummelled him into the ground like a tent peg, then piled the trunks on top of him until he was smothered. Scenes like this must have decorated the box of Kypselos.

The same room contains other Archaic finds: a limestone head of Hera (*c.* 600 BC) that probably graced the statue in her temple, a 7th-century BC Corinthian lion and the greatest collection anywhere of ancient Greek arms and armour, much of it discovered in the stadium, where it was buried as the embankments were enlarged: helmets, breastplates and the bronze blazons from the shields, which helped warriors identify who was who in battle. Note the bizarre 6th-century BC winged Gorgon figure gesturing to her stomach, her fish tail curling on the right and what look like horse legs kicking up to the left. Could it be Medusa giving birth to Pegasus? Note, too, the eerie bronze bust of a female demon, with a wing instead of an arm.

Room III holds colourful, intricately decorated terracotta fragments from Olympia's Archaic (6th century BC) buildings, particularly from the Treasury of Gela. The pediment of the Treasury of Mégara has the worn remains of a clash of the Titans. In **Room IV** we move up to the Early or Severe Classical period, with excellent painted terracottas from the 5th century: a head of Athena and a merrily pederastic Zeus striding off with Ganymede tucked under his arm, the boy holding a cockerel as a symbol of love. The story was immensely popular in Greece and Rome, as it justified to male minds not only homosexuality but the exclusion of women from society, reducing them to the role of breeders and unpaid domestics. Other exhibits are the kind that make history come alive: a helmet dedicated by Miltiades, the victor at Marathon; a Persian helmet with an inscription 'The Athenians to Zeus, having taken it from the Persians', and the contents of Phidias' workshop: bits of ivory, tools, moulds, and his cup, engraved ΦΕΙΔΙΟ ΕΙΜΙ ('I belong to Phidias').

Large, central **Room V** houses the great marble sculptures from the Temple of Zeus, carefully pieced together like a jigsaw. Key works in the study of Greek art, they were sculpted around 460 BC, when the Archaic stylization is still apparent in the description of Zeus, but Ganymede has begun to relax into the naturalism of the Parthenon marbles. The figures were sculpted in island marble, in the round, and fixed to the pediment with metal clamps.

The East Pediment, attributed by Pausanias to Paionios, shows Pelops and Oenomaos preparing for their famous chariot race that began on the banks of the Alphiós and ended at the Isthmus of Corinth. Zeus stands in the centre, Oenomaos, his wife and their charioteer Myrtos to the left, and to the right stands Pelops and Oenomaos' daughter Hippodameia, who would ride with him. In the far corners are the personifications of Olympia's river gods Alphiós and Kladeos. The composition is static and tense, but the figure of the fearful old man behind the horses of Pelops hints of the dramatic consequences of the race: two men would be dead by the end of the day, and the curse of the charioteer Myrtos on Pelops would fall on the house of Atreus.

The West Pediment, however, steals the show. The subject is the aforementioned Battle of Lapiths and Centaurs at the wedding of Theseus' friends, Peirithous and Deidameia. Apollo stands aloof in the midst of a remarkable scene of violence and turmoil: a centaur grabs the bride by the breast; another has seized a woman, but is about to be axed by Theseus; another centaur bites the arm of a man. The idea of civilization triumphing over barbarism was dear to the Greek heart; the close call at Salamis and Plataea had only happened 20 years before the pediment was carved. The sculptor, said by Pausanias to be an Athenian named Alkamenes, is also the first to show a real interest in women as women.

A third sculptor was responsible for the Parian marble *metopes* on the Labours of Heracles. These, with their very fine moulding, innovative compostion and Classical air of detachment, are a genuine preview of the Parthenon Marbles. The scene of Heracles cleaning the Augeian stables was the first time his Elean Labour was depicted in art, and the one of him supporting the world on his shoulders, as Atlas presents him with the apples of the Hesperides and Athena lends a helping hand, is sublime. Originally, like the pediment sculptures, these were brightly painted, and they were such a success that the Twelve Labours would become a favourite subject.

A small **unnumbered room** with a high ceiling, off Room IV, was especially designed for the *Nike of Paionios*, sculpted by the nephew of Phidias. It was commissioned, with no little glee, by the Messenians and Naupactians (expatriate Messenians, settled there by Athens) after the defeat of Sparta at Sphakteria in 424 BC. The femininity first expressed in the Lapith women on the West Pediment has progressed to produce a real, sensuous woman in windblown drapery. Originally the Victory had wings, and stood high on her pedestal on the back of an eagle, as if descending from heaven. **Room VI**, also off Room IV, contains Hellenistic finds, including a bust of Alexander and decorations from the Leonidaion, including its lion-head spout *sima*.

Room VIII is given over to Olympia's most famous work, the *Hermes* by Praxiteles (*c*. 330 BC) found in the Temple of Hera, carved out of the finest Parian marble and beautifully finished, standing with easy grace in Praxiteles' trademark *contrapposto* or S-shaped pose. The god holds his baby half-brother Dionysos, recently born from Zeus' thigh (a necessity after Zeus blasted his pregnant mother Semele with a thunderbolt). Zeus commanded Hermes to hide him from Hera, giving him to be raised by the nymphs of Mount Nysa. Hermes originally dangled a bunch of grapes to tease Dionysos, who reached out to grasp them. This is the only original work by Praxiteles to survive. With him Greek art entered a virtuoso stage, to be looked at and admired as art: the once deep wells of religious aspirations and panhellenic symbolism have dried up in elegant, curly-haired Hermes.

Enter the Romans in **Room IX**, with statues from the Nymphaion of Herodes Atticus: Claudius posing as Zeus; his wife Agrippina, mother of Nero; Titus and Hadrian as warriors; Faustina, the wife of Marcus Aurelius; and Antinous, Hadrian's deified favourite. The marble bull bears the dedication of the Nymphaion, from Regilla to Zeus. Lastly, **Room X** contains finds from all periods concerning the games: bases of votive statues of winners, bronze and terracotta figurines of competitors, and the 316lb stone of Bybon inscribed 'Bybon, son of Phorys, threw me above his head with one hand'. He must have been a helluva guy.

Modern Olympia

Museum of the Modern Olympic Games
*Aginárou, **t** 262 402 2544; open Tues–Sun 8–3.30; adm*

Modern Olympia is a 20-minute walk from the site over a bridge built by Kaiser Wilhelm. Nearly everything is on Kondíli Street except for the **Museum of the Modern Olympic Games**, on Aginárou, two streets up, filled with paraphernalia from the modern games since their inception in 1896.

Xenónas Bacchus >>

Shopping in Olympia

Besides the usual souvenirs, Olympia has a great bookshop, **Gallerie Orphee**, on Kondíli Street, **t** 262 402 3555. The helpful owner sells a wonderful selection of books on Greece in English and Greek music.

Where to Stay in Olympia

Olympia > *city information office, Praxitélis and Kondílis Sts, t 262 402 9011; open Mon–Fri 7.30–3*

Olympia ✉ 27065

Hotels stay open all year, and all mentioned are close to the town centre. Book ahead.

Europa, 1 Droúva, **t** 262 402 2650, *www.hoteleuropa.gr* (€€€/€€€). New, modern, the best of the best, on the hill above town, with a pool garden, parking, and a rooftop restaurant with a marvellous view.

Olympion Asty, Ancient Olympia, **t** 262 402 3665 *www.olympionasty.gr* (€€€/€€€) Also on a hill, the rival to the Europa, surrounded by greenery, with pool, tennis, a shuttle bus, Internet, and a restaurant.

Néda, 1 Kon. Karamánlís, **t** 262 402 2563, *www.hotelneda.gr* (€€/€€). Parallel to Kondíli with dark-panelled public rooms; a good winter choice.

Pelops, 2 Vareía (up from Kondíli), **t** 262 402 2543, *www.hotelpelops.gr* (€€/€€). This small modern hotel with balconies to catch the breeze really does try harder; with pleasant Greek-Australian owners who offer in-hotel activities and advice on the area.

Xenónas Bacchus, 4km west of the site at Archaía Písa/Miráka, **t** 262 402 2298 *www.bacchustavern.gr* (€€/€€). Wonderful new guesthouse with six rooms, a delightfully decked pool area, and the charming Zapándis family who know their business. Do book ahead. Their restaurant has long been a local favourite: good setting, good service, and good food stylishly served at very reasonable prices.

Ilis, Prax. Kondíli, **t** 262 402 2547, *www.olympiahotels.gr* (€€/€). Airy, white and salmon-pink, on the main street. Guests have free use of the pool at their nearby expensive sister hotel. *Open Mar–Oct.*

Hercules, **t** 262 402 2696, *www.hotelhercules.gr* (€€/€). On a quiet street just back of Kondíli; offers good value.

Posidon, 8 Stefanopoúlou, **t** 262 402 2567, *pensionposidon@yahoo.gr* (€/€). On a quiet street with a small terrace and now completely renovated with en suite baths, George and Georgia Liagouras' *pension* is as welcoming as ever and still good value.

Camping Diana, **t** 262 402 2314, *www.campingdiana.gr* (€/€). In town, with a pool; gets the most kudos.

Camping Olympia, **t** 262 402 2745 (€/€). 1km west of town on the Pýrgos road; has a bigger pool.

Eating Out in Olympia

Olympia is full of snack bars, cafés and restaurants. The locals, who like a change of scenery when they dine, suggest a trip to the *psistariás* at nearby Linária.

Aegean, dead centre of town, **t** 262 402 2904. Considerably more upscale in decoration and a great place to ogle tourists as you eat.

Cafeteria Diónysos, **t** 262 402 2932. A modest eatery on Kondíli where you can go in and have a look before choosing.

Zeus, **t** 262 402 3913. Opposite the Diónysos, with a bit of everything.

North and East from Olympia

Olympia has been a junction since ancient times. The road north into Achaía by way of **Lála** (Λάλα) is lovely but scarcely visited by foreign visitors. Before the crossroads for Pátras (west) and Lámbia (east), you pass through the last of Arcadía's once great oak forests. These stately trees, interspersed with meadows, stretch for miles in a scene resembling Poussin's Arcadia. In myth, this was the

Where to Stay and Eat North and East from Olympia

Lála ✉ 27066

Xenónas Driádes, t 697 670 2357 (€/€). Modern pink and white building just north of town with 8 studios and views. Ioánnis Galanopoúlos has cycles to loan guests. *Open all year.*

Lámbia ✉ 27063

Xenóna Lámbia Óri, t 262 408 1323, (€€/€€), A stone-built pile right in town, handy for all those tavernas.

Kéntavroi Taverna, well signposted 7km off the north–south road in Folói, **t** 262 406 2010. Not much to look at, but good food and 10 bicycles gratis to his customers. Have your hotel call ahead.

stomping ground of the centaur Folos, and you almost expect to see him in the dappled shade of this leafy paradise. The views to the east are fabulous. Just don't expect to meet many people. It is perfect cycling country and, as luck would have it, the owner of the Kéntavroi Taverna in **Folói** (Φολόη) has some.

There is a new *pension* in Lála, a market town of some size, or consider staying in **Lámbia** (Λάμπεια), for a village experience under plane trees. It has mountain views, a surprising number of *psistariá* for meat-lovers (even a combined butcher shop and restaurant), and the frescoed 14th-century Byzantine church of Ag. Triáda for dessert. East of here you can enter Achaía through its back door, at **ancient Psophis** (*see* p.197).

Alternatively, going east from Olympia into Arcadía via Langádia will take you towards the Ládon valley and into the fine Arcadian villages of **Gortynía** (*see* pp.346–56).

South of Olympia: Along the Coast to Messenía

This means crossing the Alphiós (there's a bridge west of Flókas) then turning west for the alluvial plain at **Kallíkomo** (Καλλίκωμο). The coast here is sandy but marshy, and inaccessible except by an unpaved road that you can pick up further south beyond **Káto Samikó** (Κάτο Σαμικό). Its name recalls ancient **Samikon** (signposted) which was located on a spur of the mountain that hems in the coast; a scramble up will be rewarded by impressive 5th-century BC polygonal walls.

Under the mountain, and separated from the sea by a narrow neck of land, the picturesque lagoon of **Lake Kaïafa** is the catchment basin of sulphurous waters emitted by two nymph-haunted cave springs. Various legends account for the distinctive aroma of its sources. One has it that Heracles stopped here to clean his knife after slaying the Hydra, another that the Centaur Nestor came here to bathe after being wounded by the arrows

Heracles had dipped in the Hydra's blood. Its modern name comes from yet another story: that Christ's judge, High Priest Caiaphas, stopped here to bathe, and in repugnance the waters began to reek to repel him. None of the stories has kept the Greeks from coming here to relieve skin ailments; the **spa** is on the wooded island reached by a causeway. Lake Kaiáfa's pines have been zapped by fire, the only seaside area affected by the 2007 blaze. Because of the spa, it will likely be reforested soon, one hopes.

Just south is **Zacháro** (Ζαχάρω), 'Sugar' in Greek, the name of a woman who once ran an inn here. It is a newish and lively town, and a great spot to while away a few days; its tiny train station midway between the town and the beach leaves you close to the rooms places. Down by its sandy beach, the sea is incredibly shallow and safe for children. Narrow streets are lined with summer cottages and semi-tropical gardens – a sweet enclave close to the sea and a quiet place to stay, less than a half-hour's drive from Olympia. Its other claim to notice is the fact that the mayor, hearing complaints from the local farmers that wives were impossible to find, arranged for a group of mail order brides from Russia. This effort and exchange provided material for a very popular and poignant Greek documentary: *Sugartown*.

Further south, the beach goes on and on, with access roads at **Kakóvatos** (Κακόβατος), **Neochóri** (Νεοχώρι), **Tholó** (Θολό) and **Giannitsochóri** (Γιαννιτσοχώρι). Three rich *tholos* tombs discovered at Marmari near Kakóvatos and scant signs of a Late Helladic palace in the 1910s led some archaeologists to believe this was the Pýlos of Nestor until the real thing came along; the finds from Kakóvatos are now in the National Museum in Athens. At Tholó you can pick up the road to the Néda Gorge (*see* pp.255–60), or continue south into Messenía.

★ Evelyn Rooms and Studios >>

Where to Stay and Eat South of Olympia

Kaïafa ✉ 27054

Kaiafas Lake Hotel, **t** 262 503 2954, *www.kaiafaslakehotel.gr* (€€/€). Rooms and studios set back from the lake, 2km from the sea with minibars, air-conditioning, TVs and a pool. *Open all year.*

Sidéris Rent Rooms, **t** 262 503 2634 (€/€). Right on the lake – new, modern, with air-conditioning, TVs and a lawn. Inexpensive except in August, when you can probably bargain. *Open all year.*

Zacháro ✉ 27054

Alkiónis, **t** 262 503 4582, *www.hotelalkionis.gr* (€€€€/€€). On the highway just north of town, this super new hotel has a stellar pool to make up for its location way back from the sea, parking, a good buffet breakfast, all the mod cons, and a reasonable price for its class outside of July and Aug. *Open all year.*

Evelyn Rooms and Studios , **t** 262 503 2537, *evelynshouse@gmail.com* (€€/€). Studios and rooms in a lovely grassy and shady setting with a pool, all within walking distance of the beach. This little oasis is a bargain, especially outside of July and Aug.

Banana Place Studios & Apartments, 160m from the sea, **t** 262 503 4400, *www.bananaplace1.uboot.com* (€€/€). Mr Vilionis' place is immersed in a huge banana plantation; there is volleyball, and a snack bar among other amenities. *Open 15 April–15 Oct.*

Appuntamento, t 262 503 4283 (€/€). Near Evelyn's. Simple but modern studios next to a good restaurant. *Open April–Oct.*

Theódoro Konstanópolous Rooms and Apartments, t 262 503 1724, *www.ecogreek.com* (€/€). Down in the seaside village, a 5min walk from the beach, peaceful studios among the palms and banana plants (follow the 'Rooms' signs). They sleep 2–3 and prices nosedive out of season.

Camping Tholo Beach, Tholò, **t** 262 506 1345, *campingtholo@hotmail.com* (€/€). They promise 'you are not just an unpersonal camper'. *Open April–Oct.*

Apollon Village Camping, Giannitso-chóri, **t** 262 506 1200 (€/€). Similar, but smaller and has a playground.

Ámmos Café and Restaurant, by the sea at Zacháro, **t** 262 503 2141. On the sand, with a friendly owner who specializes in fish; a great spot to watch the sun set.

Southern Elís

In ancient times, this southern third of Elis was called Triphyllía, a name you will still see occasionally. Although the Temple of Bassae is almost on the beaten track, the rest of southern Elís is anything but: the lovely Néda Gorge, just below the almost inhuman setting of Bassae, is known as 'a forgotten paradise' by the Greeks.

Kréstena to Andrítsaina

The good road running southeast of **Kréstena** (Κρέστενα) follows the route the Spartans would take to and from the Olympics; just imagine them swishing by with their long hair and red cloaks and soft bootkins. An important road, it was dotted with ancient towns, although as in Achaía there is a certain confusion over which is which. Kréstena itself is a big village near **ancient Skillus** (Σκιλλουντία) where Xenophon lived in retirement, hunting, writing and riding about the estate given to him by the Spartans. From Kréstena follow the signs for the Ναος Αθήνας, or **Temple of Athena Skillountia**, 6km to the northeast. Only the stylobate remains, but archaeologists can somehow glean from that mere platform that it was not the Temple of Athena that Xenophon built. Other ruins, including a 5th-century BC Temple of Zeus, have been found in **Markísa** (Μαρκίσα), 4.5km north of Kréstena, which some say was Skillus, or part of Skillus, or somewhere else.

Platiána (Πλατιάνα), 19km east, has long, beautifully preserved 3rd-century BC walls, a theatre, cisterns and two churches of ancient Typaneai on the ridge just south of the village, again attesting to the importance of this road in ancient times. North of Platiána, lonely in a field outside **Tripití** (Τριπητή), stands a last Gothic arch from the Frankish **Monastery of Ísovas**.

Getting to and around Southern Elís

Andrítsaina is 65km southeast of Pýrgos. Currently, there are **buses** down the Pýrgos–Kréstena–Andrítsaina road at 6am and 12.30pm, as well as from Athens twice a day. For bus **information** in Pýrgos: **t** 262 102 0600; in Andrítsaina: **t** 262 602 2239 (they don't often answer, there are so few buses).

Taxis from Andrítsaina (**t** 262 602 2380 or **t** 693 278 5998) to Bassae are €20 if you want the driver to wait. Ask about taxis at the café or the hotel. They will also take you to the Néda Gorge if you want to do the river trek, and arrange to pick you up downstream. To explore the Néda villages, however, you really need your own transport or sturdy shoes.

East of Kréstena, the road climbs slowly up the Alphiós valley, at first through parasol pines, cypresses and oleanders, under dark pine ridges. Sadly, this lovely vista ends all too soon. The Kréstena–Andrítsaina road and surroundings were devastated by the 2007 fire. Only the Andrítsaina area, its hinterland (including Bassae and its villages) and the very bottom of the Alphios valley have been saved. The picture is even grimmer a few kilometres after Andrítsaina where the fire crossed the Alphiós and went into parts of western Arcadía. The ruins of **ancient Alipheira** above the tiny modern town of **Alífira**, once lost in pines, may be easier to find now, but they would be a sad sight, best left until reforestation is under way.

Andrítsaina

Andrítsaina

Another 11km down the main road will bring you to the metropolis of south Elís, Andrítsaina (Ανδρίτσαινα), a long, multi-tiered mountain village preserved in aspic, especially the bit around the tiny *plateía* shaded by its enormous plane tree that has hardly changed from the 1960s. This is roughly when Andrítsaina's fortunes began to decline, as you may learn over a dinky cup of Greek java from the old men in Mr Thomópoulos' *kafeneíon*. For over 150 years, the village made a good living with its fleet of mules, 65-strong, taking people up to Bassae. Now the road has improved, and tour buses lurch by but rarely stop. The café itself is a relic of a Greece that is fast disappearing, with its uncompromising leather benches stuffed with horsehair. The square further east has a modest **Folklore Museum** in an old stone building. The rich library inside was donated to the town in 1840.

It may have been the contact with mule-needy philhellenes from abroad that led to the foundation here of an underground Greek school in 1764, which played an important role in sparking the independence movement in the Peloponnese. The monument in the *plateía* honours **Panagiótis Anagnostópoulos**, who was educated here. Anagnostópoulos was chief advisor to Dimítris Ypsilántis and became one of the leaders of the secret Greek revolutionary committee, the *Philikí Etairía* ('Friendly Society'), founded in Moscow by Greek expatriates after Napoleon's retreat.

Where to Stay and Eat in Andrítsaina

Andrítsaina ✉ 27061

The old *plateía* still has an old-time café and taverna; the 'new 'square just east of it with flagstones has the trendy coffee shops.

Xenónas Avgerinós and Sirrákos, t 262 602 2314, *avgerinosk@hol.gr* (€€/€€). A new attractive stone pile on the edge of town with the usual traditional décor. The rooms have fireplaces.

★ Geórgios Sieloúli >>

Theoxénia, t 262 602 2235 (€/€). By the 'new' *plateía*; a renovated relic from the 1950s, with large rooms of the usual Xénia sort: stone walls, picture windows, and great views. *Open all year.*

Xenónas Epikoúrios Apóllon, in the old *plateía*, **t** 262 602 2840 or 262 602 2408 (€/€). Maria Balkámos' guest house has five nice rooms and a large sitting room with fireplace. *Open all year.*

Kafeneíon Thomópoulos, old *plateía*, **t** 262 602 2239. A taste of old Andrítsaina.

Geórgios Sieloúli, t 262 602 2004. Beside the café, with great food, including tasty boiled goat. It packs the locals in for lunch.

Temple of Apollo Epikourios at Bassae

③ **Temple of Apollo Epikourios**
t 262 602 2275; open summer daily 8–7.30, winter daily 8.30–3; adm

The bad, dangerous road and 11km in a mule saddle from Andrítsaina did add a great deal to the appreciation of Bassae, for its beauty and for the extraordinary difficulty the 5th-century BC builders overcame to build a temple at 3,710ft. The modern road is good, but soon leaves civilization behind. Just before the sign for the wild-looking side road to Kalamáta, note the threshing floor. There are a couple of others along the way, under dry stone terraces wedged into cliffs, where eking out a living cannot have been easy.

Soon the road leaves behind these abandoned vestiges of life to enter some of the most grandiose, desolate and god-haunted country in Greece; in the old days, it was bandit-haunted as well. If nothing untoward happened, the mule riders would finally get their first breathtaking sight of the grey limestone temple, a small, defiant work of human art in a tremendous setting, yet one that harmonized with the surroundings in an unforgettable way – the hallmark of Iktinos, architect of the Parthenon.

The harmony may strike visitors again in about 2020 when rescue operations have been completed and the massive tent draped over the temple in 1982 has finally been removed. Even though the temple owes its preservation to its isolation, weather has worn it and earthquakes have jolted it. The Greek archaeological service means to restore what can be restored, and make it as anti-seismic as possible. The marbles you see lying neatly in the yard were once the roof; the tiles were all of Parian marble, which must have cost a fortune to bring here. When you enter the tent, you will notice that it is a very impressive tent, an engineering marvel in itself, especially if you come on a windy day when it angrily flaps about, or when the rain comes pelting down on it. But it does make everything dim and grey inside.

There is some confusion about the date of the temple's construction. It was commissioned by the small city of Figáleia (*see* p.258) to thank Apollo Epikourios 'the Helper' for sparing it the plague of 429 BC – the same plague that killed Pericles. This poses problems to those who believe Iktinos must have built Bassae before the Parthenon, because of its less sophisticated nature. Against that, one might argue that Iktinos had the wit to realize that the location hardly required the subtleties of entasis, nor were they possible or even desirable in the local limestone. Anyway, it seems that, having accomplished perfection in Athens, the architect felt free to innovate here. For Bassae is a very unusual temple: in its north–south orientation facing Delphi, Apollo's chief dwelling, in its Archaic-style length (125ft by 48ft, with a peristyle of six by 15 Doric columns, instead of the usual six by 13), and in the arrangement of the *pronaos*, *cella* and *opisthodomos*.

The *cella* was stripped of its Parian marble frieze in 1811–12 by a pair of cat and fox antiquarians, a German named Haller and an Englishman named Cockerell, who, inspired by Lord Elgin's 'poor plunder from a bleeding land', had already stripped the Temple of Aphaia on the Saronic island of Aegina and auctioned its *metopes* off to Munich. After bribing the local Turkish authorities, they came here and carried the 23 sections of the frieze to the then-British island of Zákynthos, and got the highest bid from the British government – a tidy sum of £19,000. To see the vigorous scenes of battling Lapiths and Centaurs, men and Amazons you'll have to go to the British Museum. It's just lucky for Greece that it became independent before Haller and Cockerell came back for the kitchen sinks.

Otherwise, the *cella* is nearly complete and, although the ropes and scaffolding won't let you enter, you can see the engaged columns (a new feature) on their bell-shaped bases (another novelty). The first four columns were Ionic, while the fifth pair are the earliest known Corinthian columns, although their capitals decorated with acanthus have been lost. They are a foot taller than the columns of the peristyle. The holy of holies, the *adyton*, was also idiosyncratic, and had an east door (possibly to admit light?) while lacking the usual wall separating it from the *cella*. The holy image was in bronze, but Pausanias wrote that it was hauled off to the *agora* of Megalópolis in 369 BC and replaced with stone.

Bassae means ravines. From here, or even better if you scramble up the side of Mount Kotilion above the tented temple, you can see the peaks of Arcadía, especially the bald pate of werewolf-haunted Mount Lýkaio rising ominously to the northeast (*see* pp.342–4).

The Néda Gorge

★4 Néda Gorge

In ancient times this was part of Arcadía and, according to Arcadian myth, Néda was one of the nymphs who cared for Zeus after his mother Rhea tricked his father Cronus into swallowing a stone instead of their newborn child. Since then, Néda and her many tributaries have carved quite a gorge, surprisingly lush and green after the stark grandeur of Bassae. Often you have to make a special effort just to get down and see the river, but it's worth it: the Néda is one of the loveliest waterways in Greece, with its numerous waterfalls, dragonflies and fantastical rock formations. In the summer, if you're adventurous, you can even walk its length down to the sea (*see* opposite).

Bassae is on the road along the top of the gorge, which is dotted with small villages. These are fragments of old Greece, ungentrified little Brigadoons, some almost abandoned outside the summer season. You can make a complete circuit around the gorge, beginning at Kaló Neró or Elía on the west coast, taking mostly unpaved roads along the south rim, wiggling your way up to Bassae, and back to the coast along the north rim. If you don't have much time, you can see many of the highlights of the gorge by car by spending the night in Andrítsaina. Visit Bassae in the morning,

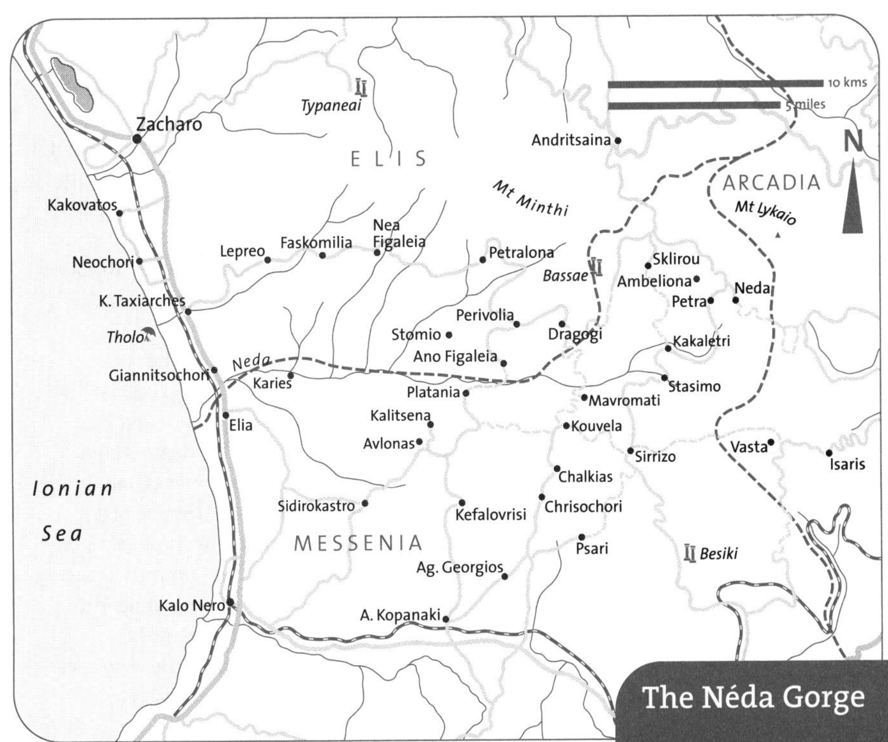

The Néda Gorge

then do the top of the Néda route clockwise, crossing the river below Dragógi. From there, follow the north rim of the gorge down via Lépreo to Káto Taxiárches.

Trekking down the Néda

Alternatively, you can walk down the Néda – literally. The whole trek takes about three days, but you can cheat and do only certain stretches. There are five points of access to the elusive river: **Pétra** (near the source); **Kakalétri's bridge** (a quiet section); the **Koúvela-Dragógi bridge** (where the river begins to become truly beautiful); the bridge on the new road between **Platanía** and **Figáleia** (the most dramatic, with a waterfall and the narrow gorge passing through pink and green rock pools downstream, perfect for bathing, and a dark cave you have to swim through); and along the riverside road between **Avlónas** and **Kariés**. After Kariés, most of the water is pumped away for irrigation, although you can continue down to the sea. Note that the trek is only possible in the **high summer** when the water is low. You'll need proper sturdy but lightweight footwear that doesn't mind the wet. Nor should you go alone; some parts require swimming and can be dangerous.

The Top of the Néda Gorge, by Car: Bassae to Koúvela via Ancient Eira

To circle around the Néda's upper reaches through tiny villages that time forgot, the route begins on the Andrítsaina–Bassae road at the turn-off for **Skliroú** (Σκληρού), 6.5km south of Andrítsaina and 4.5km north of Bassae.

This attractive stone hamlet was a hideout for Greek guerrilla bands (*klephts*) in the 18th and 19th centuries. When news got out that the Turks were letting Haller and Cockerell strip Bassae, the captains of the *klephts* gathered here to stop them, and failed miserably. For decades after, whenever the people passed the site of the battle, they would angrily toss a stone, creating a big pile considered cursed, *anáthema*.

Backtrack to the Andrítsaina road and head for **Ambelióna** (Αμπελιώνα), where film buffs can admire the birthplace of director Théo Angelópoulos. The amazingly slow pace and beautiful *tableaux* that are his trademark may be deep-seated psychological remnants of this sparse and monumental landscape, where nothing much ever happened, and certainly none of it happened quickly. Ambelióna is famous for its chestnuts; walking through its deep groves is refreshing even in the summer. If you come on 29 August, don't miss the festival of St John at nearby **Ag. Sóstis**, which offers a chance to hear traditional music.

The village of **Néda** (Νέδα), a bit farther on, has lovely views over the valley, and a mostly paved road into Arcadía, for visits to

Lykósoura and Mount Lýkaio (*see* p.342). The main road then continues to **Pétra** (Πέτρα) near the source of the Néda, at the springs of Agianatássi – the place to start if you want to trek down the whole river. As you continue south along the road, you'll see the Néda flowing on your right, near the old stone **Chapel of Panagía Kakalétri**, a fine picnic spot by a spring, just below the road. The village of **Kakalétri** (Κακαλέτρι) is further on, immersed in trees. A paved road from here leads down to a bridge over the Néda by way of the hamlet of **Marína** (Μαρίνα), pop. 6, and then continues unpaved up to Skliroú.

The citadel of **ancient Eira** was on the hill just above Kakalétri, a steep, hot 45min hike up through the thorns. When Sparta enslaved Messenía, Aristomenes (*see* box) led all the Messenians who escaped to this spot, just over the then frontier of Arcadía, and made it his base for raids into Laconía in the Second Messenian War (685–668 BC).

An Ancient Robin Hood

Although he lived 2,600 years ago, the locals are still proud of Aristomenes, 'the first and greatest glory of the Messenian name'. While the other Messenians toiled in slavery as helots, Aristomenes and his merry men harried the Spartans until they came marching up to Eira to stop them, only to suffer a defeat that so shattered their nerve that only the inspirational verses of their poet, Tyrtaios, managed to restore it:

> *Young men, fight keeping steadfastly by one another. Don't start shamefully running away and don't start to panic. Be stout-hearted and great-hearted, and when you are fighting against men, don't dwell on how great life is. Don't flee and desert your seniors, the old men, whose knees are not so nimble.*

For all Tyrtaios' words, the siege of Eira lasted off and on for eleven years. Meanwhile, Aristomenes performed remarkable acts of derring-do, at one point even penetrating into Sparta itself and the Temple of Athena Chalkiolkos, where he left a shield inscribed: 'The Gift of Aristomenes to the Goddess'. The Spartans ground their teeth in rage. A Corinthian army came to help, but Aristomenes' band came down in the dead of night and completely routed them. The Delphic oracle had promised Aristomenes that Apollo would protect his Messenian rebels until one of their billy-goats (*tragos*) drank from the Néda. The goatherds made sure it never happened. Only *tragos* in Greek also meant wild fig, and one growing on the banks drooped over so that its leaves touched the water...

Still, by all accounts, the Spartans only succeeded in taking Eira by treachery. Historians favour a tale of betrayal by King Aristocrates of Arcadía at the so-called Battle of the Great Trench. Pausanias, who read the *Messeniaca*, a lost 3rd-century BC epic, favoured a complex romantic intrigue: during a torrential storm, a Messenian woman's Spartan lover overheard her husband announce that Eira's guard had gone inside because of the rains. The Spartans then mounted a surprise attack that seriously weakened Eira. Another story tells of a secret underground passage that the Messinians used for going back and forth from Eira right under the Spartans' noses; a young girl betrayed its whereabouts when the Spartans captured her fiancé and threatened his life.

Whatever happened, when the Messenians saw that the gig was up, they escaped, many to Sicily where one of their descendants became Tyrant of Zancle and renamed the city-state Messina after his ancestral home. Aristomenes, however, was caught and marched back to Sparta, where he was tossed off the precipice of the *kaiades*. Fortuitously, his fall was broken by a ledge. He found a kindly fox and, holding its tail, was guided out of the ravine and eventually went into exile in Rhodes. But the Spartans demolished Eira to make sure no one ever used it again; if you make the scramble up you'll see a massive pile of stones and a few boulders which remain from the wall. It's a great story, but historians

today doubt that there was ever a Second Messenian War at all. Others tend to think it was a local conflict that took place here on the north fringe of Messenía, which the Spartans had failed to conquer in the First Messenian War. In this scenario, Aristomenes was a minor resistance leader, and the whole saga was invented or else greatly exaggerated after Epaminondas liberated Messenía, to create a Messenian civic myth (perhaps the only one in Greece where the gods play no role) that gave their community an identity, one denied by the Spartans for over 300 years. Tyrtaios' poems exhorting the Spartans are historical enough, but may have been twisted by the Messenians for their own ends.

Other walls of ancient Eira can be seen by the hilltop chapel of **Ag. Paraskévi** (the turn-off is 1.2km down the road to Stásimo). Beyond **Stásimo** (Στάσιμο) the road rises, with lovely views of the valley en route to **Sírrizo** (Σύρριζο), with a taverna. The next stretch of road is unpaved (4.2km) to **Koúvela** (Κουβελα), a village of tidy stone houses, famous for honey. From here a not so good road leads up to the chapel of **Profítis Ilías** for a view stretching all the way down to the coast and out to the remote Strofades islands, once home to the Harpies.

Another dirt road, in better shape this time, winds down from Koúvela to the ghost village of **Mavromáti**, where the chapel of Ag. Demítrios (the equestrian saint who replaced horse-headed Demeter) has frescoes. The river below is lovely, and there's a **bridge** here to take you up to **Dragógi** (Δραγώγι), which has something rare in the Néda villages: new houses.

The North Rim of the Gorge, by Car: Bassae to Figáleia, Lépreo and the Coast

The other approach to Dragógi is to drive directly west of Bassae. At the next village west, **Perivólia** (Περιβόλια), you'll come to a giant plane tree, where you should turn left and continue 2.9km to a rural crossroads. The unpaved road to the left doesn't look promising, but if you don't give up it will eventually take you to the very traditional but nearly empty village of Ano Figáleia (Φιγάλεια) that has superseded **ancient Figaleia**. At the crossroads as the village begins, you'll see the recently discovered remains of a **temple** (signposted) with a well-preserved altar. Walls and towers, once extending 4.5km, can be discerned on the steep cliffs.

Ancient Figaleia must have been quite a place. Although hard to imagine nowadays, it made its living as a transit point between Arcadía and the sea, sending goods up and down the Néda; in 1972 fragments of boats were found along the river. It was captured by Sparta in 659 BC, but the Figaleians recaptured it soon after. Somehow it came up with the readies to build the temple at Bassae, but it was hardly known for its piety: rather by all accounts Figaleia was a hard-drinking, wild town not averse to a little sorcery. One temple (perhaps this one?) was dedicated to Dionysos 'of the wine-mixing vessel', whose statue was placed in the middle of the vineyards, painted with cinnabar to glow red in the sun. East of town flowed the Lymakos, a tributary of the Néda, considered sacred for washing away Rhea's afterbirth (*lymata*) after she produced Zeus. There Figaleia built a Sanctuary of Eurynome, the daughter of Oceanus, which they visited once a year. Inside, the cult statue resembled a mermaid, half-woman and half-fish, and it was bound to the place by golden chains (a reminder that ancient Figaleia was in Arcadía, where gods never quite evolved into human form). The Figaleians were proudest of their two-time Olympia *pankration*-winner Arrhakion, who was choked to death in his last fight but won the wreath posthumously. His statue stood in the middle of the *agora*. What happened to his murderous opponent remains a mystery, but he probably got a statue, too.

After the temple the left fork in the road takes you to the top of the town, where the ancient fountain house (signposted) still produces water, a great picnic spot under its huge trees. Signs from here point the way (or ask) to the steep footpath for **Áspro Neró** (Υσπρο Νερό) or **White Water waterfall**, one of the most enchanting spots on the Néda; an unpaved road can also get you down (there's a bridge to the south side of the gorge where the road is excellent). Once in the river bed, plane trees provide the shade, and there are pools downstream where you can pretend to be the star of a shampoo ad. The section downriver is the steepest walled and most dramatic part of the gorge.

As you return towards Perivólia and the main road, you'll see a driveable track leading off 3km to the left to **Stómio** (Στόμιο), another lost hamlet of old stone houses. This was part of ancient Figaleia, where a cave in the wall of the gorge (near the picturesque **Chapel of the Panagítsa**) was dedicated to Demeter Melaina, 'Black Demeter'. Here Pausanias found a seated statue of the goddess with a mare's head, holding a dove in one hand and a dolphin in the other, recalling that she was the ancient goddess of the horse cult, the oak (dove) cult and the dolphin cult. She is Black Demeter because she dressed in black and took refuge here after losing her daughter to Hades and being raped by her brother Poseidon in the form of a horse. It would depress anyone. But as Demeter was also the corn goddess, her sadness drove humanity to the brink of starvation until Pan cheered her up and coaxed her out. The image in the cave was originally made of wood and caught fire, and on cue Figaleia's crops at once failed. They urgently sent to Aegina to commission the very expensive sculptor Onatas to make a bronze copy, which sorted things out.

The scenery along the main gorge road becomes distinctly greener as you approach **Petrálona** (Πετράλωνα), with a pair of cafés, a sprinkling of stone houses and a stone church, where in the afternoon the only sound is the distant tinkling of goat bells and the breeze whispering in the plane trees. **Néa Figáleia**, the next village to the west, seems like a metropolis with its *kafeneíons* strung out along the road looking down into the fertile valley.

The last village, **Lépreo** (Λέπρεο), is high over the Gulf of Kyparissía. According to the myth, ancient Lepreon was founded by Minyans, whom the Argonauts had fathered on the women of Límnos, and who sailed to Triphyllia and founded several cities. The town was named after King Lepreo, who had foolishly advised King Augeias to chain up Heracles after he cleaned out his stables; years later, when Heracles angrily came to find him, Lepreo's mother persuaded him to ask Heracles' pardon. Heracles accepted, but on the condition that Lepreo compete with him in three contests: throwing the discus, drinking the most water, and eating an ox the quickest. Heracles won the first two, but Lepreo was the first to wolf down the ox. In the excitement at having defeated the greatest hero of the Greeks, Lepreo at once challenged him to a duel, and Heracles squashed him like a fly with his club. But, in accordance with the odd logic of myth, it was Heracles who henceforth was known as *Bouphagos*, the ox-eater. Later stories associating the village with leprosy are just that, later: the disease didn't arrive in Greece until the 1st century BC.

As you enter Lépreo, a little hill resembling a giant tooth with a tiny church on top was the **prehistoric acropolis** (a yellow sign says 'archaeological site') – of the Minyans, one imagines. It also heralds the beginning of the worst of the 2007 fire damage, which the town itself escaped but not the wonderful **Hellenistic acropolis** (also signposted in yellow as 'archaeological site') at the west end of town. It sits high above, on the road to Taxiarchés. Brave the fire-ravaged forest for 1.7km until a sign points you to a short dirt road to the site. The car park ends in front of the massive eastern fortification wall. Once there, follow the path to the left and you will reach a sign describing the site's history in English. The Doric peristyle **Temple of Demeter** is the one you want to see; it is to the left of the sign in the southwest corner of the acropolis. Bits of column look as if they have been stubbed out like cigarettes around the peristyle, and there is a large altar (obviously designed for oxen barbecues) still in place. The altar looks odd tucked away on the east side of the temple when the view to the west over the Gulf of Kyparissía is so splendid, but rules are rules. Just north of the temple, you will see something not often encountered: an almost intact **Hellenistic building**, now a picturesque and unusual stable. The farmer has made use of the ancient door and window.

From Lépreo the road down to the sea passes charming churches, chickens, a lovely pine forest (and, surprise, a helipad owned by a jet-setting Greek who converted the surrounding mill into his hideaway). From here it's only a few minutes to the sea.

South of the Néda Gorge

The deep ravines of the Néda's tributaries make a quick trip down the south edge of the gorge impossible, but you could do worse than to spend a few hours in these little known byways of northern Messenía (the Néda forms its border with Elís).

Take the paved road west of **Koúvela** (*see* p.258) to pretty **Avlónas** (Αυλώνας), an up-to-date village founded in the early 19th century by a Turkish aga who couldn't bear the mosquitoes on the coast. The village bore his name, Kara-Mustafa, until 1922, when it was changed to Avlónas for an ancient city that Pausanias, Strabo and Xenophon mentioned but no one has yet located. Then head to **Sidirókastro** (Σιδηρόκαστρο), a metropolis after the preceding villages, with its big stone church topped by an incongruous blue dome, and a folk museum; and on to Agalianí and the coast. There is an unpaved road west from Avlónas to Panórama and **Kariés** (Καρυές) if you really want to hug the river, and a paved one from Kariés (near old river mills) to the sea.

If you have a couple of hours to spare, meander south of Koúvela to **Chalkiás** (Χαλκίας), an old village with slate roofs, and **Chrisochóri** (Χρυσοχώρι) and **Psári** (Ψάρι), both traditional villages with fine squares. From Psári, follow the road east towards Mélpia for 3km to the turn-off for **Besíki** (Μπεσίκι), where you can drive up part of the way, but have to continue on foot, to reach a remarkably well-preserved Mycenaean ***tholos* tomb**, 17ft in diameter. It seems rather lonely here; perhaps it was built by a family that didn't get along with the others in nearby Peristeriá (*see* p.461).

Return to Psári and continue 4km southwest to **Ag. Geórgios** (Αγ. Γεώργιος), where a giant mulberry tree shades a perfect old-fashioned *kafeneíon*. **Kaló Neró** on the coast is just east.

The mouth of the Néda, below the olive-growing village of **Eliá** (Ελιά), is the biggest nesting ground for *Caretta caretta* turtles in Greece after Zákynthos. There's an information desk in Eliá run by a turtle protection group. In the summer volunteers from Eliá and Kaló Neró mark the nests in the sands and try to protect them until the baby turtles hatch and race to the sea. Their biggest enemies aren't tourists but foxes.

To continue down the coast to Kyparissía, *see* p.461.

Where to Stay and Eat in and south of the Néda Gorge

These villages can be reached most easily from Andrítsaina, but do not forget the back door routes from Lykosoúra and Ísaris in Arcadía, both good in summer.

There are possibilities to eat in Néda, Sírrizo and Ambelióna. The village inns have mostly closed except for one in Ambelióna.

Kaló Neró (40km from Bassae if you take the Platánia–Figalía bridge) is the nearest seaside resort and offers quite a range of places to stay; Kyparissía (*see* p.461) isn't far away either.

Epoxés, Ambelióna, **t** 262 602 3991, *www.epohes.gr* (€€€€/€€€). Pretty and surprisingly sophisticated for the village – a peaceful little hideaway with a library, an attractive stone courtyard, and a restaurant promising local products on the menu. *Open all year.*

Írida Resort, Kálo Néro, **t** 276 107 1386, *www.iridaresort.gr* (€€€/€€) Attractive seaside apartments for four just north of the centre. Owner Mr Kóstas knows all about the Néda – what has been paved, and where to go. *Open all year*.

Akroyiáli, Kaló Neró, **t** 276 107 1345 (€€/€€). Comfortable standard rooms over a popular if rather barn-like restaurant right on the sea. There are pricier studios out the back.

Argolís

Cut off by mountains and the sea, Argolís may be a place apart from the rest of the Peloponnese, but in Greek history and myth it has often held centre stage – Mycenae, Tiryns, Troezen, Epidauros, Argos and Lerna are here, and, for anyone who has grazed or even snacked on the classics, the province is a full five-course banquet. For dessert there's the capital of the Argolís, ancient Mycenae's port Naúplio, the Peloponnese's most beautiful city. And, as a garnish, you'll find good beaches along the lovely coast, three buzzing islands with distinct personalities, flashy resort hotels (or old-timer inns), and a dollop of wild Peloponnesian grandeur, topped off with a volcano.

12

Don't miss

1. Myth meets history
   Mycenae p.265
2. Homer's amazing 'wall-girt' palace
   Tiryns p.292
3. A perfect Greek theatre
   Epidauros p.301
4. The prettiest city in the Peloponnese
   Naúplio p.286
5. Surreal land-scapes atop a dead volcano
   Méthana p.303

See map overleaf

Argolís

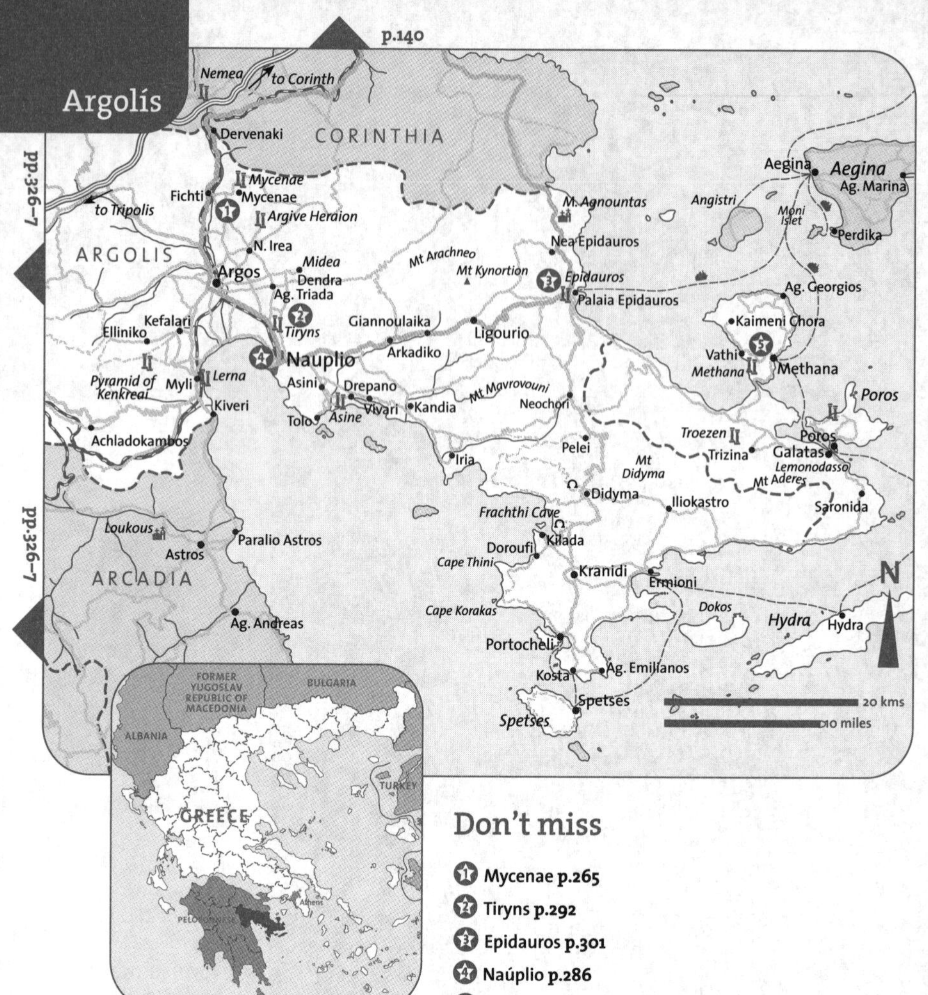

Don't miss

1. Mycenae p.265
2. Tiryns p.292
3. Epidauros p.301
4. Naúplio p.286
5. Méthana p.303

After the collapse of the Mycenaean civilization, leadership passed to Argos, a city once as important as Athens and one that, for a time, challenged the big noise from Laconía for supremacy in the Peloponnese. Even after Sparta won undisputed hegemony, Argos refused to have anything to do with its old rival, refusing even to join in the war against the Persians just because the Spartans were there. Places like Epidauros and Troezen had their own well-defined histories too: Epidauros because it was sacred, Troezen because it was cut off on the Akte peninsula. Nowadays, ferries and hydrofoils from Piraeus to Méthana and Ermióni through the Saronic Gulf make access easy (and there are hire cars available at Naúplio, Galatás, Ermióni and Portochéli) but, if you can pick and choose, the Argolís is really at its best on either side of the season, and it stays open all year.

Mycenae

The ideal approach to Mycenae from Corinth is on the Old National Road through the **Pass of Dervenáki**. The road begins to rise south of Nemea (*see* p.160), passing by way of the Nemea–Dervenáki train station, where a detour left leads to a chapel and statue of Theodore Kolokotrónis (*see* pp.344–5). The main road pierces the twin peaks of Mount Tretós ('Perforated'), where the rock resembles a giant Swiss cheese. In the adjacent gorge, on 6 August 1822, a band of insurgents and locals led by Kolokotrónis and his nephew Nikétas ambushed a Turkish force of 6,000 led by Dramali Pasha, causing over 4,000 casualties. Greek losses were minimal. Edward Trelawney, riding through Dervenáki a year later, found the gorge thick with the skeletons of men, horses, mules and camels, all gruesomely positioned just as they had fallen.

From Dervenáki the road descends to the Argive Plain; on a clear day you can spot not only the lofty castle of Argos but also Naúplio's Palamídi fortress. Next comes the busy crossroads at Fíchti, with the turn-off for Mycenae. At the end of a long, stately avenue of eucalyptus, **modern Mycenae** (Μυκήνες) turns out to be more of a cottage than the château the drumroll of trees may have suggested. But it is a pleasant village, where the people not in the tourist trade grow oranges. Beyond, the ancient citadel sits on a 1,000ft-high spur under Mounts Zara and Elias, watchful and terrible.

Ancient Mycenae: The City that Imagination Built

★ Mycenae

Supercharged with myth and history, Mycenae captures the imagination at once: the sheer barbaric power of the citadel makes it the ideal setting for the fatal playing out of the Curse of the House of Atreus. Heinrich Schliemann, the true believer, certainly thought he was unearthing those bloodstained stones when he excavated the palace in 1874. But, as at the site of his other fabulous discovery, Troy, what he actually found was much, much older, and perhaps even more intriguing than the Homeric heroes he was searching for.

The Myth

These things never happened, but are, always.
a Greek philosopher

Acrisios, King of Argos, locked his daughter Danaë in a vault, because an oracle had proclaimed that a son of hers would kill him. Zeus, smitten, visited her in a shower of gold and Perseus was born. Mother and son were then set adrift in a chest by Acrisios, and ended up on the island of Sérifos. When Perseus grew up he killed

Getting to Mycenae

By bus: There are several local **buses** a day from Naúplio and Argos, and many (15 or so) inter-provincial buses from Athens and Corinth. When train services resume south from Corinth (*see* p.142), the closest station will be Fíchti (Φίχτι), almost 2km from the site, by the Old National Road. The Schinás Café-cum-KTEL station, **t** 275 107 6206, will let you leave luggage and call a taxi for you.

By car: As well as the Old National Road, there is also a newer road from Mycenae to Naúplio. It runs in a north–south axis, but farther east, bypassing Argos while passing closer to the Heraion and Dendra.

---

the snake-haired Medusa with a little help from Hermes and Athena. He then fulfilled the oracle by accidentally killing his grandfather, and, feeling a little awkward about it, took over Tiryns instead of Argos. But one day, when he was out walking, he saw a mushroom (*mykos*) pop out of the ground, followed by a spring, and decided to start a new city called Mycenae after the mushroom. Perseus' son married Pelops' daughter, joining the two houses; their child Alcmene became the mother of Heracles, whom Zeus had fathered with the intention of making him High King of Mycenae. But jealous Hera delayed his birth long enough so that his cousin Eurystheus was born first and became king. He gave Heracles the Twelve Labours, and was killed in Attica by the sons of Heracles, who were even then plotting their return to the Peloponnese.

Finding themselves rudderless, the Mycenaeans chose Atreus, a son of Pelops, as king. Nor was it long before the infamous curse on the family – first uttered by the charioteer Myrtos as Pelops kicked him into the sea (*see* p.46) – began to take hold. Angered at his brother Thyestes' attempts to steal the throne, Atreus cooked up his nephews, served them, and then produced their heads, hands and feet for their father's dessert. It proved an effective way to keep his throne, but Thyestes laid yet another curse upon his family which fell on Agamemnon, Atreus' son. Agamemnon would lead the Greeks to Troy and win Helen back for his brother Menelaus, but first sacrificed his own daughter Iphigenia in order to gain fair winds for the fleet. His wife, Clytemnestra, did a little cursing of her own, bided her time, and duly murdered Agamemnon in his bath when he returned from Troy. That caused their son Orestes, goaded by his sister Electra, to kill his mother and her lover, Aegisthus, the surviving son of Thyestes. Orestes was hunted and haunted by the Furies until Apollo and Athena decided enough was enough and justified the matricide on the grounds that females only provided space for a foetus, so killing them didn't count as a family crime. That bit of genetic flummery absolved Orestes, who went on to become king of Sparta and died in Arcadía of a snakebite at age 70.

The barest outline of the story, first mentioned in the *Odyssey*, is complicated enough. Add 2,500 years of poets and playwrights and these stories have gathered enough critical mass to keep psychiatrists, sociologists and historians busy forever.

With so much written about them, we have to keep in mind that the Mycenaeans themselves left no written historical or mythical records. In Homer, Aeschylus and Co., what we have is the ancient Greeks' *perception* of Mycenaean culture. The oral tradition recording their Trojan expedition (some parts of the *Iliad* are said to date back to the 10th century BC) was hugely subverted by Greece's post-Mycenaean overlords in order to flatter their own warlike ways and patriarchal religion. The Trojan War occurred, but what really happened and why it happened will forever remain a mystery. That is part of Mycenae's boundless appeal to the imagination.

In Mycenae, the myths and the facts gleaned by the archaeologist's spade collide, merge and colour what we see. Heinrich Schliemann came to Mycenae seeking Agamemnon, not mere historical reality. It's hard to resist 'doing a Schliemann': looking for the bath where Agamemnon was killed, the ravine where Clytemnestra's body was hurled, and trying to figure out if those signal fires mentioned in Aeschylus really could have been seen from the citadel. Even the archaeological service gets into the act and labels tombs after Clytemnestra and Aegisthus, when the dates could not possibly jib. Oops, assuming they ever existed, of course. And about those signal fires – they could have been seen from the citadel. So it must have happened, right?

The Citadel and its History

Surrounded by half a mile of massive Cyclopean walls, Mycenae's citadel looks solid, impressive and rather barren as you approach it up the Chavos ravine from town. It is not until you walk over the ridge towards the Lion Gate and note the deep east–west Kokorétsa ravine running along behind the site to the north that you realize how defensible it was. The palace commands a view of the entire Argive Plain, and for several hundred years it commanded its political life as well.

The hill was occupied from 3000 BC on, and by 2000 BC the inhabitants may well have been Greek-speakers. For hundreds of years they used the shallow valley just west of the citadel to bury their dead. By 1600 BC or so, they were rich enough to bury their élite in what we now call **Grave Circle A**, along with a lot of weapons, more homely articles, and over 14 kilos of gold – all in all, the richest grave-find ever in Greece. Homer knew about it; he called Mycenae 'rich in gold' (πολύχρυσο). Since there are no gold mines associated with the Mycenaeans, the big question remains: where did it come from?

Informed gossip suggests that the warlike Mycenaeans either hired themselves out as mercenaries in Egypt (Egypt was known to pay in gold) or that they were one of the large bands of marauders in the Mediterranean at this date, the so-called 'sea peoples' whom the Egyptians mentioned in their written records as harassing them (the tribe called the *Akhaivasha* is associated with our Achaeans), and that they got their gold by plunder. If the Mycenaeans used Minoan ships to come and go on these expeditions, it would account for the well-off warrior society with Minoan religious and artistic habits that these graves reveal. It also nicely encompasses the Mycenaean take-over of the fabulous Minoan palaces on Crete. And there are other hints: the Mycenaean habit of burying their dead with rich goods and gold face masks certainly has an Egyptian ring to it, and many legends about Mycenaean culture suggest Egyptian connections.

The descendants of the people found in these graves went from strength to strength, their artistic and technical achievements culminating in the numerous *tholos* tombs and in the two-storey palace whose floor plan crowns the ruins. In this palace-centred culture, accounts were eventually kept in writing using the famous **Linear B** script (*see* pp.454–6) found first at Knossos in Crete. Finds at Mycenae show that trade relations extended from Egypt (ostrich eggs) to the Baltic (amber). In its period of greatest splendour, from 1400 to 1100 BC, Mycenae controlled all of the cities in the Peloponnese and beyond in some kind of federation. Roads crisscrossed the landscape connecting them.

The physical development of the citadel you see today is a 'written record' of sorts. Before 1350 BC, a palace existed, but no walls. Then Cyclopean walls were built at the same time as the palace whose ruins we see today. In 1250 BC, more walls were added, extending the citadel to the southwest and refortifying it. Changes included the construction of the massive Lion Gate. Civil expansion partly explains the changes, but they were clearly increasingly defensive in nature as well. Whether the threat was external or internal, between the Mycenaean states themselves, is anybody's guess. The further extension of the walls on the northeast to enclose a water source in about 1200 BC indicates a real fear of a prolonged siege. These fears were all too well-founded because *something* terrible and final did happen. The palace-based Mycenean culture collapsed in flames about 1100 BC, leaving remnants, but certainly no Peloponnesian-based victors.

Mycenae Site
t 275 107 6803; open daily 8–7.30; although those are the official hours year round, try to arrive before 2.30 in winter just in case, or call ahead; adm exp; the museum has toilets and a café

The Site

Declared a World Heritage Site in 1999, Mycenae's **Cyclopean walls** are simply astounding. Its huge boulders weigh, on average, six tons, and are held in place by smaller stones at their interstices.

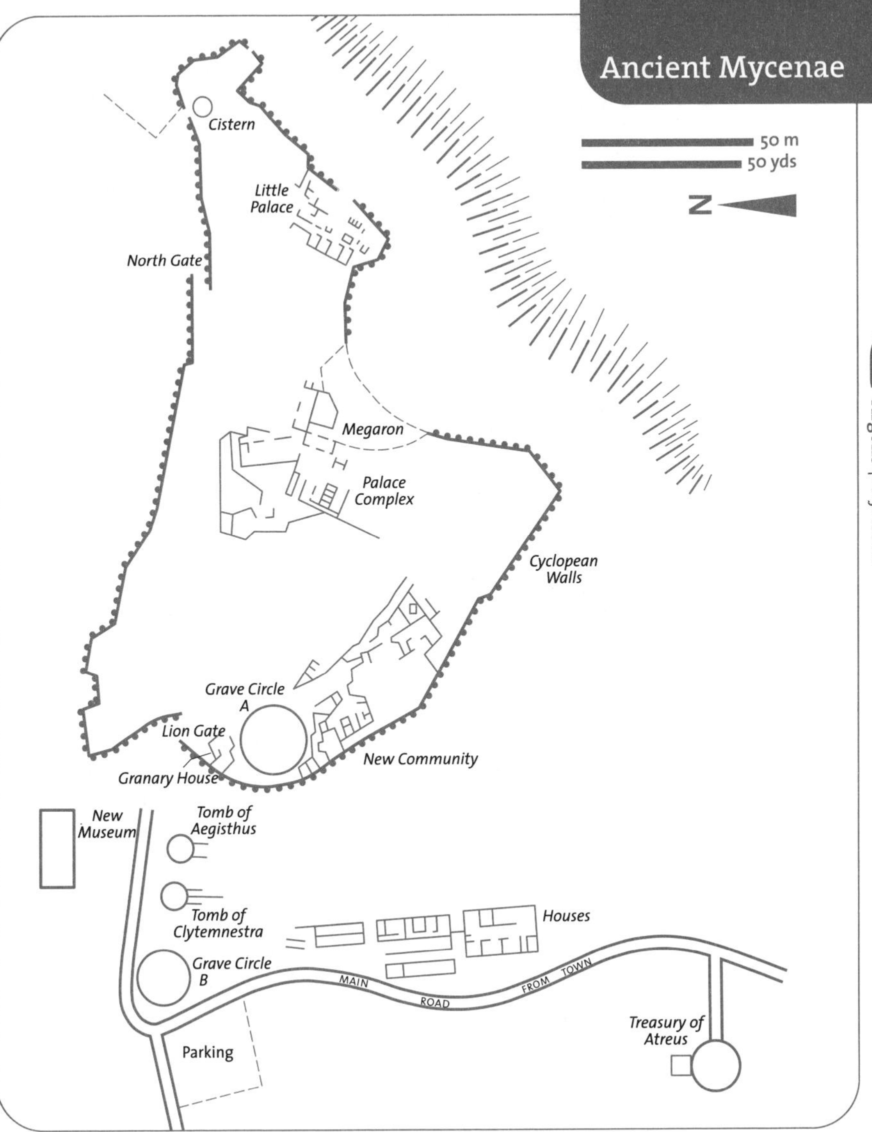

It may sound clumsy, but the results are not. Standing 15ft thick and about 50ft high in places when new, they were attributed to the giant Cyclops by awed later generations who had lost the ability to move such massive rocks.

Not all of the walls are Cyclopean. In the impressive 48ft **corridor** leading up to the Lion Gate, equally huge stones were used, but they were dressed into rectangular blocks and arranged quasi-isodomically. As you approach the gate, the citadel wall is to your left, while the wall on your right belongs to a bastion and tower built to enhance Mycenae's defensive capabilities.

The **Lion Gate** makes the perfect introduction to the citadel, conveying power, prestige, and just a touch of brute force. The gate consists of four massive monolithic stones creating an almost square opening, 10½ft high by 10¼ft wide. The gateposts narrow very slightly at the top. A sculptured relief of two (now headless) lionesses, supporting a pillar, is set in the relieving triangle of the 12-ton lintel. This fairly common Minoan heraldic motif, depicted on their seal rings, was no doubt adopted as the Mycenaean royal coat of arms, and enlarged on a scale the Minoans never attempted. The threshold was scored for better walking, and ruts for easier chariot access were created. Originally the gate had huge, hinged double doors of wood sheathed in bronze that could be bolted. Look for the pivot holes in the lintel and doorway. In the gateway to the left is a cleft, some say for guard dogs, others for guards, others for a shrine, a nice reminder that a lot of conclusions drawn about Mycenaean ruins are pure conjecture.

Immediately to the right after the gate is the so-called **granary house**. Like many buildings in Mycenae, it had two floors and may really have been a guard house. And immediately beyond this is **Grave Circle A**. Here in the summer of 1876 Schliemann believed he beheld the face of Agamemnon before it crumbled to dust as he lifted the golden mask. What a moment! He telegraphed the king of Greece at once. His date was out by three hundred years, but no matter. This royal compound, with six shaft graves, was used over a period of time and contained twelve men, five women and two children; some of the bodies were judged to be six-footers – unusually tall for the time, although Homeric heroes often had exceptional physiques. When the graves in Circle A were in use, there were no Cyclopean walls. When the citadel expanded to the southwest, the sloping ground behind the new Cyclopean wall was filled in with rubble to its present level, thus burying the original grave circle. While this was being done, the *stelae* covering the grave mounds were removed, only to be replaced inside the 85ft-diameter double circle of upright stones, capped by horizontal ones that you see today. It copied, in grander form, the original grave circle. Almost as remarkable as the fabulous treasure found by Schliemann is this testament to the deep reverence for ancestral tombs, created at a time when larger *tholos* tombs for royals had been the custom for over 200 years. A small altar was placed inside the circle of stones.

Just south of Grave Circle A is the **new community** created by the extension of the walls after 1250 BC. What we see is a labyrinth of basement foundations that would have supported one- or two-storey houses. It is likely they belonged to officials since this was a citadel, not a city. 'Houses' have been named after the finds or the finders. So many idols or cult statues were found that it is thought some buildings may have been used for religious purposes. If so, Mycenaean indoor shrines were poky affairs.

A 79ft **ramp** ascends to the upper **palace complex** and its *propylon* on the northwest side. This entrance led into a narrow corridor going south, and had two corridors off it leading east. The northernmost corridor ascended to the family quarters, which were totally obliterated by buildings in the Hellenistic period. The second and southernmost corridor led to the public rooms of the palace, the area that can be most imaginatively grasped today. Its outer court would have been open to the south, taking in a magnificent view of the Argive Plain.

The grand **staircase**, still visible, led up to this public area from the south, and was no doubt used by official visitors. They passed through the two-columned porch which faced the court (the little stairway on its north side leads to the rest of the palace) into the ***prodomos***, or vestibule, and then into the ***megaron***, the most important room in any Mycenaean palace. This was a fair-sized room (42ft by 39ft) with a circular central hearth that can still be seen; it was decorated in spirals and flame motifs. Four wooden columns sheathed with bronze held up the roof, and the area above the hearth would have been open to the sky. The floors were paved with painted gypsum tiles with linear patterns, and the walls were alive with brightly coloured frescoes. One portrayed a battle scene with Mycenaean ladies cheering on the menfolk from the ramparts. The throne must have been on the south wall, a part of the *megaron* that had fallen into the ravine by the time Mycenae was excavated, and has since been reconstructed. The rooms to the west of the open court were probably guestrooms. The **bathroom** where Clytemnestra killed Agamemnon, or at any rate a bathroom, is immediately adjacent to the *megaron* to the northeast.

East of the palace were artisans' **workshops**, and beyond that a colonnaded building called the '**little palace**' because it, too, contained a *megaron*. The exact use of some of the buildings in the upper citadel is conjectural. But we can assume store rooms, treasuries, administrative areas, all spaces required by a palace-based economy.

From this area, you can visit the **North Gate**. It was erected at the same time as the Lion Gate and, like most back doors, is not quite as grand, although built in the same style. The area furthest east was the last part of the citadel to be walled in, in order to defend a deep cistern that received water via an underground terracotta conduit from a spring, now called the **Spring of Perseus**, 500 yards outside the walls. This cistern, with its corbelled roof in the form of an inverted 'V', is one of the most impressive technical works of the Mycenaean period; 16 steps descend to a sharp turn and then there are 83 more down to the water level. It is open to the public, but you need a torch – even then it has the spooky quality of all very old underground places.

The Museum

Mycenae Museum
t 275 107 6803; open Tues–Sun 8–7.30; Mon 12–7.30; adm covered by site entrance adm; the museum has toilets and a café

The new museum is north of the Lion Gate towards the Kokorétsa ravine. The **first room**, 'The Human Presence at Mycenae', is full of wonders, displayed according to their find sites, with excellent explanations in English. Mycenae's famous clay 'dollies' are here, some soulful, others bland, others just a bit scary. Found in a shrine near Grave Circle A, some are well over 30cm high; note, curled up beside them, the solid-looking ceramic snake, a symbol so important to Mycenaean religion. Dolly number 6 has what appears to be snake hair, too. The bird vases have delicate, painted designs and lines so supple, they look as if they could come to life and sing. One case has a bit of fresco showing the elaborate skirts of the ladies, and be sure to look for the display from the artisans' quarter with un-worked quartz, rock crystals, agate, obsidian and so on. A ramp leads down to the **second room**, where the theme is 'Life to Death: Cemeteries'. Each grave offering is worth a look: small figures, whimsical toy animals, and, again, vases that seem to move from clay to life. A complete larnax with a cover, found between Mycenae and the Heraion, is quite unusual for the area. The **third room** shows objects from the site that date from after the Mycenaeans, and would fascinate in any other setting, but take a back seat to the first two rooms here. The seals, however, are worth a close look.

Southeast of the Lion Gate

Grave Circle B, somewhat earlier or contemporary with Grave Circle A, was discovered here in 1952, and produced finds almost as rich and equally fascinating. South of this are several **houses** of the 1200s BC, which may have belonged to the merchant class as they lay outside the walls; hence the so-called Oil Merchant's House. It appears he traded in aromatic oils, and rows of oil jars lined the wall when it was excavated. Other houses are named after the rich finds they yielded: the House of Sphinxes and the House of Shields. The Linear B tablets found here suggest that the script may have been used in ordinary business transactions, not just for palace inventories. Also of note are the *tholos* tombs, the most important being the so-called **Tomb of Clytemnestra** (*c.* 1300 BC), with a narrow *dromos* and quite refined in style, possibly the last *tholos* tomb built at Mycenae. Notice the single row of seats of a **Hellenistic theatre** above the *dromos*; when it was built, no one remembered the existence of the tomb. The nearby **Tomb of Aegisthus** is much earlier, as early as 1470 BC.

The Treasury of Atreus

On the road to the site, 400 yards before the Lion Gate, the magnificent Treasury of Atreus is the largest of Mycenae's nine tombs. This is the acme of *tholos* or beehive design, not to mention the largest single-span building in antiquity before Hadrian built the Pantheon in Rome. Built *c.* 1300 BC, two centuries after the first *tholos*, it was a family tomb like the others, and used many times over. A majestic 120ft entrance, or *dromos*, leads to a remarkable 34ft door, supporting a 120-ton lintel, carefully curved to match the once elaborate decorative scheme both inside and out. The triangle above the lintel, similar to the Lion Gate, shifts the weight above the door to the jambs on either side. Originally it was masked by a red marble plaque carved with spirals, fragments of which are in the British Museum, thanks to the indefatigable Lord Elgin, who visited a few decades before Schliemann. Green marble half-columns (in the Athens museum) stood on either side, and are believed by some to have been the inspiration for the Doric column and capital. The doorway has holes in the middle for a double door.

The *tholos* stands 48ft high and measures 47.5ft in diameter. Notice how the stones overlap each other to create the dome and then are capped by a single stone, a corbelled technique that required some pretty astute engineering. The small room off the *tholos*, while not unknown elsewhere, is not typical, and may have been used as an ossuary. The top of the dome would have stuck out beyond the top of the hill, and been covered over by a mound of earth. The *tholos* tombs were all robbed in antiquity, so perhaps bigger isn't always better. Pausanias, who toured the Lion Gate and *tholoi* of Mycenae in the 2nd century AD much as we do now, gets the blame for the 'treasury' misnomer: since no burials were found, he assumed they must have been store houses for the king's wealth.

Where to Stay and Eat in Mycenae

★ Belle Helene >>

Mycenae ✉ 21200

Sleeping in peaceful Mycenae means you can visit the site early in the morning before all the tour buses arrive; it's also convenient for Nemea and the Argive Heraion.

La Petite Planète, t 275 107 6240, *www.petite-planet.gr* (€€/€€). Quiet, attractive setting with a pool, and a grand view of the plain. Superb breakfast included; and the excellent restaurant uses organic produce from the family garden. Book. *Open April–Nov.*

Marion Dassis Rooms, t 275 107 6123, *www.dassis.gr* (€/€). Airy rooms in the centre (two of them for families); great bathrooms, parking at the back. *Open all year.*

Belle Helene, **t** 275 107 6225 (€/€). Built around room No.3 where Schliemann stayed in the 1870s, with memorabilia of the great archaeologist. Virginia Woolf stayed here, too. Its restaurant, with a nice terrace, is the old standby. *Open April–Oct.*

Pandelís, t 275 107 6360 (€/€). En suite rooms newly equipped with air- conditioning and heating. *Open all year.*

Atreus Camping, t 275 107 6221, *atreus@otenet.gr* (€/€). On the edge of town with shade and a small pool. *Open all year.*

Camping Mycenae, t 275 107 6121, *dars@hol.gr* (€/€). Right in town and somewhat eclipsed by Atreus; it tries hard to please. *Open Mar–Sept.*

Spíros' Restaurant and Tavern, t 275 107 6115. Traditional fare for passers-by.

The Argive Plain

The fertile Argive Plain south of Mycenae was always inhabited according to the Argives, who described themselves as 'born of the soil'. Hera won this plain from Poseidon and her sanctuary, the Argive Heraion, was one of the oldest and most important in Greece. The plain has two Mycenaean sites, a spectacular one at Tiryns and one more for specialists at Midéa, and the remains of one of the oldest known buildings in Greece at Lerna.

Argos and Pretty Castles in the Air

Some of the most famous places just don't deliver the goods. If you come at night, Argos puts on a good show with its illuminated Castle of Larissa suspended in the darkness like an ethereal beacon. In the harsh light of day, however, there is nothing ethereal about the city's box-like buildings, its tile and brick factories, and its riverbed gouged out by gravel-gathering bulldozers and festooned with garbage. Of course industry has to be placed somewhere, but surely the Inachos river, the city's mythical founder, deserves a better wreath than plastic bags and bald tyres.

Mythic Argos

When Hera and Poseidon quarrelled over possession of Argos, Inachos, the local river god, chose Hera. In revenge, Poseidon dried up the riverbed for most of the year: 'thirsty Argos' was its Homeric epithet. Phoroneos, son of Inachos, was the first king: he instituted the worship of Hera and founded the first market town in Greece, which he named Phoronicum; he taught the inhabitants how to use fire and his sister Io (*see* p.281) invented the first five vowels of the alphabet. When he died he divided the Peloponnese up between his sons Pelasgos, Iasos and Agenor. His name didn't stick to the town, however, and it became Argos. A few generations later Danaos, the great-great-great-grandson of Inachos, arrived back in Argos from Egypt and took over.

The story goes that Danaos was compelled by his brother Aegyptos to marry his 50 daughters, the Danaids, to Aegyptos' 50 sons. Not trusting his brother, he ordered his daughters to kill their bridegrooms. Forty-nine of them did just that, dutifully presenting

Getting to Argos and the Argive Plain

Argos is on the Old National Road to Trípolis. The **bus station, t** 275 106 7324, has 4 buses daily to Néa Iréa except on Sunday; from there you can walk 1km to the Heraion. The Heraion can also be reached either by car from the village of modern Mycenae or by foot on the path used by the ancient Mycenaeans.

---

their heads to their father the next morning. One, Hypermnestra, disobeyed. Her husband then killed Danaos, took over the kingdom, and everyone lived happily ever after, except perhaps the 49 daughters, who were offered to Argos' men as prizes in athletic contests. When they died, they were further punished in Tartarus by having to collect water in leaky jars for ever. Some of the details of these stories fascinate. For example, although the heads of the 49 bridegrooms were buried on Larissa, their bodies were left in the swamp at Lerna, making visiting these sites just a little more interesting, but explaining the myth just a little more difficult.

A later king of Argos, Adrastos, married one of his daughters to Polyneices, one of the twins born to the infamous Theban couple Oedipus and Jocasta. Polyneices' twin brother Eteocles had refused to share the throne of Thebes with him as promised, and Adrastos led seven Argive heroes to Thebes to redress the wrong, founding the Nemean Games along the way. Aeschylus' play, *Seven against Thebes*, was based on an epic poem, now lost; all the Argives were killed except Adrastos, who escaped on Arion his winged horse (shades of Perseus and Pegasus). Oedipus' two sons killed each other, but Cleon, the new king of Thebes, refused to bury the bodies of the dead (see Sophocles' *Antigone*). Adrastos led a band of Argive women to Athens to ask for Theseus' aid – the subject of Euripides' *The Suppliants*. Pausanias visited the tombs of the defeated Argive champions near Eleusis and, when the tombs were excavated in the 1900s, they did actually contain six bodies from the 13th century BC.

History

Argos is backed by two hills which intrude into the flat plain. The lower, rounded one was named Aspida or 'shield' because of its shape, and the 900ft conical one, now topped by the castle, was named Larissa in honour of perceived Thessalian roots. With these two defensible *acropoli*, Argos was so perfectly sited that its centre has been in exactly the same place for 5,000 years. Poseidon's curse on the Inachos river was never an insurmountable problem because the fertile plain's greatest source of water exists in aquifers. Wells have existed since time immemorial. Possibly the 50 daughters of Danaos were originally water nymphs, each presiding over a city well, toiling endlessly to draw water for the herds and gardens. In antiquity, the Argive Plain was famous for its horses.

Although powerful enough for Homer to constantly call the Greek force at Troy the 'Argives' and the 'Danaans' (after Danaos), Argos was subordinate to Mycenae for most of that era's history. It provided 80 ships for the Trojan War, led by Diomedes, son of Adrastos and the bravest warrior after Achilles. Reaching the height of its power between the 10th and 7th centuries BC, Argos was famous for its pottery, especially during the Geometric period, and also had an acclaimed school of bronze sculpture, the most famous exponents being Ageladas and Polykleitos, although Sikyon claims the latter as well.

Argos was the only city in the Peloponnese with the muscle to stand up to Sparta. As the Spartans began forming their network of conquests and alliances in the 7th century BC, Argos stood apart. Her most famous figurehead king, Pheidon, made the leap to 'tyrant' thanks to both his commercial acumen (he was the first on mainland Greece to introduce coinage, and he also improved the standard weights and measures) and his military prowess; he may have invented the hoplite shield (known as an 'argive') and in 669 BC he led the Argives to victory over the Spartans at Hysiae; he even took over the Olympic Games in 668 BC (*see* p.154). Argive–Spartan rivalry continued into the mid-6th century, when the two cities held a remarkable Wild West-style 'Battle of the Champions' of 300 Argives versus 300 Spartans on the disputed plain of Thyreatis (modern Ástros); one Spartan and two Argives survived, but the Spartans claimed that the Argives lost because the two survivors ran off to proclaim their victory while the one Spartan held the field. This resulted in an all-out battle that the Spartans won, which so infuriated the Argives that they swore to shave their heads until they regained Thyreatis. Hearing that, the Spartans vowed never to cut their hair. Coiffure aside, it permanently embittered Argos against Sparta; whatever Sparta did, Argos would do the opposite.

In the 490s BC, King Cleomenes and the Spartans tried to conquer Argos once and for all, but failed. Cleomenes burned hundreds of Argive refugees who had taken sanctuary in a sacred grove near the Heraion, an impious act that turned the gods against him; he went mad, mutilated and then killed himself. When the Spartans moved to capture Argos, now bereft of its men, the Argive women under the poetess Telesilla rallied to defend the city. The Spartans, thinking it would look unsporting to slaughter women, or even worse to be defeated by them, gave up and went home. Sir James Frazier in *The Golden Bough* thinks the Telesilla story really has something to do with the fact that Argive brides wore fake beards on their wedding nights. (But transvestite nuptials were the rage in the Peloponnese; *see* p.365.)

Thwarted of wider influence by Sparta, Argos contented herself with trying to control Nemea and the Akte peninsula, not always with much success. After sitting out the Peloponnesian War (to avoid siding with Sparta) they embraced the Macedonians, joined the Achaean League in 229 BC, but were annexed by Rome anyway. Earthquakes, barbarians and plague diminished the city during the Byzantine period. Léon Sgoúros was the last Greek to have control of the area before the Franks took over in 1212. And then the usual occurred: Turks, Venetians, Turks, Kolokotrónis, wholesale destruction by Ibrahim Pasha's troops, and independence. In its fallen state Argos even lost its status as provincial capital to Naúplio, its port. With a sigh, it rebuilt itself as well as it could and, like Candide, returned to its garden.

The City

Legend has it that Perseus buried the Medusa's head – the one that turns viewers to stone – in Argos' *agora*, although that's not what has kept the archaeologists from revealing the ancient city. Because successive inhabitants have been rebuilding on the same spot for millennia, Argos' past can only be examined piecemeal in the time it takes between an old building being torn down and a new one being put up. Only the most significant finds are preserved, leaving a few forlorn pockets of limestone ruins here and there. Exceptions are the much remodelled 5th-century ***odeion***, and the **theatre**, built around 300 BC. This was one of the largest in Greece, seating 20,000, with its 81 rows still more or less intact.

Modern Argive life revolves between two squares. One has the large 19th-century church of **Ag. Pétros** in the centre of a dozen coffee shops; the other has the arcaded **old market** on one end, and fills up completely on Friday night, Saturday and Wednesday with a vegetable and clothes market, where the spirit of old Argos is probably reflected more truly than in its ruins.

Archaeological Museum
Ólga St, **t** *275 106 8819; open Tues–Sun 8–2.30; adm*

Between the two squares, on Ólga Street, the **Archaeological Museum** has a choice selection of artefacts from Argos and around – pretty Mycenaean things, excellent Geometric pottery decorated with horses and warriors, a shard from a krater depicting the blinding of Polyphemos from the 7th century BC, a well-preserved suit of late Geometric armour (not something you see every day), clay pomegranates (a symbol of fertility), a Classical vase showing Theseus, Ariadne and the Minotaur, and Roman mosaics depicting the seasons. The entire lower level is devoted to finds from Lerna (*see* pp.283–5) – a fine Neolithic female figure from 3000 BC, dainty Early Helladic sauce boats, a three-spouted ceremonial drinking vessel, a hearth, and the clay seals found in the House of Tiles, as well as local Minyan and imported ceramics.

Where to Stay and Eat in Argos

Argos ✉ 21200

Morfeas, 2 Danáou St, **t** 275 106 8317, *www.hotel-morfeas.gr* (€€/€€). This hotel has been refurbished, with TV, air-conditioning and fridges. *Open all year.*

Mycenae, 10 Plateía Ag. Pétrou, **t** 275 106 8754, *Mycenae@otenet.gr* (€€/€). Rooms with balconies overlooking the action in the busy square below. *Open all year.*

Apollon, by the indoor market, **t** 275 106 8065 (€/€). Very basic; run by a nice lady who never stops ironing. *Open all year.*

Aegli, Plateía Ag. Pétro, **t** 275 106 7266. For a *kokonistó me patátes* or *mouskári lemonató* (veal in lemon sauce), an Argive speciality.

O Opsimos Psistaria, Korinthós St, **t** 275 102 0149. Grilled chicken in an uncompromisingly Greek provincial atmosphere. *Open eves only.*

Spiliá, just south of Argos on the highway before the turn-off to Kefalári, **t** 275 106 2300. Fake caves where you can feast on baked lamb and other traditonal dishes; half of Naúplio piles in for Sunday lunch. *Open eves and Sat and Sun lunch.*

High above Argos, conical **Larissa** has a panoramic view and a double row of walls, first built in the 6th century BC, ringing a Byzantine-Frankish-Venetian-Turkish castle made of ancient masonry from Argos' acropolis. There is a road up to it as well as a steep and overgrown footpath above the theatre if you're spoiling for a sweat (40 minutes to an hour). Note the placement of the monastery of **Panagía Katakriméni**, halfway up the hill on the site of the Temple to Hera Akraia; then have a look at the Aspida Hill (now called Profítis Ilías), site of a Mycenaean necropolis and the Argives' first acropolis.

The Argive Heraion

You can reach the Heraion from Argos by following the path taken by the ancient heroes Kleobis and Biton, who harnessed themselves to their mother's chariot to take her to the sanctuary. She was a priestess there and the usual oxen were unavailable. She was so proud of her boys that she prayed to Hera to grant them the greatest happiness humans could wish for. They slept in the temple that night and in the morning they were both dead – a rather startling insight into the ancient Greek concept of happiness.

Since oxen have always been thin on the ground here, try KTEL's horsepower. There is also a well-worn **path** from ancient Mycenae that can be followed to the Heraion by crossing the Mycenaean bridge in the Chávos ravine, about 500m south of the citadel, and heading south on foot along the side of the mountain. That's what the Mycenaeans did; this sanctuary, one of the earliest and most important of all panhellenic shrines, was situated within easy distance of all of the Argive Mycenaean settlements. For at least 2,000 years Argive Hera, titular goddess of the Argolís, was worshipped here. Her classical cult statue, made in 420 BC, was described by Pausanias: 'The statue of Hera is enthroned and very big, made of gold and ivory by Polykleitos. She wears a diadem worked with Graces and Seasons; in one hand she holds a sceptre, on the other a pomegranate...they say the cuckoo sits on her sceptre.'

Hera's Dual Nature

This royal and majestic figure is so different from the jealous wife and evil stepmother of myth that one can't help but wonder, who was Hera really? Was she heavenly, horrible or harassed? Etymologically, her name suggests 'master', 'earth' and 'sky'. She started out way back as an all-powerful nature goddess, in a direct line with the female deities familiar from Minoan and Mycenaean religion. Her primacy in the Argolid was so entrenched that Argive chronology, even in Classical times, was based on the years of service of the priestesses at this shrine. These priestesses were women of importance who served Hera all their lives and, when they died, their statues were placed in her sanctuary. Hera's peacock represented the constellations, and her white veil the Milky Way or the sun itself. It was she who embodied the annual cycle of life so important to prehistoric people. That is why she bathed every year in the spring of Kanathos (*see* p.280), to renew the crops and all life; that is why the Graces and Seasons sat on her diadem. The pomegranate in her hand signified female fertility. The cuckoo, sacred herald of rain and spring, sat on her sceptre. Her power was venerated on hilltops, and Hera ruled alone, at least until the Mycenaean civilization collapsed.

Four hundred years later, she emerged as a poor second to Zeus on Mount Olympus. Even her sacred bird, the cuckoo, was taken over by Zeus and made his attribute. The story told in Classical times was that Zeus had turned himself into this bird to 'woo' her. She found him in a storm, took pity and held him to her breast, at which moment he turned himself back into a god and raped her. Aside from what this incident tells us about sexual attitudes, it is also a telling description of a significant religious moment. In this rape and forced marriage we can actually see the shift from an earlier female-centred religion to the male-dominated Homeric and Classical one. Hera is still majestic, still venerated, but the *metopes* around the new temple on this site depicted the birth of Zeus. Her worship went underground, becoming a mystery religion, and initiates swore to keep its secrets – hence the Heraion's *telesterion*. Just as with Demeter at Eleusis, her cult was tolerated, even encouraged, because it answered a deep need, but one that was carefully controlled and regulated. Zeus and Hera struggle constantly; Hera, as a powerful mature female, threatened the new male-dominated order. Many of her symbols were trivialized, changed or misunderstood in a process that went on for centuries; the peacock became an emblem of her vanity, her white veil a symbol of her subjection to Zeus in marriage. But their original meaning is there for anyone who cares to look. And, although diminished and hemmed in, she never quite lost her primacy at the Heraion.

Myth and legend reflect the cultural attitudes of the societies which created them and there is no getting around it: ancient Greek men seem to have considered their wives a necessary evil. Zeus and Hera were the archetypal Greek couple. If their honeymoon lasted three hundred years, we have to balance that with the fact that Hera spent the rest of eternity facing his infidelities, and being depicted as a shrill, vain scold, while her husband created the only intelligent woman, a perpetual virgin, mind you, out of his own head. Hera became a shrew because that is how wives were perceived by the time these stories were put on paper. She always got a bad press. Freud developed his theories of sexuality by studying Greek mythology (no wonder that some of his theories turned out so strange). Hera's story also suggests that helping hapless cuckoos can be dangerous; a bird that lays its eggs in other birds' nests can lay cuckoo gods in other people's temples.

Contemplating the Ruins

Argive Heraion site
open 8–2.30

The fenced-in part of the dig lies on three levels; take the path to the top to survey the entire site. As you ascend, notice the enormous, rough stone blocks of the uppermost **retaining wall** built in the early Geometric period (*c.* 900 BC) to shore up the top platform. They lack the polish or order of Mycenaean walls, another reminder that a lot was lost after the palace cultures disintegrated. Once past this, you'll step on to the flat stone **paved court** which commands a breathtaking view of the entire Argive Plain. Behind is a small hilltop with remains of an **early Helladic settlement** (3000–2200 BC). A short walk will show that this hill is a natural little fortress, no doubt inhabited even earlier by Neolithic residents whose tombs have been found on the mountainside.

The fact that this was a Mycenaean cult centre suggests that this may well have been one of their hilltop shrines. The site is certainly imposing enough, and it is tempting to imagine Mycenaean priestesses among those shady olive trees beside the pavement. It was probably in this area that Agamemnon was sworn in as leader of the expedition to Troy. But the first building we know of is the **7th-century BC temple** standing just behind this top level's paving. One of the earliest peripteral buildings in the Peloponnese, it was probably only partly of stone (there was some unfathomable link between Hera and temple-building; nearly all the very first temples in Greece were dedicated to her: here, at Paleóchora, Sámos and Olympia). Only a remnant of the stylobate remains. When the temple burned down in 423 BC, it was replaced with a **new temple**, of the Doric order. Its rectangular floor plan is visible on the next level down, with its altar in front to the east.

All other structures played a supporting role to these temples. There are two ***stoas***, one of which is from the 6th century BC. It is directly under the Geometric retaining wall and has a low, square basin and tunnel for waterworks at its west end. Whatever decoration it had is gone, except for a lovely carving of two doves. The other *stoa*, from the 5th century BC, is at the lowest level towards the entrance, and is the best-preserved structure in the complex. In front of the new temple to the east (to your left if you have stayed put on the upper terrace), are the ruins of a 5th-century building with a triple row of interior columns. The fact that it is reminiscent of a similar structure in Eleusis suggests that this was the ***telesterion***, or Hall of Initiation, built for Hera's Mysteries during the Classical period. A coeval square building down one level from the new temple to the west may have been a **banquet hall** (note the three small rooms on its north side). To the west, well outside the fence, are a **Roman bath** and a ***palaestra***.

The ancients knew how to keep a secret, and the little that can be gleaned of the Mysteries shows that, however marginalized Hera

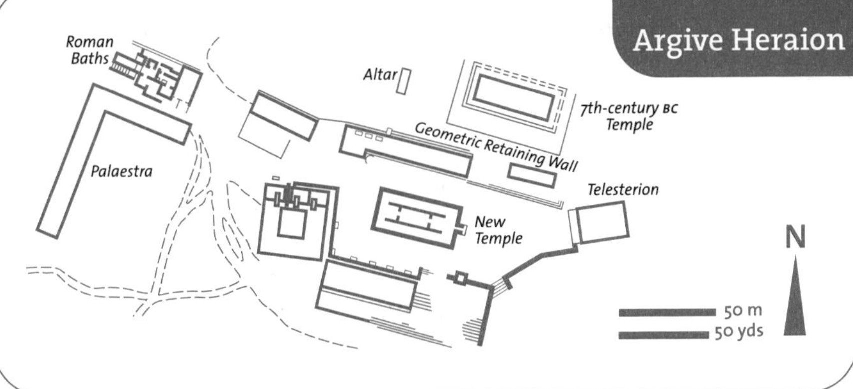

had became by the 5th century BC, the old symbols reverberated deeply and would not be denied. In many places Hera was worshipped in three aspects: *pais*, *teleia* and *chera* (the Girl, the Fulfilled and the Separated). The early Argives worshipped the moon in the form of a cow ('the cow jumped over the moon' goes way, way back) and the beast was sacred to Hera, whose Homeric epithet is *boopis* ('cow-eyed'). The myth of Io, a rain-making moon goddess (and hence a variant of Hera), survives in a form that makes Hera look bad, as usual: Io, daughter of the river god Inachos and sister of Phoroneos, was a priestess of Hera who caught the eye of Zeus. When about to be caught *in flagrante*, Zeus turned Io into a white cow; Hera claimed the cow and kept her under the surveillance of Argos, a 100-eyed giant. Zeus sent Hermes to free Io, which he did by lulling Argos to sleep and killing him. Hera then sent a gadfly after Io, who, still bovine, fled around the Mediterranean, naming the Ionian islands and Bosphorus along the way (and incidentally accounting for the spread of Hera's rites). Hera's Mysteries seem to have involved a crisis, a rupture of order (Hera the Fulfilled to Hera the Separated), perhaps ultimately going back to the withdrawal of life-giving rain in the late Argive summer. The crisis would only be resolved at the New Year Heraia festival, when the priestess led the procession in her ox-drawn cart, and Hera bathed again in the Kanathos spring, and became once more the Girl. And the rains returned, too.

East of Argos to Midea

East of Argos and south of the Heraion, the village of **Ag. Triáda** (Αγ. Τριάδα) is named for its lovely 12th-century Byzantine church. You may still hear its old name, Merbaka, believed to refer to a 13th-century Latin archbishop of Corinth, William of Meerbeke, who spoke fluent Greek and translated a number of works. Follow the signs northeast of here for **Dendra**, where Swedish archaeologists in the 1930s discovered a *tholos* tomb – the first one intact, with all of its grave furnishings (all now in Athens). Other tombs, chamber and *tholos*, have yielded the suit of armour in Naúplio, gold cups, the skeletons of four horses and other treasures. The relics of a royal cremation were found in one *tholos* tomb; some have interpreted the remains as a case of suttee, a practice vaguely hinted at in a myth or two (but then again, there is little in human experience that Greek myths *don't* contain; there's even a story about Siamese twins). The tombs belong to Mycenaean **Midea**, of which only the Cyclopean walls remain, a 15-minute walk up, immediately south of the modern village of Midéa.

South of Argos to Lerna: A Holy Cave, a Pyramid, a Hydra

Five km south of Argos, just off the main Trípolis road, **Kefalári** (Κεφαλάρι) is named for the spring that wells out at the base of a limestone cliff into pools. Called 'Erasinos' in ancient times, its waters were believed to come straight from the Stymphalian lake; the two caves here were sacred to Pan and to Dionysos, who was honoured here with a festival of Tumult. But don't come looking for Dionysian anarchy; the worst you'll get is a scrum of pilgrims from a tour bus. The larger cave, shaped like a Gothic arch and framed by maybe the world's largest bougainvillaea, is 195ft deep, spacious enough to have hosted Kolokotrónis and his army before the Battle of Dervenáki. It sheltered a lot of sheep too over the centuries, until an icon of the Virgin Mary was discovered in its depths and the tiny church of **Panagía Kefalariótissa** was built in the smaller cave to hold it. The five crystal chandeliers inside the church highlight the blue ceiling painted with little stars. Notice the single band of grapes on the white iconostasis – an extremely common motif, but at Kefalári it is especially *à propos*, given who was worshipped here first. The church's feast is on the Friday after Easter.

Most Greeks visit their shrines with a casual familiarity that is particularly evident at Kefalári, a shrine that attracts visitors from all over the country. Dressed in jogging outfits or Christian Dior, they enter to kiss the icon, take some of the holy water, say a short prayer and light a candle. And all this with hardly a break in their conversational stride. People come and go, and children are rarely hushed. The visit here is often combined with a visit to the tavernas or playground in the adjacent park. And yet there is no sense that the sanctity of the church has been in any way violated. A visit to church is simply a part of everyday life. That has to be one secret of Orthodoxy's success, and why, contrary to every other country in Europe, churches are still being built in Greece.

Kefalári highlights another phenomenon as well. This is a beauty spot, but it also has a large electric cross on the hill with a tangle of wires cascading beside the church, and a huge concrete basin with weeds wafting to indicate the speed with which the once beautiful spring rises to the surface. A lovely silver icon and a two-dimensional plywood figure of Christ wreathed in plastic flowers share the cave. This disconcerting juxtaposition of the beautiful and banal has always flummoxed visitors and has them scrambling for camera angles to cut off what they regard as the ridiculous (or, worse, photographing the ridiculous for a few laughs). But a different aesthetic is at work, the same one that led Patrick White to call Greek churches 'a combination of magnificence and squalor'. He did not intend an insult. Nor were the ancient temples all that different: consider the chains and the boar's tusk at Tegea (*see* p.337). While hardly an endangered pecies in Greece, sites like Kefalári are beginning to get the Euro treatment, all tidied up and made 'respectable'.

A mile west of Kefalári, in **Ellinikó** (Ελληνικό), the 4th-century BC **Pyramid of Kenkreaí** is impressive even if it now surveys the village football field. Six tiers of massive limestone blocks, both polygonal and squared, and part of the corbelled arch leading into its hollow centre remain. Pausanias believed it was the tomb of the Argive warriors who died at Hysiae, though excavations show it was no such thing; one archaeologist speculates that it was never completed to make a point, but served as the base of a wooden lookout tower, meant to keep an eye on the Argos road. The room underneath may have been a sleeping area for the guards. But why choose a pyramid? A returning visitor from Egypt, a mad architect? Someone reviving the old saga of the Argos' Egyptian connections? Whatever the reason, it certainly wasn't for the ease in building it. Perhaps it was a proto-folly, one of two in Argolís; there's another one near Ligourió.

One thing is for certain: this area did see its share of military comings and goings. High mountains close the Argive Plain just to the south, leaving only a narrow gap along the coast. This enabled Dimítrios Ypsilántis and his 227 troops to hold back the much superior Egyptian force of Ibrahim Pasha in 1825 and spare Naúplio the razing received by Trípolis (*see* pp.330–31). The gap is guarded by a Frankish castle on the summit of Mount Pontinós, and during the last war the Germans added another three forts.

Lerna and the House of Tiles

Four km south of Kefalári, the Trípolis road passes through the leafy village of **Mýli** (Μύλοι, 'the Mills'), the heir of **ancient Lerna**. Lerna's bottomless lake, made famous by Aristophanes, is one of several Peloponnesian entrances into the Underworld, and reputedly the place where Hades dragged down Persephone (although Enna, in Sicily, begs to differ). The potential for a mythic frisson or even a little tingle is hijacked, however, by the lake's metamorphosis into a sump pond feeding a modern waterworks. In the old days, a famous sanctuary to Persephone's mother Demeter stood on the banks in a sacred plane tree grove, and there was a later one to Dionysos, who went down to Hades via the lake to bring back his mother Semele.

Lerna was also the home of the original swamp monster, the **Hydra**, the dog-bodied, squid-like creature Heracles faced in his Second Labour. The Hydra's breath was bad enough to kill, and it had anywhere between seven and 10,000 heads; one was immortal and the others grew back, two or three at a time, as soon as Heracles, holding his own breath, lopped one off. Things reached a pretty pass when the Hydra's ally, a giant crab, came trundling out of the swamp and pinched the hero's foot. Outraged, Heracles flattened the crab with his club and called for his own ally, his charioteer Iolus, who brought a firebrand to sear the stumps as Heracles chopped off the Hydra's heads. The immortal head he buried, and he dipped his arrows in the blood, making them lethal. The land around Mýli is still swampy, and even in ancient times it was assumed that the Hydra's heads represented the many outlets of the rivers that flow into the area, and that Heracles' feat in fact represented early attempts at hydraulic engineering.

House of Tiles
t 275 104 7597; open daily 8.30–3; adm

Although it may sound like something in an American shopping mall, the main attraction today is Lerna's **House of Tiles**, signposted in a citrus grove just outside Mýli. Excavations of the low-lying mound by John Caskey and the American School in the 1950s revealed layer upon layer, a *millefeuille* of habitation from the Neolithic period (*c.* 6000 BC) to the Bronze Age.

But what caused all the fuss was the layer known as Early Helladic II (*c.* 2200 BC), a period coeval with Troy II, where Schliemann found his 'treasure of Priam'. Here Caskey unearthed a circuit wall with a row of rooms built into it, to the left of the entrance, along with the foundations of numerous dwellings, including one of hitherto unguessed-at sophistication for the time: a large (82ft by 40ft) house, the first storey made of stone, the second of mud brick, all topped by a roof of neat square tiles – hence the name, the House of Tiles. Fragments of these oldest Greek tiles are on view, as well as the floor plan of the house, which has the curious long entrance corridor found in the few other known Early Helladic buildings. Floors were of beaten clay, and plaster had just been laid on the walls, in some places divided into panels as if in preparation for paintings. One small outer room (XI) contained some 60 clay seals of delicate beauty (now in the Argos Museum) that had been affixed to jars and chests.

The House of Tiles is, in fact, the perfect prototype of the Minoan/Mycenaean palace. By the time it was built, farmers had perfected the unique Mediterranean triad of crops: the vine, olive and wheat, a discovery 'as important for the emergence of civilization as was irrigation farming in the Near East', according to Colin Renfrew. Bronze tools made life easier, even if bronze weapons made it less safe; populations expanded and began to specialize, either in farming or herding (sheep or goats, introduced from the Near East), or in metalworking or pottery. This economy required a centre to redistribute the oil and grain and pottery, as well as a leader to take charge of the contributions, which were identified by the seals. The long entrance corridor into the House of Tiles may be the original of the labyrinthine ramps and entrances that would later lead into Mycenaean palaces.

The House of Tiles was just getting its finishing touches when it was destroyed (and its tiles, bricks and seals incidentally preserved) by a devastating fire. The fact that other Early Helladic II sites were also destroyed by fire has tended to point the finger at the first wave of Indo-European arrivals. Although the invaders burned the house down, they may have adopted some of the cultural baggage of its occupants. Lerna's very ancient Sanctuary of Demeter in a sacred plane grove smacks of Minoan religious practices, and the image of the Hydra (the original of the favourite Minoan cuttle-fish/octopus motif?) may have originated with this pre-Greek civilization that continued unmolested on Crete, only to come back to the mainland full force when the Mycenaeans adopted their art.

The next inhabitants, the Early Helladic III Lernians, did something peculiar to the ruins of the House of Tiles: they built a perfectly round *tumulus* directly on top of it, surrounded by a ring of stones, as if ceremoniously *burying* it (no bodies were found). They built their own houses around this sacred mound in an apsidal form hitherto unknown in Greece, although common hundreds of years earlier on the lowest level of Troy. No one knows why. Like the early Trojans, these newcomers were also familiar with the potters' wheel; one red-brown jar found on this level was imported from Troy itself. All this adds fuel to the highly speculative theory that these invaders, perhaps even the first Greek-speakers, may have actually come from Troy.

In Mycenaean times, Lerna grew increasingly prosperous, importing pottery from Aegina, the Cyclades and Crete. Two Mycenaean shaft tombs were discovered in the House of Tiles mound, perfectly intact but disappointingly robbed in antiquity. Signs of later habitation exist, up into Roman times, but much has eroded away or been damaged by the pillboxes the Germans built here in the Second World War.

Naúplio

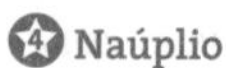
Naúplio

Blessed by nature, decorated by history and preserved with good taste, Naúplio (Ναύπλιο, pronounced Náfplio) is a rarity in the Peloponnese: a beautiful city. Sheltered in the upper pocket of the Argolic Gulf and guarded by the tiny island castle of Boúrtzi, its tall neoclassical houses rise up in tiers from Sýntagma Square to the Turkish fortress of Its Kalé. The commanding hill of Palamídi and its sprawling Venetian citadel provide a stupendous backdrop for the entire town, especially when floodlit at night.

Naúplio has seen more than its share of action, from its days as the port of ancient Mycenae to its brief fling as capital of modern Greece. But seldom has such tumultuous history produced such a harmonious result; Naúplio is not only lovely, it's also one of the few cities on the Peloponnese that demonstrates that Greece didn't really spend the period between the Middle Ages and the mid-19th century in complete suspended animation.

History: A Capital City More Than Once

Naúplio, the port of ancient Mycenae and Argos, was never large. By the Classical period, when it was a minor dependency of Argos, it had acquired the usual political myth to explain its names and significant geographical features. In this one, Naúplios was a son of Poseidon, not a surprise in view of its situation, and his son, Palamedes, fought and died in the Trojan War, but not before he

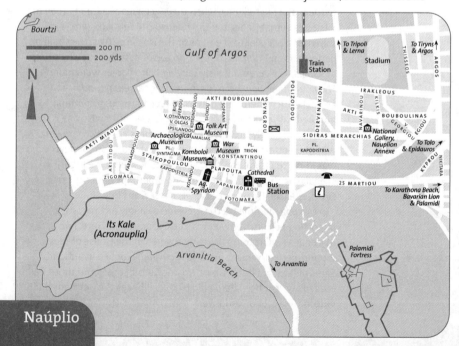

Naúplio

Getting to and around Naúplio

Naúplio is 145km from Athens. Its **bus station, t** 275 202 7323, located on Syngroú St, on the edge of the old town, has the gum-on-the-floor atmosphere which permeates all KTEL stations, but a brochure in English lists its buses to every town, beach and archaeological site in the province, as well as to Trípolis, Sparta, Corinth and Athens; special buses commute to Epidauros during the festival. The **train station** at the foot of Syngroú St by the port is a renovated railway coach. It's slow, and there are only 4 a day (for info, call **t** 275 106 7212).

It is possible to **drive** on some streets in the old town, but it's easiest to drive along seaside Bouboulínas Street, and onto the mole facing Plateía Iatroú, which offers free parking.

Car hire: Avis, 51 Bouboulínas, **t** 275 202 4160, *carrental@naf.forthnet.gr.*

Motorbike hire: Motor Traffic, 15 Siderás Merarchías, **t** 275 202 2702.

managed to invent the lighthouse, measures, scales, dice, and 11 consonants of the alphabet, to go with the five vowels invented by Io of Argos. He also donated his name to the high hill behind the city. Although little is known about Naúplio's ancient history, it did possess a spring that made it famous: Kanathos, sacred to Hera. Here she (or at least her statue) came every year from the Argive Heraion and bathed herself to renew her virginity (*see* p.279). This spring has been identified as the fountain in the courtyard of the 12th-century convent of Zoódochos Pigí (Fountain of Life), 3km out on the Epidauros road, although the virgin-wives tending it now are of an entirely different faith. Visitors are welcome if anyone would like to test the waters.

Geoffrey de Villehardouin wrested Naúplio from the Greeks in 1210 and gave it to Otho de la Roche, the Duke of Athens. New walls were built, some on ancient foundations, and Naúplio underwent the usual changes of ownership that occurred during the Frankish occupation. The Venetians bought it in 1388 from Marie d'Enghien, who was eager to sell since the town was back in Byzantine hands and not much good to her. With their usual efficiency, the Venetians assumed residence, changed its name to Napoli di Romania and repelled several Turkish attempts to take it over until 1540, when the Turks got the upper hand and made it their capital of the Morea. This was followed by a tug of war over the Acronauplía (Its Kalé): the Venetians regained it in 1686, and hoped to consolidate their position by building the tremendous Fortress of Palamídi on the heights behind it. It was completed in 1711, and the Turks, cleverly waiting until the Venetians had done all the work, took it back in 1715. The Russians occupied it briefly in 1770 during an altercation between Catherine the Great and the Sultan. The Turks then came to the conclusion that this seaside capital was attracting far too much attention from other naval powers and moved their administrative capital inland to Trípolis, although they remained fully in control of both of Naúplio's forts until 1822 when it was the turn of Kolokotrónis to capture the prize.

Not wishing to give way either to rival warlords or to the politicians who were attempting to form a government, Kolokotrónis declined to give up the fort to any of his fellow freedom-fighters until 1824. This uneasy stand-off led to bloodshed. All sides were convinced of the double-dealing of the others, and they only buried the hatchet temporarily in order to repel fresh Turkish attacks. After a lot of wrangling, Naúplio was named the new Greek capital in 1828 by Capodístria, the first president of the fledgling Greek state. The six short years of its mandate (before Athens took over) witnessed the assassination of Capodístria and the arrival of King Ludwig I's son, the 17-year-old Otto, as king of the Hellenes. His arrival in Naúplio with his Bavarian battalions in 1833 proved to be the shaky start of the modern era in Greece.

The Old Town

Some visitors to Naúplio never get beyond the café-studded **Aktí Miaoúli**, a beautiful place to sit and contemplate the sea, although here, closed in by the mountains, it looks more like a lake. If you haven't been mesmerized by the view or immobilized by ouzo, you can use the Atkí as the starting point for a seaside walk around the peninsula of **Its Kalé**, the Turkish name for the Acronauplía. If you *are* glued to your seat, then contemplate the **Boúrtzi**, the exceedingly picturesque little castle just off shore, built by the Venetians in 1471. In the case of both castles, a distant view is more romantic than a close-up. Behind Its Kalé's lovely walls the brash Xenia Palace Hotel dominates the lower town, a fitting symbol of Naúplio's new master, tourism. The Boúrtzi is a deserted hulk, waiting for a new role as the town ponders its fate. The Turks used it as a retirement home for their executioners, who didn't feel safe anywhere else; it has also been a hotel. A restaurant with gondolas would be nice.

Don't confine your explorations to the seaside. Every narrow street has handsome neoclassical houses with balconies festooned with flowers, decorated Turkish wall fountains, ruins of mosques and even a Turkish hammam; Venetian, Turkish and Greek buildings stand cheek by jowl more harmoniously than their builders ever did. There is even a Catholic church, the **Metamórphosis**, at the corner of Potamiánou and Kapodístria Streets, built by Otto I, its entrance inscribed with the names of philhellenes who died during the Greek War of Independence. At 13 Sofraní Street, a **Folk Art Museum** contains a collection of over 20,000 items covering the range of Greek traditional life, and has an excellent shop selling the same.

Folk Art Museum
13 Sofraní St,
t 275 202 8379;
open Wed–Mon 9–2

Just above it, the **War Museum** is housed in Greece's first Military Academy; displays focus on the burning of Smyrna in 1922 and the Second World War.

War Museum
Amaliás Avenue,
t 275 202 2591;
open Tues–Sun 9–2

Archaeological Museum
t 275 202 7502; open Tues–Sun 8.30–3; adm

Sýntagma Square is especially attractive, with a pretty **Turkish mosque** and the Venetian barracks housing the **Archaeological Museum**. If you've marched through Tiryns or Dendra or any of the smaller archaeological sites of the Argolís, curiosity should bring you here to see what those empty rooms and tombs once contained. The dense and eclectic collection in this revamped museum aims to explain the way of life of these ancient people, complete with video walls, computers and English translations. The first floor, devoted to prehistory, stars a unique set of Mycenaean bronze armour (15th century BC), found at Dendra, made of bronze strips to form a flounced full metal jacket, complete with a boar's tusk helmet just as Homer described it. The Mycenaean-era pottery is charming and often exquisite, full of a love of nature and a freedom of design that would disappear with this palace culture. Birds sing in sheer ecstasy, three-handled jars have debonair painted ribbons tied around each handle, and octopi and snakes look harassed, benign or playful, depending on the artist's whim. The upper floor stresses the weird and wonderful cult figures of the Archaic period, and has a good collection of Geometric pottery from the Argos area.

Kombolói Museum
t 275 202 1618; www.cs-net.gr/komboloi; open Wed–Sun 9.30am–9pm; closed Mon and Tues; adm

Sýntagma Square and surrounding streets are packed with boutiques. If you walk behind the square to Staikopoúlou Street you'll notice, amid the inviting restaurants, the first **Hellenic Parliament** building and, at No. 25, the **Kombolói (Worry bead) Museum**. The upstairs houses a collection of *kombolói*, Muslim and Buddhist prayer beads going back to 1750, in a surprising range of materials, while downstairs in the workshop you can watch replicas being made and purchase antiques or new ones (also rosaries and keychains).

Parallel to Staikopoúlou, on Kapodístria Street, is the small church of **Ag. Spyrídon** where Greece's first president, Iánnis Capodístria, was shot one Sunday morning as he walked to services. The autocratic and aristocratic Capodístria was totally unsympathetic to the anarchistic aspirations of the Maniáte clans, who had fought so hard for independence and were proving equally resistant to the idea of political unity as a final constitution was being hammered out. Capodístria arrested the great Petróbey (*see* p.402) in an effort to tame the Maniátes, and, when his kinsmen came to sue for his release, he arrested them, too. But he made the fatal mistake of allowing them the freedom of the city. As they approached him at the door of the church, he seemed to think they wanted to greet him. They did, with a *yataghan* and a bullet, the Maniáte calling cards throughout its bloody history. Behind a small glass plaque, right beside the Venetian doorway, is the hole made by the fatal bullet, a reminder that, politically speaking, Greeks can be their own worst enemies.

Into the New Town, and Palamídi

National Gallery, Naúplio Annexe
t 275 202 1915; open Mon and Thurs 10–3, Wed and Fri 10–3 and 5–8, Sun 10–2; closed Tues and Sat; adm

From Sýntagma Square, V. Konstantínou Street leads to the parks and squares that separate the old and new towns. A stunning neo-classical building at 23 Sídiras Merarchías Street is now, thanks to the Onassis Foundation, the **National Gallery, Naúplion Annexe**, fittingly filled with historical paintings on the fight for independence, the aftermath of war, and struggles of the new Greek state.

A walk in this area is very pleasant and, if you follow Syngroú or Polizoídou Street to the right, you can ascend the hill, with Palamídi looming on the left and the Grimani Bastion on the right, to **Arvanitiá**, a saddle of land between the two castles, with the Nafplia Palace hotel. This offers a panoramic view and access to Naúplio's only town **beach**.

Palamídi Fortress
t 275 202 8036; open summer Mon–Fri 8am–7pm, Sat and Sun 7.30–3; winter daily 7.30–3; adm

Arvanitiá is also the traditional way to ascend to the **Palamídi Fortress** if you have the puff to grapple with the legendary 999 stairs (there are really only 857, but that's still more than enough). By car, follow 25 Martíou St out of town and up to the castle the back way; the summer bus to Karathóna Beach will drop you close to the entrance. This was the last fortress built by the Venetians in Greece, and it was state-of-the-art: with layer upon layer of walls, eight little forts and one big fort in the centre, all beautifully made of precision-cut stone, to end up with, as Jan Morris described it, a 'Piranesi prison, whose staircases lead nowhere after all, and whose vaulted arches support nothing but themselves.' When the Turks returned, the Venetians gave it all up with scarcely a struggle.

Just up 25 Martíou Street, in the suburb of Prónoia, carved in high relief in natural rock, is the **Bavarian Lion** (on Michaíl Iatroú Street, between Sp. Giannópoulou and 28 Oktovríou Streets), a memorial created in 1834 to commemorate King Otto's Bavarian troops, who had died of the plague far from home, in a country where they were reviled and whose complexities they could never have understood. The lion is very sympathetic; it seems as if he, too, wonders what in the world he is doing so far from home, lording it over a postage stamp-sized park full of playing children.

Karathóna Beach is 2km out of town and reached by the same road that ascends to the Palamídi Fortress. This long sandy stretch, with *cantinas* and windsurf rentals, has so far escaped further development because of the proximity of the army base.

ⓘ Naúplio >
25 Martíou, t 275 202 4444, close to the bus station; open daily 9–1 and 4.30–8

Useful Information in Naúplio

Tourist police: 25 Martíou St and Anapavséos, near the Kýknos factory, **t** 275 202 1051; *open 7am–10pm*. For a list of rooms to rent in the area see *http://site.argolida-guesthouses.gr*.

Festivals in Naúplio

Other than Greek Easter and the Carnival, Naúplio holds a summer **Music Festival** with classical music under the stars. Every two years there is the **Maritime Festival** at the end of June, culminating in a Venetian evening and fireworks.

Shopping in Naúplio

Naúplio is packed full of boutiques, nearly all in the immediate radius around Sýntagma Square. On Saturday mornings, check out the market in Kolokotrónis Park.

Karonis, 5 Amalías, **t** 275 202 4446. One of the Peloponnese's best wine shops, with grappa and exquisite ouzo, distilled according to a family recipe since 1869.

Nektar and Ambrossia, 5 Farmakópoulou, **t** 275 204 3001. Organic Greek honeys.

Where to Stay in Naúplio

Naúplio ✉ 21100

Naúplio stays open all year.

Nafplia Palace, **t** 275 207 0800, *www.nafpliapalace.gr* (€€€€€/€€€€€). Reached by a lift from the old town, this sumptuous hotel in the walls of the Acronauplía has everything – heartaching views, designer rooms, spa, pools, helipad and 33 villas, some with their own pools.

Amphitryon ›

Amphitryon, Spiliádou St, **t** 275 207 0700, *www.amphitryon.gr* (€€€€€/€€€€€). The former Xenia, converted into a cool, contemporary boutique hotel full of slick gadgetry overlooking the Boúrtzi; owned by the same management as the Nafplia Palace.

Aetoma, 2 Plateía Ag. Spyridónos, **t** 275 202 7373, *http://hotel-aetoma-nafplio.focusgreece.gr* (€€€€/€€€€). Refurbished in 2006; five beautiful rooms in a traditional building, with a scattering of heirlooms. Lots of stairs. Superb home-made breakfasts.

Acronaúplia, 6 Ag. Spyrídon, **t** 275 202 4481, *www.pensionacronafplia.gr* (€€€€/€). Five renovated houses with charming period rooms (air-conditioning on request); those without their own WC are a bargain.

Marianna Pension ›

Marianna Pension, 9 Potamiánou, **t** 275 202 4256, *www.pension-marianna.gr* (€€€/€€€). Right up against the fortress wall, combining traditional decoration with mod cons like TV and air-conditioning. Great views from the terrace; parking above.

Park, 1 Dervenakión, **t** 275 202 7428, *malema@oneway.gr* (€€€/€€). Hard by the lovely municipal park and a stone's throw from the old town; plain, sympathetic, air-conditioning on request; parking is not bad.

Byron, 2 Plátanos St, **t** 275 202 2351, *www.byronhotel.gr* (€€/€€). Treat yourself up in the old town opposite Ag. Spyrídon. A beautifully renovated old building; rooms with minibars, air-conditioning on request, and lovely views.

Pension Bonne Nuit, Psarón 7, **t** 275 202 5672 (€€/€€). At the the west end of the old town. It has shared fridges and the view and location are good, but your '*bonne nuit*' may be interrupted by noise in high season.

Acropole, 9 Vas. Ólga, **t** 275 202 7796, *www.greekturism/acropol.gr* (€€/€). Old, attractive, and two streets up from the port car parks. Mr Kóskoris' card says 'with thankfulness', a message not always conveyed by hoteliers. Gently bargain, especially in the off season. The kind Mr Kóskoris is a softie.

On the edge of Naúplio are two bargains.

Económou, 22 Argonauftón, **t** 275 202 3955 (€/€). Clean if slightly shabby; some rooms have their own bath. The view to the Palamídi from their hall windows is unbeatable. Parking is easy, the Económou family are friendly and the street is quiet. Armed with a map, it's 10mins' walk to the old town.

Argolís, 32 Árgos, **t** 275 202 7721 (€€/€). It's straight out of the 1960s, with 1960s prices that can be discussed in Mr Boúras' living room. On the main street, and therefore not as quiet as the Económou. (If you're arriving by bus, there's a bus stop called Thanásenas right outside the hotel.) Mrs Boúras claims she never sleeps and accepts arrivals even in the middle of the night. A new wing offers more luxurious accommodation.

Eating Out in Naúplio

There is no shortage of places to eat in Naúplio and, if none is outstanding, most are pretty good and offer competitive prices. Along the port, Bouboulínas Street has a long line of restaurants. In the evening, narrow Staikopoúlou Street is charming.

Tou Stelára, 73 Bouboulínas, **t** 275 202 8818. Pretty blue and white décor; stresses *laderá* (vegetarian fare).

Savoúras, Bouboulínas, **t** 275 202 7704. Famous for miles around for very fresh fish and seafood dishes such as its mussels *saganáki*, therefore more pricy than average.

O Basílis, Staikopoúlou St, **t** 275 202 5344. Candles, flowers and a nice décor inside as well as out.

Ta Fanária, Staikopoúlou St, **t** 275 202 7141. On a small side alley that is a very pleasant place to sit, although their indoor area leaves a lot to be desired.

Markezínes, Staikopoúlou St, **t** 275 202 3785. Inexpensive, family-run, friendly.

★ **Aiolos** >

Aiolos, 30 V. Ólgas, **t** 275 202 6828. With tables outside in summer and an interior nicely decorated with musical instruments, this taverna offers up excellent pork in wine, tasty *imam bayildi*, and fried cheese with sesame seeds. *Eves only*.

Carrera's, Síderas Merarchías St, facing Plateía Kapodístria, **t** 275 202 4985. Great for pizza and beer.

To Sokáki, **t** 275 202 6032. A trendy coffee shop just behind the archaeological museum, deserving a special mention for its early opening hours and good breakfast, complete with bacon and eggs.

Nightlife in Naúplio

Cafés and bars fill up in Naúplio in the evening, especially along Aktí Miaoúli with its front-row seats for the sunset.

Café Benetsjanjko, Aktí Miaoúli. As picturesque as its view.

Nápoli Di Romaniá, Aktí Miaoúli, **t** 275 202 7840. A favourite of locals and foreigners alike since the 1960s.

Antica Gelateria di Roma, 3 Farmakopoúlon and Komnínou, **t** 275 202 3520. Great Italian *gelato*: try the chocolate and grappa.

Stathmós, in the municipal park, **t** 275 202 1410. Café in the renovated train station, with views of Palamídi and Its Kalé.

Nightlife centres on the restaurants and cafés. If you want more, head 2–3km west on the coastal road towards Néas Kíos, where four or five fantastical clubs lend surreal glamour to the wasteland along the beach. If you are without transport, arrange for a taxi. The current favorites are **Kinky**, **Galea**, and for Greek music the **Liquid Club**.

Tiryns

Tiryns
*5km north of Naúplio, just off the highway; the Argos–Naúplio bus passes every 30mins; **t** 275 202 2657; open summer daily 8–7; winter daily 8–3; adm*

Less visited than Mycenae, Homer's 'wall-girt' Tiryns rises only 87ft above the Argive Plain. Incongruously tucked beside an orange-processing factory and an agricultural jail, it may not look wildly impressive from the road, but get closer and you'll see why it too has been designated a World Heritage Site: its massive Cyclopean walls are absolutely extraordinary (Pausanias compared them to the pyramids of Egypt). They defend a Mycenaean palace, excavated by Schliemann in 1884, its remains laid out as neatly as an architect's plan. The historical vicissitudes of Tiryns pretty much echo Mycenae's, although its first set of walls predates Mycenae's by 50 years or so. Perhaps the legends describing it as an earlier and independent city are true. Tradition has it that Heracles was born here; he certainly resided here when King Eurystheus of Mycenae sent him on his Twelve Labours. Then again, myths can be tricky historical indicators. They also tell us that its founder Proitos had three daughters who turned into cows and rampaged through the Peloponnese. Throughout most of its history, Tiryns was somehow federated with Mycenae and subordinate to it, although it must have been a very favoured dependent: the entire citadel speaks wealth, prestige and power. After the Mycenaean turning point around 1200 BC, small shrine-rooms were built in the lower part of the citadel, very similar to those at Mycenae. Recent earthquakes have rendered sections of the walls dangerous, and you may find areas cordoned off to keep visitors from being flattened by stray boulders. But the main points of interest are still accessible.

The main entrance is formidable, but hardly straightforward. The wide **ramp** built against the east wall leads up to the citadel, and then requires a sharp right turn in order to reach an inner ramp hemmed in by massive walls. Then it's a sharp turn left, where the path to the palace passes through two gates and into a courtyard; here another sharp right turn is required to enter the **Great Propylon** leading to the **Outer Courtyard** of the palace. Turn right again, past the two small guard rooms, through the **Second Propylon** to the **Palace Courtyard**, and on via a porch and a vestibule into the **Great Megaron**. Of course, some of these twists and turns were defensive, but it may be that Mycenaeans, like the Minoans, just enjoyed building labyrinths. There may have been some ritual significance to this, since the Great Megaron at its heart was also a sacred place. Perhaps it was to impress visitors. If so, it still does.

The Great Megaron (38ft by 32ft) was set up exactly as its counterpart at Mycenae, with a circular hearth, four columns, and a throne, on the east wall this time. The walls were gaily frescoed with a boar hunt and ladies in procession, and floors stuccoed and painted with squares sporting dolphin and octopus motifs, as at Knossos; the three square doorways leading into the vestibule of the Great Megaron are exactly like ones at Knossos, too. A very early **Temple to Hera** (8th-century BC) was fitted into this area, making it hard to decipher. It's also a reminder that the classical Hera most likely began her career as a Mycenaean goddess.

The same maze-like plan can be seen in the once luxurious and frescoed **West Apartments**. Here the 20-ton monolithic slab of the **bath** has a drain and holes around it for orthostats (upright stone panels with pegs chiselled into the base to join the walls to the floor). The palace complex had decent plumbing, with four drains – another idea borrowed from the Minoans, whose craftsmen worked on numerous Mycenaean projects. Note the little T-shaped **light well** beside the bathroom and the stairwell beside it for an upper floor. A narrow corridor goes right around behind the Great Megaron to the **East Apartments**, where the courtyard and *megaron* arrangement reappear on a smaller scale. If you haven't cheated by wall-hopping, and are beginning to feel like Pacman, exit from the back door of the west apartments into the **Middle Acropolis**. While there (if it's reopened), check out the remarkably preserved **long stairway** down through the bastion to the west gate. A gap left between the top of the staircase and the landing was no doubt covered by planks, which would be removed to create a pitfall for any army that managed to crash the gate and get up all those stairs.

The famous **Underground Casement Gallery** passes underneath the first palace courtyard and links the store rooms built into the east wall. The sheer massiveness of the corbelled vaults, built with the same technique as the *tholos* tombs, is absolutely stunning. Shepherds discovered these ruins open to the east hillside and used them for generations as handy sheepfolds, which explains their lanolin-buffed and polished stones. There are similar galleries in the south wall, but they're off limits because of earthquakes. The **Lower Acropolis** was the last part to be surrounded by Cyclopean walls. Square storage chambers were cut into its walls, and two 66ft galleries tunnelled beyond it forming **cisterns** that assured Tiryns' water supply. At present, it is only for the archaeologists. About 2km into the orange groves beyond the site is the only known ***tholos* tomb** attached to Tiryns, and a fine big one it is, too. It is signposted and only a short walk from the narrow road (too narrow for tour buses so you can visit it in relative peace and quiet).

Beaches and Resorts South of Naúplio

Southeast of Naúplio runs a string of seaside towns that are a good bet for beach hotels and lazy cycling. The coast is flat except where low rocky headlands crop up, a terrain very typical of the Argolís region.

Toló (Τολό) is one of those places that no one admits they go to and yet it is full most of the time. About 10km from Naúplio, this is Coney Island, Greek-style, with a long string of hotels and campsites, bars and clubs. Toló is on a beautiful wide south-facing bay with a charming island centrepiece; nor is there any lack of jet skis, windsurfers and paddle boats to hire. The sandy beach is narrow, but it's still the best in the area.

Just to the east of town, a few minutes' walk will take you to the small rocky headland that was **ancient Asine**, a small fortified town mentioned by Homer (it got all of one word in the *Iliad*). Inhabited from the Early Helladic period, it was excavated in the 1920s by the Swedes, led by their archaeology boffin King Gustav

Getting around South of Naúplio

Buses regularly ply between Toló and Naúplio from 7am to 10pm, and many continue to Drépano; other connections are less frequent. **Boats** in Toló offer day trips. Try **Pegasus Cruises**, 10 Sekéri, **t** 275 205 9430, *www.pegasus-cruises.gr*, for cruises to Hýdra, Spétses, Naúplio by night, and Monemvasiá.

Albert, and yielded the striking clay portrait of the 'Lord of Asine' in Naúplio's museum. You can swim off the tiny beach while having a look at the remnants of its walls; doing just that inspired one of George Seferis' most haunting poems, seeking the King of Asine 'unknown, forgotten by all, even by Homer'. One of these kings of Asine made the mistake of joining Sparta to ravage the Argolís in *c.* 720 BC; in revenge, the Argives destroyed Asine utterly, and the inhabitants moved to Koróni in Messenía.

Drépano (Δρέπανο), 3km east, has a long, narrow beach that can just barely hold a candle to Toló's, but, since the town itself is set about a kilometre back from the beach on a headland, its seaside is quieter. So close to Drépano as to seem a suburb is lovely, tiny **Vivári** (Βιβάρι), a fishing port on an exquisite sea lake. Just 4km on over a headland is **Kándia** (Κάνδια), the artichoke capital of Greece. If you are in Argolís in March, April or May, be sure to try some with peas (*aginóres me bizélia*).

Where to Stay and Eat South of Naúplio

Toló ✉ 21056

In spring and autumn, Toló has juicy hotel bargains, but in winter it rolls up its streets.

Panorama Tolo, **t** 275 205 9788, *www.panoramatolo.gr* (€€€/€€). Set above the resort; friendly hotel perfect for families, with big rooms, big balconies, a big pool and big views. *Closed Nov–Feb.*

Flísvos, 13 Bouboulínas, **t** 275 205 9223, *www.flisvoshotel.gr* (€€€/€€). Air-conditioned, on the strip between the road and beach; has its own restaurant facing the sea. *Open Mar–Nov.*

Christina, 7 Bouboulínas, **t** 275 205 9001 (€€/€€). Air-conditioned, on the strip; popular for years, with a sea-view restaurant. *Open Mar–Oct.*

Epídauria, 52 Sekéri, **t** 25 705 9219, *www.epidavria.com.gr* (€€/€€). On the main street; new, air-conditioned, and nicely decorated. *Open all year.*

Ingrid Bungalows, a stone's throw east of Asine's beach, **t** 275 205 9747, *www.bungalows-ingrid.com* (€€/€€). The perfect choice for people who want the conveniences of Toló, but not the noise. New, large, attractive island-style apartments with balconies at the front and back and privacy assured by a well-kept garden. Bikes are offered free to guests who want to make the five-minute cycle into town. *Open all year.*

Barboúna, **t** 275 205 9162, *www.barbouna.gr* (€€/€). Right opposite the dune beach at the entrance to town; noisy in high season, but it has the location and the view.

Two campsites out of many: **Sunset**, **t** 275 205 9566, or **Lido**, **t** 275 205 9396.

Drépano and Vivári ✉ 21060

Danti's Beach, Drépano, **t** 275 209 2294, *www.dantishotel.gr* (€€/€€). A pretty choice with its pool and tennis court. Close to the sea, and set, as the brochure says, in a 'vegetation area'. *Open April–Oct.*

Eleni-Chrisoula Apartments, Drépano, **t** 275 202 2623 or **t** 275 209 2489

(€€/€). Plain, clean, set back from the sea amid lots of 'vegetation'. Full kitchens and air-conditioning too. *Open April–Oct*.

Plaka Beach Camping, Drépano, **t** 275 209 2194 (€/€). The best in a string of campsites, with the least number of permanently parked caravans.

Aretí >

Aretí, Vivári, **t** 275 209 2391 (€/€). The Bouzálas family's perfect little old-fashioned hotel, of the kind which are fast dying out. The view and price make up for the road that has to be crossed to get to the sea. Minibars and air-conditioning in the rooms. There are only two buses a day, but why would anyone want to leave? *Open all year*.

Christina Diamantopoúlou Rooms, **t** 275 209 2258 (€/€). Four very plain rooms right on the port with shared bath and kitchen facilities. *Open April–Oct*.

Camping Leukas Beach, Vivári, **t** 275 209 2334, *www.camping-lefka.gr* (€/€). Set on a sloping hill among poplar trees, less than a mile from town. *Open April–Oct*.

O Dimítris, Vivári, **t** 275 209 2125. A good view and good fish; on the beach.

Kándia ✉ 21110/Íria ✉ 21060

Kándia has a nice beach, fish tavernas, and not much else.

Iria Máre, 3km from Kándia, **t** 275 209 4512, *http://hotel-iria-mare.focusgreece.gr* (€€€/€€). A grand hotel-apartment complex with tennis, a huge pool, nice owners and tours in their large sailing yacht. *Open April–Oct*.

Sofia Gavrilou Studios, **t** 275 206 1162 or **t** 694 516 7611, *sofigav@otenet.gr* (€/€). Close to the sea with views; the very pleasant Sofia presides. *Open May–Oct*.

Poseidon Camping, **t** 275 209 4341, *www.posidon-camping.gr* (€/€). Just before Íria, and so attractively set in the pine forest that it may have you rushing to buy a tent.

East to Epidauros

Mountains hem in the coastal road beyond Íria and, although you can wiggle your way inland on mostly paved roads, there isn't really a compelling reason to avoid doing the obvious: taking the good 25km road by car or bus from Naúplio.

Naúplio to Ligourió

The road passes through **Arkadikó**, where you may want to keep your eyes peeled for a perfect little **Mycenaean bridge** with its single corbelled arch, a ruined ***tholos* tomb** and the impressive 5th-century BC polygonal walls of the **Acropolis of Kazarma** on the hill above, all visible from the road. Hand-carved briar wood pipes are a local industry, and you can examine them in the little shop in **Giannoulaíka**, as well as in the big bustling village of **Ligourió** (Λιγουριό). Ligourió also has a privately run **Natural History Museum**, with the only collection in the Peloponnese of fossils and rocks, mostly from Greece. The nautilus shells are especially lovely, as are the colourful minerals from Lavríon, the silver mines that financed imperial Athens; the well-arranged displays in Greek and English make you wish the owner would take over certain fusty archaeological museums. In Ligourió you'll also see a sign for its **Pyramid**; this is similar to the one at Kenkreaí (*see* p.283) but is not as well preserved; it stands 1.5km west of the centre.

Natural History Museum
t 275 302 2588; open daily 9–8; adm

Getting to Epidauros

Ligourió/Epidauros is served by four **buses** daily from Naúplio. Several buses a day go from Corinth to Palaiá Epídauros, and at least two buses daily go from there to the ancient theatre. On the map you'll see old and new Epídauros on the coast, but the Epidauros with the famous theatre is, properly, Asklepeíon Epidaúrou, signposted 2.5km east of Ligourió (the bus may also say 'Theatre'). On festival nights there are special buses from Naúplio and Athens (remember Melina Mercouri in *Never on Sunday?* – it hasn't changed much).

There is even a **ferry** from Piraeus on show nights with connecting buses, **t** 210 323 0100, *www.greekfestival.gr*.

Epidauros

A beautiful site full of pines and oleanders, Epidauros (Επιδαυρος) draws visitors from all over the world to its magnificent ancient theatre. When *it* was new, people came for quite another reason – to consult Asklepios, the god of healing, one of ancient Greece's most beloved deities. A sanctuary functioned here for over 2,000 years on two areas of Mount Kynórtion. Similar gods were worshipped under different names. Even more curiously, it was a city cult centre without a city. A little history is in order.

Chthonics, Snakes, and Politics

It all began as a Mycenaean open-air sanctuary high on Mount Kynórtion, dedicated to a chthonic god. The **chthonics** may sound like an underground rock band, but they were, in fact, very important deities. The word means 'earth' and the *chthonioi*, or 'earth ones', presided over the annual cycle of planting, growing and reaping. They were invoked and propitiated by early agricultural societies with rituals involving water and ash, the two elements quite rightly understood to be necessary for vegetative renewal. Even when the worship of Olympian gods became the norm, chthonic worship continued alongside, and in many cases, as at Epidauros, became incorporated with it. The hallmark of sacrifices to chthonic deities were ***holocausts*** (the burning of the entire animal) as opposed to the fat and thighbones burned for the ethereal Olympians. It was the vast amount of ash from holocaust sacrifices in close proximity to water sources that identified Epidauros' unnamed Mycenaean god as a chthonic one. Chthonic gods were associated with resurrection and therapeutic powers because of their ability to bring the dead earth to life. And they were always associated with **snakes**, who are, after all, equally at home under the earth and on it. They sleep underground in winter and emerge in the spring, and they have the seemingly magical ability to be reborn, sloughing off old skin to appear rejuvenated; they also haunted the cemeteries, living off the mice attracted to the grave offerings. The snake often appeared on grave stelae, especially in the Archaic period, symbolic of rebirth.

The Dream Cure and the Epiphany of the God

So how did the cure work? After being ritually purified with water from the sanctuary, and having offered a holocaust animal sacrifice on the god's altar, the pilgrim was left in the *enkoimeterion* (sleeping place) or *ávaton* (literally a 'no go' area to the unpurified) to spend the night. Asklepios, or sometimes his snake or faithful hound, appeared in a dream and revealed the cure appropriate to the illness. Priests of Asklepios interpreted the dream and proceeded with the therapy.

The many surgical instruments found at the Asklepeion indicate that they were adept medical practitioners, not just dream catchers – the famous Hippocrates was a priest of Asklepios. Procedures and case studies were recorded, and as time went on a medical library was built, open to both patients and priests. Not exactly a hospital, but not Lourdes either (although Epidauros records some 40 miracle cures), healing hinged on practical experience, but faith was the key. 'Purity is to think pious things,' was the slogan engraved over the entrance. Testimonials recorded on stone plaques by satisfied customers were left in the sanctuary. Sometimes rich gifts or buildings were donated, a custom that enhanced the sanctuary's status and size and encouraged new arrivals. Small clay votive offerings in the shape of body parts would be placed in the sanctuary, either in supplication or in thanks, by patients of more humble means, a practice that has continued in an unbroken line in Greece: the very same votives, the little stamped metal *támata*, hang from icons in Greek churches today.

If aspects of this process seem primitive, we might marvel at what has stayed the same: the god-like aura of the specialist, the shrine-like lobbies of medical buildings, dedications and donations, and the close connection between the healing arts and faith, whether in God or science. The psychology is just the same. One practice of the sanctuary might also be envied today: visitors were charged according to their ability to pay, so even a person of humble means could hope for a cure.

When Mycenaean culture collapsed, Epidauros' hilltop sanctuary was nominally given over to Olympian Apollo. Only here he was worshipped as **Apollo Maleatas**, an epithet probably referring to the earlier chthonic deity. The ritual still involved holocaust sacrifice. So it is hard to say exactly who appropriated whom.

The site might have remained just another country shrine except that, in 640 BC, the seaside city-state of Epidauros was getting nervous about the expansionist propensities of Argos. To discourage Argos, Epidauros' tyrant, Prokles, entered into an alliance with Corinth. As a compliment to Apollo, Corinth's patron, he declared the shrine of Apollo Maleatas the **Official City Cult Centre of Epidauros**, in spite of the fact that it was a 2½hr walk from the city. This proved to be an astute political move. The sanctuary just happened to be on the disputed border, so any attack on Epidauros' 'city' shrine now meant offending Corinth. Prokles further stacked the cards against Argos by instituting panhellenic games on the site timed to follow Corinth's Isthmian Games. Of course, at this point, the area also took the name Epidauros, since it was now officially the city core.

In the 6th century BC, the sanctuary expanded to the larger present site and the focus shifted to the worship of **Asklepios**, a very ancient chthonic healing deity from Thessaly, who with his companion snake would have felt at home here anyway, given the shrine's history. He was neatly incorporated into the existing cult by making him the 'son' of Apollo and the princess Koroni.

Polytheism is nothing if not elastic and eclectic. Apollo, the story goes, sent him to learn the healing arts from the centaur Cheiron, and he learned so well that he started to raise departed friends from the dead. Zeus, at Hades' request, zapped him underground with a thunderbolt. From under the earth, the benevolent Asklepios helped humans recover from the little death of illness by appearing to them in dreams. Symbolic of his status as the ancient Greek's best friend is his dog. No other god had a pet. While Apollo never officially lost precedence, it was the hope offered by the cult of the benevolent and compassionate Asklepios that made Epidauros famous from its heyday until the Christian Emperor Theodosios II closed its doors by official decree in 426. The cult of Asklepios then gave way to the Christian Son of God and snakes developed a bad name, but not before they had become the recognized symbol of the medical arts on the **caduceus**.

The Museum, Asklepeion and Theatre

Museum, Asklepeion and Theatre

*t 275 302 2009; **site** open May–Oct daily 8–7.30; Nov–April daily 8–5; **museum** open May–Oct Tues–Sun 8–7.30, Mon 12–7.30; Nov–April Tues–Sun 8–5, Mon 12–5*

This **museum** looks like a marble version of a car parts warehouse. Bits and pieces of various temples are placed here and there along with *acroterions*, votive offerings, dedicatory plaques, and so on. What with the medical instruments on display, one can almost imagine an architectural Dr Frankenstein doing his stuff in here one night and producing an entire temple by morning. The extensive ruins reflect 800 years of building and rebuilding, quite a lot of it recycled. Epidauros became a popular entertainment centre over the centuries, as various wealthy patrons added sporting facilities, *stoas*, monuments and so on. As you go north from the museum, a large 4th-century BC **hotel** is on your right; its two floors were built around four atriums. What remains are some low polygonal walls and most of the thresholds to the lower rooms. No indoor plumbing, but right beside the hotel were **baths** offering both tubs and basins and other necessities. It was built in the 3rd century, and one wonders what Epidauros' visitors did before that. The **stadium**, first used in the 5th century BC, occupies a partly artificial depression. The stone seats and starting line added in the Hellenistic period indicate the growing popularity of the shrine. There was an underground vaulted passage leading through the seats on the north side to a **Palaestra**.

The large **Gymnasium**, 230ft by 249ft, had a grand **Propylaea** or entrance on the north side. The lower parts of the walls are very well-finished limestone, showing its layout very clearly. Apparently the rest was brickwork and more perishable. A lot of its superstructure went into the construction of the Roman **Odeion**, now in ruins itself in its centre. In Roman times the *propylaea* was a Temple to Hygeia, or Health. The **Stoa of Kotys** may just have been shops, and why not? Lots of visitors were well off.

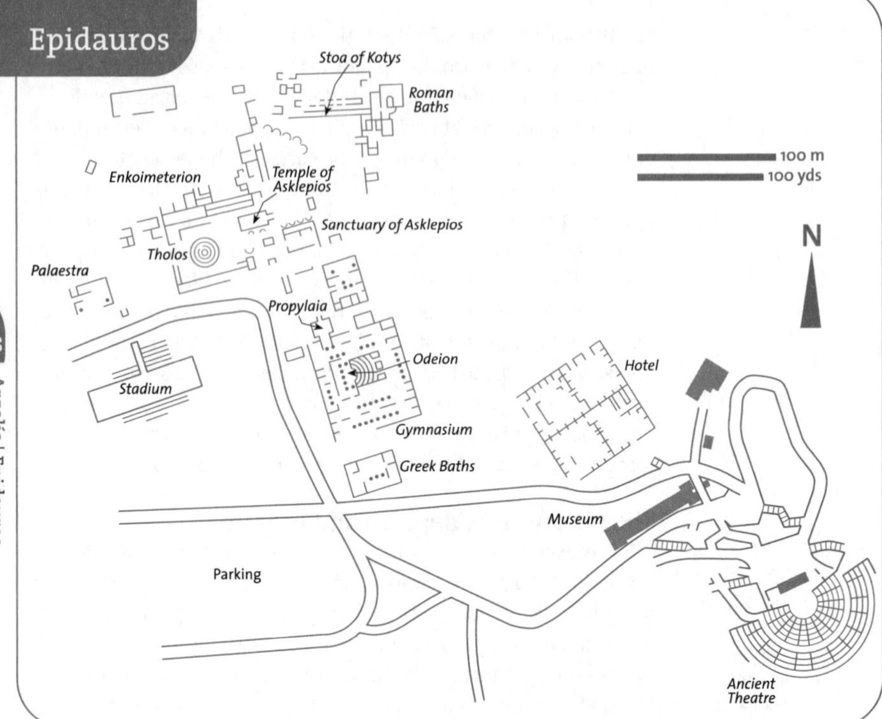

Unfortunately, the remains of the **Sanctuary of Asklepios** itself are sparse and difficult to comprehend. Surrounded by the ruins of walls, built to protect the holy of holies from the Goths in AD 395, are the remains of the old 6th-century BC complex and new 4th-century BC one. Both had an all-important temple and altar, a water source for purification, and an *enkoimeterion*. You can still make out the floor plan of the 4th-century Doric peristyle **Temple of Asklepios**; it had six columns on the front and 11 on the sides and measured a modest 43ft by 40ft, with a ramp leading to its entrance. In contrast, the 4th-century **Enkoimeterion** was large, 232ft long with two storeys at one end, allowing plenty of sleeping people to take the cure at the same time. The 6th-century BC water source was incorporated into this building.

The **Tholos** or rotunda, built in 360–320 BC by the sculptor Polykleitos, is the most intriguing building in the complex. There are drawings of it in the museum as it was when complete: it measures 72ft in diameter, and once had 26 Doric columns on the outside and 14 Corinthian on the inside. Today all that remains *in situ* is the basement, consisting of six concentric walls with openings to form a maze. The floor over this was covered with black and white diamond-shaped tiles, surrounding a circular stone which opened to give access to the subterranean maze. The most interesting theory has it that it was a sacred snake pit. Since all *asklepeions* in the Graeco-Roman world ordered a snake from Epidauros as a seal of legitimacy, they must have kept quite a serpent collection somewhere. At the time of writing the *tholos* is being partially reconstructed. The **Library** was north behind the *enkoimeterion*, and all those buildings to the north and east were **Roman baths**, gateways, and so on. The **Propylaea**, the entrance in ancient times, was on the north side of the site.

The Theatre

★ Epidauros Theatre

Designed with purposeful mathematical precision, the Theatre of Epidauros is a work of harmony and beauty, both within itself and in its relation to the landscape. Built in the 3rd century BC to accommodate 6,000 people in 34 rows, and then expanded in the 2nd to accommodate 6,000 more in another 20 tiers, it was famous even in ancient times for its astounding acoustics, which allow an actor's voice to carry effortlessly to the uppermost seats. In 2007, Nico Declercq and Cindy Dekeyser of the Georgia Institute of Technology demonstrated that the key is in the arrangement of the stone seats: placed just so, they act to suppress low-frequency background sound to enhance the high-frequency sound of the human voice.

This is the best-preserved theatre in Greece, if not the entire ancient world; the entrances, the *skene* and *proskene* in front are still pretty much as they were. Note how the seats were all carefully hollowed underneath so that the audience could tuck in their legs to allow people to pass in front. VIPs sat in the moulded seats in the first row. The circular orchestra is the only one to survive intact from antiquity, and every summer it comes to life again in modern Greek.

Epidauros Festivals

Watching a Greek tragedy or comedy in a Greek theatre in the warmth of a Greek summer evening, ideally with a soft cushion under your bottom, is an experience, even if you don't get all of Aristophanes' jokes (purchasing the English translation at the site will help). The Epidauros Festival, which began in the 1950s, takes place on weekends in July and August, concentrating on the classics of Sophocles, Aeschylus, Euripides and Aristophanes. Plays are given either the traditional or avant-garde treatment, are all in modern Greek, and are performed by either the Greek National Theatre or other companies from around Greece and Cyprus. The enormous size of the theatre means it is rarely filled up, so even if you get a seat in the gods you can move down closer once the show starts. A website in English, *www.greekfestival.gr*, lists all productions and prices. Or ring t 210 928 2900 in Athens, t 210 327 2000 for the Little Theatre, and t 275 302 2026 for the Ancient Theatre. Tickets can also be purchased at the gate, ranging from €15 to €62 (for front-row thrones). The new Insititute of Ancient Drama, a branch of Athens University, was set up in 2002 to draw students year round from all over the world to Ligourió, which promises to add yet another dimension to the town's cultural life.

Musical events of all kinds take place on July weekends at Little Epidauros at the Mikro Theatro of Palaiá Epídauros, although the calibre of the performances is not small; the likes of María Farandoúri and Paco Peña have performed here.

The Temple to Apollo Maleatas: Not for Everyone

The ruins of the older sanctuary, near the eastern summit of Mt Kynórtion, can be reached on foot, but once there you can only glimpse the **Temple to Apollo** under a shed, and cannot reach the hilltop sanctuary where all that ash was found. This complex ruin will remain closed until there is enough money to pay for guards.

Down on the Coast: Palaiá and Néa Epídauros

Still overshadowed by its famous sanctuary 10km up the road, **Palaiá Epídauros** (Αρχαιά Επίδαυρος) now concentrates on the pleasures of the sea and beach, and is not at all a bad place to spend a couple of lazy days. It has a port filled with yachts, and views closed in by a wooded headland. South beyond that, a long and very narrow sandy **beach** fronts hotels and campsites. It has to be said that the sea is not the cleanest here, especially if the wind is blowing from Aegina. On this headland, you can find another well-preserved and rather sweet 4th-century BC **theatre**. Set in an olive grove, this **Mikro Theatro** has a mere 18 tiers of seats, including ten moulded throne-like ones (*kerkides*) in the front for the big shots. Some still bear the names of the citizens who endowed them. If *plus ça change* is true, could the Mikro Theatro have been an ancient Off Broadway venue, or even a community theatre for local Epidaúron productions, even back in the days before *Oliver!*? It fills that role now, in a way, with its July music festival. On the headland, archaeologists have recently unearthed remains of the clever **ancient city** that outfoxed Argos: some Roman bits, Cyclopean walls and the foundations of a Palaeo-Christian basilica.

Néa Epídauros, 7.5km north, looks 'new' only in relation to the ruins, a village holding tight to the slopes of Mount Árkos with the remains of a Frankish castle of Nicholas de Guise guarding the gorge. Its 15 minutes of fame occurred on 20 December 1821, when Greek leaders gathered here in their first assembly to declare the country's independence in the Constitution of Epidauros. A road leads down in 2km past the orchards to the relatively quiet narrow **beach** on a pretty bay, with a blue and white church and views over mountains and cliffs. North of Néa Epídauros, 5km up the rather lonesome road to Corinth, the **Monastery Agnoúntos** is worth a stop for its remarkable 18th-century frescoes.

Where to Stay and Eat around Epidauros

Ligourió/Epidauros ✉ 21052

Avaton, Ligourió, **t** 275 302 2059, *info@avaton.com.gr* (€/€) This pleasant hotel with grass, fridges, air-conditioning and a small terraced bar has a motel feel; it lies where the road leads up to the theatre. Book ahead.

Alkion, **t** 275 302 2002 (€/€). Rooms with air-conditioning not far from the theatre and with a nice *psistaría* on the ground floor. *Open all year.*

Gefira >>

Taverna Leonides, t 275 302 2115. *The* place to dine in Ligourió; in the garden, with good food and atmosphere. It's often filled up after the show on festival evenings.

Palaiá Epídauros ✉ 21059

There are a slew of C-class hotels and four campsites on Gialási Beach south of town.

Paola Beach, t 2753 04 1397 (€€/€€). Renovated recently, with balconies facing the sea, this pleasant hotel offers good prices, especially in the low season.

Mike, directly on the port, **t** 275 304 1213, *www.mike-epidavros.com* (€€/€). Most rooms have views, and there's a popular restaurant with lovely views from the terrace. *Open all year.*

Poseidon, t 275 304 1211, *ppitsas@hotmail.com* (€€/€). With its back to Mike's; newer, whiter, balcony-rimmed, and with another good restaurant. *Open April–Oct.*

Elena and Astéria, on a quiet side street, **t** 275 304 1207 (€€/€). The Ágellos uncle/nephew team runs these comfortable, air-conditioned, side-by-side studios. *Open all year.*

Gefira, **t** 275 304 42130, *www.mike-epidavros.com* (€€/€). Set back beside the bridge, where the main north–south road and the road to the ancient theatre meet. Moderately priced (on show nights too), it is quiet, with parking and a pool. *Open all year.*

Bekas Camping, t 275 304 1714, *www.bekas.gr* (€/€). The biggest; well equipped for sports – plenty of shade too. *Open April–Oct.*

Nikolas II Camping, t 275 304 1445 (€/€). Friendly and shady. *Open Mar–Oct.*

Néa Epídauros ✉ 21054

Mariléna, t 275 303 1279 (€€/€). The better sea view. *Open June–Sept.*

Avra, t 275 303 1294 (€/€). A colourful and relaxed little hotel with a restaurant. *Open April–Oct.*

Camping Diamantis, t 275 303 1181 (€/€). With a pool, playground, wind-surfers, kitchens, supermarket, disco. *Open April–Oct.*

Akte: The Dewclaw of the Morea

If the Peloponnese resembles a sharp-clawed paw on the map, Akte is the jaggedy peninsula that dangles east like a dewclaw, dividing the Saronic and Argolic gulfs. This is the one corner of the Peloponnese that fits the Greek truism 'the land separates, the sea unites'. Along with the islands that float just off its shores, Akte is a particular favourite of the yachting fraternity. Arid Mount Adéres cuts off the north and ancient Troezen from the rest of the Argolís, but where it relents you'll find lush valleys and sandy beaches. Besides the chance to make easy day trips to the islands, Akte has charms of its own: a volcano, a devil's bridge, a lemon forest and a nearly perfect fishing village.

Méthana and the Volcano

Méthana

South of Palaiá Epídauros, the paved road riding high above the sea eventually descends to the peninsula of Méthana. Attached to the mainland by only a tenuous 100-yard-wide umbilical cord at **Stenó**, it looks like a hot air balloon on the map. In a way it is: the peninsula is made up of a volcano, or rather a cluster of volcanoes that popped out of the sea.

Getting to Méthana

A **ferry** plies the route from Piraeus, Aegina, Méthana, Póros, Hýdra, Spétses and back, five times a day in summer; less in winter. For information contact the **Méthana Port Authority**, **t** 229 809 2279, or the ticket agent in Méthana at **t** 229 809 2580. A local bus visits the villages of the peninsula three times a day.

As you pull into **Méthana** (Μέθανα), the reason for the town's nickname of *Vromolímni*, 'Stinky lake', becomes immediately apparent, a lingering reminder of its volcanic origins. Unless you actually go up to your neck in it, you'll get used to the sulphurous aura in five minutes. But getting up to your neck in it is the point: Méthana is a spa, with three **thermal springs** of various potencies to soothe your rheumatism. The rest of town oozes that old-fashioned, low-key, lie-around atmosphere that spas are heir to. It has a pretty, yacht-crammed port, sheltered by a thin strip of garden leading to a wooded islet, topped with the inevitable church. You can swim near here, but you'll do better following the narrow coastal road just north of town, to the sheltered golden sands of **Limníonas**. The steep volcanic slopes prevent the two roads that try to encircle the peninsula from succeeding, but they give on to mountain paths that are especially lovely in early summer when the orchids are blooming. Recent **digs** by the church of Ag. Konstanínos and Eléni, 1km up the east road, produced some lovely Mycenaean artefacts, although the most remarkable find in recent years is a stone head, a masculine bust, unlike anything familiarly Greek: it looks rather like one of the late Neolithic statues at Filitosa in Corsica and is now in the museum at Póros.

The paved road continues up to the tiny fishing village of **Ag. Geórgios**, then ends at what the locals call the **Baths of Pausanias** (Ag. Nikólaos on some maps), another hot spring by the shore, identified by some with the one Pausanias described as first spitting fire and then hot water, 'in the time of King Antigonas of Macedonia' (230 BC).

Vathí and up to the Volcano

The ancient city of Methana visited by Pausanias may be reached from modern Méthana by the road that cuts across to the west coast to **Vathí** (Βαθύ), a potential hideaway with its tiny beaches and handful of rent rooms. Vathí means 'deep' – the sea here plunges 1,300ft, a figure matched by the peninsula's southeast shore, reputed to be the main breeding ground for sharks in Greece; fortunately they stay down there canoodling and don't pester bathers. Some well-built Classical walls and gates to the acropolis of ancient Methana remain on the hill above Vathí at **Palaeókastro**, but the rest of the city fell into the sea after a cataclysmic eruption.

Where to Stay in Méthana

Méthana ✉ 18030

Avra, t 229 809 2382 (€€/€€). On the sea; the nicest and most comfortable of several waterfront hotels. *Open all year.*

Arsinóne (Αρσινοη), t 229 809 2900, *www.methana-hostel.gr* (€€/€). In Megalochóri, a few hundred metres up the road from Vathí, six delightful rooms sleeping up to four in the refurbished primary school.

Saronis, t 229 809 2312 (€€/€). Port-side and eager to please. *Open April–Oct.*

Small tavernas dot the waterfront to keep you from starving, and in the evening you can bop by the beach at **La Playa** disco.

The coastal road north of Vathí ascends to the Méthana peninsula's star attraction: the volcano. Leave the car or bus in **Kaiméni Chóra** ('Burnt Village'), a white hamlet wedged into the black volcanic rock. Wear sturdy shoes, take a bottle of water and a hat, and follow the path from the church of Ag. Ioánnis (marked προς Ηφαίστειο), which in 20–30 minutes and after some scrambling leads to the lip of the **volcano**. In this other-worldly landscape of savage black, red and green crags and sharp abysses, the perfect silence is relieved only by a breeze rustling in a few brave pines, the cry of a rare hawk circling overhead, and the sighing of indigo blue sea far below. The Peloponnese may be the 'Cradle of Hellenism', but here, by this pitiless primordial crater in the sizzling sun, it seems more like the cradle of the world itself. Or a sneak preview of its end.

Trizína (Ancient Troezen)

South of the Méthana peninsula, Trizína (Τροιζήνα) – Damalá on old maps – sits pretty on a deeply wooded shelf of 2,360ft Mount Adéres, blithely surveying the sea and the lemon and olive groves and cultivated flowers that make it a prosperous place today. In previous centuries this was a marshy area; the ancients planted it with clover for the famous horses they bred. You may note on the map that Trizína and environs are not politically part of the Argolís, but are administered by Piraeus; ancient Troezen never belonged to ancient Argos, and, 2,500 years later in Greece, these things still count. A few buses a day link it to Méthana and Galatás.

A Pound of Mythology, An Ounce of History

Troezen is one of the oldest cities in Greece, and its myths are tantalizingly murky and full of clues to mysteries that will probably never be resolved. Apart from the fact that Orestes came here to be purified after his matricide, Troezenian lore is outside the pale of the main Peloponnesian story cycles, and instead has close links with prehistoric Athens and, much, much earlier, with Egypt: the first man in these parts was Oros (Horus) and the name for the area was Oraia, the realm of Horus. And there was a shrine to Isis.

Originally there were two towns, Hypereia, 'High Town', and Antheia, 'Upward-looking town', founded by **Alcyone**, son of Poseidon. Alcyone then left his heir Aetios in charge while he sailed east to Caria to found Halicarnassus. Aetios was soon joined by two leaders from Pisa in Elís: **Troezen**, the son of Pelops, and his half-brother **Pittheos**, 'the wisest man of his time' and the first to teach oratory. Pausanias claims to have read a book by Pittheos in Epidauros, and he was famous for his expression 'Blast not the hope that friendship has conceived, but fill its measure high!' He unified Hypereia and Antheia to create Troezen, which he named after his brother; the original name, however, may have been *troin hezomenon*, 'the three sitters', recalling the triple kingship, or the three-throned altar Pittheos erected to Themis, who was identified with Egyptian Isis, the mother of Horus. Pittheos also founded the Sanctuary of Oracular Apollo (the Greek equivalent of Horus), the oldest shrine in Greece. It featured in a famous early real estate trade, when Apollo exchanged Troezen and Póros with Poseidon for Delphi. Poseidon's claim to his new lands, however, was disputed by Athena, until Zeus declared they had to share it, a rare compromise and one that the city commemorated on its coins. Although the Méthana peninsula was settled by the Mycenaeans, Troezen apparently was not, and these stories are believed to go back to the Early Helladic period. Whether or not Troezen was a pocket of Pelasgians or even Ionians, they perceived themselves as a people apart and had uncommonly close links to Athens, sharing the same hero.

This of course was **Theseus**, the son of Pittheos' daughter Aethra. Aethra had been betrothed to Bellerophon (like the Acrocorinth, Troezen once had a spring – the Hippocrene – formed by a kick of Pegasus' hoof) but when Bellerophon fell in disgrace and Aethra seemed doomed to virginity, her father arranged for his visitor, Aegeus, the king of Athens, to have too much to drink and mistake the door of her room for his. Later, that same evening, 'Deceitful Athena' willed that Aethra go down to the shore to make a sacrifice to Poseidon, who ravished her (when it came to Theseus' paternity, the mythographers of Athens wanted it both ways). In the morning, Aethra was miraculously back with Aegeus, who asked her to raise any child they might have in secret, and to send him to Athens only when he proved himself by lifting a boulder and taking the tokens – a sword and sandals – that Aegeus left underneath. Theseus did, of course, and subsequently performed all kinds of heroic deeds, including the slaying of the Minotaur with the help of Ariadne.

Towards the end of his career, Theseus, now king of Athens, had a son Hippolytos by Antiope, the Queen of Amazons, and sent him to his grandfather Pittheos, who adopted him as his heir. Hippolytos was devoted to physical fitness, chastity and the cult of Artemis, and he built her a temple and stadium in Troezen where he trained. Miffed by his neglect, Aphrodite caused his father's wife Phaedra to fall in love with him. In Theseus' absence Phaedra moved to Troezen where she built a temple to Peeping Aphrodite in order to spy on Hippolytos as he trained, naked, and where she perforated myrtle leaves with her dress pin in frustration.

And then the familiar story, perhaps derived from the same Egyptian source as Joseph and the wife of Potiphar, and retold in Euripides' *Hippolytos* and Racine's *Phèdre*: back in Athens, Phaedra confesses her love to her stepson in a letter and is rebuked; she hangs herself, leaving a letter for Theseus, accusing Hippolytos of attempted rape. Theseus curses his son, banishes him from Athens and calls on his divine father Poseidon to kill Hippolytos; as Hippolytos rides his chariot by the sea to Troezen, a monster (or giant wave) spooks the horses, and he is dragged to his death. Euripides introduces the concept of pardon into the story, as Hippolytos forgives his father before he dies.

This rewriting probably never washed in Troezen, where Hippolytos, whose name suggests an ancient horse god, was always far more important than Theseus. The story also has a postscript: Artemis, furious at losing her favourite, asked Asklepios to bring him back to life (in fact, a tablet in Epidauros records a gift of 20 horses from Hippolytos to thank Asklepios for his resurrection). This was the last straw for Hades, who asked Zeus to strike Asklepios with a thunderbolt, forcing him to go underground for good (*see* pp.288–9).

The 'real' history of Troezen confirms the city's special relationship with Athens. When the Persians were coming in 480 BC, the Athenians unanimously agreed with Themistocles to send their women and children to Troezen for safety – as many as 70,000 in all – and one can only guess their feelings as they watched the Athenian fleet gather in Troezen's now silted-up port before sailing to Sálamis to confront the enormous Persian navy. By all accounts, Troezen treated the refugees well; they even held free classes for the children, and erected statues of the most prominent women and children under a colonnade in the *agora*. In 1959, a tablet engraved with Themistocles' famous Decree to the Athenians exhorting them to fight the Persians was found holding up a stair in an old school. For all that, Athens captured Troezen in the Peloponnesian War, pushing the city to side with Sparta. The Franks made it one of their baronies. In 1827, the town briefly became famous again when it hosted the third Greek Assembly, which produced a third constitution ('of Troezen') and elected Iánnis Capodístria of Corfu, the then foreign minister of Russia, as the first president of Greece.

What's Left

Follow the signs up the narrow road from modern Trizína into the olive groves. In 500m, the fork in the road is marked by the **Theseus Rock**, under which the hero found the sword and sandals of King Aegeas; it was an ancient altar to Strong Zeus. The right-hand road passes first the turn-off (again on the right) for a recently discovered and excavated **Palaeo-Christian church**, made of ancient blocks, then continues over the river to the bare foundations of the **Temple of Hippolytos** and a 3rd-century BC ***asklepeion***. It preserves some of its plumbing (water being an important part of the cure) and a curious room that may have been a morgue.

The ancient Temple of Aphrodite Kataskopeia, 'Peeping Aphrodite', built by Phaedra to watch Hippolytos, is believed to be on the site of the ruined Byzantine church of the **Episkopí** ('overseer' or bishop). There's no sign of the holy myrtle leaves or the Stadium of Artemis, or indeed of most of the temples recorded by Pausanias. One was a Museion, or Sanctuary of the Nine Muses, built by Ardalos, the inventor of the flute. Just to show the ancient Greeks had a sense of humour, it had an altar dedicated to Sleep.

If you return to the Theseus Rock and take the left fork, you'll pass a prominent **tower** from the old city walls, 2nd-century AD on the bottom, medieval on top. Shortly beyond, a grove of enormous plane trees marks the **Devil's Gorge**; after entering Hades at Lerna to fetch his mother Semele, Dionysos brought her up through this cleft in the hills. Yet you'll be hard pressed to find a more idyllic place, where nymphs seem to lurk just behind the ferny, drippy boulders and crystal pools, fed by what is tentatively identified as Troezen's 'golden stream that never dries'. The small **bridge** here is the heir of the ancient aqueduct and, fittingly, a Sanctuary to Pan once stood nearby. Pan's cloven-hoofed kinsman, the Devil, built the bridge, or so they say, and demanded a toll. Someone painted his picture on the wall. A third road from modern Trizína heads up the slopes of Adéres for the **Monastery of Ag. Dimítrios** (1.5km), with fine frescoes restored in the 17th century, and excellent views across to Póros.

Galatás and Póros

Just east of Troezen at Galatás (Γαλατάς) you'll find the 'Greek Grand Canal', which just separates the Peloponnese from the island of Póros. Although the latter is far more fashionable, **Galatás**

Getting to and around Galatás and Póros

A **car ferry** (every 30mins) or summer **water taxis** flit across the strait to Póros. KTEL **buses**, **t** 229 804 2480, in Galatás leave from opposite the ferry dock, three times a day for Epidauros (the theatre), Naúplio, Méthana and Trizína. **Port authority**: **t** 229 802 2274.

Pops Car Rental, **t** 229 801 4714, *www.popscar.gr*, in Galatás, does the business if you need a car; motor bikes are for hire in front of Koulis Rent Rooms. There are also plenty of **taxis**.

On Póros, **buses** go as far as Russian Bay and the monastery, passing most of the beach hotels.

---

has the better view – of Póros Town and its dense pile of houses, churches and bell towers peeking over one another's shoulders over the strait, or *póros*, in Greek. Galatás for its part is an easy-going, workaday place, stretched thinly along the waterfront. Although you'll see little evidence of dairy products (*gála* means milk), its residents are still more concerned with their orchards and flowers. There are two beaches to the east: **Pláka** (2km) and **Alykí** (signposted, 4km) on an unpaved road, with a good taverna. Near the Alykí turn-off, at the sign for the Cardassi restaurant, begin the citrus groves nicknamed the **Lemonódassos**, or lemon forest. They say the blossoms from one lemon tree can scent an entire garden; on a warm spring day, a stroll here with 30,000 is a full dose of aromatherapy. Follow the trails up to the delightful taverna for a glass of lemonade. Ask the owner about locating **Artimos** – the submerged ruins of a Temple of Artemis, just east.

Póros

If there is one dream which I like above all others it is that of sailing on land. Coming into Póros gives the illusion of that deep dream.
Henry Miller, *The Colossus of Maroussi*

If you sail through the straits from Galatás on a large ferry you can see what people on the second floors are watching on TV.

The Minoan presence on Póros is remembered in the myth of **Skylla**, whose father the king had a lock of hair that made him immortal. When Minos of Crete besieged Póros, Skylla caught sight of him and fell in love with him, then cut off her father's magic lock while he slept and brought it to Minos. Minos killed the king and easily took Póros, but he was revolted by Skylla's betrayal and left for Crete without her. Desperate, Skylla swam after him, but she was attacked by her father's avenging spirit in the form of an eagle, and drowned in the bay which bears her name (Askéli).

In antiquity Póros was named **Kalavria** (Χαλαυρια), 'gentle breeze', and served as the headquarters of a 7th-century BC maritime amphictyony that operated under the protection of Poseidon, who had a famous sanctuary here. Little remains of it today beyond the memory of the orator, Demosthenes, who, unlike today's Greeks, didn't think Macedonia was quite Greek and roused his native Athens against the expanding influence of Philip II. Briefly silenced by Athens' defeat by Philip at Chairóneia (338 BC), Demosthenes continued his defiance of Philip's successor, Alexander, and, after Alexander's death in 322, led another revolt against the

Macedonians. This time Alexander's general Antipater lost all patience and went after him. Demosthenes fled to Póros and sought sanctuary at the Temple of Poseidon, only the Macedonians impiously burst in, swords raised. But Demosthenes died proving his pen was mightier: he had bitten off the poison he had concealed in the nib.

Póros' **Russian Bay** recalls the events of 1828–31, when British, French and Russian emissaries gathered on Póros for a conference on Greece. The Russians were close to the first president Capodístria, one-time foreign minister to the Tsar – too close, thought many revolutionaries from Hýdra and Póros. Tensions rose significantly in 1831, when Admiral Miaoúlis, overseeing the national fleet at Póros from his flagship *Hellas* (an American-built warship that cost twice the national budget), was ordered by Capodístria to loan Russia the *Hellas*. Instead, the honest admiral blew it up in the Strait of Póros; it broke his heart, but averted a civil war.

From Póros Town to the Temple of Poseidon

Póros (Πορος) consists of two islands: larger **Kalávria**, pine-forested and blessed with innumerable quiet sandy coves, and little **Sferiá**, a volcanic bubble that popped out of the sea in 273 BC. Picturesque **Póros Town**, the capital and port, clambers all over Sferiá, topped by a pair of landmarks – the **clock tower** of 1927 and the blue-domed campanile of the cathedral, **Ag. Geórgios**. This has 20th-century wall paintings by Konstantínos Parthénis, who lived on Póros from 1909–11. Cadets attend the **Naval Training School**, housed in the buildings of the first arsenal of the Greek state. A small **Archaeological Museum** in Plateía Koryzí contains artefacts from the island and ancient Troezen, including a lion spout gutter from the Temple of Aphrodite that played a prominent role in Euripides' tragedy *Hippolytus*. Another favourite thing to do in town is cross over to **Galatás** and swim at the beach by the **Lemonódassos**, the massive lemon forest 2km southeast.

Archaeological Museum
t 229 802 3276; open Tues–Sun 9–3

Sferiá is joined by a bridge to Kalávria at the **Sinikismós** ('settlement' – settled by Asia Minor refugees in 1923). Kalávria has Póros' **beaches**, backed by pines: **Neórion**, **Megálo Neórion** and pretty Lovers' Cove (**Limenáki tis Agápis**) are west, towards Russian Bay. The latter was named for warehouses and a ships' biscuit bakery (now partly ruined) built by the Russian navy in 1831, which they used into the 1900s.

Other beaches, **Askéli** and **Kanáli**, are to the east of Sinikismós. From Kanáli the road continues into the trees to the 18th-century **Monastery of Zoodóchos Pigí**, with a miraculous spring, a lofty 17th-century gilt iconostasis made in Cappadocia and the tomb of Admiral Miaoúlis; below is a charming pebble beach, **Kalávrias**.

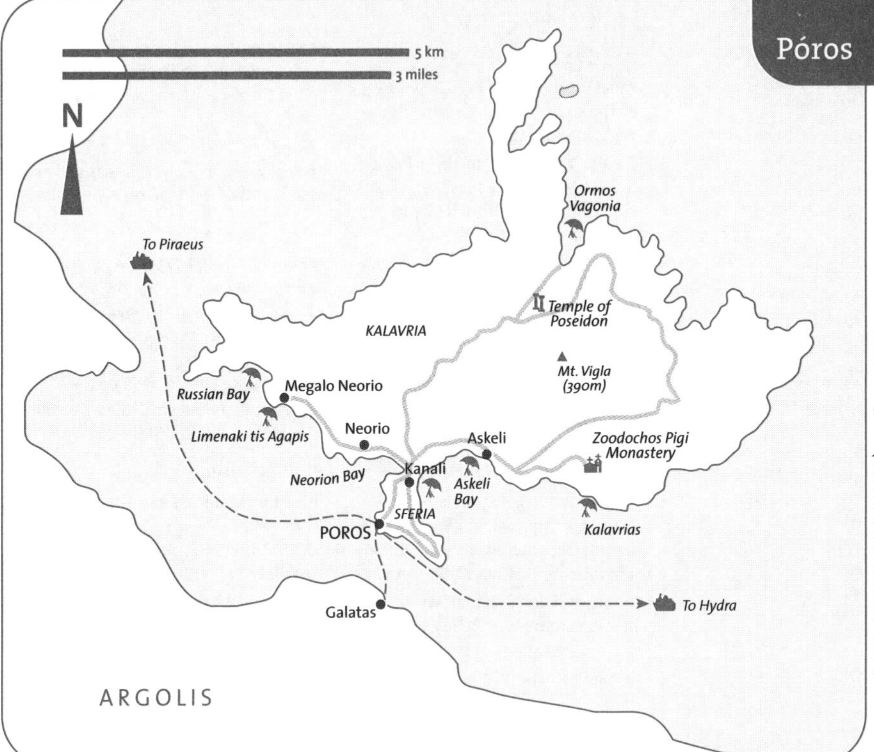

From the monastery you can drive up to the plateau of Palatia and the scant remains – the locals call it 'the five stones' – of the once celebrated Doric **Temple of Poseidon**. First built in brick by the Mycenaeans, it was rebuilt in marble *c.* 500 BC; when Pausanias visited it, he saw the tomb of Demosthenes in the precinct. All this is dust in the wind (and most of the marble is now in Hýdra), but the view across the Saronic Gulf is spectacular. A narrow road descends to the northern beach of **Vagonia**.

Although it's out of print, keep an eye peeled for *In Argolis*, a delightful book about Póros written by George Horton, editor of the *Philadelphia Enquirer* who became US consul in Greece and helped organize the first modern Olympics in 1896. In 1922 he was in Smyrna, and helped to save the lives of thousands of Greeks; he wrote *Blight of Asia* about the experience, a book that influenced US foreign policy of the day.

Useful Information on Póros

Tourist police, on the waterfront, **t** 229 802 2462.

Where to Stay and Eat in Galatás and on Póros

For a complete list of apartments and rooms, call **t** 229 802 5577, *www.poros.com.gr*.

Galatás ✉ 18020

Papassotiríou, **t** 229 804 2841 (€€/€€). By the sea in town; offers meals as well. *Open all year.*

Galatia, **t** 229 804 3728 (€/€). Right on the sea, with the best views of Póros; pure Greek 1970s, from lobby to awnings. *Open all year.*

O Vláchos. The best taverna; the real McCoy, with tables by the sea.

Póros Town ✉ 18020

Sto Roloï >

Sto Roloï, 13 Chartzopoúlou-Karrá, **t** 229 802 5808, *www.storoloi-poros.gr* (€€€€/€€). Under the clock tower, romantic hotel-apartments in a 200-year-old stone house with a pool.

Diónysos, near the ferry, **t** 229 802 3511, *www.hoteldionysos.com* (€€€/€€€). Attractive old building with cool, stone-walled rooms, air-conditioning and satellite TV. Low off-season rates.

Manessis, **t** 229 802 2273, *www.manessis.com* (€€/€€). Tidy, by the port in a neoclassical-style building.

Seven Brothers, just back from the waterfront, **t** 229 802 3412, *www.7brothers.gr* (€€/€€). Convenient and comfortable, with air-conditioning.

Nikolaos Douros, 9 Dimósthenous (first road right after the high school), **t** 229 802 2633 (€/€). Pleasant rooms with air conditioning, TV and a view.

Caravella, on the waterfront, **t** 229 802 3666. Greek and international dishes made from organic produce.

Karavolos, behind the cinema, **t** 229 802 6158. The 'Snail' is popular for its good Greek fare. Get there early to find a table.

Kathestos, by the post office, **t** 229 802 4770. Simple taverna that serves some of the best food on Póros.

Neórion ✉ 18020

Pavlou, **t** 229 802 2734, *www.poros.com.gr/pavlou* (€€€/€€). The best choice here, and at the lower end of the price scale; it has a lovely pool and tennis courts.

Mortzoukos, **t** 229 802 3924. Very good food; try the stuffed pork or the mouthwatering soufflé.

Askéli ✉ 18020

Christina Studios, **t** 229 802 4900, *www.poros.com.gr/christina* (€€€/€€€). Close to the beach, with lovely sea views from the big balconies.

New Aegli, **t** 229 802 2372, *www.newaegli.com* (€€€/€€€). Resort hotel with a real Greek flavour, pool, beach and water sports; all rooms have sea views.

Sirene, near the monastery, **t** 229 802 2741, *www.hotelsirene.gr* (€€€/€€€). The most luxurious on Póros, with two salt-water pools, and its own beach. *Open April–Oct.*

Panorama, **t** 229 802 4563. One of the island's best tavernas, serving very reliable Greek staples.

To the Tip of the Akte Peninsula

The road east of the Lemonódassos to the tip of the Akte peninsula is equally lovely, especially early in the morning or at twilight, when Póros and its baby islands and rocks are stained violet in the mirror of the sea. Only a handful of villas are scattered among the undulating coastline, dotted with cypresses and olive groves. Very few places as beautiful, and as easily accessible from Athens, have escaped the cement mixer; the lack of beaches may have something to do with it. There are signs of big resort construction under way once the road curves south, however, and Hýdra with its equally arid sidekick Dókos heave into view. And unless you have business along this dreary stretch of marshy, scrubby, beach-dotted coast, consider the scenic if unpaved road west from here along the spine of Mount Adéres. You can pick it up at **Saronída** (Σαρονίδα), 8.5km from Galatás, take it to **Iliókastro** (Ηλιόκαστρο) and on to Ermióni: it is isolated and offers great views of the Argolís, although on the hottest days a heat haze interferes.

Ermióni, Portochéli and Kósta

Ermióni and Portochéli, the resorts on Akte's southerly nub, are big ports of call among pleasure sailors and favourites among Athenian weekenders because they are so easy to reach by sea from Piraeus. Ermióni and its coast bask in the reflected glow of glittering Hýdra, while Portochéli's satellite Kósta is the nearest landfall to the stylishly laid-back island of Spétses. The reflected glow is such that Sean Connery and Vladimir Putin among others have invested along the coast, which sweaty-palmed estate agents are keen to package as 'Greece's Côte d'Azur'.

Ermióni (Ερμιόνη) occupies a long, narrow headland; one side has the handsome waterfront and port, where selling ice cubes to floating gin palaces is big business, while the other side, known as

Where to Stay and Eat in Ermióni, Portochéli and Kósta

Ermióni ✉ 21051

Philoxenia, t 275 403 1218 (€€/€€). Near ancient Hermione; handsome studios that are quiet and well furnished. If no one's there, ask at Taverna Ganossis right on the port, **t** 275 403 1706 (the food is pretty good, too).

Akti, t 27 5403 1241 (€/€). A modest waterfront choice. *Open April–Oct.*

Psitariá To Bitsi, near the pines. Succulent grilled meats on a terrace.

For fish, trawl the tavernas at Mandráki.

Around Ermióni

Paladien Lena-Mary, 7.5km south at Petrothálassa Beach, **t** 275 403 1450, *lenamary@otenet.gr* (€€€€/€€€€). Well-equipped luxury compound that could be anywhere; popular with the French. *Open April–Oct.*

Portochéli ✉ 21300

Porto Heli, t 275 405 3400, *www.akshotels.com* (€€€€€/€€€). Supplies all the beach amenities; rooms have kitchenettes, satellite TV, and so on. *Open all year.*

Kalithea Studios, 4 Kalithéa, **t** 275 402 2157, *www.studioskalithea.gr* (€€€/€€). On a hill overlooking the port, attractive studios offering a quiet alternative to the bustle of downtown Portochéli. *Open all year.*

Poseidon Sports and Studios, t 694 710 2425, *www.poseidon-sports.com* (€/€). Attractive, shipshape wi-fi-equipped British-owned studios, with a barbecue terrace and green philosophy. Their water sports centre is 10mins away on the beach. They also hire out bikes. *Closed Dec and Jan.*

Porto, t 275 405 1410 (€/€). Portside, if you're stuck. *Open all year.*

Ostria, t 275 405 3625, *www.ostria-bay.gr*. Fashionable if pricey seaside café-bar-restaurant with an imaginative menu and a great wine list; for a special night out.

En-Plo, t 275 405 1489. Popular place to end the day nibbling *mezédes* as the sun goes down.

Kósta ✉ 21300

Lido, t 275 405 7393, *www.lidohotel.gr* (€€€/€€). Plain, motel-like, right on the beach between the water taxis and the swimming beach; fine for a night or two – and a godsend if you miss the last water taxi to Spétses. *Open April–Sept.*

Getting to Ermióni and Portochéli

KTEL **buses** from Naúplio run to Ermióni and Portochéli four times a day.

The ports are frequently linked to one another and Piraeus daily, all year, by **Saronikos Flying Dolphin**, **t** 210 419 9200. For information in Ermióni call the **port authority**, **t** 275 403 1243, in Portochéli, **t** 275 405 3333. You can rent a car in Ermióni from **Pops**, **t** 275 403 1880, *www.popscar.gr*. They deliver in Portochéli too. Ermióni **taxis**: **t** 275 403 1060 or **t** 275 404 1660.

Mandráki, has pretty rocks you can swim off under white island-style houses, followed by a rank of seafood restaurants. The French are especially fond of it; there are big self-contained resort hotels on either side. The sparse ruins of **ancient Hermione**, with some stones from a Temple to Poseidon, lie scattered in a pine grove at the tip of the headland, but fluorescent blue birds called European rollers steal the show as they flit over the sea. Hermione's claim to fame is that it was the only ancient city in Greece to hold nautical games – boat races and diving (or swimming), all in honour of Dionysos of the Black Goat. Up at **Iliókastro** (Ηλιόκαστρο), 8km north, are polygonal walls and the ruins of a Temple of Demeter and Persephone at **ancient Eileoi**.

Set on a beautiful, sheltered little bay perfect for water sports, **Portochéli** (Πορτοχέλι) was built on the site of ancient Halieis, and there are fine views back from the ancient acropolis prominent across the bay. Portochéli was a fishing village that caught the fancy of the yachters, and is one of the very few ports in Greece that manages to feels suburban, thanks to the roads and car parks that separate it from the sea. Its tentacles have spread north towards **Ververóda** (Βερβερόντα) and south to **Ag. Emilianós** (Αγ. Αιμιλιανός), home to sprawling all-in resorts.

Kósta (Κόστα), several kilometres south and the base for water taxis to Spétses, is in the loop, but offers a much nicer atmosphere, partly because the water taxi quay is isolated on the far left, leaving the rest of the area quiet and natural. There is a lovely beach with a terraced restaurant, a small hotel and not much else. The fact that so many wealthy Athenians have villas on the headland to the west of the beach may explain why Kósta has not gone ballistic: the élite who live here have *méson* (influence) where it counts.

Hýdra

Hýdra (ΥΔΡΑ) is a long, grey, very fashionable rock with an outrageously picturesque town of stone and pastel mansions rising steeply over the harbour. As the last sea captains and merchants moved out, artists, writers and their camp followers moved in, inspired by the scenes of Hýdra in *A Boy on a Dolphin* (1957) starring Sophia Loren, and *Phaedra* (1962), Jules Dassin's

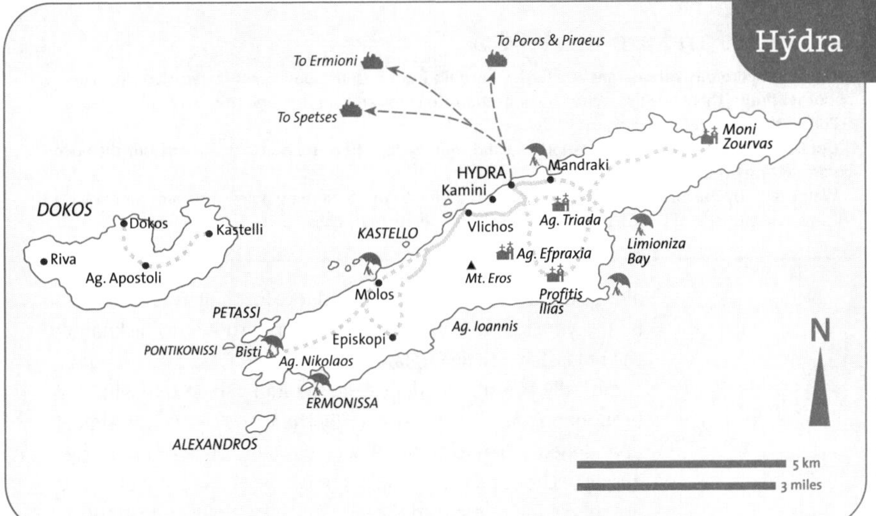

remake of *Hippolytus*, with Melina Mercouri. Known as the Greek St-Tropez, Hýdra is wonderfully free of cars and motorbikes (except for two rubbish trucks), functioning instead on donkey power. It has a hopping night scene, but was snoozing when God was handing out beaches.

History

The first permanent population on Hýdra didn't arrive until the 15th century, when it was settled by Greeks and Albanians from Épirus, fleeing the growing ambitions of Serbia under Stephen Dusan. By necessity, they turned to the sea to survive: building up a fleet of 150 merchant ships, nearly monopolizing the corn market from the Black Sea to Europe, with a bit of smuggling and piracy on the side. By the late 18th century, Hýdra was for all purposes an autonomous state, to which the Turks turned a blind eye as long as it paid its taxes. It boasted a wealthy population of 25,000, and the sailors Hýdra sent as a tribute to the Sultan were prized – especially the Albanians, who made fortunes running the British blockade in the Napoleonic Wars.

Hýdra did so well under the Ottomans that the outbreak of the War of Independence in 1821 left its captains lukewarm, until their rivals on Spétses had chalked up a few victories and the people of Hýdra threatened to revolt. Once the decision to fight was made, however, they threw themselves wholeheartedly into the fray. Merchants (notably the Koundouriótis family) converted their fleets into warships and, under such leaders as Tombázis and Miaoúlis, commander-in-chief of the Greek navy, the Hydriots terrorized the Turks. Fire ships were their secret weapon: at night, some 20 daredevils would sail a decrepit vessel full of explosives

Getting to and around Hýdra

Up to 20 **hydrofoils, catamarans** and **ferries** sail daily from Piraeus, some going 'express' to Hýdra in about 1½ hours; there are also frequent connections to Póros and Spétses, and from Ermióni.

Port authority: t 229 805 2279.

Donkeys wait by the quay to transport you and your luggage to your hotel (always work out the price before setting off).

Water taxis by the quay ferry up to 10 people at a time to the swimming holes at Kamíni, Mandráki and Vlíchos, and the islet of Dokós; they have fixed fares and are fairly cheap if you join the crowd.

---

alongside Turkish ships, light it and row for their lives in an escape boat. Hýdra's arch-enemy, Ibrahim Pasha, grudgingly nicknamed the bold island 'Little England'.

Ironically, the independence Hýdra fought so hard to win brought an end to its prosperity. By the 1950s Hýdra was almost abandoned, when fortune's wheel was oiled once again by the arrival of Greek painter Hadjikyriákos Ghíkas, the pioneer of the artists' colony that paved the way for today's glitterati; in 1960 Leonard Cohen bought a house, and still returns periodically.

Hýdra Town

Just arriving is an extraordinary experience. The island looks like an arid rock pile until your vessel makes a sharp turn, and – *voilà*, the sublime port, the pearl in the oyster shell, the scene that launched a thousand cruise ships. The typically three-storey grey and white mansions, built in the late 18th century by Venetian and Genoese architects, attest to the loot amassed by Hydriot privateers and blockade runners; nearly all have terraces atop cisterns, where the owners used to hide their treasures. Some of the mansions are now hotels, while others have found assorted uses: the **Athens School of Fine Arts** has a branch in the old Tombázi mansion, and the **Skolí Eborikís Naftilías**, Greece's oldest school for merchant marine captains, is housed in the Tsámados house.

Lázaros Koundouriótis Historical Mansion
t 229 805 2421; open Mar–Oct Tues–Sun 10–4.30; adm

Museum and Archives of Hýdra
t 229 805 2355; open daily 9–4.30 and 7–9; adm

The loveliest mansions – and the largest – belonged to the Koundouriótis family, Albanians who could barely speak a word of Greek but who contributed two leaders to the cause: the fat, jovial Geórgios, who was elected president of the executive for 1823–6, and Lázaros, who converted his merchant fleet into warships at his own expense. In 2001, after decades of restoration, the big yellow **Lázaros Koundouriótis Historical Mansion** was opened to the public as an annexe of the National Historical Museum in Athens, preserving its original walls and ceilings; it holds costumes, antiques and a gallery with paintings by Constantínos Byzántios. On the left side of the harbour, the **Museum and Archives of Hýdra** contains a rich collection of portraits of Hydriot captains and heroes, folk paintings, ships' models and weapons.

The Man who Captivated Nelson

Before becoming commander-in-chief of the Greek navy, Miaoúlis (Andréas Vókos, 1769–1835) was elected admiral by the fleet, in recognition not only of his seamanship, but of his exceptional integrity – a rare trait in 1821, when many Greek leaders had no qualms about jeopardizing the entire enterprise for their own profit. Miaoúlis (who took his *nom de guerre* from the Turkish word for a felucca, *miaoul*) instead devoted his fortune to the war. The Greeks tell the story that Nelson once captured Miaoúlis on one of his more piratical adventures, but Miaoúlis in turn captured Nelson with his charm, and was released with a pat on the back.

He needed all the charm he could muster to deal with the difficult, independent-minded sailors of Hýdra and Spétses, who were accustomed to the medieval system that gave each crew member a right to the profits and a say in all matters; if the majority disagreed with a captain's decision, even if they were about to do battle, they would go on strike. The fact that Miaoúlis avoided mutiny, kept his ships together and harried the massive, well-organized Egyptian invasion fleet of Ibrahim Pasha for four months was an accomplishment in itself, even if it ultimately failed. Afterwards, while all but a handful of Greek admirals refused to sail without being paid in advance, Miaoúlis struggled to relieve the besieged city of Messolóngi, and always outfoxed the enemy when he had a fighting chance. After handing over his command to Lord Dundonald in 1827, when the real power in Greece had shifted to Britain, France and Russia, he bowed out of the entangled politics after the war with a bang (*see* 'Póros', p.310) and is fondly remembered on his native island in the Miaoúlia (20 June).

The churches in Hýdra also reflect the island's former wealth and influence. The most beautiful is the 18th-century **Panagía tis Theotókou**, next to the port, with a lovely marble iconostasis and silver chandelier; the cells of its **convent**, now used as town offices, encompass a serene marble courtyard (quarried from Póros' Temple of Poseidon). There's also a little **museum** of ecclesiastical items. From the church, climb up Miaoúlis Street to the lovely square of **Kaló Pigádi**, site of two 18th-century mansions and two deep wells that supplied the town with fresh water.

The one real beach on Hýdra is a good 20-minute walk away at **Mandráki**, by the old docks; alternatively, dive off the lovely rocks at **Kamíni**. On Good Friday, Kamíni is packed with Hydriots and visitors who come to watch the moving candlelit procession of Christ's bier, the *epitafiós*, which culminates here by the sea.

Around the Island

Other excursions require more walking or a donkey ride, a guaranteed way to escape the idle throng. At **Kastéllo**, behind Hýdra, are the ruins of a thick-walled castle near the shore. **Vlíchos**, a 6km walk west of town, is a pretty hamlet with a rocky beach, a picturesque little bridge and a good taverna; water taxis from the port also make the trip. Pines and coves for swimming make **Mólos** a popular place for outings and for spotting Joan Collins, who often spends the summer here.

Hýdra was a pious place, and has a disproportionate number of religious houses per capita. Mule tracks lead south from Hýdra Town in about an hour to the **Profítis Ilías Monastery** (1813) and the nearby **Convent of Ag. Efpráxia** (1863), where the nuns make embroideries. Start early in the day, and take a bottle of water to reach the **Monastery of Ag. Triáda** (1704; men only) and the **Convent of Ag. Nikoláos** (1724), both above **Mandráki** – the latter has a frescoed church and superb views. Furthest of all is the **Monastery of Zourvas** (1814) near the lighthouse, with great views, a two-hour walk from Ag. Triáda. There's also a clutch of hunters' lodges at **Episkopí**, in Hýdra's fire-scarred pine forest.

Dokós

From Hýdra it's an hour by caique to Dokós, an islet named after the family of Hydriot captains who once owned it. It has been inhabited off and on since the late Neolithic period, and two families live on the island today; there's a **beach** and excellent snorkelling in a pretty bay, often used by passing yachties. In 1975, a shipwreck dated to 2200 BC (Early Helladic II) – the oldest ever found in Greece – was discovered, with its cargo of ceramics made just before the introduction of the potter's wheel.

Inland are ruins of the walls and towers of the **Kástro**, built in the 7th century and last used by Morosini. Quarries yield *marmarópita*, a hard grey and red marble, often used in building.

Useful Information on Hýdra

Tourist police: Vótsi Street, **t** 229 805 2205. *Open summer only.*

Hýdra Festivals

20 June: The Miaoúlia.
July: Festival of Marionettes.

Where to Stay on Hýdra

Hýdra ✉ 18040

Be warned: it is sheer madness to arrive in Hýdra in the summer without a booking. Most of the hotels are small, and have better rates if you stay at least three days.

Bratsera, **t** 229 805 3971, *www.greekhotel.com* (€€€€/€€€€). Combines traditional design with glamour in a beautifully converted sponge factory. Most rooms overlook the colonnaded pool and lantern-lit restaurant. *Closed Nov.*

Angelica, 42 Miaoúli, **t** 229 805 3202, *www.angelica.gr* (€€€/€€€). Calm, a 5min walk from the port. Lovely shady terrace. *Open all year.*

Ippokampos, 100m from the port, **t** 229 805 3453, *www.ippokampos.com* (€€€/€€€). Restored mansion, with a pretty courtyard.

Leto, **t** 229 805 3385, *www.letohydra.gr* (€€€/€€€). Two minutes from the port, a traditional mansion with antique-furnished rooms, including some sleeping four. *Open Mar–Dec.*

Miramare, at Mandráki, **t** 229 805 2300, *www.miramare.gr* (€€€/€€€). Stone bungalow complex, linked to the port by boat; overlooking the island's sole bit of sand. *Open April–Oct.*

★ Miranda >>

Miranda, **t** 229 805 2230, *www.mirandahotel.gr* (€€€/€€€). Another elegant 19th-century sea captain's town house, with stunning Venetian painted ceilings. *Open May–Oct.*

Mistral, **t** 229 805 2509, *www.mistralhydra.gr* (€€€/€€€). An old stone tower mansion, with simple but attractive rooms in mint condition.

Orloff, near the port, **t** 229 805 2564, *www.orloff.gr* (€€€/€€€). Beautifully restored 19th-century mansion, its nine rooms individually designed and set around a courtyard; excellent breakfast. *Open Mar–Oct.*

Phaedra, a few minutes from the port on level streets, **t** 229 805 3330, *www.phaedrahotel.com* (€€€/€€€). A former carpet factory converted into lovely spacious doubles and suites.

Kondylenia >>

Hýdra, 2 steep mins from the clock tower, *hydrahotel@aig.forthnet.gr*, **t** 229 805 2102 (€€€/€€). You'll need your mountain goat skills to stay here; warm welcome and fine views from a historic mansion.

Delfini, by the hydrofoils, **t** 229 805 2082 (€€/€). 11 rooms. *Open April–Oct.*

Erofili, 2mins from the port, **t** 229 805 4049, *www.pensionerofili.gr* (€/€). A young couple run this child-friendly *pension* with a vine-shaded courtyard.

Eating Out on Hýdra

Geitoniko (aka **Christina**), **t** 229 805 3615. Courtyard setting in an old stone building; excellent traditional cuisine – good stewed dishes – at fair prices.

Iliovassilema (or **Marina's**), Vlíchos Beach, **t** 229 805 2496. Delicious food (sea urchin spaghetti) and superb sunsets; take a water taxi (*c.* €10).

Paradosiakó, near the Alpha Bank, **t** 229 805 4155. Recommended especially for its *mezédes*.

Porfyra, **t** 229 805 3660. For reasonably priced stuffed vegetables, lamb and home-made desserts.

Sto Steki, by the clock tower, **t** 229 805 3517. Serves home-cooked favourites from moussaka to lobster; try the famous fish soup. *Open all year.*

Vigla, **t** 229 805 4154. Verandas with lovely views; serves excellent seafood. From €32.

Kondylenia, 15mins' walk from town on Kamíni Beach, **t** 229 805 3520. Outstanding, with views over the quaint harbour; try the squid in tomato sauce or the sea urchin dip. Around €35.

Nightlife on Hýdra

Hýdra comes into its own at night, but bring a wad of euros if you want to join the party.

Ydronetta, **t** 229 805 4160, *www.ydronetta.gr*. Cool bar on the west end of town with lovely views and swimming platforms in beach-poor Hýdra, with romantic music and sunset cocktails – and dance music late.

Amalour, Tombázi, **t** 229 805 3125. With a mix of jazz and Greek music.

Pirate, south end of the harbour, **t** 229 805 2711. The classic, open till it's time for breakfast in July and August.

Nautilus, west of the harbour, **t** 229 805 3563. Where the Athenians head for trendy Greek music, often live.

Disco Heaven, **t** 229 805 2716. Perched high on the west side of the harbour; the evergreen favourite.

Spétses

Spétses (ΣΠΕΤΣΕΣ) is a beautiful, low-lying pine-scented island in the Argive Gulf, the furthest from Athens, a factor that long kept it more relaxed than its more accessible sisters. For all that, it's an old hand at tourism: since the First World War Athenian families have come every summer for its safe beaches and climate. The island still attracts visitors lured by the luscious descriptions of John Fowles' *The Magus*, as well as a merry mix of British and Athenians, nearly all on motorbikes – it's a lot noisier than Hýdra and considerably less posey, although the opening of new boutique hotels seems set to make it a more upmarket place.

History

Although discoveries at Ag. Marína indicate that Pityoussa, as Spétses was called, has been inhabited since 2500 BC, it stayed out of the spotlight for the next 4,000 years. No one is even sure how the island got its name; the best guess is that the Venetians called it 'Spice,' or *spezie*. Like the other Saronics, Spétses was eventually repopulated with refugees from Albania and Épiros; the first shipyards date from the early 17th century. By the 19th century Spétses was renowned for its seamanship and, like Hýdra, prospered from the derring-do of its merchants and sea captains.

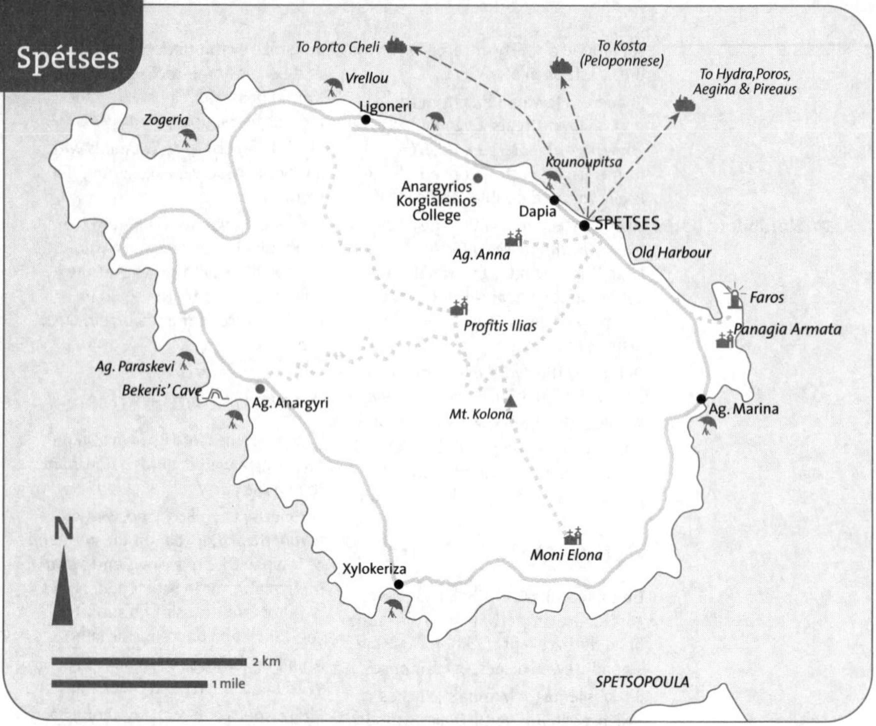

'Old Spice' made the history books by helping to ignite the War of Independence. During the years of Napoleonic blockade-running, the Spetsiots established a small fleet ready to take on the Turks, and the island raised the flag of war on 13 March 1821, under the influence of **Laskarína Bouboulína**, the wealthy, twice-widowed mother of seven, and the only female member of the revolutionary Friendly Society, the *Philikí Etairía*. Her flagship, the *Agamemnon*, was the finest in the country, and on 4 April the indomitable lady admiral, leading her 'brave lads', won Greece's first naval victory, capturing three Turkish ships as she led her fleet of eight vessels over to Naúplio to help blockade the port. She personally led the attack against the seaside fortifications; if the hottest fighting was happening on shore, Bouboulína would abandon ship for a horse and sabre. She stayed there until Naúplio fell in 1822, then participated in the blockade of Monemvasía; later she personally intervened to save the women and children of the Pasha's harem

Getting to and around Spétses

By sea: Several **hydrofoils**, **catamarans** (2hrs) and **ferries** (4hrs) connect daily with Piraeus and other Argo-Saronic islands year-round; there are also frequent boats from the nearby port of Kósta.

Port authority: t 229 807 2245.

Note: **cars** aren't allowed on the island. **Bicycles** and **scooters**, however, are for hire everywhere. There are four **taxis** on the island and two **buses** run from the Dápia to Anárgyri, and from Hotel Possidonion to Ligonéri. **Sea taxis** (at the Dápia) and caiques can take you to the beaches along the coast; book one at t 229 807 2072. **Horse-drawn carriages** for hire along the waterfront add a touch of elegance, but don't go any further than Ligonéri or Ag. Marína and agree on a price before setting out.

---

during one of the worst Greek atrocities of a war filled with atrocities: the massacre at Trípolis in the Peloponnese.

Spétses Town

Spétses, the capital and port, is not your typical Greek island town: where most are very dense, it spreads out leisurely amid orchards and gardens, into a score of neighbourhoods. Some of the oldest houses – proud neoclassical captains' mansions – are inland, safely invisible from the waterfront. Another distinctive feature is a love for black and white pebble mosaic pavements (*choklakía*). One commemorates the revolt of 1821 on the **Dápia**, the elegant square that sweeps down to the new quay. Bristling with cannon, the Dápia was once the town's frontline defence, but now it plays a more peaceful role as the vortex of Spétses' café society. On the esplanade there's a she-means-business statue of Bouboulína, who was assassinated in 1825 in her mansion nearby – over a dispute over her son's elopement with a local girl. The mansion was restored and is run by her great-great-great-grandson as the delightful **Bouboulína Museum**; here are her weapons and headscarf, a model of the *Agamemnon* and a portrait of Bouboulína looking improbably dainty. Apparently she is still the only woman admiral, ever.

Bouboulína Museum
t 229 807 2416, www.bouboulinamuseum-spetses.gr; open mid-Mar–Oct; 45min tours daily 9.45–8; adm

Behind Bouboulína's statue stretches the Edwardian façade of one of the first tourist hotels on any Greek island, the **Hotel Possidonion**, built in 1914 by philanthropist Sotíris Anárgyro who, after making his fortune in the tobacco trade in New York, decided to make that of Spétses; when it was built it was considered the most luxurious hotel in the Balkans, and it may soon undergo renovation. A dedicated Anglophile, he also founded the **Anárgyrios Korgialénios College** in 1927, on the English public school model. John Fowles taught here, a not altogether happy experience, and made it his model for the Lord Byron School in *The Magus*. Closed in 1983, it's now used as a centre for seminars. Anárgyro's other contribution to the island, Spétses' **pine forests**, were sadly much damaged in fires in 2000 and 2005. Anárgyro's **mansion**, built in 1903 (behind the Roumani Hotel), is a turn-of-the-century bombast modelled on an Egyptian temple.

Spétses Museum
t 229 807 2994; open Tues–Sun 8.30–3; adm

Spétses' **museum** is housed in the handsome mansion (1795) of Hadziyiánnis Méxis, another ship-owner and revolutionary; it has many of its original furnishings, archaeological finds, a box holding Bouboulína's bones, the 'Freedom or Death' flag of the War of Independence, and ships' models, paintings and figureheads.

The picturesque **Paléo Limáni**, or Old Harbour, is shared by fishermen, yachts, caique-builders and the oldest church, **Ag. Nikólaos**. On its pretty white bell tower the Spetsiots raised their defiant flag in 1821 – a bronze cast is displayed opposite and a pebble *choklakía* in the courtyard tells the tale. When they heard the Turks were sailing over to crush their revolt, the inhabitants created mannequins out of barrels and flowerpots, dressing them in red fezes and Turkish-appearing uniforms, and set them up along the quay. Seeing them from a distance, the Turkish commander thought that the island had already been taken, and sailed by.

Further east, near the **Fáros** (lighthouse), the church of **Panagía Armáta** was built after a Spétses fireboat sent the invading Turks fleeing on 8 September 1822, an event celebrated annually with gusto during the **Armáta**; inside, a painting by Koútzis commemorates the triumph. Just beyond is **Ag. Marína Beach**, looking across to **Spetsopoúla**, owned by the Niárchos family, whose late *paterfamilias* Stávros was one of the 'Super-Greeks' of the 1960s and '70s, and whose financial and romantic doings in the tabloids were only overshadowed by those of arch-rival Aristotle Onassis – in fact, one of Niárchos' six wives was an Onassis ex. Many believe he was the original for Fowles' enigmatic Colchis. Sometimes the 325ft Niárchos yacht is moored here, nearly as big as Spetsopoúla itself. Two other fine churches are up the hill at **Kastélli**, where the houses are mostly ruined: the 17th-century **Koimistís Theotókou** has frescoes, and **Ag. Triáda** a superb carved iconostasis (*ask the tourist police for keys*).

Around the Island

It's 26km around Spétses' pretty coast, embellished with pebbly beaches and rocky swimming coves. Heading clockwise, the first likely place for a swim is **Xylokeríza**, with a pleasant shingle beach that rarely gets crowded. The opposite holds true of **Ag. Anárgyri**, the only other settlement on the island, on an irresistible bay, rimmed with trees, bars and tavernas. From the beach it's a short swim or walk to **Bekeris' Cave**. You can enter from the sea or there is a low entrance by land; go in the afternoon, when the sun illuminates the stalactites inside.

Continuing clockwise, some caiques continue to **Ag. Paraskeví**, a delightful pebbly cove, watched over by the **Villa Jasemia**, the house Fowles used as the residence of his endlessly tricky Magus. A hop over the rocks at the west end is Spétses' official naturist beach. **Zogeriá**, further west, is a pretty, double-coved bay, a hardish slog from the road. In the north, the beaches of **Vréllou** (aka Paradise) and shady **Ligonéri** are nicest.

Useful Information on Spétses

Tourist police: on the far side of the Dápia, above OTE (telephone office), **t** 229 807 3100 or **t** 229 807 3744.

Athens Centre, **t** 210 701 2268, *www.athenscentre.gr*. Runs summer cultural programmes on Spétses.

Where to Stay on Spétses

Spétses Town ✉ 18050

Unless you arrive for Easter, August or the Armáta (8 Sept), you can generally find a room; ask at one of the tourist offices on the Dápia.

Economou, near the town hall, **t** 229 807 3400, *www.spetsesyc.gr* (€€€€€/€€€€€). Large studios in a traditional, renovated mansion with a pool.

Nissia, on the seafront, 500m from the Dápia, **t** 229 807 5000, *www.nissia.gr* (€€€€€/€€€€€). 'Traditional residences' in a 1920s industrial building, with a magnificent pool, excellent restaurant and fully equipped studios and maisonettes.

Orloff Resort, 2km from town, **t** 229 807 5444, *www.orloffresort.com* (€€€€€/€€€€€). Bright white apartments around a pool, with marble baths, Internet, the works.

Villa Christina, in town, **t** 229 807 2218, *www.villachristinahotel.com* (€€/€€). A central, charming and deservedly popular little place.

Villa Kriezi, 5mins' walk from town, **t** 229 807 4086, *adlogothetis@yahoo.gr* (€€/€€). En suites with TV and air-conditioning; many have sea views.

Mimosa, close to the Old Harbour and Ag. Marína beach, **t** 229 807 4087, *www.spetsesdirect.com* (€€/€, including breakfast). Good-value studios.

Klimis, on the east end of the waterfront, **t** 229 807 2334 (€/€). Pleasant seafront rooms over a pastry shop. *Open all year.*

Ag. Anárgyri ✉ 18050

Acrogiali, **t** 229 807 3695, *www.acrogiali.com* (€€€/€€€). Has beautifully designed suites with plasma TVs, Persian rugs and Korres beauty products in a lush Mediterranean garden, overlooking a pool. *Open April–Oct.*

Eating Out on Spétses

Spétses Town

Exedra, in the old harbour, **t** 229 807 3497. Renowned for its seafood, including pasta with lobster.

Kipos. Well priced, with barrelled wine and a delightful garden setting, off the main square.

Lazaros, uphill from the Dápia, **t** 229 807 2600. Full of character; good for vegetarians and meat-eaters, but they also have fish. *Closed lunch.*

Patralis, 10mins' walk along the front to the right of the main harbour, **t** 229 807 2134. Very popular. Try fish *à la spetsiota*, baked with tomato, olive oil, garlic and pepper.

Stelios, **t** 229 807 3748. In addition to fish fresh from the nearby market, come for excellent vegetarian dishes and a wide choice of set-price menus.

★ Tarsanas >>

Tarsanas, in the old harbour, **t** 229 807 4490. A big favourite (*book in summer*). Owned by a fishing family and serving *mezédes* and fresh seafood, including a superb fish soup. *Closed Mon–Fri in low season.*

Ag. Anárgyri ✉ 18050

Tassos. An example of how wonderful Greek food can taste; try the house speciality, 'lamb in a bag'.

Nightlife on Spétses

There are two outdoor cinemas in summer; otherwise Spétses Town starts to swing at around 1am.

Back towards Naúplio

The main road north of Portochéli passes through the pleasant but otherwise unremarkable market town of **Kranídi** (Κρανίδι). Just south of town, a road branches west along unpaved roads to the little beaches at **Doroúfi** (Δορούφι) and **Thiní** (Θυνί), and **Cape Kórakas**, the last one being especially lovely. But a second road west of Kranídi that leads to **Kiláda** (Κοιλάδα) is the one for seafood-lovers. Kiláda is that *ava rara*, an unspoiled fishing village. Although the phrase itself is often the kiss of death, Kiláda has two things going for it: terrible beaches, and the fact that it really is a professional fishing village, full of no-nonsense boats, and of everyone either catching fish or selling them at the restaurants that line the seaside. So tuck in (and keep it under your hat).

This little bay may be one of the oldest fishing holes in creation, too. Visible from Kiláda's esplanade is the gaping maw of the huge **Frachthi Cave** (Σπηλιά Φραγχθι), where the oldest skeleton yet found in Greece (8000 BC) was unearthed. The cave is an awesome sight and should have you arranging a ride over with a fisherman, or following the dirt road around the bay, or taking the road to it just south of **Foúrni** on the main road. Get as close as you can, take a torch and a buddy and walk the last bit. There is a water source inside the cave, and lots of bats. The cave, inhabited from the Mesolithic to Neolithic eras, has proved of fundamental importance in dating other sites in the Mediterranean and Europe, but nothing very old remains inside. Equally little remains of the Mycenaean settlement of Masis, which once stood nearby.

After Foúrni, the main road ascends towards **Dídyma**, a village off to the right of the road. Your eye, however, will be drawn to the left, where the flank of the mountain is scarred by a startling enormous **hole**. Actually there are two holes. The sign pointing to the access road calls them *spiliá* (caves). The local story is that they are craters left by meteors, although geologists say they are karstic sinkholes. Access to the smaller one, measuring 80m in diameter, is by way of a subterranean passage (signposted Ag. Geórgios), leading down to a natural ledge that supports two little 15th-century churches, apparently built to encourage God to keep the stars in the sky where they belong. The wilder second one, a few minutes' walk up the slope, measures 90m. Once past the holes, the road climbs into a saddle of 3,678ft **Mount Dídyma**, affording big views over the Argolic Gulf; even bigger views await if you take the road to the right that zigzags 10km up to the church on the summit.

North of Dídyma, there's a turn-off after 14km for **Peleí** (Πελεή) – an unpaved road that continues with more grand views down to the coast east of Naúplio. If you wait another 6km, there's a paved but less scenic road from **Neochóri** that does the same thing.

Arcadía

In spite of possessing a familiar name, Arcadía, along with Achaía, is one of the best-kept secrets of the Peloponnese, a place that seemed ancient even in ancient times, that defies not a few Greek stereotypes and gets under your skin in mysterious ways. Lacking big-league attractions, it is full of sublime minor ones, where the getting there is often half the fun. Most visitors making the circuit around the Peloponnese scarcely set foot in it, although in the past few years, with the new highway to Trípolis, Greeks in the know have made it a favourite weekend bolt hole. Now it can be hard to find room at the inn on a Friday night.

13

Don't miss

See map overleaf

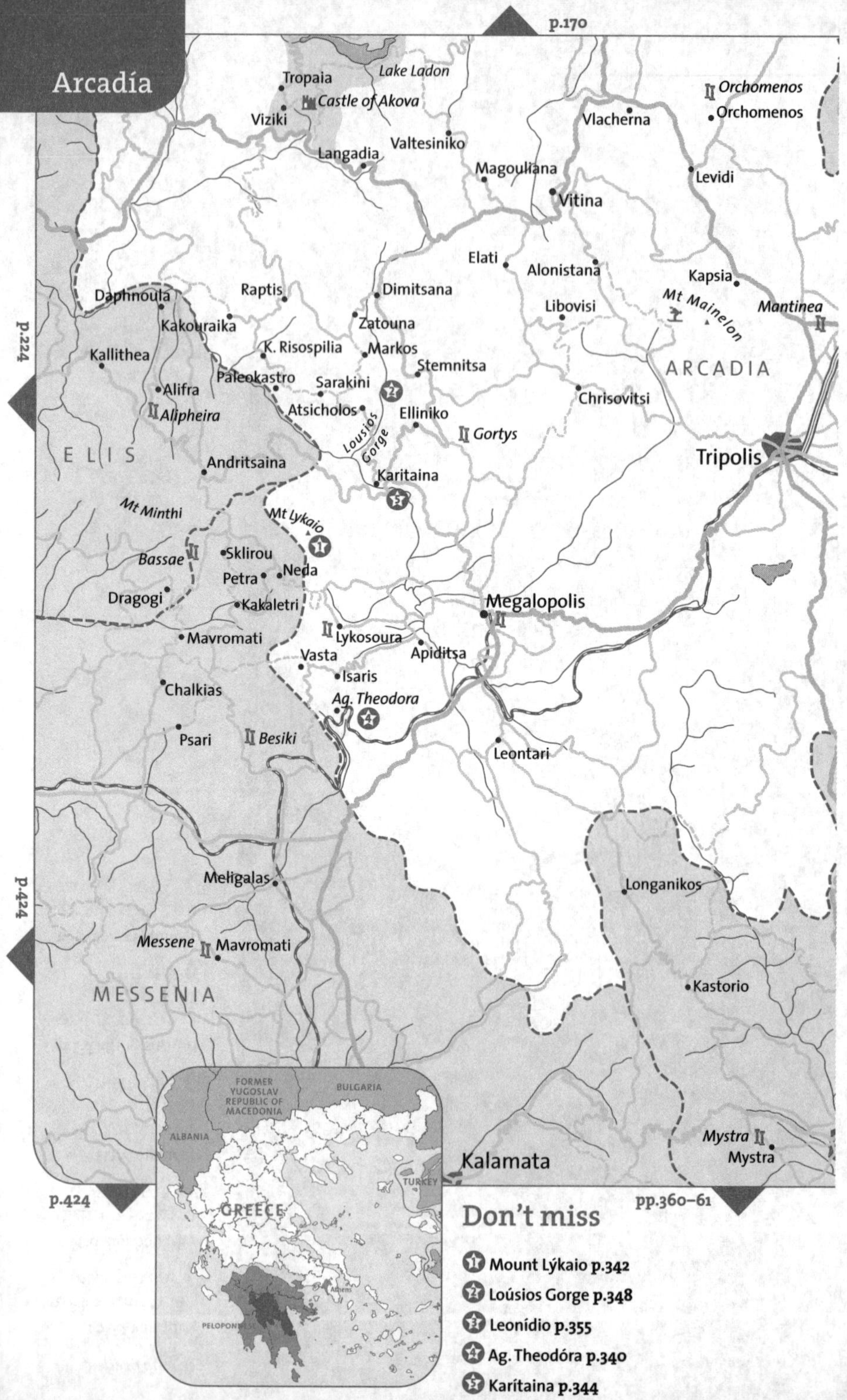

Arcadía
p.170
p.224
p.424
p.424
pp.360–61
Lake Ladon
Tropaia
Castle of Akova
Viziki
Langadia
Valtesiniko
Vlacherna
Orchomenos
Orchomenos
Levidi
Magouliana
Vitina
Elati
Alonistana
Kapsia
Mt Mainelon
Mantinea
Libovisi
ARCADIA
Raptis
Dimitsana
Daphnoula
Kakouraika
Zatouna
K. Risospilia
Markos
Kallithea
Stemnitsa
Paleokastro
Sarakini
Alifra
Alipheira
Atsicholos
Elliniko
Chrisovitsi
Lousios Gorge
Gortys
Tripolis
ELIS
Andritsaina
Karitaina
Mt Minthi
Mt Lykaio
Bassae
Sklirou
Petra
Neda
Dragogi
Kakaletri
Megalopolis
Mavromati
Lykosoura
Apiditsa
Vasta
Isaris
Chalkias
Ag. Theodora
Psari
Besiki
Leontari
Meligalas
Longanikos
Messene
Mavromati
MESSENIA
Kastorio
FORMER YUGOSLAV REPUBLIC OF MACEDONIA
BULGARIA
ALBANIA
GREECE
TURKEY
Athens
Mystra
Mystra
Kalamata
Don't miss
1 Mount Lýkaio p.342
2 Loúsios Gorge p.348
3 Leonídio p.355
4 Ag. Theodóra p.340
5 Karítaina p.344

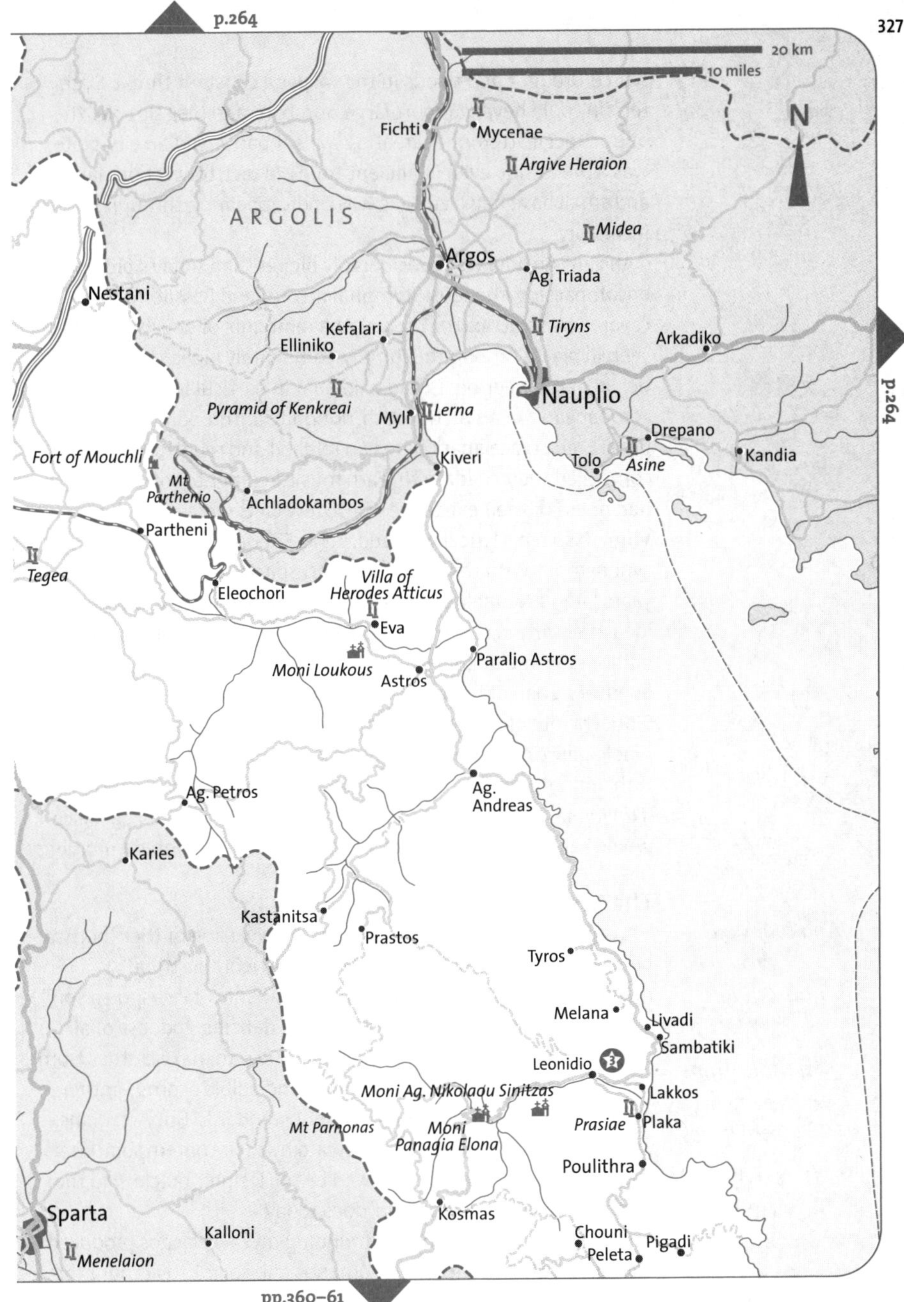

Yet Arcadía can look forbidding, even dreary, from the highway. With the exception of the eastern coastal strip of Kynouría (a modern add-on), the province is a combination of wild forested mountains scored by rivers and deep gorges, and flat, sometimes featureless, alpine valleys drained by sink holes. Arable land is scarce, drought and floods in the valleys a constant threat. Such terrain could never support large numbers, and Megalopolis, the one artificial attempt at creating a great pan-Arcadian city-state, was a mega-flop even in ancient times. In fact, towns both large and small have had a curious way of disappearing throughout its history.

Ancient Arcadía was considerably bigger than today's province, encompassing Pheneós, Stymphalía, Lousí and Bassae. Mostly covered by scrub and oak forest, the remnants of which can still be seen in places among the Johnny-come-lately pines, it was once rich in game, deer, bears and wild boar in particular – suitable company for Arcadía's uncouth, not quite anthropomorphized gods. Ever a place apart, here Pan reigned and rough shepherds compelled their children to learn music in order to soften the harshness of their existence. These few facts were enough for Virgil to spin his lyrical web and, in his *Eclogues*, Arcadía became synonymous with the idealized, gentle pastoral life. Some 1,500 years later, a Neapolitan poet, Jacopo Sannazaro, revived Virgil's idea in his *Arcadia*, a Renaissance bestseller that went through 66 editions; his melancholy hero inspired Shakespeare's Jaques, Spenser's Colin Clout and other affable rural misfits, while Sir Philip Sidney wrote of eclogue-singing shepherds in his *Arcadia*. The whole genre of rural idylls struck a powerful chord in France in the 18th and 19th centuries, all the way down to Mallarmé's *Après-midi d'un faune*. But the real Arcadía is far more stunning and, as Alice would say, curiouser, than Poussin's and Claude's painted imitations.

The Strange History of Arcadía

And black earth produced god-equalling Pelasgos

in mountains with long hair of tall trees

that a mortal race might come to be.

Asios of Samos (7th or 6th century BC)

Arcadía is so old that the Arcadians' own version of their 'born before the moon' origins may well reflect Neolithic tribal memories. They claimed to be the descendants of Pelasgos, a son either of Mother Earth or Eurynome, the dancing goddess of all creation. Pelasgos taught the Arcadians how to make clothes from sheep skins, to build rude huts and to find edible acorns – rather modest achievements, even by ancient standards. But Arcadians would always be considered backward by their contemporaries. The name 'acorn-eaters', bestowed by the Delphic oracle, had the same connotation as 'hayseed' does today.

In the grand tradition of the 'founding myth', Pelasgos produced enough sons (Mantineos, Orchomenos and so on), to account for pretty well all ancient Arcadía's cities. His daughter Kallisto was impregnated by Zeus, turned into a bear by jealous Hera and promptly killed by Artemis. As she lay dying, Kallisto produced a son, Arkos, thus explaining the name Arcadía to everyone's satisfaction. Kallisto was rewarded for her starring role by being made into a constellation – the Great Bear, while Arkos became the

Little Bear. Another of Pelasgos' offspring, Lykaion, added a new cultural element when he introduced human sacrifice on Mount Lýkaio (*see* pp.342–3).

While not ignoring the Olympian gods, primitive Arcadía clung to earlier local cults and gods long after they had evolved into more sophisticated, rationalized entities elsewhere. The details of Arcadian lore have all of the weirdness and fascination of stories recounted around an evening camp fire: werewolves on Mount Lýkaio, the statue of a rapist set up near Orchomenos, the sea rising at landlocked Mantinea, Olympian Demeter sporting a horse head in Figalía. Taken together, even the unflappable Pausanias lost his cool: 'Now that I have reached Arcadía, I have decided to treat [these stories] from the point of view that [they] told their stories in riddles and not out of stupidity.' Nonetheless, as a religion junkie, he was hooked by the quirks and described them in loving detail. Goat-legged Pan, amoral and only half-human, more a force of nature than a benevolent deity, could only have been conceived in Arcadía, and set its tone and tune.

There was a large Mycenaean presence in Arcadía and, significantly, their culture didn't disappear as abruptly after 1100 BC as it did on the coast. Whether the torch was held by the natives or by refugees from the coastal cities, or both, is anybody's guess. What is a fact is that traces of the Mycenaean language found in the oldest written Arcadian dialect made John Chadwick and Michael Ventris realize that Linear B (*see* pp.454–6) must indeed be Greek.

In historical times Arcadian cities were never powerhouses. More often than not they were pawns in the rivalries of the likes of Sparta and Athens. The lack of usable land (and perhaps the independent highland spirit) constantly pitted local settlement against local settlement in wars that benefited no one in the long run. Thebes and Macedonia occupied Arcadía, partly to counter Sparta. Rome arrived and erected its usual decorations; the barbarians came and caused their usual destruction. The Franks built castles, the Turks took them away, and the wild, rugged area of Gortynía came into its own as a base of Greek resistance.

Orientation: Exploring Arcadía

Upland Arcadía divides itself naturally into three main areas: Trípolis and its plain, Megalopolis and surroundings, and Gortynía; plus there is also the east coast.

Improvements in roads and accommodation make exploration of Arcadía easier than ever. The new highway and the Artemísion tunnel have cut the Athens–Trípolis journey to 2½ hours. The train is more dramatic but takes twice as long. Travel by public transport is possible but requires careful planning to avoid being stranded. Distances are not great, but they can seem much longer because of the twisting roads and frequent stops while shepherds clear the way of sheep or goats. Mules or horses would be the perfect way to travel the mountains, but so far no entrepreneur has thought of it. They should, though, because even today Zeus the Rainmaker asserts himself by periodically sending several kilometres of the road engineers' best efforts sliding down the mountain, just to show who's still boss here.

In this last period, Arcadía had a large population. The plain of Trípolis became the Turkish administrative capital of the Peloponnese, the large mountain villages filled with freer spirits whom the Turks were content to leave more or less alone, and some even smaller villages housed entire clans of klephts or freedom-fighters whom the Turks never did find. After the revolution, rural Arcadía was left to its own devices and has generally suffered a slow but steady decline in population, losing people either to bigger Greek cities or to the United States.

Trípolis

Smack in the heart of the Peloponnese and home to 22,000, Trípolis (Τρίπολη) is Arcadía's capital and its farming and industrial heavyweight, producing textiles, building materials and leather products. They say its climate is one of the worst in Greece, too hot in summer, too cold and rainy in winter, and those are the residents talking! Listening to the way they go on about their upland city you would think they lived in Winnipeg or Mongolia, and not a mere 45km from the blue Aegean. Like most provincial capitals, it's a transportation hub, only Trípolis takes this a step further – the three squares in the centre are giant traffic roundabouts, with major roads radiating out in every direction. This makes passing through an adventure as well as something of a necessity. One gets the feeling that the Tripolisiótes on their lonely plain rather enjoy compelling everyone travelling across the Peloponnese to run the gauntlet. This is a town without suburbs, a dense, concentrated hive; and it can feel like New York, too, after you've spent a week in the wilds of Arcadía. The climate is not that bad.

History

Trípolis' history is short and bleak. It was the small village of Droboglitsa when the Turks took over in the 1700s and made it the home of the Pasha of the Morea. They renamed it Tripolitsá, Three Cities, for the three ancient cities of Mantinea, Tegea and Pallantio – whose stones went into its building. By the late 18th century, Trípolis had 10,000 people, three quarters of whom were Greek, most of them involved in business, some of them very prosperous. When Veli Pasha arrived in 1807 with 12,000 Albanian and Turkish soldiers it became the biggest Turkish stronghold on the Peloponnese. That made it a prime target for Kolokotrónis (*see* pp.344–5) when the War of Independence broke out. He gathered his forces, attacked, and took the town in 1821. Over 10,000 people sheltering behind or defending its walls were slaughtered in the subsequent three-day orgy of looting, torturing and slave-taking

Getting to and around Trípolis

Trípolis' **Arcadías bus station, t** 271 022 2560, at 50 Naúplio St, offers the following connections: Athens, 17 daily; Megalópolis 9; Pýrgos 2, Andrítsaina 2. This station also serves Stemnítsa and Dimitsána twice a day but not on weekends, Vitína several times a day, Alonístaina twice, and Karítaina (bottom of the castle hill only) twice. For Messénia and Laconía, the **KTEL bus station, t** 271 024 2086, is 400m east of the Arcadías station, opposite the train station. Buses are as follows: Sparta, 8 daily; Kalamáta, 12 daily; Pýlos, 5 daily.

Local buses from Plateía Áreos leave every hour to Mantinea and Tegéa.

The **train station, t** 271 024 1213, is 400m east of Plateía Kolokotrónis. Expect better connections with Árgos and Corinth to the north and Kyparissía–Kalamáta to the south thanks to the new, faster rail line just being completed at time of writing. For up-to--date information: **t** 1110 or *www.ose.gr*.

All **roads** lead to and out of the centre of Trípolis, but once you get there, expect some confusion and next-to-impossible parking.

---

that in those days passed as army pay. Kolokotrónis noted in his memoirs that when he entered Trípolis and crossed it from wall to wall, his horse's hooves never touched the ground, so thick were the layers of bodies. The plunder financed the war – one reason for Kolokotrónis' success and independence is that he invested his share wisely, in the banks of the then British Ionian islands. The Turkish reprisal, a few months later, was the massacre of 25,000 Greeks on Chíos, and the enslavement of 47,000 more. Ibrahim Pasha got Trípolis back in 1825 and started his own reign of terror. When he was driven out, he destroyed the town, or what was left of it. Not an inch of its old walls stands today.

The Town and its Museum

The Trípolis that rose out of the blood and ashes is a lively place and one full of young people, thanks to Greece's largest military training base. The shopping magnet for the outlying villages, it has some lovely squares, excellent restaurants and two or three parks, including an extensive pine forest on the west side of town. Its drab building block architecture won't win any prizes, but the town museum designed by Ziller, the courthouse and the Malliaropoúlio theatre are three lovely neoclassical exceptions to the rule.

A magnificent **statue of Kolokotrónis** in his famous Frankish helmet lords it over **Plateía Áreos**. They say Kolokotrónis was so sensitive about his modest stature that he went everywhere on horseback, even up to the porch of the church on Sundays. That may be a cheap shot, but he has certainly ridden into history; all of his statues do seem to be equestrian.

Archaeological Museum
6 Evangestrías St, between Kolokotrónis and Ag. Basileíou Squares, ***t*** *271 024 2148; open Tues–Sun 8.30–2.30; adm*

Trípolis' very under-rated **Archaeological Museum** displays finds from all over Arcadía, neatly arranged by era from the prehistoric to the Roman, with plenty of helpful pictures showing the areas of the finds (something that more museums should do). It does not have a guide book, but it does list the general contents of each numbered room in the foyer with clear descriptions in English. When they get around to numbering the rooms (and they promise they will), the system will work perfectly.

There are wonderful finds from prehistoric Arcadía. Two clay storage jars are unique to this museum. One of them is about a yard high, the other slightly smaller, each with four handles. They are surprisingly sophisticated, with attractive ripple-like patterns in the clay. Those 'acorn-eaters' obviously had enough taste to enjoy artistic, not just utilitarian, creations. Along with Stone Age tools, there is a choice array of those tasty little Neolithic fertility figurines or 'Venuses' so typical of the era.

The Mycenaean pottery, found in the tombs at Paleókastro on the Alphíos river, is exceptional. In the main floor room, notice especially the fair-sized pot from tomb 7 with braided handles, fish and birds, and every kind of Mycenaean 'filler' design from wavy to straight lines and checkerboard squares. And, this being Arcadía, some of these finds raise a lot of questions about the Greek 'dark age'. For example, look at the smallish round-lidded pot from tomb 22 in the same room, adorned exclusively with a pattern of lines and weaving type motifs, that looks almost completely Geometric, but is Mycenaean. And how about those big fibulas that so many books said that Dorians introduced and Mycenaeans never wore? Apparently they did in Arcadía – perhaps because, here in the mountains, cloaks were of necessity heavier? This museum suggests a seamless continuity of habitation in Arcadía and gently reminds us that the more we learn about Greek history, the less we know.

In the room to the far right of the entrance, called 'Arcadian sanctuaries', are many of the votive offerings found in Arcadian shrines. They are small, sympathetic, and give some idea of the hope and devotion evoked by these shrines. There's a room of Roman artefacts, too, many hailing from Herodes Atticus' villa at Eva, near Ástros.

ⓘ Trípolis >>
13 Demitrakopoúlou near Plateía Áreos, **t** *271 023 1844, kenkalprax@tri.forthnet.gr; open Mon–Fri 8.30–12.30; also see www.arcadia.ceid.upatras.gr/arkadia for an archaeological site map, articles on the area's wines and more*

Trípolis Festivals

Trípolis celebrates its **Independence from the Turks** on 23 September, and is famous for its **Easter celebration** in Plateía Áreos.

Shopping in Trípolis

While in Trípolis, stock up on some of the fine Arcadian **wines**. This is one of the Peloponnese's finest growing areas, home to vineyards of the well-known Cambas label but also some terrific smaller ones such as the Tsélepos estate near Tegea (*see* p.60). Try their Mantinía, an excellent white wine made from aromatic *moschofílero* grapes.

Where to Stay and Eat in and around Trípolis

Trípolis ✉ 22100

Trípolis' hotels are open all year and most are either recently renovated or in the process. This is quite a change and means there is no budget hotel in town. The tourist office they can help you find rooms in Arcadía's villages.

Mainalon Resort, Plateía Áreos, **t** 271 023 0300, *www.mainalonhotel.gr* (€€€€/€€€€). On the pedestrianized main square, this old standby has undergone such a facelift that it's now listed as one of Greece's top 150 hotels, complete with velvet and chandeliers. There's parking out back.

★ Climataria Piterou >>

★ Mélathron >>

Anaktorikon, 48 Konstantínou, **t** 271 022 5545, *anaktorikon@aias.gr* (€€/€€). Adequate, with the usual mod cons, and easy parking, but noisy late-night bar next door.

Galaxías, Plateía Ag. Vassilíou, **t** 271 022 5195 (€€/€€). Currently the cheapest hotel in town.

Kápsia ✉ 22100

Archondikó Kaltezióti, **t** 271 023 5822, *www.kaltezioti.gr* (€€€€€/€€€€). Handsome stone hotel complex in a lovely mountain setting, with a large outdoor pool and gym. Its summer prices compete with Trípolis' hotels. Handy for the ski area and Kápsia Caves too.

Levídi ✉ 22002

Anatolí, **t** 279 602 2123 (€€/€). A perfectly adequate small hotel on the southern outskirts. The six rooms have tiny kitchens. Easy parking.

Eating Out in Trípolis

The Tripolisiótes do eat and drink well. Deligiánni Street, one block south of Plateía Áreos, has been closed to traffic and is the favourite local watering hole.

Climataria Piterou, 11a Kalávriton, **t** 271 022 2058. Serves wonderful pork with celery and other delicious dishes.

Dionyssos Tavern, next door, **t** 271 022 7268. The competition keeps both of them on their toes. Famous for casserole dishes.

Pequéro, Plateía Áreos, **t** 271 023 7413. A recent addition with a Spanish name, but its Greek cuisine is popular with local gourmands and visitors alike.

Locanda, Ag. Konstantínou, **t** 271 022 2678. Good *mezédes*, a fireplace, and a family atmosphere.

Mélathron (Μέλαθρον), 2km north on the Levídi highway, **t** 271 024 2148. A well-run complex, its unprepossessing location belying its upscale amenities. Dine around a kidney-shaped pool, where patrons can take a dip (*small fee*). Delicious specialities like wild boar or chicken with pasta.

Around Trípolis: The Flood Plain and Water Wars

Ancient Tegea, **Mantinea** and **Orchomenos** occupy the same smallish flood plain, partially indented by low, barren hills. Dry and brown in summer, it was likened by one writer to a lunar landscape, an effect heightened by the scarcity of buildings. While not wholly inaccurate, it doesn't do the area's austere beauty justice, and ignores its transformation into an emerald bog every spring. The shepherds and farmers of these cities shared the same hills, had the same trying difficulties with flooding and drought, and unfortunately the same obsession to destroy each other whenever possible. Their very proximity, with no more than 35km between them, in the relative isolation of Arcadía, makes the absurdity of Greek city-state rivalry especially poignant. Low-lying Mantinea and Tegea would dam the others' river exits in order to flood their cities and grazing lands. Since most buildings were of mud brick, it was an unedifying spectacle. No wonder the ruins of these three cities are not extensive. Still, they are the busiest archaeological sites in Arcadía, visited mainly by earnest tourists who want a dose of 'culture' provided that it lies close enough to a main road.

Do visit the **Kápsia Caves**, a complex just getting ready to open as a show cave at the time of writing. Reckoned to be one of Greece's best, it has a 'Hall of Wonders' measuring 200ft by 230ft, with a ceiling up to 33ft high. Arcadía may have been water-starved, but swallow (or sink) holes like this one, and their surrounding tunnels, have left spectacular evidence of aeons of activity by underground river systems.

As a footnote, there was a fourth city on the flood plain, **Pallantion**, just south of Trípolis. It was quarried so extensively in the building of Trípolis that only its name has survived, tacked on to a modern village. But few names can claim a similar legacy, for this was the birthplace of the mysterious King Evander, son of Hermes and an Arcadian nymph, who founded a colony called Palatine on a hill overlooking the Tiber, a generation after the Trojan War; if true, Pallantion was the origin of our word 'palace.' The Roman emperors, at least, believed in the connection, and accorded Pallantion privileges because of it.

Mantinea: The Case of the Disappearing City

Mantinea
always open

Mantinea lies 12km due north of Trípolis off the Levídi road; the church of **Ag. Foteiní** (1978), a wonderful hotchpotch of titbits from ancient Mantinea, marks the spot. A Minoan-Classical-Byzantine ratatouille of a building, it is right opposite the ancient *agora*. The church is dedicated to 'the Virgin, the Muses and Beethoven' and many Greeks dislike it, claiming that it is a 'folly' in every way and a disgrace to Orthodoxy. That, of course, merely puts Ag. Foteiní and its architect, Konstantínos Pappatheodórou, in the grand Arcadian tradition.

According to Homer, Mantinea sent warriors to Troy. Excavations on **Gourtsoúli**, the rounded low hill just north of the theatre, indicate an **acropolis** inhabited from the Geometric until the Classical period. During the Persian wars, Mantinea fought alongside Sparta, but, like all of Sparta's subject cities, it tried to get out from under the big thumb whenever the coast looked reasonably clear. It took its chances with Athens during the Peloponnesian War, and in 418 BC Sparta and Athens fought in a decisive battle so close to Mantinea that it has gone down in history as the First Battle of Mantinea. Athens (and Mantinea) lost. By this time, Mantinea had moved on to the flat plain where its ruins now lie, by the then meandering Ophis (Snake) river, and surrounded itself with high, mud-brick walls – another bad decision, but that wasn't obvious until 385 BC when they rebelled against Sparta again. The Spartans trooped up, camped on high ground near the city, surveyed the situation and for once used their imagination instead of their famous phalanx. King Agesipolis of Sparta simply dammed up the natural outflow of the Ophis, waited for the water to rise, and literally dissolved the city's defences. He then dispersed the citizens into small villages. The Mantineans regrouped and raised their mud-brick walls again after the Battle of Leuktra (371 BC) with the blessing of their new patron Epaminondas of Thebes, but this time they prudently built the lower courses with stone. These walls were elliptical, about 4km in circumference, and had 122 towers and 10 gates. Mantinea, whose rulers were doggedly thick, turned against Thebes just in time to be soundly trounced by Epaminondas in 362 BC in the Second Battle of Mantinea. In 223 BC the Macedonians took over and dissolved the city – politically this time. Built up again by the Romans in AD 125, it became a centre for the worship of Hadrian's deified boyfriend Antinous. Pausanias remarked that 'the Emperor Hadrian was extraordinarily enthusiastic about him'. The Mantineans equated his worship with Dionysos. Those were the days...

Poseidon and the Sea at Mantinea

Like all Greek cities, Mantinea was full of shrines. One, the famous temple to Horse Poseidon, offers no ruins to speak of, but still says a lot about Arcadian religion. It was just south of the walls, but close enough to be regarded as part of the city. Many archaeologists place it at present-day Miliá. Entrance was strictly forbidden, or *avaton*. A simple length of wool was tied across the entrance to remind the faithful, and usually that was enough. But when one Aipytos crossed its threshold he was immediately struck blind by a wave from the sea, and died on the spot. Now, off-limits shrines were fairly common in ancient Greece, but that sea wave and even Poseidon himself seem just a tad out of place on this land-locked plain.

One theory obtains that Poseidon was an earlier all-powerful Arcadian god who was supplanted by the cult of Zeus, then more or less relegated to the position of a sea god in the Homeric Olympian pantheon, a watered-down version of his former self, if you like. This theory of former glory fits in well with the many legends about Poseidon's loss of contests for supremacy with other gods or goddesses – Athena in Athens and Hera in Argos come to mind. It also might explain his non-aquatic symbol – the horse, which is the equivalent in symbolic potency to Zeus' bull. Even as an Olympian, Poseidon controlled earthquakes and rivers, very important powers where earthquakes could and did alter drainage, and rivers determined wealth. Whatever the reason, in water-fixated Arcadía, which either had too much or not enough, he never lost his supremacy and remained a very important deity.

With Poseidon now firmly in place in Arcadía, the sea-rising at Mantinea should not be hard to swallow as simply a miracle. But it may have a basis as an actual phenomenon. In March 1999, after heavy rains and snow, the slightly raised highway ran through a completely marine landscape for miles around Nestáni and the Artemísion tunnel. Modern drainage techniques make this an unusual occurrence now, but it was not rare in ancient times. A vast expanse of water like this may have given rise to the story that Poseidon could raise the sea on to alpine valleys at will, especially since the resulting water was not good to drink.

Hadrian was so taken with this Temple to Poseidon, a ruin by the time he saw it, that he built a new temple around it. In honour of the old rule, he assigned guards to ensure that no workmen ever so much as peeked into the old sanctuary as they built. Was this a political manoeuvre to gain favour from the locals as he introduced his dubious new cult to Antinous, was it genuine respect, or perhaps a bit of both?

The Ruins

Mantinea is one of the oldest excavated sites in Greece, dug up in 1887–8 by Fougères, who used Pausanias and the stunted growth of wild hashish as his guides. What civic buildings have been brought to light are right in the middle of the present-day farming community. The low hump of the **theatre** is the most prominent ruin, with many of the large polygonal stones of the ***cavea*** in place as well as two stairs on its outer circumference. The two identical **temples** mouldering directly in front, beyond the 'stage', are Roman. Immediately to their south is a ruined **Temple to Hera**, and just to their north is the **Hero's Shrine to Podares**, a monument that shows a certain greatness of soul since he was their leader in the *losing* battle against Thebes in 362 BC. The entire area in front of the theatre is the **Agora**, which still has traces of paved roads that crossed it, and of the **Bouleuterion** on its south side and colonnades on its north. This *agora*, sparse though the ruins are, gives an idea of what a mixed conglomeration of shrines and buildings could rub shoulders in a small area. Mentally add a score of plaques, statues, memorials, shops and chattering groups of Mantineans plotting their next blunder and you get the picture. Many stones from the lower courses of the city's **walls** can be found in surrounding fields.

Orchomenos

The small valley of Orchomenos, lying in moody Wild West scenery between Levídi and Vlachérna, is reached from the Trípolis–Pátras highway. Orchomenos never moved entirely onto its frequently flooded plain, and so has bequeathed some ruins to posterity. Founded by its namesake, an offspring of Lykaion, it was called 'rich in sheep' by Homer, and there are still quite a few kicking around. In its Mycenaean heyday, it controlled a very large area. In the Classical period, Orchomenos often made alliances with Sparta or Athens merely to spite arch rival Mantinea. In the Roman age it still minted its own coins. The small **acropolis** on a hill overlooking the plain is worth a visit for the view from the small **theatre**. There are two **temples**, to Apollo and to Artemis, higher up, plus a ***bouleuterion*** with a *stoa* and a cistern.

The small defile to the east has **Venetian watch towers** guarding the ancient and medieval road to Pheneós, now passable only by four-by-fours, mules and hikers. It was on this road that Pausanias saw the monument to Aristokrates, who had raped the virgin priestess of Singing Artemis. Not only were monuments awarded for this, but the act itself seems to have been considered so natural that the Orchomeniótes decided to reduce the odds on a repetition by switching the employment prerequisites: young virgins were replaced by old married women well past their prime. The priests at Delphi made a similar change with their Pythia.

Tegea

Tegea, 7km south of Trípolis on the Sparta road, was probably a conglomerate of villages rather than a city. Famous in the ancient world for its dauntless warriors, Tegea considered itself especially favoured by the goddess Athena and built a splendid temple in her honour. One story goes that during the 600s BC, when the Tegeans were proving less than enthusiastic allies, the Spartan army came marching north to put things right. In a crude but typically Spartan gesture, they came bearing the chains they intended to use to truss up the rebellious Tegeans and drag them home as slaves. With Athena's help, of course, the Tegeans completely routed the Spartans in the 'Battle of the Fetters'. The chains were triumphantly hung up in her temple alongside a tooth from the Caledonian boar. Sparta's humiliating defeat taught her a lesson, and she tried a subtler tactic and made pacts instead, with herself, naturally, as *hegemon* or leader (Sparta would defend their ally if attacked, and their ally would contribute troops to Sparta's wars and help them suppress the z). Even Athena couldn't prevent Tegea from being a vassal state of Sparta by 560 BC. The Tegeans tried to throw off the Spartan yoke on various occasions, didn't succeed, then astutely decided to side with them in the Peloponnesian War, unlike Mantinea.

After Leuktra in 371 BC, Tegea joined the Arcadian League and stayed loyal to Thebes in 362 BC, again unlike Mantinea. It flourished under the Romans, and was destroyed by Alaric in the 5th century. The city sank into oblivion until 1209 when it was made made a barony by the Franks and reborn as Nikli, a name we will encounter again in the Máni (*see* p.400).

The Ruins

Ancient Tegea covered a large area, and only a small part has been excavated. What civic buildings have been brought to light are in the middle of a workaday farming community which probably in many ways resembles the ancient city. The famous **Temple of Athena Alea**, whose substructure is complete, is not far from the museum. Built in 370 BC and decorated by the great Skopas, it replaced an Archaic temple and was second in size in Greece only to the Temple of Zeus at Olympia. It must have been striking, with a Doric peristyle (six by 14 columns) and an internal colonnade of Corinthian half-columns with Ionic above, all made of marble from Dolianá to the southeast. The East Pediment depicted the Caledonian boar hunt and the virginal huntress Atalanta, who was a native of Tegea and made good in spite of the fact that her parents had exposed her as a baby because she was not a male. The West Pediment depicted the fight between Telephos and Achilles. Sadly, there is no sign of the chains, or the boar's tooth: Augustus took the mighty cuspid to Rome to punish Tegea for siding with Antony and Cleopatra.

Remnants of Tegea's **Agora** are to the west. The 2nd-century BC **theatre** is a 20-minute walk from the temple and somewhat difficult to see because the church of **Palaiá Episkopí** (built in 1888) was erected inside its *cavea*. This church replaced the earlier Byzantine chapel of Nikli and used some of its stones in its walls, as well as preserving its mosaic icons, still venerated today.

The Museum of Tegea and a Hmm on Herms

Museum of Tegea
t 271 055 6540; open Tues–Sun 8.30–3; adm

This newly expanded museum has marble **thrones** from the theatre, some of the ***acroteria*** from the Temple of Athena Alea and part of its altar, all pretty standard fare. But two sets of stone **herms**, each about two feet high, are unique to this museum. Both consist of stone columns stuck together, one set having human heads on each column, the other, mere triangular appendages. In the Classical period, herms were placed at crossroads all over the Greek world, but their usual form was a column with a human head and *membrum virile* that you could hang your hat on (or use to tempt vandals, in the infamous case of Alcibiades in Athens during the Peloponnesian War). Their function was prophylactic or protective, which is why they were also outside houses.

A speculative history of the god Hermes' development has him starting out as an upright stone road-marker, developing from that into a guardian of travellers, then simply into a guardian, and evolving from there into his role as messenger of the gods and deliverer of souls to Hades. He became the patron saint of merchants because he guarded them on their travels, hence the name Ermoú for the high street in virtually every Greek town today. While he was often anthropomorphized in the Classical period, Hermes never entirely shed his non-human form, and existed simultaneously as a stone column. In primitive Arcadía, though, where he originated, he kept his original form even longer than elsewhere.

The Megalópolis Valley

At intervals in its history, areas of the large Megalópolis valley would spontaneously catch fire because lignite deposits lie so close to the surface. It was only a matter of time before this bonanza would be exploited in power-starved Greece. Two huge power plants have made 'Megalópolis blossom on its fertile plain',

Getting to and around the Megalópolis Valley

Megalópolis' KTEL **bus** station, **t** 279 102 2238, one block from the main *plateía*, serves Trípolis (nine daily); Kalamáta (several daily); Andrítsaina (two daily). A daily local bus goes into the villages of Karítaina and Lykósoura; Vásta just gets one on Fridays. Happily, the taxis congregate around in the main *plateía*.

---

according to the rosy view of the National Tourist Organization. As you wind up or down a beautiful road in the surrounding hills, you'll catch sight of these ugly fire-breathing behemoths at every turn. They rule the valley, digging huge pits to fuel themselves, and spewing out pollution at Athenian levels that stays when the wind doesn't blow. But all those air-conditioned beach hotels would be sad without them.

Under the smoke stacks, **modern Megalópolis** (Μεγαλόπολη) is a tiny, unassuming company town with a quiet, lazy, nothing-much-ever-happens-here atmosphere; to sit in its central *plateía* is to take a time machine back to the 1960s. The most exciting annual event is the setting up of three huge red plastic eggs with yellow chicks every Easter.

Ancient Megalopolis

After the Theban general Epaminondas defeated Sparta at Leuktra in 371 BC, he founded two new cities, Messene and Megalopolis, both intended to act as bulwarks against future Spartan aggression. Megalopolis was to be a capital for the newly formed Pan-Arcadian League and, to populate this ancient Brasilia, Epaminondas simply emptied 38 small Arcadian cities. Anyone reluctant to move was either dragged there or killed, an inauspicious start for the 'Great City' and perhaps the reason why the League lasted only a few years, and why many of its citizens secretly preferred Sparta, which had at least left them slaves in their own cities. Many of these reluctant Megalopolites would later support the Macedonian army when it invaded.

In spite of a wholesale introduction of local cult statues and shrines, which made visiting the city so fascinating for Pausanias, its inhabitants continually slipped off home whenever possible, thus turning the Great City into a 'Great Desert', as Strabo wittily observed. Briefly repopulated in Roman times, Megalopolis then sank into oblivion, never really famous for much except its size. The signposted **ruins** lie on both banks of the Hellisón river, 1km north of town. The main attraction is the **theatre**, the largest in Greece, seating 21,000. Built in the 4th century, it had 59 rows of seats divided by 10 aisles and an orchestra 99ft in diameter, although the only spectacle you're likely to see from the *cavea* is the belching saga of the power plants. Right in front of the theatre are the ruins of the square **Bouleuterion** of the Pan-Arcadian League, a nice symbolic reminder of the shambles of the league itself. Across the river, in the fields, are scanty remains of the city, as yet unexcavated in any major way.

Around Megalópolis

Megalópolis is not *quite* as bad as it first looks, and it can be a useful base for the fascinating remains of ancient Lykósoura as well as two of the Peloponnese's strangest shrines: Ag. Theodóra and the summit of Mount Lýkaio itself. These, along with the castle of Karítaina to the northwest, are not visited as much as they deserve. The 2007 fires have devastated a wide swath of forest and scrub in the hills west of town but not the actual sites described below.

Collecting unusual Greek shrines like these has a lot of the charm of bird-watching or rock-climbing – the goal gives you a great excuse to get out into nature. The journey to these shines offers lovely and quite different scenery. While it is just possible to rush down to Ag. Theodóra and then reverse to take in the other two in a single day, it would not be advisable unless you just want to say you did it. But Lykósoura and Mount Lýkaio are feasible in a one-day duet. Lunch possibilities are limited, so pack a picnic. The starting point for all three is the village of **Apidítsa** (Απιδίτσα), 8km south of Megalópolis on the Kalamáta road.

Ag. Theodóra: the Saint who Turned into a Church

Ag. Theodóra

Apidítsa has a sign for Ag. Theodóra. Go 8km or so up to **Ísaris** (Σσαρης), where the 2,788ft height provides a panoramic view of the Arcadian mountains and Taíyetos; then a twisty little road winds 6–7km down from **Vásta** (Βάστας) through an isolated forest to the church beside the river. The large car park and kiosks touting church bric-a-brac come as a surprise. An even bigger jolt awaits when you notice that the tiny stone 10th-century church of Ag. Theodóra has no fewer than 17 large oak trees growing from its slate roof. Walking around the church, you'll see all these trees have only a single root, about as thick as your wrist, to the left of the entrance. The rest are all thin as hairs and have somehow threaded their way *inside* the church walls between the roof and ground to form the miraculous canopy.

Some claim that the origin of this miracle is the spring upon which the church was built, but the 'real' story began in the 9th century when each local family had to provide one son for a year to guard a nearby (now defunct) convent. Having no son nor the money to pay a substitute, Theodóra's parents dressed her as a man and sent her on guard duty. A young nun became pregnant, and was thrown into a guarded room until she revealed her lover's name. Only Theodóra showed her sisterly compassion. For this kindness she was accused of the crime and condemned. The nun, trying to protect her real lover, said nothing. Too ashamed to reveal her identity, Theodóra uttered only one prayer before she died: that her body become a church, that her flowing hair become trees and that her blood become a rushing river. When the horrified executioners realized their error, they immediately built this little church.

Lykósoura: the Oldest City in the World

Lykósoura
t 279 108 1344; ***site*** *open daily 8–2.30;* ***museum*** *is closed indefinitely for want of a guard*

For Lykósoura (Λυκόσουρα), head about 2km northwest of Apíditsa, and then turn left (west). The ruins and small museum are at the top of a short, steep road on the south edge of town. The sign is there, but small.

Arcadians claimed to be the oldest inhabitants of the Peloponnese, and ancient Lykosoura was touted as the oldest city in the entire world. It was so respected that, when the Thebans gathered all of the other Arcadian citizens to inhabit Megalopolis, only the Lykosouriótes were spared the ignominy of being forced to leave their homes. Goat-legged Pan had an early oracle here before Apollo took over the prophecy business, and as late as Roman times a flame was kept eternally lit in front of his shrine for old times' sake. By the Classical period, visitors (like so many today, in search of authenticity) thronged to the Mysteries celebrated at the Temple to the Mistress, or Despoina, Arcadía's answer to the Persephone legend. In this version, Demeter had turned herself into a mare in an attempt to escape Poseidon's advances, but he promptly turned himself into a stallion, and the result was the winged horse Arion and 'Despoina', the maid, whose real name only intitiates knew. The Mysteries probably were similar to those at Eleusis, with vegetative symbols, baskets of fruit and so on, but with the more theriomorphic, primitive undertone so dear to an Arcadian's heart. How else could all those small clay figurines with human bodies and animal heads found in Despoina's *megaron* be explained? What intrigued punters in the old days was a mirror hung on the wall by the temple's entrance, which blurred the reflections of those gazing into it but revealed the cult statues a treat. Even back then, it never hurt to give the folks a thrill and a story to tell back home. The ladies' dress code was inscribed in the *stoa* north of the temple: no provocative dress, no rings, no rich materials, no make up and no fancy hairdos. The only gold and silver allowed was that which was intended for donation to the sanctuary.

As you arrive, the **acropolis** covers the entire hill in front of you. To your right, the Temple of the Mistress and attendant buildings are underneath the museum. To your left, a path opposite the museum leads to other significant buildings including a bath and fountain that probably belonged to a hotel.

The **Temple of the Mistress**, built in 180 BC to replace an earlier, smaller 4th-century one, measures 70ft by 28ft. It had six Doric columns on a paved mosaic porch and three altars in front. On the south side an intriguing **'wall' of stepped stones** goes up the hill. First taken to be a retaining wall, the steps are now believed to have been seats for spectators, whose eyes would have been glued to the unusual small doorway built into the side of the temple – surely something significant must have manifested itself during the Mysteries to account for this departure in design. The cult statue of Demeter and the Maid seated on a throne, with Artemis-cum-hound to the left and Anytos, the Titan who raised the Maid, to the right, was carved by Damophon of Messene out of a single block of stone. If true, the temple must have been built around it; its total height was 19ft and it fitted into the temple with only 19 inches to spare at the back and very little on the sides. Parts of this intricate monument are in Athens, and some in the small, unopen **museum**. The remains of the **long *stoa*** are beside the temple, and on the hillside in front of the temple, going up to the museum level, stood the multi-levelled ***megaron*** of Despoina, where votive offerings were left. Many parts of the city walls are intact but buried in undergrowth; some sections can be seen from modern Lykósoura's main street, on the road to Lýkaio.

Mount Lýkaio: Haunt of Ancient Werewolves

Mount Lýkaio

Et in Arcadia Ego. As the expression goes, death exists, even in Arcadía. But even without stories of werewolves and human sacrifice as an incentive, the isolated top of Mount Lýkaio (Λύκαιο), or 'Wolf' Mountain, would be worth visiting. From Lykósoura, drive up past **Áno Kariés** (Υνω Καριές) to the top of the mountain. Much of the road is unpaved after Áno Kariés, but it is a good road. You can drive there, or it's about an hour's hike.

Think of the entire mountaintop as a shrine complex, albeit a sparsely built one. The setting itself inspired the worship. The stupendous view reveals at least a third of the Peloponnese on a clear day, giving the sensation of being on top of the world, and a slightly alien world at that. The dome-like summit, the traces of deserted terraced fields, stone walls and slate-grey huts, all combine to create an austere backdrop for a shrine that goes back to some of the earliest Greek rain-making rites. The Arcadians adamantly claimed that Zeus was born here, not in Crete, and appealed to him at all times, but especially during drought. Somewhere up here was a spring called Hagnos. The priest of Lykaion Zeus dipped an oak branch in it, a mist would arise, cover the mountaintop, and then it would rain – sympathetic magic, pure and simple, the imitation of the desired end.

Yet it was rumoured all through antiquity that human sacrifices were also offered on the altar to the rain god, a rite initiated by Lykaion, son of Pelasgos. Legend had it that, when a child was sacrificed, it changed into a wolf as its blood splashed on the altar. Zeus, according to more civilized Greeks, took umbrage at this, and turned Lykaion himself into a wolf and struck his house with lightning. This failed to get the message across, and, when Lykaion's sons brazenly offered Zeus a bowl of umble soup made from the guts of one of their brothers, he was so disgusted that he released too much rain – a flood, in fact, to kill off all humanity. But even these extreme measures failed to do the trick. Besides Deucalion and Pyrrha (the Greek Noah and his wife), a band of Parnassians survived the flood, migrated to Arcadía and, as soon as there was another drought, revived the wicked rites. (No one seemed to mind the fact that Zeus comes out in this attempt to reconcile different traditions as a deranged schizophrenic.) A system of sorts developed: a shepherd, chosen by lot, would eat the soup prepared from the human sacrifice and turn into a werewolf. If he didn't kill anyone, he would regain his human shape after eight years. One famous ex-werewolf, Damarchus, even went on after his eight-year stint to win the boxing event at the Olympics.

The **altar** in Classical times was flanked by two columns surmounted by golden eagles which faced east and the rising sun. The image seems more Hollywood than holy, but the two column bases and part of a column are still there to back up the story. Strange taboos surrounded this shrine. Part of it, no doubt the part struck by Zeus' lightning bolt, was fenced in by stones and no one was allowed to enter, at the risk of losing their shadow and dying within a year. Even animals wandering in lost their shadow.

Ascending from **Áno Kariés**, you come to a flat area containing the confusing ruins of a 4th-century ***stoa*** and small **hotel**, a **Temple to Pan**, a **stadium**, and the very obvious **hippodrome**; you may be inclined to think prizes should have been awarded just for getting here. The road then ascends above the hippodrome and divides. The left fork goes to the summit with the **altar** and ***temenos*** where a wrong move might cost you your shadow. Look for the ruins near the little **church of the Prophet Elijah** (the Christian version of the weather god). The other fork continues quite a way, to the very scarce remains of the Archaic **Temple of Parnassian Apollo**, located just north of the church of **Ag. Ioánnis**, which incorporates much of its ancient stones. The temple was also a weather shrine. They say a boar was sacrificed annually in Megalopolis and brought here to encourage the god to bring rain. Its bones and thighs were burned on the Altar of Apollo and the rest was cooked and eaten.

A dirt road between Áno Kariés and ancient Lykaio (look for the sign) leads 11km north to join the Andrítsaina–Karítaina road, 12km west of Karítaina. Try this one in summer only.

The Castle of Karítaina: 'the Toledo of Greece'

Northwest of the Megalópolis plain, the dramatic, picture-perfect castle of Karítaina (Καρίταινα) crowns a prominent, cone-shaped hill. The site of ancient Brenthe, it came into its own in 1254 when Hugues de Bruyères built the castle as the seat of his barony and bulwark against the Slavic bands then living wild in Skorta, just to the north. Skorta, the medieval misnomer of ancient Gortys, was host to outlaws all through history and a constant bane to the people living in the fertile valleys below. Hugues' son, Geoffrey, the Sire de Caritaine, was the flower of chivalry, whose romantic exploits get full treatment in the *Chronicle of the Morea*: captured by the Greeks and held in Constantinople along with his lord, William de Villehardouin, Geoffrey charmed the emperor and was able to arrange for William's ransom. 'The very birds sang songs of lamentations' when he died in 1275.

Although the castle itself looks impregnable, the Franks never gained full control of the area and sold the castle in 1320 to the Byzantine Despot Andrónikos II Paleológos. The Turks took over from 1460 until the War of Independence, when Kolokotrónis made it his headquarters. The last warlike use of the castle occurred when the Germans constructed gun emplacements inside to control the Andrítsaina road against the Greek resistance, who, like the medieval Slavs, made good use of the wild country as hideout and base. The castle, a fine example of feudal fortifications, can be reached by a short (if steep) path. In the east curtain wall, the gate has a square niche over it, no doubt for the de Bruyères coat of arms. It is flanked on the north by a square tower topped by three stone brackets, which would have held a platform for showering missiles on attackers. Inside, an ascending vaulted passage leads to the triangular *enceinte*. On the south side, the ruins of a large, vaulted hall has four north-facing windows and a vaulted cistern in front. The walls dramatically overhang the river 650ft below.

Theodore Kolokotrónis: Klepht and Warrior

Locals claim that Karítaina castle is haunted by de Bruyères; if so, the wrong ghost is in residence. The dominating spirit here was the more powerful and charismatic Theodore Kolokotrónis. On the old 5,000 drachmae note, Kolokotrónis was on the front and the bridge and castle on the back, and there is no better place than in the shadow of its walls to tell his story.

Born in Messenía in 1770, to a clan that had never submitted to the Turks, the intelligent, talented and shrewd Kolokotrónis became a *kapi* (head or leader), as his father had been before him, at the age of 15. Klephtic bands like his can be likened to Scottish Highland clans, in their sense of identity, cohesion and the close web of family relationships. Kolokotrónis inspired great love and devotion, and when the uprising in the Máni started he at once went to Karítaina and gathered his followers, many

of whom called him king. He was largely responsible for most of the great victories in the Peloponnese during the War of Independence. He took Trípolis from the Turks in 1821, defeated Dramali at Dervenáki in 1822 and was sent to lead the fight against Ibrahim Pasha, even although the other Greek leaders, warriors and politicians alike, were as sceptical of his motives as he was of theirs.

Kolokotrónis fortified Karítaina at his own expense in 1825 and made it his headquarters. He took to wearing a Frankish helmet he found buried there; it would become his trademark. The period of Ibrahim Pasha's reign of terror was the low point of the war, and the only time he almost lost hope. Ibrahim insisted on papers of submission from the terrified towns and, fearing death or worse, they gave them up. Then Kolokotrónis came promising the same for any town that did not take back their submission. He realized that these 'submissions' would be used politically by the Ottomans to claim that ordinary Greeks were against independence. His earlier cry of 'fire and axe to every place that does not listen to the nation' became a terrible reality to the so-called collaborating villages burned by his troops. It seems as if every Arcadian town has a story of Kolokotrónis arriving either to encourage – or to punish.

It was a brutal and horrible phase in a brutal and horrible war, fought out under medieval, not Marquess of Queensberry, rules. At this time Kolokotrónis was offering a dollar apiece for Turkish heads, an echo of the Turks' own method of verifying and rewarding their soldiers' kills. Many a headless body, including that of Kolokótronis' own father, was buried by a family while the head joined the pile in the enemy's gruesome trophy display. Kolokotrónis was not unaware of the awfulness, but simply believed that he had to fight fire with fire. From Karítaina he conducted a resourceful guerrilla war against Ibrahim without enough men, supplies or ammunition until the decisive Battle of Navarino ended the nightmare. After the war, Kolokotrónis found favour with Capodístria, but after his assassination was arrested, charged with treason and condemned to death – a not uncommon fate for Greek military leaders. He was pardoned five months later by King Otto because of his service and because his amazing popularity would have made it imprudent to do otherwise.

Loyal soldier, warlord, rogue, hero, 'Kolokotrónis, with all his faults and virtues, is one of the leaders of our race,' wrote Kazantzákis, and his frank autobiography makes gripping reading to anyone who wants to understand the complexities of modern Greek history and the Greek character. One thing is certain: he had style. When Kolokotrónis met King Otto on his arrival in Naúplio, he grandly offered him 'his' Karítaina as a personal gift. What more royal gesture could there be than that from one 'king' of a castle to another? And what better example of submission to the new Greek political reality? When he died in Athens in 1843, he was affectionately known to all as the Old Man of the Morea.

Underneath the castle, the **village of Karítaina** is just as picturesque, made up of medieval churches and old stone houses with little wooden balconies on narrow winding streets. Karítaina has a small population now, but towards the end of Turkish rule it was a prosperous town of over 35,000 with a soap and silk industry, grain fields, and water mills. It keeps two other souvenirs of the Franks: at the bottom of the village, there's the 11th-century Byzantine **church of the Panagía** with a separate bell tower, the only Frankish-Italian architectural innovation that caught on in the Peloponnese. The second is the **bridge** crossing the Alphiós river on the road to Andrítsaina. Originally it had six arches, with a tiny chapel built on a middle pier; it was reduced to four when it became a paved road in modern times. During the Second World War, the Germans tunnelled into it with the intention of blowing it up; they didn't succeed, but they did weaken the structure. So now it sits in ruins under the modern bridge, a forlorn reminder of a more harmonious method of spanning rivers.

Where to Stay and Eat in the Megalópolis Valley

Megalópolis ✉ 22200

The hotels in Megalópolis are central and open all year. They cater to businessmen, and for that reason alone they will probably be enchanted if you stay.

Paris, 9 Ag. Nikolaou, **t** 279 102 2410 (€/€). Old-fashioned, family-run, and just renovated with TV, fridges and air-conditioning.

Hotel Pan, t 279 102 2270 (€/€). If the Paris is full, this one does the business at an even lower price but without air-conditioning.

O Antónis. Fine food in the main *plateía*.

Ísaris ✉ 22025

Archondiko Ísari, t 279 102 1101, *www.archontikoisari.gr* (€€€€/€€). A beautifully decorated traditional building with a garden. The common room has a fireplace; rooms have all the mod cons. Its price in summer can match the Isareikó Spíti below, but is higher in winter.

Isareiko Spiti, t 279 108 1200, *isari@otenet.gr* (€€/€). Offers simple rooms in a traditional *xenóna*, towering over the main square. Their restaurant is famous in the area, especially for cockerel with pasta and *kayianá*, a special tomato omelette. *Open all year*.

Ag. Theodóra ✉ 22025

Psistariá Nerómylos, t 279 108 1208. Just downstream from the church, offering food cooked in an old-fashioned wood-burning oven. *Open all year*.

Karítaina ✉ 22022

Xenónas Brenthe, t 279 103 1650 (€€/€€). Double or triple rooms opposite the town hall. Their café is surprisingly trendy and your best bet for refreshment after a hike to the castle.

Kondopoúlos' Rooms, t 279 103 1262 (€/€). Two plain but central rooms very near the castle. *Open all year*.

To Castro, t 279 103 1113. Good food in a traditional setting.

Gortynía

Named for ancient Gortys, this corner of Arcadía teems with rushing rivers, offers rugged alpine scenery and several stupendous monasteries. Here the Ládon, the Erýmanthos, the Loúsios and the Boufágos rivers all leave precipitous north–south ravines and pour into the quieter, fertile Alphiós valley. The forested, craggy mountains provided hide-outs, refuges in times of trouble, and bandit enclaves all of the time. This is Kolokotrónis country. Under the Turkish occupation, these hills were 'home base' to the resistance; no Turk ever entered willingly. But today you can, any time of year. This area has become a popular winter destination, especially with Mount Maínelon just to the east. Gortynía invites lingering; Vitína, Dimitsána and Stemnítsa make wonderful bases, while the more adventurous may prefer the *xenónas* in the hamlets. Ideally, spend a few days and loop back around on the spectacular Vitína–Stemnítsa road.

Stemnítsa

Lively medieval Stemnítsa (Slavic for 'forested area') has a long main street overlooking the Loúsios Gorge and the Megalópolis

Getting to and around Gortynía

By **car**, Dimitsána is 65km from Trípolis, 40km from Megalópolis and 71km from Olympia. Side roads will increase the distance, but add to the pleasure. **Taxis**, useful for visiting the monasteries, can be got in Dimitsána, **t** 693 214 0116/**t** 697 757 5955; and Vitína, **t** 279 503 1100/**t** 279 502 2619.

A sporadic **bus** service connects Gortynía's villages with Trípolis (**t** 271 022 2560), Megalópolis and Kalávrita. Vitína gets several a day; Dimitsána and Stemnítsa, two a day; Alonístaina and Chrissovítsi, one a day. **Hikers** will love the Loúsios Gorge, and **cyclists** will enjoy the 24km road linking Vitína (west of town) to Stemnítsa via Eláti.

Valley, and the most beautiful and harmonious collection of stone houses anywhere in the Peloponnese, stacked in tiers on a precipice. These houses are substantial, with solid walls on the lower floors (store rooms and animal pens) and living quarters on top. Although the going may be steep, Stemnítsa rewards exploration on foot. Keep your eyes open for some of its 18 churches, especially the 12th-century **Panagía ee Baféro**, **Ag. Nikólaos** and the 15th-century **Zoodóchos Pigí**.

Stemnítsa was Queen for a Day in 1821, when it was declared the capital of Greece. Many Peloponnesian towns had this honour, showing just how unclear the geography of the new Greek state was during the revolution, but Stemnítsa was *numero uno*. Always famous for its metalwork, it now has a **school for gold- and silversmiths**, attracting students from all over Greece. Housed in a renovated five-sided building in the centre, the school looks quite grand with its black and gold double doors. Several shops sell its creations. Stemnítsa is also famous for its sweets, especially ones called *skaltsoúnia* (little socks), a clam-shaped pastry filled with walnuts and honey and then covered in sugar powder.

Dimitsána

The 'balcony of the Loúsios', lovely Dimitsána is dramatically piled on a high hill overlooking the gorge. Resolutely medieval, its streets are cobblestoned and tilted towards a central stepped path for the animals, a slope which also allows winter rains to run off more easily and away from the houses. It is built on ancient Teuthys, the walls of which survive here and there among the handsome stone buildings of the upper town. Important even in the 11th century and a major centre of learning during the Turkish occupation, today's Dimitsána, with a population of 1,000, is the main town in the Gortynía, with banks, a post office and local law courts. It has made a real effort to attract tourists without losing its charm, not always an easy task, especially because of its limited parking, a real headache on winter weekends.

Dimitsána museum
t 279 503 1219; open Mon–Fri 9–1.30

A small **museum** displays Dimitsána's rare old books, a collection much diminished during the War of Independence when their pages and bindings were pirated by desperate guerrillas to make cartridge cases. A major source of the town's prosperity was its

water mills, over 90 of them, serving as tanneries, grain mills, *nerotrivés* to wash blankets and rugs, distilleries making *tsipoúra* (Greek schnapps), and, from 1700 on, gunpowder works for the revolution. The **Water Mill Museum** has several restored mills, videos in English, and sells a good cultural map of the area with explanations about gunpowder. For a fine view of the gorge, walk towards the Dimitsána hotel to the belvedere by the road.

Water Mill Museum
t 279 503 1630; open summer Wed–Mon 10–2 and 5–7; winter Wed–Mon 10–4; adm

The Loúsios Gorge: Monasteries and Ancient Gortys

Loúsios Gorge

The narrow **Loúsios Gorge** extending from Dimitsána to Karítaina (*see* p.344) is wild, beautiful and crisscrossed in places by unpaved roads, which unfortunately are slowly being asphalted, meaning tour buses will eventually be able to enter. But don't be lulled into thinking the gorge has been tamed. A group of hikers lost their lives in seconds in the spring of 2007 after a sudden storm caused the river to rage.

The best place to see the river is from ancient Gortys; the best place to see the entire gorge is from Dimitsána or Zátouna; and the best way to explore it is to take the gorge roads to the **monasteries**. You can get to the Prodrómou monastery from Stemnítsa and the Philosóphou from Zátouna and Márkos, but both, along with the Emialón, can be reached from the road between Dimitsána and the Dimitsána hotel (*see* box, over). This road is safe, even in rain. If you choose only one monastery, choose Philosóphou, just for its location.

Moní Emialón
t 279 503 1273

Moní Emialón, the most accessible of the three, is built into a rock face, 3km south of Dimitsána; a paved road from the water mill museum also goes there. Built in 1625 on the ruins of an older monastery, it is worth a look, and would be considered spectacular were it not for its two neighbours. Robes for visitors hang neatly at the entrance. Large **Moní Prodrómou** was founded in 1167, also at the base of a huge rock, in the east side of the gorge. Its frescoes date from the 16th century. Note the bullet holes in the door: Kolokotrónis used it as a refuge and headquarters, and it was also a hospital for the wounded during the War of Independence. Some of the monks fought in these battles and the monastery, once very wealthy, gave much of its gold to the cause.

Moní Prodrómou
t 279 503 1279

Moní Philosóphou
t 279 508 1447

Moní Philosóphou is perched so close to the west edge of the gorge that it looks ready to spill into it at any moment. To get there, the gorge road passes over the Loúsios on a lovely old stone bridge. What you see on arrival is the church of the 'new' monastery of 1691, with excellent wall paintings inside from the same period. The cells have disappeared. The guest house is being rebuilt as a small hostel by the government, but it's no place for sleepwalkers. The old monastery, built in 927, is 400m away, clinging to a niche at the base of a huge rock.

Ancient Gortys is best reached by a good 4km road from **Ellinikó** (Ελληνικό), although it's possible to get there from Karítaina via **Atsícholos** (Ατσίχολος) and from Stemnítsa in good weather. Park beside the Loúsios river near the old stone bridge and explore. The site itself is extensive. Gortys' **acropolis**, within ruined walls from the Macedonian period, is a half-hour walk above Atsícholos. Other ruins on the west bank of the river that beg exploration include the ***asklepeion*** where Alexander was said to have dedicated his breast plate and spear. Legend had it that the Loúsios, 'the wash', was the place where Zeus' swaddling clothes were rinsed, giving it a certain spiritual cachet. It was also said to be the coldest river in the world, so you can put your picnic wine or beer bottles in to cool before you do the archaeology bit.

West of Dimitsána: An Excursion into the Alphiós River Valley

Take the paved road from Dimitsána across the Loúsios river, a route that offers great retrospective views of the town and glimpses of the graceful, if no longer used, stone bridge over the river. Just before the attractive village of **Zátouna** (Ζάτουνα) at the 4km mark is a **belvedere** with the best panoramic view, bar none, of the Loúsios Gorge. From Zátouna you can go a bit south to **Márkos** and on to the Philosóphou monastery, or go west to **Ráptis** (Ράπτης) and **Kakouráika** (Κακουράικα), even crossing the river to **Daphnoúla** (Δαφνούλα) and returning via Andrítsaina. This would allow a side trip to Bassae (*see* p.253).

The south side of the Alphiós after Zátouna is Mycenaean country. Tombs were found near **Paleókastro** (Παλαιόκαστρο) on the lower reaches of the river. This road passes through small working mountain villages that do not see a lot of tourism, and are reminders that agricultural life in Arcadía is a hard scrabble, made even harder by the extensive fire devastation on both sides of the Alphiós in 2007.

Northwest of Dimitsána: Langádia, the Ládon, and Ancient Thelpousa

On the main road to Olympia, **Langádia** (Λαγγάδια) makes you think of one of Italo Calvino's fantastical *Invisible Cities*. It is famous for its tall stone houses, but it's their almost perpendicular, vertiginous setting (*langádia* means ravine) that makes them so spectacular, clinging grimly to their precipitous slope in a rather bleak, forbidding landscape. Even in death, the inhabitants cannot escape the vertical: the town cemetery is built on four levels, counting the church.

Langádia offers interesting side trips. The first takes you 13km west, then 2km north, to **Vizíki**, and then even further north to the lake formed by the **Ládon Dam**. A 3km detour due east of Vizíki on a dirt road (ask for *to kástro* in town) leads to the picturesque ruined Frankish castle at **Akova** (and film buffs might like to know that director Costa-Gávras was born just south of here, in Loutrá Iraía).

For the second possibility, head 22.5km west of Langádia, and turn north for a scenic drive up the Ládon to **ancient Thelpousa**. Once you find the sign, go 500m on the signposted road, past a small farmhouse, then turn left for 200m, and left again (don't go farther up the hill) for 50m. You will be rewarded with a ruined Roman bath and a marvellous view over the Ládon river. The river is quite wide here and has plenty of sand bars, reminiscent of Milton's 'by sandy Ladon's lilied banks'. He may have gilded the lilies, but the sandy part is right. Continue up the main road to get a look at the dam and power station.

Vitína and Mount Maínelon

Vitína (Βιτίνα), while still pleasantly small (pop. 600), has been something of a tourist centre because of its dry and cool climate. Its stone houses, of a peculiar grey-black stone indigenous to the area, sit in a flat open meadow under Mount Maínelon and its towering firs, a stunning sight in the winter snows; surrounding pastures are dotted with surreal bush sculptures made by munching goats. The villagers here are are inordinately proud of the fact that Vitína has always had a Greek name, whereas most villages in the area sported Slavic ones at some point (early Slavic immigration is still a sensitive topic and a subject best avoided or only referred to obliquely over an evening ouzo). Small shops flog Vitína's famous cheese, honey and, above all, wood carving, ranging from the mesmerizingly tacky to beautiful pieces in olive wood.

Mount Maínelon (6,500ft), like Mount Kyllíni, was sacred to Pan. Its wooded slopes once crawled with tortoises and, although they were ideal for making lyres, no one touched them because they belonged to the god. Maínelon's newest charmed species are the snow bunnies who crowd the slopes at **Ostrakína** wherever there is enough snow. With six runs or so, Maínelon's **Ski Area** is not yet ready to challenge the Chelmós resort, but there are plans to expand the runs, and a snack bar, café and ski rental shop are open in season. The 10km road up the mountain south of Levídi is almost always ploughed. The 14.5km road from Vitína is sometimes snowbound, but in the process of being improved. Ask at your hotel. There is a 50-bed **refuge** at Ostrakína and lots of gorgeous scenery for non-skiers to enjoy. For information, contact the helpful **Trípolis Alpine Club**.

Maínelon Ski Area
t 279 602 2227, www.mainalo-ski.gr

Trípolis Alpine Club
6 Ag. Konstanínou St, t 271 023 2243

North of Vitína to Magoúliana and Valtesiníko

Magoúliana (Μαγούλιανα), 10.5km northwest of Vitína, is 'the balcony of the Morea', the highest inhabited village in the Peloponnese. Its coffee shop under the large plane trees certainly has the view to prove the 'balcony' part. Drop by the church of the **Panagía** in the lower town to view the iconostasis carved by the village wood-workers, a reminder that this is a local craft honed over many centuries into an art. After Magoúliana, the road ascends steeply, affording the kind of views you usually get from a small plane rather than a car. It then descends to the alpine village of **Valtesiníko** (Βαλτεσινίκο), once a going concern in the Frankish period, and on to meet the Vitína road 4km east of Langádia.

South of Vitína through the Forest to Stemnítsa

The magnficent road linking Vitína (just west of town) and Stemnítsa should not be missed. It winds majestically through a full-grown forest, where that old saw about sentinel pines is absolutely true for miles and miles. Near the 12km mark, an unpaved road detours east to **Libovísi** (Λιμποβίσι), the village that the Kolokotrónis clan called home. Back when this was a large village, the Turks could not even find it. A one-room **museum** has been set up in a typical home of the period, complete with a Kolokotrónis *fustanella* in a glass case and family pictures. The family church has been disappointingly renovated and white-washed. And that's about all. This village, once populated by 60 families, has returned to nature. The scenery and views are grand. One thing is sure, the clan did not make their living by growing spuds: this is a hide-out, pure and simple.

Libovísi museum
open whenever the caretaker is in residence; free

Another side road, 17km south of Vitína, goes east 5km to **Chrisovítsi** (Χρυσοβίτσι), a plain village, but worth the detour to see its alpine valley, reminiscent of Pheneós, but on a smaller scale. It was here that Kallisto (the most beautiful) was said to have been raped by Zeus and produced Arkas (the bear), the eponymous hero of Arcadía. The main forest road then leads past some seriously posh private mountain retreats and on to Stemnítsa.

Where to Stay and Eat in Gortynía

These hotels tend to be more expensive in winter. On holidays and winter weekends, it's essential to book.

Stemnítsa ✉ 22024

Country Club Trikolónion, t 279 502 9500 or **t** 210 688 9249, *www.countryclub.gr* (€€€€€/€€€). Once a grubby inn, now a chic designer boutique hotel.

Stemnitsa Restaurant, t 279 508 1371. In the main square beside the bell tower. Traditional hearty mountain fare, and not expensive either.

Maria Baroutsa. This *zacharoplasteío* opposite the Trikolónion Hotel makes wonderful sweets including *skaltsoúnia*.

Dimitsána ✉ 22007

Try the 'little rooms' places for an atmospheric experience. Their facilities are good; most offer kitchenettes, bathrooms, even TVs, and some have little common rooms with fireplaces as well. Dimitsána is famous for its bread and *mizíthra* cheese. Everything is open all year.

Dimitsána >

Dimitsána, **t** 279 503 1518, *www.dimitsanahotel.gr* (€€€€/€€). Located on the south side of town, this beautifully situated and renovated hotel still belongs to the municipality. It has 30 roomy rooms and views of the gorge. *Open all year.*

Georgos Belisaropoulos, **t** 279 503 1617 (€€/€). Several rooms with a view high up in the main part of town.

Vasilís Tsiápa >

Vasilís Tsiápa, **t** 279 503 1583 (€€/€). Rooms in the centre with kitchenette, bath and TV, in a wonderful old stone house, with a living room and fireplace overlooking the Loúsios Gorge; parking nearby.

The Zygoumi family, **t** 279 503 1409 (€/€). Three rooms in the centre.

O Tholos, **t** 279 503 1514. The Polýxronos family offers good food in a barrel-vaulted room in the centre of town. *Open Thurs–Sun in winter and daily in summer.*

Baroutadiko, opposite the *tholos*, **t** 279 503 1629. A small, more stylish restaurant with a bar upstairs.

Psistaria Demitsana, **t** 279 503 1680. Small, family-run, at the bottom of the town hill; has great charcoal-grilled lamb.

Vitína ✉ 22010

Art Mainalon Hotel, **t** 279 502 2217, *www.artmainalon.gr* (€€€€/€€€). Right in the centre, traditional woodsy style with balconies and very well appointed, and full of art, as its name suggests.

Archondikó Nikolopoúlou, **t** 279 502 2274, *www.arxontikonikolopoulou.gr* (€€€/€€). An inn with all the mod cons, in a traditional building with a beautifully decorated interior. Some rooms have kitchenettes. There is a garden and parking too.

Villa Valos, **t** 279 502 2210, *www.villavalos.gr* (€€€/€€). Not quite as cosy and relentlessly traditional as some newer hotels, this old standby is large, roomy and has its own old-fashioned charm. It has ample parking, a fireplace, a big garden and is within easy walking distance of the town centre. *Open weekends and holidays only in winter.*

Aigli, **t** 279 502 2216 (€€/€€). A central hotel, renovated, with a restaurant and bar. *Restaurant open Thurs–Sun only in winter.*

Sinoi, **t** 279 502 2354 (€€/€€). The Telonís family have added on and renovated and are now offering doubles and triples with fireplaces. Right in town.

Taverna Klimataría >>

Taverna Klimatariá, **t** 279 502 2226. An old favourite; two dining rooms, each with a fireplace and lots of dishes to choose from.

Oinotherapevtério Vitínas, **t** 279 502 2898. Also in town, with a fireplace.

Vitina Club, 1km west of town, **t** 279 502 2960, *www.vitina-club.gr*. A popular new restaurant with extensive grounds backed by pines, a large pool for a pre-lunch dip, and a café upstairs offering home-made pastries and cakes. The view is superb. They are adding wooden chalets (€€€/€€) with kitchenettes, but so far they seem like orphan 'add ons'. As if admitting that, they offer 30 per cent off the hotel price if you eat at the restaurant. *Open all year.*

Hotels and Xenónas in the Small Villages of Gortynía

Chalet Eláti, 6km south of Vitina, **t** 279 502 2900, 694 737 9410, *www.sale-elati.gr* (€€€€/€€€). Book ahead for one of these attractive chalets in a gorgeous forest setting with a pool, not far from Kolokotrónis' hideaway. They rent bicycles in an area perfect for bike touring. *Open all year.*

Xenónas Theoxénia, 9km south of Vitína in Alonístaina (Αλονίσταινα) ✉ 22100, **t** to 271 043 1363, *www.theoxenia-arcadia.gr* (€€€/€€€). Ensconced in a small village in a narrow pass, this lovely renovated neoclassical house is in a pretty setting and has a very attentive owner. *Open all year.*

Plataníti, Alonístaina ✉ 22100, **t** 271 043 1100, *www.hotelplataniti.com*

(€€€/€€€). Charming rooms in a stone mansion with an excellent breakfast promised. *Open Fri–Mon, all year.*

Kentrikón-Maniátis, west of Vitína on the road to Ancient Olympia in Langádia ✉ 22003, **t** 279 504 3221, *www.maniatis-hotel.gr* (€€€/€€€). A pleasant hotel above an excellent taverna with fireplace and its own barrelled wine. The same people offer new studios in town if you plan to stay a while. *Open all year.*

Agnántio Studios, Langádia ✉ 22003, **t** 279 504 3671, *www.hit360.com/agnantio/gr* (€€/€€). Three beautiful studios decorated in the traditional style of the area; they can sleep up to five and offer views of the gorge. *Open all year.*

Xenónas Kosmopoulos, west of Vitína in Valtesiníko ✉ 22026, **t** 279 508 2350 (€€/€€). A lovely old stone house with wooden floors, by a forested mountain. *Open all year.*

The Arcadian Coast: Kynouría and the Tsakonians

Cut off from the rest of Arcadía by the wild sierra of Mount Parnon (6,345ft at its highest), the eparchy of Kynouría was *terra incognita* until recent years, even more isolated than the Máni, accessible only by mule path or by sea. And, like the Maniates, who claim Spartan descent, the Kynourians are believed to be a race slightly apart. Herodotus wrote that they were Ionians, and their soft, rich language, Tsakoniká, still widespread a century ago, has been intensely studied by linguists as a kind of oral fossil; a German professor named Thiersch, who devoted his life to it, found that, while many words were similar to ancient Dorian, its basic structure predates even the Dorians, with elements going back to the early-Bronze Age Pelasgians. The name Tsakonía may be a corruption of Laconía; by 1573, at any rate, the Tsakonians are recorded by the chaplain of the Imperial Ambassador to Constantinople as 'a people not understood by the rest of the Greeks'. A number of older people still speak Tsakoniká fluently, and there is a proposal to teach it in the schools. It may be too late. Kynouría's isolation has ended: a coastal road has been dynamited into the crinkle-crankle coast as far south as Poúlithra, and the master-blasters are back every summer, extending it another few yards south towards Kápsala in Laconía. Still, except for the occasional yacht flotilla drifting over from Spétses, Kynouría is as yet relatively unknown.

From Trípolis to the Coast

The main road to Kivéri on the coast heads straight east, towards 4,000ft **Mount Parthenío** (on your right), the second Arcadian mountain sacred to Pan, and one where the goat-footed one made a famous cameo appearance: in 490 BC, as the professional Athenian runner Pheidippides was carrying news of the Persian invasion to Sparta he encountered Pan, who called him by name.

Getting around the Arcadian Coast

Buses from Trípolis and Athens go down the coast: for information in Athens, **t** 210 513 2834; in Tyrós, **t** 275 704 1467; in Leonídio, **t** 279 102 2255.

Unlike the Spartans, Pan offered to help, and was duly seen by the outnumbered Athenians at Marathon, panicking the Persians. *See* box, **Laconía**, p.368.

By the road, about 3km east of **Agiorgítika** (Αγιωργίτικα) are the ruins of **Mouchli**, a Byzantine fort inherited by the Franks and destroyed in 1460. Another 12km east lies **ancient Hysiae** (Υσιαι), on the frontier between Tegea and Argos, where in 669 BC the Argives defeated the Spartans (*see* p.276). In 417 BC the Spartans came back and wiped it off the map – all except for some handsome polygonal walls around the acropolis, a mile or so from Hysiae's modern incarnation, **Achladókambos** (Αχλαδόκαμπος). It's named for the wild pears that once grew here in abundance, now rare amongst the cultivated nut and olive groves and fruit orchards. Stop for a coffee at the roadside *kafeneíon* 3km further down for the mighty view over the Argolic Gulf, and to steel yourself for the loop-the-loops curling down to **Kivéri**, with little roadside shrines rather alarmingly marking each bend in the road.

Parálio Ástros and Herodes Atticus

South of Kivéri, a corniche road skirts the cliffs high over the sea before descending to the orchards of the Thyreatic plain and the village of **Parálio Ástros** (Παράλιο Υστρος), out on a spit of land shared by a minor Frankish castle and the even scantier ruins of ancient Nisi. Now newer villas mingle with old stone houses, overlooking a horseshoe port with a marina, while on either end of the village are a sandy and a pebbly beach; if one is wind-whipped, the other is guaranteed to be calm. Three km inland, **Ástros** is famous for its peaches; here the **Archaeological Museum of Kynouría**, in an old school, has five rooms of finds, including a set of Imperial Roman busts, from the Villa of Herodes Atticus.

Archaeological Museum of Kynouría
t 275 502 2201; open Tues–Sun 8.30–3

There are two things to see just up the Trípolis road. Four km from Ástros, the picturesque **Moní Loukoús** stands next to a ruined Roman aqueduct; the nuns have a beautiful garden and delightful little Byzantine church from the 1100s, a collage of ancient bits, with reliefs embedded in the walls next to ceramic plates. The source of some of its stone was the **Villa of Herodes Atticus** at **Eva**, on the other side of the Trípolis road (signposted and visible through the fence). The richest man of his day, it seemed, came down here to get away from it all, but didn't exactly rough it; the villa, with its atrium, the three porticos with mosaic floors and the baths (fed by the aqueduct), extended at least 3,500 square metres.

From Ástros a paved road twists up to **Prastós** (Πραστός), in Turkish times the centre of Tsakonía and the subject of numerous ballads. When Ibrahim Pasha came he destroyed all its houses save the one he was staying in. The Tsakonians rebuilt, but the town is deserted yet again except for Kýrios Pétros and his wife, who watch its 42 churches gently moulder away. In still lively **Kastánitsa** across the ravine – close as the crow flies – are some of the best-decorated churches in the area, and wonderful stone houses, one now housing an upscale *xenónas*. The roads in the area are being paved, making the mountain trip from Ástros to Kastánitsa via Plátanos a tempting detour.

South of Ástros and **Ag. Andréas** (with a road down to its sandy beach), the mountains close in to the sea. The road chiselled into their flanks sails dramatically high over the sea; out of season you can go for miles and not see another vehicle. Little shingle coves offer a chance for a swim or a quiet place to sleep, in a handful of rooms or on campsites. The cliffs give way briefly at **Tyrós** (Τυρός), the centre of the Tsakoniká language, to allow for terraces of olives, a beach (rooms and tavernas), and some ruined windmills. Further south, a byroad leads up to **Mélana**, which claims to be a 'typical Dorian village' if you've ever wondered what they look like. The coastal road then passes sandy coves at **Livádi** and at **Sambatikí**, with a few places to stay and eat, before the road winds down to a dramatic change of scenery at Leonídio.

Aubergine Heaven: Leonídio and Poúlithra

A vertical wall of red cliffs rings whitewashed **Leonídio** (Λεωνίδιο) and its emerald coastal oasis, the lush 'garden of Dionysos' according to Pausanias. Vines, however, are no longer the main crop: this is the home of long, pale, purple-striped *tsakónikis melanzánas*, the *ne plus ultra* of European aubergines, so unique that they have the EU status of AOC wines – a protected name of origin. Tiny ones are used to make a sweet called *melitzanáki leonidíou*, on sale in town. A late August aubergine festival attracts chefs from across Greece. Leonídio is a fine old town (note the typical Greek welcome sign, Καλας ηλθατε, written in Tsakoniká, Καουρ εκανετε), but not one designed for all the motor traffic that funnels through its long narrow main street, around the tightest corners. A series of mirrors manages to prevent collisions, and the incredible bottlenecks caused by any bus or truck that wanders through offer much amusement to *kafeneíon* habitués.

Most visitors stay by the sandy beaches, **Lákkos** and **Pláka**, guarding either end of aubergine-land; Pláka, the site of **ancient Prasiae**, with its little port, eight friendly geese, tavernas and long, sheltered sandy beach, wins the charm prize, a great place to hole up in for a few days and do nothing. If you like folk art, Leonídio is

Fire in the Sky

Leonídio comes into its own at Easter, when it holds one of the most charming celebrations in Greece. On Good Friday, the young girls in the town's five parishes gather wild flowers, vying to make the most beautiful *epitaphioi* (the palanquins bearing the figure of the dead Christ) for the solemn procession. Holy Saturday, as usual, is quiet, although tension mounts as evening falls and everyone prepares to go to church with their candles (the children with their special football team or Barbie doll models) to pass the flame from one to another as the priest declares that Christ is risen; fireworks and cherry bombs explode – that much is typical throughout Greece. But in Leonídio, at the very moment of the Resurrection, over 500 colourful balloons, the *aerostata*, each about 5ft high and with a flame in its basket, are released and ascend to the stars like Chinese lanterns; the effect is breathtaking.

The next day, the town turns the municipal gardens into a huge holiday feasting area, treating all comers to the usual Greek feast of lamb and *kokoréstsi* (the innards, coiled like rope around the skewer, and delicious), wine and red-dyed eggs. In the afternoon the head priest reads the Gospel in Tsakoniká in the main square; afterwards the young men and women of Leonídio, in their traditional dress, start off the dancing to age-old Tsakoniká music, and it can go on all night.

Yiánnis Katsígris
t 275 702 2015

proud of its self-taught wood-engraver, **Yiánnis Katsígris**, who specializes in striking portraits of Orthodoxy's warrior saints that resemble detailed brass rubbings; ring him if you'd like to see his work.

At one point, however, make the loop south of Leonídio: a so-so unpaved road leads up the cliffs, dotted with ruined hermitages, and the **Moní Ag. Nikoláou Sínitzas**, a monastery built by a cave where a giant fig tree (*síntza*, in Tsakoniká) once grew. On a clear day you can see Spétses, Spetsopoúla and Hýdra floating in the Argolic Gulf. The icons inside date from the 17th century. Circle down from here to **Poúlithra**, with another long white sandy beach, tavernas, and places to stay and eat. The mountain villages above Poúlithra – **Peletá** and **Pigádi** – have lovely views, and from **Choúni** there's a panoramic if unpaved road direct to Kosmás.

From Leonídio to Kosmás

Until the dauntless road engineers conquer the mountains, the only way to head south of Leonídio is by way of the scenic mountain road to Kosmás. After about 20 minutes, you'll suddenly see, hanging high overhead, one of the most stunning of the many vertiginous monasteries in the Peloponnese, the shining white **Moní Panagía Élona**, founded around 1500 to house a miraculous icon. Frequently looted and burned, the church was last rebuilt in 1809, and in 1821 the monks played their part in the War of Independence. The icon – supposedly one of the 70 painted by St Luke – was stolen in a Topkapi-like raid in 2007 and miraculously recovered – a real coup for the Greek police, who returned it in an elaborate and widely televised ceremony. Besides the superb natural setting, Élona (a convent since 1972) has a chapel containing a beautifully and imaginatively carved iconostasis as well as the famous icon, all clad in silver, and a holy spring.

Moní Panagía Élona
open dawn to dusk; ring the bell if necessary

From Élona the road continues up to **Kosmás** (Κοσμάς), 'the balcony of Kynouría' (3,772ft). Surrounded by orchards, Kosmás has a perfect main square encircling its stone church, surrounded by a ring of *kafeneíons* (and a local potter) and a splashing lion's head fountain, all shaded by enormous plane and horse chestnut trees; it will be even nicer if the planned rerouting of the main road now running through the *plateía* ever happens. The ancient name of the region was Maleas, and when a small Archaic bronze statue was found in the village it was named Apollo Maleatis and carted off to grace the National Museum in Athens. The road continues into Laconía and Geráki (*see* p.382).

Where to Stay and Eat on the Arcadian Coast

Parálio Ástros ✉ 22001

Crystal, t 275 505 1313, *hotelcrystal@hotmail.com* (€€/€€). One block from the sandy beach. The rooms have air-conditioning, TV and fridges. There is a café bar and the friendly owners speak excellent English. *Open all year.*

Houdís Holiday Houses, Parálio Ástros, **t** 275 505 1444, **t** 697 398 1384, *houdis-houses@hotmail.com* (€€/€€). Modern maisonettes in an olive grove by the sea, sleeping up to five. Oval pool and tennis too. Very reasonable for what is on offer. *Open April–Oct.*

Camping Astros, north of town by the beach, **t** 275 505 1500, *platisd@altecnet.gr* (€/€). Very shady.

Taverna Remezzo, by the marina, **t** 275 505 1494. Tasty food – onion soup, a wide variety of salads, seafood, pizzas and more. *Open 20 May–20 Oct.* (There's a good *mezepoleíon* next door, to warm up with an *ouzáki*.)

Avra. On the sea, and the best place for fish.

Kastanitsá ✉ 22001

Xenonas Andoníon, t 275 505 2255, *www.sun-mountain-snow.gr* (€€/€€). Renovated old house in the centre, very correct and well done. Nice view across the ravine too. *Open all year.*

O Parnon, t 275 505 2243. A good restaurant and grill house in the main *plateía*. Watch the passing mules and donkeys while enjoying the local cooking.

Paralía Tyroú ✉ 22300

Kamvissis, t 275 704 1424 (€€/€). Most rooms have sea views. *Open all year.*

Oceanis, t 275 704 1244, *www.okeanis hotel.gr* (€/€). Smaller; all rooms have fridges and phones. *Open all year.*

Four Stars Rooms, t 275 704 1437 (€/€). All the Kótsyfa family's rooms have balconies with sea views and air-conditioning. *Open all year.*

Zaritsi Camping, t 275 704 1429, *www.zaritsi.gr* (€/€). In a sandy cove north of town, with a restaurant, bar, kitchen, and water sports. *Open April–Oct.*

Taverna Manoleas, Livádi, **t** 275 706 1092 (€/€). Simple rooms to rent all year and delicious traditional aubergine dishes.

Leonídio ✉ 22300

Ta Kamaria, t 275 702 2757 (€€/€). A bit isolated over in Lákkos, these are furnished flats in a large garden, with lots of space for activities. An excellent family choice, but they prefer you stay three days or more. *Open all year.*

★ Diónysos >>

Diónysos, Pláka Beach, **t** 275 7023 455 (€/€). Tidy and blue, occupying a former ice factory; nearly all rooms overlook the beach. *Open all year.*

N. Troúbas Rooms, Pláka, **t** 275 702 3660 (€/€). A bargain.

Restaurants in season will regale you with dishes starring the King of Eggplants.

★ Michael-Margaret >>

Michael-Margaret, Pláka, **t** 275 702 2379. Of the many places to eat in Pláka, this is the standout. The view is fabulous, the food excellent. The local ducks gather peacefully among the cat population every evening, all more interested in titbits than inter-species rivalry.

Poulíthra ✉ 22300

Níkos Spanoudákis, t 275 705 1325 (€€/€). Nice seaside studios. *Open all year.*

Akrogiali, t 275 705 1262 (€/€). Traditional, with quiet studios and a lovely view of the sea. *Open all year.*

Andréas Stágias, t 275 705 1466 (€€/€). Air-conditioned studios and flats, sleeping up to four. *Open all year.*

Taverna Zavalis, t 275 705 1341. In a pretty setting by the beach, with home cooking.

Meraklis, t 275 705 1480. New, by the port; specializes in *mezédes*, fresh fish and aubergine dishes.

Kosmás ✉ 22300

While in Kosmás, try the local honey, made from thyme and chestnut blossoms.

Maleatis Apollon, t 275 703 1494, in Athens **t** 210 561 2978 (€/€). In the main *plateía*; a handsome *xenónas* in a restored stone mansion of 1876, with friendly owners and traditional rooms sleeping up to four; all come with a kitchenette. Good restaurant too. *Open all year.*

Kosmas Studios, t 275 703 1483 (€/€). Well-equipped rooms with kitchenettes and TVs; warm in the winter and cool in the summer.

Taverna Elatos, t 275 703 1427. Next to the lion fountain; try the charcoal-grilled lamb, local pasta and tasty dishes from the oven. *Open in summer only.*

Laconía

Laconía's mountains divide it neatly into four eparchies: Sparta, coastal Gýthio, Ítalo (the Inner Máni) and Epídauros Limerá (Monemvasiá). Monemvasiá's position as the Gibraltar of the East ensured it a unique history; the Máni, that ultimate refuge of the unwanted and hunted, is in a dazzling class by itself, as is Mystrá, last outpost of the Byzantine Empire. But it was the Spartans, the most famous Peloponnesians of all, who made their name synonymous with Laconía.

14

Don't miss

1. **A notorious temple**
   Temple of Artemis Orthia p.368
2. **The last outpost of Byzantium**
   Mystrá churches p.376
3. **Tower houses in a timewarp**
   The Máni p.400
4. **A city on a mighty rock**
   Monemvasiá p.384
5. **A colourful fishing port**
   Gýthio p.403

See map overleaf

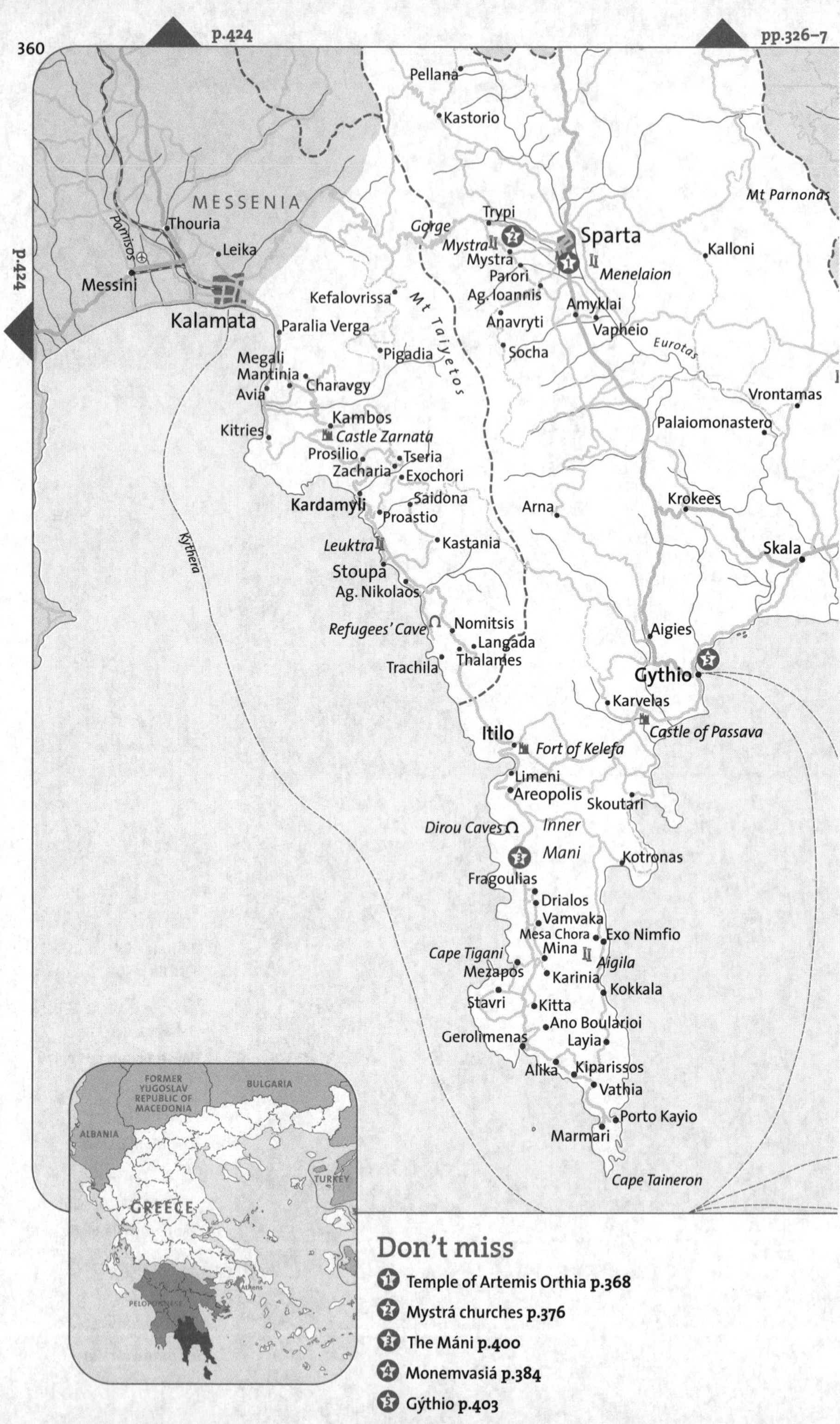

Don't miss

1. Temple of Artemis Orthia **p.368**
2. Mystrá churches **p.376**
3. The Máni **p.400**
4. Monemvasiá **p.384**
5. Gýthio **p.403**

pp.326–7

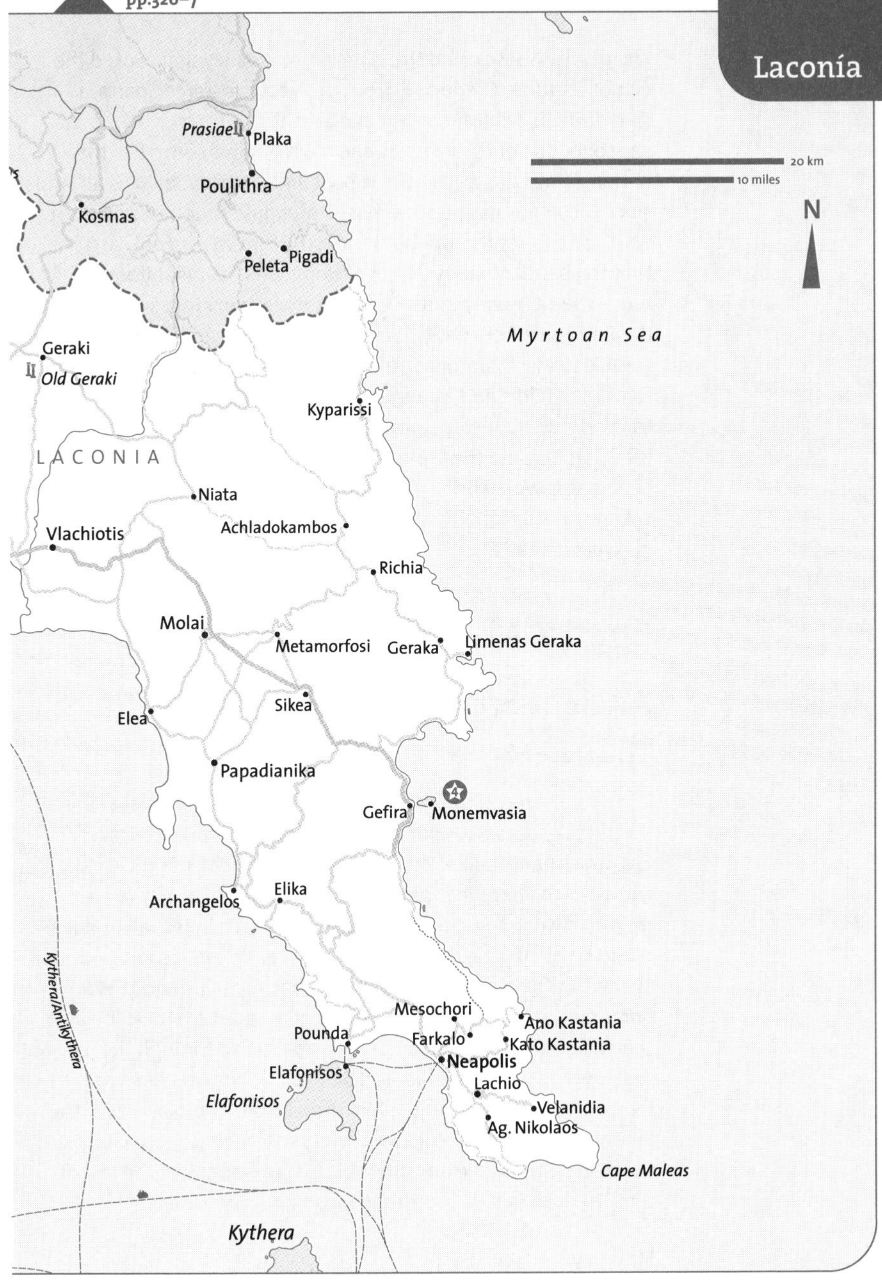

When he arrived in Laconía, Kazantzákis was so overcome by the sheer power of its beauty that he proposed a theory about the relationship between the landscape and the human soul. Surely some kind of cultural gene or propensity was at work, he mused, that allowed the Mycenaeans to see only the green and fertile valley, and the Spartans only the implacable rocky chasm of

Kaiádas. How else could the same Eurótas valley that evoked the cult of perfumed, seductive Helen also have fostered Sparta, a single-minded culture of war and death?

Laconía, one of the loveliest and most original corners of the nation, brings out a little of the poet and philosopher in us all. And since Laconians have been Greece's proudest, toughest and most warlike *hombres* throughout its long history, we can only assume that the hard and flinty gene has dominated its inhabitants in much the same way as its two great mountain ranges have dominated its horizons. Spine-chilling Taíyetos and its rough-and-tumble sidekick Párnonas stretch their mighty vertabrae south to form the middle and eastern peninsulas of the Peloponnese, giving the prefecture a wealth of coastlines on the Messenian Bay, the Laconian Bay, and the Cretan and Myrtóan seas. Some 95,000 people still live in the time-honoured Laconian way, in small villages, most of them utterly unspoiled and served by an excellent network of roads.

Sparta, Mystrá and the Taíyetos

Ancient Sparta: Hollow in More Ways than One

The very name still has the power to make you stop slouching, sit up and take note; say Sparta and words like 'simplicity', 'bravery', 'patriotism' and 'militarism' immediately come to mind. Get to know it, and words like 'paranoia', 'weird' and '1984' may replace them. How one sees Sparta is a kind of Rorschach test all by itself.

Tracing its cultural development is not easy. The 'laconic' Spartans, after a brief cultural fling in the Archaic period, seldom bothered to immortalize their thoughts in print or stone. It was their enemies, the Athenians, looking at Sparta through the lens of their own experiment in radical democracy, who made Sparta famous. The very gaps in the historical record, combined with the Spartan mystique, have allowed every succeeding age, including our own (witness the amazing success, and excess, of the recent film *The 300*) to give Sparta the meaning it chooses.

History

Homer called the area that would become Sparta 'Hollow Lacedaemon'. Tucked down in the Eurótas (pronounced Evrótas) river valley, between the towering Taíyetos range to the west and the rugged Párnonas range to the east, it was inhabited in Neolithic times and went on to become an important Mycenaean centre. From here Paris stole Helen from Menelaos, igniting the

Getting to and around Sparta

Sparta is 246km from Athens. Nine **buses** a day from Athens' Kifissos station, **t** 210 512 4913, go to Sparta via Corinth and Trípolis. Sparta's **bus station**, **t** 273 102 6441, is on Lykoúrgou Street about 10 blocks east of Paleológou; Sparta is linked by two buses a day with Kalamáta, five with Gýthio, three with Areópolis, three with Monemvasiá and Neápolis, two with Geráki, three with Geroliménas, and one with Pýrgos Diroú, one direct and two via Areópolis. Beware of diminished service on weekends.

Taxis: Sparta has many and there are stands in all the main *plateías*. Radio taxis: **t** 273 102 4100.

Car hire: Kottáras, 54 Menélaou, **t** 273 102 8966. *www.kottaras-car-rentals.com*.

Trojan War. The Spartans were part of the Dorian push into the Peloponnese some time after 1200 BC. But while most of their fellow Dorians settled down, built splendid cities, fostered the plastic arts and founded colonies, Sparta, more single-minded and never big on foreign travel or civic architecture, focused instead on Messenía, her unlucky neighbour to the west, and conquered her in two bitter wars, lasting from 743–724 BC and 685–668 BC. About the same time, they also put in place the world's very first constitution, the great **Rhetra**, supposedly handed to them by Lykourgos, one of their early legendary kings. Like all future constitutions, it both encapsulated and perpetuated the ethos of the nation.

The Spartan Constitution (Rhetra)

When a sanctuary of Zeus Sullanios and Athena Sullania has been established the people divided into tribes and obai, *and the thirty men, including the kings, appointed as a Gerousia, then the Apellai [a feast of Apollo] shall be celebrated from time to time between Babyka and Knackion [names of a bridge and river]. Thus questions shall be introduced and withdrawals made. To the Assembly of the citizens shall be given the final authority.*

The lynchpin of this 8th-century document was the total equality between free citizens, the **Spartiates**, who lived in a loose conglomeration of five townships around their low acropolis. One arresting feature was the dual kingship, one king being chosen from the **Agiad** family and and one from the **Eurypontids**, two clans who traced their ancestry back to Heracles and were forbidden by law to intermarry. Once elected, the kings functioned as judges, religious leaders and, above all, military commanders. Two other governing bodies complete the broad picture. Male Spartiates (the peers or *homoioi*) formed a citizen assembly, the **Apella**, which annually chose five **Ephors** who swore to uphold the kings, provided they acted constitutionally. The real power was held by the **Gerousia**, a senate made up of 28 members and the two kings. Membership in the Gerousia was for life, restricted to a group of aristocratic families and to men over 60 years old. Candidates for the Gerousia would be named, and judges, hidden out of sight behind a stone, would decide who had received the loudest approval, just like the applausometer once so popular on American television. It sounds great: citizen equality, respect for elders, permanent institutions. And the Rhetra has had its share of ardent admirers, many of whom were especially impressed by its vaunted immutability, an immutability that King Lykourgos went to extremes to ensure. The story goes that, before travelling to Delphi to get Apollo's blessing on the Rhetra, he made the Spartans swear by terrible oaths that they would not change a word of it until he returned. Once the Rhetra was duly blessed, Lykourgos starved himself to death, thus ensuring that no amendments could be made and that Spartan culture would not develop one iota from that day forward. There are even stories that he asked that his ashes be scattered at sea to prevent anyone from returning his body to Sparta and using that as an excuse to change the Rhetra.

The guarantee of equal assets and responsibilities to each free citizen has a hollow ring when you consider that the Spartiates were always a small minority in Sparta (even at their height they only numbered nine or ten thousand), and that their so-called freedom was based on the ruthless subjection of the majority, who were to be as immutably subject as the Spartiates were to be immutably 'free and equal'. Both the indigenous population and semi-Dorian Messenians, having been made *untermenschen* under the Spartiate jackboot, were divided into two classes. The luckier ones, the ***perioikoi***, were tradesmen, artists and craftsmen allowed to live in free towns, with very limited self-rule, no citizen rights, and an obligation to provide troops for Sparta's army. The vast majority were despised **helots**, slaves with no rights at all, but whose presence was absolutely necessary to perpetuate Spartan society.

To say that the Spartiates were unloved by their subject people would be an understatement. It is recorded that, when on campaign, the Spartan army placed two rows of sentries, one looking outward to the visible enemy and one looking inward to the piled arms cache every evening, to make sure their own *perioikoi* and, later, helots (who were brought into service as the number of Spartiates declined) did not grab them and revolt. To maintain their conquests and keep their many subject people in line, a militaristic society, with paranoid tendencies and grandiose visions of its own worth, was inevitable. Sparta boasted that she needed no walls around her city; her soldiers were her walls. How true. By the Classical period, the Spartan social system had created Spartiates with a fortress mentality par excellence (*see* box, opposite).

By around 500 BC, Sparta had gained control of most of Arcadía, Argolís and Elís. She was the force to be reckoned with in the

The Life of the Spartan Elite

Every Spartiate was a soldier, liable for military service until 60, with preparation for his role beginning from the cradle. A ***Leske*** or group of citizens appointed by the state decided if a newborn child should live or be thrown from **Kaiádas**, a rocky ravine of the Taíyetos. The criterion was physical fitness. Each new male citizen was allotted an equal share of state land to be worked by state-owned helots, allowing him the freedom and wealth to become a part of the state military machine.

Boys were taken from their mothers at age seven and raised in barracks until age 20. Brutal games, including beatings where the victors or *vomoníkes* (βομονίκες) were the ones who did not flinch, theft exercises where being caught was severely punished, and even a spell in the infamous Spartan secret police (where helots were hunted and killed) were all part of the educational programme, the *agoge* instituted by Lykourgos, aimed at creating the perfect warrior (*see* pp.51–4). Retreat in battle was not an option. 'Either return with your shield or on it,' was the Spartan motto, and shame or death awaited anyone who disobeyed. The concept of the **'beautiful death'** in battle led to the heroics at **Thermopylae** in 480 BC when Leonidas, a Spartan king, and a band of 300 Spartans fought to the last man defending the pass against the Persians. That was the upside of the Spartan military achievement. The downside was the fear this same military ethos inspired in their fellow Hellenes. The disciplined **Spartan phalanx**, the only army to march lock-step into battle to the sound of pipers, struck terror into its fellow Greeks, whose armies were made of everyday citizens and whose major preparation for battle was a pep talk from their current leader.

And **Spartan women**? If dying in battle was the only way to have your grave *stele* commemorated by name for a man, the only way for a woman was to die in childbirth. In death they were equal: heroes of the state. Much has been made of the freedom Spartan women enjoyed in relation to their Athenian counterparts. True, they seem to have been more outspoken, but that is not saying much in view of the highly regimented society they were 'freer' in. They were encouraged to exercise and even to compete naked in games, or so the shocked but interested Athenians said, but the reason for this was hardly related to women's lib. Healthy women produced healthy citizens. Women were just as fanatical about military matters as the males and full of contempt for 'tremblers', as perceived cowards were called. Spartiates who did not come up to scratch were purposely exposed to highly public female scorn.

Spartan marriage customs show just how far off the ancient norm Spartan society became. The bride, her hair shorn, was dressed in male attire and left lying in a darkened room where her new husband would visit her without fanfare, exercise his conjugal rights, and then immediately return to his barracks. They would continue to meet in this clandestine fashion until the man was 30 and was allowed to live with his wife and any offspring these meetings might have produced. Why? There are a lot of theories. Some suggest it was a ritual enactment of a bride kidnapping from more primitive times, or even an act of ritual humiliation. Since homosexuality was common, even encouraged, in the Spartan army, perhaps it was simply a way to make sex with a female more familiar or palatable. It was certainly a way of ensuring that the Spartan man kept his mind on soldiering, rather than on hearth and home.

Peloponnese, coercing other states to form alliances with her, or to fight and be beaten into submission. She became Athens' great rival, until the outbreak of hostilities in 431 BC began the Peloponnesian War. Throughout history, her reluctant allies abandoned ship whenever they could, creating a lot of trouble for future students trying to remember who was allied with whom and when.

Many great Athenians, including Socrates and Xenophon, admired Sparta, even during the Peloponnesian War when they were on opposing sides. True, most chose to admire her from a comfortable distance or had a personal bone to pick with the

Athenian *polis*. Socrates, like many people with a deep distrust of if not contempt for some aspects of democracy, still preferred to live (and die) in one. Democracy was messy, the Spartan system brutal but neat. Philosophers, utopian idealists and socialists of all stripes have idealized the Spartan ethos, praising parts of it and then justifying the whole. 'Spartan simplicity' still has a positive ring, and in war Spartan virtues of unquestioning obedience are praised. Certainly too many 20th-century social experiments have taken a leaf out of the Spartan notebook, from eugenics to brutal military training to suppression of minorities on the basis of their 'natural' inferiority. *See* **Topics**, pp.51–4, for more on Spartan habits.

Sparta won the Peloponnesian War, but did not know quite what to do with her victory. On one occasion she invaded Corinth, broke up the Isthmian walls and...went home. Sparta fought wars in order to contain the power of others who might upset the status quo in her own territory, rather than for dominance. Like other states who exist by suppressing their majorities, Sparta lived in terror of an interior revolt.

Myth and legend aside, it was really only a matter of time before Sparta declined. Constantly at war, the population dwindled, and there was no provision in the constitution allowing the formation of new citizens. Never innovators, they refused to adjust to the times; made for war, they could not adapt to peace. The Spartan surrender on Sphaktería in 425 BC (*see* p.448) had already put paid to the myth of fighting to the last man. Epaminondas of Thebes proved that Sparta could be defeated in 371 BC and built the cities of Megalopolis and Messene to contain their aggression. After that the Macedonians conquered the Spartans; they were defeated in battle by the Achaeans in 222 BC and forced to join their League.

By the Roman period, the Spartans were reduced to living on their fame. Tourists crowded into the brand new colosseum-style amphitheatre built around the Temple to Artemis Orthia to see the young boys beaten, a spectacle designed to show just how tough the Spartans had really been, way back when.

Modern Spárta

Today's Spárta (Σπάρτη) occupies the same spot as the ancient and medieval city. It is the centre for a thriving agricultural industry, producing olive oil, figs, honey, tomatoes and oranges, oranges, oranges.

Founded by decree in 1834 by King Otto, and designed in a grid system with German efficiency, it was built to hold 100,000 citizens, in the clear hope that Sparta would regain some of its old glory. Perhaps its open and pleasant atmosphere can be attributed to the fact that only 18,000 actually live on the broad orange-tree-lined streets. Some have lovely neoclassical buildings.

The two principal avenues are north–south Paleológou and east–west Lykoúrgou, the names pretty compliments to Spárta's medieval and ancient heroes. **Paleológou Street** is the showplace, with a palm-studded median sprinkled with round-clipped bushes. Most of the hotels are in the area, along with restaurants and banks and the **Art Gallery**, by the Cecil Hotel. Plainer, everyday **Lykoúrgou Street** has the archaeological museum to the east (*see* p.369) and the main *laikó* or villagers' shopping district west of the square that knots the two streets together. Sparta also has a **library**, a white marble pile with an extensive collection of English books on Greece, and on Laconía. The **Museum of the Olive** is in a renovated stone building two blocks south of the city hall. Here three floors reveal the fascinating history of the tree and olive production through the ages. They host travelling exhibits, too.

Art Gallery
*Paleológou and Thermopilón, by the Cecil Hotel, **t** 273 108 1557; open Tues–Sun 8–3; closed Mon*

Library
*135 Lykoúrgou, **t** 273 102 6853*

Museum of the Olive
*129 Óthonos-Amalías, **t** 273 108 9315, www.oliveoilmuseums.gr; open Wed–Mon 10–6; closed Tues, adm*

Spárta's lively atmosphere reflects both the pride and confidence her citizens feel for their inland capital. Far from any other large town, Spártans stay at home and have made the best of their city. The setting helps. It may be far from the sea, but to the west the Taíyetos range rises so abruptly that it looks like a painted theatrical backdrop of Himalayan proportions. This effect is magical in the winter and spring when the entire upper 'wall' is covered in snow, a dramatic contrast to the flat valley full of olives and citrus trees.

The Remnants of Ancient Sparta

The day will come when you will seek the traces of Sparta, and not find them.
Thucydides

Thucydides (*see* left) was right; there's not a lot to see. The Spartans left the big civic building projects to the Athenians. But the **acropolis** is a great place for a stroll. Walk north on Paleológou Street and follow the signs past the track and field stadium and the brightly painted nursery school-cum-playground (modern Sparta's answer to early state education is wildly incongruous in this particular setting!). The low acropolis is a lovely park with wide flagstone paths and olive groves; bits and pieces of ancient stones add accents here and there.

Of the Temple of Athena Chalkioikós, so called because it was lined with bronze sheeting, there is not a trace, but it lives on in memory because of a famous example of Spartan delicacy. In 470 BC Pausanius, a Spartan commander, was accused of treason and took refuge there. The Spartans couldn't flout the rule of sanctuary, so they filled in the doorway with stones, his mother apparently laying the first one, and waited. Just before Pausanius starved to death, they hauled him out to breathe his last so he would not pollute the sanctuary. That sort of ingenuity employed to avoid offending a deity was much admired at the time.

A large **Roman theatre** was built on the south side of the acropolis in the Imperial period. Some of it is still there. Its orchestra

The Spartathlon

It's 246km from Athens to Sparta, and although Herodotus doesn't mention runner Pheidippides' time making the journey in 490 BC (*see* Arcadía, p.353), he commented that 'he arrived the next day'. His account inspired John Foden, an RAF Wing Commander, who retraced the historic route; he ran it in 36 hours, and in 1983 set up the first Spartathlon race. Now Greece's most prestigious extreme sport, this ultra-marathon takes place every last Friday in September, the estimated date of the original run; it starts at 7am at the Acropolis gate and involves a gruelling night-time run over Mount Parthenío, often in the rain, along a rocky path illuminated by battery-run flashlights. On average, only a third of the contestants make it to Sparta before the 36-hour limit. In the first year, Iánnis Koúros of Trípolis won in 21hrs and 53mins, three hours ahead of the competition, and in 1994 he set what looks like an unbeatable record – an astonishing 20 hours 25 minutes. He has even lobbied for a genuine recreation of Pheidippides' feat – that the runners, once reaching Sparta, should turn around and run back to Athens. In 2007, American Scott Jurek, the second fastest man after Koúros, won for the second time. And the prize for one of the world's toughest foot races? An olive branch, a medal, and a glass of water from the Eurótas river.

was 82ft in diameter and its *cavea* 459ft. It most closely resembles the theatre at Megalópolis and was the third largest theatre in Greece, seating 16,000. Large holes were found for wooden posts to hold up shades during the performances. If the Spartans during their glory days had a theatre of any kind, it has yet to be found. On the acropolis are traces of the **walls** built to keep out the barbarians after AD 267, as well as the ruins of the 10th-century **Basilica of St Níkon**, which provide a pleasant rest stop and a reminder that this was the site of medieval Lacedaemonia until it moved to Mystrá. In a little street park near the Roman theatre is a ruin said to be the **Memorial to Leonidas**, the hero of the famous last stand at Thermopylae. His modern statue, looking heroic and sporting a great pair of legs, stands at the north end of Paleológou Street; this is where the gruelling Spartathlon ends (*see* box, above).

Temple of Artemis Orthia
under renovation at the time of writing

The **Temple of Artemis Orthia**, an easy walk from the centre, is signposted just south of the Eurótas bridge on the north side of town. Until the renovation, this was an uncharacteristically shabby site for tidy Sparta, almost as if a certain amount of shame about what went on here has lingered. This may reflect a certain disdain for what is partly a Roman ruin, but it may also be a place that everyone in today's Sparta would rather forget. A *temenos* existed here from the 10th century BC, a temple from two centuries later. The existing remnants date from the 6th century BC: the remains of a *cella*, a *proanos* and two Doric columns can be traced on the east side, and its oblong altar can be seen east of the temple.

In the historical period it was said that Artemis' statue was found standing (*orthia*) in a thicket, and its discovery coincided with an outbreak of madness, murders and epidemics. These could be stopped only by offering human sacrifice to the goddess. By Spartan times, the 'sacrifice' was somewhat mitigated. Young boys were flogged and prizes given to the ones who did not flinch or posthumously to the ones who died. Passing the cruel test at Artemis Orthia was an important Spartan rite of passage. One macabre detail has the statue of Artemis being held by a priestess. If the flagellation slackened, she would seem to bend under the weight of the displeased goddess until the beatings became more severe. Other contests, such as singing or oratory, suggest a less bloody side to the rites. Many clay masks were found at the site. Masks and flagellation suggest early fertility rituals *à la* Pheneos (*see* p.178), as do the sickles that were embedded in stone on the winners' trophies. The hillside above the temple accommodated spectators. After AD 100, the Romans built the horseshoe amphitheatre whose scant remains can just be deciphered. In this construction, the temple occupied the place of the raised stage, and the altar, where the whipping took place, was right in the middle of the orchestra.

The Archaeological Museum

Archaeological Museum
*On Lykoúrgou, just west of Paleológou St, **t** 273 102 8575; open summer 8–7.30; winter 8.30–3; closed Mon; adm*

The museum, a neoclassical building of 1875, is set in a large garden populated by the usual bevy of headless statues. It's not large, but it covers the ground in Laconía from prehistoric finds at Diroú to some very interesting Mycenaean artefacts and Roman art. The few rudimentary explanations in English and Greek may make you feel that no one much cares whether you come or not, but there are one or two unique finds. In the entrance hall are the distinctive **stone plaques** inset with sickles and inscribed with the names of 'victors' of the contests held at the festival of Artemis Orthia. These particular ones date from the 4th century BC. There is also a statue base of a *vomoníkes*, a young lad who had endured the flogging and won the prize. The first room left of the entrance offers two cases of **clay masks** from the Sanctuary of Artemis Orthia, many dating from the 7th and 6th centuries BC. These are uncanny; one theory is that they are copies of wooden masks worn in the ceremonies. The museum has over a hundred of them, indicating their importance, if not their significance. The ones on display are fascinating in their sometimes bizarre expressions, and yet some seem to represent real faces.

In the second room to the right are some powerful Achaic stone **votive offerings** either to chthonic (underworld) deities or heroized ancestors. Note the double-handed cup, the snake motifs and the horses and dogs as well. Were they clan signs? On the right wall are plaques of snakes, which always seem to be more in evidence when Mycenaean sites are in the area. The so-called **Statue of Leonidas** is in the third room to the right. It was found in the Temple to Athene Chalkioikós, dates from the 5th century BC and is a nice example of the Spartan military ideal.

Ancient Sites close to Sparta: the Menélaion, Amýklai and Vapheío

Menélaion
adm free

The **Menélaion** is 5km southeast of Sparta and easier to get to than to explain. Take the road north out of town, and immediately after the Eurótas bridge turn right (south) for 3.3km on the road to Geráki until you see the sign. A rather poor road goes up the 1.3km to the site. A large Mycenaean settlement existed here, but what you see is the curious **Sanctuary of Menelaos and Helen**, built on three artificially raised ramps, topped by the remains of an Archaic temple, and giving a stupendous view over the entire valley and of Sparta itself. Its dominant position recalls the Argive Heraion, and its function and local importance may well have been similar.

The Sanctuaries of Apollo and Vapheío are in modern **Amýklai**, about 7km south of Sparta, on the west bank of the Eurótas. Amýklai is very old and very sacred; its name is believed to have derived from a deity known as Mlk-Mnuklos, from the area of Palestine and Cyprus, two early Mycenaean trading partners. To reach the **Sanctuary of Apollo**, look for the small sign indicating a left turn and head one kilometre east; the last 500m are attractively flagstoned and planted with poplars. This pleasant low hill overlooking the valley is the kind of place the Mycenaeans favoured, and the discovery of sub-Mycenaean (12th century BC) and Geometric votives here suggest a continuous cult site. Only a few large stones, erected at a later date, survive. The sanctuary surrounded the tomb of Hyakinthos, a pre-Greek deity, as the ending *-inthos* indicates (as in the Minoan *labyrinthos*). The Greeks incorporated him into their pantheon by making him a young friend whom Apollo killed by mistake and whose blood created the flower. Apollo buried him here with honours, instituted the Hyakinthia festival, celebrated every July, and then took over his name, thus becoming Apollo Hyakinthos, and everybody was happy. The Hyakinthia was famous for its cult hymns to Apollo called *paeans*. Plutarch wrote that these were brought to Sparta

The Real Helen

There is a lot more to Helen than meets the eye in the *Iliad*, where she is basically just a prize to be stolen or recovered. In her earliest manifestation she was clearly a fertility goddess, and the most likely theory has her as the focus of a local vegetative tree cult where her fetish, or statue, was annually 'stolen' (causing the land to be barren) and then 'returned' (causing the land to blossom). As myths were rationalized, her mystic disappearance and return became an abduction, a *casus belli*, and her return an ego-thumping victory for her male champions. How else can one explain that she finished up a divinity, and that her abduction even in the *Iliad* was viewed as virtually a natural phenomenon? Some scholars believe the whole House of Atreus cycle, taken over by the Dorians of Argos, was actually a Laconian import or echo of a Laconian myth. The whole evolution of worship from the Mycenaean period is a fascinating can of worms. Even the rough and tough Spartans considered the saga of utmost importance: one of their most treasured relics was a piece of shell from the egg from which Helen, daughter of the swan-raped Leda, was hatched.

from Crete in the 7th century BC, and Cretan Linear B tablets do attest to a god called Paean (whereas Apollo and Aphrodite have never been found in Linear B). Sometimes the few facts we have about early Greek religion are rather like one of those logic problems that start 'Mrs Smith was not from Tilsbury and sat next to Mr Brown, her cousin, in a southbound train'. A small church now occupies the spot.

The **Vapheío** turn-off is just a little further south and 3km in from the road. Watch out for farm tractors. The *tholos* tomb, while huge, is deep in a pit and almost totally destroyed except for the lower courses. While famous for the two magnificent golden cups it yielded (now in the National Museum in Athens), the tomb itself is for Mycenaean *tholos* fanatics only.

North of Spárta: (possibly) the Palace of Menalaos at Pellána

Pellána (Πελλάνα), 26km north and a bit west of Spárta, has a cluster of evocative *tholos* tombs to show for itself on the brow of a hill, but what has the archaeologists really excited is the nearby area where they have been unearthing a 46ft by 105ft Mycenaean **palace**, perhaps the very one from which Paris stole Helen. It was surrounded by workshops and store rooms, encircled by 2km of Cyclopean walls (only the foundations remain) and reached by a monumental road. Theodóros Spyrópoulos, who has been digging since 1980, is utterly convinced this is Homeric Lacedaemon, and claims that he has found ten times as many finds as at Mycenae itself. Pellána is still a work in progress, but if the tombs themselves were not enough reason to go, then the drive through typical Laconian farmland makes the detour a delight. By the time you get to **Kastório**, a fine upstanding Laconian farming town with an attractive main *plateía* (an excellent spot to stop for lunch), you are in very pleasant country indeed. Pellána is the stuff of bucolic idylls; even the cows look happy. The archaeological site is a three-minute walk from Constántia Sigálo's little coffee shop-cum-snack bar. She was born in the area, and like many of the people hereabouts would not trade her life for the bustle of Spárta, let alone Athens. You can join the Spárta–Trípolis road again west of Pellána at Sellasía.

Useful Information in Spárta

ⓘ Spárta >
EOT: City hall, Gortsológou St and main plateía, ***t*** *273 102 6771; open Mon–Fri 8.30–2*

Bookstores and kiosks sell the annual newspaper *Laconian Traveller*, which is full of information.

Also see *www.lakonia.org*.

Sports and Activities in Spárta

There are lots of these and, in keeping with Spárta's past, they tend to be athletic. First and foremost there is **walking**. Spárta has done a lot for hikers, publishing trail maps and making efforts to improve the old mule paths. For local information and a booklet with all the trails and refuges, contact the **Alpine Club of Spárta**, 97 Gortsológou, ✉ 23100 Spárta, **t** 273 102 2574. The autumn **Spártathlon** (*see* p.368) hosts athletes from abroad. Contact the **International Spártathlon Association**, 7 Kédrou St, ✉ 210033 Athens, **t** 210 322 7756, *www.spartathlon.gr*. And there is the **Spartakías**, **t** 273 102 9082, a cycling event for young people from all over Greece every September.

From June to September, a full cultural programme is offered at the **Sainopoúleion Amphitheatre**, 5km south, an outdoor theatre offering ancient Greek drama, music, and modern plays. Contact the **Sainopoúleion Foundation**, 86 Paleológou St, 23100 Sparta, **t** 273 102 8878 or **t** 273 108 2470.

Where to Stay in Spárta

Spárta ✉ 23100

Menelaion, 91 Paleologou, **t** 273 102 2161, *www.menelaion.gr* (€€€/€€). Built in 1935 in the neoclassical style, this newly renovated hotel in the town centre offers an attractive pool with a popular restaurant surrounding it, and an aura of refined luxury.

Sparta Inn, 105 Thermopylón, **t** 273 102 1021, *www.spartainn.gr* (€€/€€). Comfortable enough, with two small swimming pools.

Laconía, 61 K. Paleológou, **t** 273 102 8951, *www.lakonia.gr* (€€/€). Recently renovated to a high standard, with all mod cons and free Internet in the rooms. Good buffet breakfast.

★ Cecil >

Cecil, 125 K. Paleológou, **t** 273 102 4980 (€€/€). Small, popular, and totally renovated. But the new air-conditioning hasn't affected one iota of the warm hospitality offered by its very welcoming owners, Katerína and Ioánnis Katránis. They are a fund of information on Laconía, too.

Eating Out in Sparta

The Spartans of old favoured black broth flavoured with pig's blood and vinegar; fortunately the new ones don't. Remember, too, that Mystrá and Paróri are not far away. As in every Greek city, the locals often patronize tavernas in outlying villages, just to get a change of scene.

Taverna Lámbrou, 82 Paleológou. Good traditional Greek soul food. This is one of the last of the old-fashioned eateries that catered to villagers coming into town for the day. They served *patsás* (sheep's stomach soup) from early morning and home cooking for lunch. They never did open at night because everyone had gone home by then. *Open noon–3pm only.*

Diethnés, 105 Paleológou, t 273 102 8636. Has been around for a while, and serves reasonable food at reasonable prices; with a small garden at the back.

Elyssée, 113 Paleológou, **t** 273 102 9896. Near the Diethnés; similar in style and content, not surprisingly since the owners are brothers. It seems to be a tad more popular with the locals.

Dias, in the Mániatis Hotel at 72–6 Paleológou, **t** 273 102 2665. A genteel pastel setting and a pretty good reputation, especially with Sparta's young set.

Il Posto, 104 Lykoúrgou, **t** 273 108 1181. Mr Papadákis has a milk bar with a wonderful difference. Along with the usual good stuff, he serves delicious American-style pancakes and may be the only shop in the Peloponnese where a coffee refill is actually offered – and on the house too. It must be all those years in America. Bravo!

Entertainment and Nightlife in Sparta

Ministry Music Hall, 84 Paleológou St, **t** 273 108 1288. This café is full of trendy young men, and those are just the waiters. It is the kind of place that makes anyone over 30, or less than perfectly dressed, want to scuttle by. It is open morning, noon and night for the fashion victims who want to see and be seen to the beat of contemporary music. Ask here about which clubs are currently 'in'. The habitués will know.

Mystrá

From Sparta, it's a lovely 6km drive through lush gardens to Mystrá (Μυστράς). The modern town, with its red-tiled roofs and stone walls backed by groves of cypresses, recalls that Byzantine Mystrá was known as the 'Florence of the East'. The tiny ***plateía***, however, is pure Greek, spread around a majestic plane tree with water flowing from its bole. Just past this tree a sign marks the popular trail, part of the E4, that leads 2.5km up the mountain on a cobblestoned path to the hamlets of **Tauyéti** (Ταυγέτη) or **Barsiníkou** (Μπαρσινίκου).

The main road turns right at the *plateía*. As it does so, an imposing **bronze statue of Constantine Dragátses Paleológos**, the last emperor of Byzantium, guards the ascent. Mystrá is his town. The yellow Byzantine flag with its black double-headed eagle (one head for Rome, the other for Constantinople) flies from practically every building; signs are written in Byzantine lettering, and even lamp-posts sport the double eagle. It isn't just for the foreigners; Mystrá and Constantine have an almost sacred significance to Greeks. Legend states that the emperor has been preserved in marble in a secret cave, awaiting the moment when the Greeks return to Constantinople (Greeks rarely say Istanbul), an ambition most have relinquished in practice, but almost none in dreams.

The ghost town of Mystrá is a couple of miles above the modern village, set high on an outcrop of Taíyetos. This was the last sigh of Byzantium, where the last imperial Despot ('Despot' was the title of an imperial prince, and is still used for bishops in the modern Greek church) held on for three years after the fall of Constantinople. Now cypresses, olives and flowers grow where 40,000 people once lived, their memory kept alive by the grace of their churches and the bittersweet splendour of their frescoes, painted in the twilight years of Byzantine civilization with the intense spirituality that informs all Byzantine art, yet with a vitality, colouring and delicate charm as if they were harbingers of spring instead of death.

A strange mountain he discovered, cut off from the range on high above Lakedaimonia and about a mile beyond there indeed he much preferred as the place to make his stronghold.

The *Chronicle of the Morea*

History

The Spartans may not have needed walls, but the French certainly did. In 1249, after finally subduing the fierce Melingi Slavs in the southern Peloponnese, William II de Villehardouin, the most philhellene of the Franks, found just above Sparta a perfect 2,037ft pedestal for his castle, located at the mouth of the Gorge of the Melingi, with impossible cliffs falling to the south. He called it after the Greeks' piquant name for the mountain, Myzithra (goat cheese), and it became his favourite residence; the lushness of the Eurótas valley must have kindled atavistic memories of France.

Getting to Mystrá

Buses from Spárta to Mystrá leave every hour between 8am and 8pm from the bus station or from Lykoúrgou St, two blocks west of the main square. They all go to the site's lower gate. This same bus can also drop you at the two local campsites and at modern Mystrá. Some but not all of these buses will take you up to the site's top gate. Since the two gates are over 2km apart, and the site is very steep, it may make sense to take the bus to the top, enter there and then walk down through the ruins, returning to Spárta from the stop near the bottom gate. A shady cobblestoned path goes from the west end of Lykoúrgos St along the river bank to the first houses of Mystrá, perfect for an early or late afternoon stroll. For **taxis** in Mystrá call **t** 273 108 3450 or **t** 273 108 3318.

William kept his 'strange mountain' until he was captured by the Byzantines in the Battle of Pelagonia (apparently they discovered him hiding in a haystack, and recognized him by his buck teeth). After three years in the clink in Constantinople, the assembly of his barons in 1262 finally agreed to pay the heavy ransom: Mystrá, Monemvasiá and the Máni – but only because, in the absence of the lords in battle, their wives got to vote, and they tipped the 'yeas'. When the Franks tried to recapture the citadel a couple of years later, the citizens of Sparta, who until then had camped out in the ruins of the classical city, decided to relocate, literally, stone by stone to higher ground, just under the castle walls. By the end of the century, the monasteries and their libraries in this isolated outpost began to attract scholars. Eventually, as Constantinople became more and more vulnerable, Mystrá would take over as the intellectual and artistic centre of the dying empire of Byzantium.

In 1348, as conditions in the Peloponnese grew more settled, Emperor John VI Cantacuzenós made Mystrá the seat of the Despot of the Morea, ruled by his cultivated son Manuel; Emperor John himself, one of the greatest scholars of his time, visited Mystrá when he abdicated, and died here in 1383.

Ruling the Morea wasn't an easy task; harassed by Franks and Turks, the Despots brought in Albanian mercenaries in such numbers that occasionally they too became a threat. The ethnic mix of the Despotate made for interesting times – Slavs in the mountains, Albanians mostly on farms, Greeks and a fair number of Jews in the towns, and Franks. As policy, the Despots always married Frankish princesses from Achaía, just as the Frankish lords took noble Greek wives. After the Cantacuzenoí came the Paleológoi Despots: two Theodores, the brother and nephew of the great Emperor Manuel II, who himself favoured Mystrá with two visits. By this time, thanks to Gemistos Plethon, the little city had established itself as an important centre of scholarship and philosophy. The younger Theodore's brother, Constantine Dragátses, served as Despot before becoming the last Byzantine emperor; another brother, the conniving Demétrios, allowed the Turks to take Mystrá in 1460.

Mystrá was occasionally the seat of an Ottoman pasha, but the next period of prosperity only returned when Morosini regained it for Venice in 1687, and made it an important silk-manufacturing town, with a population of 42,000. It fell again to the Turks in 1715 and was burned badly twice, in 1770 by the Albanians in the employ of the Sultan and in 1825 by the Egyptian troops of Ibrahim Pasha. By this time travellers confused it with Sparta itself; others came to seek the Mystrá described by Goethe in *Faust*, the place where Classical Beauty – epitomized by Helen – meets Romance (Faust) and gives birth to Euphorion, ready to die for Liberty.

In 1831, when King Otto founded modern Sparta, many of the ancient stones went back down to the plain to build the new city. Salvage work by the French at the turn of the century and restorations in the 1930s saved the churches. As a last sad note, Mystrá was damaged again by fighting in 1944 between Greek partisans. Thirty families stuck around until 1952, when the archaeological service moved them out.

Last in Byzantium, First in the Italian Renaissance

Back in the 11th century, just as Aristotle and scholasticism were being introduced into the budding universities of the West, the University of Constantinople's Michael Psellos was already 'reopening the well-spring' of Plato and neoplatonism. Even in the heart of the very spiritual Byzantine Empire, this study of the pagans was recognized as legitimate; after all, Christianity as a system of belief and logic was a product – the very last one – of Classical Greece, and Plato as well as Aristotle laid much of the groundwork for the early doctors of the Church. Psellos' most brilliant successor at the university was George Gemistos Plethon (1355–1452), who scandalized the Orthodox establishment by taking the Classicism rather too far in his Platonist lectures. Sent to Mystrá by his friend Emperor Manuel II Paleológos to keep him from being charged with heresy, Plethon went happily enough – to be in the heart of Classical Greece, near Sparta, suited him just fine.

Quixotically, though he lived at the tail-end of ancient Greek civilization, Plethon's increasingly esoteric philosophy was devoted to the idea of returning Greece to its glory days. His free school in Mystrá attracted scholars from all over, among them the famous Bessarion of Trebizond and Isidore of Kiev, both of whom later became cardinals in Italy, and George Scholários, who would become the first Patriarch of Constantinople under the Sultans. Plethon also saw himself as the advisor of the Despots and Emperor, and sent them briefs on how to rule the state. These helpful hints were not unlike Machiavelli's advice to the Medici: like the Spartans, they should train an army of citizens and not rely on foreign mercenaries to defend them; peasants, not the Church or nobility, should own the land they tilled; exports should be kept to a minimum in the name of economic self-sufficiency. Plethon had no patience with ascetic, dogmatic Christianity, and criticized Greek monks for avoiding their political duty, believing rather that 'saintly is he who acts in the midst of society'. The monks hated him; the Emperor thought his reforms were utopian.

Plethon's most lasting legacy was the year he spent with John VIII Paleológos at the Council of Florence (1438–39), during the Emperor's doomed attempt to reconcile the Eastern and Roman churches – in the hope that the Pope would send aid against the Turkish threat. Like a relay runner, Plethon passed the baton of Platonic scholarship from East to West, where it was still practically unknown; he lectured Florentine humanists and left them his treatise, *On the Differences between the Platonic and Aristotelian Philosophies*. This in turn inspired Cosimo de' Medici to sponsor a Latin translation of Plato and found the first Platonic academy, which would, among many other contributions to the Renaissance, inspire the complex allegories of Botticelli. Plethon also introduced

the *Geography of Strabo* to the west, which soon overturned the medieval Ptolomeic system and inspired Columbus.

Plethon was revolutionary for his belief that human conceptions of divinity were not fixed, but changed according to time and place. Some of his comments look forward to Vico: 'Cycles of time produce, and will always produce, similar ways of life and similar activities from age to age. Nothing new has ever yet come into existence.' His last work, *On the Laws*, completed at age 90, urged the creation of a new religion, one that placed Zoroaster as the first divine intermediary of wisdom, followed by Pythagoras, Plato and Christ; he also sought to combine Christianity with symbols from Classical polytheism – Christ infused with the spirit of Apollo. These paths would be pursued in Renaissance Florence by the Medici's 'natural magician' Ficino and by Pico della Miradola. It was a blessing for the old man to die the year before Constantinople fell to the Turks. As soon as he was safely dead, George Scholários, the future Patriarch, burned his writings – some say as a horrified friend, some say as a bitter rival – and the Church made his name *anáthema*. But in homage to his reputation in Italy, the Prince of Rimini, Sigismondo Malatesta, recovered Plethon's body in 1464 while serving with the Venetians, and gave him a fancy tomb in Rimini's cathedral, with an epitaph lauding 'the greatest philosopher of his time'.

The Site

Mystrá's churches

Mystrá

t 273 108 3377; open summer daily 8–7.30; winter 8.30–3; adm exp; keep your ticket, wear sturdy shoes, and come in the morning when the sunlight illuminates the best frescoes in the Perívleptos

Mystrá is famous for its surviving churches, and each is strikingly individual. The Despots never had money to build lavishly, but their architects had verve and imagination, and made good use of local stone and brick. They couldn't afford mosaics, but attracted the best painters in late 14th-century Byzantium to supply the frescoes. Frustratingly, next to nothing is known about these artists, or how they came to transfigure and humanize the usually remote Byzantine cast of holy characters, and to do so without compromising their spiritual essence.

Steep Mystrá is divided into three levels; the oldest and uppermost, built around Villehardouin's castle, has an entrance that can be reached by bus or car (*see* 'Getting to Mystrá', p.374). The main entrance at the bottom leads through a vaulted passage in the walls into the **lower town**. Take the path to the left, where you'll find the ruins of **Lascaris House**, once one of the grandest mansions in Mystrá, and the little chapel of **Ag. Geórgios**, and the **Perívleptos**. The latter is a picturesque 14th-century cross-in-square church set against a vertical rock face, which gave rise to its irregular plan, and the entrance is through a small rock passage at the back. The Frankish elements – the pretty bell tower and polygonal apses, and lily and lion embedded there – point to Despot Manuel Cantacuzenós and his wife Isabella de Lusignan as the founders. A second plaque refers to its restoration under the Venetians, in 1716.

The **frescoes** of the Perívleptos are not only among the most beautiful in Greece, but also, unlike the other churches in Mystrá, they were all painted during a single period, if by three or four different hands. The irregular plan led to a complex iconography, lavish with incidental detail: note the playing children in the

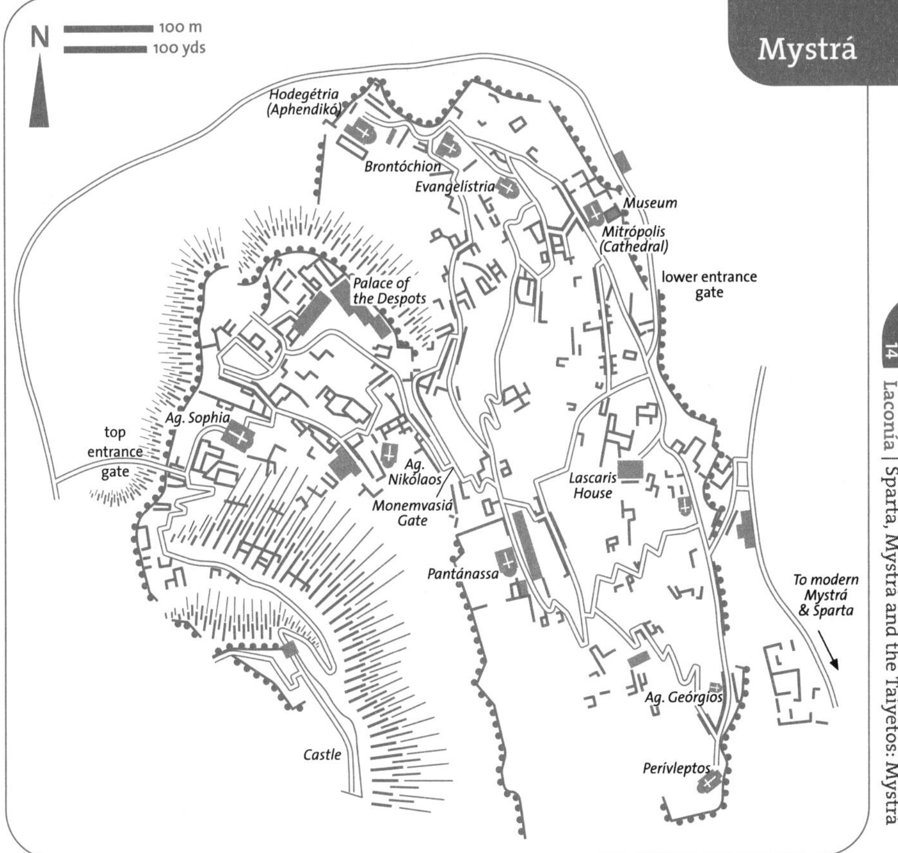

foreground of the *Entry into Jerusalem*, the beautifully coiffed angels, the fish and tiny people swarming in the river in the *Baptism of Christ*, and the interest in creating an illusion of space in architecture and landscapes. There are striking parallels with the great Sienese master Duccio di Buoninsegna in the *Descent from the Cross*.

A steep path from the Perívleptos ascends to the **Pantánassa**, the loveliest of Mystrá's churches, set by a Frankish-style bell tower with a little melon dome above a convent and a narrow flower-filled courtyard, tended by a handful of nuns, the last residents of Mystrá. The church was founded by John Phrangópoulos, chief minister of the Despot, and dedicated in 1428, the culmination of the Mystrá style. It has the same plan as the Aphendikó (*see* pp.378–9): a five-domed cross-in-square set on top of a basilica. The apses are even higher and narrower, windows more numerous, the architectural features emphasized in masonry. The narthex is frescoed with grisly martyrdoms, while the inner doorway sports Islamic Kufic designs, apparently made by a Greek who simply liked the calligraphy and tried to imitate it. In the main body of the church, the poorly preserved frescoes on the lower level were added in the 17th and 18th centuries; the upper ones, as in the Perívleptos, show a love of detail, softer modelling of the figures and bright colours. The *Entry into Jerusalem* is especially fine.

From here the path leads up to the **Monemvasiá Gate**, under an impressive battlemented house from the 15th century. Above, in what was once the main square of Mystrá, stands the massive **Palace of the Despots**. Travellers in the 18th and 19th centuries believed it was the Palace of Menelaos. Begun by the Franks, work was continued by the various Despots; after 1400 the Palaeológoi added the vast throne room, once stuccoed and painted and heated by no fewer than eight fireplaces; its Gothic windows are Venetian in inspiration. The church to the left, **Ag. Nikólaos**, was built during the Turkish period while to the west, up from the Palace of the Despots, is **Ag. Sophía**, built as the *katholikón* of a small monastery by the first Despot Manuel Cantacuzenós (1348–40). It represents the simpler style of Mystrá church, the cross-in-square, but with unusually tall and narrow proportions and two exterior colonnades, a feature common in Constantinople but rare in Greece. Only a few frescoes have survived, plus some of the once elaborate marble paving.

Palace of the Despots
currently undergoing restoration

From here you can continue to the very top and Villehardouin's **castle** (*kástro*) where he and his wife Anne-Ange Comnene ('as beautiful as a second Helen of Menelaos', according to the *Chronicle of the Morea*) held a chivalric Franco-Greek court. The castle still follows the lines of the original, and it's easy to understand why the Franks were loath to give it up. Most of what you see today was rebuilt by the Turks. The walk is hard work on a hot day; if you have a car, save your ticket and drive up. The views are spectacular.

From the Despots' palace, the path descends back through the Monemvasiá Gate, past the 14th- or 15th-century **Evangelístria**, another cross-in-square church, used as a mortuary chapel and ossuary. At the bottom, turn left for the **Brontóchion**, once a vast monastic complex built by the archimandrite Pachomios. It has two large and impressive churches. The older, octagonal-domed **Ag. Theódori** (1290s) was probably copied from the Ag. Sophía in Monemvasiá. A unique feature, however, is the east façade, with its triple broken roof and bands of grey stone and red ashlar; the west is similar, but hidden by a later narthex. The frescoes have been badly damaged.

The second church, the **Hodegétria**, 'she who points the way', now better known as the **Aphendikó**, was built 20 years later and designed to be even more impressive, as if to remind the citizens of Mystrá of their imperial lineage. The view from above onto the

Aphendikó's garden of tiled roofs is perhaps the best way to appreciate the architectural sleight of hand that fused a tall basilica with a Greek cross, topped with five domes. The interior, with its marble facings, is elegantly proportioned, and the frescoes are excellent: saints and Hierarchs, and lively scenes of the *Miracles of Jesus*. In the north chapel of the narthex are the tombs of Pachomios and the Despot Theodore II Paleológos, showing him dressed as a Despot and as a monk (it wasn't uncommon for Byzantine rulers to abdicate and enter a monastery). Copies of chrysobulls (imperial decrees) to the Brontóchion are on the walls.

The last church, back down by the gate, is the **Mitrópolis** or cathedral, dedicated to Ag. Demítrios and built in 1291 when the Bishop of Lacedaemonia transferred his seat to Mystrá. It is the most confusing church in town: originally built as a basilica and divided into three barrel-vaulted aisles, it suffered from an insensitive 15th-century bishop named Mathew who whipped off the roof and beheaded the upper rank of frescoes to give it a women's gallery and five domes. The heavy bell tower was built over a chapel in the style of the Aphendikó. In a corner of the courtyard, a Roman sarcophagus decorated with maenads and griffons was used as the basin of a fountain; it is the only Classical artefact ever found in Mystrá. Inside, the Mitrópolis has a marvellous marble iconostasis carved with dragons. The inscriptions on the columns were left by various bishops, describing their good deeds for posterity. The frescoes were painted at various periods: the *Miracles of Jesus* and the *Saints*, the *Cycle of Feasts*, the *Passion* and *Resurrection*, while the *Last Judgement* in the narthex is the most recent fresco, showing the *Preparation of the Throne* (the *Etoimasiá*) and scenes of hell, where lusty women are punished with coiling snakes. The lone *Virgin and Child* in the apse recalls the mosaic in Venice's Torcello cathedral. A marble double-eagle plaque on the floor marks the spot where the gentle-natured Constantine Dragátses was crowned the last emperor of Byzantium in 1449; because most of Orthodoxy was still furious over his brother John's attempt to unite the Eastern and Western churches, he would never have a proper coronation in Constaninople's Ag. Sophia. Four years later, he died defending Constantinople from the Turks, shedding his imperial regalia to fight like a common soldier. His body was never identified, and he became the marble fairytale prince in his countrymen's dreams.

There is a small **museum** up the stairs in the Mitrópolis' courtyard, with architectural fragments, icons, part of a silk dress and a plait of hair recovered from a noblewoman's tomb, jewellery, a relief of the arms of Isabella de Lusignan, a fine 12th-century plate showing an eagle attacking a hare, and a very peculiar metal cross, with branches sprouting baby crosses.

A Short Detour into the Taíyetos

There are at least two good reasons to visit nearby Parόri (Παρόρι), less than 2km south of Mystrá: it offers restaurants by a small waterfall and a 20-minute walk into a typical, albeit miniature, Taíyetos gorge with the tiny church of **Panagía Langadiótissa** (Παναγία Λαγγαδιότισσα), the Virgin of the Gorge. The atmosphere is suitably eerie, especially towards dusk when bats flit about. There are caves high up on your right and a small stream in the narrow gorge below; the church, itself inside a cave, has a platform in front to sit and contemplate the scenery. Some say this gorge was the infamous Kaiádas where the Spartans tossed unwanted children. There is another candidate on the Sparta–Kalamáta road, but this one has practicality on its side. It is simply closer to Sparta: getting rid of imperfections would not have seemed important enough to Spartans to warrant a long journey. Three hundred metres past Parόri, a 5km footpath twists up the mountain (cobblestoned for the first 3.5km) to lofty **Anavrytí** (Αναβρυτή) which offers restaurants, an inn, and walks for the intrepid and not so intrepid (*see* box, opposite). Anavrytí can be reached by car via Ag. Ioánnis up a steep secondary road with spine-chilling hairpin turns. This road was hand-crafted in desperation by the villagers themselves, fed up with having only mule paths to their land and village. It corkscrews up the steep hill with hardly a guard rail in sight. The straight road from Parόri back to Mystrá offers a marvellous daytime view of the castle, and a spectacular perspective for its evening illumination at weekends.

Where to Stay and Eat in and around Mystrá

Mystrá ✉ 23100

Pyrgos Mystra, 3 Manousáki, **t** 273 102 0770, *www.pyrgosmystra.com* (€€€€€/€€€€€). In one of Mystrá's most beautiful settings, a dreamy, exquisite little hotel in a mansion of 1850, with no expense spared on the fittings. Lovely home-made breakfasts, too.

Byzántion, t 273 108 3309, *www.byzantionhotel.gr* (€€/€€). With its arched balconies, the Byzántion fits its setting. A new pool in the garden is a great addition to the facilities. *Open April–Oct.*

Christina Vachaviólou (Βαχαβιόλου), behind the hotel, **t** 273 102 0047 (€/€). Three plain rooms in an old-fashioned house; communal baths and fridge, plus an apartment that can sleep four in a modern wing.

Camping Mystrá, t 273 102 2724 (€/€). A tiny campsite with a small pool and playground. *Open all year.*

★ Castle View >>

Castle View, **t** 273 108 3303 (€/€). Larger campsite, with a slightly bigger pool; it has three small bungalows at a very reasonable price. *Open April–Oct.*

Vourlókas, t 273 108 2666. In Mystrá's main *plateía*, with cannons and a pretty side garden. This is the nicest taverna in town.

Marmara, t 273 108 3319. On the road to the site with a terrace overlooking Spárta, piano music on weekends, and pretty hefty prices.

★ Xenía Tourist Perípteron >>

Xenía Tourist Perípteron, by the lower gate, **t** 273 102 0500. Attractive, modern and not expensive, with a bar/coffee shop on one floor and a pizzeria-restaurant above. A huge mulberry tree shades its terraces, both overlooking the entire valley, showing 'hollow Lacedaemon' at its best. There is no better place to be at dusk.

Roads over the Taíyetos

The great spine of the southern Peloponnese is a force to be reckoned with. 'Look at the Taíyetos and your chest expands, petty calculations vanish, you are ashamed of the tiny, meaningless life that you have led,' as Kazantzákis put it. In myth, Taygete was one of the seven Pleiades, who fled the attentions of Zeus by turning into a hind; her son Lacedaemon, 'the lake demon', was the ancestor of the Spartans. Significantly, she felt so unmaternal towards the little bruiser that she immediately hanged herself on the mountain that took her name.

Nor has the mountain lost its allure for famous suicides. In the spring of 1998, Dimítris Liandínis, respected professor, writer and philosopher, took his own theory about death to the extreme. A local since birth, he ascended Taíyetos, immured himself in a small cave, and waited to die. Seven years later, his body was found. Many admire his theory that man's only freedom is to choose when to die. Others shudder.

Even if you don't have the time or energy for a mountain walk, you can get a spellbinding taste of the Taíyetos on the 60km route over the celebrated 4,265ft **Langáda Pass**, on a road built in 1940 between Spárta and Kalamáta. This pass is no longer the only paved road, but it is the widest and most direct, and offers some of the best views. Just past **Trýpi** (Τρύπη) the road enters a sinister gorge, steep and forbidding enough to be called *Kaiádas* by some. A little church dedicated to the **Panagía** marks the top of the pass, which is also the watershed of the Eurótas and Néda rivers and the boundary between Laconía and Messenía. A more circuitous road further south snakes over from **Aigiés**, 5km north of Gýthio, via **Saidóna** (Σαιδόνα), **Kastaniá** (Καστανιά) and on to Stoúpa in the Outer Máni. This one is for the adventurous.

Hiking on Taíyetos and Mount Párnonas

The highest reaches of Taíyetos, such as the path over the mountain and down to Kardamýli, are best left for hardened hikers with proper equipment and maps (the RO4D Taíyetos map is a good one). But there is plenty of scope for duffers near Sparta. Many of the old paved mule paths, the *kalderími*, have been repaired and rebuilt. Roads occasionally cross these paths, a paved one at Anavrytí, and unpaved ones to Tauyéti (Ταυγέτι), Sochá (Σοχά) and to the Alpine Club refuge near the highest peak of Taíyetos, Profitís Ilías, (7,897ft), so that it is possible to combine driving and hiking. Profitís Ilías is named for its church; many people hike to its summit on the evening of 19 July for the annual service.

Mount Párnonas, east of Sparta, also offers good walks. Although not as majestic as the Taíyetos, Laconía's number two range is easier to reach, thanks to a forest road to the 6,348ft summit from Vamvakoú (Βαμβακού); driving north from Spárta, take the turn-off 12km up the Trípolis road. From Vamvakoú a path leads up in two hours (or the unpaved road twists for 26km) to the mountain refuge Arnomousga (4,593ft) run by Spárta's Alpine Club (35 beds, kitchen facilities: t 273 102 6518 or t 273 102 7500 to book). From here you can drive or walk (3hrs) to the summit, which goes by the name Megáli Toúrla or Krónion. The lonely villages of Párnonas are famous for their mountain teas; stop and try some.

Where to Stay and Eat in the Taíyetos

Trýpi/Anavrytí/Árna/Paróri

✉ 23100

Xenóna Geodí, Árna, **t** 273 102 0703, *www.geodi.gr* (€€€€/€€€€). This nicely decorated, upscale *xenóna* is for hikers with deep pockets. The owners speak English and know their area well, arranging for walks and activities. *Open all year.*

Kaiádas, Trýpi, **t** 273 109 8338 (€/€). A simple hotel for passers-by with a spine-chilling name. On a cliff, of course.

Anavrytí, Anavrytí, **t** 273 102 1788 (€/€). Plain, nice and a bargain in a great location, if you can just brave either the road or footpath to it. Do book ahead. *Open all year.*

O Kéramos, Paróri, **t** 273 108 2855. Serves traditional Greek oven dishes in a pretty leafy setting in town beside a waterfall.

Geráki: A Mini-Mystrá

Southeast of Spárta, the Eurótas wends through some rather empty, undulating countryside with olive groves and farms, dignified by views over the Taíyetos backbone. In the Middle Ages, the strategic hotspot between Mystrá and Monemvasiá was Geráki (Γεράκι). Captured by the Franks in 1245, William II de Villehardouin gave it as a barony to Guy de Nivelet. Geráki ('falcon') evokes courtly visions of Guy and his falconer riding off to hunt where Japanese pick-up trucks now trundle through olive groves. Along with Mystrá, the Franks had to hand it over to the Byzantines in 1262, after the Battle of Pelagonia; Geráki was thereafter ruled by the Despotate of Mystrá and followed its history.

Modern Geráki is a dense white hill town, piled atop the ancient city of Geronthrai, famous in Spartan times for its festival in honour of warlike Ares. Scattered in the vicinity there are no fewer than four (locked) churches with 13th-century frescoes. The best one to seek out is the **Evangelístria**, a tall little domed church with fairly well-preserved frescoes; visit Old Geráki first and ask the caretaker about the key.

Old Geráki and churches
contact Mr Kourís, t 697 701 7597

Old Geráki, the medieval village that grew up directly under De Nivelet's castle, is 4km above the modern town, a kind of third-division Mystrá, abandoned in the 1800s. The motorcycle-riding, mobile-phone-toting Greek-only-speaking caretaker, Mr Kourís, is to be found up in the castle area. He is also your man if you want to see the locked interiors of any of Geráki's churches, especially the ones in the lower village; have your hotel phone Mr Kourís ahead of time. If that is too much trouble, the brick exteriors of these little churches both in and below the castle are well worth a visit. Wear sturdy shoes; the paths are rocky.

Three frescoed churches worth a look are, like all Geráki's churches, tiny and far more typical of the period than the churches in that imperial hothouse orchid, Mystrá. The first is **Ag. Paraskeví**, a cross-vaulted church built by the French, with traces of their 13th-century sculptural decoration and Greek frescoes from the 15th century. The back wall has portraits of the donors. The simple, aisleless **Zoodóchos Pigí** has paintings from the same period: note the priests dedicating the church, and John the Baptist, sadly contemplating the head in his hands, and a lovely enthroned Virgin – Geráki's painters were good on facial expressions.

Castle
open Tues–Sun 8.30–3

The most remarkable Franco-Greek fusion is at the top, in Guy de Nivelet's **castle**, still emblazoned with his moon and star coat of arms; it has superb views towards the Taíyetos, Mystrá and the Máni. Inside its walls, the little basilica of **Ag. Geórgios** boasts the only Gothic tabernacle in Greece, a curious, rugged work carved in the stone, with little knotted columns and decorated with the Villehardouin fleur-de-lys and Nivelet stars. Note too the ancient column and relief.

South of Geráki

South of Geráki, towards Skála and Gýthio, **Vrontamás** (Βρονταμάς) is proud of its houses by Ernst Ziller. Some 3km south is the turn-off to the surprisingly deep and wild Eurótas Gorge that houses the cave monastery called **Palaiomonástero** (Παλαιομονάστηρο), dedicated to Ag. Nikólaos, Ag. Nikítas and the Virgin. Besides a remarkable setting, it has some 12th-century frescoes and a grim history. Ibrahim Pasha burned alive the 500 villagers who sought refuge here on 15 September 1825, in one of the worst atrocities of the War of Independence. The massacre is solemnly commemorated every September.

Eastern Laconía: Epídauros Limerá

With the exception of Monemvasiá, the eparchy of Epídauros Limerá, or far east end of Laconía, is the back of beyond, stretching from the formidable slopes of Mount Párnonas down to storm-tossed Cape Maléas. There are plenty of beaches rimming the Lakonikós (Laconian) Gulf, but they are smacked by the wind much of the time, and more suited to the sea turtles who nest there; the Eurótas delta is one of the most important wetlands in the Peloponnese. It may be grim-looking for humans, but some 210 species of birds who pass through and the 60 species who nest here like it well enough. Some are rare, like the black pelican, the imperial eagle, the *basilonótamos* (on the rivers), and a unique fish, the *Tropidophoxineius Spartiaticus*.

Down the Myrtoan Coast

'Down the coast' is a bit of a misnomer: south of Poúlithra (in Arcadía), your chances of touching the sea are strictly limited by

Getting to Kyparíssi

Local **buses** make the trip to Kyparíssi once or twice a day from Molái, **t** 273 202 2209. The easiest way to reach Kyparíssi by **car** is to take the turn-off to Metamórfosi (Μεταμόρφωση) from either Molái or Sikéa on the Spárta–Monemvasiá road, and continue 40km through Achladókambos (Αχλαδόκαμπος), Lambókambos (Λαμπόκαμπος), Chárakas (Χάρακας) and then down, down, down to Kyparíssi (Κυπαρίσσι).

---

the eastern, sometimes utterly barren flanks of Mount Párnonas. But if you like long, lonesome drives over the wild mountains, scooting along at eagle level, this is the place for you. At least half of the roads are paved, and the little ports at the end of them are their own reward.

The extra effort it takes to reach **Kyparíssi** (pop. 400) makes it a place to linger. Surrounded by majestic, if rather terrifying mountains, the road winds down to the first white houses piled on the slope, all with tidy red tile roofs and gardens, next to a silvery plain of olives. It has a perfectly clear sea and pebbly beach, a few *kafeneíons*, a couple of shops and tavernas and that's it – as close to an island as you can get.

With your map, you can backtrack towards **Metamórfosi**, turning left after **Achladókambos** at the crossroads for **Richiá** (Ρειχιά). After this the asphalt gives out for a few kilometres, until you come to the left turn for the coast and the **Evanglístrias convent**, perched high above the sea, with lovely views. The main road from Richiá continues to **Géraka** (Γέρακα) and its fjord-like port, **Liménas Géraka**, with its three little tavernas and coves just south of the village. Within easy striking distince of Monemvasiá, however, it doesn't quite have the faraway feel of Kyparíssi.

Monemvasiá

Monemvasiá

Charm'd magic casements, opening on the foam

Of perilous seas, in faery lands forlorn.

Keats

Monemvasiá (Μονεμβασιά) is one of the natural wonders of the Peloponnese – a mighty Gibraltar floating just off the coast, an unassailable rock-berg moored to the coast by a bridge. No matter how many photos you may have seen, the Rock still startles, especially in October, when the upper plateau is a massive carpet of cyclamens, dyeing it a soft purple. The town of Monemvasiá, once home to 40,000 to 50,000 people, is invisible from land, tucked around on the south side of the rock facing the sea. It had only one entrance (*moni emvasis*), and getting through that one gate, if one came with unfriendly intent, was next to impossible. This sense of total security, similar to that of Venice in her lagoon, allowed the Monemvasiótes to create the Greek equivalent of an Italian medieval republic, ruled by an oligarchy of *archons*, who were also merchants and pirates as the need arose. For besides its made-to-order defensive potential, the Rock overlooked the main sea lane between the Bosphorus and the West.

Getting to Monemvasiá

Buses from Athens, **t** 210 512 4913, go direct to Monemvasiá (by way of Skála) twice daily, and there are three daily from Spárta. KTEL in Monemvasiá: **t** 273 206 1752. **Parking** along the road outside the gate can be exasperating, and you may get ticketed. In the summer (weekends only in winter), a **minibus** run by the municipality links the medieval town with the mainland (at the beginning of the causeway) daily every 15 minutes in high season, a bit less frequently in winter.

History

According to Pausanias, the first settlement here was Akra Minoa, founded perhaps by the Minoans as a trading counter, although as yet no trace of them has been found. It defended the ancient city of Epídauros Limerá. In AD 375 a mighty earthquake rent the Rock from the mainland, leaving a sandy isthmus between it and the shore. The present town of Monemvasiá was founded by Byzantine Emperor Maurice in 585, and it soon drew in the inhabitants of Epídauros Limerá and other less secure places, fleeing the invasions of Slavs and Avars. The mainland was given over to growing food for the city, while its vineyards produced the most prized wine of the Middle Ages; the Italians called it *malvasia* (there are still at least ten streets in Venice named after it), while in England, where tongues slurred it into 'malmsey', it was shipped to the court in butts big enough to drown in, as the Duke of Clarence demonstrated. The Monemvasiótes were feisty and independent enough to contribute ships, along with Naúplio and Athens, in a doomed expedition against the iconoclast Emperor Leo III in 727. The impregnability of their defences was severely tried in the 800s by the Saracens from Crete; they stood up to an onslaught of the Norman army from Sicily in 1147. By this time the emperors, especially the Comnenes, had seen the wisdom of granting the Monemvasiótes all manner of privileges to keep their loyalty.

As the Rock was the key to the southeast Peloponnese, this loyalty was a thorn in the side of the Franks in the 1240s. To besiege and blockade Monemvasiá, William de Villehardouin borrowed four manned ships from the Venetians. After three years, when the Monemvasiótes were reduced to eating cats and dogs, they offered to surrender, but on the condition that they kept all their privileges. William agreed; with the Rock under his belt, he could now capture Sparta and the Máni and control the entire Morea – with the exception of the ports of Methóni and Koroní, the price Venice extracted for her aid. After 14 years, when Monemvasiá returned to the Greeks as part of William's ransom, it became the port of Mystrá, a golden period when libraries and over 40 churches were founded. When Mystrá fell in 1456, the last Despot, Demétrios Paleológos, took refuge here, then fled as the Turks approached and was captured; the Monemvasiótes bluffed the Turks into not attacking them.

But this now isolated Greek outpost knew it would only be a matter of time before the Turks returned, and the Monemvasiótes knew they could hardly face them alone. They sought help from a Catalan pirate, Lopez de Baldaja, whose arrogance quickly led to his dismissal; they next tried Pope Pius II, but his attempts to impose his rule saw his representatives sent home after four years. In 1464, the Monemvasiótes turned to their ancient enemies, the Venetians. They confirmed the privileges of Napoli di Malvasia, as they called it, and strengthened its walls. But Venice was in decline herself, and in 1537, after Suleiman the Magnificent defeated the combined forces of Venice, Charles V and the Pope at Préveza, a treaty was signed handing Monemvasiá and Naúplio over to the Turks. The Venetian who wrote the treaty was later beheaded as a traitor in Venice, but the terms allowed the citizens to leave peacefully if they wished, and many did, taking their cannons, bells and vine-roots to Crete and Santoríni. That was the end of the malmsey. The Turks, who came when the cyclamens were out, named their new acquistion Menekschе, the 'Violet City'.

The Venetians made several attempts to regain Monemvasiá in the 17th century. Their technique – bombing the fort and starving out the defenders – failed to make them any friends among the locals, but it finally succeeded in 1690, after Francesco Morosini captured the rest of the Morea. The Venetians repopulated the town with Cretans, Albanians and many of the families who left in 1540. There was a building boom of churches and palaces. In 1715, the Turkish army that had reconquered the rest of the Morea turned up at Monemvasiá's door, and the Venetian governor surrendered the Rock without a fight. The resigned Venetians didn't even cut off his head.

Monemvasiá knew its last minute of glory in 1821 when, after a four-month siege that starved out its Turkish garrison, it became the first fortress captured by the Greeks in the War of Independence. One of the leaders was the famous *kapitana* from Spétses, Laskarína Bouboulína (*see* p.320). Although many of the old families moved back, the Rock went into decline as people abandoned their old houses for more spacious lodgings on the mainland in Géfira. Today 90 per cent of the population lives there, while the Byzantine and Venetian mansions in Kástro, protected by a preservation order that forbids even an overhead wire, are a powerful reminder of the Rock's past. Over the past 30 years, about half of the crumbling stone palaces have been immaculately restored as holiday homes, hotels, trendy bars and restaurants.

The Kástro

Géfira (Γέφυρα), or 'bridge', is Monemvasiá's mainland extension and a typical Greek seaside town, dignified with a beautiful view.

Monemvasiá's Poet

The sky is seven times blue. This clarity
is the primordial truth, my last will.

A plaque and bust mark the house near the entrance of the Kástro where Yánnis Rítsos, one of the major figures of 20th-century Greek poetry, was born in 1909. His family was one of the most important in Monemvasiá, but his life was sad: his father went insane and died, and his mother and brother died of tuberculosis when he was twelve, leaving him in the care of relatives. He went to law school in Athens, but ended up in a tuberculosis sanitorium; when he got out, he worked as an actor and dancer. In 1934 he joined the Greek Communist Party, and wrote his first poems, taking up the themes of socialism and suffering, and using vivid images from his personal experience. His most important pre-war work, *O Epitáfios* (*The Funeral Procession*) was dignified by a public burning in front of the Acropolis.

Rítsos joined the partisans and fought the Nazis, and against the monarchists in the Civil War that followed. In 1949 he was arrested and spent four years on Makrónisi, the bleak prison island in southeast Attica. His poems of the period celebrated the partisans, and Míkis Theodorákis (then in his left-wing period) put *O Epitáfios* to music, and the songs became anthems for the country's left-wing rallies. But Rítsos' work was far more than just political: he wrote mythological monologues, and shorter verses that were dry and ironic. His irony served him well in 1967, when he was arrested again by the military *junta* and sent back to Makrónisi: it was like a reunion of old acquaintances, he commented. He later went into exile, and his poetry remained banned in Greece until 1972. When he died in 1989, he was buried in Monemvasiá's little cemetery.

The walls and acropolis of **ancient Epídauros Limerá**, founded by the Argives, can still be seen in the fields north of Géfira, although most of the stone was reused for the Kástro. There's a long crescent of sand, 6km north of Géfira, the **Paralía tou Xifía**; there's another beach, **Porí**, 4km south of Géfira as well.

A causeway from Géfira leads to the **Kástro**, as the locals call the town on the Rock. The road passes the **cemetery**, the last resting place of Yánnis Rítsos (*see* box, above). Beyond are traces of the elaborate fortifications destroyed in order to build the road, but the entrance is through a single **gate**, and cars are not allowed. They wouldn't fit, anyway. The massive wooden doors of the gate, once closed every evening at sundown, are scarred by bullets.

Within, the cobbled main street is little more than an alley, lined with arty tourist shops and bars. It leads straight back to the main landmark of the lower town: the tall bell tower and church of **Christós Elkómenos** (the 'dragged Christ'), named for an icon that was so marvellous that the Emperor Isaac II had it stolen for a church near Constantinople in the 12th century. The curious marble relief over the door, of two peacocks grabbing a snake with a cow's head in between, is a relic of the original 11th-century church; other ancient marble bits were incorporated into the portal as well in the Venetian restoration of 1697. The church was badly damaged by the Turks in 1770 to punish the Greeks for joining the Orloff revolt, and only repaired after 1821, when it was given a neoclassical veneer. According to legend, the church's two painted thrones were placed there for the first king and queen of Greece.

The adjacent monastery, now the parish house, is marked by a Lion of St Mark over the door. The square also has a cannon dated 1763, a cistern (Monemvasiá has no springs, so every house had a cistern) and a Turkish mosque, now the local **Archaeological Collection**, containing fragments from Ag. Sophía and other buildings, reliefs and everyday items found up in the castle, as well as information on the town. Below the square you can wander down to the **Portello**, or little sea gate, to swim off the rocks.

Archaeological Collection
t 273 206 1403; open summer Tues–Sun 8–7.30, Mon 12–7.30; winter Tues–Sun 8–3, closed Mon; adm

Wandering about the lower town, you'll find Byzantine, Venetian and Turkish houses, built and rebuilt so often that it's hard to distinguish which is which. The Kástro's most popular church, the white 17th-century **Panagía Chrysaphítissa**, is down by the sea along the eastern walls; it was built to house an icon from Chrysapha, a village near Spárta, when it was given its marching orders by the Virgin. The Monemvasiótes built a chapel to house the icon, the people of Chrysapha took it back, suspecting foul play; but the icon flew back to its new home and Chrysapha had to settle for a substitute. The tiny chapel next to it is dedicated to a holy spring, although the water is now salty. Another church, **Panagía Myrtidiótissa** ('The Virgin of the Myrtle') is near the Elkómenos bell tower, and is the finest example of the Italo-Byzantine style in town. It has an elaborately carved iconostasis, originally in the Elkómenos (the church is usually locked, but you can see it through the window).

The Upper Town

From Panagía Myrtidiótissa, a path zigzags steeply up to the 1,000ft plateau. For centuries, thousands of people were dependent on supplies brought up along this path, and it was carefully designed to make access difficult for an attacker. It also defeated the locals; the last resident turned out the lights in the Upper Town in 1911. The door of the gate in the upper walls is marked with bullet holes, while a little plaque above informs all comers that 'Christ reigns here'. Anyone who didn't give a hoot and got past that would have to ascend a vaulted passage, lined with guardrooms and prison cells full of nasty traps, while defenders poured hot oil from the roof.

Although the walls up here are fairly intact, much of what stood inside them is a desolate, overgrown ruin. The great exception is **Ag. Sophía**, a beautiful cross-in-square church with an octagonal drum and round dome, balanced on the very lip of the precipice. Although attributed to Emperor Andronicos II in the late 1200s, it may well be older – no one can make out the inscription of its foundation. Unlike most Byzantine churches, Ag. Sophía has a two-storey loggia, built during the first Venetian period. Note the prettily carved capitals in the windows. The frescoes, mostly badly

Ag. Sophía
open during the summer 8–7.30; in winter, ask at the archaeological museum; they give keys to groups, so try to link up with one

damaged, are from the 13th century: you can make out the Pantocrator in the dome, the bishops and an angel. A single column and traces of mosaic pavement mark the site of the cloister. Although the houses are all ruined, you can still see their cisterns, and the citadel, up at the highest point – the last resort if the rest of the rock fell.

Useful Information in Monemvasiá

Malvásia Travel, t 273 206 1752, *malvtrvl@otenet.gr, malvtrvl@spa.forthnet.gr*, is in the centre of Géfira, on the Sparta–Monemvasiá road, 50m from the main *plateía*. It is also the town KTEL station and the place to go for information about rooms as well as car or moped rental.

Where to Stay and Eat in Monemvasiá

Monemvasiá Kástro ✉ 23070

Try not to bring too much luggage! A number of Venetian mansions have been tastefully restored and are open all year.

★ Ardamis >

Ardamis, t 273 206 1886, *www.ardamis.gr* (€€€€/€€€€). An 800-year-old tower, beautifully converted into rooms and suites with plenty of exposed beams and stone vaults, with a massive veranda over the sea for soaking up the views. They also have a pretty café.

Lazareto, t 273 206 1991, *lazareto hotel@yahoo.com* (€€€€/€€€). Large rooms and suites, with minibars and sea views; in the old Venetian quarantine station 700m before the Kástro's gate.

Zambelli Suites, t 273 206 1212, **t** 694 620 7515 (€€€/€€€). Three large rooms/studios for two to three people with kitchenettes, and a seating area. *Open all year*.

Byzantinó, t 273 206 1254/61351, *byzantino@yahoo.gr* (€€€€/€€). A choice of rooms, some large and furnished with antiques, some smaller under vaulted roofs. Prices vary widely, depending on the view.

Dina, t 273 206 1311 (€€€/€€). Rooms and studios, somewhat cheaper than the norm for the Kástro.

Malvasia, t 273 206 1323 (€€/€€). Three buildings (follow the signs), with rooms and suites, all air-conditioned with beautiful traditional furnishings. One, the Stelláki mansion, is the most imposing in town.

Matoula, t 273 206 1660. The oldest and prettiest garden restaurant; delicious *dolmádes* in lemon sauce overlooking the wine-dark sea. Go early; it's popular.

Kanoni, t 273 206 1387. Greek and international dishes plus a sea view. Open for coffee.

Géfira ✉ 23070

Among the advantages of staying in Géfira are the view of the big Rock, easy parking and lower prices. The disadvantage is the mosquito problem. Most bedrooms have screen windows, but coils are a good bet.

Pramataris, t 273 206 1833, *www.pramatarishotel.gr* (€€/€€). Well located by the beach and bridge with lovely sunrise views of the Rock, English speaking and friendly. They also have two apartments. *Open all year*.

Filoxenia, t 273 206 1716, *www.filoxenia-monemvasia.gr* (€€/€€). Overlooks the rocky town beach; its balconies offer fine views of the Rock. *Open Mar–Oct*.

Petrino Rooms, t 273 206 1136 (€€/€€). By the sea; a stone building with traditionally styled rooms with balconies. One of the prettiest places to stay. *Open all year*.

Akrogiáli, t 273 206 1056. The tables overlook the sea with enchanting views of Monemvasiá. Excellent local fare.

Taverna Pipenellis, t 273 206 1044. Two km south of town; no view, so they have to try harder in the kitchen, with *mamma* doing the business at the range.

Géfira. A seafront restaurant popular with discerning locals.

Monemvasiá Nightlife

The trendy bars in Kástro close at 3.30am, but by then the fun crowd has taken to the clubs out along the Spárta road one kilometre out. There's a new club even further up the road, of uncertain name, open in winter.

South of Monemvasiá: Neápolis, Elafónisos and Cape Maléas

The Peloponnese's easternmost prong, the Vátika peninsula, is wild and arid on the east side, and windblown and marshy on the west. None of its man-made attractions is particularly compelling – Elafónisos with its beautiful beaches, and Kýthera, the island of the goddess of love, are the main lures.

Neápolis and Cape Maléas

The road from Monemvasiá over the mountains has a certain austere charm, which is more than could be said of **Neápolis** (Νεάπολη). This 'new city' was born after Greek independence, when the farmers came down from the hills and settled on the fertile plain in sprawling hamlets, lumped together in 1845 as Neápolis. In ancient times this was Boeae (pronounced *Ví-e*), founded by Boias, one of the 101 descendants of Heracles, and just like modern Neápolis its population was drawn from the older Mycenaean settlements. An important Spartan port during the Peloponnesian War, and member of the Laconian League in Roman times, it became Vátika under the Byzantines, a name you will still see for the 12 surrounding villages. Today Neápolis looks to the sea: most of the action is concentrated along the waterfront, the sea views nicely closed in by Elafónisos and Kýthera. Leaving is actually the main reason for coming, although a surprisingly slick, cheesy strip of clubs north of town confirms that nocturnal Neápolis is the Las Vegas of the Vatíka peninsula, at least for the under-30s.

The best swimming in the area – and it's good – is out on Elafónisos (*see* opposite), but if you want to potter about this world's end, you could take the road above Neápolis to **Mesochóri** (Μεσοχώρι), a medieval village now all but abandoned, where the Byzantine chapel of Ag. Theodóri has the remains of fine frescoes. The next village, **Farkaló** (Φαρκαλό), 'the Balcony of Vátíka', with its stone houses and Byzantine churches, was the capital of the 12 villages in the Middle Ages, and it remained the most important town in these parts in Venetian and Turkish times. From here you can circle around to **Áno Kastaniá** (Ανω Καστανιά), at the top of a

Getting around South of Monemvasiá

Buses, t 273 402 3222, link Neápolis to Athens and Sparta at least three times a day, and go to Poúnda (for Elafónisos) four times a week, weekdays only.

Ferries, t 697 763 3567, to Elafónisos leave from Poúnda (opposite the island) regularly from 7am to 1am in summer, and from 7am to 7pm in winter.The *Andréas II*, **t** 273 402 4004, comes and goes to Kýthera three times daily in summer, less in winter. The *Mirtidiótissa*, **t** 273 402 9120, does the business every Tuesday.

Neápolis **port authority: t** 273 402 2228.

---

gorge, with a road winding down to a quiet sandy beach, and **Káto Kastaniá** (Κάτω Καστανιά) with a clutch of little Byzantine chapels. A beautiful cave was recently discovered near here, although it's still off limits to the public.

If you aren't subject to vertigo, and the wind isn't blowing your car off the road, another option is to take the paved road above **Láchio** and zigzag up the mountain (in itself a great place to watch the sunset behind Kýthera), then twist and turn down steeply again through Gothic pinnacles of rock to the remote but rather large village of **Velanídia** (Βελανίδια) 17km away, with a scattering of Byzantine chapels on the way. Or head south to **Ag. Nikólaos**, with a tiny fisherman's cove below called **Ag. Lías**; then continue down on a mostly unpaved road to **Cape Maléas** itself. This is also liable to be on the gusty side, and was dreaded by ancient sailors; the storms here blew Odysseus off course to the land of the Lotus-Eaters, which everyone has been looking for ever since. The cape, once the site of a Sanctuary of Poseidon, is marked by the white chapel of **Ag. Iríni**, built high on a terrace above the sea, where a single hermit lived in the early 1800s, living off the alms from passing sailors. Another landmark is the chapel of **Ag. Geórgios**, built into the cliff near the lighthouse.

Elafónisos: A Little Island with Big Beaches

The Venetians called this rocky island Cervi for its deer head shape, and the name in Greek, Ελαφόνησος, means the same thing. In AD 174 Pausanias saw a monument there dedicated to Kinadi, commander of Menelaos' ship to Troy. It was linked to the mainland until a few centuries ago, but became island enough (it's only 300m from Poúnda) for the Venetians and the Venieri family to hold on to it even after the Turks occupied the Peloponnese, and for it to follow the fortunes of its much bigger neighbour, Kýthera, passing to the British in 1815, then ceded to Greece in 1864. But don't expect to see any signs of this exciting past. What the little island does have are the best **beaches** in this part of the world: the gorgeous white crescents of sand and dunes on a transparent sea at **Símos** and **Leúki** (in the south, linked by a small road or caique) and the sands of **Nisiá tis Panagías**, with its cluster of baby islets just offshore (5km south of the port, linked by a paved road).

Where to Stay and Eat South of Monemvasiá

Neápolis ✉ 23053

Limira Mare, t 273 402 2236, *www.limiramare.gr* (€€€/€€). By the sea, with air-conditioning and water sports. *Open April–Oct.*

Vergina, t 273 402 3445, *www.verginahotel.com* (€€/€). More modest. *Open all year.*

Aïvali, t 273 402 2287 (€€/€). Air-conditioned rooms north of the centre on the sea. *Open all year.*

Elafónisos ✉ 23053

Elafónisos Mare, t 273 406 1349, *www.elafonisosmare.gr* (€€€€/€). This well-equipped and modern complex is set back a bit from the sea in its own garden, but has good sea views from the second floor. There is one studio; and prices vary according to the room size. *Open May–Oct.*

Asteri tis Elafonissou, t 273 406 1271 (€€/€€). In town, back from the sea; offers rooms with fridges. *Open all year.*

Lafotel, t 273 406 1138, *www.elafonisos.org* (€€/€€). Well-appointed and right on the beach. *Open May–Oct.*

Elafonissos, t 273 406 1268 (€/€). Smack on the beach, offering breakfast, a lunch barbecue and bar in the evenings. *Open Easter and June–Oct.*

The dunes, lakes and lagoons on the mainland opposite Elafónisos are important wetlands, where birds and the occasional loggerhead turtle come to nest. You'll find similar areas up the west coast of the peninsula, with dirt roads leading down to long, empty stretches of sand; aim for **Archángelos**, a fishing village with a long beach and a hotel. **Eléa** on its little cape, with views across to the Máni, also has a few places to eat, and rooms.

Kýthera

Tucked under the Peloponnese, Kýthera (ΚΥΘΗΡΑ), the isle of the goddess of love, is a wonderful slice of traditional Greece, on the way to nowhere. It owes a good part of its attraction to that fact.

The opening of the Corinth Canal in 1893 doomed even the minor commercial importance Kýthera once had by virtue of its position between the Ionian and Aegean seas. In the 20th century most of the population drifted over to the other side of the world; some 100,000 people of Kýtheran origin now live in Australia or 'Big Kýthera', as the 3,000 who remain in Greece call it.

If it can't quite match the shimmering luxuriance of Watteau's sumptuous masterpiece, *Pèlerinage à l'Île de Cythère*, the island does have stunning beaches and a handful of 'sights', and cliffs and meadows decorated with yellow *sempreviva*, 'eternal life', which the locals dry and hang around the house.

History

After Cronus, son of Gaia, took his golden sickle and castrated his father, Uranos, he cast the bloody member into the sea. This gave birth to Aphrodite, who according to Hesiod's *Theogony* rose out of

Getting to and around Kýthera

By air: There are two flights a day from Athens in season; **airport information**: **t** 273 603 8395; tickets from **Olympic Airways**, 49 El. Venizélou, Pótamos, **t** 273 603 3362.

By sea: Kýthera has two ports, **Diakófti** and **Ag. Pelagía** (sometimes used in high winds). In season there are ferries from Neápolis, on the nearby mainland (*see* p.391); year-round connections on **ANEN Lines** between Piraeus, Neápolis, Gýthio, Kalamáta, Antikýthera and Kíssamos (Crete); contact **Porfyra Travel** (*see* p.397) for schedules. **Port authority**: Diakófti, **t** 273 603 4222; Ag. Pelagía, **t** 273 603 3280.

From Kapsáli, a caique visits nearby beaches and Avgó Island, **t** 273 603 1222.

By road: There are no **buses**, but **taxis** charge set fees. **Hire cars** (and **motorbikes** and **scooters**) from **Panayiotis** in Kapsáli and at the airport, **t** 273 603 1600, *panayioti@otenet.gr*; and cars from **Cerigo**, at the airport and in Chóra, **t** 273 603 1363; **Active**, in Ag. Pelagía, **t** 273 603 3749, *mact@aias.gr*; and **Anna**, in Ag. Pelagía, **t** 273 603 4153, *romadica@otenet.gr*.

the foam on her scallop shell at Kýthera, accompanied by Eros and Himeros (Desire). She apparently found it far too puny for her taste and drifted off east to Paphos, Cyprus. A sanctuary dedicated to Aphrodite on Kýthera was the most sacred of all her temples in Greece, but scarcely a trace remains today. Aphrodite was called Astarte by Kýthera's first settlers, the Phoenicians, who came for its murex shells, the source of a reddish purple dye for royal garments – hence the island's other ancient name, Porphyrousa.

The Minoans, the first in Greece to worship Aphrodite, made Kýthera a trading counter. Its location between Crete and the mainland, and between the Aegean and Ionian seas, was a busy neighbourhood, and the island was in great demand: Kýthera has been invaded 80 times in recorded history. Particularly frightful were the 10th-century incursions of the Saracens based on Crete, which caused the island to be abandoned until Nikephóros Phokás reconquered Crete.

From the 12th century, the Eudaimonoioannis family from Monemvasiá ruled Kýthera. The Venetians occupied the island in 1204, but with the help of Emperor Michael Palaeológos, Kýthera was regained for the Eudaimonoioannis and served as a refuge for Byzantine nobles until 1537, when Barbarossa stopped on his way home after his unsuccessful siege of Corfu and devastated the island. The Venetians took over again in the 16th century and in their slurry Italian accents redubbed the island Cerigo. In 1864 Kýthera was ceded to Greece by the British with the other Ionians.

Chóra (Kýthera)

Chóra (Χωρα), the capital of the island, is a pretty-as-a-picture-postcard blue and white Greek village hanging above the sea, guarded by a ruined 16th-century **Venetian castle**, built over a Byzantine fort of 1150. Its location was supposedly selected by pigeons, who took the tools of the builders from a less protected site; inside the walls, the residence of the former governor houses the island's Venetian and English archives and two churches built by the Venetians, Catholic **Panagía Myrtidiótissa** and Orthodox **Panagía Orfáni**. Ten old **Venetian mansions** in Chóra still retain their coats of arms, and a small **Archaeology Museum** has artefacts from Minoan times to gravestones from the English occupation. From June to October the **Tzannes Gallery** displays paintings of the island by New Yorker-Kýtheran George Tzannes.

Archaeology Museum
t 273 503 1739; open Tues–Sun 8.30–3

Tzannes Gallery
t 273 603 8292; www.tzannesart.com

Below Chóra, **Kapsáli** (Καψαλι) is the most developed resort on the island, with its two pebble and sand beaches, one very sheltered and boaty, the other a bit more exposed. Kapsáli's **Avgó** (egg) **islet** is said to be the spot where Aphrodite was born.

Kálamos, just east, is within walking distance. One of its churches, **Ag. Nikítas**, has a pretty bell tower, and there is a restaurant and some rooms for rent by the square. Dirt roads continue across the rugged landscape to various beaches; the nearest is pebbly **Chálkos**, set in a beautiful, almost enclosed bay.

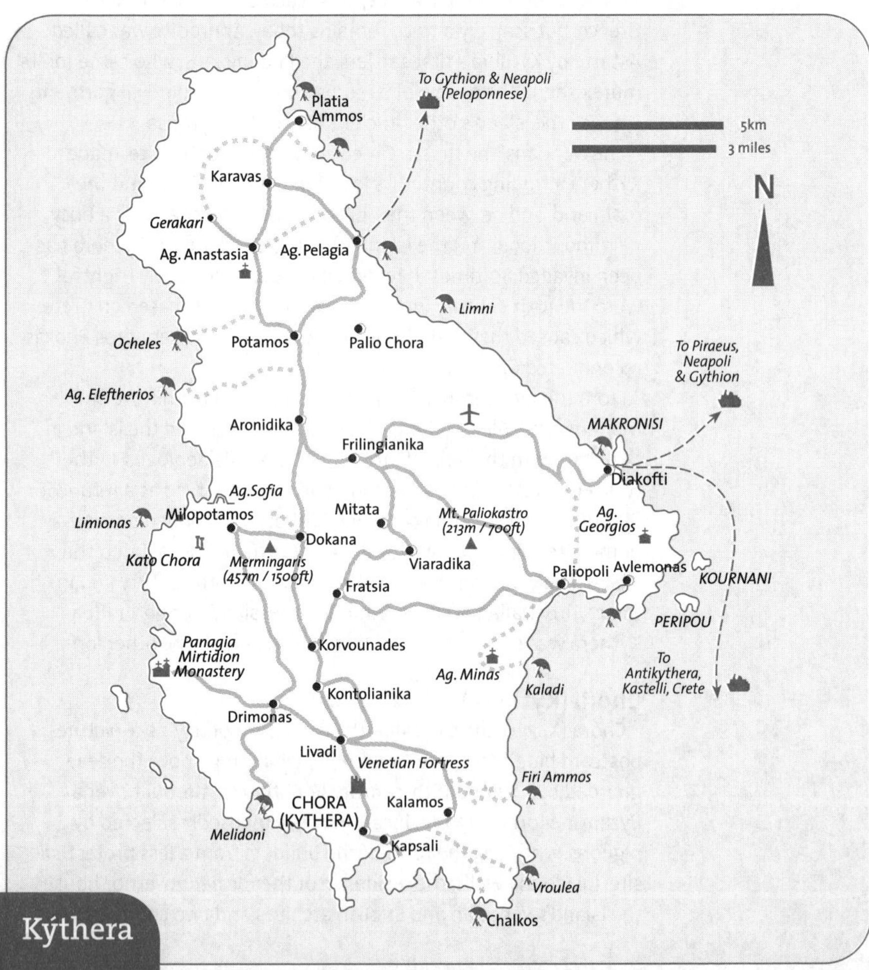

Northwest of Chóra

Five km north of Chóra, **Livádi** (Λιβάδι), the commercial centre of the island, has a landmark 13-arched bridge built by the British in 1822 and proudly heralded as the largest in Greece – until 2004, when the Gulf of Corinth bridge stole its thunder. If it seems unaccountably grand for the setting, the story goes that its size is a result of the British engineer's romance with a local girl and his desire to prolong his stay on the island. Ring ahead to visit the Roússos ceramic workshop, where the tradition of Kýthera pottery is kept alive, now into the fourth generation.

Roússos ceramic workshop
t 273 603 1124

Heading east from Livádi, you'll come across a good collection of Byzantine and later artefacts in **Káto Livádi**'s museum. A 4km dirt road leads on to the dramatic beach of **Fíri Ámmos** ('red sands'), popular with snorkellers. West of Livádi via **Drimónas**, the 19th-century **Monastery of the Panagía Mirtidíon** and its carved bell tower are magnificently set on the wild west coast among cypresses, flowers and peacocks. The monastery is named after a gold-plated icon of the Virgin and Child, discovered in the myrtle. Two islets just below are said to be pirate ships that the Virgin petrified for daring to attack her church.

Káto Livádi museum
t 273 603 1731; open Mon–Fri 8–2.30

North of Drimónas, **Milopótamos** (Μιλοπόταμος) is the closest thing to Watteau's vision of Cythère, a pretty village with a waterfall, criss-crossed by tiny canals. The lush valley is called the Neraída, or Nymph; an old watermill lies along the path to the waterfall **Foníssa**, 'murderer', named after a girl who took her life by jumping into it. On quiet evenings in the café you can hear the nightingales sing. The nearby fortified ghost town of **Káto Chóra** was built by the Venetians in 1560 after Barbarossa destroyed Palió Chóra (*see* below), its gate guarded by a well-preserved relief of the Lion of St Mark gripping an open book (a sign that the town was in Venice's favour), bearing the angelic words '*Pax Tibi, Marce, Evangelista Meus*'. Inside are ruined houses and churches, some with frescoes (but mostly locked). A road descends steeply to one of the island's best secluded beaches, white sandy **Limiónas**.

A road from Káto Chóra leads down to the Ag. Sofía Cave. In the past, the cave housed a church, and inside there are frescoes and mosaics, as well as impressive stalactites and stalagmites; some say it tunnels all the way under Kýthera to Ag. Pelagía. To the south, **Mitáta** is a great place for picnics, surrounded by lovely green countryside; the cool, clear water of its spring is delicious. It's also a good spot to purchase thyme honey.

Ag. Sofía Cave
usually open summer Mon–Fri 3–8, Sat and Sun 11–5, but check in the village

The East Coast

Paliópoli (Παλαιόπολις) is a tiny village on the site of ancient **Skandeia**, the city mentioned by Thucydides. There was a Minoan trading settlement here as well, from 2000 BC until the rise of the

Mycenaeans; their long-ago presence has bestowed archaeological status on the long and lovely Paliópoli beach, which has kept it pristine except for a taverna. In ancient times, devotees would climb to the splendid Temple of Urania Aphrodite, 'Queen of the Heavens', to pay their respects to the daughter of Necessity, whom even Zeus could not control. The Christians destroyed it and built the church of **Ag. Geórgios**, re-using the temple's Doric columns.

In nearby **Avlémonas** (Αβλέμονασ), a fishing village and resort, locals can direct you to the 'ruins' of Helen's throne where she first met Paris as well as the sea baths of Aphrodite. Nearby are boulders grooved by the Mycenaeans to channel blood from sacrifices, and an ancient cave dwelling resembling a five-roomed house, with an early example of a column used for structural support. The coast is guarded by a small octagonal **fortress** built by the Venetians, who left a few rusting cannons inside. The island's most stunning beach, **Kaladí**, is 2km away: the road stops at a blissful little chapel, from where a steep rough track leads down to the glorious pebbly beach.

North of Avlémonas, **Diakófti** (Διακόφτι) is the island's main port and very low-key resort with the island's only white sand beach, sheltered by a pair of islets, **Makronísi** (now linked by a causeway to shore) and **Prasonísi**.

Palió Chóra and the North

Palió Chóra (or Ag. Dimitríou) is a Byzantine ghost town, founded by Kýthera's Eudaimonoioannis in their native Monemvassian style. Set high on the rocks, it had 800 people and 72 churches and was carefully hidden from the sea – Barbarossa only found it by capturing some locals and torturing them until they told him where it was. Beside the ruins of the fort is a terrible 100m (330ft) abyss, **Kakiá Langáda** – 'bad gorge', where mothers threw their children before leaping themselves, to avoid being sold into slavery. There are a few frescoes in the haunted churches, but because of the dark memories the site was never again inhabited.

Palió Chóra is near **Potamós** (Ποταμός), which, despite its name, has no river. It is the largest village in the north, very authentic, and on Sunday people from across the island gather at the big weekly market. West of Potamós, **Ag. Elefthérios** is a lovely secluded beach, and a pretty place to watch the sunset.

From the pretty village of **Karavás**, the road continues to the fine beach, taverna and rooms at **Platiá Ámmos**. **Ag. Pelagía** (Αγ. Πελαγία), Kýthera's northern port looking across to Elafónisos, also has a long pebble beach and a few more facilities, if not a lot of boats, since many have diverted to Diakófti. There are better beaches to the south, including **Kalamítsa**, 2km away on a dirt road.

Useful Information on Kýthera

Porfyra Travel, Livádi, **t** 273 603 1888, *www.kythira.info*. For ferry tickets, accommodation, etc.

Glass-bottomed boat tours, around Kýthera's and Elafónisos' beaches and caves. Contact **Spiros Kasmiatis**, **t** 697 402 2079.

Kýthera Festivals

Early Aug: Two-day wine festival in Mitáta.

6 Aug: Traditional dance party in Avlémonas.

Oct: Photographic meetings, with exhibitions around the island.

Where to Stay and Eat on Kýthera

For a complete list of rooms on the island, see *www.kythera.gr*.

Chóra (Kýthera) ✉ 80100

Margarita, off the main street, **t** 273 603 1711, *www.hotel-margarita.com* (€€€/€€€). A dozen attractive rooms in a 19th-century mansion. New French owners promise croissants, quiches and English tea. *Open all year.*

★ Nostos >

Nostos, **t** 273 603 1056, *www.nostos-kythera.gr* (€€€/€€€). In the centre, a 19th-century residence with seven antique-filled rooms and a café. *Open all year.*

Xenonas Keiti, **t** 273 603 1318 (€€€/€€). Beautiful 18th-century mansion that has hosted at least two Greek prime ministers on their visits to the island.

Castello, near the fortress, **t** 273 603 1069, *www.castelloapts-kythera.gr* (€€/€€). Three studios and six rooms leading off a walled garden.

Belvedere, **t** 273 603 1892. Pizzeria-cum-grill house with a great view.

Zorba's, **t** 273 603 1655. Old-fashioned local classic – the best in Chóra.

Kapsáli ✉ 80100

Raikos, between Chóra and Kapsáli, **t** 273 603 1629, *www.raikoshotel.gr* (€€€/€€€). One of the island's posher places, light and bright, with a pool and water sports. *Open May–Sept.*

Iannis Avgerinos, on the beach, **t** 273 603 1189 (€€/€€€). Rooms and apartments converted from fishermen's huts, in an olive grove.

Daponte Stella, **t** 273 603 1245 (€€/€€). Peaceful and private, with access to the gorgeous secluded beach of Sparagário.

Poulmentis Rooms, **t** 273 603 1003 (€€/€€). Clean and comfortable.

Filio, just inland in Kálamos, **t** 273 603 1054 (€/€). Rooms to rent at a charming taverna, one of the very best on the island, where locals go to sample traditional Kythniot cuisine.

Hydragogio, **t** 273 603 1065. Dine under the trellis of this excellent restaurant, run by a young Belgian couple, with a wide choice of vegetarian specialities. *Closed Oct–April.*

In summer, Kapsáli has most of the island's nightlife; try the music cocktail bars **Mercato** and **Fox Anglais**.

Livádi ✉ 80100

Mylos Studios, **t** 210 417 1913 (€€€/€€€). Studios of character, in an 18th-century windmill.

Aposperides, **t** 273 603 1656, *www.greek-tourism.gr/kythera/aposperides* (€€/€€). A pristine hotel.

Grigoria Rooms, **t** 273 603 1124, *www.greek-tourism.gr/kythera/grigoria* (€€/€€). Rooms and studios with the pottery-making Roússos family; guests are welcome to help themselves to free garden vegetables.

Pierros, **t** 273 603 1014 (€/€). Inexpensive rooms and one of the oldest and most traditional tavernas, with home cooking and kind prices.

Avlémonas ✉ 80100

Manti, 150m from the beach, **t** 273 603 3039, *www.manti.gr* (€€€/€€). Handsome rooms and apartments.

Maria Varda, **t** 273 603 1727, *www.kythera.gr/wheretostay/varda* (€€/€€). New building with sea views and four new flats. *Open April–Oct.*

Skandeia, near Paliópoli, **t** 273 603 3700. Greek specialities served under an enormous plane tree.

Sotiris, **t** 273 603 3722. Taverna in a square overlooking the sea, preparing great seafood caught by the owners.

To Korali, **t** 273 603 4173. Friendly little fish taverna.

Diakófti ✉ 80100

Sirene Villas, right on the sea, **t** 273 603 3900, *www.sirene.gr* (€€€/€€€). For peace and quiet, with big verandas and kitchens.

Manolis, **t** 273 603 3748, on the beach. Good fish taverna, with interesting extras like pittas filled with cheese and greens. *Open eves only in winter.*

Mitáta ✉ 80100

★ Michális >

Michális, **t** 273 603 3626. Informal taverna with panoramic views. People come from across Kýthera to eat island specialities, including cockerel and rabbit, prepared with vegetables from their own garden.

Pótamos ✉ 80100

Xenóna Pitsinades, south in Aroniádika, **t** 273 603 3877, *www.pitsinades.com* (€€/€€). Six traditionally decorated rooms with arches and vaults in restored 150-year old house. *Open mid-June–mid-Sept.*

Ag. Pelagía ✉ 80100

9 Muses, **t** 273 603 3155, *www.greek-tourism.gr/kythera/9muses* (€€€/€€€). Near the beaches, with sea views from every room.

Venardos, **t** 273 603 4100, *www.venardos-hotels.gr* (€€€/€€€). Smart hotel built around a pool, with a spa offering aroma- and thalassotherapy.

Romantica, **t** 273 603 3834, *www.romanticahotel.gr* (€€€/€€). A minute from the beach, pleasant rooms and apartments sleeping up to four, plus a pretty pool.

Amir Ali, inland at Karavás, **t** 273 603 4346. A café in a gorgeous setting near a spring, named after a Turkish tax collector who died here. *Closes sunset.*

The Máni

There are really two Mánis. The **Outer Máni**, the part that belongs to Messenía, stretches from Kalamáta to Ítilo, a marvellous blend of hills, bays and seaside villages, all backed by the jagged Taíyetos range. Its largest and most beautiful town is Kardamýli. And while not lushly fertile, the Outer Máni's olive groves and plane-shaded *plateía* assume paradisaical proportions in comparison with the **Inner** (or **Deep**) **Máni**, the part that belongs to Laconía. This has Gýthio as a gateway, but its core is the tower-studded middle finger of the Peloponnese, where the Taíyetos hunker down in a no-frills cascade of barren limestone south to Cape Taíneron. There is virtually no water, and hardly any arable land except around Areópolis and by Cávo Grósso. In spring, these barren rocks have an ephemeral covering of green, and the entire Inner Máni becomes a yellow and pink rock garden. But the rest of the year, it displays grey rocks, prickly pear and seared grass, with tenacious olives

Visiting the Máni

By **car**, the Outer Máni can be traversed easily in a day in the 80km from Kalamáta to Areópolis, although to do so would be to miss a lot of its charm. The Inner Máni is also a small enough area to drive around in one day, and many visitors do just that, using Gýthio as a base. From Gýthio to Areópolis it's 25km, and from Areópolis to Cape Taíneron a mere 36km. If time permits, a day or two in three or more places would be ideal.

In the high season, **book accommodation**. In the off season, finding somewhere to stay is easy. Many of the hotels are traditional, and run by local people who have a story to tell, making the choice of accommodation part of the experience.

knuckled down in rocky terraces – so stunted that they never impede the view. The landscape is austere, almost inhuman. But so beautiful and alien is this mountain desert surrounded by pounding surf on both sides that even the dustiest historical account waxes poetic. No wonder the Máni is famous for its dirges. These isolated regions produced a unique and warlike culture which reached its heights in the 17th and 18th centuries, and was still going strong until well after 1850.

History

The Máni has been inhabited since Neolithic times, as finds in the caves at Diroú prove. In the Bronze Age, both Phoenician traders and Mycenaeans were a presence, and it was important enough for Homer to mention eight of the Máni's cities (Iri, Enopi, Kardamýli, Ítilo, Messe, Las, Kranai, Elos and Augeia). After 1200 BC it was subject to Sparta. Early in this period, **Cape Taíneron** was already an important shrine to chthonic Poseidon, and its *temenos* a place of asylum, meaning that a lot of tough customers could roam the area with impunity. The Máni remained relatively prosperous in Roman times, boasting several cities of the **Free Laconian League**, a league, like so many in Peloponnesian history, founded to impede Spartan ambitions. Even when sidelined, Sparta was the Hannibal Lecter of the Peloponnese, and great care was always taken to make sure it stayed de-fanged. While many citizens of the Máni were no doubt going peacefully about their business, Taíneron was already garnering a dark reputation as the gathering point for a motley crew of adventurers, always ready to hire themselves out to anyone making landfall at the cape and offering enough gold. During the Byzantine period it was not showered with attention, partly because of its isolation and partly because of its increasingly wild reputation. At this point, remnants of the **Slavic tribes** then roaming the Taíyetos settled and began assimilating with the already independent-minded natives.

Who were the Maniátes? Some theories based on linguistic analysis suggest that the bulk of Maniátes are remnants of the Spartans fleeing Slavic invasions. The eight-syllable *myrologia* ('dirges') of the Inner Máni display Dorian origins. Some suggest that they were remnants of the Frankish principality, fleeing medieval Nikli and other centres in Arcadía when the Turks came. Certainly their hierarchical and warlike social system has Spartan and feudal overtones. Cretan refugees from the Turkish conquest of their island in the late 1600s definitely added to the mix, and probably to that one could add just loose ends from anywhere and everywhere else. The Máni's isolation and Greece's turbulent history combined to make this a cultural melting pot, or rather a constantly bubbling cauldron.

A Note on Maniáte Churches and Towers

Maniáte churches are fascinating. All are small, but their exteriors and interiors are lovingly decorated, often with childlike charm. The Máni is simply so rich in them that the most dilapidated have been left to moulder away, doubling as animal shelters, bird houses and bat caves. Some churches resemble piles of enormous stones, but are decorated with care inside. Ag. Pandaleímonos in Boulárii is a good example of the type, as is the Sássaris family church near Mézapos. There has been an effort recently to signpost churches and monuments. Churches in isolated spots are invariably locked; ask at your hotel or in the nearest village coffeehouse about keys.

Towers exist everywhere: all alone as watch towers, in company with one-storey houses, or most commonly with two-storey houses. Villages resemble medieval Italian hill villages – Kítta or Váthia look like miniature San Gimignanos. Since the 'Franks' were actually mostly Italian in the last part of their Peloponnesian interlude, and the Venetians from Koróni and Methóni were a constant influence, there may have been some borrowing. Certainly in the beginning the towers were home-made versions of the Venetian watch towers that dot the Peloponnese – no-nonsense affairs, meant to give height, not to display wealth. They become more elaborate as their owners grew richer, and some of them take on the trappings of little castles. This effect is heightened by the tendency, as time went by, to put walls around the house and tower, creating an inner courtyard, and to add a church as well. These tower complexes exist in the Inner Máni, but they positively proliferate in the richer Outer Máni. The stone work could be rough, almost megalithic, as if the Cyclops had come to town. But this, too, changed over time and became more sophisticated, especially among the Maniáte clans with pretensions, and there were a lot of those. You would be on precarious ground dating buildings by their architectural style, however; what makes the Máni so remarkable is that their 'medieval cities' were built from 1600 on and were being added to as late as 1850.

★ Máni tower houses (box, above)

The earliest **churches** date from about the 6th century, although there is evidence that the Máni was not totally converted until the 800s when a bishopric was established. At that point the Máni was under Byzantine control to the extent that they could at least map it and give it the name '**Castle Maina**', which it has retained until today. The most arresting etymological theory derives Maina from *manes* (or *mánii*), the name given the Furies, those frightening female harridans at home in Taíneron and Hades, and who were worshipped in Arcadía and elsewhere. Our words 'maniac' and 'manic' come from the same root, a fitting etymology for the warlike culture.

With no real authority in place, except in a castle or two, the law of the sword, cannon and gun prevailed. Barbarian invasions, unrest and plagues in the rest of the Peloponnese sent a growing number of refugees to the area. Farming alone could not possibly have sustained the population and, by the late Byzantine period, it wouldn't have suited their temperament either. More lucrative activities such as **piracy** and the **slave trade** blossomed. The Franks came and fortified the castle of Maina, but did not attempt many inroads into the hinterland. And thus, over time, the free-wheeling, weapon-toting Maniátes developed their own social system. An aristocratic few, the **Nikliáni**, had the political clout, and their houses sprouted high, narrow towers with tiny openings for guns, and often a platform on top for a cannon. The lower strata were called **Achamnómeri**; they had very few rights, and were not only obliged to help the Nikliáni in their wars, but were forced to live in low, tower-less houses with flimsy roofs within shooting range of the towers, so retribution would be swift if they rebelled. That certainly explains the compact quality of Maniáte tower villages.

In the Máni, the lawless, war-like ethos joined seamlessly with the church in a symbiotic relationship that can only be marvelled at for its sheer chutzpah. There are tiny churches everywhere, and when fighting made going to church difficult, churches were added to the tower compounds. Ritual was observed, and a Maniáte was perfectly capable of devoutly making the sign of the cross in front of a church he was trying to blow to smithereens if it sheltered a rival. It speaks volumes for life in the Máni that there are no large churches at all.

Turf wars over scarce land resources may explain how the fighting became institutionalized into **vendettas** with elaborate rites of correct behaviour regarding truces, treatment of women and so on. Certainly by the time outsiders visited the Máni and began to record its strange ways, etiquette and murder went hand in hand, and the vendetta was an accepted, even glorified way of life. The birth of a male was announced as the birth of a new 'gun' in the family, and the Maniátes raised the presence of death to the heights of poetry in their wonderful ***myrologia***. These were long-drawn-out extempore funeral songs chanted by black-garbed women (*mirologístres*) that could go on for hours, in praise of the dead, in lamentation against 'fate' (*myrologia* means 'fate words'), and, in the many cases of violent death, actively encouraging revenge. Their creators counted on formulaic phrases and patterns that gave time for the addition of new phrases that would apply specifically to the deceased. They were as practised and passionate in their recitals as any Homeric bard.

God made so many good things, but one thing failed to make,
A bridge athwart the sea, and a stair to the underworld,
That one might cross, one might descend and go to the world beneath,
And see the young folk where they sit, the old folk where they lie,
And see the little children, how they fare without their mothers.

During the **Turkish period**, the Máni was one of those enclaves where entering was so hazardous that it was avoided whenever possible. By this time the aristocratic Nikliáni had fragmented into small family clans, and tiny villages could house two or even more clans, their towers bristling with cannons and guns, implacably at war, and yet so close together they could shout insults at each other with ease. In other cases, clan families held somewhat larger areas like the Grigorákis clan around Skoutári and the

Mavromichális clan at Tsímova (Areópolis) and Liméni. Many of them grandly claimed to descend from Byzantine royal houses.

The Turks tried various strategies to control the Maniátes. In 1669, they allowed them 'privileges' denied to other Greeks: to ring their church bells, put crosses on their belfries and pay lower taxes. They also rescinded the child tax law, so Maniáte first sons did not have to become Janissaries as they did in the rest of Greece. Of course, they were just making a virtue of necessity, because no one was about to enter the Máni to enforce the law. The Turks contented themselves with building forts at Kelefá and Pórto Káyio, just to keep their hand in, and to try to counter growing Venetian influence in the Máni. Their hope was that they could cater to one or two important clans and rule through them. It was actually a time of prosperity for the Máni. The wily Maniátes took the privileges, and plotted against the Turks with all and sundry at the same time. They were a virtual recruitment centre for Venetian and Russian efforts to harass the Sultan. They sent legations to the pope, legations to Napoleon – in fact legations were sent to anybody who might help them against the Turks.

Like other freedom fighters in Greece, they were left in the lurch again and again as the **Great Powers**, influenced by larger political interests, briefly helped, then pulled out and left them to suffer Turkish reprisals. But the Maniátes never gave up. By 1776, the Turks, somewhat at their wits' end, formally invested all local powers in **Beys**, chosen from the Máni's important clans. In return for collecting taxes and keeping order, these Beys were offered protection from other clans by the Turkish Capitan Pasha of the area. Not surprisingly, the Maniáte Beys, or the best of them, did manage to wrest more privileges from the Turks while doing very little in return. It was a dangerous job: out of the seven Beys from 1776 to 1821, three were executed by the Turks, and three summarily dismissed. The last Bey was the famous **Petróbey** of the Mavromichális clan. Like the Kolokotrónis family in Arcadía, they provided many 'guns' for the War of Independence when it came.

Ironically, the victory they fought so hard for would turn out to be the death knell for their own way of life. Constitutional rule and a foreign king did not sit well with Maniátes, who would have preferred to carry on as before, or even to enlarge their territory. Well after members of the Mavromichális clan had assassinated Capodístria, Greece's first president, the young King Otto's advisors decided that the Maniátes needed to be 'civilized'. The entire area was far too well fortified and full of potential rebels. One of the king's first edicts was that the towers in the Máni and Arcadía had to go. Arcadía complied, but the Máni didn't. When King Otto sent his Bavarian troops down to the Máni on a tower-destruction mission, the entire army were captured by the Maniátes, stripped naked and held for ransom. A typical example of the Maniáte sense of humour is the price they asked the king to pay: 20 cents a soldier, 10 cents an officer, and two dollars for a donkey.

Eventually even the Máni was brought to heel, but not until the tower order, luckily for posterity, was rescinded. Taming the Máni was a slow process. Even now, a very high proportion of its citizens are in the armed forces, the airforce in particular. And the Máni has produced more than its share of the political families that are still a force in the Greek government. The common expression in Greek, to hold something *Maniátiko*, means holding an implacable grudge that demands revenge. *Mirologístres* still exist, although diminished in ranks. And reading the death notices in the local paper proves that poetic eulogies have not yet gone out of style in the Máni. One family in Areópolis buried a loved one recently and commissioned a *mirologístra*. Her lament 'broke the heart of the rocks', the satisfied funeral-goers proclaimed.

Water is now piped into the Inner Máni, making it difficult to comprehend just how barren it was. For years, the young defected to the cities en masse, leaving the old folks behind in the crumbling ruins of their tower houses. How many years longer will those old women in black be seen sitting in front of low tower doors, with huge Kelvinator refrigerators sent by the kids gleaming in the depths behind? A few young people are coming back to help with the new tourist boom; there is building going on everywhere, and fortunately almost all of it in the native style. Right now, the Máni, sitting at the start of a new millennium, still looks back to the old. This is a good time to visit, before it changes utterly.

The Inner Máni

Gýthio: Gateway to the Inner Máni

Gýthio

Not many towns can claim they were founded by two gods settling a dispute over a pot. Heracles was miffed because the priestess at Delphi refused to purify him after one of his forays into mayhem and murder. In a huff, he stole the tripod she sat on while receiving oracular messages from Apollo, thus leaving her without a pot to 'see' in. Apollo wouldn't take that insult sitting down, and fisticuffs broke out between himself and the Peloponnese's greatest hero at Pheneós. Zeus stepped in, reclaimed the tripod for Delphi and made the boys shake hands. As a sign of their new bond, they were to build together a new city – Gýthio.

Perhaps that explains why Gýthio is bathed in Apollo's sun and why it has produced citizens as rough and tough as Heracles all through its bold, bad history. Gýthio was a Mycenaean settlement; *tholos* tombs have been found at nearby Mavrovoúni, and were

Getting to and around Gýthio

The Gýthio (Γύθειο) **bus** station, **t** 273 302 2228, is close to the sea on the Sparta road. At last glance there were six buses per day to and from Athens (**t** 210 512 4913) via Corinth–Trípolis–Spárta; two for Kalamáta via Ítilo; and four for Areópolis and Geroliménas, passing the campgrounds at Mavrovoúni and Passava. You can even get to Váthia on some days. For Monemvasiá, you'll have to take a bus 17km up the Spárta road to Xánia, and wait for a connecting bus.

Ferries to Kýthera are supposed to be daily, and to Crete three times a week; contact the Rozákis Travel Agency (*see* box opposite) to be sure; they can also help with **car rentals** (unavailable further south). **Taxis**, **t** 273 302 2601, wait opposite the KTEL station. **Port authority**: **t** 273 302 2262.

apparently used by the Germans as bunkers during the Second World War. During the Classical period it was Sparta's port and a town of *perioikoi* (*see* p.364), famous for its murex molluscs that produced their prized purple dye, the imperial colour. The town came into its own when the Romans created the Free Laconian League, to act as a buffer against Sparta.

Today Gýthio claims 4,000 inhabitants, and tourism is big business. Overlooking a curved bay, its picturesque pastel houses tumble down the hill from the ancient acropolis, Laryssion. Houses, hotels and restaurants decorate one side, and the Gulf of Laconía decorates the other. Twenty years ago, this was a shabby town in a beautiful setting, where depressing neoclassical hotels with peeling paint and problematic plumbing were necessary evils for anyone awaiting a ferry to Crete or Kýthera. Not any more. The hotels have been renovated and joined by newer rivals, giving Gýthio one of the best collections in the Peloponnese. Gýthio did, after all, host one of the most consequential honeymoons in history, when Paris spent his first night with Helen on the tiny island of Kranai, now **Marathonísi**, before departing for Troy.

The fishing port is huddled to the south, over by the causeway that ended Marathonísi's days as an island in 1896. The good **beaches** are either to the north towards Monemvasiá, past the headland, or 2km to the south towards Areópolis, beyond Mavrovoúni. Shod in plastic beach shoes to avoid the sea urchins who also enjoy the rocks, you can have a pleasant swim off pine-studded Marathonísi and to visit its Museum of the Máni at the same time.

Museum of the Máni
t 273 302 2676; open Tues–Sun 8.30–2.30

The **Museum of the Máni** is housed in the renovated fortress tower of Zanetbey Grigorákis, built in the late 18th century, when this was still an island. It is a good introduction to the Máni, with portraits of the locals as well as foreign visitors during the Turkish period. On the main floor, look for the flag flown by the Eastern Máni during the War of Independence. There is a wonderful portrait of the great Petróbey, mustachioed, and smoking a *chibouk*, a pipe so long its bowl goes right down to the floor. Big pantaloons, tightly fitting calf leggings and slippers complete the picture of the great man 'at home'. The top of the tower offers pictures and floor plans of typical Maniáte towers, with explanations in Greek and English.

Roman theatre
adm free

The **Roman theatre** is signposted, if you look carefully, on the coastal road north of town. It makes a nice destination for an evening *vólta*. Even before its marbles were hauled off by all and sundry it was tiny, the entire *cavea* a mere 246ft across. Several tiers of seats remain, including some of the front-row VIP seats with backs, and the foundations of *skene*. For a climb and a view, go up into the town behind the causeway and look for the flights of stairs up to **Laryssion**. There is nothing to see in the way of ruins, but you get the same view the Romans did.

ⓘ Gýthio >
***EOT booth**: 20 Vas. Georgiou, not far from the Aktaion Hotel, **t** 273 302 4484; open year-round Mon–Fri 8–2.30*

Useful Information in Gýthio

Rozákis Travel Agency, t 273 302 2207, on the waterfront near the docks, are very helpful for every need.

Andreíkos bookshop by the bus station has books on the Máni. The more you know, the more interesting...

Where to Stay in Gýthio

Gýthio ✉ 23200

All hotels are on the road overlooking the sea. Gýthio's campsites are lined up like soldiers for inspection along the sandy beach at Mavrovoúni.

Aktaion, t 273 302 3500, *www.hotelaktaion.gr* (€€€/€€). A perfect gem of a period renovation, from its reception to its air-conditioned bedrooms. *Open all year.*

Gythion, t 273 302 3452, *www.gythionhotel.gr* (€€/€€). Built in 1864 as a club, where poker was first introduced to Greece, this small hotel has spacious rooms, and a piece of the cliff-face jutting into its attractive reception area. *Open April–Oct.*

Kranai, t 273 302 4394, *kranai@ath.forthnet.gr* (€€/€). Renovated with a wonderful façade; traditional rooms in a variety of sizes and shapes following the original plan. *Open all year.*

Leonidas Rooms, t 273 302 2389 (€€/€). Near the bus station, with air-conditioning and TV. *Open Feb–Nov.*

Pension Saga, t 273 302 3220 (€€/€). Modern, family-run, and pleasant. *Open all year.*

★ Xenia Karlafi's Rooms >

Xenia Karlafi's Rooms, by the causeway to Marathonísi, **t** 273 302 2719 (€/€). Fridge and cooking facilities. Mrs Karlafí has the knack of making her guests feel at home. She will tell you that her 'hotel' started by accident many years ago when two desperate people knocked on her door needing a place to stay. With true Maniáte hospitality, she and her husband gave them their own bed, refusing payment. The visitors left some much-needed cash on her pillow and her guest house was born.

Gythion Beach Camping, t 273 302 2522. Says he's open all year.

Meltemi, t 273 302 2833, *www.campingmeltemi.gr*, and **Máni Beach, t** 273 302 2522. Both popular choices. *Open April–Oct.*

Eating Out in Gýthio

There is no shortage of restaurants in Gýthio. If a great dining experience is elusive, a good one is not, and all of the restaurants have terraces on the seafront.

Saga, t 273 302 3220. Run by Mr Kolokotróni and his French wife; has a good reputation and a pleasant décor complete with fireplace.

To Akroyiáli, t 273 302 2943. Claims to have an astounding 80 different dishes on any day.

Psarotavérna Constantínos Drakoulákos, t 273 302 4086. Near the Hotel Kranai; a picturesque choice for fish with its old blue wooden chairs.

Touristikó Períptero, t 273 302 2282. Start your evening with an ouzo in this trendy spot by a lovely park on the sea right in front of the KTEL station.

From Gýthio to Areópolis

The road stretches west past the campsites and then into a series of small scrub- and pine-clad hills, one crowned by the **Castle of Passava** (9.5km). This was one of a string of castles built by Geoffrey de Villehardouin in 1254 to keep the Máni; the Franks had to abandon it to the Byzantines by 1263. The Turks took over, then the Venetians for a time, and then the Turks again. It was not a lucky castle. As in Corinth, the Turkish population lived here along with the soldiers. In 1780, in retaliation for the execution of a family member, Zanet Grigorákis of Gýthio and his clan overran the castle and killed all the 700 Turkish men, women and children who lived there. *Myrologia* praised the deed, of course. Astonishingly, this same Zanet was subsequently made an offer by the Turks that he couldn't refuse – to become the Máni's third Bey, or die. The Turks may have been thinking of the *Arabian Nights* story of Achmed the Moth, the prince of burglars who was made chief of police by Harun-al Rachid. That is how he became Zanetbey in 1784 and ruled in the Máni until 1798, when schmoozing with Napoleon got him fired. He fled for his life, but even then he never stopped stirring up trouble for the Turks, even from exile.

For the best view of the castle and its virtually intact 40ft-thick walls, head north towards the village of **Karvelás** (Καρβελάς) and then look back. Alternatively, make the 15-minute scramble up the hill for a closer look. There was a cobblestoned path, but it is so overgrown that finding your own way is best. The ruins inside are Turkish, although many ancient stones from Homer's city of Las are built into the underground cisterns. The panoramic views, especially from the higher west wall, will reward the effort. After Passava, a road goes south to the very good beach at **Skoutári**, a couple of towers and tavernas, but not much else, then continues, unpaved, to **Kótronas** and the east coast of the Inner Máni.

As the road continues to Areópolis, the hills become more scoured and barren, the flat dinner-plate leaves of prickly pear, a trademark of the Inner Máni, often the only touch of green. Ten kilometres or so after Passava there is a marked turn-off for the large Turkish **fort of Kelefá**, built in the 1670 to keep an eye on the east–west and coastal roads leading to Areópolis. It is an ugly, no-nonsense fortress, covering nearly four acres, and rarely visited. Four kilometres after the turn-off, we come to Areópolis.

Areópolis, Ítilo and the Diroú Caves

Called Tsímova in the old days, and renamed 'the city of Ares', as a compliment to Petróbey Mavromichális and his contribution to the War of Independence, small and compact **Areópolis** is a perfect introduction to the Inner Máni. Its narrow streets evoke the old days, especially at Easter when they echo with exploding

Getting to and around Areópolis

The KTEL **bus** station, **t** 273 305 1229, is housed in the Europa Grill in Areópolis' *plateía*. There are two daily buses to Geroliménas and Váthia in summer (three a week in winter) and one daily to Kótronas. Four buses a day go to Gýthio, three daily to Kalamáta with a change at Ítilo, and three to Sparta; fewer at weekends. There is a bus to the caves at Diroú leaving at 11am and returning at 12.40pm, just enough time to see the caves if there is no queue. **Taxis** come in handy here. There is a stand in the main square, **t** 273 305 1442, **t** 697 719 3548. Prices are roughly €7.50 for Diroú, €23 for Váthia, and €4 for Liméni Beach.

---

firecrackers at all hours of the day and night, pretty much as they must have during a clan war. Areópolis' workaday main square, **Plateía Athanáton**, is dominated by a huge bronze statue of Petróbey himself, looking splendidly ferocious and entirely at home among the small business emporiums and pick-up trucks that line the streets. This *plateía* is just off the main highway and is the centre of business for the town, and for all points south as well.

The beautiful old town stretches to the west, down the narrow street which leads to Plateía 17 Martíou and the church of the **Taxiarchón**, the town landmark with its wonderful stone reliefs of angels, suns, eagles, lions and signs of the Zodiac inside and out and its high bell tower, added on in 1836. Stroll past this square and continue west, and in ten minutes you come to cliffs overlooking the sea. The marvellous view extends as far south as the forbidding bulge of Cávo Grósso. Note the low stone walls everywhere, the tiny fields, and remember that this was the *fertile* area of the Inner Máni. Some of the more famous **towers** are signposted.

North of Areópolis: Ítilo and Liméni

Ítilo (Οιτιλο), 10km north of Areópolis, is on the hillside opposite Kelefá (*see* p.406) and is remarkable only because it is the nominal capital of the Inner Máni. Burned in 2007, this area shows just what a wildfire can do even in an area famous for its sparse vegetation. At the southern end of Ítilo's bay, **Liméni** (Λιμένι) was the chief stronghold of the Mavromichális clan, and here **Petróbey's tower** stands perfectly preserved. Petros Mavromichális became Bey in 1815. He impressed the English traveller Colonel Leake as a 'gentleman', praise indeed from Leake, who had a very jaundiced view of the Máni. While he was Bey, he and his clan plotted with the *Philikí Etairía* (that revolutionary group of expatriate Greeks, *see* p.26), and it was Petróbey who stood outside the church of the Taxiarchón in Tsímova and declared the Máni's independence. Forty-nine members of his family would die during the subsequent fighting, not an unusual statistic in the Máni during this war. It was his arrest that led his clan to assassinate Capodístria in Naúplio. Petróbey himself survived incarceration and returned to the Máni to fight another day, this time for the Greek government – when it suited his own plans for the area, of course.

The Caves at Diroú and the Museum

Eleven kilometres by car from Areópolis, but considerably less by mule path, the caves at Diroú lie hidden on the south side of a large bay. In 1826, Ibrahim Pasha, aware that Maniáte forces were near Kalamáta, sailed into this bay with his ships and 1,500 men, who rushed up from shore and invaded Tsímova. Here the church bell privilege proved its worth: the bells rang out and the Maniáte women rushed to the defence of their city with such ferocity that they were able to contain the troops until Kolokotrónis arrived with reinforcements. Ibraham was forced to turn tail, leaving 500 men on the shore to face Maniáte retribution. This bloodstained spot is now a pleasant pebble beach that you might want to use while waiting for your turn to visit the caves during the high season.

Vlycháda
t 273 305 2222; open June–Sept daily 8.30–5.30; Oct–May daily 8.30–3; adm exp

Discovered by a fisherman in 1900 and first explored in 1949 by Ioánnis and Anna Petróchilos, the cave of **Vlycháda** is part of a large subterranean lake system in which, so far, over 5km of passages and great halls have been explored. Parts of it are open to the public, who float through in small boats, a journey that in spite of the sardonic guides and all the tourist hype is awe-inspiring. The cave is labyrinthine, to say the least, and only certified speleologists are allowed in unaccompanied. The water temperature inside the cave averages 18°C, and at its deepest point is 100ft. There are stalactites in fantastic shapes and colours, and even stalagmites under the water, formed before sea levels rose and covered them. Fossils over two million years old have been found.

Alepótripa
t 273 305 2233; open Tues–Sun 8.30–3; adm

Museum
t 273 305 2233; open Tues–Sun 8.30–3.30; adm

Of the other two caves, **Alepótripa** (the 'foxhole'), discovered in 1958, and **Kataphýgi** (the 'refuge'), only the former is open. Its 'great hall' alone measures 330ft by 100ft. The Alepótripa yielded extensive Neolithic remains and rock paintings, which are very rare in Greece. These finds feed the small **museum** and continually push the date back for man's first step on the Máni.

Useful Information in Areópolis

Areópolis has a **bank** and a **post office**; villages further south are served sporadically by travelling ones.

Shopping in Areópolis

Areópolis is the place to buy *síglino*, a smoked pork that was a Máni staple and is extremely popular to this day, either by itself, in baked dishes or in omelettes. Orange-flavoured sausages and *díples*, a fried pastry smothered in honey and walnuts, are also favourite Máni fare, and are available in the square. For real tourist tat, look by the turn-off to the Diroú Caves. But any shoe store in Areópolis can provide you with *tsaroúkia*, the Greek slippers with pompoms worn by the Evzones guarding Sýntagma Square in Athens. Here they are still worn by some.

Festivals in Areópolis

Areópolis celebrates Independence Day a week earlier than the rest of Greece, on 17 March, the day the Máni rose up. There is a church service and dancing in the square. This is a good time to get a look at the Maniáte flag and its two mottos: 'Freedom or

Death', from the War of Independence, and 'Return either with your Shield or on it', from Sparta.

Where to Stay and Eat in and around Areópolis

Areópolis ✉ 23062

Londas Traditional Hotel, **t** 273 305 1360, *www.londas.com* (€€€/€€). A beautiful renovation of a Maniáte tower; a chance to live like a modern Petróbey. *Open all year.*

Trapéla, **t** 273 305 2690, *www.trapela.gr* (€€€/€€). 12 nicely decorated rooms in a stone building near the main *plateía*, with all mod cons and a very nice receptionist. *Open Mar–Oct.*

Máni, **t** 273 305 1190, *www.hotelmani.gr* (€€€/€€). This hotel's attractive new stone wing has transformed it. Each room has a balcony, and two have fireplaces; there is another nice one in the lobby, too. *Open all year.*

Xenónas Tsímova, **t** 273 305 1301 (€€/€). Across the street from the Taxiarchón church. Mr Versákos, the friendly owner, has quite a little war museum in his salon, and is proud of the fact that Kolokotrónis not only slept here but sent the family a thank-you note. Like many Maniátes, his family are of Cretan extraction. His stories are classic Maniáte tales, elaborately woven for appreciative audiences. Try to find a translator. He has two apartments with kitchen and bath, generally inexpensive depending on when. *Open all year.*

Kourís, **t** 273 305 1340 (€€/€). Ten modern rooms with TV, air-conditioning and minibar in the main *plateía*; the bargain choice and a fine one for a night or two. *Open all year.*

Nicola's Place, in the square, **t** 273 305 1366. Don't be put off by the awful pictures of what's on offer. The dynamic Démitra takes a real interest in her cooking and has built up a reputation that can overcome them.

O Barba Petros, **t** 273 305 1205. In an old stone building en route to Plateía 17 Martíou; well established, popular.

March 17 restaurant, Plateía 17 Martíou. A renovated stone house, complete with marble table-tops and a huge gilt mirror.

Ioánnis Alépis, **t** 273 305 1276. Near the main square; the best *souvláki* here.

Ítilo ✉ 23062

Alevra's Tower Guest House, **t** 273 305 9388, *www.alevrastower.gr* (€€/€€). Up on a hill; large rooms for three people, complete with kitchen, a pool in the garden and a view of the bay. *Open May–Oct.*

Liméni ✉ 23062

Limeni Village, **t** 273 305 1111, *www.limenivillage.gr* (€€€€/€€€). High above Liméni, this new stone complex, with pool, classy lobby and tour buses, is the Máni *à la* Palm Beach, and almost as unreal as the plaster of Paris tower houses flogged by the tourist shops. Getting down to the pool is a hike, getting to the beach even more so. *Open all year.*

Tákis, **t** 273 305 1327. Tucked away in the corner of the village, the taverna has good food and you can swim just under it in a very pretty sheltered area.

Elixírion, on the north side of the bay at Karabotási, **t** 273 305 9275, *www.mani-elixirion.gr* (€€/€€). Stone built, attractive newish hotel by the sea. A bit isolated, although that is part of its charm. *Open all year.*

Diroú ✉ 23063

Sole e Mare, **t** 273 305 2240, *sole1991@otenet.gr* (€€€€/€€€). This very attractive hotel is close to the sea and caves, has a pretty pool, and a pleasant owner. *Open all year.*

Panorama, **t** 273 305 2280, *www.clickhere.gr/hotels-greece/mani/panoramamanien.htm* (€€/€€). Walking distance from the caves and sea; air-conditioned, too. The owner promises fresh fish from his taverna downstairs. *Open April–Oct.*

Diros, at the crossroads to Diroú, **t** 273 305 2306 (€€/€). A plain hotel offering air-conditioning and screens, but a long way from the sea. *Open all year.*

Villa Koulis, 7km south of Diroú, **t** 273 305 2350 (€€/€). Built of traditional stone, in a big garden; large, with balconies and kitchens, and run by the nice Strilákou family. *Open all year.*

South of Diroú: Into the Bad Mountains

South of Diroú, the tail end of the Taíyetos becomes the Kakovoúnia, the 'Bad Mountains'. They don't look more evil than any of the others in the Máni, and Patrick Leigh Fermor puts forth a convincing argument that the alternative name for the region, *Kakovoúlia*, the 'Land of Evil Council', is a misinterpretation of *Kakkavoula*, the 'Cauldroneers', recalling the Maniáte habit of converting their three-legged cauldrons (where they made their Spartan black broth) into helmets when they attacked a passing ship; there are records of them doing that into the 18th century.

There is no road over the Bad Mountains until Álika and Pórto Káyio, although one or two hikers' paths exist. The best of these is from **Karínia** (Καρύνια), south of Mína, over to **Éxo Nímfio** (Εξω Νήμφιο). This leaves the western 'Shadowy Coast' and the east 'Sunny Coast' quite separate. Well-marked small towns are hemmed in by the sea on one side and the mountains on the other.

The main road goes south 9km to the turn-off for **Mézapos**. For a close look at several small villages, try the small parallel road that takes you through **Fragoúlias** (Φραγούλιας), **Dríalos** (Δρύαλος) and **Vámvaka** (Βάμβακα) to **Mína** (Μίνα). Vámvaka's lovely cruciform church, with elaborate cloisonné brickwork, dates from 1075. The network of stone walls snaking down the bald mountain behind these villages is a reminder of the once intensive efforts at farming. Three hundred metres past the turn-off to Mézapos, on the right, is the church of **Ag. Nikólaos**, a nice combination of tower house and church.

Mézapos, Tigáni and Cávo Grósso

Sleepy, out-of-the-way **Mézapos** (Μέζαπος) was a pirate centre once, and an important stop for the ferries that plied the Inner Máni before the road was built. Now it is almost deserted. The only sign of life in winter are black-clad old women sitting in rickety wooden chairs, their backs against sunny walls. Down by the mole to the right is a small, almost perfectly circular bay completely surrounded by high cliffs. Aside from its tempting swimming, several historians claim that Odysseus' wandering did not, in fact, take him far from Greek shores, and identify this bay with the one in which the Cyclops hurled rocks down at the terrified sailors.

Mézapos offers fine views of **Tigáni** (Τιγάνι), a long, bone-white causeway of jagged rock that curves a kilometre out into the bay and radiates out at the end to support the imposing ruins of a castle. The name *tigáni*, 'frying pan', describes it perfectly. Behind it, the 1,000ft cliffs of **Cávo Grósso** rise to the south in one of the grandest spectacles the Máni has to offer. These precipitous limestone cliffs are riddled with caves, called *thyrides* or 'windows' by locals. The same word means 'safe deposit boxes' in Greek banks

– apt, because these almost inaccessible *thyrides* were used by Maniáte pirates expressly to stash their loot. The top of the cape is a fairly smallish flat area by anyone else's standards, but it's the great plain of the Inner Máni.

Tigáni, which seems so close and imposing from Mézapos, can best be reached on foot from **Stavrí**, on the heights of Cávo Grósso. The going is tough. Tigáni's arm is pock-marked with salt pans, 365 of them, an old song claims. Gathering salt was a big industry at one time, and villagers still use the pans for their own supplies.

Tigáni's imposing castle was the famous Byzantine **Castle Maina** and quite a place in its heyday. It may have been started as early as the 6th century by Justinian. Its 2,460ft perimeter encloses cisterns, incomprehensible ruins, and the foundations of a large (by Máni standards) Byzantine church, 72ft long. This was probably the cathedral for the bishopric formed in the 9th century. Cyclopean walls from about 1300 BC show that Tigáni has seen a lot of forts in its day. It is probably the site of Homer's 'dove-haunted Messe'. Whether it was also the site of the William de Villehardouin's Castle of the Grand Maina is still moot. If it was on the mainland, as some contend, it is hard to see how any one wanting to control the area could ignore Tigáni, so the Franks must have been here, too. But it is hard to care about details when faced with the awe-some beauty of this spot. If the walk to the castle is too daunting, at least take the road from Stavrí towards Tigáni to the end and enjoy the view. Tigáni has garnered innumerable stories, including one about a princess who was loved by Death. He came and swept her away, leaving his horse's hoofprint on the stairs to the castle. In the Máni, Death was admired for the invincible war lord he was.

Kítta and Geroliménas

Midway between Mézapos and Geroliménas, **Kítta** (Κοίτα) offers not only a view over the Cávo Grósso area, but also a marvellous collection of tower houses and churches. Its name could come from *città*, or city in Italian, reinforcing the theory that the Italians inspired the Máni's towers. Kítta was settled by Niklians from Arcadía when the Frankish empire collapsed, or so the story goes. In 1805 it had 22 towers and was the biggest settlement in the Inner Máni. Now, it has even more towers, reminding us that, incredibly, many of these towers were only built in the 1800s. From Kítta it is possible to take the main road to Geroliménas or a circular route around Cávo Grósso, or a side road to Boulárioi, another bristling tower town.

Geroliménas (Γερολιμένας), with its good-sized shingle beach, is what passes for civilization in these parts, with a dense cluster of restaurants and hotels along with traditional houses. It became important only in the 1800s, when, for a while, it rivalled Mézapos.

The cliffs of **Cávo Grósso** loom like a curtained backdrop over the bay, and create quite a shadow in the late afternoon. It is a pleasant place to stay, useful for exploring **Upper** and **Lower Boulárioi** (Μπουλάριοι) on the mountain. Between them, the two Bouláris have an astonishing 21 churches from the 10th to the 18th centuries; the most important is the domed, cruciform 11th-century church of **Ag. Strátigos**, containing marvellous frescoes.

Kipárissos, Váthia and Pórto Káyio

The road goes on to **Kipárissos** (Κυπάρισσος), where a detour to the sea by the river bed will take you to a beach with an overgrown headland on its left. This was Roman **Kenipolis**. Underground water made the establishment of a busy Roman town possible, and it is still something of an oasis today, with small gardens and robust olive trees. On the beach and out on the headland are the ruins of Temples to Aphrodite and to Demeter, and of other buildings. On the inner slope of the headland are the remains of the 5th- or 6th-century **Basilica of St Peter's** mouldering in a private garden (try asking for the '*Archaíos Naós tou Agioú Pétrou*'). At 70ft by 62ft, it was a fair size, and one of the Máni's earliest churches. This deserted headland with its weed-choked ruins can create a certain *frisson*, as if ghosts still linger here. Look out for uncovered well heads, or you may become one of them.

The road then climbs to **Váthia** (Βάθεια), an especially photogenic nest of tower houses, this time crowning a hill. Its towers were rented for a time by the National Tourist Organization, but are abandoned at the moment, while the lease is sorted out. The inhabitants of Váthia were apparently involved in a feud that lasted 40 years. The village is so compact that it is hard to imagine how even complicated rules of etiquette could have handled the usual truces, breaks for holidays, harvesting and so on in such a tiny area. The road continues south to a point so narrow that a single glance encompasses the wonderful small bays of **Marmári** to the west, and **Pórto Káyio** (Πόρτο Κάγιο) to the east. Pórto Káyio, the port of quails (probably from the Italian *Porto Quaglio*) was a popular hunting ground for these birds as they migrated. A Turkish **fort** of 1669, along with a few lovely Mystrá-style stone houses and a little monastery with a spring, grace today's settlement up on the north side of the bay. The Turkish grip was slippery, however, and they kept losing the fort to the Venetians and others. On 29 March 1942, Allied forces were evacuating to Crete when a single German Stukka divebombed the battleship. The returning hail of bullets from the ship missed the plane, but hit the castle, the last time it was ever involved in a battle. Pórto Káyio, with its little tavernas, is a popular spot in summer for lunch and a swim.

Where to Stay and Eat South of Diroú

Stavri/Geroliménas/Pórto Káyio ✉ 23071

Pirgos Tsitsiri, Stavrí, **t** 273 305 6297 or **t** 273 305 6296 (€€€/€€). A renovated tower house with some thoughtful extras: larger windows, and a terrace in the courtyard. Its breakfast room is a barrel-vaulted basement; its position on the Cávo Grósso makes it ideal for rambling. The owner can tell you how to get to Tigáni. *Open all year.*

Kyrímai, Geroliménas, **t** 273 305 4288, *www.kyrimai.gr* (€€€/€€). On the rocks by the sea, new, gorgeous conversion of seaside towers and well appointed throughout; considered one of Greece's top hotels.

Xenonas Laoúla, Geroliménas, **t** 273 305 4271, *www.gerolimenas.net* (€€€€/€€). Seven renovated rooms next door to Kyrímai, with the same great view of the bay and Cávo Grósso. If the five-minute walk to the town's pebble beach does not appeal, there is a wooden dock off the rocks in front. *Open all year.*

Psamáthous, Pórto Káyio, **t** 273 305 2033, *www.portokayio.com* (€€/€€) Rooms are built in local style; all have air-conditioning, fridges, and are close to the narrow beach. *Open all year.*

Akroyiáli, Geroliménas, **t** 273 305 4204, *www.gerolimenas-hotels.com* (€€/€). On the beach, run by an industrial chemist, Mr Theodorakáki, and his Canadian wife, a stone sculptor. Their terraced restaurant by the sea has a good reputation. They have added a wing with pricier apartments, and have restored a trio of old tower houses as **O Gerolimenas Traditional Hotel**. *Open all year.*

Porto, Pórto Káyio, **t** 273 305 2033. A fish taverna on the beach run by a member of the Grigorákis clan. For dessert, it offers an art gallery with 'subjects from the Máni'.

Kótronas ✉ 23062

Kótronas Bay Bungalows, **t** 273 302 1340, *www.kotronasbay.gr* (€€€/€€). Roomy bungalows sleeping up to four, with kitchens, in a lush garden across the road from its small pool and the sea. Owner Maria Panagákou cooks up a storm in the restaurant and hosts a radio cookery programme as well.

Up the Sunny Coast

At this point, most visitors head back up the 'Sunny' east coast and back to Gýthio. The intrepid may wish to carry on to Cape Taíneron, an isolated piece of real estate with a unique history.

Five km north of Pórto Káyio, **Láyia** (Λάγια) has a large collection of tower houses, some of them very old – you can recognize them by their tapered tops. At 1,300ft up, it offers a vista and a coffee shop. Northwest of Láyia are the quarries of *antico rosso*, a red-hued marble that was much sought after even in Mycenaean times; some of it graced the Treasury of Atreus in Mycenae. The road north is hemmed into an extremely narrow space between mountain and sea. Three km past **Kokkála** (Κοκκάλα), turn left at **Éxo Nímfio** (Εξο Νήμφιο) and drive up to **Mésa Chóra** (Μέσα Χώρα), then make the hike up to the **Moní Panagías Kournoú**, a monastery on the mountainside by a never-failing spring. The rare water source made this isolated spot the site of the small city long ago. The ruins of two Doric temples, all that is left of **ancient Aígila**, sit on a plateau about 500m beyond the monastery. Perhaps one of them is the Temple to Demeter, where Aristomenes, the great 7th-century BC Messenian rebel leader who had a penchant for stealing Spartan women and holding them for ransom, tried his luck with the priestesses. Unluckily for him, the women were in the midst of a religious service and were armed with the roasting spits they intended to use to skewer and barbecue the sacrificed animals after the service. They used their skewers on the men instead; Maniáte women were forces to be reckoned with no matter what the era. **Kótronas** (Κότρωνας), at the top of the east coast, has a sandy beach, with good views down the east coast and taverns, but seems awfully civilized after the journey south. Kótronas is on the site of ancient Teuthrone. From here, roads go back inland to Areópolis or around the cape north to Skoutári.

Cape Taíneron and the Underworld

From Pórto Káyio an unpaved road continues south to the ruined church of **Ag. Asomáton**. Set on a little oval bay, Ag. Asomáton occupies a rectangular building believed to date from Hellenistic times; its name (the 'bodiless') refers to the Archangel Michael, who, in the Orthodox Church, is the *psychopompeion*, the gatherer of dead souls. His presence here is no accident: 60 yards away is the cave once occupied by the famous **Sanctuary of Poseidon** at Taíneron, which was both *asyla* and *avaton* (not to be violated and not be trodden). Isolated, like most spots holy to this god of the elements, it had, besides the usual priests, a resident *psychopompeion*, escorter of souls of the dead and representative of the border-crossing god Hermes, bearing his chthonic staff, the *kerykeion*, with its stylized copulating snakes. Here a murderer, with the aid of the *psychopompeion*, could summon up the soul of his victim and placate him with a sacrifice.

This sanctuary also had a connection with other marginal types – outlaws, mercenaries (in Hellenistic times this was greatest 'man market' in Greece) and escaping helots. The destruction of Sparta in an earthquake in 464 BC was attributed to the wrath of Poseidon after the Spartan Ephors had impiously dragged helots out of this sanctuary and murdered them, an act that shocked the entire Greek world, and was the subject of a lost play by Eupolis called *The Helots*. Traces of the sanctuary can be seen: cuttings on the north side of the cave entrance, where *stelae* recorded the emancipation of slaves, and numerous foundations cut in the rock. These were used for the construction of huts, where supplicants could stay; apparently there were quite a few at any given time. Cilician pirates, however, were not impressed and destroyed the sanctuary in the 1st century BC. These days the busy café and camper vans somewhat spoil the 'end of the world' feeling in high season.

A path leads in half an hour to the lighthouse of **Cape Taíneron** (or **Matapán**), the southernmost point in continental Europe with the exception of Tarifa in Spain. Sacred places marking transitional planes of existence are often marginal, on the edge of the world, so to speak. Anthropologists like to demonstrate this with a Venn diagram, two circles representing This World and The Other, slightly overlapping in the centre, where communications between the two are possible and where ritual takes place. This is especially potent at Taíneron, where the above and underworld met at the **entrance to Hades**, locally known as η σπηλια του αδη. (It's on the other side of the cape and accessible only by boat; ask around at Marmari.) This was one of the most famous of Hades' ventilation shafts, favoured by mortals on quests, although these were not always crowned with success. Theseus and his friend Peirithous descended through here to rescue Persephone; through here Heracles dragged the three-headed dog Cerberos in his Twelfth Labour; Orpheus descended here in search of his Eurydice; and Psyche went down to find Aphrodite's beauty kit.

The Outer Máni

The Outer Máni (the part belonging to Messenía) is remarkable for its small Byzantine churches (*see* p.400), stunning scenery and beautiful seaside towns such as Kardamýli and Stoúpa. With its blend of olive trees, cypresses, limestone mountains and blue sea, this is a Mediterranean landscape at its most classic, particularly the area from Kardamýli to Ítilo.

Cut off in the old days by the rocky prominence of Mount Kaláthi and capes Kitriés and Koúrtissa, today's main road from Kalamáta heads for hills marked with guard towers here and there until Kámbos and points south. If you have time, a secondary coast road branches off from **Paralía Vérga** (Παραλία Βέργα), going 8km south via Avía to Kitriés with tavernas and pretty beaches; from either of these you can ascend east and rejoin the main road.

Kámbos and the Castle Zarnata

The village of **Kámbos** is set in a fertile upland plain of olive trees and meadows that even attracted the Mycenaeans, although it isn't typical of their haunts; yet a *tholos* tomb was excavated near Kámbos in 1888. To the south, Kámbos is overlooked by a low, perfectly conical hill occupied by the romantic fairytale **Castle Zarnata**. Circular walls, as high as 33ft, tonsure the lower part of the hill; high up on the 'crown' stands a circular fortified keep, topped by a square Maniáte tower. Come in the spring if you can, when the area bursts into a riot of colour. Bits and pieces of prehistoric and ancient debris stud the hill, suggesting it was Homeric Enope and Classical Gerinia; the Máni's ruins can only hint, as there is very little written or verifiable historical data. The present castle started out as a Byzantine fort, and the Franks are probably responsible for the outer wall. In the early 1400s Thomas Paleológos, the last Emperor's brother, had control. In those days the castle contained many small houses with gardens, each with its ground floor or underground cistern.

When the Turks came, they razed the castle and houses. The terrified citizens fled to Táranto in southern Italy where they have remained, still speaking Greek with a mixture of Italian. In 1670, the Turks rebuilt the castle to keep an eye on the Maniátes. They tried to ensure their supremacy (and safety) with 51 cannons, six pointing in all directions from the top of the hill. Its outer wall had a walkway and six towers, two round and four square. They added a mosque with an imposing minaret, a type of 'tower' not often seen in the Máni, and the Pasha built himself a nice little house near the top of the cone, to remind everyone who was now top of the heap. The Venetians got it for a while after 1690, not by outfacing all those cannons but by treaty, and, in their organized way, mapped the area and gave the little settlements around the castle Latin names (like 'Malta', just west of the castle).

During the period of the Beys, when Greeks were top dogs, the ruined square tower and house you see were built. They were occupied by the first and fourth Maniáte Beys, of the Koutífari and Koumandoúrou families. The Koumandoúrou clan would have a significant impact on modern Greek history. Alexander Koumandoúrou, whose tower house is so prominent on your right just south of town (signposted and hard by the huge Mycenaean *tholos* tomb), was prime minister an astounding 10 times over a period of 16 years in the late 1800s, suggesting that 19th-century Greek politics had a lot in common with Maniáte vendettas. No wonder he felt at home. His importance is reinforced by the fact that large Koumandoúrou Square on Piraeus Street in Athens is *still* named after him. In modern Greece that is praise indeed. Kámbos is still a big town by Maniáte standards, but its castle sits abandoned and forlorn. Its cisterns are used for animal fodder, and the little church of **Zoodóchos Pigí**, inside the castle walls, is practically derelict, although it has a wonderful wooden iconostasis and frescoes of zodiacal signs, flying horses and sea beasts.

Around Kámbos

Six kilometres north of Kámbos at Charavgý, a paved road will take you up and up to **Vérga** (Βέργα), for a great view of the Messiniakós Gulf and Kalamáta. Continue up the road and you arrive, inevitably in Greece, at a church of **Profítis Ilías**, at about 4,265ft. Instead of turning left to Vérga on this same road, it is possible to turn right after 4.5km, past Ag. Geórgios monastery and up on unpaved roads into the fastness of the Taíyetos. The scenic road through **Pigádia** (Πιγάδια, 'spring') and **Kefalóvrissa**

Getting to and around the Outer Máni

Kardamýli's **bus station**, **t** 272 107 3642, is in Evángelos Troupákis' ouzerie in the centre of town, making waiting for a bus part of the holiday. There are three to four **buses** a day to and from Kalamáta, and three from Ítilo, that pass through Stoúpa as well. In summer a shuttle bus runs hourly between Kardamýli and Stoúpa from 9am to 4pm.

Taxis are plentiful: in Kardamýli call Níkos, **t** 697 233 0915. The taxi drivers hang about at Mr Troupákis', hopefully drinking coffee, not ouzo. A taxi ride to Stoúpa is €7–8. **Best Car Rent a Car**, **t** 272 107 3940, is in Kardamýli on the main street. For information in Stoúpa, ask at **Travel Agency Zorbas**, **t** 272 107 7735, *www.zorbas.de*, on the north end of the beach. They can help with car, moped, bike and motor boat hire.

(Κεφαλόβρυσσα, 'spring head'), their names reminders of the all-important water source that settlements in these mountains depended on, can even take you to the Sparta road just west of the Kaiádas. Ask in Kámbos about this road before trying it. It is as isolated as it is tempting – for the adventurous, or hikers.

Kardamýli

Six kilometres south of Zarnata, you'll suddenly find yourself circling down like an eagle, with a tremendous view of the Víros Gorge cutting deep into the Taíyetos, and the small coastal plain of Kardamýli. Anyone who approaches from these heights and is not moved by its combination of tiny island, indented coastline, stone houses and rugged hills has the soul of a peanut. When you draw nearer, you'll find Kardamýli a little symphony in stone. In spring, the flowering shrubs and aromatic bushes will make you wish you were all nose. Happily it lacks a coastal road, and the various side roads going to the sea are never too busy. The town shore is rocky, and although swimming is certainly possible, especially off the dock on the little port, there is also a sand and pebble beach stretching north for quite a way, within walking distance of town.

Even in the Mycenaean period, Kardamýli was desirable real estate. In the *Iliad*, Agamemnon, trying to mitigate Achilles' famous wrath, offered it to him along with a few other cities. The fact that he didn't jump at the chance shows just how mad he was. Augustus was in a sufficiently expansive mood to offer Kardamýli as a gift to Sparta, so it could have a port of its very own (Roman benevolence didn't run to giving them Gýthio back). Sparta accepted with alacrity. If you consider the hike from Sparta over the Taíyetos by mule path, it was a gift only a Spartan could have construed as a favour. All this, however, was mere prelude for Kardamýli's great historical moment, a moment which produced the wonderful conglomeration of 'Old Kardamýli' and much of the existing town as well. Most of it was built in the late 1700s. Yet these medieval-looking settlements, especially the Troupákis, Moúrtzinos and Petréas enclaves, represent the acme of Maniáte tower-complex building, and the feudal way of life.

Old Kardamýli

Following the signs to 'Old Kardamýli' will take you up the river bed to the main gateway of the **Moúrtzinos Compound**, now minus its massive wooden door, although the holes for the bar that crossed it can still be seen. Inside the courtyard is the church of **Ag. Spyrídon**, built at the beginning of the 18th century, or so they say. Dates are tricky in the Máni. Its 56ft Frankish bell tower sports ornamental designs showing the sun, moon, stars, and the double-headed eagle, a lovely mixed bag of symbols. The Maniátes are also fond of decorating their lintels, windows and doorways; usually these are in sandstone, but here they are marble. The church's eight-sided dome is all Byzantine, its slightly pointed arched window Frankish.

At this period the houses, too, displayed not only superior workmanship and wealth (the use of ceramic tiles for the roof, rather than slate, meant money), but a mixture of Byzantine, Latin and even Turkish architectural styles that is dazzling in its own right. Inside the courtyard is a two-storey house, which like all Maniáte houses has narrow windows topped by an arch, and, in the corner, the important defensive tower, with its many wooden floors packed with all the paraphernalia needed in times of siege. This one has a ground-floor store room and a stairway up to its entrance. Unlike the houses, the towers were all business, and not very comfortable. Various other store rooms, sleeping quarters and a spring or cistern for gathering rainwater make up the rest. In short, a medieval castle in miniature. These families controlled what trade there was, functioning as self-proclaimed customs houses, and oversaw all aspects of life in their area; all in all, it was a more genteel existence, for the wealthy at least, than in the parched Inner Máni. Kolokotrónis was a guest here. (He slept in more places than Napoleon or George Washington.) And, like everyone else, he probably slept on the floor: as in many village houses in Greece until after the Second World War, bedding was folded up in the corner by day and spread out on the floor at night.

The Moúrtzinos family not only had a resident priest – handy in times of vendettas – but a full-time paid storyteller as well. And all of this in a not very well fortified situation. That makes you wonder if defensive necessity didn't at some point just give way to a glorious medieval fantasy. But probably not. Those other towers overlooking the complex probably belonged to allied families. In any case, the Moúrtzinos would have owned other towers at strategic points in the area.

Twice a day the church bell would ring and the wooden doors were thrown open to welcome a queue of citizens and retainers who came for meals that may have been cooked in the small ruin just to the left, inside the main gate. This Maniáte custom was widespread. The Grigoráki family in Gýthio were also famous for this kind of hospitality. In a second courtyard, also with its own defensive tower, lie ruins of the olive press and mill stones. The **enclave of the Petréas family**, just to the southeast, is composed of three fortified towers, various living quarters and store rooms, a small family cemetery and a spring with an arched entrance that dates from 1734. Many old compounds are still inhabited by family members, who have renovated them with varying degrees of aesthetic success, and some offer a good idea of what Maniáte life must have been like.

The Dioscouri, the twins Castor and Polydeuces, were familiars of Kardamýli, hatched from the same clutch as Helen and Clytemnestra by a brooding Leda some time after Zeus' notorious visit to her in the guise of a swan. The girls went on to raise Cain elsewhere in Greece, while the boys, generally depicted in flowing white gowns with stars in attendance around their heads, remained special deities for the Lacedaemonians. They became the protective gods of sailors and protectors of hospitality, their famous benevolence no doubt stemming from the happy situation of the town which raised them, and the fact that they were not forced into early disastrous dynastic marriages like their sisters. They also played the role of knights errant, and often proved their worth in battle – this was the aspect the Spartans, and later the Romans, especially admired. The Spartans also associated them with their twin kingship. When they died, Zeus turned them into the constellation of Gemini. The fact that stars and heavenly motifs have always been a popular Outer Máni motif on lintels and doorways may be just coincidence, but it is nice to think it a tribute to two home boys who made good. The **graves of the Dioscouri** (Mycenaean tombs, carved in the rock) can be visited on the path up from Old Kardamýli to Ag. Sophía church.

Around Kardamýli: Walking and Hiking

With Kardamýli as a base, the possibilities only depend on what shape you are in and how much time you have. Get a copy of the municipality's map called *Hiking Routes and Walking Times*; it is very helpful, especially in separating couch potato routes from mountain goat ones.

You can walk through the entire gorge: paths go from **Prosílio** (Προσήλιο) ①, 8km north of Kardamýli, east to **Tséria** (Τσέρια) ② or **Zachariá** (Ζαχαριά) ③, and thence into the gorge. Alternatively, the two-hour walk to and from Kardamýli to Ag. Sophía church is not too strenuous, and it takes you past the aforementioned 'graves of the Dioscouri'. Stick to the river bed and you can go to the **Monastery of the Saviour** (Sotíros) and back in two hours. Another four–five-hour walk starting at **Exochóri** (Εξοχώρι) ④, way above town, takes you into the gorge and back to Kardamýli, via great scenery, ruined mills, a cave or two, and some springs.

Go south of Kardamýli a bit and then up to **Proástio** (Προάστιο) ⑤, which has the greatest ratio of religious to secular buildings of any village in the Máni, an amazing one church or monastery for every eight houses. From there walk back north along the hillside to Kardamýli. The really keen can hike up to the church of Profítis Ilías on top of the Taíyetos (*see* p.381); the less so can take the car road up from Stoúpa and walk as much of the route as they please. Taking a taxi part way and walking back is a good idea. Consider a walk (or drive) 2km south of Kardamýli. Just after the turn-off to Proástio, look for a small sign saying **Vatsinídi Cave** (Σπήλαιο Βατσινίδι), a sea cave, its land entrance 50m from the road.

Stoúpa

Stoúpa has a beautiful sandy beach in a picture-perfect semicircular bay that is both its honeypot and its curse. Tourists swarm to Stoúpa, and they have brought intensive development in their wake, creating a dense hive of attractive seaside dwellings that overpower the beach and the hinterland. With its blue waters and shallow sea it is still a wonderful choice in the off season, but a less attractive one in August when the beach might be hard to find under the bodies. In winter, Stoúpa is pretty much deserted except at weekends. If peace and quiet is your goal, leave Stoúpa in the high season and head for Kardamýli.

Past the north end of Stoúpa's beach, but on the road into town, is the beautiful little bay of **Kalógria** with a smaller beach. Here Níkos Kazantzákis lived between 1917 and 1918, trying to run a lignite mine with a certain Macedonian miner and inveterate skirt-chaser named George Zorba, in the saga that would one day become *Zorba the Greek*. The residents insist that many of the other characters in the novel were portraits of the locals.

Around Stoúpa

Ancient Leuktra sits on a table-topped rock just north of Kalógria. Experts claim it was also the site of the Castle of Beaufort built by William de Villehardouin, which he had to return to the Greeks along with Mystrá. The ruins of both are sparse, but the setting is great. Straight up from Stoúpa, a scenic route leads into the mountain to **Kastaniá** (Καστανιά), **Saidóna** (Σαιδόνα), and after that the sky's the limit. This road can take you to the other side of the Taíyetos in good weather.

On no account miss the small secondary road leading several kilometres south to Trachíla, starting from the seaside town of **Ag. Nikólaos** (Αγ. Νικόλαος), 2km south of Stoúpa. Ag. Nikólaos has tavernas and coffee shops, but otherwise is not up to much; however, the white rocky prominence in front of **Trachíla** (Τραχήλα), which has summer fish tavernas, is worth the trip. The view is lovely and the stones form a kind of miniature Tigáni (*see* p.410). This entire strip of seaside is riddled with caves, once used as hideouts (*katafígia*) and by hermit monks. Traces of Neolithic inhabitants have been found in many of them.

Between Stoúpa and Ítilo

The road between Stoúpa and Ítilo is lined with hedgerows of prickly pear, with great views of the sea, and passes through a series of charming villages, each one with at least one show-stopper of a medieval church. In **Nomitsís** (Νομιτσής) it's the frescoed chapel of the **Anárgiri**, while the practically twin villages of Thalámes and Langáda are both worth exploring. The church in **Thalámes** (Θαλάμες) is little **Ag. Sophía**, from the 13th century. Its car park sports what looks like an ancient statue base – an ancient something-or-other in any case – just to set the tone. (Don't expect the locals to enlighten you. They have been looking at old stones all their lives and are not impressed.) The entire village is built on top of ancient Thalámes. But even if it weren't, the plane-shaded terrace of Mr Pávlos Michaléakos' Oasis café, surrounded by old stone houses, is worth a stop. For the ultimate experience, see if you can persuade him to make you a delicious omelette with *síglino*, the smoked pork the Máni made famous.

Langáda (Λαγκάδα) has a number of gorgeous stone houses and **Ag. Sotíros**, a marvellous little church containing icons from the 10th century. Towers rise in tiers up the hill, including the sign-posted **Pýrgos Kapetsino**. The tile roofs on many houses here have an unusual turned-up edge. A little farther south at **Ag. Níkon** (Αγ. Νίκον), the church of the same name deserves a look, and the coffee shop in the main square, hard by the heroic monument crowned by an eagle, just begs a visit.

The road continues south to Ítilo; *see* p.407.

Where to Stay in the Outer Máni

Kardamýli ✉ 24022

Farángi, Exochóri, **t** 272 107 3372, *www.faraggi-hotel.gr* (€€€€/€€€). A lovely hotel overlooking the gorge, a few kilometres due west of Kardamýli. All mod cons, a sitting room with fireplace, and a stunning view.

Kalamítsi, **t** 272 107 3131, *www.kalamitsi-hotel.gr* (€€€/€€€). On the bay south of town. Rooms with mini-bars and separate studio bungalows in an idyllic setting overlooking cypresses, olives, and then the sea. Sir Patrick Leigh Fermor, whose book made the Máni famous, had a house on the bay. *Open April–Oct.*

Nótos, just north of town, set back from sea, **t** 272 107 3991, *www.notoshotel.gr* (€€€/€€€). A very nice studio complex in the native style with parking and nice views. *Open all year.*

Anniska Apartments >

Anniska Apartments, **t** 272 103 6001, *www.anniska-liakoto.com* (€€€/€€). Modern seaside apartments in three buildings, run by a Greek-Australian family. There is a large common terrace, and a binder in every room describes local attractions, including hiking trails with maps. *Open May–Oct.*

Traditional Hotel Patriarcheas, **t** 272 107 3366 (€€/€€). Up from the main road north of town, by the historical centre; huge rooms, with ceiling fans, balconies with views, and refrigerators in the corridors. *Open May–Oct.*

The Castle, **t** 272 107 3226, *tokastro@otenet.gr* (€€/€). Traditional; small rooms with balconies in a garden, each complete with fridge and tiny kitchen. *Open May–Oct.*

Léla's Pension and Taverna >

Léla's Pension and Taverna, **t** 272 107 3541 (€€/€). Five rooms above the seaside taverna with fabulous sea views and good food served at old-fashioned tables on different levels, and a room with fireplace for the winter. Book early; it has a loyal and regular clientele. *Open Mar–Oct.*

Ioannis Dimitríou Rooms, **t** 272 107 3367 or **t** 697 681 9386 (€/€). Three rooms with common kitchen and bath near the old town and mini-market. The friendly host, one of the few (only 20 per cent) Australian emigrants to return to the Máni, has written a book about Hellenic settlement in Australia; he knows a lot about his home town too. *Open all year.*

Olympía Koumanákou Rooms, **t** 272 107 3623 (€/€). Behind Léla's, a bargain with a common kitchen, a garden, and very friendly hosts. *Open all year.*

Joan Stephanéa Rooms, **t** 272 107 3242 (€/€). On the main road, by the bus station. Three rooms, with en suite baths and a shared kitchen. Mrs Stephanéa is related to just about everybody and will help the 'roomless' using her family network – a good person to know in August. *Open all year.*

Stoúpa ✉ 24024

Stoúpa, **t** 272 107 7308, *www.zorbas.de/english/apps/hotel.php* (€€/€€). Modern, nice, set back from the beach; much cheaper out of season; minibars in each room. *Open all year.*

Leuktron, **t** 272 107 7322, *www.lefktron-hotel.gr* (€€/€€). Beside the Stoúpa and very like it. *Open April–Oct.*

Apartments Kalógria, **t** 272 107 7479, *www.web-greece.gr/kalogria* (€€/€€). Right on the beach at Kalógria, with wonderful views. The Balaktári family offer rooms with fridges, and very good off-season prices as well. *Open April–Oct.*

Camping Kalógria, **t** 272 107 7319 (€/€). Close to Kalógria beach, on the other side of the road; lots of shade. *Open June–Sept.*

Eating Out in the Outer Máni

Kardamýli

Amán, **t** 272 107 3266. A new, nicely decorated café beside Léla's.

O Kýpos tis Kardamýlis, **t** 272 107 3516. Just behind Kikí's; tables set out in a large garden under grape vines.

Stoúpa

Akrogiáli, **t** 272 107 7335. The blue and white terrace is the perfect place to view the bay over a plate of fresh fish.

Taverna Panoréa, on the Stoúpa–Kalógria road, **t** 272 107 7360. Not right on the sea, so tries harder with Greek nights and an English library where you can exchange books.

To Pefko, **t** 272 107 7452. A terrace and fireplace. Coffee or food available day and night.

Psistariá Stoúpa, **t** 272 107 7516. At the north end of the bay; grilled meat on a terraced site full of pine trees overlooking the bay.

Messenía

Down in the southwest corner of the Peloponnese, Messenía is the luxuriant land of King Olive. Here, groves in thick canopies produce not only fine oil but fat, tapering, purply brown Kalamáta olives that make a much-appreciated addition to any Greek salad and are grown according to a secret farming technique. Everyone in Messenía owns a few trees, and, although you may find smaller hotels that stay open after October, they come with the caveat that it may be hard to find the owners during the harvest.

For the visitor today, the prefecture offers some of the most beautiful sandy beaches of the Peloponnese, enough historical attractions for a decent dose of culture, and a convenient airport in the capital, Kalamáta.

15

Don't miss

1. A Mycenaean palace in a valley
   Nestor's Palace **p.452**
2. Castles, islands, wetlands, legends and a modern city
   Bay of Navaríno **p.447**
3. Massive Classical walls
   Ancient Messene **p.430**
4. Flowers, the best beach and a Venetian castle
   Methóni **p.442**
5. Paradise for windsurfers
   Finikoúnda **p.442**

See map overleaf

Messenía

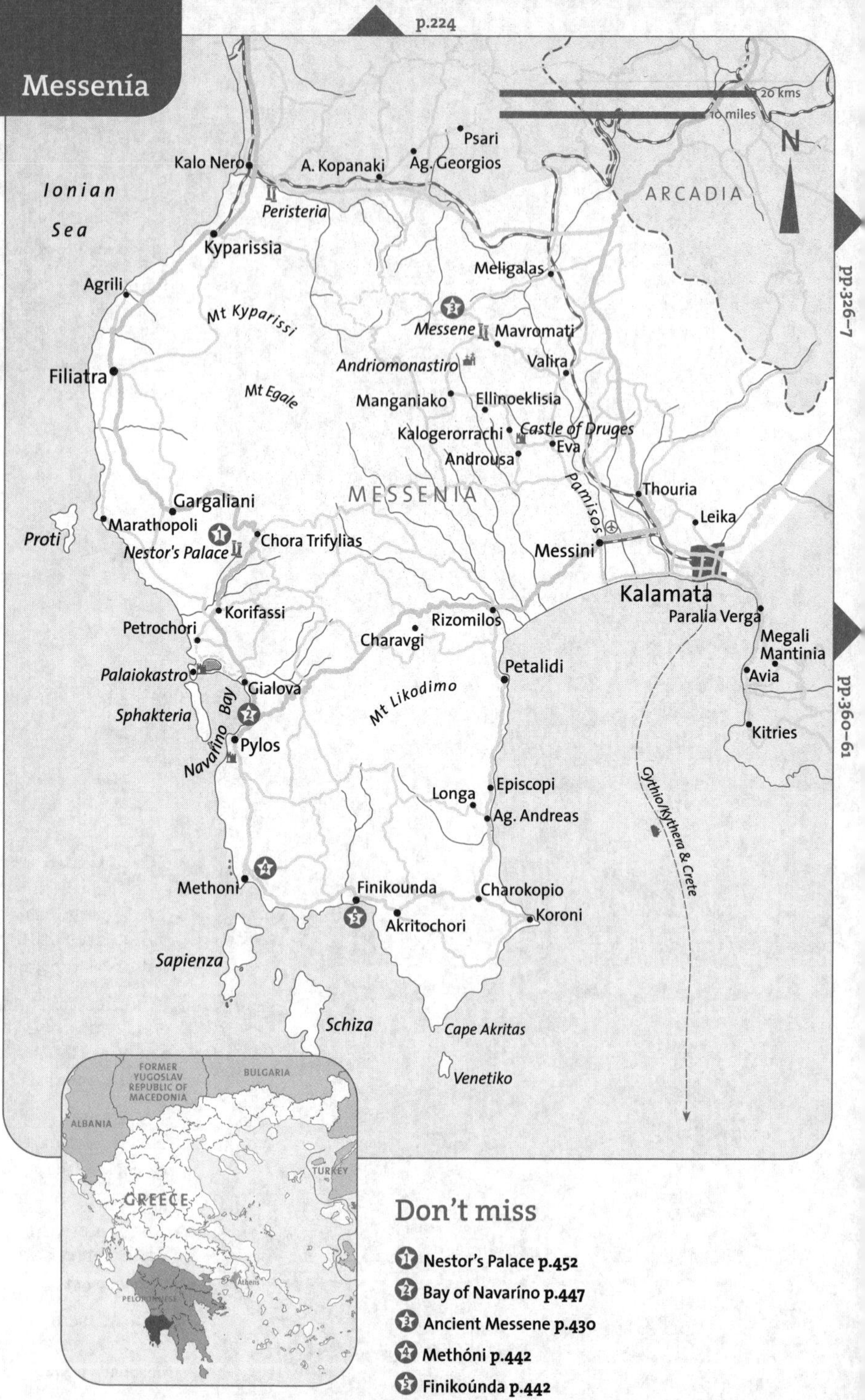

p.224

pp.326–7

pp.360–61

20 kms
10 miles
N

Ionian Sea
ARCADIA
MESSENIA

Kalo Nero
A. Kopanaki
Ag. Georgios
Psari
Peristeria
Kyparissia
Agrili
Mt Kyparissi
Meligalas
Messene
Mavromati
Andriomonastiro
Valira
Filiatra
Mt Egale
Manganiako
Ellinoeklisia
Kalogerorrachi
Castle of Druges
Eva
Androusa
Pamisos
Thouria
Leika
Gargaliani
Marathopoli
Proti
Nestor's Palace
Chora Trifylias
Messini
Kalamata
Paralia Verga
Korifassi
Petrochori
Rizomilos
Charavgi
Megali Mantinia
Avia
Palaiokastro
Gialova
Petalidi
Sphakteria
Navarino Bay
Mt Likodimo
Pylos
Kitries
Episcopi
Longa
Ag. Andreas
Gythio/Kythera & Crete
Methoni
Finikounda
Charokopio
Akritochori
Koroni
Sapienza
Schiza
Cape Akritas
Venetiko

FORMER YUGOSLAV REPUBLIC OF MACEDONIA
BULGARIA
ALBANIA
TURKEY
GREECE
Athens
PELOPONNESE

Don't miss

1. Nestor's Palace **p.452**
2. Bay of Navaríno **p.447**
3. Ancient Messene **p.430**
4. Methóni **p.442**
5. Finikoúnda **p.442**

While o'er Messenía's beauteous land,
Wide-watering streams their arms expand,
Of nature's gifts profuse;
Bright plenty crowns her smiling plain

The fruitful tree, the full-eared grain,
Their richest stores produce.
Large herds her spacious valleys fill,
On many a soft-descending hill
Her flocks unnumbered stray;
No fierce extreme her climate knows,
no chilling frost nor winter snows,
Nor dog-star's scorching ray.

Euripides, from a lost play

As well as olives, this fertile prefecture is also famous for its figs. However, only a few vestiges remain of Messenía's once famous mulberry groves, introduced by the Byzantines and greatly encouraged by the Venetians, but systematically destroyed by the Turks during the War of Independence. Messenía also has its share of rugged mountains, although in this book the most dramatic bit – the Outer Máni – is with the rest of the Máni (*see* pp.415–22).

In the *Iliad*, Messenía was the fief of Nestor, 'flower of Achaean chivalry', whose calm reason provides a foil for the hotheads at Troy. When the Dorian 'sons of Heracles' divided the Peloponnese into three portions, Messenía, symbolized by a fox, was occupied by Kresphontes, whose dynasty soon merged with the natives, who had close kin and religious ties with the Arcadians. Unlike the bossy Dorian states of Argos and Sparta, Messenía didn't have a central kingship but was divided into small, self-governing units. By the 8th century BC, this state of affairs was far too mellow for the military perverts next door, and after a long war Messenía was captured by the Spartans. Their subjugation wouldn't remain the *fait accompli* the Spartans wished, and in the 4th century BC they became free to share fully in the historical vicissitudes of the Hellenistic and Roman periods. In the Middle Ages, contact and trade with Venice brought prosperity, then bitter battles with the Turks; during the War of Independence, Messenía witnessed the sea battle at Navaríno that led directly to Greek independence.

Kalamáta: Castles, Kerchiefs and the *Kalamatianó*

Kalamáta, the second city of the Peloponnese, is actually a nice town of 44,000, with a vibrant cultural life, galleries, plentiful parks and a smart marina for its yachts. A manufacturing centre and oil

Getting to and around Kalamáta

Kalamáta is 235km from Athens, 60km from Sparta. The **airport**, **t** 272 106 9442, complete with car hire offices, is 6km west of town, and receives charters only, except for a flight from Thessaloníki three times a week.

The **train station** is in the town centre at 1 Frantzí St, **t** 272 109 5056 (**t** 1110 for train times). There are daily trains as follows: three to Athens, four to Pátras, seven to Pýrgos, 12 to Meligalás, and two to Kyparissía.

The **KTEL bus station**, **t** 272 102 2851, is at the north end of Artémidos St near the New Market. Buses are as follows: Athens 11 per day via Megalópolis and Trípolis and the Isthmus; Pátras two per day via Pýrgos; Sparta two per day; Mavrományi (ancient Messene) two per day; Koróni eight per day; Pýlos nine per day; Finikoúnda three per day (where you can change for Methóni); Areópolis four per day.

The **city bus depot** is near Plateía 23 Martíou. Bus no.1 goes down Aristoménous and east along the waterfront as far as the Filoxenía Hotel every 12 to 15 minutes.

For a **taxi** in the centre, **t** 272 102 1112; on the seafront, **t** 272 102 8181. There are taxi stands at the rail and bus stations. For a 24-hour radio taxi: **t** 272 102 1112.

For **car hire**, see **Maniates Travel** (p.428), **Avis**, 2 Késseri St, **t** 272 10 2 0352, or **Best Car**, 125 Nedóntos, **t** 272 109 3240, *bestcar@hellasnet.gr*. For **motorbikes**: **Alpha**, 143 Vironos St, **t** 272 109 3423, *www.alphabikes.gr*.

Or catch a **boat**: **Anen Lines**, **t** 272 102 0704, sails its F/B *Mirtidiótissa* from Kalamáta to Kíssimos in Crete once weekly.

port (olive oil, that is) as well as a port for the other fruits of Messenía, Kalamáta is also something of a resort, although it has difficulty competing with the holiday centres to its south on either finger of the Peloponnese. The swimming is good, especially out by the Filoxenía hotel's pebble beach, where the usual grey-white pebbles mingle with unusual pure black mud stones, the kind that are perfect for mosaics. Still, foreigners usually stay only out of necessity, while waiting for a train or a charter flight.

Laid out in a grid by French engineers in 1829 after Ibrahim Pasha's destruction, Kalamáta has the usual traffic-clogged streets and parking nightmares, exacerbated by the fact that this is a long, narrow city, stretching almost two kilometres from its medieval castle down to the port. Adding to that, its seaside thoroughfare is also the main road into the Máni, which makes it almost a highway; when you find yourself frustrated and stymied in the concrete city centre, it is hard to remember that Kalamáta's claims to fame are its olives and figs. This is the place to buy ceramic pots, a big industry here, or a silk headscarf, a last memory of Messenía's once prosperous mulberry groves. Kalamáta is as famous for these as it is for the *Kalamatianó*, a circle dance popular all over Greece.

The Kástro, Archaeological Museum, and Beaches

Frankish castle
open in daylight

Kalamáta's **Frankish castle** sits on a low hill at the north end of the town away from the sea. It looks good once you find it, and the old part of Kalamáta encircles its *enceinte*. The castle sits on top of **ancient Pharai**, whose history is as obscure as its ruins. Suffice it to say that the Mycenaeans were here (Telemachus dropped by looking for his father) and it suffered the same fate as all other Messenian cities during the Archaic and Classical periods – squeezed firmly under the thumb of the Spartans. Later, the

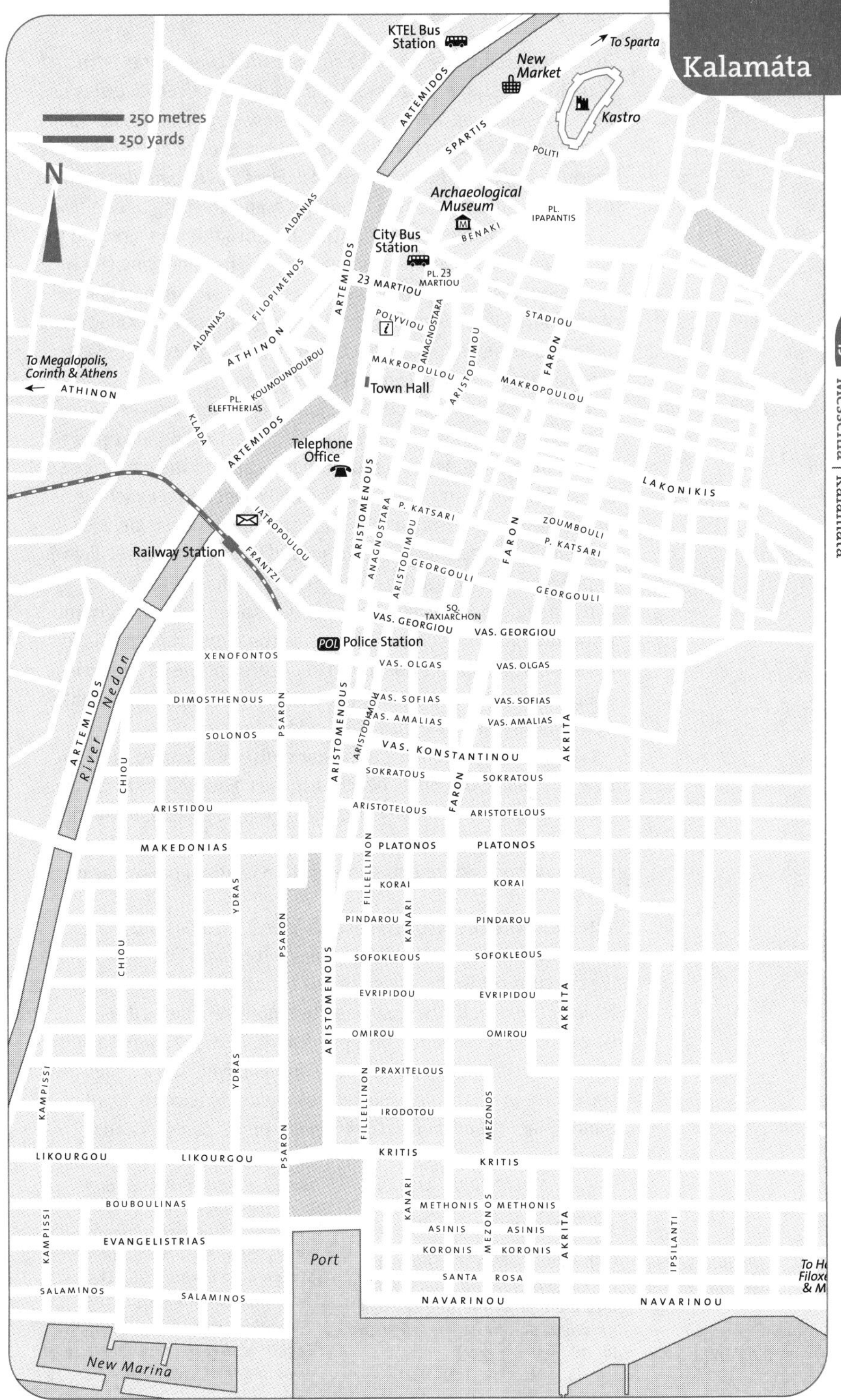
KTEL Bus Station
To Sparta
New Market
Kastro
250 metres
250 yards
N
ARTEMIDOS
SPARTIS
POLITI
Archaeological Museum
BENAKI
PL. IPAPANTIS
ALDANIAS
City Bus Station
PL. 23 MARTIOU
23 MARTIOU
FILOPIMENOS
ARTEMIDOS
POLYVIOU
ANAGNOSTARA
STADIOU
ALDANIAS
ATHINON
FARON
ARISTODIMOU
To Megalopolis, Corinth & Athens
ATHINON
KOUMOUNDOUROU
MAKROPOULOU
Town Hall
MAKROPOULOU
PL. ELEFTHERIAS
KLADA
ARTEMIDOS
Telephone Office
ARISTOMENOUS
LAKONIKIS
IATROPOULOU
P. KATSARI
ZOUMBOULI
FARON
P. KATSARI
Railway Station
FRANTZI
ANAGNOSTARA
ARISTODIMOU
GEORGOULI
GEORGOULI
SQ. TAXIARCHON
VAS. GEORGIOU
VAS. GEORGIOU
Police Station
XENOFONTOS
VAS. OLGAS
VAS. OLGAS
ARTEMIDOS
River Nedon
DIMOSTHENOUS
PSARON
ARISTOMENOUS
VAS. SOFIAS
VAS. SOFIAS
VAS. AMALIAS
VAS. AMALIAS
SOLONOS
ARISTODIMOU
AKRITA
VAS. KONSTANTINOU
CHIOU
SOKRATOUS
SOKRATOUS
FARON
ARISTIDOU
ARISTOTELOUS
ARISTOTELOUS
MAKEDONIAS
FILELLINON
PLATONOS
PLATONOS
YDRAS
KORAI
KORAI
KANARI
PSARON
PINDAROU
PINDAROU
CHIOU
ARISTOMENOUS
SOFOKLEOUS
SOFOKLEOUS
AKRITA
EVRIPIDOU
EVRIPIDOU
OMIROU
OMIROU
PRAXITELOUS
KAMPISSI
YDRAS
FILELLINON
IRODOTOU
MEZONOS
PSARON
LIKOURGOU
LIKOURGOU
KRITIS
KRITIS
KANARI
BOUBOULINAS
METHONIS
METHONIS
KAMPISSI
ASINIS
ASINIS
MEZONOS
AKRITA
IPSILANTI
EVANGELISTRIAS
Port
KORONIS
KORONIS
SANTA
ROSA
SALAMINOS
SALAMINOS
NAVARINOU
NAVARINOU
New Marina

Byzantines built a castle and a small church over Pharai. Both were in poor shape long before the Franks came, but Geoffrey de Villehardouin was not slow to see the low acropolis' possibilities and in 1208 he built a fortress with the outer *enceinte*, inner redoubt and keep that you see today. His son William was born here. The castle then passed through many grasping hands, from Slavs (1293) back to the Franks (the Duke of Athens in 1300), to the Paleológoi and Byzantines in 1423, then to the Venetians, the Turks, the Venetians, and so on. No wonder it is the worse for wear. Walking inside is restricted; the last big earthquake in Kalamáta in 1986 put some ominous cracks in the walls and devastated the imposing metropolitan church nearby.

Archaeological Museum
t 272 102 6209; open Tues–Sun 8.30–3; closed Mon; adm

Near the castle on Benáki Street, the **Archaeological Museum**, with explanations in English, covers the Classical period up to the War of Independence. The museum is located in the handsome old Benáki mansion, and its excellent small collection is exactly what one would expect from anything that involves one of Greece's great philanthropic families. A new and larger museum is already in place next door but the moving date is still uncertain.

In the Middle Ages, the city was called Kalámai. It got its name *kalamáta* (good eyes) when an icon of the Virgin, remarkable for her sympathetic eyes, was found in the area of the city. You can check out the truth of this in the **Church of the Apostles** in Plateía 23 Martíou, where the icon holds pride of place.

Kalamáta's last dramatic appearance in war occurred nowhere near the castle, but on its **beaches**. In 1941, 7,000 Allied troops fell into German hands here before they could be evacuated by the Royal Navy. Every year, Kalamáta has hosted reunions of these soldiers whose war ended so abruptly in German prison camps.

The Velanidiás Monastery: A View and an Icon

While still inside Kalamáta proper, on the main Sparta road, look for the turn-off to the village of **Leíka** (Λαίκα), then immediately look for the sign to the now deserted **Móni Velanidiás** (Μόνι Βελανιδιάς). It offers the best panoramic view of Kalamáta and the castle. The monastery got its name in 1884, when an icon fell out of the centre of a lightning-blasted oak (*velanídi*), a rather Nordic hiding place for an icon in Greece. They prefer caves as a rule.

ⓘ Kalamáta ›
EOT: 6 Polyviou St, t 272 108 6868, www.messinia.net.gr; open Mon–Fri 7.30–2.30

Useful Information in Kalamáta

The **tourist office** gives out maps of the city, but only if you can find them first. The office is near the City Hall (*to dimarchío*); once there, ask them for Polyvíou St, a block south of Plateía 23 Martíou.

Maniates Travel, 1 Iatropoúlou St (near the train station), **t** 272 102 5300, *maniatis@kal.forthnet.gr*, helps with hotels, car hire and tours. Branches in Stoúpa, **t** 272 107 8062 and Chráni (south of Petalídi, **t** 272 503 1233).

Be sure to look for the informative English weekly *This Week in Messenía*, *www.messiniathisweek.ws*.

Festivals in Kalamáta

On 23 March, Kalamáta celebrates **Independence Day** two days before the rest of Greece. No two areas joined the fray at the exact same moment, and any city that feels it 'jumped the gun', so to speak, is very proud of it. Politicians could, and do, spend an entire week going from town to town in the Peloponnese in March celebrating various Independence Days.

Easter in Kalamáta is famous for its noise: local youths stuff pipes with gunpowder (*saítes*), spin them around and hurl them with a bang.

In the open-air theatre near the castle, Kalamáta hosts an acclaimed **International Festival of Dance** from mid-July to mid-August.

Where to Stay in Kalamáta

Kalamáta ✉ 24100

Hotels here are open all year. Many are on Navarínou St, the long coastal road leading to the Máni, served by the no.1 bus. The top ones are in that indeterminate, anonymous style demanded by tour operators, with lots of highly paid genuine Greek dancers ready to provide a 'real' Greek night.

★ Filoxenía >

Filoxenía, Navarínou-Paralía, in a little park on the beach on the east edge of town, **t** 272 102 3166, *www.grecotel.gr* (€€€€€/€€€). This newly renovated, well-run hotel has an indoor pool and a large outdoor pool, steps away from a fine pebbled beach and the sea. It offers tennis, parking, and interesting offers in the off season. Visiting politicians of all stripes call it home when trawling for votes in the Máni.

★ Taverna Kostéa Anavrití >>

Rex, 26 Aristoménous, **t** 272 109 4440, *www.rexhotel.gr* (€€€/€€€). 45 well-equipped rooms in a beautifully renovated neoclassical building near the bus station and castle. Only a few parking spaces, though.

Flísvos, 135 Navarínou, **t** 272 108 2282 (€€€/€€€). On the coastal strip midway between the Filoxénia and the centre; a total renovation in 2007 has added style as well as TVs, air-conditioning and minibars.

Haícos, 115 Navarínou, **t** 272 108 2886, *www.haikos.gr* (€€/€€). Slightly closer to the centre, with pretty much the same on offer as the Flísvos.

Vyzántio, 13 Sidir. Stathmoú St, **t** 272 108 6824 (€€/€). 100m from the station. It may not be dead quiet, but it is dead handy and well run. It's also hard to find; ask at the train station.

George, Frantzí St and Dágre St, **t** 272 102 7225 (€/€). A seven-room bargain by the train station with air-conditioning, TV, and a shared fridge.

Ávra, 10 Santa Rosa (near Fillellínon Street), **t** 272 108 2759 (€/€). Quiet and simple (shared bath), just a street back from Navarínou.

Cafe Island, Avías, t 272 105 8008 (€/€). Hate cities? Try these good rooms over a good Greek-Italian restaurant on the busy seaside strip south of town. Phone ahead. Bus service and parking. *Open April–Oct.*

Eating Out in Kalamáta

Most restaurants of note in Kalamáta are either on Navarínou St, around the marina to the west of the port, or in busy Avías and Kitriés, Kalamáta's southern seaside suburbs. The first, where the busy road separates most restaurants from their seaside terraces, makes work a death-defying dodge for the waiters.

Psaroúla (Ψαρούλα), on the beach at 14 Navarínou, **t** 272 102 0985. For fresh fish and friendly service.

Taverna Kostéa Anavrití, Megáli Mantinía, **t** 272 105 8062. High on a hill above Avías, this village taverna is popular with Kalamáta people who make the trek, and locals too. Delicious meat dishes and *mezédes*, all washed down with local wine. Megáli Mantinía can be reached from the road to Kardamýli as well.

The marina west of Kanári St, beyond the port, offers easy parking and restaurants overlooking the yachts. They look swish, but prices are similar to Navarínou St, minus the noise. These places are so untouristy they have yet to anglicize their signs:

Liméni (Λιμένι), **t** 272 109 5670.

Pyrofáni (Πυροφάνι), **t** 272 109 5386.

Kanná (Καννά), **t** 272 109 1596.

New Messíni to Ancient Messene, through the Blessed Land

Just west of Kalamáta and the airport, the modern but excruciatingly dull town of **Messíni** (Μεσσήνη) is located in one of Greece's prime rice-producing areas. Originally named Nísi, it has shanghaied the proud name of ancient Messene, and the turn-off for the same is about the only reason to cross into the city limits.

The direct route to ancient Messene passes through **Éva** (Ευα), 8km north of Messíni, a town once sacred to Dionysos and named after the cry '*evoi! evan!*' of his maenads. It then continues north of Lámbena and then left to Mavromáti. But there is a tempting back way through part of medieval Messenía starting at **Androúsa** (Ανδρούσα), 2.5km west of Éva. Here a down-at-heel, gypsy-haunted Frankish pile known as the **castle of Druges** commands a splendid view over the Messenían plain, known since ancient times as Makária, the 'blessed land', a wide glimmering plain of olive groves, dotted by cypresses, the whole watered by the Pásimos, the mightiest river in the south Peloponnese. Today the Plain of Makária is one of the most densely populated rural areas in Greece; 2,500 years ago it was the unhappy land of the helots, toiling away to feed the Spartans.

Byzantine churches dot this once wealthy area, starting with the single-nave church of **Ag. Geórgios** in Androúsa itself. Go north-west up through **Kalogerórrachi** (Καλογερόρραχη) and on towards **Ellinoeklisía** (Ελληνοεκλησία) for the ruined 14th-century **Samarína Monastery**, founded by the Empress Theodora; its church, Zoodóchos Pigí, perhaps the most beautiful in all Messenía, was built over an ancient temple and incorporates some of its columns under the dome. From here, continue northwest towards **Manganiakó** (Μαγγανιακό), where you'll come to the dirt road to Petrálona. Along it lies the **Andriomonástiro** (Ανδριομονάστηρο), another imperial monastery, this one built by Andronicus II Paleológos above the spring that still provides Androúsa with its water. From Petrálona, head northeast to Mavromáti and back even further in time to Messene.

Ancient Messene

Ithóme means 'step', and at 2,630ft it was a giant one, a natural citadel over the Plain of Makária to the south and the Plain of Stenýklaros to the north. Underneath it, in a fold closed off by the austere slopes of Mount Eva, lies ancient Messene, still enclosed in its magnificent late Classical walls. Within these, on the map, modern **Mavromáti** (Μαυρομμάτι) resembles a few grains of rice

Getting to Messene

There are two daily **buses** from Kalamáta in summer but sometimes only three a week in winter.

lost in a large frying pan, barely keeping alive the promise of the oracle: 'The bright bloom of Sparta shall perish and Messene shall be inhabited for all time.' Since 1986, excavations directed by Pétros Themelís of the University of Crete have identified all of the buildings mentioned by Pausanias (except for the Temple of Isis and Serapis) and many have been or are currently in the process of being restored.

History

Legend says **Queen Messene**, daughter of King Triopas of Argos, built the Altar of Zeus Ithomatas on Mount Ithóme and thus founded the city – one of the few Greek women ever to do such a thing. By the 10th century BC Messene herself was worshipped alongside Zeus. In the 8th century BC, when the Spartans coveted Messenía, their devious minds came up with one of the kinkiest provocations of all time to justify a war. A group of young Spartans in drag went to a symposium of Messenian worthies, first pretending to entertain them, then pulling out the daggers hidden under their skirts. But the Messenians were quicker and killed the phoney girls, which was enough for Sparta to self-righteously declare what has since been known as the **First Messenian War.**

The Messenians, under their king, **Aristodemos**, fought long and hard, but eventually the Spartans cornered them on Ithóme. It was a long, bitter siege. Aristodemos was credited with inventing some sort of long-lost secret weapon that enabled the Messenians to hold their own against the Spartan hoplites on the steep slopes, but even so the Spartans were numerically superior, the Messenians in grave danger and the auguries bad. Aristodemos, remembering Agamemnon's sacrifice of his daughter Iphigenia, announced that he would sacrifice his pure virgin daughter on the Altar of Zeus Ithomatas for the sake of victory. The night before, her lover removed her from the ranks of the virgins in the hope of sparing her life, but Aristodemos killed her anyway in a spate of paternal fury.

The Messenians then asked the Delphic oracle how they could defeat the Spartans, and were told that whoever first dedicated a hundred tripods to Zeus on Ithóme would be the victor. The Messenians set to work, making great bronze tripods, but word leaked out to the Spartans, who defied their reputation for stupidity by quickly whipping up a hundred toy tripods and sending them up to the sanctuary in the bag of one of their spies. When the Messenians saw them, they simply gave up and abandoned the citadel, except for Aristodemos, who killed himself on the same spot where he had killed his daughter.

Sparta's defeat by Argos at Hysiae in 669 BC encouraged the Messenians to revolt under their gallant hero Aristomenes (*see* pp.257–8) with aid from Argos, Elís and Arcadía. Although many historians think this **Second Messenian War** was highly romanticized, the **Third Messenian War** (465–459 BC) certainly wasn't. In 465 BC, when Sparta was devastated by an earthquake, the helots saw their chance and attacked; the quick-thinking Spartan king Archidamos rallied the surviving Spartans in battle formation and held the ruined city; the helots retreated to Ithóme and made a stand. This was Sparta's worst nightmare, and she asked Athens for help against the helots, invoking a treaty the two powers had signed after the Persian Wars. After a good deal of soul-searching, Athens sent 4,000 hoplites. Their presence at Ithóme brought out the tremendous differences in their cultural attitudes, until Sparta, growing nervous at the 'adventurous and revolutionary' behaviour of the Athenians, sent them home because 'they weren't needed after all'. Although Sparta eventually reconquered Ithóme, Athens, now insulted, sided with the helots and resettled them in Nafpaktos (across the Gulf of Corinth) and allied herself with Sparta's enemy Argos, beginning a cold war that set the stage for the Peloponnesian War in 431 BC.

Messene's Founding Father: Epaminondas

Ancient Greek and Roman writers regarded Epaminondas of Thebes as one the greatest men of all time. He was accomplished in music and philosophy, but it was his military prowess that made him famous. While his 4th-century compatriot Pelopídes founded the Theban Sacred Band (a hand-picked company of 150 pairs of lovers – the ultimate buddy system, inspired by the Spartan model), Epaminondas was the first to deploy his troops in a deep phalanx to draw in the enemy infantry, leaving them vulnerable to his cavalry, which would suddenly pounce and demolish them. It worked at treat in 371 BC at Leúktra, when 1,400 Spartan hoplites were killed in 'the most famous of all battles won by Greeks over Greeks', according to Pausanias. Philip II of Macedonia studied Epaminondas closely; Philip's son, Alexander, would use his deep phalanx and cavalry tactics to conquer the world.

In 369, Epaminondas invaded the Peloponnese for the first of four times to drive nails into Sparta's coffin, leading the Thebans and their allies to victory after victory. To help bottle up the Spartans in Laconía, he founded Messene, choosing fortress-like Ithóme as the spot that would hurt Spartan pride the most. He repatriated the Messenians living in Nafpaktos and elsewhere; he was present when the first sacrifices were made to Zeus Ithomatas, and joined in the prayer that all the Messenian heroes, in particular Queen Messene and Aristomenes, would return in spirit now that their people were free. His planners laid the new city out in a Hippodamean grid, which was considered the most apt for a democracy, because it give all citizens equal plots of land and equal access to the public and sacred buildings (Piraeus and Rhodes are two earlier examples). All Greece guaranteed the autonomy of the new city – except bad fairy Sparta, of course, which looked on with impotent fury. 'The most painful thing is the prospect, not of being deprived unjustly of our territory, but of seeing our own slaves become master of it,' growled one of Sparta's kings. The Spartans finally killed Epaminondas even as his army defeated them one last time, at Mantinéa in 362 BC. The Messenians, for their part, never forgot him, and accorded their founding father heroic honours.

In 369 BC, Epaminondas (*see* box, left) founded Messene, which Diodorus Siculus wrote was built in 85 days – an exaggeration perhaps, although speed was of the essence, not only through fear of Sparta (hence the 9km of walls), but also because the Messenians were keen to make up for their four lost centuries; they built like crazy, held games in honour of Zeus, and participated fully in the complicated alliances and betrayals that characterized the Hellenistic age. Loathing and distrust of Sparta dictated most of their policies, but not always.

The walls proved their worth on three occasions: in 295 BC against the famous Demetrios Poliorketes 'the Besieger'; then in 214 BC, against an even stronger Macedonian army led by Demetrios, son of Philip V, who was killed with nearly all of his phalanx when citizens of both sexes bombarded them with boulders and tiles; and then again in 202 BC, when the Spartans made their last play to take back the Peloponnese under their tyrant Nabis. On this occasion, they were repulsed by the great general of the Achaean League, Philopoemen of Megalopolis, who later annihilated the Spartans at Gýthio and would have razed Sparta to the ground had not the Romans stood in his way. But gratitude was as sadly lacking in Messene as in Athens: in 183 BC, a demagogue led a faction to revolt against the Achaean League; Philopoemen attacked them, was captured, thrown in prison and forced to take poison. By 146 BC the Romans had the city in their pocket, and in AD 395 the Goths overran the town and it faded from history.

The Site

Ancient Messene site
currently open daily from 8am to sunset, adm free, but this may change when the fencing of the lower site is completed and it gets 'civilized' with guards and adm

Museum
t *272 405 1201; open Tues–Sun 8.30–3; adm*

Mavromáti is a bucolic little place, offering a fine overview of the ruins, and a peaceful spot for an overnight stay in the boondocks. Its still-functioning fountain is ancient, fed by Messene's famous spring, **Klepsydra**, brought down by an aqueduct from Ithóme. Just north of the village is the **museum**, with statues and architectural fragments from the site. Next to this, a road descends to the ruins and the car park near the **Theatre**. This was built to a revolutionary design, the *cavea* cupped in an artificial slope supported by a semi-circular wall, made from the same fine limestone blocks as the city walls, with pointed entrances every 65ft. This was the first known example of what a modern designer would call the 'fortified look', a style that become popular in large free-standing Roman theatres and amphitheatres. Part of the *skene* and the stairway up to the *parados* remain intact. A stretch of **street**, just over 6ft wide, was found in front of the second western arch, with slabs covering one of the Messene's main drains.

No one felt like going to the theatre any more by the time of Diocletian (early 4th century AD), and some of its blocks were used for the restoration of the nearby **Fountainhouse of Arsinoe**, which received water from the Klepsydra. The fountainhouse was still used into the Byzantine period; a coin of Leo VI (d. 912) and a quantity of Byzantine pottery from as late as the 13th century confirm that Messene carried on quietly for centuries. Little remains of the **Agora**, its northern extent marked by a semicircular *exedra* and a great 330ft *stoa*, shaped like a Greek P. Fragments from its temples of Poseidon and Aphrodite, described by Pausanias, are in the museum.

The real hot spot in the ancient city was the nearby **Asklepeion**. The Messenians regarded Asklepios not as the god of healing (none of the usual votives of body parts was found here), but as an important member of their royal family, in the time before the Dorian invasion. In 214 BC, they erected this Asklepeion over a 7th-century *asklepeion* and Sanctuary of Orthia in a flurry of patriotic pride after the defeat of the Macedonians. As Pausanias describes it, it was a sculpture gallery and civic centre; statue bases (originally there were over 140) cluttered the space around the temple and altar. No one is quite sure of the dedication of the **Doric temple** with its large altar in the middle of the Asklepeion, but it held a giant chrysolith (gold and marble) statue of the heroine goddess Messene, so it was probably hers.

A quadrangle of *stoas* (200ft by 215ft) surrounded the temple. Three important buildings in a row were attached to the east end. The **Ekklesiastérion**, a roofed and elegant little theatre, was used for meetings of the Assembly as well as for concerts. It was surrounded by a strong retaining wall and the floor of its orchestra was paved in Roman times with red, white and blue stone. Next is an imposing gateway or **Propylaia** with three doors (preserving cuts for the bolts and hinges). Beside this is the **Bouleuterion** (or Synedrion), where the councillors or *synedroi* of the independent cities of Messene met; a continuous bench running along three sides of the room could seat 76. Ajacent were the **Archives of the Secretary of the Synedroi**. Remnants of 5th–7th century Christian settlement lie just east, along with a Hellenistic cemetery with the cist graves of people killed in the Spartan attack in 201 BC.

The **west wing** of the **Peristyle Court** held what we might call 'terrace temples': a row of four **cult rooms** that once held statues by Damophon, a 2nd-century BC native of Messene who was responsible for Demeter's statue at Lykósoura (*see* p.341) and who was chosen to restore Phidias' Zeus at Olympia after an earthquake. A roof shelters the best-preserved cult room, dedicated to **Artemis Orthia** (or Phosphoros, the 'light-bearer'), where the body of Damophon's statue of Artemis was found, along with bases for statues of priestesses and initiated girls. According to Pausanias, the cult room dedicated to Epaminondas held a statue of the city's

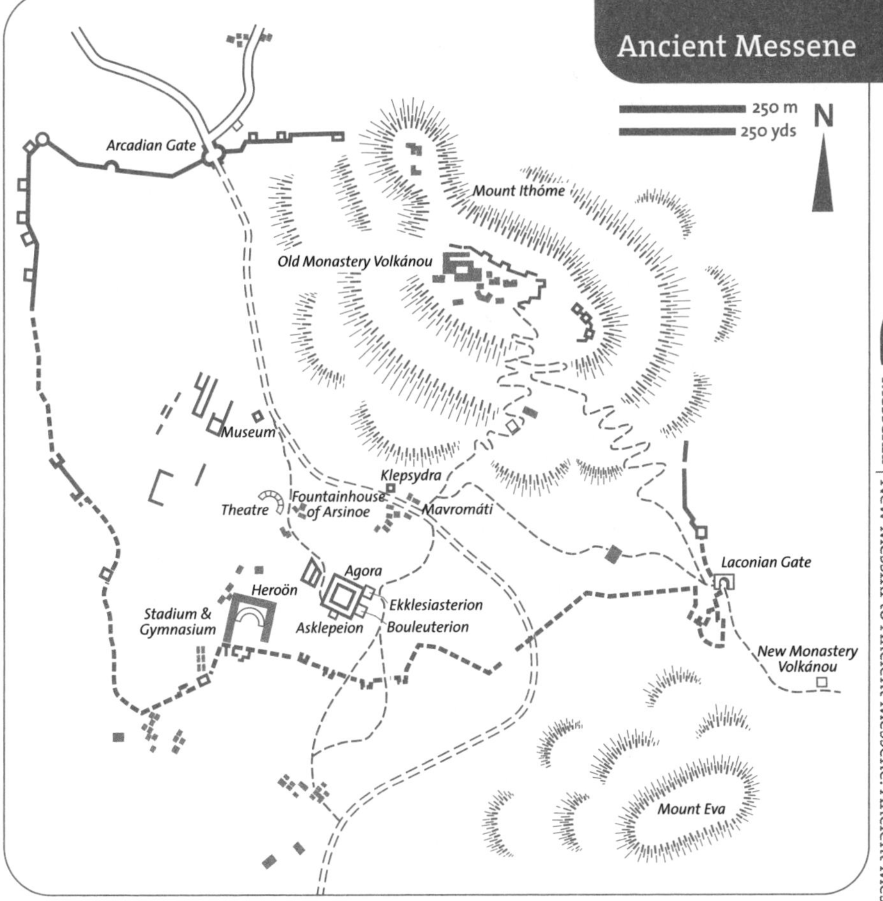

founder in iron, as a sign of the tremendous respect Messenians felt for him. The stout **northern wing** contained public dining halls that were later converted into the **Sevasteion** or Caesareion, dedicated to the worship of the goddess Roma and the emperors, with two compartments divided by a monumental staircase.

Northwest of the Asklepeion are the ruins of the original **Sanctuary of Orthia**, with a square-shaped *cella*, and west of that are the poorly preserved remains of a **Sanctuary of Demeter and the Dioscouri**, where a large quantity of votive deposits were found. Its east end was demolished for a drainage channel in 1960; problems with flooding on the site were resolved when this and the ancient drains were restored. The rectangular foundations of **Hellenistic baths** are just east of the Asklepeion; cuttings for clay tubs and some of the terracotta pipes have survived, as well as a hoard of bronze coins, many in identical pairs: the charge for a bath was two pennies. Near the baths stood a rectangular funerary monument, or **Heroön**, erected in the mid-2nd century BC.

A column found here was inscribed with honours from seven cities to Damophon for his talent, generosity, and skill at restoring cult monuments.

Some 80 yards east of the Asklepeion, a very late but lavish Roman building known as the **Room with Opus Sectile** was uncovered, the interior faced with marble, the floor paved in a marble *opus sectile* pattern. It was destroyed in the late 4th century AD, perhaps by the Goths; a statue of Artemis Laphria was found in the ruins. Excavations are continuing to the east of the Asklepeion, where a street over another drain was found, along with a stone ***hecataión***, or column, its sides sculpted with three aspects of Artemis, a nice reminder than even in Roman times her function as a seasonal fertility symbol was not wholly forgotten. South of the Asklepeion is the **Heirothysion** (*heirothyta* were the parts of an animal eaten after a sacrifice), used by magistrates responsible for running Messene's festivals. According to Pausanias, this held statues of the Olympian gods, a bronze statue of Epaminondas, and the tripods that appear on Messene's coins and were given as prizes in the Ithomaian Games (a generous gesture, considering the story of Spartan trickery). Among the finds inside was a stone inscribed with two lines of music. The most popular attraction in the vicinity was the now vanished 'tomb' of Aristomenes.

South of the Heirothysíon are the well-preserved **Stadium** and **Gymnasium**, built as a single unit. Entrance to the complex was by way of a Doric **Propylaea**, with four columns; note the ruins of a stair on the south side, made in late antiquity out of statue bases, and carved with a board for playing dice. The Stadium had stone seats (including fancy ones for members of the festival committee) and its horseshoe curve is surrounded on three sides by ***stoas***: a double one on the north and single ones on the east and west. The one on the east, built on the cheap without iron clamps and dowels, has completely collapsed. The Gymnasium, abutting the west *stoa*, had a **Sanctuary of Heracles and Hermes**, and between the columns you can see statue bases for various *gymnasiarchs*, or coaches. Many prominent Messenians chose to face eternity from the vicinity of the stadium; the biggest tomb, the late Hellenistic **Heroön of the Stadium**, belonged to a wealthy high priest named Saethidas. The lofty podium is intact, and there are plans to restore the shattered fragments of the little Doric funerary monument.

The Mighty Walls of Messene

Messene's 9.5km circuit of walls are the most spectacular of Classical-era Greece, their ashlar limestone blocks so finely and precisely cut (from quarries on Ithóme) that all subsequent fortifications look a bit shoddy. Pausanias was suitably impressed: 'If you take the walls at Ambrosos in Phokis and at Byzantium and at Rhodes, which are extremely well-walled cities, the Messenian walls are stronger still.' Standing only 20ft high in most places, they take advantage of the escarpments in the terrain, rendering most ancient siege machinery and scaling ladders impractical. Thirty square or horseshoe-shaped towers stand at the most vulnerable points. The walls were designed to enclose enough farmland to keep the city from starving during a long siege (with Sparta nearby, no precaution was too great), although nowadays the land looks so scrubby it's hard to imagine. Enough survives of the complete circuit to trace it entirely, but best preserved is the northwest section, by the circular **Arcadian Gate**, up the main road from the museum. This gate, with its mighty limestone lintel half-fallen, was the symbol of the city for early travellers. Two niches in the gate held herms, and restoration work in the 1990s revealed a number of funerary monuments along the road, dating from the 2nd to the 6th century AD; the finds are in the museum. With minimal scrambling you can walk along the top of the walls below the gate and pretend you're an ancient Messenian on patrol.

The second best preserved gate, the **Laconian Gate**, can also be reached by car on the road winding up through the centre of Mavrométi (signposted). From the gate you have a fine view of the walls rising precipitously up the slopes of Ithóme. If you follow the road through the gate you'll soon come to the impressive 'new' **Monastery Voulkánou** (Μονή Βουλκάνου), which in the 15th century briefly belonged to the Knights of St John; their coat of arms decorates the gate.

Mount Ithóme

Off the road to the Laconian Gate is a zigzagging path and unpaved road to the flat top of Mount Ithóme. Homer made it sound like a ladder, but it's not quite that steep. Strabo considered Ithóme the strategic equal of the Acrocorinth; when Philip V of Macedon was contemplating the conquest of the Peloponnese, he was advised 'if you hold the horns (the Acrocorinth and Ithóme), you will hold the ox (the Peloponnese)'. Yet this landmark twice (in the First and Third Messenian Wars) proved to be an Alamo for its defenders. Their ancient citadel is long gone, the ruins scant, the view sublime. Blood was often spilled on Ithóme, and it wasn't all in battles. Like many tall and peculiar mountains (most notably Mount Lýkaio, *see* p.342), it was associated with Zeus in his primordial weather god guise, and not only him; all of Ithóme was a raw realm of birth and death. On the way up are the foundations of a **Temple of Limnatis**, dedicated to Artemis Laphria, who as in Pátras (*see* p.208) demanded cruel animal holocausts. Similar nastiness took place another 300m further on, on the south slope of Ithóme, in a **Temple of Eileithyia and the Kouretes**, dedicated to the goddess of childbirth; in local myth the nymphs Neda and Ithome bathed baby Zeus in the Klepsydra spring and tended him while the Kouretes banged their shields to cover the baby's cries, to keep his cannibalistic father from swallowing him. The bench found inside is a hallmark of a sanctuary to the chthonic deities.

On the summit of Ithóme, the abandoned 13th-century Monastery Voulkánou was built over Queen Messene's **Sanctuary of Zeus Ithomátas**. On the east side, some ancient foundations may be seen; the discovery of a leg from a Geometric-era tripod confirms the shrine's antiquity. Like Zeus Lykaios in Arcadía, Zeus Ithomatas is associated with human sacrifice; here Aristodemos sacrificed his daughter or, according to another account, killed 300 Spartan captives, including their king Theopompos. Messenian coins showed the cult statue, holding a thunderbolt in one hand and an eagle in the other. There was another statue of Zeus, as a baby, which the Messenians had kept in Nafpaktos and brought back when Messene was founded.

Meligalás

If you go through the Arcadian Gate, it's 9km to the land of 'milk and honey', **Meligalás** (Μελιγαλάς), the largest village of the rich northern Plain of Stenýklaros. Although in the misty past it was the seat of Kresphontes and the 'sons of Heracles', no sign of their city has ever been found. What you can see, however, is the famous triple **Mavrozoúmenos bridge**, built over the Pámisos where it is formed by the conjunction of the Mavrozoúmenos and Ámphitos rivers. The piers of the bridge are from the 3rd or 4th century BC; the seven arches are Turkish.

West to Pýlos

If you leave modern Messíni westwards on the Pýlos road, stop at the tiny village of **Charavgí** where a narrow but good road can take you past little houses, drying figs, and on towards a spectacular little gorge (a sign says 'Polylímnio and waterfalls' in English). You have to walk the last bit as it is steep, but it is worth the effort. If you get lost, follow the signs to Ag. Ioánnis. Consider a picnic.

Where to Stay and Eat around Messene

Mavromáti ✉ 24002

Rooms Lykoúrgos, t 272 405 1297 (€/€). The pleasant Athanosokopoúlou family have five rooms available, with views, balconies, fridges and air-conditioning.

Pension Zeus, t 272 405 1426 (€). Two rooms with kitchenettes.

There is a good restaurant and one or two souvenir shops, along with Mr Grumpy at the other 'rent room' place, and a lot of archaeologists currently working at the site.

Down the Coast to Koróni

Messenía's easterly coast, facing the Gulf of Messenía, is lined with good beaches, with views across the water to the jagged profile of the Taíyetos. Thanks to the airport at Kalamáta, package holiday flats and campsites have sprouted among the little farms and villages, which now stock foreign newspapers. Historically, this coast has played musical chairs with names even more than the Greek norm. The first town, **Petalídi** (Πεταλίδι), sprawls 15km southwest of Messíni. It has pretty good swimming on either side and a nice, rather old-fashioned main square by the sea that hosts the local farmers' market every Saturday. Originally named Aepeia, it was renamed Korone in 369 BC by Epimelides, after his home near Thebes. The name stuck, but migrated south (*see* below). Some bits of Aepeia/Korone are on the hill behind town, while a rich, dark age settlement, one of the most important in Greece, was excavated at nearby Nikchória; a significant find was a 'chieftain's house' where sacrifices had taken place. In August 1828, General Maison landed at Petalídi with 14,000 French troops, an event which encouraged Ibrahim Pasha to leave the Peloponnese once and for all 10 months after the Battle of Navaríno.

Episcopí, 10km south of Petalídi, is almost entirely made of holiday flats and studios, while picturesque Ag. Andréas, a few miles beyond, is much less cosmopolitan but more of a real place, with its charming little spick-and-span port and beaches shaded by lofty eucalpytus trees. This was the ancient port of **Longa** (Λογγα), where the **Shrine of Apollo Korythos** was famous for its therapeutic properties. It was rebuilt four times, from the Geometric period on; in the Christian era, the temple was replaced with a basilica, which was later replaced by the current church of Ag. Andréas. As you head south, vines and cypresses line the road as you approach the crossroads at **Charokopió** (Χαροκοπειό), a fine old-fashioned Messenian village. Koróni is just 4.5km to the east.

Koróni

Although badly damaged in the 1860 earthquake that shook this coast, Koróni (Κορώνη) is still a wonderful, quirky old place full of character, a bit of Greece that time forgot. Yet it has everything a place should have: a long sandy beach at Zága, a picturesque Venetian castle, a piquant old town reminiscent of an island port, piled on narrow, steep, zigzagging streets, and splendid views across the Messiniakós Gulf to the Máni.

Koróni's history closely parallels that of Methóni on the opposite end of the peninsula, only it went through even more name-changes. It was originally ancient Asine, a colony founded by

Getting to and around Koróni

Koróni and the seaside towns are linked by **buses** from Kalamáta. In Koróni the KTEL bus stop is in the square behind the seafront: buy tickets at the astonishing news-stand of master hoarder Tákis Stampatópoulis, **t** 272 502 2231. In August, you can find **boat excursions** across the Gulf to Stoúpa and the Diroú caves in the Máni (*see* p.408).

refugees from Asine near Argos who were sent packing when they sided with Sparta. In the 9th century AD, more refugees, this time from ancient Korone (today's Petalídi) fled here, when marauders trickled into their territory. They took the town name with them, and rebuilt Asine's acropolis as their citadel, which in turn was taken over by the Franks in 1204 and Venetians in 1207. The Venetians rebuilt the castle and, like Methóni, considered it an 'Eye of the Republic'; it was also an important port for olive oil and the red dye cochineal, made from beetles who infest prickly pear. In 1500, when Bayezit II appeared with a Turkish fleet fresh from crushing Methóni, the disheartened inhabitants gave up without a fight, and the Sultan packed them all off to live in Kefaloniá, which still belonged to Venice.

In 1532, the famed Geneose admiral Andrea Doria captured Koróni in the name of the Holy Roman Emperor, but the dread pirate admiral Barbarossa came fast on his heels, forcing Doria to evacuate; those left behind were slaughtered. In 1685, Francesco Morosini (who superstitiously always dressed in red and never travelled without his cat on the poop deck) captured Koróni for Venice and in turn massacred its 1,500 Turkish defenders. Again the Greeks and Venetians came back, and again they had to leave in 1718 when the Turks regained Koróni.

The picturesque **castle**, scene of so much trouble, sits on the bluff, its round bastions surrounded by water on three sides. The curtain walls are made from stones of ancient Asine, while the Venetians added the romantic Gothic gate, reached by a cobbled ramp from the north. Inside the walls are tiny houses and churches (one, Byzantine **Ag. Sophía**, is built over a Temple of Apollo). The locals say there's a network of secret underground passages as well, so take care while wandering about. A stair leads down to a little plateau occupied by the church of the **Panagía** (host to another miraculous icon), a palm grove and a small building containing a **historical and archaeological collection** that you can skip without feeling very guilty. Long, sandy **Zága Beach** begins below the walls to the south.

On the north side of the castle, the **medieval town** spills down narrow cobbled streets to the **port**. A fondness for primary colours, folk art and flowery gardens adds to its charm (even the garbage bins are brightly painted), along with the fact that cars can't squeeze into many of its lanes. The port, lined with fish tavernas and ouzeries, ends in an elegant neoclassical square; walk beyond this for a wonderfully romantic view of the castle on its rock, rising over the waves, guarded by cypresses, golden in the setting sun.

Where to Stay and Eat on the Coast to Koróni

Petalídi ✉ 24005

Sunrise Village, **t** 272 203 2120, *www.sunrise-greece.com* (€€€€/€€€). An all-in family resort, with a lagoon-style pool, playgrounds, gym and health club, and a diving centre; English-speaking instructors and reasonable fees. The restaurant serves Greek and Cypriot cuisine. *Open Mar–Oct*.

★ Erató Studios and Apartments >

Erató Studios and Apartments, **t** 272 203 1719 or **t** 272 203 1965, *erato@kal.forthnet.gr* (€€/€). Up in a residential neighbourhood, 100m from the main *plateía*. Spotless, and all with kitchenettes and verandas; the warm and welcoming Mrs Níkki will make you feel like her personal guest.

Petalídi Beach Camping, **t** 272 203 1154, *www.campingpetalidi.gr* (€/€). With bungalows.

Ag. Andréas ✉ 24100

A peaceful port with an island atmosphere.

Francisco, **t** 272 503 1396, *www.francishotel.com* (€€/€€). Pretty, modern, with a restaurant, a large pool and kids' pool on the lawn; walking distance from town. *Open May–Oct*.

Akroyáli, **t** 272 503 1266, *www.akroyaliganios.gr* (€€/€€). This friendly, large white and blue old-style hotel at the port has been transformed. All rooms now have a fridge, TV, and air-conditioning. Some have kitchens. The staff speak English. *Open April–Oct*.

Camping Ag. Andreas, **t** 272 503 1881, *www.aab.gr* (€/€). Well-shaded sites by the sea. *Open April–Oct*.

Koróni ✉ 24004

Auberge de la Plage, **t** 272 502 2401, *www.delaplage.gr* (€€/€€). Overlooking Zága Beach; offers a great location, views, a pretty garden, air-conditioning, minibus, and steps down to the beach.

Panayiótis Gialelís Flats, **t** 272 502 2334 (€€/€€). On the same cliff road over the beach, two comfortable flats which can sleep up to four; a garden too. *Open all year*.

Tákis Stampatópoulis, **t** 272 502 2231 (€€/€€). Studios sleeping up to four with no extra charge on a farm with views stretching to Africa. Contact him at the store that doubles as Koróni's bus station.

Diana, **t** 272 502 2312, *www.dianahotel-koroni.gr* (€€/€). Down near the port, this pretty neoclassical hotel is tasteful, air-conditioned, and immaculate, even if the rooms are on the small side. *Open all year*.

Marinos Bungalows, **t** 272 502 2522 (€/€). On the north entrance to town; guests enjoy a lovely view over the sea and town. Rooms have air-conditioning and kitchens. Animals are welcome: a bargain and the owner speaks English too. *April–Oct*.

Christos Mállios Rooms, **t** 272 502 2229 (€/€). Past the neoclassical *plateía* under the castle. Air-conditioned rooms in a restored neoclassical building, with high ceilings and a shared kitchen; the same owners also have a new building just behind, with moderately priced flats sleeping four. *Open April–Oct*.

Spíros Lagadítis, **t** 272 502 2146 (€/€). Above the waterfront Parthenon Restaurant; rooms with fridges and air-conditioning. *Open Mar–Dec*.

Koroni Camping and Bungalows, **t** 272 502 2884, *koroni-camping@hotmail.com* (€/€). North of town, with a pool under a big palm tree, a playground, restaurant, and bungalows furnished with TVs and kitchenettes. *Open April–10 Oct*.

Memi Beach, **t** 272 502 2130, *magos@hol.gr* (€/€). Simpler, along Zága Beach. *Open May–Sept*.

As usual, most of the restaurants and bars are on the waterfront. Try **Flísvos** (Φλοίσβος) for seafood, or **Ifigénia** next door for *mezédes*, moussaka or a big 'farmer steak'. Koróni is hardly trendy, but it has a **Dodóni** on the waterfront, a member of the chain that scoops out Greece's finest ice cream.

The Southwest Coast

Finikoúnda

Finikoúnda

Although this squared-off westernmost prong of the Peloponnese isn't as mountainous as the other two, the southern coast is craggy enough and dotted with little islands. There's one point, however, midway between Koróni and Methóni, where a river has melted the rocks and made a series of sandy beaches. In the early 1970s, the village by the beaches, **Finikoúnda** (Φοινικούντα), was a fishing port with a Phoenician-sounding name, a vaguely Spanish air and the same climate as Ierápetra on the south coast of Crete. A few beach bums found their way to this isolated, sheltered haven, followed by campers and watersports-lovers, a holiday company or two, some palm trees, and whoosh! sleepy town is now busy resort.

The once shabby coastal road has been widened and improved, but cuts a brutal straight swath through the back of Finikoúnda, bringing new developments and campsites to the once lonely coast. Finikoúnda has a sandy in-town **beach**, prettily framed by headlands and Schiza Island, and a broader one, **Anemómilos**, just over the hill to the west, with a taverna, campsite and the **Surf Station**, offering catamarans, windsurfers, lessons and other gear from March until the end of October.

Surf Station
t 272 307 1133

Schiza Island, closing off the sea view to the west, offers a goal for sailors, with its low white cliffs, wild goats, and a sheltered cove on its southwest side. It's also a target for Greek airforce bombers, so don't venture over unless you're sure the coast is clear. The little low islet of **Ag. Mariáni**, west of Schiza, is crowned with a new chapel that is visited on 17 July. Lastly, to the east, off the southern point of **Cape Akítas**, the islet of **Venetikó** has a little lighthouse, a dramatic rocky coast and a rudimentary beach.

Methóni

Methóni

In the extreme southwesternmost corner of the Peloponnese, Methóni (Μεθώνη) is a pleasant sun-soaked town with white streets charmingly lined with red and green hibiscus trees. Venetian walls still enclose its great thumb-shaped promontory, now inhabited only by lizards; its once bustling harbour, partly sheltered by the Inoússai islands, is now a long, sandy beach. As much as a town can, Methóni has retired from history, with a sigh of relief, for this is one of those places where every stone has been stained with blood.

History

In Homer, Methóni was Pedasos, 'rich in vines', one of the seven cities offered by Agamemnon to the sulking Achilles. In the 7th century BC, the Spartans allowed a group from Naúplio (exiled by Argos for their support of Sparta) to settle Méthoni as *perioikoi*, the class able to perform the commercial and artisan tasks forbidden to the Spartan overlords and the Messenian helots. The Messenians didn't mind the Argives, and allowed them to remain after they became independent. In the 4th century AD, Methóni was recorded as a Byzantine bishopric, but in the troubled times that followed it became a nest of pirates, and was razed by the Venetians in 1125. Yet the Venetians coveted Methóni, or Modon as they called it, and claimed it with the capture of Constantinople in 1204 as part of their 'quarter and a half' share of the Byzantine Empire. In the meantime, Geoffrey de Villehardouin, anxious to grab a piece of the action in the east, had landed in Methóni by chance in a storm. While he waited to sail, it occurred to him that the ill-prepared Greeks could hardly stand up to his mounted knights, even though they were only a handful, and he managed to capture the entire Peloponnese. So when the Venetians came to claim Methóni in 1207 they found Villehardouin well ensconced. Both sides retreated to a Benedictine monastery on the island of Sapiénza and the changeover was accomplished amicably, by treaty. It was the only time that would ever happen.

Venice used Greece's islands and ports as stations for her Eastern fleet, but none was as important to her as Methóni, 'the receptacle and special nest of all our galleys, ships and vessels'; along with Koróni, it was the *Oculi capitales communis*, the 'Eyes of the Republic'. Venice's trade routes to the Black Sea and Middle East converged here, and every year two convoys would set sail together as far as Methóni – 20 galleys resembling triremes, rowed by free men, accompanied by an escort of light warships. On board were not only goods to trade, but pilgrims bound for the Holy Land. At Methóni they would pick up water and provisions, and silk and wine to barter; on the return trip they picked up bacon; Methóni supplied nearly all of Venice. Relations with the locals were good, and the Greek light horse, or *stradioti*, were given responsibility for land defences. The only sore point derived from the Venetian insistence that they shave their beards. The most famous commander of the *stradioti* was Graítzas Paleológos, who fought so bravely against the Turks in the 1450s that he became the commander of all the Serenissima's cavalry. When the Turks took the Peloponnese, the Venetians were confined within their walls, here and at Koróni and Pýlos.

In 1500, the Turkish fleet of Sultan Bayazit II, manned with 100,000 Janissaries, cut off all Methóni's supply routes.

Nevertheless, the 7,000 defenders held out for a month and fought back so fiercely that Bayazit was on the verge of sailing away, especially once five Venetian supply ships slipped past the Turks' blockade. In Methóni, the besieged were so thrilled by the arrival of food and munitions that they forgot to man the walls. The Turks noticed and stormed Methóni, and beheaded every male over the age of 10, until the waves ran red with blood. When word reached Venice that Methóni had fallen, the ruling Council of Ten burst into tears. In 1531, Fra Bernardo Salviati, a nephew of the pope, led the Knights of St John to Methóni, on the chance that, if they liked it, they could seize it and stay there instead of Malta. The Knights mistook the Greeks for Turks, pillaged their houses and carried off all their women to Malta (there *are* reasons why the Greeks are traditionally mistrustful of the West). The Venetians were more earnest, and recaptured Methóni on their sixth attempt in 1685 under Morosini, who so impressed the Turks with his flamboyant red clothes and courage that they surrendered. But in 1715 Venice lost Methóni, again through a muddle: the Turks were besieging the walls, and the Commander of the Fleet, Hieronymus Dolphin, came to succour the defenders. A Turkish fleet appeared on the horizon and Dolphin made an undignified dash for it, and once more the Venetian and Greek defenders were massacred.

In 1825, during the War of Independence, the Greek admiral Miaoúlis sailed into Methóni and directed his trademark fireships at the fat Turkish frigates. All caught fire, but so did Methóni when the powder in the cargo ships exploded. Not long afterwards, Ibrahim Pasha landed his troops here, beginning their rampage of the Peloponnese, and the town remained Turkish until 1828, when it was liberated by the French under General Maison. During the Second World War, the castle played its most recent role, housing an Italian garrison.

The Venetian Castle

Venetian castle
open daily 9am–7pm

Even in its damaged state, the castle is still a bold sight, surrounded by the sea on three sides and a wide dry moat on its landward side, now used by the locals to gather wild *hórta* for their salads. Two reliefs of the **Lion of St Mark** in the walls smile down upon them; note that the books they hold are open, a sign of favour (places that had rebelled or were otherwise in the Republic's bad books would get scowling lions with closed books).

The moat is spanned by a handsome 14-arched stone **bridge**, built by the French to replace the original wooden structure, which leads to a fancy **monumental gate** built by the Venetians in 1700, adorned with a pair of Corinthian columns and reliefs of war-like trophies. Inside are two more **gates**, one with a neatly made round hole on the side that looks as if it were a measure for cannonballs.

In the masonry you can see the Classical stone of the ancient city, completely cannibalized by the Venetians. The medieval town that once stood inside the walls was cannibalized in turn by the French in 1828 when they built the new town, leaving only a ruined Latin church and a Turkish bath.

Through the old sea gate, a causeway leads to the picturesque **Boúrtzi**, the little octagonal Turkish fort built on the spot where the last hapless Venetians and Greeks were cornered and beheaded in 1500. In the late afternoon sun it takes on a rich pink hue.

Après castle, stop at the ungentrified coffee shop just opposite the entrance, one of a dying breed that sells everything from drinks to playing cards. Methóni's big sandy **beach** is only a few steps away.

Sapiénza: Strawberry Trees and Neutrinos

Sapiénza, the large uninhabited island south of Methóni, means 'wisdom' in Italian, and a long-gone Benedictine monastery that once stood there was the scene of the negotiations in 1209 between the Villehardouins and the Venetians that gave the doge Methóni and Koróni. Although its small ports have often provided shelter (and bases for attacking Methóni), many ships didn't quite make it, coming to grief on its rocks. One, a Venetian galley filled with the pilfered granite columns from the Great Peristyle built by Herod in the 1st century AD in Kessaria, Palestine, was wrecked on Sapiénza's north cape, **Karsí**. This, and other wrecks, give opportunities for fascinating diving, and at the time of writing there are plans to make Karsí an underwater park.

The cliffs of Sapiénza, some low, some high and craggy, make for lovely sailing. Near Karsí there's a pier by the sandy beach **Ámmos** where a path, overgrown in places, leads through a valley containing a unique arbutus forest. Arbutus are low shrubs that form part of the typical Mediterranean *maquis*; in autumn, red strawberry-like fruit and white blossoms appear at the same time in their dark green foliage. Here, isolated for thousands of years in the middle of Sapiénza, they have grown into large trees, standing up to 40ft high. So much pollen has accumulated over the centuries that it has formed a unique orange 'rock' in the middle of the island called *spartólaka*. Sapiénza is also home to 200 mountain goats from Crete, the *kri kri*, which are now almost extinct on their native island.

At the end of the path, on a height overlooking the south of the island, stands a handsome **lighthouse**, built by the English in 1890. It has a cold spring at the front if you need a drink; if it's open, you

Getting to Sapiénza

Captain Fótis Zampólas, **t** 697 353 2754, based in Methóni, will pick up passengers almost any time of year with his caíque from Methóni or Finikoúnda for a trip to Sapiénza island. The cost is about €25 per person for a 4–5 hour excursion; groups cost much less.

can climb up the tower for the stupendous view. Just below are two sea rocks known as the Two Brothers, and just beyond them is one of the deepest places in the Mediterranean, an abyss called the *fréar tis Mesogeíou* or **Well of Inoússes**, plunging 16,801ft.

Down on a plateau (12,467ft below sea level), Greek, Italian, Swiss, German and Russian physicists have constructed a 1,345ft **submarine telescope** to study stardust – neutrinos and sub-atomic muons – deep down where they are unaffected by cosmic rays. There are only a few such instruments in the world; this one is named NESTOR, not after the King of Pýlos, but short for Neutrino Experimental Submarine Telescope with Oceanographic Research.

Festivals on the Southwest Coast

On **Clean Monday** (the first day of Lent), Methóni celebrates a comical mock wedding in the main square, Του Κουτρούλη ο γάμος, with phoney priests, men playing the roles of bride and groom, and a big party.

Where to Stay and Eat on the Southwest Coast

Finikoúnda ✉ 24006

Try to avoid driving into Finikoúnda in high season if at all possible; parking is a headache, and even moving can be difficult in summer.

Finikoúnda, **t** 272 307 1208 (**t** 272 307 1408 or **t** 272 307 1308 during olive season) (€€/€). In town with parking; quiet if smallish rooms around a courtyard, with a shady upstairs terrace. Optional buffet breakfast. *Open all year.*

Aktí Studios, **t** 272 307 1316 (€€/€). Just off the beach in town; a nice, friendly place immersed in bougainvillaea, with a few precious parking places. *Open April–Oct.*

Porto Finissia, **t** 272 307 1457 (€€/€). On the east end of the beach; lovely views, air-conditioning and a friendly owner. *Open May–Oct.*

Korakákis Beach, **t** 272 307 1221, *www.finikounda.com* (€€/€). Offers parking, air-conditioning and fridges. *Open April–Oct.*

Dímitra Tomará Rooms, **t** 272 307 1323 (€€/€). Above the fishing port, studios sleeping up to three, with overhead fans and balconies. Block-booked in high season but a bargain in the colder months. *Open all year.*

Camping Loútsa, **t** 272 307 1169 (€/€). Níko Tsónis' at Loútsa Cove on the east end of town is a friendly favourite, with a restaurant and family atmosphere. *Open April–Oct.*

Camping Ámmos, **t** 272 307 1262, *www.finikounda.com* (€/€). Closer to town, on the sea and n the way to Koróni. *Open April–Oct.*

All the restaurants have seaside terraces.

Oméga, **t** 272 307 1227. One of the better and most popular ones.

Ta 5 F, **t** 272 307 1242. For seafood.

Kýma, **t** 272 307 1224. There are good 'ready' dishes made by mama; it's also one of the few restaurants that remains open all year.

Héllena House, **t** 272 307 1235. On the point, with big views through the trees; perfect for an evening drink.

ⓘ Methóni >>
www.methoni.gr

Methóni ✉ 24006

Methóni has a stellar website (see left), and offers a wide range of accommodation. It doesn't quite close down after mid-October but, as always in Messenía, expect skeletal service 'during the olives'.

Methóni Beach >

Methóni Beach, **t** 272 302 8720, *www.methonibeachhotel.gr* (€€€/€€€). This totally renovated old Xenia is right on the beach and all rooms but one have the 'view'. At least have coffee on the terrace.

Achilléus, 100m from the beach, **t** 272 303 1819, *Achilles@ath.forthnet.gr* (€€/€€). Air-conditioning, TV and fridges; a friendly in-town hotel with large, airy, well-furnished rooms, some with balconies. *Open all year.*

Odysseus, **t** 272 303 1600 (€€/€€). Comfortable, with all mod cons plus a decent restaurant. *Open all year.*

Furnished Apartments Melina, **t** 272 303 1505 (€€/€). These are terrific new and clean studio apartments, each one separate, with a garden in front, and right on the town beach. Each apartment is different. All are nice and the owner friendly. *Open all year.*

Ánna, on the main street, not far from the sea, **t** 272 303 1332 (€€/€). A homey place with a deep shady tunnel to its door, and a terrace.

O Fáros, **t** 272 303 1229 (€€/€). Close to the beach; four very well-furnished studio flats with kitchenettes, air-conditioning and TV that sleep up to four; prices drop dramatically out of season.

Castéllo, **t** 272 303 1280 (€€/€). Modern, near the sea, with views over the castle; good value for its category, with plain rooms and breakfast in the garden. *Open May to Oct.*

Municipal Campsite, **t** 272 303 1228 (€/€). A bit basic. *Open May–Oct.*

Akrogiali 'Fish House', **t** 227 230 31520. Blue and white and right on the beach (practically in the castle moat), this well-known old standby will have you wondering which to photograph first, the seafood or the setting.

Meltémi, **t** 272 303 1187. By the brand new seaside *plateia*; this is one of the nicest; an old-fashioned taverna which offers fish, good *mezédes* and barrelled wine. The owner closes for a siesta from 4–6pm, so come early for lunch.

Navaríno Bay

22 Navaríno Bay

Navaríno Bay is one of the most beautiful, fragile and evocative areas of the Peloponnese. The bay is three and a half miles long and two miles wide, affording one of the best natural harbours in the Mediterranean. The beach at Giálova, almost dead centre, offers the most comprehensive view of the complicated topography: stand on its mole at sunset when the hills turn purple and the water slowly melts from blue to rose to gunmetal grey. From this vantage point, modern Pýlos tumbles down the hill around the Turkish castle to the south. In front, Sphaktería Island broods lengthwise across the large bay. Its barren rocks and low-lying hills stretch from the 1,300m-wide southern sea channel at Pýlos town to the much narrower and shallower northern strait. Above this strait, the ancient medieval fortress dominates the sloping hill. Just beyond that, a headland marks the Voïdokoiliá, 'the cow's belly', an exquisite, perfectly round bay, and Mycenaean tombs.

The bay's temperate climate and harmonious blend of low hills, cliffs, islands and sea make it a magnet year-round. Happily, it has retained its quiet charm; it's just far enough from Athens and Pátras to discourage short-term visitors and, except for the sandy Voïdokoiliá, the beaches at Methóni, Finikoúnda and Koróni are

Getting to and around Navarino Bay

Pýlos is 324km from Athens and 51km from Kalamáta by the overland route. The KTEL **bus station** on the main square, **t** 272 302 2230, has a regular service to Giálova, Chóra and Kyparissía (five per day), Methóni and Finikoúnda (four per day), Kalamáta (nine per day) and Athens (two per day; a 5hr trip). At the time of writing, you can only get to Koróni via Kalamáta.

Car hire is possible through the hotels.

For a **taxi**, call **t** 272 302 2555. The **water taxis** have a stand on the pier. If no one is there, try the waterfront Aetos Café, where the owners often congregate. Prices to visit the bay, Golden Beach and the war memorials vary according to the time of year, the owner's mood and the number of passengers. Unless you get a deal, you can give Sphaktería a miss. Other than the 'monuments' to the dead, it has only a few Cyclopean walls on its heights and not much else.

better. This peace and quiet may be short-lived: two massive holiday complexes, one at Petrochóri and one south of Giálova, are in the works, complete with golf courses and every amenity proven to attract the all-in resort crowd.

Which voice should you choose?
Níkos Kazantzákis

A Short History of Navaríno Bay

The entire bay was Mycenaean country, overlooked by Nestor's Palace, discovered on the low hill of Epáno Englianó. Well-signposted *tholos* tombs are everywhere, suggesting a conglomeration of small settlements that all owed allegiance to the palace on the hill. When it was destroyed after 1200 BC, the centre of habitation relocated to the northern part of the bay, on the more defensible hill now crowned by the medieval castle. In the Classical period it was called Koryphasia, and fortified. On its northern side is the large so-called Cave of Nestor, inhabited from time immemorial; under it, settlements tumbled down to the Voïdokoiliá Bay, the main centre for well over two thousand years. The Slavs and Avars had their innings here between the 6th and 9th centuries, leaving the name Avarino-Navaríno to posterity, and not much else. In 1278, Nicholas II of St-Omer built the wonderful

Two 'Untoward Incidents' in Navaríno Bay

Navaríno Bay is famous for two blunder-filled defeats that made history. The first occurred during the Peloponnesian War, in the summer of 425 BC, and involved some incredible misjudgements on the part of the Spartans. Never great sailors, and even worse swimmers, the Spartans were always nervous of the Athenians, who were good at both. So when the Athenians came to Navaríno Bay and decided to fortify Koryphasia and leave behind five triremes to guard it, Spartan antennae were quivering. They decided to send their own allied ships to the bay and at the same time to obliterate Koryphasia by land, thus ending the threat to their soft Messenian underbelly. They landed 420 men on the island of Sphaktería to keep an eye on the big fort and deny the Athenians its use, while they deployed the rest of their army on the mainland. The Athenians, from their bird's eye perch on Koryphasia, saw them coming, and called for more ships, which somehow escaped the Spartans' notice until they sashayed into the bay from both entrances, and trounced the Spartan navy.

That left the 420 Spartans stranded on barren Sphaktería with shields as sun shades, and not much else; a pretty pickle, and a warning to future generations that spying from islands has its downside. Sphaktería's narrow 2¾-mile length was never well wooded, and has only one brackish well. The Athenians were not much better off in their fort, surrounded by Spartans. Talks were held and food

sent to the stranded Spartans, until the talks broke down. Even then a few brave helots swam over the guarded straits at night with supplies stuffed in skins. Things remained at an impasse for 72 days, until fresh Athenian troops arrived under Kleon and attacked the island from all sides at once. The fact that the Athenians were less than eager to engage the enemy although they outnumbered them by 25 to one speaks volumes for the Spartan reputation.

Fighting valiantly, but unable to ward off this concentrated horde of adversaries, the Spartans sent a lone swimmer to the mainland for advice. The laconic reply was: 'The Lacedaemonians order you yourselves to consider your own situation, provided that you do nothing dishonourable.' After a fierce battle, the 292 Spartans left alive came up with their own interpretation of 'dishonour' and surrendered. The propaganda value of this defeat was all out of proportion to the number of soldiers captured. Suddenly the Spartans were no longer invincible. The Athenians rushed to grab Spartan gear as souvenirs (one shield is in the Agora Museum in Athens), the captives were hauled off to Athens to be put on display (shades of Rome) and the magnificent Victory of Paionios was erected at Olympia for all the Greek world to see. It didn't seem so then, because the Spartans did win the war, but this untoward incident was the beginning of the end for the Spartan mystique. It would continue to haunt them and give joy to their many enemies until they passed from the scene altogether.

The next 'incident' occurred on 20 October 1827, when the British, French and Russian fleets had massed together near Navaríno Bay under the command of Admiral Codrington. He had been given the unenviable task of 'guaranteeing the autonomy of Greece' while somehow not offending the Sultan, an unachievable order if ever there was one. This double-barrelled policy (many Greeks would say double-dealing) foreshadowed subsequent relationships between the Great Powers and Greece, right up to and including the Cyprus crisis in 1974.

The mere presence of the fleet sent Ibrahim Pasha packing, but still left 82 Turkish warships bristling with 2,438 guns and 16,000 of Ibrahim's men riding anchor in the bay, while the allied fleet of 26 ships and 1,270 guns cooled its heels in the open sea, eager for action. Negotiations on land had hit a stalemate; the allies called for an armistice which was promptly accepted by the Greeks and ignored by the Turks who figured they had nothing to gain by accepting and knew that the dithering by the Powers helped their side. What they hadn't taken into account was the philhellenic bias and the enterprising spirit of the allied admirals. Using the Turkish refusal to sign the armistice as a pretext, they came sailing into the bay through the southern gap (they would later claim that the Turks shot first) and proceeded to annihilate the Turkish fleet. By nightfall the Turks were left contemplating their ruined fortunes, and the watery grave that now held 6,000 men and 53 ships. The allies were left sitting pretty with only 145 dead and every timber of their compact fleet intact. The French and Russian governments did not even bother to conceal their delight at what the British, weeping crocodile tears, would refer to as an 'untoward event' in parliament, thus washing their hands of responsibility, while quite prepared to reap the kudos for their helping hand.

It was the battle that ended the war and guaranteed Greek independence, and if you're in Pýlos on 20 October you can take part in the wonderful celebration marking the Battle of Navaríno. Navies from the three allies send ships full of sailors in full dress uniforms to decorate the square for several days, flags fly, politicians show up to bask in reflected glory, and ordinary citizens line up to take the water taxis to the three separate burial grounds of the heroic allies, or to see the rotting timbers of the Turkish ships hard by Sphaktería if the sea is calm. Interestingly, the British monument is on the tiny island of Chelonáki ('little turtle') in the middle of the bay, well away from Sphaktería and the other monuments, as if even in perpetuity they are not sure to what extent they want to claim participation in the 'incident'.

castle that now crowns the hill. At that time, the surrounding area was called Porte des Joncs, a tribute to the rushes (*joncs*) growing prolifically in the wetlands below. This castle bore the brunt of Genoese, Venetian, even Austrian attentions and then fell to the Turks in 1501. But the Turks felt too exposed here and in 1572 moved lock, stock and mosque to the so-called 'new castle', **Neókastro**, which guarded the southern gap of Navaríno Bay, which in any case was being used by the bigger ships of this era.

In 1825, the Neókastro became the headquarters of Ibrahim Pasha, when he made his devastating sweep through the Peloponnese in an attempt to add it to his already extensive lands in Egypt. A large part of his strategy was to eliminate as many Greeks as possible; the ones he didn't kill were captured and sold as galley slaves in a slave market he set up in Navaríno. He remained there until the naval forces of France, Great Britain and Russia began to focus on Navaríno. Discretion forced him to abandon the fort, just before the decisive Battle of Navaríno ended his hopes for good. The modern town of Pýlos slowly took on its present pleasant shape after the War of Independence.

Modern Pýlos

Pýlos is a small, pleasant, sleepy town (except on 20 October) built amphitheatrically around the enormous rectangular **Plateía ton Trion Navárkon** (Three Admirals Square) which is open on its west side to the sea. Aside from being the roller blade and skateboard centre, this is also the place to come for a drink while lounging under the huge plane trees. The centrepiece is a large **Monument to the Battle of Navaríno** with Admirals Codrington (British), de Rigny (French), and von Heydon (Russian) looking majestically at the sea, the *kafeneíons* and the fruit stand respectively. This square, framed in arcaded neoclassical and *faux* neoclassical buildings, is all the orientation you need to plumb the depths, or heights rather, of Pýlos (you'll find lots of staircases leading up to the town on the north). If the modern town seems to exude a Gallic atmosphere, that is because it was designed by the French, who occupied the castle for some time after liberation.

The quay offers a great view of the entire bay, and especially the dramatic cliffs and islands by the southern shipping gap. This is where the battleships moor for the 20 October festivities. Pýlos is a popular sailors' destination and yacht flotillas are made welcome by the town, which sometimes throws parties for them in the *plateía*. There is no really good swimming in the town itself, although ladders are built into a cement platform just south of the mole and there is a postage-stamp-sized beach in its corner. Hotel guests in town make good use of both. For beaches, head to Giálova, 6km to the north, or Methóni, 11km to the south.

Town museum
***t** 272 302 2448;*
open Tues–Sun 8.30–3, closed Mon; adm

The Town Museum and the New Castle

The small **town museum**, just south of the *plateía* on the road to Methóni, offers a pleasant interlude. It has minor finds from some of the many Mycenaean and Hellenistic tombs in the area. They are especially proud of some Hellenistic glass on display from the area of Tsopánis Ráchi (shepherd's hill). Some of the large clay pots are lovely as well.

Neókastro
t 272 302 2010; open Tues–Sun 8.30–3; adm

The large **Neókastro** crowns Pýlos to the southwest on the Methóni road. In spite of its size, the castle is not especially obvious unless you take the shore road to the Karalís Beach Hotel. From the sea, however, it dominates the town. It is nicely wooded on the outside, and well laid out with cobblestone paths on the inside. The Turks began it in 1572, and the entire Turkish population lived inside its walls. The Venetians gave it their own particular signature when they held sway from 1686 to 1718. A bloodcurdling massacre of the Turks took place in 1821, before it played its most famous role as the headquarters of Ibrahim Pasha. Its great walls now have the same, almost too perfect atmosphere as Palamidi in Naúplio. Inside, the Turkish barracks hold a **museum of engravings** from the War of Independence, no doubt a very satisfying change of function to its many Greek visitors; unfortunately the engravings are labelled only in Greek. The church of the **Metamórphosis tou Sotírou** (the Transfiguration) in the middle of the castle was a mosque, speedily 'metamorphosed' into a church after independence.

The Voïdokoiliá, the Old Castle, and Nestor's Cave

The Old Castle has too few visitors, whereas **Voïdokoiliá** (Βοϊδοκοιλιά) has far too many. It's not hard to understand why: under a steep headland this perfectly round shallow bay (hence the name 'Cow's Belly') that was once the ancient harbour of sandy Pýlos is an enchanting sight. You'll see it on the postcards, deserted and pristine, the way it was a few years ago when it belonged to a few sheep or herons.

Now that Voïdokoiliá is no longer a secret, perhaps the only way to keep tourists from destroying it is to cordon the area off from cars entirely. If you want to be part of the solution not the problem, leave your car on Golden Beach or at Petrochóri, pack a picnic and refuse bag for debris, and walk to Voïdokoiliá and the castle. Go early to enjoy it alone, for a while anyway.

On the main road just north of Giálova, there is a signposted road to Golden Beach and St Omer's Castle, now better known as the Old Castle or **Palaiókastro**. If you drive, go slowly and be careful where you park; this is an important nesting area and chameleon territory. Walk past the narrow sea channel between the castle and Sphaktería. The path to the castle is on the sea side, near the channel, and its entrance is obvious from this vantage point. It is an easy enough if steep 25-minute climb, rewarded with wonderful views along the way. The castle has crenellated walls (partly built on Cyclopean or Classical bases), square towers, and an inner and outer court. Quite an array of wild creatures call it home and seem, understandably, to resent intrusions. But don't worry; their reaction is a startled stare and a hasty retreat. Old castles on the Peloponnese seem to be the exclusive haunt of gypsies (although not in this case) and of birds and foxes, all of them endangered species in their own way.

It is possible to clamber down to the Voïdokoiliá from the north side of the castle and have a look at **Nestor's Cave** en route. (If that seems too precarious, retrace your steps and walk to Voïdokoiliá from sea level along the footpath at the base of the castle hill, on the landward side.) Because the stalactites were thought to resemble animal hides, this was supposed to be either a stable for Nestor's cows, or the place where Hermes hid Apollo's herd after he stole them. Certainly it appealed in the Stone Age, and there were settlements near it in both the Mycenaean and the Classical periods. The wonder is that some shepherd or shepherdess has not yet found an icon in its depths and claimed it for Christendom.

There is a path to the headland north of Voïdokoiliá and a Mycenaean ***tholos* tomb**, said to belong to Thrasymedes, the son of Nestor. The Messenians made it a hero shrine; excavators found an entire sacrificed bull inside, as well as 4th- and 3rd-century BC votives. If you continue along this path beyond the *tholos*, you can also scramble down to a small **beach** on the open sea.

The Wetlands: The Giálova Lagoon

The wetlands at the north end of Navaríno Bay are fed by two rivers and encompass Voïdokoiliá and the area right up to the old castle. The Institute of Marine Biology and the Sea Turtle Protection Society have undertaken to safeguard it from increasing salinity and human encroachment; it is a Natura 2000 site. Loggerhead turtles (*Caretta caretta*) nest here, and the lagoon is the only habitat of the African chameleon in Europe. These insect-eaters change colour and lay their eggs in the sand, making them very vulnerable. Some 245 species of birds have been sighted here: the bay is home to coots, cormorants, terns, herons, osprey and flamingos, while the marsh attracts glossy ibises, grebes and black-winged stilts, which breed in the area.

Nestor's Palace

Nestor's Palace

Pýlos is practically synonymous with Nestor, the respected, hospitable, garrulous, rather humourless old trout who ruled for three generations. At Troy his 90 ships were second only to

Agamemnon's, but in the *Iliad* he is more than a warrior; he is also a sage and peacemaker – a thankless task with that unruly lot. But as a reward he got to be one of the very few Achaean chieftains who arrived home safely. Homer occasionally contradicted himself on the location of Nestor's Palace: in the *Iliad* he places it on the banks of the Alphiós, in Elís, and in the *Odyssey* he says Telemachus found it near the shore, but later on he places it on a crag overlooking a plain. As far back as the 3rd century BC, scholars were arguing over the precise location. In 1939, Carl Blegen, fresh from excavating Troy with the University of Cincinnati, turned his attention to finding Nestor's Palace. His first hunch, the Hill of Epáno Englianó, 14km north of modern Pýlos, was right on the money. Unfortunately the dig had scarcely begun when war broke out, and Blegen had to wait until 1952 to finish the task.

A Mostly Mythic History

Pýlos was the home of **Melampos the Magician**, the first mortal to practise as a physician. He was the first to build temples to Dionysos, the first to mix water with his wine and, because he understood the language of the birds, he was the first 'seer' or *mantis*. Many later seers in Classical times traced their genealogies back to Melampos; the Spartans in particular employed his descendant, Teisamenos, whose entrail-readings accurately led them to five great victories, including Plataea.

Melampos was brought to Pýlos by **Neleus**, son of Poseidon, who settled the city with Achaeans and Aeolians and chased out the natives. Neleus had twelve children. The youngest was **Nestor**, who was the only member of his family to receive Heracles when he showed up in Pýlos, asking to be purified after murdering a house guest. Heracles never forgot a kindness or an insult, and, when he later attacked Pýlos for aiding King Augeas of Elís, he killed the entire royal family except Neleus and Nestor.

Pýlos was rebuilt by the Eleans, but they insulted Neleus and stole the horses he sent up to compete in an Olympic chariot race. To retaliate, he sent Nestor to raid their cattle, provoking a general war, in which Nestor was the hero and won nearly all the events in the following funeral game, as he informs everyone in the *Iliad*. After he returned to Pýlos from Troy, he entertained Telemachus who came to ask about his father Odysseus, but otherwise bows out of history, living peacefully among his sons.

Or was it all domestic bliss? In the great Mediterranean upheavals following Troy, it seems that the descendants of Neleus went east again, this time to Ionia in Asia Minor. 'We left steep Pylos, the town of Neleus, and arrived in ships in the Asia we longed for; with insolent force we settled at lovely Colophon, leaders of trouble and violence,' as the poet Mimnermos wrote in the 7th century BC. Were they the original Ionians, the clever people who invented philosophy and mathematics? The tradition was there at any rate: in the 5th century BC, Panyassis, the father of the historian Herodotus, wrote a lost epic about the founding of the Greek colonies in Ionia by Neleus and Kodros of Athens. The Spartans often used their 'sons of Heracles' myth to justify their foreign policy, and although the Messenians never had a chance to do the same with their Ionian connections, the Athenians certainly did: their shared Ionian past was used to justify their aid to the Greek cities in Ionia – inciting the Persian Wars.

The Palace

Nestor's Palace
t 276 303 1358 or t 276 303 1437; open July–Oct daily 8–7.30; Nov–June daily 8–3; adm; save money with a combined ticket to the site and the Chóra museum

Fitting in nicely with the peaceful reputation of Nestor's reign, 'his' palace has none of the awesome Cyclopean walls of Mycenae or Tiryns, although from its hilltop residents could see all who approached. It was built around 1300 BC (according to legend, by Nestor's father Neleus), and went up in flames along with Mycenae and Tiryns after 1200 BC. Although the highest walls are only waist-level, the palace is our best preserved example of a Mycenaean royal residence, surrounded by its store rooms and magazines. The large roof sheltering the remains from the elements seems to disappoint many visitors, but it does add a note of realism: the palace was originally roofed, after all, if in wood. The residence and state apartments were two storeys high, stone on the bottom and half-timbered in the Tudor manner on top, the walls made of rubble braced in timber. The exterior walls were faced with squared limestone blocks, and the interior ones were plastered. Important ones were frescoed.

The original entrance is the one still used today, with an **outer and inner *propylon***. To the right of the outer entrance was a **guard room**, while directly to the left, with an outward facing door, are the two **archive rooms**, with remains of a staircase leading to an upper floor, which may have been a watchtower. Here Carl Blegen unearthed a cache of hundreds of **Linear B tablets** in the very first hour of digging in 1939 – unfortunately on the same day that Italy invaded Albania. Preserved by the tremendous conflagration that destroyed the palace, these tablets were the very first found on mainland Greece. One can well imagination Blegen's excitement, and his keen disappointment when the war brought the excavations to an abrupt end, while the tablets were spirited away to spend the war in an Athenian bank vault.

Linear B tablets (along with the older, rarer Linear A) had already been found by Arthur Evans at Knossos on Crete. Blegen at first shared Evans' opinion that both were etched in a long-lost language, and their presence at Pýlos was evidence of Minoan imperialism. That is, until Michael Ventris, an architect with a bent for languages (and who as a boy had heard Evans lecturing at the British Council in Athens in 1936), put his mind to the task of deciphering Linear B. At first he thought the language might be Etruscan but, when he reached an impasse, he turned to Greek. He taught himself the language, and results were encouraging, only the script still didn't fit because of the endings. In 1952, John Chadwick, a Cambridge expert on ancient Greek, heard Ventris explain his difficulties with word endings on the radio, and at once realized that they fitted the ancient dialect that had survived in the hills of Arcadía. When Ventris and Chadwick deciphered the tablets conclusively in 1952–3, it forced a rewriting of history: what were Linear B and Greek doing in Crete? Mycenaean incursions had never been considered until then. Other examples of Linear B were found by Wace at Mycenae in 1952; there are a few fragments at Tiryns, and on pots in Thebes, where clay tests proved much to everyone's surprise that they were Cretan imports.

The language was syllabic – fine for the number-crunchers, but basic enough to ensure no lyric poetry would ensue. The location of the archive rooms at the palace entrance suggests that they were tax collection offices. The tablets concern taxes, debts, distribution of goods and other administrative business – not compelling reading, but a fascinating insight into the operation of a palace economy. The most startling discovery was a reference to Dionysos, which undercut the long-held belief that he was a young, not entirely Greek god who immigrated from Thrace. It also jibes nicely with stories about Melampos the Magician.

A Little Linear B

Forget, for a moment, the cold facts of Linear B and the lists of arrowheads, broad two-sided spears, chariots, captives and slaves attached to the palace that the warlike Mycenaeans recorded. Concentrate instead on the entrancing glimpse into everyday life these clay tablets allow. Suddenly we see people who named their domestic animals 'Darkie', 'Bawler', 'Winey', 'Dapple', and those perennial favourites, 'Whitefoot' and 'Blondie'. We find out about their occupations: there were spinners, weavers, wool spinners, fullers (the king or *wanax* had his own personal fuller for his extensive wardrobe), carpenters, masons, shipwrights, caulkers, bronzesmiths, goldsmiths, bow-makers, perfume-makers, charcoal-makers, woodcutters, shepherds, goatherds, cowherds and swineherds. Iron wasn't unknown, but it is mentioned only once. It was still the Bronze Age, after all.

We know that the Mycenaeans favoured perfumes made from sage, roses and cypress. We know they had doctors – one was given a land grant by the wanax. Potters did pretty well, too; one had a large estate ceded to him. And no wonder: Nestor's Palace required more dishes than Buckingham Palace and the White House put together, and almost everything was stored in ceramic pots. We know they favoured footstools, and had ebony chairs with ivory inlay, and above all we know their *wanax* liked to keep lists of everything in his kingdom, all in separate baskets with a clay seal on the top stating what lists each basket contained, whether it was the breastplate list, a wagon wheel list or the pig list. Filling a file required 'paper' consisting of small damp pieces of clay and a narrow wooden cursor, used to draw some of the 87 complicated signs in a legible script before the clay dried.

There is a mystery here: no dates. Were the accounts only for one year? Conventional wisdom suggests that they were temporary annual palace lists (that's why the clay was unbaked: it didn't have

to last) that would later be written up on wood or some vegetable matter, now long crumbled to dust. Frankly, that seems unlikely. The script clearly could be painted more easily than it could be incised, and wood or papyrus must have been less cumbersome. So why not just use those? Nobody knows. But quite a few scribes must have been scratching away to have created the hundreds of tablets that quite by accident were fired along with the palace.

Oddly enough, no word for 'scribe' has been deciphered. Were they mere nonentities, or was this strange new invention envied and admired? Certainly no budding Shakespeare ever wrote a sonnet, and no grave stone or monument has ever been found written in Linear B. It would do a treat for a shopping list, though. Michael Ventris sometimes attempted correspondence in Linear B. It sounds nerdy, but when you read the exciting book written by Chadwick it's hard to resist attempting a few scratches or brush strokes yourself. There were signs for the five vowels, and signs for 12 consonants combined with each of these vowels, as well as ideograms, number signs and the like. There were lots of confusing and arcane little rules to be mastered by the scribes: for example the sign for 'r' and 'l' was the same, so Pylos was py ros; double consonants were broken into syllables and then written, so the 'tri' in 'tripod' would be rendered 'ti ri' and so on.

The numbers can be fun: (12,345)

There are lots of ideographs: (man, woman, horse, spear)

(tripod, cup, amphora, wheel)

And then there are the phonetic letters themselves. Some look like objects: for instance, *o* was a throne; *za* looks the the Egyptian life sign, *au* looks like a little pig, and *ki* like a cocktail with a swizzle stick. But they were sounds.

Bronze – *kha(l)ko(s)* – was *ka ko*:

A tripod – *tripo(s)* – was *ti ri po*:

A priestess – *(h)iereira* – was *i je re ja*:

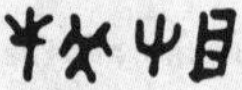

A shepherd – *po(i)me(n)* – was *po me*:

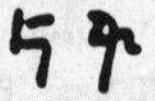

Once past the gates is the large **inner court**, which was open to the sky. To the left is a **waiting room** with a bench; wine jars and cups found in the adjacent room suggest visitors were served wine while they waited. When the king was ready to receive them, they would continue straight into the state rooms or *megaron*, where all the walls were colourfully frescoed: the **entrance porch**, the **vestibule** (where a stair led to an upper floor) and the **throne room**, the grandest in the palace, 36ft by 43ft. Similar to Mycenae, this has a round hearth in the centre, and bases where four wooden fluted columns once supported a gallery (see the picture on the plan that comes with your ticket). An opening over the hearth would have allowed light in and smoke out. The walls were frescoed

with lions and griffons (a creature that appears on a gold seal found in one of the royal tombs, and was painted on the walls of the Mycenaean throne room of Knossos). The floor was divided into squares, each colourfully decorated with geometric or wavy designs. The throne, inlaid with ivory, stood against the right wall, where you can see a shallow trough that may have allowed the king to offer a libation without getting up. Pýlos exhibits the same maze-like quality of other Mycenaean royal houses. The vestibule was the only entrance to the throne room, and to reach the surrounding rooms required backtracking through the vestibule and down the narrow corridors on either side. Five small rooms off the left corridor were **pantries**, the source of all the crockery in the museum. Those off the right corridor, and directly behind the palace, were used as **oil magazines**. The tablets found in the two back rooms were descriptions of the various olive oils, their flavours and qualities. Even back then Greeks were connoisseurs.

If you walk back through the vestibule to the inner courtyard and turn left, you'll enter the section of the palace known as the

Queen's Megaron. The small hall has a round hearth, and there's a room with a drain (possibly a **lavatory**), and a little room everyone remembers best: a **bathroom**, complete with painted terracotta bathtub on a base. When Telemachus was a guest here, he received special treatment from Nestor's daughter Polykastra:

bathing him first, then rubbing him with oil.
She held fine cloths and a cloak to put around him
when he came godlike from the bathing place

A gateway from around the corner of the bathroom leads towards a pair of courts and a multipurpose second building, identified as the palace **arsenal** and **workshop**, with a little **shrine** similar to the small cult rooms found at Mycenae. A large room to the north of this was the **wine magazine**, where clay seals were found identifying the sources of the large jars. The city of Pffilos was spread along the slopes of the hill. On the west side of the palace, separated by open courts, is a second **residence**, tentatively identified as the original palace, its throne room perhaps later used as a banquet hall. It had its own **wine store** as well, to the north. Royal ***tholos* tombs** have been found to the north and south of the palace; one, about 100m northeast of the gate, has been restored.

The topography of ancient Messenía has been an ongoing subject of study since 1958 in the University of Minnesota Messenía Expedition; since 1990, the Pýlos Regional Archaeology Project (*http://classics.uc.edu/prap*) under the direction of Jack Davies of the University of Cincinnati has spent each summer surveying and investigating the 40 square kilometre area around Pýlos, and has already doubled the number of known ancient sites.

Chóra and the Archaeological Museum

Four km north of the palace, the market village of **Chóra Trifylías** (Χώρας Τριφυλίας) is distinguished by a big square full of cafés and a small but important Archaeological Museum In **Room I**, your eye is at once drawn to the **gold cups** found in the *tholoi* of Peristeriá, glittering in their central case with **gold jewellery**, a diadem and bee beads, nautilus shells and tiny owl rivets, all done in loving detail. Cases on the left side hold the more utilitarian Mycenaean finds from Myrsinochóri, Nikchória and Voroúlia: double axes, arrowheads, seal impressions, tweezers, a rhyton with three deer heads, and good if surly-looking octopi to the right of the door. **Room II** is dedicated to artefacts from Nestor's Palace. Compared to Mycenae, its tombs yielded few precious works in gold, jewellery, bronze and ivory, but all are of a high quality, and all are in the National Museum in Athens. Here at Chóra you'll find cupboards of **crockery**, with 20 different kinds of cups and plates; nothing fancy, but handy for royal banquets. The star attractions

Archaeological Museum
t 276 303 1358; open summer Tues–Sun 8–7.30; winter Tues–Sun 8–3; closed Mon; adm; combined ticket available with Nestor's Palace

are remnants of the brightly coloured frescoes: there's a war scene showing the boar tusk helmet and a rather gruesome spearing of a warrior, doves, a bull leaper and a lyre-player. Were the squiggly lines borders, rivers, or simply decorations? No one knows.

Room III has more finds from the palace of Nestor: stone horns of consecration reminiscent of those found in Knossos, giant storage *pithoi*, loom weights, chimney pipes, a rhyton decorated with a palm tree, stacks of what look like tea cups, an ancient clay *souvláki* grill and a fine vase decorated with stylized ivy. The pots show signs of the intensity of the fire that destroyed the palace (and preserved the Linear B).

Where to Stay and Eat in Navaríno Bay

Pýlos ✉ 24001

Karalís Beach, **t** 272 302 3021 or **t** 272 302 3504 (€€€/€€€). Quiet and nice; tucked under the new castle about an 8min walk south of the main plateía. Rooms have balconies overhanging the sea and offer fantastic views of the bay and southern gap. No beach, though; the word is often added to Greek hotel names to let people know they are on the sea. The location draws plenty of non-guests to the rooftop café. *Open April–Oct.*

Hotel Phillip, **t** 272 302 2741 *www.hotelpylos.com* (€€€/€€). Nice rooms and studios for up to four with a sea view. Sitting pretty in the north part of town where the road from Kalamáta meets the Giálova–Pýlos road. The restaurant terrace, where you can enjoy excellent beef *stifádo* and creamy *scordaliá* among other delights, has a stellar view of the sea. *Open all year.*

★ Zoe >>

Karalís, **t** 272 302 2960, *www.hotel-karelis.com* (€€/€€). New, tastefully built in the neoclassical style; two minutes up from the square. Only the main road lies between it and a marvellous sea view. *Open all year.*

Miramare, **t** 272 302 2751 (€€/€€). A 4min walk south of the *plateía*; pleasant, and right by the bathing ladders. Some rooms have terrific views. There are fridges, air-conditioning, and pleasant hosts. Perhaps some day they will rethink the purple colour scheme. There is a road in front, but it's a quiet dead end. *Open April–Oct.*

12 Gods Rooms, **t** 272 302 2179, *www.12gods.gr* (€/€). One of the nicest of the 'rent room' places that congregate in this area just north and up from the *plateía*. A lovely terrace overlooks the sea. *Open April–Oct.*

Diethnés, **t** 272 302 2772. Has been by the quay for years and is a good bet.

Giálova ✉ 24001

Giálova (Γιάλοβα), 6km north of Pýlos, used to be a run-down, raggle-taggle little settlement. But now it has a lovely flagstoned street that ends in an attractive pier, a sandy beach and several small restaurants.

Thanos Apartments, **t** 272 302 2115, *www.appthanos.com*. Double rooms (€€€/€€€) and bigger, pricier studios with kitchens dot a pleasant olive grove on a hill with a view of the bay end; there's a lovely swimming pool. *Open all year.*

Zoe, **t** 272 302 2025, *www.hotelzoe.com* (€€/€€). Enchanting views over a garden of native trees and vegetation, with the bay in the background. The rooms are small, the balconies large, and the hospitality offered by the Giannóutsos family superb. They have made a tiny paradise here and are fully involved in efforts to save the wetlands. There are now large studios on offer as well and a small pool to be shared with hotel residents. Their restaurant, where the talented Mr Giannóutsos is chef, is one of the best, supplied by their organic garden and local fishermen. It is not expensive either, but do book ahead. *Hotel open all year; restaurant May–Oct.*

Camping Erodios, on Golden Beach, **t** 272 302 8240, *www.erodioss.gr* (€/€). Large, state-of-the-art, in a perfect setting on the beach with every facility, including a restaurant and 10 large air-conditioned villas with screens (€€/€). It is also right beside the wetlands, so expect frog serenades and take mosquito coils.

Petrochóri ✉ 24001

Petrochóri (Πετρωχόρι), the jumping-off point for Voïdokoiliá, is still a pleasant town, but it has been growing at an alarming rate in the last few years.

Navarone complex, **t** 272 304 1571, *www.hotelnavarone.gr* (€€/€€). Above the town on a small hill facing the sea (a 15min walk away); new stone buildings, barrel vaulted arches and arcades, tennis, and a pool. *Open April–Oct*.

Up the Ionian Coast: Chóra to Kyparissía

Northwest of Chóra, the main road makes its way up through hilltop **Gargaliáni** (Γαργαλιάνοι), where an electric sign welcomes visitors, especially the crowds that pour in for the enormous Wednesday market, making enormous traffic snarls. Gargaliáni has lovely views over the fishing village of **Marathópoli** (Μαραθόπολη) and the island of Próti, which floats off shore like a giant beaver. If it's time for lunch or a swim, you could do much worse than to take the road at the north end of Gargaliáni down to one of Marathópoli's seafood tavernas. In fact, you might even prefer to take the secondary road between Giálova to Filiatrá. It skirts the sea in places and passes through some of the most gorgeous open scenery in Messenía, including the huge watermelon estates that provide Europe with its first taste of the ambrosial fruit every June. Stop at the spacious O Grigóris in **Ag. Kyriakí** and you can watch them load up, eat, and swim in its tiny pristine bull's-eye port.

Regular boats from Marathópoli go out to **Próti**, which in ancient times had a little market town mentioned by Strabo, and stout walls to prove it. The island's small sandy beach is just below at Vourliá. Seafarers would take shelter in Próti's eastern bays; one is known as Gramméno or 'written' bay for the inscriptions sailors carved in the rock, wishing their ships a safe voyage. The boat from Marathópoli supplies a handful of monks at the Monastery Theótokou, named for an icon found on the shore in 1984. This one was first painted in the late 18th century, then painted over in 1832; the anniversary of its discovery, 23 September, is an excuse for a big *panegýri* with a fish feast. Próti was long an island for hermits and ascetics, the last of whom died only a few years back, so perhaps it's not surprising it still has a few icons on the loose.

North of Marathópoli and Gargaliáni is more of the low hilly country that the Mycenaeans liked best. To the east are the nubby peaks of Mount Egáleo, the largest range in Messenía, that reaches

Getting around the Ionian Coast

There are four daily **trains**, **t** 276 102 2283, from Pátras or Kalamáta to Kyparissía. Its **bus** station, **t** 276 102 2260, near the train station, has four buses daily from Athens (via Trípolis) and Kalamáta, three from Pýlos and two from Pátras, fewer on weekends. **Taxis**: **t** 276 102 2666.

its peak at 3,937ft; when the Mycenaeans were here, the slopes were covered with thick oak forests, of which only a few copses remain among the *maquis* and scrub.

Down below, orchards and olive groves surround **Filiatrá** (Φιλιατρά), a farmers' market town. These are a dime a dozen in the Peloponnese, but Filiatrá has a sparkle that catches the eye even if you're just passing through: first, the bell towers of the churches have brightly painted island-style domes. Second, the big *plateía* in the centre has a cast iron fountain decorated with cherubs riding lizards and turtles. At the south edge of town stands a miniature version of the **Unisphere** from the 1964 New York World's Fair. On the north side of town, you'll find a 40ft model of the **Eiffel Tower**, painted white. If you're intrigued, there's more: Mr Fouraráki, the artist behind the tower and globe, left his third work, a fairytale castle called the **Pýrgos ton Thaumaton** in the seaside hamlet of **Ágrili**, 6km north of Filiatrá.

Kyparissía and Peristería

The landmark on this coast and capital of the eparchy of Trifylia, **Kyparissía** (Κυπαρρισία) is a modest resort, famous for sunsets and sandy beaches, some of which are also popular with mama loggerhead turtles. Near the sea, a defensible 500ft crag, **Mount Psychro**, attracted Epaminondas when he was looking for a port for ancient Messene. When the Avars and Slavs invaded in the early Middle Ages, so many refugees from Arcadía poured in that the town became known under the Franks as Arkadía. The lure, as always, was Mount Psychro, now covered with needle-sharp cypresses and a **castle**; get there by way of a signposted road from the main square. Ruined along with the rest of the Kyparissía by Ibrahim Pasha, it has a big keep built with masonry from the time of Epiminondas to the Franks; on a clear day you can see the Ionian island of Kefaloniá. Around the castle are little medieval streets, stairways and houses with pan-tiled roofs, the prettiest part of Kyparissiá and a favourite place to spend the evening.

Peristeriá *tholos* tombs
the guardian should be there 8.30–3 except Mon; mostly he is

Before Epaminondas, the Mycenaeans were here, and buried their important dead inland at the three *tholos* tombs in **Peristeriá** (Περιστερία). The signpost just north of Kyparissía on the main road says 4km, but the gate is actually 5.5km away. Peristeriá has a perfect Mycenaean setting: rolling hills over a quiet river valley, a beautiful and unspoiled landscape. From the winding road, you'll see the knob of a corbelled dome protruding from the ground like

Where to Stay and Eat on the Ionian Coast

Marathópoli ✉ 24400

Ártina, **t** 276 306 1400, *www.artina.gr* (€€/€€). Lovely, modern, on the sea, with views over Próti island; all rooms have balconies, TVs and air-conditioning, and there's a restaurant. *Open all year.*

Camping Próti, **t** 276 306 1211, *www.camping-proti.gr* (€/€). With a swimming pool and playground. *Open May–10 Oct.*

Filiatrá ✉ 24300

Limenari, **t** 276 103 2935, *limenari@otenet.gr* (€€/€€). Down by Filiatrá's beach, 50m from the sea, with a pool, restaurant, and air-conditioning. *Open all year.*

Kyparissía ✉ 22500

Kyparissia Beach, **t** 276 102 4492, *www.greek-tourism.gr/peloponese/kyparissia/kyparissiabeachotel* (€€/€€). In a garden by the sea; large air-conditioned rooms with TVs, and balconies facing either the mountains or sea. *Open all year.*

Kanellakis, **t** 276 102 4464, *www.hotelkanellakis.gr* (€€/€€). Stylish, with an attractive pool area and a beautifully landscaped setting; 100m from the sea. *Open all year.*

Tsolaridis, **t** 276 102 2145, *tsolaridis@otenet.gr* (€€/€€). A startling purple and white confection, impossible to miss; along with its kitschy charms, this newish hotel has a truly lovely terrace and rooms equipped with air-conditioning and TVs. *Open all year.*

Ionian, **t** 276 102 2511 (€/€). Further from the sea, with TVs and air-conditioning. *Open all year.*

Camping Kyparissía, **t** 276 102 3491, *www.campingkyparissia.com* (€/€). The only one; right down by the sea. *Open April–10 Oct.*

For dinner try the beach tavernas or the three little restaurants up by the castle, with lovely views (the latter open in evenings only in the off season).

an *omphalos* or stone breast. The three *tholoi* here, the source of the gold cups and jewellery in the Chóra museum, were discovered by accident in 1960, when a dog fell through one of the domes. The archaeologist Spíros Marinátos reconstructed the best-preserved one: it stands 33ft high, with a 25-ton lintel and a faint relief of a dove (*peristéri*) and olive branch, preserved under glass on the door jamb.

Language

Greek holds a special place as the oldest spoken language in Europe, going back at least 4,000 years. From the ancient language, Modern Greek, or Romaíka, developed into two forms: the purist or ***katharévousa***, and the popular, or Demotic ***demotikí***, the language of the people. These days few purist words are spoken but you will see the old *katharévousa* on shop signs and official forms. Even though the bakery is called the *foúrnos*, the sign over the door will read ΑΡΤΟΠΟΛΕΙΟΝ, 'bread-seller', while the general store will be the ΠΑΝΤΟΠΟΛΕΙΟΝ, 'seller of all'. You'll still see the pure form on wine labels as well. At the end of the 18th century, writers felt the common language wasn't good enough; archaic forms were brought back and foreign ones replaced. Upon independence, this somewhat stilted, artificial construction called *katharévousa* became the official language of books, documents and even newspapers.

The more vigorous and natural Demotic soon began to creep back; in 1901 Athens was shaken by riots and the government fell when the New Testament appeared in *demotikí*; in 1903 several students were killed in a fight with the police during a *demotikí* performance of Aeschylus. When the fury subsided, it looked as if the Demotic would win out until the Papadópoulos government (1967–74) made it part of its puritan 'moral cleansing' of Greece to revive the purist *katharévousa*. The debate was settled in 1978 when Demotic was made the official tongue.

Greeks travel so far and wide that even in the most remote places there's usually someone who speaks English. Usually spoken with great velocity, Greek isn't a particularly easy language to pick up by ear, but it is very helpful to know at least the alphabet – so that you can find your way around – and a few basic words and phrases.

For food vocabulary, *see* pp.48–50.

The Greek Alphabet

See also 'Transliteration and Pronunciation', p.66.

		Pronunciation	English Equivalent
Α	α	*álfa*	short *a* as in 'father'
Β	β	*víta*	*v*
Γ	γ	*gámma*	guttural *g* or *y* sound
Δ	δ	*délta*	always a hard *th* as in 'though'
Ε	ε	*épsilon*	short *e* as in 'bet'
Ζ	ζ	*zíta*	*z*
Η	η	*íta*	long *e* as in 'bee'
Θ	θ	*thíta*	soft *th* as in 'thin'
Ι	ι	*yóta*	long *e* as in 'bee'; sometimes as *y* in 'yet'
Κ	κ	*káppa*	*k*
Λ	λ	*lámtha*	*l*
Μ	μ	*mi*	*m*
Ν	ν	*ni*	*n*
Ξ	ξ	*ksi*	*x* as in 'ox'
Ο	ο	*ómicron*	*o* as in 'cot'
Π	π	*pi*	*p*
Ρ	ρ	*ro*	*r*
Σ	σ/ς	*sígma*	*s*
Τ	τ	*taf*	*t*
Υ	υ	*ípsilon*	long *e* as in 'bee'
Φ	φ	*fi*	*f*
Χ	χ	*chi*	*ch* as in 'loch'
Ψ	ψ	*psi*	*ps* as in 'stops'
Ω	ω	*oméga*	*o* as in 'cot'

Diphthongs and Consonant Doubles

ΑΙ	αι	short *e* as in 'bet'
ΕΙ	ει / ΟΙ οι	*i* as in 'machine'
ΟΥ	ου	*oo* as in 'too'
ΑΥ	αυ	*av* or *af*
ΕΥ	ευ	*ev* or *ef*
ΗΥ	ηυ	*iv* or *if*
ΓΓ	γγ	*ng* as in 'angry'
ΓΚ	γκ	hard *g*; *ng* within word
ΝΤ	ντ	*d*; *nd* within word
ΜΠ	μπ	*b*; *mp* within word

Greekspeak

Sign language is an essential part of Greek life, and it helps to know what it all means. Greekspeak for 'no' is usually a click of the tongue, accompanied by raised eyebrows and a tilt of the head backwards. It could be all three or a permutation. 'Yes' is usually indicated by a forward nod, head tilted to the side. If someone doesn't hear you or understand you they will shake their heads from side to side quizzically and say '*Oríste?*' Hands whirl like windmills in conversations, and beware the emphatic open hand brought sharply down in anger.

A circular movement of the right hand usually implies something very good or in great quantities. Greek people also use exclamations which sound quite odd but actually mean a lot, like *po, po, po!*, an expression of disapproval and derision; *brávo* comes in handy for praise, while *ópa!* is useful for whoops! look out! or watch it!; *sigá sigá* means slowly, slowly; *éla!*, come or get on with you; *kíta!* look.

Useful Phrases

Yes	*Né/málista* (formal)	Ναί/μάλιστα
No	*Óchi*	Οχι
I don't know	*Then kséro*	Δεν ξέρω
I don't understand... (Greek)	*Then katalavéno... (elliniká)*	Δεν καταλαβαίνω... (Ελληνικά)
Does someone speak English?	*Milái kanís angliká?*	Μιλάει κανείς αγγλικά?
Go away	*Fíyete*	Φύγετε
Help!	*Voíthia!*	Βοήθεια!
My friend	*O fílos moo* (m)	Ο φίλος μου
	Ee fíli moo (f)	Η φίλη μου
Please	*Parakaló*	Παρακαλώ
Thank you (very much)	*Evcharistó (pára polí)*	Ευχαριστώ (πάρα πολύ)
You're welcome	*Parakaló*	Παρακαλώ
It doesn't matter	*Thén pirázi*	Δεν πειράζει
OK, alright	*Endáxi*	Εντάξει
Of course	*Vevéos*	Βεβαίως
Excuse me (as in 'sorry')	*Signómi*	Συγγνώμη
Pardon? Or, from waiters, **What do you want?**	*Oríste?*	Ορίστε?
What is your name?	*Pos sas léne?* (pl & formal)	Πως σάς λένε?
	Pos se léne? (singular)	Πως σέ λένε?
How are you?	*Ti kánete?* (formal/pl)	Τί κάνεται?
	Ti kánis? (singular)	Τί κάνεις?
Hello	*Yásas, hérete* (formal/pl)	Γειάσας, Χέρεται
	Yásou (singular)	Γειάσου
Goodbye	*Yásas* (formal/pl), *andío*	Γειάσας, Αντίο
	Yásou	Γειάσου
Good morning	*Kaliméra*	Καλημέρα
Good evening/goodnight	*Kalispéra/kaliníchta*	Καλησπέρα/Καληνύχτα
What is that?	*Ti íne aftó?*	Τι είναι αυτό
What?	*Ti?*	Τί
Who?	*Piós?* (m), *piá?* (f)	Ποιός?, Ποιά?
Where?	*Poo?*	Πoυ?
When?	*Póte?*	Πότε?
Why?	*Yiatí?*	Γιατί?
How?	*Pos?*	Πώς
I am/You are/He, she, it is	*Íme/íse/íne*	Είμαι/Είσαι/Είναι

We are/You are/They are	*ímaste/ísaste/íne*	Είμαστε/Είσαστε/Είναι
I am hungry	*Pinó*	Πεινώ
I am thirsty	*Thipsó*	Διψώ
I am tired/ill	*íme kourasménos/árostos*	Είμαι κουρασμένος/άρρωστος
I love you	*S'agapó*	Σ'αγαπώ
good	*kaló*	καλό
bad	*kakó*	κακό
so-so	*étsi ki étsi*	έτσι κι έτσι
fast	*grígora*	γρήγορα
big	*megálo*	μεγάλό
small	*mikró*	μικρό
hot	*zestó*	ζεστό
cold	*krío*	κρύο

Shops, Services, Sightseeing

I would like...	*tha íthela...*	Θα ήθελα...
Where is...?	*poo íne...?*	Που είναι...?
How much is it?	*póso káni?*	Πόσο κάνει?
bakery	*foúrnos/artopoleíon*	φούρνος/αρτοπωλείον
bank	*trápeza*	τράπεζα
beach	*paralía*	παραλία
church	*eklisía*	εκκλησία
hospital	*nosokomío*	νοσοκομείο
hotel	*xenodochío*	ξενοδοχείο
hot water	*zestó neró*	ζεστό νερό
kiosk	*períptero*	περίπτερο
money	*leftá*	λεφτά
museum	*moosío*	μουσείο
pharmacy	*farmakío*	φαρμακείο
police station	*astinomía*	αστυνομία
policeman	*astifílakas*	αστυνομικάς
post office	*tachithromío*	ταχυδρομείο
plug (electrical)	*príza*	πρίζα
plug (bath)	*tápa*	τάπα
restaurant	*estiatório*	εστιατόριο
sea	*thálassa*	θάλασσα
shower	*doush*	ντους
student	*fititís*	μαθητής, φοιτητής
telephone office	*Oté*	ΟΤΕ
toilet	*tooaléta*	τουαλέτα

Time

What time is it?	*ti óra íne?*	Τί ώρα είναι?
month	*mína*	μήνα
week	*evthomáda*	εβδομάδα
day	*méra*	μέρα
morning	*proí*	πρωί
afternoon	*apóyevma*	απόγευμα
evening	*vráthi*	βράδυ
yesterday	*chthés*	χθές
today	*símera*	σήμερα

tomorrow	*ávrio*	αύριο
now	*tóra*	τώρά
later	*metá*	μετά
it is early/late	*íne norís/argá*	είναι νωρίs/αργά

Numbers

one	*énas* (m), *mía* (f), *éna* (n)	ένας, μία, ένα
two	*thío*	δύο
three	*tris* (m, f), *tría* (n)	τρείs, τρία
four	*téseris* (m, f), *téssera* (n)	τέσσερεις, τέσσερα
five/six	*pénde/éxi*	πέντε/έξι
seven/eight/nine/ten	*eptá/októ/ennéa/théka*	επτά/οκτώ/εννέα/δέκα
eleven/twelve/thirteen	*éntheka/thótheka/thekatría*	έντεκα/δώδεκα/δεκατρία
twenty	*íkosi*	είκοσι
twenty-one	*íkosi éna* (m, n), *mía* (f)	είκοσι ένα, μία
thirty/forty/fifty	*triánda/saránda/penínda*	τριάντα/σαράντα/πενήντα
sixty	*exínda*	εξήντα
seventy/eighty	*evthomínda/ogthónda*	ευδομήντα/ογδόντα
ninety	*enenínda*	ενενήντα
one hundred	*ekató*	εκατό
one thousand	*chília*	χίλια

Months/Days

January	*Ianooários*	Ιανουάριος
February	*Fevrooários*	Φεβρουάριος
March	*Mártios*	Μάρτιος
April	*Aprílios*	Απρίλιος
May	*Máios*	Μάιος
June	*Ioónios*	Ιούνιος
July	*Ioólios*	Ιούλιος
August	*Avgoostos*	Αύγουστος
September	*Septémvrios*	Σεπτέμβριος
October	*Októvrios*	Οκτώβριος
November	*Noémvrios*	Νοέμβριος
December	*Thekémvrios*	Δεκέμβριος

Sunday	*Kiriakí*	Κυριακή
Monday	*Theftéra*	Δευτέρα
Tuesday	*Tríti*	Τρίτη
Wednesday	*Tetárti*	Τετάρτη
Thursday	*Pémpti*	Πέμπτη
Friday	*Paraskeví*	Παρασκευή
Saturday	*Sávato*	Σάββατο

Driving/Transport

a car	*éna aftokínito*	ένα αυτοκίνητο
a motorbike	*éna michanáki*	ένα μηχανάκι
a bicycle	*éna pothílato*	ένα ποδήλατο
Where can I buy petrol?	*poo boró n'agorásso venzíni?*	Πού μπορώ ν'αγοράσω βενζίνη?

Where is a garage?	*poo íne éna garázh?*	Που είναι ένα γκαράζ?
a map	*énas chártis*	ένας χάρτης
Where is the road to...?	*poo íne o thrómos yiá...?*	Που είναι ο δρόμος γιά...?
Where does this road lead?	*poo pái aftós o thrómos?*	Που πάει αυτός ο δρόμος?
Is the road good?	*íne kalós o thrómos?*	Είναι καλός ο δρόμος?
EXIT	*éxothos* (*th* as in 'the')	ΕΞΟΔΟΣ
ENTRANCE	*ísothos* (*th* as in 'the')	ΕΙΣΟΔΟΣ
DANGER	*kínthinos* (*th* as in 'the')	ΚΙΝΔΥΝΟΣ
SLOW	*argá*	ΑΡΓΑ
NO PARKING	*apagorévete ee státhmevsis*	ΑΠΑΓΟΡΕΥΕΤΑΙ Η ΣΤΑΘΜΕΥΣΙΣ
KEEP OUT	*apagorévete ee ísothos*	ΑΠΑΓΟΡΕΥΕΤΑΙ Η ΕΙΣΟΔΟΣ
the airport/aeroplane	*to arothrómio/aropláno*	το αεροδρόμιο/αεροπλάνο
the bus station	*ee stási too leoforíou*	η στάση του λεωφορείου
the railway station	*o stathmós too trénou*	ο σταθμός του τρένου
the train	*to tréno*	το τρένο
the port/port authority	*to limáni/limenarchío*	το λιμάνι/λιμεναρχείο
the ship	*to plío, to karávi*	το πλοίο, το καράβι
a ticket	*éna isitírio*	ένα εισιτήριο
I want to go to ...	*thélo na páo ston* (m), *sti n* (f)...	Θέλω να πάω στον, στην...
Where is...?	*poo íne ...?*	Που είναι...?
How far is it?	*póso makriá íne?*	Πόσο μακριά είναι?
When will the... leave?	*póte tha fíyi to* (n), *ee* (f), *o* (m)...?	Πότε θα φύγει το, η, ο...?
How long does the trip take?	*póso keró pérni to taxíthi?*	Πόσο καιρό παίρνει το ταξίδι?
Please show me	*parakaló thíkste moo*	Παρακαλώ δείξτε μου
the (nearest) town	*to horió (to pió kondinó)*	Το χωριό (το πιό κοντινό)
here/there	*ethó/ekí*	εδώ/εκεί
near/far	*kondá/makriá*	κοντά/μακριά
left	*aristerá*	αριστερά
right	*thexiá*	δεξιά
north	*vória*	βόρεια
south	*nótia*	νότια
east	*anatoliká*	ανατολικά
west	*thitiká*	δυτικά

Glossary

acropolis fortified height, usually the site of a city's chief temples
acroteria figures on pedestals on the top and corners of a pediment
agíos, agía, agii saint or saints, or holy (Ag.)
agora market and public area in a city centre
aktí coast
ámmos sand
áno/apáno upper
amphora tall jar for wine or oil, designed to be shipped (the conical end would be embedded in sand)
áno upper
avaton holy of holies, where only the priests could enter
bouleuterion council chamber
cavea concave seating of an ancient theatre
cella innermost holy room of a temple
choklakía black and white pebble mosaic
Cyclopean describes walls of stones so huge that only a Cyclops could carry them
chthonic pertaining to the underworld
dimarchíon town hall
entablature all parts of an architectural order above the columns
entasis convex curving of a column that gives the illusion of its being straight
EOT Greek National Tourist Office
eparchía eparchy, an Orthodox diocese, now used to refer to an area outside a big city
exonarthex outer porch of a church
helot a Spartan serf
herm pillar with bust of Hermes and phallus (used to mark borders)
heroön a shrine to a hero or demigod, often built over the tomb
hoplite foot soldier with a large circular shield, often interlocked with other hoplites to form a unit called a phalanx
iconostasis in an Orthodox church, the decorated screen between the nave and altar
kalderími stone-paved pathways
kástro castle or fort
katholikón monastery chapel
káto lower
kore Archaic statue of a maiden
kouros Archaic statue of a naked youth
ktíma estate, property, domaine
krater large bowl for mixing wine and water
larnax a Minoan clay sarcophagus resembling a bathtub
limáni port
limenarchíon port authority
límni lake
loútra hot spring, spa
megaron Mycenaean palace
metope sculpted panel on a frieze
moní monastery or convent
monopáti footpath
narthex entrance porch of a church
néa new
nisí/nisiá island/islands
odeion concert hall (originally roofed)
ósios Blessed
paleo old
palaestra wrestling area in a gymnasium
panagía the 'all holy' Virgin Mary
panegýri saint's feast day
pantokrátor the 'Almighty' – a figure of the triumphant Christ in Byzantine domes
peripteral building surrounded by a colonnade supporting the roof
píthos (pl. ***píthoi***) large ceramic storage jar
plateía square
polis city-state
pótamos river
pronaos temple porch
propylon entrance gate; a ***propylaea*** has more than one door
pýli gate
pýrgos tower
rhyton drinking horn
skála port; also stair
spílio cave or grotto
spíti house
stoa portico not attached to a large building; in an *agora*, often lined with shops
temenos sacred precinct of a temple
tholos circular building; often a Mycenaean beehive tomb

Further Reading

Alpha Beta (*The ABC*) ***of Greek Wines***, published annually by Oínos O Agapitós, describes all the wines of Greece, with a picture of their labels, their prices, their origin, and all for the price of a bottle.

Andrews, Antony, *Greek Society* (Penguin, 1967). Good introduction to ancient Greek society, divided into bite-sized topics.

Andrews, Kevin, *Castles of the Morea*. This is *the* castle book. It's hopelessly expensive; try your local library. Even more interesting is the book Andrews wrote about travelling in the Peloponnese writing about castles during the Greek Civil War: *The Flight of Icaros* (Penguin, 1984).

Angelomatis-Tsougarakis, Helen, *The Eve of the Greek Revival: British travellers' perceptions of early 19th-century Greece* (Routledge, 1990). Attitudes on the verge of the War of Independence.

Burckhardt, Jacob, *The Greeks and Greek Civilization* (HarperCollins, 1998). One of the world's first and greatest cultural historians lectured on the ancient Greeks, but never published his work; it was too controversial. Now reconstructed from his notes by Oswyn Murray, it offers a very different, challenging view of Classical Athens in its heyday.

Camp, John M., *The Athenian Agora: Excavations in the Heart of Classical Athens* (Thames and Hudson, 1992). Fascinating, well illustrated story of 60 years of excavations by the director of the project.

Castleden, Rodney, *Minoans: Life in Bronze Age Crete* (Routledge, 1990).

Chadwick, John, *The Decipherment of Linear B* (Cambridge University Press, 1991). A detective story, following the intricate and ingenious way in which Michael Ventris set out to break the code that was Linear B.

Cheetam, Nicolas, *Medieval Greece* (Yale University Press, 1981, out of print). A former diplomat sheds light on the strange Frankish interlude in the Peloponnese, and on the dark age between the Romans and the Franks.

Constantinidou-Partheniadou, Sofia, *A Travelogue in Greece and a Folklore Calendar* (privately published, Athens 1992). Modern customs and superstitions.

Clogg, Richard, *A Short History of Modern Greece* (Cambridge University Press, 2002). Best, readable account of a messy subject.

Dalby, Andrew, *Siren Feasts: A History of Food and Gastronomy in Greece* (Routledge, 1996). Very detailed account of the ancient Greek diet and feasts.

Davidson, James, *Courtesans and Fishcakes* (Fontana Press, 1998). Mr Davidson knows his onions. It is just erudite enough for you to read all the gory details about ancient Greek sexual gymnastics (and lust for seafood), without having to hide the book when Aunt Jane comes to call.

Drews, Robert, *The Coming of the Greeks* (Princeton, 1988). If, like Butch Cassidy and the Sundance Kid, you find yourself asking 'Who were those guys?', read this careful accounting of the evidence of Indo-European migrations to Greece.

Fermor, Patrick Leigh, *The Mani* (Penguin, 1984). One of the most beautiful books ever written about the Máni, about the Peloponnese, and about everything else.

Finley, M. I., *The World of Odysseus* (New York Review of Books Classics, 2002). On the Mycenaean world's history and myth.

Forrest, W. G., *A History of Sparta 950–192 BC* (Norton, 1969). A compact account of antiquity's totalitarians, although it presumes you didn't snooze during Classics class.

Graves, Robert, *The Greek Myths* (Penguin, 1955, but often reprinted). The provocative classic, seen through a poet's eye, with his beguiling, occasionally crackpot footnotes.

Greenhalgh, Peter and Eliopolis, Edward, *Deep Into Mani* (Faber and Faber, 1985). A *tour de force* and labour of love. Hard to beat, terrific on the *myrologia*, an excellent read.

Harrison, Jane Ellen, *Themis: A Study of the Social Origins of Greek Religion* (Meridian Books, Cleveland, 1969) and *Prolegomena to the Study of Greek Religion* (Merlin Press, London, 1980). Reprints of the classics.

Kazantzákis, Níkos, *Travels in Greece* (Faber & Faber, 1966). Written as a series of newspaper articles just before the Second World War, Kazantzákis' travels in the Peloponnese are filled with brooding tension and perception.

Koliopoulos, John and Veremis, Thanos, *Greece: The Modern Sequel: From 1831 to the Present* (Hurst and Company, 2002). Two Greek history profs' fascinating account of modern Greece; has caused a lot of Greeks to look with new eyes at their recent past.

Lazarakis, Konstantinos, *The Wines of Greece* (Mitchell Beazley Classic WIne Library, 2005). The most up-to-date book in English on the subject.

Lazenby, J. F., *The Spartan Army* (Aris & Phillips Ltd., 1985). Sounds boring, and some of the battle explanations are for the military-obsessed, but he also provides real insight into the Spartan mentality and what's more, you can trust what he says.

Leontis, Artemis, ed., *Greece: A Traveler's Literary Companion* (Whereabouts Press, 1997). Insightful selection of Greek short stories: a great introduction into the obsessions of modern Greece.

McKirahan Jr., Richard D., *Philosophy Before Socrates* (Hackett Indianapolis, 1994). Know your pre-Socratics and discover there really isn't anything new under the sun.

Mazower, Mark, *Inside Hitler's Greece* (Yale Nota Bene, 2001). In-depth study of life in Greece during the Occupation.

Meier, Christian, *Athens: A Portrait of the City in Its Golden Age* (Pimlico, 2000). Wide-ranging and knowledgeable overview.

Miller, Henry, *The Colossus of Maroussi* (W. W. Norton, 1975). Simply one of the best books ever written about Greece, on the eve of the Second World War.

Osborne, Robin, *Greece in the Making 1200–479 BC* (Routledge, 1996). Excellent account of Archaic Greece, incorporating all recent scholarship.

Pausanias, *Guide to Greece* (two volumes), trans. Peter Levi (Penguin, 1971). This is the ultimate source on the Peloponnese; if the first flick through seems mind-bogglingly boring, skip the histories and read the descriptions. Peter Levi's detailed footnotes show just how much Pausanias got right.

Rice, David Talbot, *Art of the Byzantine Era* (Thames & Hudson, 1963).

Runciman, Steven, *The Great Church in Captivity* (Cambridge University Press, 1968). One of the few westerners who can explain the Greek Orthodox church to woefully ignorant westerners; in this case, he examines its tricky role under the Turkish Occupation.

Sagan, Eli, *The Honey and the Hemlock* (Princeton University Press, 1991). This is a study of democracy using the Athenian model. It sounds dull, but isn't; after all, why bother with the cradle of civilization if we don't want to know what happened after the baby got out? The really scary part is how little we have changed.

Saitas, Ioannis, *Greek Traditional Architecture: The Mani* (Melissa, Athens).

Slater, Philip E., *The Glory of Hera* (Princeton University Press, 1968). A well-written, witty and gripping Freudian analysis of Greek mothers, their inferior status and how it affects their boys – which will have you taking a closer look at repetitive destructive behaviour, and the myths of Heracles, Perseus, Bellerophon, Dionysos. Don't miss.

Spivey, Nigel, Greek Art (Phaidon, 1997). Intriguing account of the evolution of ancient Greek art and its political undercurrents.

Storace, Patricia, *Dinner with Persephone*, (Pantheon, New York, 1996/Granta, London, 1997). New York poet full of exquisite insights on the contemporary scene.

Trypanis, Constantine, *The Penguin Book of Greek Verse* (Penguin, 1971). From Homer to modern times, with prose translations.

Ware, Timothy Callistos, *The Orthodox Church* (Penguin, 1993). All you've ever wanted to know about the national religion of Greece.

Woodhouse, C.M., *Modern Greece: A Short History* (Faber & Faber, 2000).

Index

Main page references are in **bold**. Page references to maps are in *italics*.

2nd edition published 2008

Cadogan Guides is an imprint of
New Holland Publishers (UK) Ltd
London • Cape Town • Sydney • Auckland

New Holland Publishers (UK) Ltd
Garfield House
86–88 Edgware Road
London W2 2EA

80 McKenzie Street
Cape Town 8001
South Africa

Unit 1, 66 Gibbes Street
Chatswood, NSW 2067
Australia

218 Lake Road
Northcote
Auckland
New Zealand

cadogan@nhpub.co.uk
www.cadoganguides.com
t 44 (0)20 7724 7773

Distributed in the United States by Globe Pequot, Connecticut

Cover photographs: © Jim Zuckerman/CORBIS, © Walter Bibikow/JAI/CORBIS
Photo essay photographs © Tim Mitchell, except p.9 New Acropolis Museum © N. Daniilidis
Maps © Cadogan Guides, drawn by Maidenhead Cartographic Services Ltd and Angie Watts
Cover and photo essay design: Sarah Gardner
Editor: Linda McQueen
Proofreading: Daphne Trotter
Indexing: Isobel McLean

Printed in Italy by Legoprint
A catalogue record for this book is available from the British Library

ISBN: 978-1-86011-396-3

Please help us to keep this guide up to date. We have done our best to ensure that the information in this guide is correct at the time of going to press. But laws and regulations are constantly changing, and standards and prices fluctuate. We would be delighted to receive any comments. Authors of the best letters will receive a copy of the Cadogan Guide of their choice.

Peloponnese & Athens touring atlas

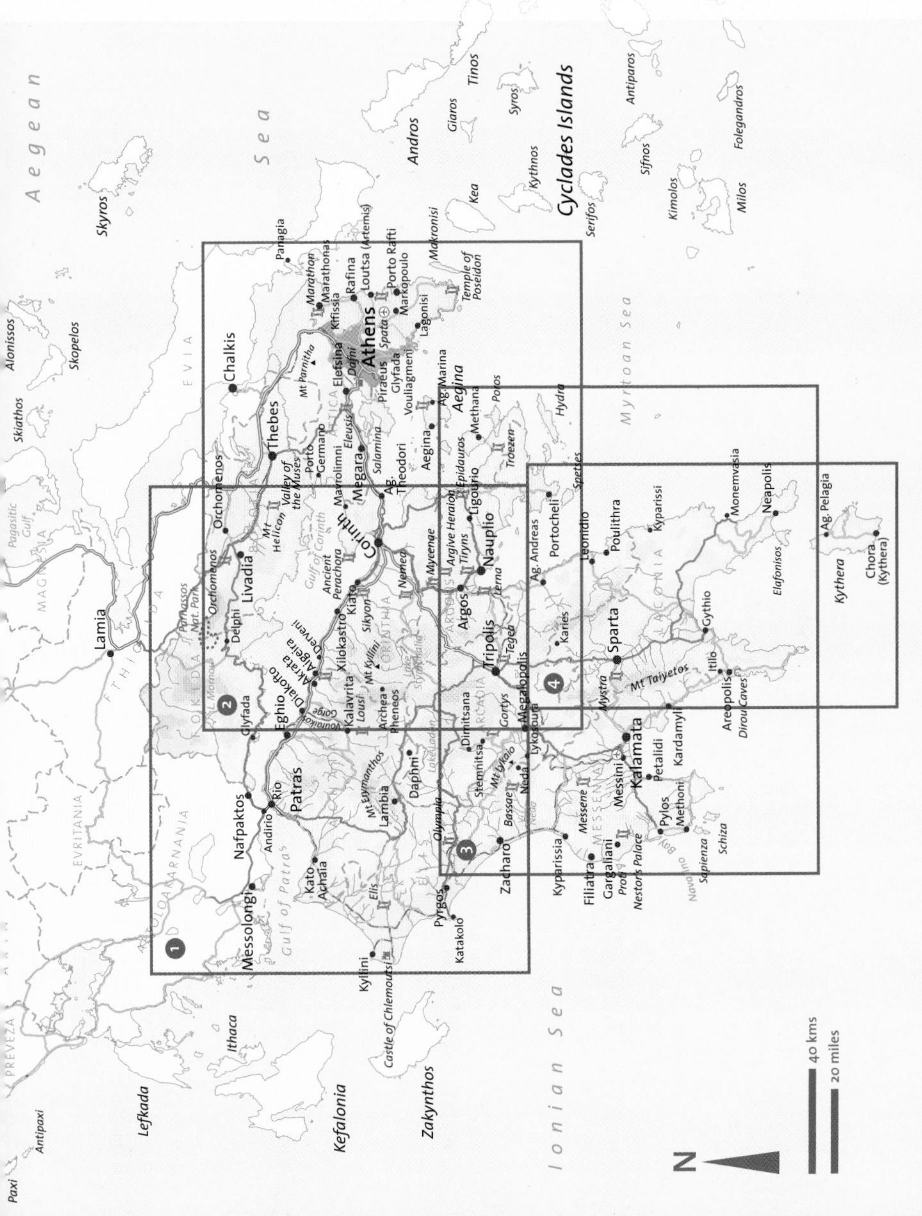

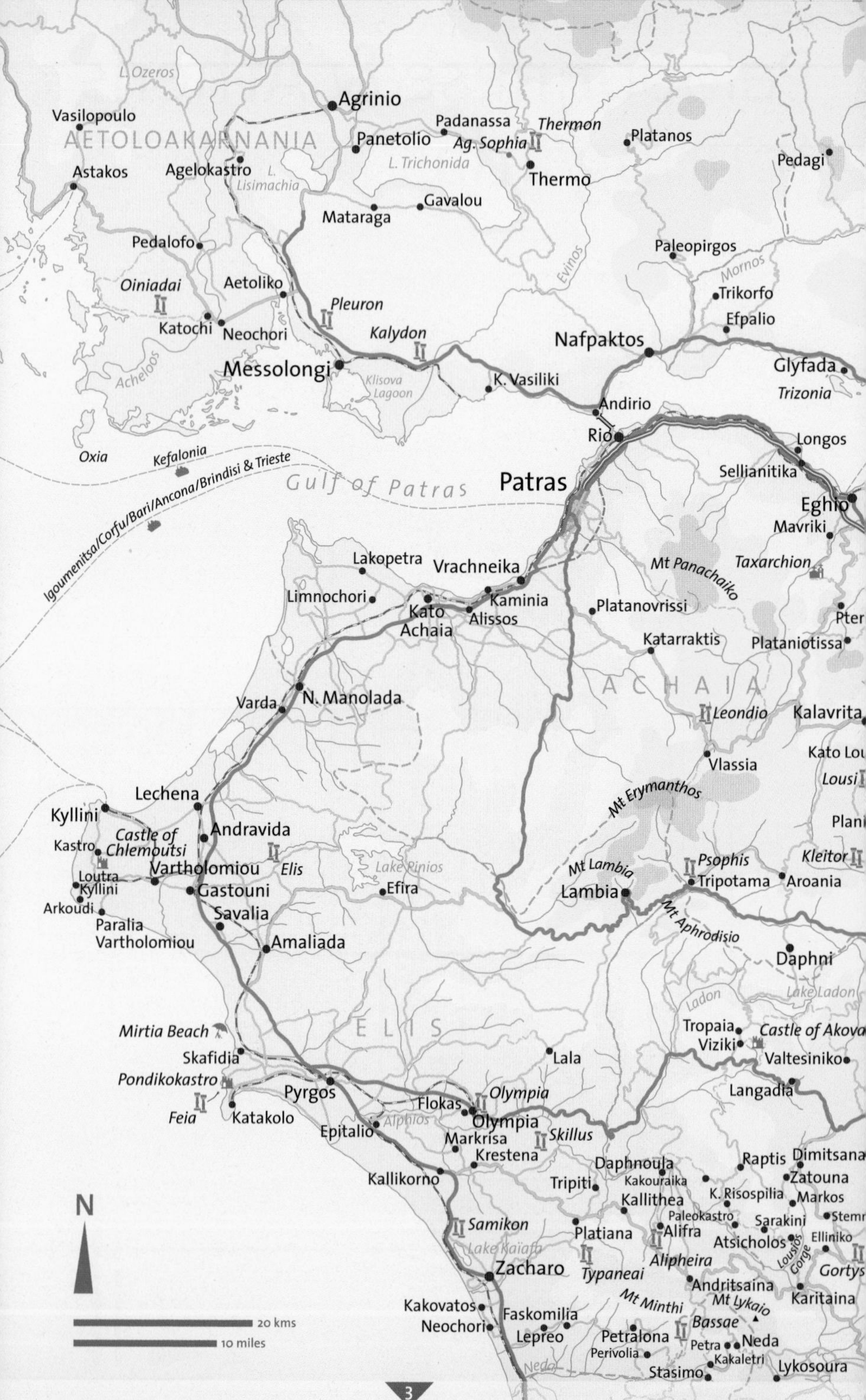

Agrinio
Vasilopoulo
AETOLOAKARNANIA
Panetolio
Padanassa
Thermon
Ag. Sophia
Platanos
Pedagi
Astakos
Agelokastro
L. Trichonida
Thermo
Mataraga
Gavalou
Pedalofo
Paleopirgos
Oiniadai
Aetoliko
Trikorfo
Pleuron
Efpalio
Katochi
Neochori
Kalydon
Nafpaktos
Messolongi
Glyfada
K. Vasiliki
Trizonia
Andirio
Rio
Longos
Oxia
Kefalonia
Gulf of Patras
Patras
Sellianitika
Igoumenitsa/Corfu/Bari/Ancona/Brindisi & Trieste
Eghio
Mavriki
Lakopetra
Vrachneika
Mt Panachaiko
Taxarchion
Limnochori
Kaminia
Kato Achaia
Alissos
Platanovrissi
Katarraktis
Plataniotissa
ACHAIA
Varda
N. Manolada
Leondio
Kalavrita
Vlassia
Mt Erymanthos
Lechena
Kyllini
Andravida
Castle of Chlemoutsi
Kastro
Elis
Vartholomiou
Loutra Kyllini
Lake Pinios
Psophis
Kleitor
Gastouni
Efira
Mt Lambia
Lambia
Tripotama
Aroania
Arkoudi
Savalia
Paralia Vartholomiou
Amaliada
Mt Aphrodisio
Daphni
Ladon
Lake Ladon
ELIS
Mirtia Beach
Tropaia
Castle of Akova
Viziki
Skafidia
Lala
Valtesiniko
Pondikokastro
Langadia
Pyrgos
Olympia
Feia
Katakolo
Flokas
Epitalio
Alphios
Skillus
Markrisa
Krestena
Dimitsana
Raptis
Daphnoula
Zatouna
Kallikorno
Kakouraika
Tripiti
K. Risospilia
Markos
Kallithea
Paleokastro
Sarakini
Samikon
Platiana
Alifra
Atsicholos
Elliniko
Lake Kaiafa
Lousios Gorge
Typaneai
Alipheira
Zacharo
Gortys
Andritsaina
Mt Minthi
Mt Lykaio
Karitaina
Kakovatos
Faskomilia
Bassae
Neochori
Lepreo
Petralona
Petra
Neda
Perivolia
Kakaletri
Stasimo
Lykosoura
N
20 kms
10 miles
3

1

FTHIOTIDA
FOKIDA
BOEOTIA
CORINTHIA
ARGOLIS
ARCADIA

Polidrosos
Amfiklia
Elatia
Atalandi
Mt Giona
Eptalofos
Parnassos National Park
Mt Parnassos
Lidoriki
Amphissa
L. Mornou
Orchomenos
Orchomenos
Kastro
Davlia
Arachova
Chrisso
Delphi
Chaironeia
Moni Koimiseos Theotokou
L. Copais (drained)
Itea
Distomo
Osios Loukas
Livadia
Oracle of Trophonios
Andikira
Aspra Spitia
Eratini
Galaxidi
Ag. Nikolaos
Aliartos
Askra
Thespies
Mt Helicon
Valley of the Muses
Thespai
Elopia
Livadostra
Aliki
Helike
Eleonas
Diakofto
Platanos
Akrata
Aigeira
Aigeira
Mavra Litharia
Derveni
Vouraikos Gorge
Mamousia
Kalamias
Voutsimos
Pyrgos
Aiges
Mega Spileo
Panagia ton Katafigion
Gulf of Corinth
Halcyonic Gulf
Zachlorou
Ambelokipi
Tsivlos
Monasteri
Evrostina
Xilokastro
Sikia
Melissi
Riza
Pellene
Selliana
Agridi
Exochi
Peristera
Ag. Varvara
Rethi
Zemeno
Sterna
Strava
Ancient Perachora
Mavrolimni
Perachora
Mt Gerania
Kiato
Nerantza
Vrachati
Solo
Kato Trikala
Ano Trikala
Souli
Cave Lakes
Zarouchla
Mt Chelmos
Sikyon
Velo
Perigiali
Lechaion
Korakou
Corinth
Vouliagmeni
Loutraki
Corinth Canal
Isthmia
Isthmia
Goura
Mt Kyllini
Krioneri
Paradisi
Gonoussa
Assos
Ellinochori
Ag. Georgios
Archea Pheneos
Pheneos
Titani
Corinth
Mosia
Bouzi
Examilia
Kyras Vrisi
Ag. Theodori
Kleitoria
Stymphalia
Aprokambos
Chalkio
Soulinari
Acrocorinth
Kastania
Kaliani
Daphni
Kenchreai
Stymphalos
Phlious
Kaledzi
Xilokeriza
Loutra Elenis
Aidonia
Koutsi
Kleonai
Lafka
Lake Stymphalia
Galatas
Nemea
Nemea
Mapsos
Koutsomoudi
Chiliomodi
Kandila
Dervenaki
Sofiko
Orchomenos
Orchomenos
Mycenae
Mycenae
Vlacherna
Fichti
Argive Heraion
M. Agnountas
Magouliana
Levidi
Vitina
N. Irea
Midea
Nea Epidauros
Mt Arachneo
Palaia Epidauros
Alonistana
Argos
Dendra
Mt Kynortion
Nestani
Ag. Triada
Mt Mainelon
Mantinea
Libovisi
Kefalari
Giannoulaika
Epidauros
Elliniko
Tiryns
Ligourio
Nauplio
Arkadiko
Pyramid of Kenkreai
Chrisovitsi
Myli
Lerna
Asini
Drepano
Mt Mavrovouni
Fort of Mouchli
Neochori
Tripolis
Mt Parthenio
Tolo
Asine
Vivari
Kandia
Kiveri
Achladokambos
Pelei
Iria
Partheni
Tegea
Eleochori
Didyma
Megalopolis

2
2
3

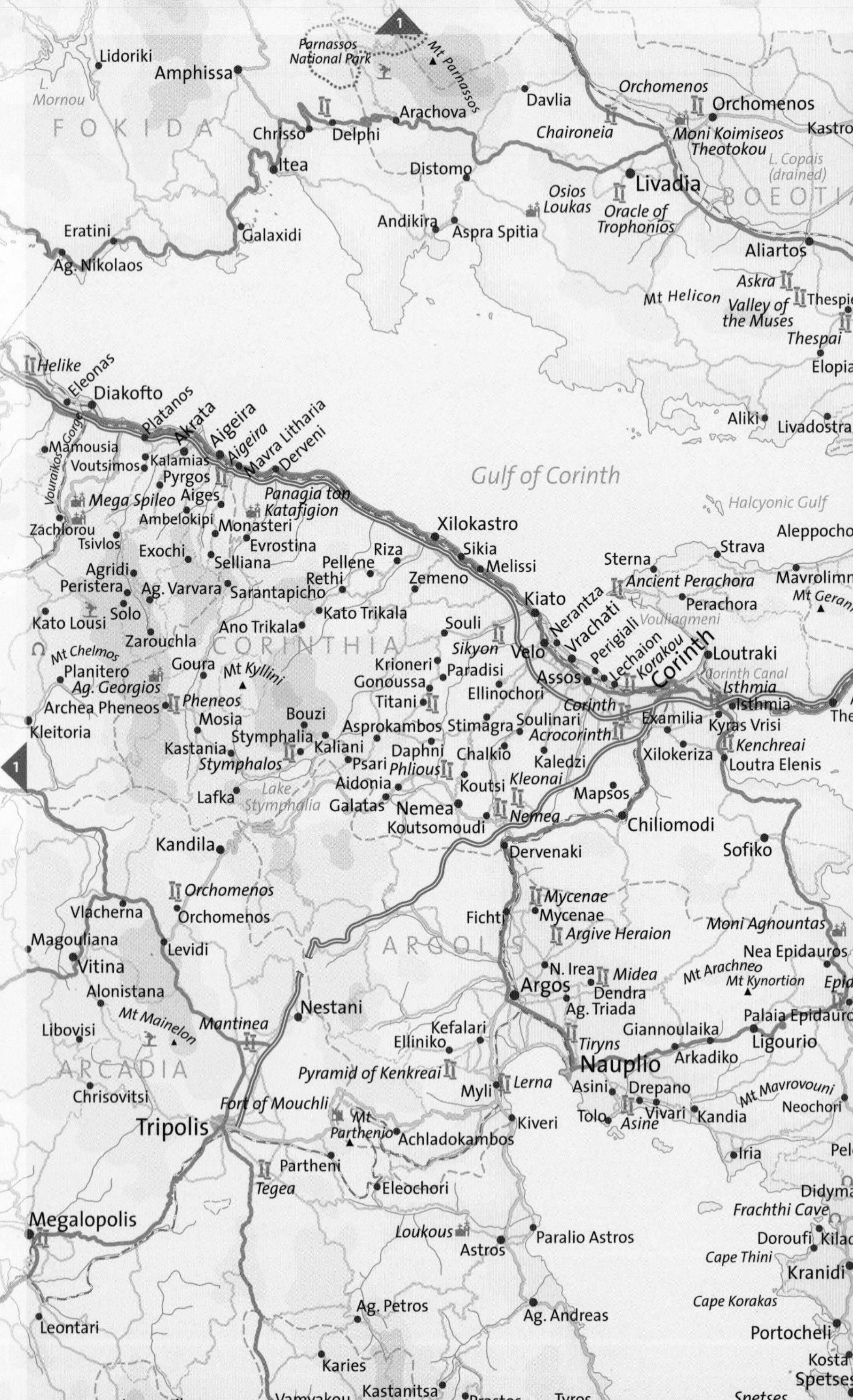

1
Parnassos National Park
Mt Parnassos
Lidoriki
Amphissa
L. Mornou
FOKIDA
Chrisso
Delphi
Arachova
Davlia
Orchomenos
Orchomenos
Kastro
Chaironeia
Moni Koimiseos Theotokou
L. Copais (drained)
Itea
Distomo
Livadia
BOEOTIA
Osios Loukas
Oracle of Trophonios
Andikira
Aspra Spitia
Eratini
Galaxidi
Ag. Nikolaos
Aliartos
Askra
Mt Helicon
Valley of the Muses
Thespies
Thespai
Elopia
Helike
Eleonas
Diakofto
Platanos
Akrata
Aigeira
Aigeira
Mavra Litharia
Derveni
Aliki
Livadostra
Mamousia
Vouraikos Gorge
Voutsimos
Kalamias
Pyrgos
Aiges
Gulf of Corinth
Mega Spileo
Panagia ton Katafigion
Halcyonic Gulf
Zachlorou
Ambelokipi
Monasteri
Xilokastro
Tsivlos
Evrostina
Aleppochori
Exochi
Selliana
Riza
Sikia
Sterna
Strava
Agridi
Pellene
Melissi
Peristera
Ag. Varvara
Rethi
Sarantapicho
Zemeno
Ancient Perachora
Mavrolimni
Kiato
Nerantza
Mt Gerania
Kato Lousi
Solo
Kato Trikala
Perachora
Ano Trikala
Souli
Vrachati
L. Vouliagmeni
Zarouchla
CORINTHIA
Perigiali
Mt Chelmos
Sikyon
Velo
Lechaion
Korakou
Loutraki
Corinth
Goura
Mt Kyllini
Krioneri
Planitero
Gonoussa
Paradisi
Assos
Corinth Canal
Ag. Georgios
Ellinochori
Isthmia
Archea Pheneos
Pheneos
Titani
Corinth
Isthmia
Kleitoria
Mosia
Bouzi
Asprokambos
Stimagra
Soulinari
Examilia
Kyras Vrisi
Stymphalia
Kaliani
Acrocorinth
Kastania
Daphni
Chalkio
Kenchreai
Stymphalos
Psari
Phlious
Kaledzi
Xilokeriza
Loutra Elenis
1
Aidonia
Koutsi
Kleonai
Lafka
Lake Stymphalia
Galatas
Nemea
Mapsos
Nemea
Koutsomoudi
Chiliomodi
Kandila
Dervenaki
Sofiko
Orchomenos
Mycenae
Orchomenos
Mycenae
Vlacherna
Fichti
Argive Heraion
Moni Agnountas
Magouliana
Levidi
ARGOLIS
Nea Epidauros
Vitina
N. Irea
Midea
Mt Arachneo
Argos
Mt Kynortion
Epidauros
Alonistana
Dendra
Nestani
Ag. Triada
Palaia Epidauros
Mt Mainelon
Mantinea
Libovisi
Kefalari
Giannoulaika
Ligourio
Elliniko
Tiryns
ARCADIA
Arkadiko
Nauplio
Pyramid of Kenkreai
Myli
Lerna
Asini
Drepano
Mt Mavrovouni
Chrisovitsi
Neochori
Fort of Mouchli
Vivari
Kandia
Tolo
Asine
Tripolis
Mt Parthenio
Kiveri
Achladokambos
Iria
Partheni
Tegea
Eleochori
Didyma
Frachthi Cave
Megalopolis
Loukous
Astros
Paralio Astros
Doroufi
Kilada
Cape Thini
Kranidi
Cape Korakas
Ag. Petros
Ag. Andreas
Leontari
Portocheli
Karies
Kosta
Spetses
Kastanitsa
Vamvakou
Prastos
Tyros
Spetses
Longanikos
3

Martino
Nea Artaki
EVIA
Gla
Loukisia
Chalkis
L. Yliki
L. Paralimni
Vasiliko
Lefkandi
Amarinthos
Aliveri
Lepoura
Krieza
Eretria
(Nea Psara)
Dilesi
Vagia
Tanagra
Thebes
Asopia
Skala Oropou
Dystos
Zarakes
Amphiaraion
Ag. Apostoli
Kalamos
Almyropotamou
Panagia
Leuktra
Avlona
Malakasa
Temple of Nemesis
Plataea
Erithrai
Ag. Merkourios
Kapandriti
Ramnous
Eleutherai
Osios Meletios
Mt Kitheronas
Porto Germano
Inoi
Mt Parnitha
Ag. Triada
Dekelia
L. Marathonas
Kato Souli
Ag. Marina
Nea Styra
Marathonas
Aigosthena
Vilia
Palaiochori
Tatoï
Kifissia
Marathon
Psatha
ATTICA
Fili
Acharnes
Ano Losia
Nea Makri
Mandra
Elefsina
Metamorfosi
Mt Pendeli
Eleusis
Aspropirgos
Ag. Andreas
Rafina
Megara
Dafni
Dafni
Athens
Megalonisos
Pikermi
Salamina
Paloukia
Loutsa
(Artemis)
Kinetta
Paxi
Ambelakia
Peania
Mt Ymittos
Koutouki
Selinia
Brauronia
Andros/Tinos
Mykonos
Piraeus
Spata
Salamina
Koropi
Porto Rafti
Markopoulo
Glyfada
Voula
Saronic Gulf
Diapori
Vouliagmeni
Vari
Varkiza
C. Kavouri
Keratea
Lagonisi
Souvala
Temple of Aphaia
Aegina
Ag. Marina
Anavissos
Saronida
Thoriko
Aegina
Moni Islet
Perdika
Lavrio
Makronisi
Angistri
Cyclades/Dodecanese/ E. Aegean Is./Crete/Cyprus
Ag. Georgios
Temple of Poseidon
C. Sounion
Kaimeni
Kea
Vathi
Methana
Methana
Poros
Temple of Poseidon
Troezen
Poros
Zoodochos Pigi
Syros
Mt Didyma
Trizina
Galatas
Lemonodassos
Mt Aderes
Iliokastro
Saronida
N
Serifos
Ermioni
Dokos
Hydra
20 kms
10 miles
Hydra
Ag. Emilianos

1
Flokas
Olympia
Alphios
Olympia
Skillus
Markrisa
Krestena
Kallikorno
Samikon
Lake Kaïafa
Zacharo
Magouliana
Vitina
Alonistana
Mt Mainelon
Nestani
Mantinea
Libovisi
Dimitsana
Raptis
Zatouna
Daphnoula
Kakouraika
Tripiti
Kallithea
Markos
Paleokastro
Stemnitsa
ARCADIA
Chrisovitsi
Platiana
Alifra
Alipheira
Atsicholos
Lousios Gorge
Elliniko
Gortys
Fort of Mouchli
Tripolis
Mt Parthenio
Typaneai
Andritsaina
Karitaina
Parthenì
Tegea
Nea Figaleia
Mt Minthi
Mt Lykaio
Kakovatos
Faskomilia
Neochori
Lepreo
K. Taxiarches
Tholo
Bassae
Perivolia
Dragogi
Neda
Megalopolis
Giannitsochori
Neda
A. Figaleia
Platania
Karies
Elia
Mavromati
Lykosoura
Avlonas
Kalitsena
Kouvela
Apiditsa
Chalkias
Isaris
Ag. Theodora
Kefalovrisi
Psari
Beziki
Ag. Petros
Kalo Nero
A. Kopanaki
Ag. Georgios
Leontari
Kyparissia
Peristeria
Karies
Meligalas
Vamvakou
Agrili
Mt Kyparissias
Longanikos
Pellana
Messene
Mavromati
Andriomonastiro
Valira
Kastorio
Filiatra
Mt Egaleo
Manganiako
Ellinoeklisia
Castle of Druges
Kalogerorrachi
Eva
Androusa
Trypi
Marathopoli
Gargaliani
MESSENIA
Thouria
Sparta
Mystra
Mystra
Pamisos
Leika
Parori
Menelaion
Chora Trifylias
Messini
Kefalovrissa
Ag. Ioannis
Amyklai
Proti
Nestor's Palace
Mt Taiyetos
Anavryti
Vapheio
Kalamata
Korifassi
Paralia Verga
Socha
Petrachori
Rizomilos
Pigadia
Eurotas
Palaiokastro
Gialova
Avia
Charavgy
Petalidi
Sphakteria
Mt Likodimo
Navarino Bay
Kambos
Kitries
Castle Zarnata
Pylos
Tseria
Zacharia
Exochori
Navarino
Longa
Episcopi
Kardamyli
Saidona
Krokees
Ag. Andreas
Proastio
Leuktra
Kastania
Kythera
Stoupa
Methoni
Finikounda
Charokopio
Ag. Nikolaos
Akritochori
Koroni
Nomitsis
Refugees' Cave
Langada
Aigies
Sapienza
Trachila
Thalames
Karvelas
Cape Akritas
Castle of Passava
Schiza
Itilo
Fort of Kelefa
Is. Venetiko
Limeni
Areopolis
Skoutari
Dirou Caves
Kotronas
Fragoulias
Drialos
Vamvaka
Exo Nimfio
Cape Tigani
Mina
Aigila
Mezapos
N
Ionian Sea
Stavri
Karinia
Kokkala
Kitta
Cavo Grosso
Ano Boularioi
Gerolimenas
Layia
Alika
Kiparissos
Vathia
Porto Kayio
20 kms
Marmari
10 miles
Cape Taineron

2
3
4
ARGOLI
LACONIA
Myrtoan Sea
Argos
N. Irea
Midea
Dendra
Ag. Triada
Mt Arachneo
Mt Kynortion
Nea Epidauros
Epidauros
Palaia Epidauros
Angistri
Aegina
Ag. Georgios
Kaimeni
Vathi
Methana
Methana
Poros
Temple of Poseidon
Zoodochos Pigi
Poros
Troezen
Trizina
Galatas
Lemonodassos
Mt Aderes
Mt Didyma
Saronida
Kefalari
Elliniko
Giannoulaika
Ligourio
Tiryns
Arkadiko
Nauplio
Pyramid of Kenkreai
Myli
Lerna
Asini
Drepano
Mt Mavrovouni
Neochori
Tolo
Asine
Vivari
Kandia
Kiveri
Achladokambos
Iria
Pelei
Didyma
Iliokastro
Eleochori
Frachthi Cave
Loukous
Astros
Paralio Astros
Doroufi
Kilada
Cape Thini
Kranidi
Ermioni
Is. Dokos
Hydra
Cape Korakas
Hydra
Ag. Andreas
Portocheli
Kosta
Ag. Emilianos
Spetses
Spetses
Kastanitsa
Prastos
Tyros
Melana
Livadi
Sambatiki
Leonidio
Moni Ag. Nikolaou Sinitzas
Lakkos
Mt Parnonas
Moni Panagia Elona
Prasiae
Plaka
Poulithra
Kalloni
Kosmas
Chouni
Peleta
Pigadi
Geraki
Vrontamas
Palaiomonastero
Kyparissi
Niata
Achladokambos
Vlachiotis
Skala
Richia
Molai
Metamorfosi
Geraka
Limenas Geraka
Gythio
Elea
Sikea
Papadianika
Kythera/Antikythera
Gefira
Monemvasia
Elika
Mesochori
A. Kastania
Pounda
Farkalo
K. Kastania
Elafonisos
Neapolis
Lachio
Velanidia
Elafonisos
Ag. Nikolaos
Cape Maleas
Gythio
Kythera
Platia Ammos

3
Kranidi
Ermioni
Cape Korakas
Portocheli
Ag. Emilianos
Kosta
Spetses
Spetses
Ag. Petros
Ag. Andreas
Karies
Kastanitsa
Prastos
Tyros
Vamvakou
Longanikos
Pellana
Kastorio
Melana
Livadi
Sambatiki
Leonidio
Lakkos
Moni Ag. Nikolaou Sinitzas
Mt Parnonas
Moni Panagia Elona
Prasiae
Plaka
Poulithra
Myrtoan Sea
Trypi
Mystra
Mystra
Sparta
Menelaion
Kalloni
Kosmas
Chouni
Peleta
Pigadi
Kefalovrissa
Parori
Ag. Ioannis
Mt Taiyetos
Anavryti
Amyklai
Vapheio
Socha
Eurotas
Pigadia
Geraki
Kyparissi
Vrontamas
Palaiomonastero
LACONIA
Tseria
Zacharia
Exochori
Kardamyli
Krokees
Niata
Achladokambos
Kastania
Leuktra
Stoupa
Vlachiotis
Skala
Richia
Ag. Nikolaos
Nomitsis
Refugees' Cave
Langada
Trachila
Thalames
Aigies
Molai
Metamorfosi
Geraka
Limenas Geraka
Gythio
Karvelas
Sikea
Elea
Itilo
Castle of Passava
Papadianika
Limeni
Fort of Kelefa
Areopolis
Skoutari
Kythera/Antikythera
Gefira
Monemvasia
Dirou Caves
Kotronas
Elika
Fragoulias
Drialos
Vamvaka
Cape Tigani
Mina
Exo Nimfio
Mezapos
Aigila
Stavri
Karinia
Kokkala
Kitta
Cavo Grosso
Ano Boularioi
Gerolimenas
Layia
Alika
Kiparissos
Vathia
Porto Kayio
Marmari
Cape Taineron
Mesochori
A. Kastania
Pounda
Farkalo
K. Kastania
Elafonisos
Neapoli
Lachio
Velanidia
Elafonisos
Ag. Nikolaos
Gythio
Cape Maleas
Platia Ammos
Ag. Pelagia
To Kalamata, Crete & Gythio
Potamos
Palio Chora
Is. Kythera
Diakofti
Milopotamos
Paliopoli
Avlemonas
Mirtidion Monastery
Livadi
Antikythera & Crete
Chora (Kythera)
Kapsali
N
20 kms
10 miles